D1613604

The SAGE Handbook of
Gender and Education

The SAGE Handbook of
Gender and Education

Edited by

Christine Skelton,
Becky Francis
and Lisa Smulyan

(2006)

SAGE Publications

London ● Thousand Oaks ● New Delhi

SAGE Publications Ltd
1 Oliver's Yard
55 City Road
London EC1Y 1SP

SAGE Publications Inc.
2455 Teller Road
Thousand Oaks, California 91320

SAGE Publications India Pvt Ltd
B-42, Panchsheel Enclave
Post Box 4109
New Delhi 110 017

British Library Cataloguing in Publication data

A catalogue record for this book is available from
the British Library

ISBN-10 1-4129-0792-6   ISBN-13 978-1-4129-0792-7

Library of Congress Control Number: 2006922117

Typeset by C&M Digitals (P) Ltd, Chennai, India
Printed in Great Britain by The Cromwell Press Ltd, Trowbridge, Wiltshire
Printed on paper from sustainable resources

Contents

Acknowledgements

We wish to thank all those who have contributed to making this collection such a powerful statement of the field of gender and education. We are grateful to Marianne Lagrange of Sage for commissioning the project and to her and Emma Grantmills for their support throughout. We particularly wish to thank Professor Miriam David for chairing the Review Panel, and indeed the consultants whose expert advice and guidance has ensured the high quality of this volume. And, finally, we thank our family and friends for their patience and encouragement during the book's production.

Review Panel

Chair
Professor Miriam David, Institute of Education, London, UK

Panel
Professor Diane Anderson, Department of Educational Studies, Swarthmore College, Swarthmore College, PA, USA

Dr Louise Archer, Department of Educational and Professional Studies, King's College London, London, UK

Dr Shereen Benjamin, School of Education, University of Edinburgh, Edinburgh, UK

Dr Loraine Blaxter, School of Health and Social Studies, University of Warwick, Coventry, UK

Dr Carolyn Jackson, Department of Educational Research, Lancaster University, Lancaster, UK

Professor Kay Johnston, Department of Education, Colgate University, Hamilton, NY, USA

Dr Kevin Kumashiro, Director, Center for Anti-oppressive Education, Washington, DC, USA

Professor E. Stina Lyon, Faculty of Arts and Human Sciences, London South Bank University, London, UK

Dr Heather Mendick, Institute for Policy Studies in Education, London Metropolitan University, London, UK

Professor Martin Mills, School of Education, University of Queensland, Brisbane, Australia

List of Contributors

Sandra Acker is a Professor in the Department of Sociology and Equity Studies, Ontario Institute for Studies in Education of the University of Toronto. She has worked in the United States, Britain and Canada. She is a sociologist of education, with interests in gender and education, teachers' work and higher education. Her book publications include *Gendered Education* (Open University Press, 1994), *The Realities of Teachers' Work: Never a Dull Moment* (Continuum, 1999), and (co-edited with Elizabeth Smyth and others) *Challenging Professions: Historical and Contemporary Perspectives on Women's Professional Work* (University of Toronto Press, 1999). Recent research has considered the spread of the research culture and its impact on academics in faculties of education; gender and academic leadership in Australia, Britain and Canada; and the tenure process in Canadian universities.

Madeleine Arnot is Professor of Sociology of Education, Fellow of Jesus College, Cambridge University, and the Academy of Social Sciences. She has published extensively on gender, class and education, social change and equality policy making. Her current research focuses on gender values in relation to democracy and citizenship education, education for all and poverty alleviation, and refugee education. Her recent publications include *Closing the Gender Gap: Postwar Education and Social Change,* with M. David and G. Weiner (Polity Press, 1999*); Challenging Democracy: International Perspectives on Gender, Education and Citizenship* (co-edited with J. Dillabough, RoutledgeFalmer, 2000); *Reproducing Gender? Essays on Feminist Theory and Educational Politics* (RoutledgeFalmer, 2002); and *Gender and Education Reader* (with M. Mac an Ghaill, Routledge, 2005)

Jo Boaler is an Associate Professor at Stanford University, specializing in mathematics education and gender. She is a former secondary-school teacher of mathematics and has taught in diverse, London inner-city comprehensive schools.

Her PhD dissertation won the national award for educational research in the UK, and she is the author of numerous articles and four books. Dr Boaler specializes in the impact of different mathematics teaching approaches upon student understanding, achievement and equity. Her book, *Experiencing School Mathematics,* won the Outstanding Book of the Year award for education in Britain. Her latest book, with Cathy Humphreys, *Connecting Mathematical Ideas,* is a collection of video cases and accompanying lesson notes and analyses.

Nancy Brickhouse is Professor and Associate Director of the School of Education at the University of Delaware. Her writings on gender and science education have been published in a variety of outlets, including *Journal for Research in Science Teaching, Journal of Curriculum Studies and Science Education,* and in *International Handbook of Science Education,* edited by Ken Tobin and Barry Fraser, and published by Kluwer. She has recently completed a project with Danielle Ford, 'Bringing Young Girls into Science', funded by the National Science Foundation.

Angela Calabrese Barton, is an expert in urban science education, and feminism and science education. She received her PhD in curriculum, teaching and educational policy from Michigan State University in 1995. Her work has been published in *Educational Researcher, American Education Research Journal, Educational Policy and Practice, Journal of Research in Science Teaching, Science Education,* and *Curriculum Inquiry,* among others. Her most recent book, *Teaching Science for Social Justice* (Teachers College Press), won the 2003 AESA Critics Choice Award. Her other recent book, *Re/thinking Scientific Literacy,* won the 2005 AERA Division K Award for Exemplary Research.

Bagele Chilisa is an Associate Professor at the University of Botswana. Her research focus is on educational policies, gender, research methodologies and indigenous knowledge systems. She has co-authored the following books: *Gender, HIV/AIDS and Life Skills Education in Community Junior Secondary Schools in Botswana* (UNICEF, Nairobi) and *Gendered School Experiences: Impact on Retention and Achievement, in Botswana and Ghana* (DFID, London). Some of her work appears in *Gender and Education Journal* (UK) 2002, 14(1): 21–35; *International Journal of Educational Development* (UK) 2001, 21(5): 433–46; *Transformation, the Journal of Inclusive Scholarship and Pedagogy* (USA) 2001, X(11): 115–16; *International Journal of Educational Assessment* (UK) 2000, 7(1): 61–81; and *International Journal of Qualitative Studies* (USA) 2005, vol. 18(6): 659–84.

R.W. Connell is University Professor in the Faculty of Education and Social Work, University of Sydney. Author or co-author of *Ruling Class Ruling*

Culture, Class Structure in Australian History, Making the Difference, Gender and Power, Schools and Social Justice, Masculinities, The Men and the Boys and *Gender*. R. W. Connell is past president of the Sociological Association of Australia and New Zealand, and a contributor to journals in sociology, education, political science, gender studies and related fields. Current research concerns gender equity, globalization and intellectuals, and social theory on a world scale.

Professor Bronwyn Davies was appointed to the School of Education at the University of Western Sydney in 2003 and is Chair of the Narrative Discourse and Pedagogy Research Group. She is well known for her work on gender and classroom research and her writing on aspects of post-structuralist theory. More recently, she has been working on body/landscape relations, critical literacy and a critique of neo-liberalism as it impacts on subjectivities at work. Recent books include *Gender in Japanese Preschools. Frogs and Snails and Feminist Tales in Japan* (Hampton Press, 2004); *A Body of Writing 1989-1999* (Alta Mira Press, 2000); *(In)scribing Body/landscape Relations* (Alta Mira Press, 2000); second editions of *Shards of Glass. Children Reading and Writing Beyond Gendered Identities* (Hampton Press, 2003) and *Frogs and Snails and Feminist Tales. Preschool Children and Gender* (Hampton Press, 2003). *Frogs and Snails* has also recently been translated into Swedish by Christer Wallentin, as *Hur flickor och pojkar gör kön*.

Dr Kevin G. Davison is Lecturer in Education, and Research Development Coordinator, with the Department of Education, at the National University of Ireland, Galway. He teaches sociology of education for the Higher Diploma in Education program, as well as qualitative research methodologies for the postgraduate program. He currently researches and publishes in the area of masculinities, bodies, boys and literacies, as well as research methodologies in the postmodern condition. In addition to serving as guest co-editor on three special theme issues on boys, masculinity and education for *Journal of Men's Studies, Canadian Journal of Education* and *McGill Journal of Education*, he is co-editor, with Blye Frank, of a collection soon to be published by Althouse Press, *Masculinities and Schooling: International Practices and Perspectives*, and he is the author of the forthcoming book, *Gender Gravity and the Postmodern Push: The Pressure of Gender and Bodies on Curriculum* (Edwin Mellen Press).

Sara Delamont is Reader in Sociology at Cardiff University, where she has taught since 1976. She was the first woman to be president of BERA in 1984. Her historical research has focused on the education of clever women, using structuralist perspectives, and is presented in *Knowledgable Women* (1989). Her most recent book is *Feminist Sociology* (2003). She is currently doing an ethnography of capoeira teaching in the UK.

Jo-Anne Dillabough is an Associate Professor in the Department of Educational Studies; a Faculty Associate (2005–06) at the Peter Wall Institute for Advanced Studies, University of British Columbia, Vancouver, Canada; and a Spencer Research Fellow. Her co-edited book with Madeleine Arnot, published by RoutledgeFalmer, is *Challenging Democracy: International Perspectives on Gender, Education and Citizenship* (2000). She is also co-editor (with A.H. Halsey, H. Lauder and P. Brown) of *Education, Globalization, and Social Change* (in press, Oxford University Press). Her scholarly work has been concentrated in three inter-related areas of study. The first of these areas could be broadly described as the sociology of education and social theory, particularly in relation to critiques of democracy and the study of marginalized communities. The second area comprises the socio-cultural analysis of youth, economic disadvantage and social exclusion in Canada and cross-nationally. A third more recent interest is the relationship between youth exclusion, international human rights' issues and critical analyses of the law. Her approach across the entire corpus of this work could be characterized as that of a cultural sociologist specializing in microcultural sociological and qualitative approaches in the study of social inequality. Jo-Anne has published widely in the sociology of education, and was the recipient of the National Doctoral Award in Curriculum Studies for the most distinguished Canadian dissertation in that field. She currently holds two large-scale SSHRC (Social Sciences and Humanities Research Council) grants and a Spencer Foundation grant.

Jannette Elwood is Professor of Education at Queen's University, Belfast. Her research and teaching lie in the area of examinations and assessment. She has led nationally funded research projects into gender differences in UK examinations at 16+ and 18+. She advises UK and international policy makers and awarding bodies on the impact of assessment and testing systems on boys' and girls' performance. Her recent publications include 'Gender and Achievement: What Have Exams Got to Do with It?', *Oxford Review of Education* (2005) 31(2):l; and *Equality Awareness in Teacher Education in Northern Ireland: Summary of Final Report* (2004), published by the Equality Commission, Belfast (with P. McKeown, T. Gallagher, R. Kilpatrick, C. Murphy and K.Carlisle).

Debbie Epstein is Professor of Education at Cardiff School of Social Sciences. She has published widely on sexualities in educational settings. Her current research is on HIV/AIDS, gender and sexuality in southern Africa and also on globalization and higher education. Her most recent publications include *Silenced Sexualities in Schools and Universities*, co-authored with Sarah O'Flynn and David Telford, and *The Academic's Support Kit* (a boxed set of six books), co-authored with Rebecca Boden and Jane Kenway.

Becky Francis is Professor of Education at Roehampton University. Her research interests include the construction of social identities in education, educational policy and social exclusion, feminist theory, and gender and achievement. Her recent authored books include *Understanding Minority Ethnic Achievement: Race, Gender, Class and 'Success'* (with Louise Archer, Routledge, 2006); *Reassessing Gender and Achievement* (with Christine Skelton, Routledge, 2005); and *Boys, Girls and Achievement; Addressing the Classroom Issues* (RoutledgeFalmer, 2000). Becky has also co-edited several readers concerning issues of theory and practice in gender and education.

Dr Blye W. Frank is Professor in the Division of Medical Education in the Faculty of Medicine at Dalhousie University in Halifax, Nova Scotia, Canada. His research interests are in the areas of social justice; inequities in health care; social accountability in health; feminist, post-structural and queer theory; and masculinities and sexualities.

Jane Gaskell is Professor and Dean at the Ontario Institute for Studies in Education at the University of Toronto. Her research on gender and education began with her thesis on young working-class women, their aspirations and their views of the women's movement. Her subsequent work on gender issues in education includes 'The Women's Movement in Canadian and Australian Education: from Liberation and Sexism to Boys and Social Justice' (with Sandra Taylor), *Gender and Education*, 2003, 15: 149–66; 'White Women as Burden: on Playing the Role of Feminist 'Experts' in China' (with Magrit Eichler), *Women's Studies International Forum*, 2000, 24: 1–15; *Gender In/forms Curriculum: from Enrichment to Transformation* (edited with John Willinsky, 1995, Teachers College Press); *Gender Matters from School to Work* (1991, Open University Press); and *Women and Education* (edited with Arlene McLaren, 1991, Detselig Publishers).

Professor Tuula Gordon is a Fellow and Deputy Director of the Helsinki Collegium for Advanced Studies. Her research interests include young people's transitions, citizenship and nationality, gender, education and methodology. She has published in all these fields – for example, 'Girls in Education: Citizenship, Agency and Emotions' (*Gender and Education,* 2006, 18:1); *Making Spaces: Citizenship and Difference in Schools*, with Janet Holland and Elina Lahelma (Palgrave and New York University Press, 2000); *Democratic Education: Ethnographic Challenges*, with Dennis Beach and Elina Lahelma (eds) (Tufnell Press, 2003); 'Imagining Gendered Adulthood: Anxiety, Ambivalence, Avoidance and Anticipation', with Janet Holland, Elina Lahelma and Rachel Thomson (*European Journal of Women's Studies,* 2005, 12:1).

Dr Carole Leathwood is a Reader in Education in the Institute for Policy Studies in Education, London Metropolitan University. She specializes in research in post-compulsory education, with a particular interest in issues of gender, class and 'race', including the marketization of further education, gender and new managerialism, widening participation in higher education, and critical analyses of educational policy. She is the Ireland/Britain editor of *Women's Studies International Forum* and an associate editor of *Gender, Work and Organisation*.

Diana Leonard is Professor of Sociology of Education and Gender at the Institute of Education, University of London. She has published extensively on the sociology of gender and the family, including *Familiar Exploitation: A New Analysis of Marriage in Contemporary Western Societies* (with C. Delphy, Polity, 1992, reprinted 1996), and has conducted research on 'gender and learning' among 10-year-olds, 'violence resilient secondary schools', 'domestic responsibilities of 9–16-year-olds' and, currently, the long-term consequences of single- and mixed-sex schooling. Her other interests include diversity in the experiences of doctoral students (see *A Woman's Guide to Doctoral Studies*, Open University Press, 2001)and a report on the experiences of international students in UK higher education for UKCOSA: The Council for International Education (2003).

Fengshu Liu is a PhD candidate at the University of British Columbia working on the topic, 'Identity construction of rural women in today's China: a life history approach'. Before coming to the West and starting her journey as a social researcher, she was Dean of and teacher in the English department of a Chinese higher education institution. She co-edited several textbooks on English teaching and English writing during that period. Currently, her research interests include, *inter alia*, rural studies, gender studies, higher education, moral education, the only-child generation, identity politics and youth studies. In the past three years, she has published on basic education in China's rural areas, parental expectations of the only child, and Chinese culture and its implications for education.

Glenda MacNaughton has worked in the early childhood field for 30 years. She is currently an Associate Professor in the Faculty of Education at the University of Melbourne, where she established and now directs the Centre for Equity and Innovation in Early Childhood. Her years in early childhood have included work across all sectors as a practitioner and a manager, and she has been a senior policy adviser to government in the UK and Australia. Her most recently published book explored the politics of knowledge and activism in early childhood. She is currently researching how gender, class and race intersect and construct young children's learning; how teachers explore contemporary issues in the early childhood curriculum; and staff–parent relations in early childhood.

Professor Meg Maguire works in the Centre of Public Policy Research in the Department of Education and Professional Studies at King's College London. She teaches and researches issues of policy and practice in urban contexts, including social justice issues, teachers' lives, and age and ageism in education settings. She is also deputy editor of *Journal of Education Policy*.

Catherine Marshall is Professor in the Department of Educational Leadership at the University of North Carolina at Chapel Hill. She writes about the politics of education, qualitative methodology, women's access to careers, and values in education. She is author or editor of numerous books, including *Rethinking Educational Politics*; *Leadership for Social Justice: Making Revolutions in Education; Designing Qualitative Research;* and *Feminist Critical Policy Analysis,* Vols I and II. AERA presented the Willystine Goodsell Award to Dr Marshall in 2003 for her career of scholarship and activism on behalf of women and girls. She heads Leadership for Social Justice, a grass-roots group pushing to put equity research into action. Her next book will be on educator activists.

Dr Wayne Martino is an Associate Professor in the Faculty of Education at the University of Western Ontario, Canada. He has been researching boys, masculinities and schooling for the past decade, and his work has been published in refereed journals in Australia, the UK, Canada and the USA. His book, *So What's a Boy?: Addressing Issues of Masculinity and Schooling* (with Maria Pallotta-Chiarolli, Open University Press, 2003), dealt specifically with documenting boys' experiences in Australian schools. He has published a range of books on boys, masculinities and schooling, including *What About the Boys?: Issues of Masculinity and Schooling* (with Bob Meyenn, Open University Press, 2001) and *Boys' Stuff: Boys Talking About What Really Matters* (with Maria Pallotta-Chiarolli, Allen & Unwin, 2001), as well as textbooks and source books for English teachers: *Gendered Fictions* (with Bronwyn Mellor, Chalkface Press, 1995); *From the Margins: Exploring Ethnicity, Gender and Aboriginality* (Fremantle Arts Centre Press, 1997); and *Gender and Texts: A Professional Development Package for English Teachers* (with Chris Cook, AATE, 1998). His latest books are *'Being Normal is the Only Way to Be': Adolescent Perspectives on Gender and School* (with Maria Pallotta-Chiarolli, UNSW Press) and *Gendered Outcasts and Sexual Outlaws* (with Chris Kendall, Haworth Press).

David James Mellor is a doctoral student at Cardiff University School of Social Sciences. Working with an emphasis on subjectivity, dominance, culture and the everyday, his research focuses on gendered heterosexuality and the cultural pedagogies of heterosexuality. He is currently completing his thesis, which is about children's understandings of and investments in romance and romantic love.

Ann L. Mullen is an Assistant Professor of Sociology at the University of Toronto, Scarborough. She also currently holds a National Academy of Education/Spencer Postdoctoral Fellowship. Originally from California, she received a B.A. from the University of California at Berkeley and Master's and Doctorate degrees in sociology from Yale University. She has also studied in France and Brazil. Dr Mullen was awarded the American Educational Research Association Dissertation Fellowship and the Postdoctoral Research Fellowship. Before beginning her current position, she served as a Senior Research Associate at the Institute of

Educational Sciences at the US Department of Education. Her research focuses on several facets of the complex relationship between post-secondary education and social inequality, including enquiries into the importance of institution type and field of study as critical sorting mechanisms. Recent publications include 'Who Goes to Graduate School?: Social and Academic Correlates of Educational Continuation after College,' in *Sociology of Education* (with K.A. Goyette and J.A. Soares, 2003) and 'Who Studies the Arts and Sciences? Social Background and the Choice and Consequences of Undergraduate Field of Study' (with K.A. Goyette), forthcoming in the *Journal of Higher Education*.

Carrie Paechter is Professor of Education at Goldsmiths College, London. Her research interests include the intersection of gender, power and knowledge; the construction of identity, especially with regard to gender, space and embodiment in and outside schooling; and the processes of curriculum negotiation. She regards herself as a Foucaultian post-structuralist feminist in orientation and writes regularly on issues of research methodology in this context. Her latest book, *Being Boys, Being Girls: Learning Masculinities and Femininities* (Open University Press), will appear in 2007.

Diane Reay is Professor of Education at Cambridge University. She is a sociologist working in the area of education but is also interested in broader issues of the relationship between the self and society, the affective and the material. Her priority has been to engage in research with a strong social justice agenda that addresses social inequalities of all kinds. Her research has a strong theoretical focus, and she is particularly interested in developing theorizations of social class and the ways in which it is mediated by gender and ethnicity. Her most recent book, *Degrees of Choice: Class, Race and Gender in Higher Education* (with Miriam David and Stephen Ball, Trentham Books, 2005), employs a Bourdieurian analysis to look at inequalities in access and participation in higher education.

Dr Emma Renold is a senior lecturer in Childhood Studies at the Cardiff School of Social Sciences, Cardiff University. Her main research interests focus on young children's school-based gender and sexual identities, the identity work of children in residential care, gender-based bullying and sexual violence, and researching sensitive topics with children and young people (particularly participatory and visual methods). Some of these areas are explored in her recent book, *Girls, Boys and Junior Sexualities* (RoutledgeFalmer).

Jessica Ringrose is a Postdoctoral Fellow in the School of Social Sciences, Cardiff University. Her current research, funded through the Social Sciences and Humanities Research Council of Canada, focuses on femininity, class, ethnicity, and issues of aggression and bullying in popular culture and schooling. Her publications in this area can be found in *Feminism* and *Psychology*. She is also interested in students' experiences of grappling with race, class and gender-inclusive feminist pedagogies in higher education, and she has published on this theme in *Resources for Feminist Research* and *Working Through Whiteness: International Perspectives* (State University of New York Press).

Tracy Robinson-Wood is a Professor in the Department of Counseling and Applied Educational Psychology at Northeastern University. Her research focuses on the intersections of race, gender, culture, class and spirituality in psychosocial identity development. She is the author of the textbook, *The Convergence of Race, Ethnicity, and Gender: Multiple Identities in Counseling*. Her current research projects include a qualitative investigation of white mothers of non-white children, and resistance, coping and racial identity in young Black women.

Harilyn Rousso is President of Disabilities Unlimited Consulting Services, an organization that provides consultation, training and research on disability equity issues to promote equal opportunity for people with disabilities. An educator, social worker, psychotherapist, writer, painter and advocate, she has worked in the disability rights field, with a particular emphasis on issues of women and girls with disabilities, for more than 20 years. Ms Rousso is the founder of the Networking Project for Disabled Women and Girls of the YWCA/NYC, the executive producer of the documentary *Positive Images: Portraits of Women with Disabilities*, and the author of numerous publications on gender and disability, including *Double Jeopardy. Addressing Gender Equity in Special Education* (SUNY Press, 2001) and *Strong Proud Sisters: Girls and Young Women with Disabilities* (Center For Women Policy Studies, 2001).

Dr Sue Saltmarsh is a Postdoctoral Research Fellow working with the Narrative, Discourse and Pedagogy Research Group in the School of Education at the University of Western Sydney, Australia. Her research concerns the discursive production of subjectivities and social relations, with particular reference to issues of educational consumption, institutional violence and social justice. Her postdoctoral research focuses on the function of texts and textual practices in the gendered and racialized production of young people's subjectivities in the outer metropolitan region of Greater Western Sydney. Her PhD in critical and cultural studies was awarded the Macquarie University Vice Chancellor's Commendation and the Australian Association of Researchers in Education Doctoral Thesis Award 2005.

Jo Sanders is Director of the Center for Gender Equity in Camano Island, Washington, USA. She specializes in gender and technology issues in education. She has written many books, chapters and papers on the topic and has spoken widely in professional venues among educators in the USA and abroad. For more information, see her website at www.josanders.com.

Tesha Sengupta-Irving, a former secondary mathematics teacher, is a doctoral candidate in mathematics education at Stanford University in Palo Alto, California. She is interested in how student collaboration can create more equitable and open conceptions of mathematics and how that promotes the engagement of historically marginalized student communities in the discipline.

Charol Shakeshaft, PhD, is Professor in the Department of Foundations, Leadership, and Policy Studies at Hofstra University, where she teaches courses on gender, statistical analysis, evaluation methodology, and school safety. Charol Shakeshaft has been studying equity in schools for more than 25 years, documenting gendered practice in the classroom and in school administration. She is an internationally recognized researcher in the area of gender patterns in educational delivery and classroom interactions. Her work on equity in schools has taken her into school systems across the USA, Australia, China, Japan, Canada and Europe, where she has helped educators make schools more welcoming to females. Dr Shakeshaft has recently completed a three-year national study of the relationships between a school-based risk prevention programme and risk behaviors of sixth to eighth-grade students and a three-year National Science Foundation project to promote interest in science careers among seventh- and eighth-grade girls, particularly girls of color from low-income families.

Christine Skelton is Professor of Education at Roehampton University and Director of the Centre for Research in Education Policy and Professionalism. Her research interests include the construction of gender identities in teachers and pupils in the primary and early years sectors. Her published works include *Reassessing Gender and Achievement* (with Becky Francis, Routledge, 2005); *Boys and Girls in the Primary Classroom* (edited with Becky Francis, Open University Press, 2003); and *Schooling the Boys: Masculinities and Primary Education* (Open University Press, 2001).

Lisa Smulyan is a Professor and Chair of the Department of Educational Studies at Swarthmore College, where she teaches courses in educational foundations; adolescence, gender and education; and school and society. Her work focuses on the role of gender in teachers' and administrators' personal and professional lives. Her most recent book is *Balancing Acts: Women Principals at Work.*

Elaine Unterhalter is a Senior Lecturer in Education and International Development at the Institute of Education, University of London, where she coordinates the masters degree in education, gender and international development. She is one of the coordinators of the Beyond Access project, which works with Oxfam GB and the Department for International Development (DFID) in the UK to generate and share new knowledge about the Millennium Development Goals, gender and education. Her recent work includes *Beyond Access: Transforming Policy and Practice* *for Gender Equality in Education* (co-edited with Sheila Aikman) and *Gender, Schooling and Global Social Justice* (2006).

Linda M. von Hoene is the Director of the Graduate Student Instructor Teaching and Resource Center at the University of California, Berkeley. She received her PhD in German from the University of California, Berkeley, with a dissertation entitled, 'Fascism and Female Subjectivity: The Lure of Fascism for the Female Subject in Psychoanalytic Theory, German Literature and Film'. She has published articles and book chapters on the intersection of second language acquisition and feminist, psychoanalytic and post-colonial theory. She is currently co-authoring a book with colleagues at Berkeley on instructional design and student motivation that will be published by Cambridge University Press.

Valerie Walkerdine is Professor of Psychology in the School of Social Sciences, Cardiff University. She has published extensively, including *Mass Hysteria: Critical Psychology and Media Studies* (with L. Blackman), *Challenging Subjects: Critical Psychology for a New Millennium,* and *Growing up Girl: Gender and Class in the 21st Century* (with H. Lucey and J. Melody). Her latest book on children, relationality and multimedia will be published by Palgrave in 2006. Her current research focuses on neo-liberalism and subjectivity, and subjectivities and work identities in transition in South Wales and Sydney. She is also working toward a theory of relationality. Valerie is founding editor of the *International Journal of Critical Psychology.*

Janie Victoria Ward, EdD, is an Associate Professor of Education and Human Services, and Chair of the Africana Studies Department at Simmons College in Boston, Massachusetts. She is Co-Principal Investigator (with Wendy Luttrell, Harvard Graduate School of Education) of Project ASSERT (Accessing Strengths and Supporting Effective Resistance in Teaching), a participatory research study designed to explore cultural beliefs and presuppositions that underlie discourses of gender, race and class expressed by adults working with urban youth. The author of four books, and many chapters and articles, Janie's research interests focus on the psychosocial development of African-American children and youth.

Michelle Webber is an Assistant Professor of Sociology at Brock University. She researches and publishes in the areas of feminist pedagogy, gender and higher education. Her teaching subjects include sociology of education, qualitative research methods, sociology of gender and introductory sociology. With co-editor Kate Bezanson, she has published *Rethinking Society in the 21st Century: Critical Readings in Sociology* (Canadian Scholars Press, 2004). Her current research focuses on the regulation of academics through disciplinary mechanisms such as merit pay and the tenure process.

Michael L. Wehmeyer, PhD, is Professor of Special Education; Director, Kansas University Center on Developmental Disabilities; and Associate Director, Beach Center on Disability, all at the University of Kansas. Dr Wehmeyer is engaged in teacher personnel preparation in the area of severe, multiple disabilities, and directs multiple federally funded projects conducting research and model development in the education of students with intellectual and developmental disabilities. He is the author of more than 170 articles or book chapters and has authored, co-authored or co-edited 19 books on disability and education-related issues, including issues pertaining to self-determination, transition, universal design for learning and access to the general curriculum for students with significant disabilities, gender equity and students with intellectual disabilities, and technology use by persons with cognitive disabilities. He is past-president of the Council for Exceptional Children's Division on Career Development and Transition and is editor-in-chief of the journal *Remedial and Special Education.*

Gaby Weiner is currently Honorary Professor at Edinburgh University. Her previous posts included Professor of Teacher Education and Research at Umeå University in Sweden (1998–2005) and Professor of Educational Research (1992–98) at South Bank University, London. She has written and edited a number of publications on social justice, gender, race and ethnicity, including *Feminisms in Education* (1994), *Equal Opportunities in Colleges and Universities* (with M. Farish, J. McPake and J. Powney, 1995), *Closing the Gender Gap: Postwar Educational and Social Change* (with M. Arnot and M. David, 1999), and, most recently, *Kids in Cyberspace: Teaching Antiracism Using the Internet in Britain, Spain and Sweden* (with C. Gaine, 2005). She is also responsible for two book series: Gender and Education (with R. Deem) and Feminist Educational Thinking (with L. Yates and K. Weiler). She is currently completing a book on the uses of auto/biography to educational research.

Michelle D. Young is the Executive Director of the University Council for Educational Administration (UCEA) and a faculty member in the Department of Educational Leadership and Policy Analysis at the University of Missouri-Columbia. Her scholarship focuses on the preparation and practice of school leaders and school policies that facilitate equitable and quality experiences for all students and adults who learn and work in schools. Young is the recipient of the William J. Davis award for the most outstanding article published in a volume of the *Educational Administration Quarterly.* Her work has also been published in the *Review of Educational Research,* the *Educational Researcher,* the *American Educational Research Journal,* the *Journal of School Leadership,* the *International Journal of Qualitative Studies in Education,* and *Leadership and Policy in Schools,* among other publications.

Introduction

Christine Skelton, Becky Francis
and Lisa Smulyan

Since the upsurge of second-wave feminism in the 1960s, research into the experiences of girls and women in education has continued unabated. During this time, 'feminism' has fractured into 'feminisms' in order to recognize the plurality and diversity of the perspectives the concept embraces. And the field of gender and education has continuously expanded to take in the wide range of locations where gender has been found to influence experiences and structures. During the early days of second-wave feminism, it was efforts of feminists in the West that raised awareness of the educational inequities faced by women and girls, but at this point in the twenty-first century feminists from across the world are pointing to how gender shapes educational opportunities in specific contexts. Importantly, where gender was once contested as an issue that educational policy makers needed to be concerned about (Arnot, 1985), today it is accepted as a significant factor that requires consideration by educational providers. At the same time, interest in masculinities began to proliferate in the 1990s, and it is somewhat ironic to note that far more attention began to be given by policy makers in Western countries to gender when 'boys' became the focus of attention!

It has been a privilege for us to edit this book, which brings together leading scholars on gender and education who are able to provide an up-to-date and indispensable guide to the field. We have also been fortunate in being able to draw on the expertise of a consultation panel led by Professor Miriam David, who reviewed the chapters and offered supportive advice to authors to ensure that this handbook reflects the 'internationality' of current theoretical and methodological perspectives. The scope of this collection testifies to the range and diversity of contemporary work on gender and education, and to the power, relevance and dynamism of this feminist body of knowledge.

The book is divided into five sections. The first deals with theory and methods, and includes chapters that contextualize the work in other sections of the book. Chapters in this section examine what we mean by 'gender', 'masculinity' and 'femininity', and expound on the theorization of these concepts, as well as the application of theory to the field of gender and education. Furthermore, feminist fields of pedagogy and methodology are outlined, and policy movements discussed in relation to gender and education. Section Two addresses gender in the various educational sectors, and includes a chapter on single-sex education. In the third section, authors focus on different curriculum subjects, elucidating gender issues which are specific to particular subjects, as well as how more generic gendered constructions have an impact in relation to these subjects. Section Four concentrates on identity construction within educational settings. Various facets of identity and their interrelation with gender are examined,[1] in addition to chapters focusing specifically on the construction of masculinities and femininities in the classroom. Finally, Section Five addresses gendering of educational institutions and practices, with particular attention to the gender issues faced by teachers. We are confident that in representing such diverse areas of theory and research there will be something within this collection to interest everybody researching and teaching gender and education or related fields.

In the analysis of these various areas and issues, theoretical tensions are sometimes articulated which are indicative of theoretical dilemmas currently challenging feminists and social scientists concerned with social justice. These include, for example, tensions between postmodern and deconstructive theories which stress the determinism of discourse and deconstruct grand narratives, and feminist notions of agency and emancipatory projects. Another struggle represented in these chapters centres on how to conceptualize recognition of both the structural power and impact of gender, while also acknowledging the diversity, fluidity and contradiction of individual gender identities. This also relates to the challenge of adequately articulating the influence of multiple aspects of identity and location, while still forcefully arguing the profound bearing of gender for educational experiences and outcomes. The rich and wide-ranging critique offered in this collection powerfully illustrates how the privileging of the masculine (albeit a particular construction of the masculine) across education demands a feminist analysis and response.

This book provides faculty and students at undergraduate and postgraduate levels with a unique international resource as they continue their own explorations of the field of gender and education. Recently, there has been a preoccupation with issues of identity in gender studies, and a wariness of making recommendations due to the postmodern turn in academic theory. This has led to a dearth of international, comprehensive collections on different theoretical positions on equity issues in schools, a gap which this collection addresses. The book reviews and synthesises key contemporary topics and themes from a range of theoretical and methodological perspectives, providing a dynamic and critical interrogation of issues in gender and education. As the authors and editors worked on this volume, they discovered that researchers and educators around the world did not always have the opportunity to read and share in conversation across national or regional boundaries. Chapter topics expanded and became richer and more complex as authors engaged with international references and perspectives. In the same way, readers will develop a broader and more nuanced understanding of the issues in the field of gender and education as they use this book.

REFERENCES

Arnot, M (ed) (1985) *Race and gender: equal opportunities policies in education.* Oxford: Pergamon.

NOTE

1. It might be argued that all gender research ought to take other factors of identity aside from gender into account, and, indeed, work across the chapters in this collection is attuned to such nuance. However, by including chapters with a specific focus on aspects such as 'race', sexuality and social class, we sought to ensure that these issues are given due space.

Gender Theory and Methodology

INTRODUCTION

It is a truism that feminism is a 'broad church', to the extent that there is debate about what holds the various strands of 'feminist' thought together. Within this rich and vibrant seam of theory, there are multiple constructions and contestations over 'feminist' epistemologies, and indeed over the nature of that which is core to our concerns: gender itself. These debates around feminist theory and practice are found in gender and education research, as in other areas of feminist work. This section sets out to address the themes and debates which contextualize the rest of the book. It addresses what it is that we might mean when we refer to gender, and the theorizing of its expression (as masculinity and femininity). It also provides overviews of other areas which are integral in informing research discussed in other parts of the book – gender and methodology; feminist pedagogy; global perspectives on gender and education; policy pertaining to gender and education, and the application of theory in gender and education research. All the chapters elucidate key arguments emerging in these different areas, illustrating the dynamic and contested nature of the field, but also the power, passion and advanced theorizing and which infuses contemporary feminist (and 'pro-feminist') work in gender and education.

The section begins with a chapter examining the category 'gender' which this collection addresses. Gender essentialist and social constructionist positions are outlined, and tensions emerging from 'theoretical slippage' between sex and gender explored. Becky Francis concludes her discussion in Chapter 1 by considering the implications for feminist educational research. Such theoretical challenges are taken up in R.W. Connell's chapter on masculinities. Connell reflects on the theorization of masculinity, not least the author's own influential contribution concerning multiple versions of masculinity, and the controversies arising. In Chapter 3, Valerie Walkerdine and Jessica Ringrose examine the psychic tensions resulting from the production of classed femininities within a neoliberal context, and the role of education in the transmission of neoliberal discourse and versions of selfhood.

The various theoretical positions informing these chapters, and other work in gender and education, are teased out and analysed in Jo-Anne Dillabough's chapter. She provides an overview of theoretical approaches from socialization theories to those underpinning the recent 'cultural turn' in gender and education theory, illuminating the diversity and complexity of the field. Feminist methodologies and their application in the field of education are explored in Chapter 5. Catherine Marshall and Michelle D. Young celebrate the creativity and radicalism of gender research in education: they chart how this work has 'pushed the boundaries' in both methodological approach and subject matter, challenging dominant epistemologies rather than simply 'adding women'. In Chapter 6 Gaby Weiner explores the idea of whether a feminist pedagogy exists and what it might look like.

A global perspective and context is brought to the preceding debates by Elaine Unterhalter in Chapter 7. Elaine documents the educational inequalities that are endemic across the globe, and outlines the various movements and approaches that have sought to address these issues. Finally, in Chapter 8, Meg Maguire provides analysis of the ways in which policy movements inform, and are informed by, issues in gender and education. She uses the recent focus on boys' educational performance, and neoliberal policy drives of the 'standards agenda', as contemporary examples of formative policy drives in the West and ways in which these inform and compound gender issues.

The Nature of Gender

Becky Francis

Why is it that across education, and in society as a whole, girls/women and boys/men tend to behave in different ways? What causes these patterns of behavioural difference? And just as importantly, why are there so many individuals, or instances, that do not 'fit' these trends, and where males and females behave similarly? In any book of this stature examining issues of gender and education, it is necessary to discuss the concept/s of 'gender' that we are working with. Of course, the other subject of this book, 'education', is itself a very broad and sometimes controversial term. The purposes and methods of education continue to raise philosophical, political and ethical debates; and indeed the *boundaries* of the application of the term (i.e. what counts as education?) remain contentious. Yet the broad meaning as concerned with learning and teaching is relatively clear. The concept of gender, however, is a recent development in the study of people and society, and has been contested from a variety of quarters since its inception (e.g. Butler, 1990; Pinker, 1994; MacInnes, 1998). As well as the diverse competing explanations for the patterns of gender/sex difference across society, there are differing interpretations of 'gender' among theorists.

This chapter aims to tease out some of these theoretical and political trajectories. It begins by briefly charting some of the alternative explanations provided for behavioral differences between girls/women and boys/men. The notion of gender (as opposed to sex) is then discussed, outlining the critiques that have been applied to the concept and some of the tensions emerging.

DIFFERENT EXPLANATIONS FOR GENDERED BEHAVIOR

That there are patterns of behavior and social organization that differ according to sex/gender is not in doubt. These patterns differ radically between societies, and even between generations, social classes, and ethnic or religious groups within the same society. But, globally, societies maintain a notion of sex/gender, and tend to use these categories as organising principles (MacInnes, 1998). Even relativists, such as Judith Butler (1990), who challenge the *category* sex/gender recognize the powerful effects that labelling a person as male or female has. As feminists have charted, the majority of societies elevate men – and the activities/attributes associated with men in that society – over women and their related activities and apparent attributes. Numerous activities have been shown to be seen as the appropriate domain of women in one society and of men in another, but as feminists have pointed out, where they are practised by men, the activities tend to have higher status (Delphy and Leonard, 1992).

However, explanations for these gendered practices of social power, status and organization are highly diverse. Some see them as the inevitable product of inherent, biologically programmed differences between men and women. Others see them as due to socio-political historical developments. Many readers will observe that these contrasting perspectives boil down to what Rose (2001) refers to as 'that tired dichotomy of nature versus nurture' (p256). Rose maintains that we should rather conceive human behaviour as defined by a different dichotomy; that of specificity and plasticity. But as he acknowledges, most competing theories of gender difference have been firmly located on either side of the former debate, grounded in a view of gendered behavior as either innate or socially constructed. These positions tend to be intertwined with political standpoints. So, for example, Western feminists have tended to support a social constructionist view of gender difference (which is more amenable to seeing gendered relations as open to change), whereas conservatives and men's movement proponents are inclined to see gendered behaviour as due to inevitable biological differences, which render efforts to alter such behaviour misguided and/or pernicious (see Francis and Skelton, 2005, for elaboration).[1] I shall briefly discuss some of the key theoretical positions that support these perspectives, as well as the criticisms directed at each.

Perspective 1: innate difference

The view that the sexes are 'just naturally different' can be found across disciplines, including within feminism (some radical and *differance* feminists have supported this idea, often maintaining that women's biological differences from men and ensuing behaviors should be celebrated). However, as perspectives in their own right, and particularly in their application to educational theory, evolutionary psychology and related 'brain difference' theories stand out in their determinist stance on sex/gender.

Evolutionary psychologists see gender differences in behavior as reflecting innate sex differences that were configured during prehistory. In this view, our human (gendered) capacities and behaviors were developed according to Darwin's principle of the 'survival of the fittest' to best ensure the survival and propagation of the human race – and contemporary gendered behavioural trends can be explained in these terms. Hence we are predestined to gendered expressions of behavior, which are fixed and inevitable. These theories have been applied particularly commonly to aspects of sexuality, to argue that present-day trends in women's and men's sexual behavior can be explained as the result of men and women having evolved different reproductive strategies (e.g. Buss, 1994; Wright, 1994; Birkhead, 2001).

However, many biologists and neuroscientists (as well as social scientists) have been extremely critical of the evolutionary psychology approach. Steven Rose, for example, rejects the evolutionary psychology view of a fixed 'architecture' of the (gendered) human brain, and famously accuses evolutionary psychologists of having 'a Flintstones view' of the human past based on 'endless speculation' (cited in Hill, 2000). Rose (2001) maintains that evolutionary psychologists ignore plausible social and local explanations for the phenomena they discuss due to their (political) project of seeking adaptionist explanations for all social occurrences.

Proponents of 'brain difference' theories cite research examining brain activity and structure, maintaining that such activities are gendered, and that this in turn reflects the inherent nature of gender differences. Typically, it is noted that the corpus callosum (the bundle of nerves that links the two sides of the brain) tends to be thinner in boys, apparently limiting the communication between the two cerebral hemispheres. This, brain difference theorists maintain, is why men often respond to certain problems by using only one side of their brain, while women tend to use both sides. This difference is seen to be manifested in men taking a linear approach to problem solving, and women taking a more holistic approach; and also to be expressed by developmental differences such as girls learning to talk sooner. These suppositions are then extended to explain phenomena such as women predominating in the humanities and communications subjects, and men in the sciences, or to argue that males and females have different ways of learning (e.g. Gurian, 2002).

Yet, as Browne (2004) and Whitehead (2002) discuss, findings on 'gendered' brain activity are not nearly so consistent or conclusive as is often implied by those evoking them. Even a proponent of gendered patterns, Baron-Cohen (2004), asserts that the diversity across genders is just as significant as comparative patterns. Studies of the brain are in their relative infancy, and no one can yet be sure what impact brain differences have, or the ways in which they are manifested (Rose and Rose, 2001). Further, neuroscientific evidence has shown that the brain develops through social interaction, and as a result of environmental/circumstantial factors (e.g. Karmiloff-Smith, 2001; Gerhardt, 2004) such findings contest the views of 'brain difference' theorists who see brain differences between the sexes as natural and unalterable. Such studies suggest that any brain differences between men and women may be at least partially caused by their different experiences (Paechter, 1998).

Perspective 2: difference as socially constructed

In contrast to those approaches that see gendered expressions of behavior as inevitable and 'natural', there have been theorists who point to the role of the social in producing such behaviors. Many 'first-wave' feminists pointed to the role of socio-economic practices and expectations embedded in the legal system and in social conventions and institutions as constraining women's lives and behaviour (e.g. Wollstonecraft, 1985[1792]). Education was seen as having a central role to play in perpetuating these inequities – both in terms of access (for example, female exclusion from educational sectors such as higher education, and from access to certain curriculum subjects), and form (e.g. the sorts of subjects girls were taught; teaching methods and expectations).

'Second-wave' feminists frequently drew on 'sex role' perspectives to explain gender relations. Social learning theory explained gender identity as learned by children via social institutions such as family, school, the mass media, and so on (Sharpe, 1976; Stanworth, 1981). An alternative view was forwarded by cognitive-development theorists, who suggested that children's understanding of their gender identity depended upon their stage of cognitive development (Kohlberg, 1966; Emmerich *et al.,* 1977). Both these perspectives saw gender identity as connected to social learning and perception, and as potentially shifting, rather than as inherent. However, these 'sex role' theories have been criticised for not being able to account adequately for social change, and for presenting individuals as passive recipients of socialization.

Social constructionist analysts of gender have been less open to accusations of determinism due to their concern with contradiction and change – social constructionists attend to nuance, and microaspects of local interactions. Many social constructionists see individuals as biologically sexed, with consequences flowing from this bodily difference in terms of the way others interact with them (for example, that others have different expectations of individuals and approach them in different ways depending on their apparent ascribed sex; see, for example, Oakley, 1972; Paechter, 2006). In this way, gender differences in behavior and experience are perpetuated. Other social constructionists go further, seeing biological sex itself as socially constructed (e.g Kessler and McKenna, 1978, 1997; Davies, 1989; Butler, 1990, 1997). This is particularly the case for those influenced by post-structuralism.

Post-structuralism has appealed to many feminists for a number of reasons (for discussion, see Fraser and Nicholson, 1990; Ramazanoglu, 1993; Francis, 1999). Foucault's explanation of power as operating through discourses[2] was able to clarify the phenomena of resistance and contradiction which had proved so problematic for sex role theory, due to sex role theory's aforementioned tendency to present selves as fixed recipients of socialization via which social relations are reproduced. It also enabled the untangling of some of the theoretical complexities that had challenged feminism in the 1980s, such as the way in which power is constituted between women (and between men), as well as between women and men (e.g. hooks, 1982; Hill-Collins, 1991; Mirza, 1997). Foucault's theorization of people as positioned in and produced by discourse can also explain the gendered nature of society as produced by gender discourses that position all selves as men or women, and present these categories as relational (Davies, 1989). In this view, 'maleness' and 'femaleness' are simply produced by discourse; sex itself is socially/discursively constructed (Butler, 1990; 1997). Therefore, some feminists argue that the terms 'women' and 'girl' are misleading and redundant, implying a fixity and homogeneity that do not exist.

That gendered behavior is to some extent socially constructed is irrefutable, given that these behaviors, and those assigned appropriate to one gender or the other, vary between cultures and historic periods. However, as we saw above, many commentators believe that gendered behavior is to some extent grounded in innate difference. And just as social constructionists critique socio-biologists and evolutionary psychologists for applying a sex-determinist view even to phenomena that could have social explanations, so the latter group accuse social constructionists of political reasons for attributing such phenomena to the social (e.g. Hoff-Sommers, 2000; Gurian, 2002). These commentators point to the constancy of sex/gender as a factor of delineation across cultures to support their stance.

PROBLEMATIZING SEX/GENDER CATEGORIES

So we have seen the ways in which theorists have explained trends in behavior according to sex/gender. But what of the category itself? In analysing social relations, feminists in the 1960s and 1970s began by analysing 'sex' as a variable, or analysing human behavior according to apparent sex difference. However, there were problems with this approach. Not everyone is clearly identifiable by sex. As researchers from Kessler and McKenna (1978) to Butler (1990) have observed, not everyone falls easily into the categories of 'male' or 'female', for a variety of reasons. Yet despite this, sex is usually assumed to be an unproblematic, straightforward, 'common-sense' categorization. And as we have seen, it is a common presumption that inherent, 'natural' gender differences in behavior result directly (and inevitably) from biological sex (Hawkesworth, 1997). Such essentialist connotations rendered the use of 'sex' as an analytical category uncomfortable for many feminists.

An apparent solution to this problematic terminology emerged when the concept of *gender* was appropriated from linguistics for sociological use by Anne Oakley in the 1970s (Oakley, 1972). The word 'gender' has been used to describe and analyse the behaviors resulting from sex identification, from a social constructionist or social-learning perspective. Those using the term 'gender', then, did so in order to indicate that differences in behaviour according to sex/gender identification were a social, rather than biologically driven, phenomenon.

The terms 'male' and 'female' (relating to biological sex) have largely been replaced, then, with 'masculinity' and 'femininity' (relating to gender) in feminist and profeminist discussions of human behaviour. In recent years, attention has been drawn to the ways in which the individuals constituting the groups referred to as 'women/girls' and 'men/boys' have different ethnic, social class, religious and sexual identities, as well as different characteristics traditionally attributed to 'personality', such as charisma, and confidence. This recognition of diversity, and the impact of multiple factors of identity on the socially constructed self, has led many researchers of gender identity to refer to 'masculinities' and 'femininities' in plural (rather than to 'masculinity' and 'femininity'), in order to reflect the different ways in which masculinity and femininity are constructed or performed by different individuals (see the influential work of R.W. Connell, 1995, for discussion).

However, this plural terminology has been criticized by some for evoking typologies, directly or by suggestion (MacInnes, 1998; Francis, 2000; Whitehead, 2000). In education, it has indeed been the case that some researchers have listed various 'types' of masculinity or femininity as being manifested among pupils (e.g. Mac an Ghaill, 1994; Sewell, 1997). Elsewhere I have argued that a notion of different categories of masculinity or femininity, often with a 'hegemonic masculinity/ femininity' at the top of a hierarchy, and other forms of masculinity or femininity below (e.g. Connell, 1995), suggests something more fixed than is the case (Francis, 2000). Work with pupils from minority ethnic groups illustrates that performances of gender by these pupils do not constitute 'a different sort of masculinity/ femininity' according to ethnicity – the construction of gender as relational (and the feminine as subjugated) holds across ethnic groups, but the behaviors deemed acceptable according to gender differ according to ethnicity. Hence minority ethnic pupils have different discursive resources available to them, and are also positioned differently in Western gender discourses (Archer, 2003; Archer and Francis, 2005; Francis and Archer, 2005). As Kerfoot and Whitehead (2000) point out, the notion of multiple masculinities and femininities, including hegemonic gender models, seems to reify gender as something stable that can be dissected and categorized.

A further problem is that the application of 'masculinities' and femininities' categories appears to be based on a conflation of 'sex' and 'gender' which underpins much work adopting 'gender' as a concept (Francis, 2002). As MacInnes (1998) observes, in the literature it only ever appears to be *boys* that fit, or are described as performing, the various categories of masculinity; and girls the various types of femininity. MacInnes (1998) asks why, if gender is purely notional and socially constructed, girls are rarely described as having masculine characteristics, or expressing one of the 'types' of masculinity, and vice versa? Hood-Williams (1999) was a leading British critic of what he saw as 'theoretical slippage' between sex and gender. He agrees with MacInnes that, in the literature on gendered behavior, it is always males who 'do' masculinity(ies), and girls who perform 'femininities'. If gender is relational, just as a lack of masculinity denotes femininity, a lack of femininity must denote masculinity. Yet women and girls are rarely described as constructing their masculinity or behaving in masculine ways, and vice versa (see also Halberstam, 1998; Francis, 2000). So people's performance of 'gender' appears intractably connected to their 'sex' in this literature. Hood-Williams expresses his key argument thus:

> The paradox is this: in sex/gender two contradictory notions are in place. The first is that sex determines gender. It is for this reason that it is men and only men that are always masculine. … But if sex determines gender what is the point of the concept of gender? If gender is always collapsing back onto sex why not just talk sex? The second is that sex does not determine gender; gender is a social construction [… But …] What would gender be 'about' if it flew off and left sex behind? Where would be the maleness of masculinity? The paradox is that gender must be, and cannot be, determined by sex. Neither makes sense.
>
> (1999: 861)

There are, of course, other criticisms of the concept of 'gender' and its application. MacInnes (1998) maintains there is no 'gender' at all, only sex difference, which is having less and less effect on life outcomes as we are less prey to biology (hence MacInnes predicts 'the end of gender/sex' as a relevant category). Paechter (2006) argues that the division of sex (biological) and gender (social) evokes a dualism that is unrepresentative of the lived reality and experience of the sexed body. Hence she maintains that the (sexed) body necessarily holistically affects social experience and behavior ('gender'), and hence that educational researchers must acknowledge and attend to the impact of the body in education (Paechter, 2006). Judith Butler (1990) maintains a completely different interpretation, agreeing with MacInnes that there is no distinction between sex and gender, but seeing the category as purely socially constructed, rather than located in physical sex. Like earlier researchers (e.g. Kessler and McKenna, 1978), Butler (1990) argues that the dualism of sex (male/female) is false, and that many people cannot obviously be identified or classed as male or female via traditional classifications. She maintains that sex itself is performative. There is no real 'essence' of gender/sex; rather, it is the various *acts* of gendered behaviour that perpetuate the notion of gender/sex; The categories 'male'/'female' are illusory constructions.

This theoretical conundrum remains central to feminist research. As Hawkesworth (1997) observes, application of a model where gender is seen as in some way tied to, or resulting from, reproductive sex organs (what she calls the 'base/superstructure' model) impedes feminism because it perpetuates biological determinism. In this way, 'the ideology of procreation' (Hawkesworth: 663) seeps back into feminist theory, preventing escape from essentialist accounts of behavioral difference between men and women as linked to inherent, dualistic biological differences (and hence inevitable and inescapable).

Hawkesworth's (1997) critique of various treatises on gender was in turn attacked by Scott (1997) for being unhelpfully critical, and for seeking to impose an impossible and undesirable unity and conformity on feminist theory by erasing all paradox and contradiction. This defence of the problematic and/or contradictory is reminiscent of Davies' (1997) desire of 'having her cake and eating it too' in terms of feminist theorizing. Yet, although it is futile and erroneous to maintain that there should be a single, unitary feminist approach, I believe that to embrace complete incoherence risks fragmenting and undermining the feminist theoretical project (Francis, 1999). Analyzing the conflation of sex and gender (and attempting to move the debate forward) is also particularly important for other reasons. One is the point made earlier, that such conflation links us to a biological essentialism that social-constructionist feminists would seek to avoid. Moreover, because females behaving in non-traditional ways are rarely conceived as 'doing masculinity', and males behaving in non-traditional ways are not perceived to be 'doing femininity' (as a consequence of this conflation between sex and gender), it tends to be the gender-*traditional* behaviour of males and females which gets seized upon and analyzed by researchers of gender and behavior. This may over-represent and reify gender difference, rather than deconstruct it (Francis, 2000; Skelton and Francis, 2002). In this way, such work could serve to support, rather than undermine, popular gender discourses based on notions of 'natural' difference.

REFLECTIONS FOR GENDER RESEARCH IN EDUCATION

If gender is socially constructed rather than inherent, gendered traits are not tied to biological sex (Butler, 1990; MacInnes, 1998). It follows that girls/women can and do behave in 'masculine' ways, and males in 'feminine' ways (see Halberstam, 1998; Mendick, 2005). The reluctance of feminist researchers to label certain behaviours in girls as 'masculine', and certain behaviours in boys as 'feminine' has some understandable explanations (Skelton and Francis, 2002). For one thing, branding behavior such as aggression as 'masculine' and passivity as 'feminine' might be seen to reify what are shaky and contested characteristics of either gender (for example, not everyone might agree that passivity is feminine: interpretation might vary somewhat between cultures, social classes, generations, etc. Further, behavior tends to be interpreted in gendered ways according to the ascribed sex of the subject concerned – what might be read as aggression in a man might be read as manipulativeness/bitchiness in a woman). For another, such identification of behavior with the opposite gender can seem perniciously stereotyping. For example, Hill-Collins (1990) and Wright *et al.* (2000: 87) have argued that the equation of the assertive behaviors of some Black girls with masculinity 'reinforces specific "controlling images" of Black women as "non-feminine"' (Collins, 1990). And it can seem plain offensive to call a girl masculine, or a boy feminine, due to our own deeply held constructions of gender difference (Francis, 2000). Yet, arguably, we ought to be reflecting on and challenging such constructions.

A further problem that emerges is how to analyze gendered classroom behavior without reference to 'girls' and 'boys' that evokes their biological sex category (Jones, 1993). One approach is to see this categorization as to do with pupils' sex/gender identification, which is socially constructed (Mendick, 2005). The argument that in the vast majority of cases this self-identification will correspond with biological genitalia can be countered by the point that this sex duality is in itself socially constructed (Butler, 1990; 1997), and that in any case the exceptions deconstruct the ability to generalize confidently. On the other hand, what is more problematic for education researchers is that, in actuality, it is usually we researchers, rather than respondents, who categorize children according to gender. And indeed the education system freely and pervasively categorizes pupils as boys and girls, making it difficult for pupils to resist such identification within an education context.

Arguably, the challenge for us as educational researchers is to reflect carefully on these issues in relation to our own practices, and to take up Halberstam's (1998) invitation to extend her work on 'female masculinity' (and male femininity) into the education environment. Doing so will require close analysis and reflection on the social construction of behavioural expressions (such as aggression and manipulation) as gendered. And in analyzing such non-gender-traditional behavior, researchers will need to be attuned to the costs and consequences of such behaviors in an educational environment. As Walkerdine (1990) eloquently argues, the psychic pain and labour involved in taking up the position of 'the Other' are extensive. We know that it can be hard and costly for boys and girls to take up their traditional gender positions – stultifying free expression, violently suppressing one's emotions (boys), the self-violence of passivity (girls). Yet how much harder to stand against the tide and display behaviors traditionally associated with the opposite sex, when all our own self-development and the societal apparatuses and discourses have been driving us toward the construction of a gender-appropriate identity and the behaviors that delineate this? Walkerdine (1990) and Walkerdine *et al.*'s (2001) work demonstrates the psychic and emotional costs in adopting the position of the Other, and that of Davies (1989) and Reay (2002) demonstrate poignantly the danger of marginalisation and bullying that non-gender-traditional classroom behaviour can provoke for children. They allude to harrowing examples of the marginalization and rejection of pupils due to their inability/refusal to conform to 'normal' gender codes. Perhaps this is another reason researchers have tended to avoid the labelling of non-feminine behaviour as 'masculine' and vice versa – we are instinctively wary of the shadow of pathologization (Skelton and Francis, 2002). But, conversely, these examples highlight the imperative that we pursue these conundrums further in order to enable more precise and inclusive theorization of gendered constructions of identity.

REFERENCES

Archer, L (2003) *Race, masculinity and schooling.* Buckingham: Open University Press.

Archer, L and Francis, B (2005) They never go off the rails like other groups: teachers' constructions of British-Chinese pupils' gender identities and approaches to learning. *British Journal of Sociology of Education*, 26: 165–82.

Baron-Cohen, S (2004) *The essential difference.* London: Penguin.

Birkhead, T (2001) *Promiscuity: an evolutionary history of desire*. Cambridge: Harvard University Press.

Browne, N (2004) *Gender equity in the early years*. Maidenhead: McGraw-Hill/Open University Press.

Buss, D (1994) *Evolution of desire: strategies for human mating*. New York: Basic Books.

Butler, J (1990) *Gender trouble*. New York: Routledge.

Butler, J (1997) Performative acts and gender constitution, In Conboy K, Medina N and Stanbury S (eds) *Writing on the body: female embodiment and feminist theory*. New York: Columbia University Press.

Cealey Harrison, W and Hood-Williams, J (1998) More varieties than Heinz: social categories and sociality in Humphreys, Hammersley and beyond. *Sociological Research Online*, 3(1): www.socresonline.org.uk/socresonline/3/1/8.html.

Connell R (1987) *Gender and power*. Cambridge: Polity Press.

Connell R (1995) *Masculinities*. Cambridge: Polity Press.

Davies, B (1989) *Frogs and snails and feminist tales*. Sydney: Allen & Unwin.

Davies, B (1997) The subject of post-structuralism: a reply to Alison Jones. *Gender and Education*, 9: 271–83.

Delphy, C and Leonard, D (1992) *Familiar exploitation*. Cambridge: Polity Press.

Emmerich, W, Goldman, S, Kirsh, B and Sharabany, R (1977) Evidence for a transitional phase in the development of 'gender constancy'. *Child Development*, 48: 930–6.

Foucault, M (1980) *Power/knowledge: selected interviews and other writings, 1972–1977*. New York: Pantheon.

Francis, B (1999) Modernist reductionism or post-modernist relativism: can we move on? *Gender and Education*, 11: 381–94.

Francis, B (2000) *Boys, girls and achievement: addressing the classroom issues*. London: Routledge.

Francis, B (2002) Relativism, realism, and reader-response criticism: an analysis of some theoretical tensions in research on gender identity. *Journal of Gender Studies*, 11: 39–54.

Francis, B and Archer, L (2005) Negotiating the dichotomy between boffin and triad: British-Chinese constructions of 'laddism'. *Sociological Review*, 17: 495–522.

Francis, B and Skelton, C (2005) *Reassessing gender and achievement*. London: Routledge.

Fraser, N (1995) From redistribution to recognition? Dilemmas of justice in a post-socialist age. *New Left Review*, 212: 68–93.

Fraser, N and Nicholson, L (1990) Social criticism without philosophy: an encounter between feminism and postmodernism, in Nicholson L (ed) *Feminism/postmodernism*. London: Routledge.

Gerhardt, S (2004) *Why love matters: how affection shapes a baby's brain*. London: Routledge.

Gurian, M (2002) *Boys and girls learn differently!* San Francisco, CA: Jossey Bass.

Halberstam, J (1998) *Female masculinity*. Durham, NC: Duke University Press.

Hawkesworth, M (1997) Confounding gender. *Signs*, 22:670–685.

Hill, D (2000) Back to the Stone Age. *Observer Review*, 27 Feb 2000: 1.

Hill-Collins, P (1991) *Black feminist thought*. New York: Routledge.

Hoff-Sommers, C (2000) *The war against boys (how misguided feminism is harming our young men)*. New York: Simon & Schuster.

Hood-Williams, J (1998) Stories for sexual difference. *British Journal of Sociology of Education*, 18: 81–99.

Hood-Williams, J (1999) Book review: 'The end of masculinity'. *Sociological Review*, 46: 860–3.

hooks, b (1982) *Ain't I a woman?* London: Pluto Press.

Jones, A (1993) Becoming a 'girl': poststructuralist suggestions for educational research. *Gender and Education*, 9: 261–9.

Karmiloff-Smith, A (2001) Why babies' brains are not Swiss army knives, in Rose H and Rose S (eds) *Alas poor Darwin: arguments against evolutionary psychology*. London: Vintage.

Kerfoot, D and Whitehead, S (2000) Keeping all the balls in the air: further education and the masculine/managerial subject. *Journal of Further and Higher Education*, 24: 436–57.

Kessler, S and McKenna, W (1978) *Gender: an ethnomethodological approach*. Chicago: University of Chicago.

Kohlberg, L (1966) A cognitive developmental analysis of children's sex-role concepts and attitudes, in Maccoby E (ed) *The development of sex differences*. Stanford, CA: Stanford University Press.

Mac an Ghall, M (1994) *The making of men*. Buckingham: Open University Press.

MacInnes, J (1998) *The end of masculinity*. Buckingham: Open University Press.

McKenna, W and Kessler, S (1997) Comment on Hawkesworth's 'Confounding gender': who needs theory? *Signs*, 22: 687–91.

McNay, L (2000) *Gender and agency*. Cambridge: Polity.

Mendick, H (2005) A beautiful myth? The gendering of being/doing 'good at maths'. *Gender and Education*, 17: 205–19.

Mirza, H (ed) (1997) *Black British feminism*. London: Routledge.

Oakley, A (1972) *Sex, gender and society*. London: Temple Smith.

Paechter, C (1998) *Educating the Other*. London: Falmer.

Paechter, C (2006) Reconceptualizing the gendered body: learning and constructing masculinities and femininities in school, *Gender and Education*, 18: 121–35.

Parsons, T (1956) The American family: its relations to personality and to the social structure, in Parsons T and Bales R (eds) *Family: socialisation and interaction process*. London: Routledge & Kegan Paul.

Pinker, S (1994) *The language instinct*. New York: William Morrow.

Ramazanoglu, C (ed) (1993) *Up against Foucault*. London: Routledge.

Reay, D (2002) Shaun's story: troubling discourses of white working-class masculinities. *Gender and Education*, 14: 221–33.

Rose, H and Rose, S (2001) Introduction, in Rose H and Rose S (eds) *Alas poor Darwin: arguments against evolutionary psychology*. London: Vintage.

Rose, S (2001) Escaping evolutionary psychology, in Rose H and Rose S (eds) *Alas poor Darwin: arguments against evolutionary psychology*. London: Vintage.

Scott, J (1997) Comment on Hawkesworth's 'Confounding gender'. *Signs,* 22: 697–702.

Sewell, T (1997) *Black masculinities and schooling*. Stoke-on-Trent: Trentham.

Sharpe, S (1976) *Just like a girl*. Harmondsworth: Penguin.

Skelton, C and Francis, B (2002) Clever Jack and conscientious Chloe: naturally able boys and hardworking girls in the classroom. Paper presented at the British Educational Research Association Annual Conference, University of Exeter.

Stanworth, M (1981) *Gender and schooling*. London: Hutchinson.

Walkerdine, V (1990) *Schoolgirl fictions*. London: Verso.

Walkerdine, V, Lucey, H and Melody, J (2001) *Growing up girl*. London: Virago.

Whitehead, S (1999) Masculinity: shutting out the nasty bits. *Gender, Work and Organisation*, 7: 133–7.

Whitehead, S (2002) *Men and masculinities*. Cambridge: Polity.

Wollstonecraft, M (1985 [1792]) *Vindication of the rights of women*. London: Penguin.

Wright, C, Weekes, D and McGlaughlin, A (2000) *'Race', class and gender in exclusion from school*. London: Falmer.

Wright, R (1994) *The moral animal: why we are the way we are*. New York: Pantheon.

NOTES

1. Of course, not all analyses of gendered behavior take a position on 'where gender comes from', as some approaches simply comment on existing social relations without necessarily exploring origins. An example would be functionalist analysis. Functionalist sociologists such as Talcott Parsons (1956) argued that the different roles of men and women (men as 'breadwinners'; women as homemakers) are complementary, and are perpetuated because they are the most effective way to ensure the social and economic functioning of society. (This male-centric and socially classed view was roundly critiqued by feminists in the 1960s and 1970s.)

2. Foucault (1980) does not see power as a possession to be held by one group at the expense of others, but rather as borne by 'discourses' (textual narratives which present and produce the word and selves in particular ways). In this way, selves may be positioned and repositioned in discursive relations, sometimes as powerful, and sometimes as powerless. And as well as being positioned in discourses, selves may also be active in discursively positioning others.

Understanding Men: Gender Sociology and the New International Research on Masculinities[1]

R.W. Connell

INTRODUCTION: DEBATES ABOUT MEN AND BOYS

In the last decade, there has been an upsurge of concern with issues about men and boys. In the public realm, there have been social movements focused on the reform or restoration of masculinity, such as the 'mythopoetic' movement, the Million Man March and the Promise Keepers (Messner, 1997). In education, there has been much talk of boys' 'failure' in school and the need for special programs for boys (Connell, 1996; Gilbert and Gilbert, 1998). In health, there has been increasing debate about men's health and illness (Sabo and Gordon, 1995; Schofield *et al.*, 2000). A popular therapeutic movement addresses men's problems in relationships, sexuality and identity.

In a way, this is surprising, because men remain the principal holders of economic and political power. Men make up a large majority of corporate executives, top professionals, and holders of public office. Worldwide, men held 93% of cabinet-level posts in 1996, and most top positions in international agencies (Gierycz, 1999). Men continue to control most technology and most weaponry; with only limited exceptions, it is men who staff and control the agencies of force such as armies, police and judicial systems.

This used to be thought 'natural', either prescribed by God or a consequence of biology. Essentialist views of gender are still popular, and are constantly reinforced in the media. However, they are increasingly under challenge, not only in biology (Fausto-Sterling, 1992), but also in everyday life. The rise of the women's liberation movement, and the many feminisms that have followed on from it, produced a massive disturbance in the gender system and people's assumptions about gender.

Questions about men are inevitable, once this disturbance began, because gender is a living system of social interactions, not a stack of watertight boxes. What affects the social position of women and girls must also affect the social position of men and boys. Large numbers of men now acknowledge that their position is under *challenge*, that what they once took for granted about must be rethought. They may or may not like it, but they cannot ignore it.

NEW SOCIAL RESEARCH

This cultural disturbance about gender and the position of men has given impetus to the social-scientific work on masculinities that has been accelerating since the mid-1980s.

Realization that masculinities are socially constructed goes back to early psychoanalysis, and in the social sciences first took the shape of a social-psychological concept, the 'male sex role'. The 'role' approach emphasized the learning of norms for conduct, and has been popular in applied areas like education and health. But sex role theory is inadequate for understanding diversity in masculinities, and for understanding the power and economic dimension in gender (Connell, 1987). Accordingly, recent research on men and masculinities has moved beyond the abstractions of the 'sex role' approach to a more concrete examination of how gender patterns are constructed and practised.

'Constructionist' research has used a range of social-scientific methods to explore the situationally formed gender identities, practices and representations of men and boys. The studies range from quantitative surveys (Metz-Göckel and Müller, 1985; Zulehner and Volz, 1999) to close-focus ethnographies (Klein, 1993), life-history studies (Messner, 1992; Messerschmidt, 1999), and studies of organizations (Collinson *et al.*, 1990) and cultural forms such as films, novels and plays (Buchbinder, 1998).

While most of the research has been done in those countries which account for the bulk of social-science research — the USA, Britain and Germany — concern with these issues has spread far beyond the metropole. Two semiperipheral regions — Scandinavia and Australasia — have been fertile in ideas and research on masculinity (Holter and Aarseth, 1993; Donaldson and Tomsen, 1998; Law *et al.*, 1999). Research on men and patriarchy is building up in South Africa, following the end of apartheid (Morrell, 1998). Critiques of traditional patterns of masculinity have developed in Japan (Nakamura, 1994), where a men's center with a reform agenda has recently been established. Issues about men, sexuality and fatherhood have been debated and researched in Brazil (Arilha *et al.*, 1998).

Discussions of these questions have now moved into international forums. In 1997, UNESCO sponsored a conference on masculinity, violence and peacemaking, which drew participants from Russia and the rest of Eastern Europe as well as other parts of the world (Breines *et al.*, 2000). In 1998, FLACSO convened a conference on research and activism about masculinities across Latin America and the Caribbean (Valdés and Olavarría, 1998). An International Association for Studies of Men has been established. The *IASOM Newsletter*, and journals such as *Men and Masculinities* now serve as forums for international research.

SIGNIFICANT CONCLUSIONS

We now have a growing library of studies from around the world, across a number of the social sciences, in which researchers have traced the construction of masculinity in a particular milieu or moment. They include studies of marital sexuality, homophobic murders, a body-building gym, street gangs, a clergyman's family, an insurance office, a high school, a film, a political movement, professional sports, a police station, a literary genre, and a media debate (Cornwall and Lindisfarne, 1994; Connell, 2000). I call this the 'ethnographic moment' in masculinity research, in which the local and specific is emphasized.

Though each study is different, there are many common themes. Some of the most important findings of this research may be summarized in the following six theses.

Multiple masculinities

Historians and anthropologists have shown that there is no one pattern of masculinity that is found everywhere. Different cultures, and different periods of history, construct masculinity differently. For instance, some cultures make heroes of soldiers, and regard violence as the ultimate test of masculinity; others look at soldiering with disdain and regard violence as contemptible. Some cultures regard homosexual sex as incompatible with true masculinity; others think no one can be a real man without having had homosexual relationships.

It follows that in large-scale, multicultural societies there are likely to be multiple definitions of masculinity. Sociological research shows this to be true. There are, for instance, differences in the expression of masculinity between Latino and Anglo men in the USA, and between Greek or Lebanese and Anglo boys in Australia. The meaning of masculinity in working-class life is different from the meaning in middle-class life, not to mention among the very rich and the very poor.

Equally important, more than one kind of masculinity can be found within a given cultural setting. Within any workplace, neighborhood or peer group, there are likely to be different understandings of masculinity and different ways of 'doing' masculinity. In the urban middle class, for instance, there is a version of masculinity organized around dominance (e.g. emphasizing 'leadership' in management), and another version organized around expertise (e.g. emphasizing 'professionalism' and technical knowledge). Recent German discussions have spoken of 'multi-optional masculinities' to emphasize the potential diversity (*Widersprüche,* 1998).

Hierarchy and hegemony

Different masculinities do not sit side-by-side like dishes in a smorgasbord; there are definite relations between them. Typically, some masculinities are more honored than others. Some may be actively dishonored; for example, homosexual masculinities in modern Western culture. Some are socially marginalized; for example, the masculinities of disempowered ethnic minorities. Some are exemplary, taken as symbolizing admired traits; for example, the masculinities of sporting heroes.

The form of masculinity which is culturally dominant in a given setting is called 'hegemonic masculinity'. 'Hegemonic' signifies a position of cultural authority and leadership, not total dominance; other forms of masculinity persist alongside. The hegemonic form need not be the most common form of masculinity. (This is familiar in school peer groups, for instance, where a small number of highly influential boys are admired by many others who cannot reproduce their performance.) Hegemonic masculinity is, however, highly visible. It is likely to be what casual commentators have noticed when they speak of 'the male role'.

Hegemonic masculinity is hegemonic not just in relation to other masculinities, but in relation to the gender order as a whole. It is an expression of the privilege men collectively have over women. The hierarchy of masculinities is an expression of the unequal shares in that privilege held by different groups of men.

Collective masculinities

The gender structures of a society define particular patterns of conduct as 'masculine' and others as 'feminine'. At one level, these patterns characterize individuals. Thus, we say that a particular man (or woman) is masculine, or behaves in a masculine way. But these patterns also exist at the collective level. Masculinities are defined and sustained in institutions, such as corporations, armies and governments – or schools (for a striking example in educational research, see Mac an Ghaill, 1994). Masculinities are defined collectively in the workplace, as shown in industrial research; and in informal groups like street gangs, as shown in criminological research.

Masculinity also exists impersonally in culture. Video games, for instance, not only circulate stereotyped images of violent masculinity, but they also require the player to enact this masculinity (symbolically) in order to play the game at all. Sociological research on sport has shown how an aggressive masculinity is created organizationally by the structure of organized sport, by its pattern of competition, its system of training and its steep hierarchy of levels and rewards. Images of this masculinity are circulated on an enormous scale by sports media, although most individuals fit very imperfectly into the slots thus created.

Active construction

Masculinities do not exist prior to social behavior, either as bodily states or fixed personalities. Rather, masculinities come into existence as people act. They are accomplished in everyday conduct or organizational life, as patterns of social practice.

Close-focus research has shown how we 'do gender' in everyday life; for instance, in the way we conduct conversations. A similar insight has thrown new light on the link between masculinity and crime. This is not a product of a fixed masculine character being expressed through crime. Rather, the link results from a variety of men — from impoverished youth gangs on the street to white-collar criminals at the computer — using crime as a resource to construct particular masculinities.

Masculinities, it appears, are far from settled. From bodybuilders in the gym, to managers in the boardroom, to boys in the elementary school playground, a great deal of effort goes into the making of conventional masculinities. And this is true also of nonconventional masculinities. Recent research on homosexual men shows that for these men, too, identity and relationships involve a complex and sustained effort of construction.

Internal complexity

One of the key reasons why masculinities are not settled is that they are not simple, homogeneous patterns. Close-focus research on gender, both in psycho-analysis and ethnography, often reveals contradictory desires and logics. A man's active heterosexuality may exist as a thin emotional layer concealing a deeper homosexual desire. A boy's identification with men may coexist or struggle with identifications with women. The public enactment of an exemplary masculinity may covertly require actions that undermine it. Close-focus research on men's sexuality (e.g. Dowsett, 1996) is a rich source of evidence on tension and contradiction. Masculinities may have multiple possibilities concealed within them.

The complexity of desires, emotions or possibilities may not be obvious at first glance. But the issue is important, because these complexities are sources of tension and change in gender patterns.

Dynamic

From the fact that different masculinities exist in different cultures and historical epochs, we can deduce that masculinities are able to change. In the layering of masculinities, we see one of the sources of change; and in the hierarchy of masculinities, we see one of the motives. Historians have traced changes in masculinity as struggles for hegemony; for instance, redefining patterns of managerial masculinity in British manufacturing industry as economic and technological change rearranged the balance of power (Roper, 1994).

To speak of the 'dynamics' of masculinity is to acknowledge that particular masculinities are composed, historically, and may also be de-composed, contested and replaced. There is an active politics of gender in everyday life. Sometimes it finds spectacular public expression in large-scale rallies or demonstrations. More often, it is local and limited. But there is always a process of contestation and change, and in some cases this becomes conscious and deliberate. This has happened, for instance, in the 'men's movements' of contemporary North America.

Compared with earlier understandings of men and masculinity, the 'ethnographic moment' has already had important intellectual fruits. This is not to say, however, that it is beyond criticism.

CRITIQUE AND NEW DIRECTIONS

Among the problems of masculinity research are problems of definition. Hearn (1996) has raised doubts about the usefulness of the concept of 'masculinities', and, more recently, (1998a) has spelt out the very diverse, and to some degree incompatible, positions that have been adopted in men's theorizing of men. Clatterbaugh (1998), working through definitions of 'masculinity', has found them mostly vague, circular, inconsistent, or in other ways unsatisfactory.

Hearn and Clatterbaugh are undoubtedly right: there are real difficulties in defining 'masculinity' or 'masculinities'. These terms are certainly used in inconsistent ways by different authors. They are often used in ways that imply a simplified and static notion of identity, or rest on a simplified and unrealistic notion of difference between men and women. Social science has put a lot of effort into mapping masculinities as actual patterns of conduct or representation. But in the language of the mythopoetic movement, 'masculinity' stands for an ideal existence of men, or a deep essence within men, set against the disappointing empirical reality – and this is a usage that seems to have had more resonance outside the academy.

Hearn and Clatterbaugh are both inclined to drop the concept of masculinities because they think the real object of concern is something else – 'men'. If, as Clatterbaugh (1998: 41) puts it, 'talking about men seems to be what we want to do' why bother to introduce the muddy concept of 'masculinities' at all?

But then, why would we talk about 'men' in the first place? To talk at all about a group called 'men' presupposes a distinction from and relation with another group, 'women'. That is to say, it presupposes an account of gender. And whichever conceptual language we use, we need some way of talking about men's and women's involvement in that domain of gender. We need some way of naming conduct which is oriented to or shaped by that domain, as distinct from conduct related to other patterns in social life. Hence the need for a concept of 'masculinities'.

Under the influence of Foucault, a school of gender researchers has studied how discourses ranging from medicine to fashion have classified, represented and helped to control human bodies, emphasizing how systems of knowledge function as part of an apparatus of power. The approach has been particularly fruitful in relation to sport, where the interweaving of cultural images of masculinity with the management and training of bodies has been powerfully effective (Rowe and McKay, 1998).

Foucault's work on power/knowledge is employed by Petersen (1998) and Star (1999) as the basis for a tilt at the whole basis of research and analysis on masculinity. Implausibly claiming that masculinity research neglects power (which is, in fact, a central theme in the field), Petersen more accurately argues that much of the discussion of masculinity smuggles in a kind of gender essentialism. Others too have noticed this: how the concept of 'hegemonic masculinity' tends to become a fixed personality type, something like the once-famous 'Type A personality'. Given this tendency, all the objectionable things men do − rape, assault, environmental degradation, dog-eat-dog business practices, etc. − can be loaded into the bag of 'hegemonic masculinity'. And the more extreme this image becomes, the less it has to be owned by the majority of men.

But the broader critique of masculinity research for assuming fixed identities, or stability in masculinity, is not accurate. Research on the social construction of masculinities has placed a good deal of emphasis on the uncertainties, difficulties and contradictions of the process (Messner, 1992; Thorne, 1993; Connell, 1995a). Whether the outcomes are stable or unstable, mostly fluid or mostly fixed, is surely an empirical question, not one to be settled in advance by theory. To adopt a view of gender as only performance, identities as inherently fragmented and shifting, is to lose a great deal. Butler (1990), the main proponent of a 'performative' account of gender, is strikingly unable to account for work, child care, institutional life, violence, resistance (except as individual choice) and material inequality. These are not trivial aspects of gender.

There are some cases, both in research and in practice (e.g. in work concerning domestic violence), where patterns of masculinity are quite tough and resistant to change (Ptacek, 1988). There are other situations where masculinities are unstable, or where commitment to a gender position is negotiable. In the innovative educational work of Davies (1993), for instance, the way people are positioned within discourses of gender is something that children in school can learn about, and can learn to change. It is possible to teach this skill, to develop classroom exercises where it becomes visible and discussable. In quite practical ways, Davies shows how both boys and girls can move into and out of a masculine identity or subject position.

Recognizing this possibility raises important questions about when, and why, people hold on to a certain subject position, adopt or reject the possibility of movement. The importance of material interests in accounting for men's gender conduct is forcibly argued by McMahon (1999) in a critique of journalistic, psychological and academic talk about the 'new man' and the 'new father'. Much of this talk turns out to be fantasy; most men have little interest in changing the patterns of child-care and housework.

The question of material interests and material practices has emerged in several recent contributions. Godenzi (2000), one of the few people to have offered a serious economic analysis of masculine practices, points to the diverse and sometimes indirect strategies by which men protect their interests in the face of challenges from women. Hearn (1996), like McMahon, emphasizes the material interests at play in gender practice, and raises the politically vital question of what mechanisms bind men together as a group. Hearn's (1998b) research on men's violence to women is an important example of how material practices – indeed, practices addressed to bodies – can be linked to the construction of meaning, the making of ideology. Holter (1997) presents a sophisticated 'social forms analysis', showing that gender, masculinity and femininity are historically specific features of social life. They arise not from a timeless dichotomy of bodies but from the specific course of development of the large-scale structures of modern society. The argument emphasizes the role of institutions – the family, and the workplace under industrial capitalism – as keys to the problems of gender.

But we cannot now speak of 'capitalism' without thinking of its global dimension, and this points to another important critique of research on masculinities. The 'ethnographic moment' has been wonderfully productive, but gender relations themselves are no longer local. The history of imperialism and globalization means that to understand specific masculinities we must look to large-scale contexts, ultimately to global contexts.

Moodie's (1994) superb study of black labor in South African gold mining provides a classic demonstration of this point. The Witwatersrand gold mines, products of colonial settlement financed by metropolitan capital, employed a large black labour force supervised by whites. Initially, most of these workers were peasant proprietors who migrated temporarily to the mining district, and used their wages to build up the resources to establish a peasant household. A particular pattern of masculinity was associated with this adjustment to the colonial economy, which gave a good deal of authority to the women back in the homeland, as economic partners, and allowed the custom of 'mine wives', that is, homosexual and domestic relations with younger miners, as part of the accepted life of mineworkers. By the 1970s, the old moral economy of the mines was breaking down. Peasant agriculture was becoming unviable, mining wages were rising, and a more urban workforce was recruited. The old pattern of black masculinity was now displaced by one associated with the process of proletarianization, and closer to the European-derived masculinity of the Afrikaner elite: vehemently heterosexual, more open to violence, treating women more as economic dependents, and more insistent on masculinity as bodily superiority.

What is shown in this specific case is broadly true. The development of global social structures has meant an interaction between the gender orders of colonizers and colonized, sometimes resulting in hybrid or novel gender patterns (Altman, 1996). Globalization has, further, created new institutions which operate on a world scale, and which provide new arenas for the construction of masculinities: transnational corporations, global markets, global media and intergovernmental institutions.

In these complex and large-scale social processes, new patterns of masculinity may emerge. I call these 'globalizing masculinities', appearing as they do on a global stage, oriented to a global gender order. Within the contemporary world gender order, the emerging hegemonic form seems to be a masculinity based in multinational corporations and international capital markets, which I call 'transnational business masculinity' (Connell, 1998).

Briefly, the most powerful group of men in the world are transnational businessmen and the politicians, bureaucrats and generals associated with them. The masculinities of these milieux are historically based on the bourgeois masculinities of the rich countries (Roper, 1994; Donaldson, 1998; Wajcman, 1999). But some new patterns seem to be emerging: a shift toward mobile career structures with very conditional loyalties, a personalized rather than dynastic approach to marriage, and the abandonment of commitments to social responsibility through the welfare state or corporate welfare.

While the embodiment of transnational business masculinity has yet to be studied in detail, two points leap to the eye. One is the immense augmentation of bodily powers by technology (air travel, computers, telecommunications), making this, to a certain extent, a 'cyborg' masculinity. The other is the extent to which international businessmen's bodily pleasures escape the social controls of local gender orders, as their business operations tend to escape the control of the national state; along with globalization of business has gone the rapid growth of an international prostitution industry.

USES OF SOCIAL RESEARCH ON MASCULINITIES

Social research is useful at three levels: increasing understanding, solving practical problems, and guiding long-term change.

A better understanding of masculinities and men's gender practices is worth having simply because gender is an important aspect of our lives. If we value living in knowledge rather than in ignorance, this is a significant subject for education, research and reflection. And if we are to think about it at all, we need to think about the whole of the gender equation and all the groups included in it. So there is a purely intellectual purpose for research that illuminates the lives of men and the forms and dynamics of masculinities.

There is also a hard practical purpose. Contemporary masculinities are implicated in a range of toxic effects. These include effects in the lives of men themselves: high levels of injury, such as those caused by road crashes (four times as high among young men as among young women, in Australia (Walker *et al.*, 2000); patterns of ill health and mortality resulting from poor diet, drug abuse and inadequate use of health services (Schofield *et al.*, 2000); high levels of victimization (men are the majority of victims of reported violence) and imprisonment (about 90% of prison inmates are men in countries like Australia and the USA); and patterns of conflict among men that easily lead to violence (Tomsen, 1997).

They also include toxic effects in the lives of others: rape and domestic violence against women, homophobic violence and racism (Tillner, 1997; Hearn, 1998). They include patterns which may link these two types of effects, such as closed horizons in education, that is, the rejection by many boys of humanities as areas of study, and of personal issues as topics of reflection (Martino, 1994).

In dealing with these problems at a practical level, one is constantly led beyond the immediate situation; for instance, a campaign against men's violence against women is led toward issues of prevention as well as immediate response (Hagemann-White, 1992). Research on masculinities may also be important in opening new possibilities in gender relations (Segal, 1997).

Research on the multiple forms of masculinity, for instance, may help people to recognize the diversity of masculinities, the open-ended possibilities in gender relations – and thus to see alternatives for their own lives. Here masculinity research fruitfully interacts with research on more democratic family forms and workplaces; for instance, Risman's (1998) study of 'fair families' in the USA.

Studies of men and masculinities may also help to identify men's interests in change. There have been two polar positions here: the idea that men share women's interest in changed gender relations, and the idea that men as the dominant group have no interest in change at all. The real position is more complex. Men as a group gain real and large advantages from the current system of gender relations; the scale of this 'patriarchal dividend' is indicated by the fact that men's earned incomes, worldwide, are about 180% of women's.

But some men pay a heavy price for living in the current system, as the observations just made on toxicity go to show. Particular men, or particular groups of men, share with certain women an interest in social safety, in prevention of discrimination, in more inclusive and less hierarchical economies. It is possible to define, for many issues, bases for coalitions for change.

Many people think that activism around issues of masculinity must follow the model of feminism; that it requires a general 'men's movement' mobilizing for gender reform. As I have argued in more detail elsewhere (Connell, 1995b), there are reasons why this model might not be appropriate. Given both the material interests of men, and the hierarchy of masculinities, the democratic reconstruction of the gender order is more likely to divide men than to unite them (in gender terms).

Yet there are many arenas where reform of men's gender practices can be undertaken with some chances of success. Health is an important case. It is possible to pursue men's health programs as part of a 'backlash', antifeminist politics, competing for funding with women's health initiatives. But it is also possible to pursue health issues for men in cooperation with women's health initiatives, creating coalitions around shared interests in reducing violence, alcoholism, road trauma and other toxic consequences of contemporary masculinities.

History is not a one-way street. Things can get worse, and in the growing gender disparities of the former communist countries, and the decline of the welfare state in the West, we see examples of decline, not advance, in gender equity. But a more democratic gender order is possible, and some groups of men are working toward it (Pease, 1997; Segal, 1997). If we are to realize democracy in the gender order, many men must share the burden, and the joy, of creating it.

REFERENCES

Altman, D (1996) Rupture or continuity? The internationalisation of gay identities. *Social Text*, 48: 77–94.
Arilha, M, Unbehaum Ridenti, SG and Medrado, B (eds) (1998) *Homens e masculinidades: outras palavras*. São Paulo: ECOS/Editora 34.
Breines, I, Connell, RW and Eide, I (eds) (2000) *Male roles and masculinities: a culture of peace perspective*. Paris: UNESCO.
Buchbinder, D (1998) *Performance anxieties: re-producing masculinity*. Sydney: Allen and Unwin.
Butler, J (1990) *Gender trouble: feminism and the subversion of identity*. New York: Routledge.
Clatterbaugh, K (1998) What is problematic about masculinities? *Men and Masculinities*, 1: 24–45.
Collinson, D, Knights, D and Collinson, M (1990) *Managing to discriminate*. London: Routledge.
Connell, RW (1987) *Gender and power*. Cambridge: Polity Press
Connell, RW (1995a). *Masculinities*. Cambridge: Polity Press.
Connell, RW (1995b) Politics of changing men. *Socialist Review*, 25: 135–59.
Connell, RW (1996) Teaching the boys: new research on masculinity, and gender strategies for schools. *Teachers College Record*, 98: 206–35.
Connell, RW (1998) Masculinities and globalization. *Men and Masculinities*, 1: 3-23.
Connell, RW (2000) *The men and the boys*. Berkeley, CA: University of California Press.
Cornwall, A and Lindisfarne, N (eds) (1994) *Dislocating masculinity: comparative ethnographies*. London: Routledge.
Davies, B (1993) *Shards of glass: children reading and writing beyond gendered identities*. Sydney: Allen & Unwin.
Donaldson, M (1998) The Masculinity of the hegemonic: growing up very rich. *Journal of Interdisciplinary Gender Studies*, 3: 95–112.
Donaldson, M and Tomsen, S (eds) (1998) Australian masculinities. Special issue of *Journal of Interdisciplinary Gender Studies*, 3 (2).
Dowsett, GW (1996) *Practicing desire: homosexual sex in the era of AIDS*. Stanford, CA: Stanford University Press.
Fausto-Sterling, A (1992) *Myths of gender: biological theories about women and men*. 2nd edn. New York: Basic Books.
Gierycz, D (1999) Women in decision-making: can we change the status quo?, in Breines, I Gierycz D and Reardon BA (eds) *Towards a women's agenda for a culture of peace*. Paris: UNESCO, 19–30.
Gilbert, R & Gilbert, P (1998) *Masculinity goes to school*. Sydney: Allen and Unwin.
Godenzi, A (2000) Determinants of culture: men and the economic power, in Breines, I Connell R and Eide I (eds) *Male roles and masculinities: a culture of peace perspective*. Paris: UNESCO.
Hagemann-White, C (1992) *Strategien gegen Gewalt im Geschlechterverhaeltnis: Bestandsanalyse und Perspektiven*. Pfaffenweiler: Centaurus-Verl.-Ges.

Hearn, J (1996) Is masculinity dead? A critique of the concept of masculinity/masculinities, in Mac an Ghaill, M (ed) *Understanding masculinities.* Buckingham: Open University Press.

Hearn, J (1998a) Theorizing men and men's theorizing: varieties of discursive practices in men's theorizing of men. *Theory and Society,* 27: 781–816.

Hearn, J (1998b) *The violences of men: how men talk about and how agencies respond to men's violence to women.* London: Sage.

Holter, ØG (1997) *Gender, patriarchy and capitalism: a social forms analysis.* Oslo: Work Research Institute.

Holter, ØG and Aarseth, H (1993) *Menns livssammenheng [Men's life patterns].* Oslo: Ad Notam Gyldenhal.

Klein, AM (1993) *Little big men: bodybuilding subculture and gender construction.* Albany, NY: State University of New York Press.

Law, R, Campbell, H. and Dolan, J (eds.) (1999) *Masculinities in Aotearoa/New Zealand.* Palmerston North: Dunmore Press.

Mac an Ghaill, M (1994) *The making of men: masculinities, sexualities and schooling.* Buckingham: Open University Press.

Martino, W (1994) Masculinity and learning: exploring boys' underachievement and under-representation in subject English. *Interpretations,* 27: 22–57.

McMahon, A (1999) *Taking care of men: sexual politics in the public mind.* Cambridge: Cambridge University Press.

Messerschmidt, JW (1999) *Nine lives: adolescent masculinities, the body, and violence.* Boulder, CO: Westview.

Messner, MA (1992) *Power at play: sports and the problem of masculinity.* Boston: Beacon Press.

Messner, MA (1997) *The politics of masculinities: men in movements.* Thousand Oaks, CA: Sage.

Metz-Göckel, S and Müller, U (1985) *Der Mann: die Brigitte-Studie.* Hamburg: Beltz.

Moodie, TD (1994) *Going for gold: men, mines, and migration.* Johannesburg: Witwatersrand University Press.

Morrell, R (1998) Of boys and men: masculinity and gender in Southern African studies. *Journal of Southern African Studies,* 24: 605–30.

Nakamura A (1994) *Watashi-no danseigaku [My men's studies].* Tokyo: Kindaibugei-sha.

Pease, B (1997) *Men and sexual politics: towards a profeminist practice.* Adelaide: Dulwich Centre Publications.

Petersen, A (1998) *Unmasking the masculine: 'men' and 'identity' in a sceptical age.* London: Sage.

Ptacek, J (1988) Why do men batter their wives?, in Yllo K and Bograd M (eds) *Feminist perspectives on wife abuse.* Newbury Park, CA: Sage, 133–57.

Risman, BJ (1998) *Gender vertigo: American families in transition.* New Haven, CT: Yale University Press.

Roper, M (1994) *Masculinity and the British organization man since 1945.* Oxford: Oxford University Press.

Rowe, D and McKay, J (1998) Sport: still a man's game. *Journal of Interdisciplinary Gender Studies,* 3: 113–28.

Sabo, D and Gordon, D (eds) (1995) *Men's health and illness: gender, power, and the body.* Thousand Oaks, CA: Sage.

Schofield, T, Connell, RW, Walker, L, Wood, JF and Butland, DL (2000) Understanding men's health and illness: a gender relations approach to policy, research and practice. *Journal of American College Health,* 48: 247–56.

Segal, L (1997) *Slow motion: changing masculinities, changing men.* 2nd edn. London: Virago.

Star, L (1999) New masculinities theory: poststructuralism and beyond, in Law, R Campbell H and Dolan J (eds) *Masculinities in Aotearoa/New Zealand.* Palmerston North: Dunmore Press, 36–45.

Thorne, B (1993) *Gender play: girls and boys in school.* New Brunswick: Rutgers University Press.

Tillner, G (1997) Masculinity and xenophobia. Paper to UNESCO meeting, Male Roles and Masculinities in the Perspective of a Culture of Peace, Oslo.

Tomsen, S (1997) A top night: social protest, masculinity and the culture of drinking violence. *British Journal of Criminology,* 37: 90–103.

Valdés, T and Olavarría, J (eds) (1998) *Masculinidades y Equidad de Género en América Latina.* Santiago: FLACSO.

Wajcman, J (1999) *Managing like a man: women and men in corporate management.* Sydney: Allen & Unwin.

Walker, L, Butland, D and Connell, RW (2000) Boys on the road: masculinities, car culture, and road safety education. *Journal of Men's Studies*, 8: 153–69.

Widersprüche (1998) Special issue: *Multioptionale Männlichkeiten?*, no 67.

Zulehner, PM & Volz, R (1998) *Männer im Aufbruch: Wie Deutschlands Männer sich selbst und wie Frauen sie sehen.* Ostfildern: Schwabenverlag.

NOTE

1. This article first appeared in the journal *Social Thought and Research* (2001) vol 24, nos 1 and 2.

3

Femininities: Reclassifying Upward Mobility and the Neo-Liberal Subject[1]

Valerie Walkerdine and Jessica Ringrose

INTRODUCTION

Second-wave feminism ignited a new interest in girls' and women's education, and innovative research in the field. Ground-breaking studies, such as those by Elena Belotti (1975), Dale Spender (1982), and Carole Gilligan (1982), documented how girls' experiences and perspectives were being systematically belittled and marginalized by their male pupil peers, teachers, and the school system itself. While some studies focused on the way in which educational resources are disproportionately directed at boys, and the discriminatory practices and attitudes in educational environments that worked to 'teach girls their place', others attacked the masculinist epistemology underpinning the very construction of knowledge. Within this emerging body of work, two key understandings of gender predominated: socialization and 'sex role' models (in which gender roles are reproduced via social institutions; see also Chapters 1, 3 and 4 in this volume), and work developing cognitive psychology approaches about the learning of gender identities (and in Gilligan's case, challenging previous androcentric assumptions reflected in prior work in the field). What such work held in common was a tendency to see gender identities as fixed, and also to treat girls as a homogeneous group, as though their experiences were unified (for elaboration and critiques of such positions, see Davies, 1989). Hence these readings presented a single version of female experience. Problems with this approach are now well rehearsed: it ultimately relies on dichotomous biological sex distinctions (Connell, 1987); and it depicts subjects as either passive dopes of cultural forces or, for those whose behavior does not conform to the appropriate gender role, 'failed products of socialization' (Pilcher and Whelehan, 2004). Although manifestations of gender 'role' in girls and women were usually seen as 'femininity' – socially produced rather than biologically inherent – girls' individual experiences and identity constructions did not tend to be closely examined.

However, during the 1980s, these positions came to be critiqued from two different directions. On the one hand, Black, White working-class, and lesbian feminists attacked the privileging and colonization of a White, middle-class, heterosexist model of experience by Western feminists, and their lack of recognition of inequalities and differences of 'standpoint' between women. Simultaneously, structuralist and post-structuralist perspectives were challenging the notion of a coherent and fixed individual subject. There was a consequent explosion in the study of identities and, with this, of research on the experiences of different groups of girls (and boys). In recognition that people do not all share or experience the same constructions of gender, and to evoke gender's fluidity, this research is often referred to as work on 'femininities' and 'masculinities' in the plural (although this terminology has in turn been challenged as surreptitiously essentialist – as 'femininities' tend to be exclusively applied to females and 'masculinities' to males – and as evoking typologies (MacInnes, 1998; Francis, 2000; Whitehead, 2002)).

Our work has taken up this analysis of different constructions of subjectivity among girls and young women as mediated by education, and has examined the social structures, discourses, representations and practices through which class, ethnicity and gender become manifest. Valerie Walkerdine and colleagues have developed various theoretical applications as tools in this work, including post-structuralist and psychoanalytic readings. In this chapter, we seek to illustrate these approaches, focusing particularly on gender and social class. In recent writings, one of us (Valerie) has become increasingly interested in the gendered nature of neo-liberal subjectivity, and the classed and gendered constraints that are incited yet masked by neo-liberal discourse. We shall develop our analysis of these themes in the sections that follow. But first, we need to contextualize our analysis with a brief note on work around education and social class.

In the 1950s and 1960s, there was considerable emphasis in Britain on the possibility of escape from the working class on the basis of an upward mobility made possible by educational success within state grammar schools. Discussions of upward mobility focused entirely on the working-class boy (Douglas, 1964; Halsey et al., 1980). This fitted neatly with a clear concern about the male manual worker as the bearer of working-class identity. Women have tended to be excluded from notions of radical working-class identity (Reay, 1998). Indeed, many media portrayals have presented women as the driving force for respectability and upward mobility and, as Beverley Skeggs (1997) demonstrates clearly, the issue of respectability is an important one for working-class women in the present, who are marked more by the categorization of their sexuality (rough/respectable/slut) and by the possibility of entry into upward mobility through their production of themselves as worthy of marriage to a middle-class man. While for many working-class men and women in the post-war period, there was a conflict between working-class belonging and educational and occupational aspiration, it was women who were always positioned more ambivalently in relation to class in the first place, and whose combination of pain and desire went largely unrecognized. At the turn of the millennium, a very different political and economic landscape configures the place of gender and class differently.

In this chapter, we want to explore how we might understand reclassification, and how shifting discourses of femininity operate in the fantasies of upward mobility, through education, work and consumption, that are central to the production of neo-liberal subjectivity. As the recent study by Walkerdine *et al.* (2001) makes clear educational attainment for girls in Britain is still deeply and starkly divided on traditional class lines, so that the possibility of entering the new female professional labor market is still incredibly difficult for working-class young women. On the other hand, the number of working-class women entering service work has increased. This kind of work, together with the increase in access to university, provides the possibility of a life envisaged as much more tied to the possibilities of being traditionally related to middle-class status. Yet current educational debates around girls' achievements in school and later in work contribute to what we would call a post-feminist and post-class discourse of unambiguous female success, where celebrations of 'presumptive' gender equity are taken as proof that meritocratic principles for attaining bourgeois success have worked (Foster, 2000; McRobbie, 2001, 2004; Ringrose, forthcoming; Walkerdine *et al.*, 2001). Qualities of reinvention and making over the self, which are core psychological characteristics for the adaptation to market forces required by neo-liberalism, contribute to the individualization and so called feminization of both work and upward mobility. In this climate, girls and women become the new 'poster-boy' for neo-liberal dreams of upward mobility. The discourse of female success has led to an intensification of fantasies of self-transformation and increased incitements to make over the self as middle-class. Neo-liberalism inscribes the feminine as a bourgeois sign in new ways, creating new sites of contradiction in forging a legitimate feminine identity, particularly for working-class women. It is these discourses and narratives through which 'upward mobility' is to be lived for women in the present that we explore.

CLASSIFICATION

Regarding the history of social class classification (see Walkerdine, 2003, for elaboration), there are two issues of relevance to us here: the first is an understanding of the historicity of the use of class in technologies of subjectification and the second is the way in which the economics of capitalism have and have not changed. When we and others wish to hang onto the use of class in relation to subjectivities, it is because the exploitation and oppression which class politics signals, though changed, have not ceased, and no other political discourse has emerged to explain or mobilize around these issues, that is, the issue of inequalities associated with social and economic difference. It is how such differences, and the oppression and pain that they bring can be spoken, that we need urgently to address inside a political space that seems to deny its existence at the very moment that class is taken to be an anachronistic concept. However, a theorization of class as a universal concept of sociology, an overarching discourse of the subject, is rendered deeply problematic by post-foundational theorizing within the social sciences and humanities. The issue becomes one of how it is possible to think about both the place it has in the making of subjects now and the possibility of talking about exploitation and oppression in terms of social, cultural and economic differences which have not gone away and which therefore need to be understood as a central part of any politics in the present. So, our interest here is the discourses and narratives through which class has been understood and the place of those in producing modes of subjectification and subjectivity, including the meaning and possibility of upward mobility, and analyzing how these are gendered in particular ways. We want to suggest that modes of regulation are shifting from practices of policing and external regulation to technologies of self-regulation in which subjects come to understand themselves as responsible for their own regulation, and the management of themselves is understood as central to a neo-liberal project in which class differences are taken to have melted away. The neo-liberal subject is the autonomous liberal subject made in the image of the middle class.

Neo-liberalism and the psychology of success and failure

By the late twentieth century, analysts of social class were incessantly heralding embourgeoisement and the 'end of the working class' (Gorz, 1982). It is these processes that, we could argue, have reached their zenith in what has been termed neo-liberalism. By now, the subject is understood by many sociologists (e.g. Giddens, 1994) as having been completely freed from traditional ties of location, class and gender and to be completely self-produced. The affluent worker has given way to the embourgeoisement of the population, and so the end of the working class is taken to have arrived. Freed from the ties of class, the new workers are totally responsible for their own destiny, and so techniques and technologies of regulation focus on the self-management of citizens to produce themselves as having the skills and qualities necessary to succeed in the new economy. The sets of political and economic changes which have led to neo-liberalism (the loss of power of trade unions, the end of jobs for life, the increase in short-term contracts, etc.) have emerged alongside a set of discourses and practices already well in place, but in which certain discourses and practices of class which stress class as oppositional have been replaced by those which stress that the possibility of upward mobility, particularly for women. Here a narrative of escape from traditional familial and domestic arrangements bolsters a neo-liberal dream of reinvention through education and work-based identities (Walkerdine, 2003).

In the contemporary economic context, the nature of work is being transformed in terms of the kind of work available, and its contractual basis and gendered nature, and the forms, imperatives and distributed outcomes of education are also in a period of major transformation. Jobs for life are being replaced by a constantly changing array of jobs, small businesses and employment contracts. In such an economy, it is the flexible and autonomous subject who must be able to cope with constant change in work, income and lifestyle and with constant insecurity. It is the flexible and autonomous subject who negotiates, chooses and succeeds in the array of education and retraining forms that form the new 'lifelong learning' and the 'multiple career trajectories' that have replaced the linear hierarchies of the education system of the past and the jobs for life of the old economy (cf. Giddens's (1991) 'reflexive project' of the self as a key marker of this new period of history; Gee's (1999) 'shape-shifting portfolio person'; du Gay's (1996) 'entrepreneur of oneself'). It is argued that these times demand a subject who is capable of constant self-invention.

Such a subject is presumed by, as well as being the intended product of, contemporary forms of education and training. While self-realization is what is expected of the life project, one in which success is judged by the psychological capacities to succeed and the ability to handle uncertainty, in fact, the never knowing where work will come from produces an almost inevitable failure that will be lived as a personal failing. Hence the necessity for forms of counselling and therapy intended to prop up the fragile subject, to keep the illusion of a unitary subject intact (Rose, 1999). Containing this kind of subject and the containment of fracturing and fragmentation is a key task for neo-liberal and globalized economies that are no longer willing to provide long-term forms of support. We no longer have a large manufacturing base which provides the pivot for an understanding of social stratification based on class divisions. What used to be the working class is now dispersed into service industries based on individual contracts, piecework, home work and work in call centres, with jobs for life having disappeared. Women's employment is divided between those who have education and skills to enter the professional and managerial sector and those who leave school with little or no qualifications and enter a labor market defined mostly by poorly paid, often part-time work, little job security and periods of unemployment. We are witnessing the complete collapse of civil society; thus, the attempt to develop further the psychological and social characteristics of the Robinson Crusoe economic man of liberalism (even if that man is now female) has to be created at this conjuncture as a subject who can cope without strong community roots or ties. Hence the desire to make subjects responsible for their own lives through networks of 'social capital'.

Femininity as bourgeois sign and the feminization of upward mobility

In this context of neo-liberalism and 'choice biographies', upward mobility becomes a central trope of class/ification, where women and the qualities ascribed to femininity have a central place. As we have seen, work in the last 20 years on femininity has moved us very far away from fixed, sex roles and socialization theory (Henriques *et al.*, 1984) We shift from universalized, essentialist sex-role models that bind sex to gendered qualities (i.e. girl to femininity), to the post-structural imperative to locate femininity and masculinity as a complex set of gendered/sexualized representational discourses, practices, signs and subject (dis)locations, of which idealized/normative forms exist (Butler, 1990; 1993). Femininity as a sign is to be traced as socially and historically specific and mediated in complex ways: 'being, becoming, practising and doing femininity are very different things for women of different classes, races, ages and nations' (Skeggs, 1997: 98).

Walkerdine's work has consistently explored how it is bourgeois feminine characteristics that are idealized and then taken as normal through a pathologization of the working class, and particularly working-class women and mothers as threats to the moral order who must be monitored, controlled and reformed (1991; 1996: 148). Skeggs (1997: 99) traces how femininity was seen to be 'The property of middle class women who could prove themselves to be respectable through their appearance and conduct ... [and] use their proximity to the sign of femininity to construct distinctions between themselves and others'. This various work makes it is possible to see how the feminine as representation has operated as a bourgeois sign, with working-class women marked as 'Other'. But where, historically, the set of practices in which an idealized/normalized femininity was sustained was in a private/public split, with women ensconced in the maternal/domestic sphere, this traditional split has collapsed with the mass entry of women into higher education and masculine domains of work throughout the Western world (Pateman, 1988). The content of the feminine/bourgeois coupling has shifted dramatically in the context of neo-liberalism, brought about by late modernity and globalization.

The desegregation of gender in many jobs and the shifting nature of work into service industries brings the distinction between 'men's and women's work' into question, radically disrupting the social construction of gender (Cohen and Ainley, 2000). The qualities of re-invention, adaptation, flexibility and malleability by outside market forces that are in demand are ones that are traditionally feminine. The gender shifts we are witnessing require that both men and women increasingly perform what Lisa Adkins (1995) calls an 'aesthetics of femininity' in most types of work. The feminine is, therefore, marshalled in new ways in processes of neo-liberal subject formation. But this feminization of upward mobility means a complex set of masculine and feminine qualities are to be balanced in attaining bourgeois identity. Indeed, responding to Adkins' (1995) thesis that workers are required to perform an 'aesthetics of femininity', Diane Reay suggests that in education (a key site in the production of upward mobility), with its 'growing emphasis on measured outputs, competition and entrepreneurship, it is primarily the assertiveness and authority of masculinity rather than the aesthetics of femininity that is required and rewarded' (2001: 165). So the task is to somehow juggle traditionally feminine and masculine attributes. This is the new work of 'doing' bourgeois femininity that girls and women must perform.

We are all familiar with the tropes of the supermom and women 'having it all' (Erwin, 1996) that exist as bourgeois ideals of femininity at present. The feminist political dilemmas of housewife versus career woman and the struggles for educational and workplace access and child-care provision have been replaced by a renaissance woman who juggles a thriving career (attained through the right modes of education) with motherhood. And although she may buy maternal services from the less successful and pathologized working-class woman, this depends on her own (or family's) financial power to do so, devolving responsibility increasingly onto the individual. Those working in girlhood studies suggest these myths of unambiguous female success are bolstered by educational debates that use girls' superior achievements in school vis-à-vis boys' to proclaim the future is female, and make sweeping claims about gender equity and girl power (Walkerdine *et al.*, 2001; Aapola *et al.*, 2005 Ringrose, forthcoming). Many dichotomies, including clever/pretty, private/public and rational/irrational, are apparently resolved in these new bourgeois fantasies of femininity – a new vision of a Stepford fembot who excels in the traditionally feminine terrains of the home and the shopping mall as well as in the masculine domains of education, the office and the gym. This is a 'post-feminist' fantasy where women and girls are celebrated as benefactors of equal opportunities who can also retain their femininity, while processes of regulation into the neo-liberal economic order are masked within the psychological discourses of individual adaptation and entrepreneurship. But are the dilemmas of striving for bourgeois femininity resolved – or do we find a set of complex contradictions about upward mobility, painful and traumatic in the wake of a discourse of female success, which leads us back to the inevitability of the individual's failure to succeed in the bid to reinvent the self? Isn't navigating this brave new postfeminist 'gender order' merely the latest chapter in a long-established incitement to women to become producers of themselves as objects of the gaze, to make themselves over as appropriately bourgeois and feminine in the constitutive terms of the moment? (Connell, 1987).

The make-over as site of neo-liberal reinvention

The concept of the 'make-over' has been a staple of women's magazines for many years (see Walkerdine, 2003, for elaboration). It constitutes a central motif of upward mobility toward bourgeois ideals. The make-over is hardly new, but we would argue that these incitements have intensified and work in important ways to normalize the neo-liberal ethos of continuously maximizing, bettering and reinventing the self. A cursory look at any television guide reveals the massive proliferation of this theme. In scores of do-it-yourself programs, television viewers are incited to rearrange their homes and gardens to make them fashionable, even if they have little money, by utilizing leftover pots of paint and scraps from the garden shed or storeroom. But where the centrality of formations of femininity as bourgeois sign, the failures of working-class women to approximate these ideals, and the proliferation of psychological discourses to address and regulate these failures become most striking is in the programs designed to make-over the working-class family, mother, female body and psyche.

Many of these shows focus on the unhealthy lifestyle choices and socialization environment of primarily working-class families, and the working-class mother figures as specific objects of failure and scrutiny. This is evident in the range of nanny shows that are popular at the moment: 'Super Nanny' (C4), 'Little Angels' (BBC3), 'The House of Tiny Tearaways' (BBC3), and the US 'Nanny 911' (FOX). In these newest twists on Foucault's panopticon, psychologists monitor families through close-circuit TV, while mothers typically wear earpieces to receive the proper parenting strategies. These woman psychologists are the new bourgeois gods, bearers of middle-class manners, who dole out rebukes and praise into the waiting receptacle for change – typically, a working-class, and often single, mother. Single, working-class mothers are also usually the target of the make-over in the series of body/eating-focused shows, where poor women are ridiculed for being obese and for pushing obesity onto their children because they do not under-stand the basic foundations of nutrition (or own a juicer, the right cookbooks or membership at a gym).[2]

And let us not forget the masculine subject in all of this. The massive popularity in the USA and the UK of 'Queer Eye for the Straight Guy' (BRAVO/LivingTV) points out the increasing necessity for men to be made over into middle-class, consuming subjects of an increasing market for gay men (the rise of the 'metrosexual'), which involves heterosexual men adopting traditionally feminine burdens of self-surveillance, fastidious grooming, and domestic and culinary skills, usually in order to get or keep a woman.

So, what was once understood as upward mobility now takes on a different and more central place, a place in which both women and men are incited to become self-reflexive subjects, to be looked at and in that sense feminized and in charge of their own biography in Rose's sense, but in which the feminine takes on a particular significance. We have the erosion of a discourse of the working class, which is also pushing onto women the old place of the displacement of radicality onto a middle-class conservatism, while at the same time bringing in values of flexibility, adaptability, and making over the self – the values of a psychology and interiority usually ascribed to women. Women can thus become understood as the carriers of all that is both good and bad about the new economy in the sense that the erosion of a discourse of classed identity can also be seen as a feminization. We are certainly not witnessing any lessening of inequality or exploitation – far from it – but we would claim that this inequality is differently lived because low-paid manual and service workers are constantly enjoined to improve and remake themselves as the freed consumer, the 'entrepreneur of themselves'. And it is fantasies of working-class women's transformation in particular that have become a drama of desire and failure played out in living rooms around the nation, shoring up the limits and impossibilities of living a neo-liberal subject position at present.

Education, mobility, defences and desires

Walkerdine (1996) and Skeggs (1997) make similar points about the unremitting nature of what Skeggs calls the 'doubts and insecurities of living class that working-class women endure on a daily basis' (p167). But what we want also to argue is that there are very different struggles for working-class women depending on how they forge an identification with bourgeois femininity. Education plays a central role in how one is to stake out a bourgeois identity, profoundly shaping how the fissures and ruptures in attempting to make-over the self into middle class are actually to be lived.

In the 1991 documentary film 'Didn't She Do Well?' Walkerdine explored narratives of upward mobility presented by a group of professional women who had grown up working class in Britain at different historical moments and who had all made a transition to the middle class by virtue of education and professional work. The film showed how what Pheterson (1993) calls 'daily routine humiliation' elicits considerable pain and a whole defensive organization, sets of desires, avoidances, and practices designed to make the pain bearable or go away. It provokes pursuing other possibilities of being, to develop practices of coping, hoping, longing, shame, guilt and so forth. But these are understood as personal failures when all there is available to understand them is an individual psychological discourse. A common theme for these women was the issue of what we might call 'survival guilt', in which they felt that it was not acceptable for them to have survived and prospered when their families, and particularly their fathers, had suffered greatly, and their families had to live in poverty, illness, and doing without. What is clear about some of their narratives is that they do not want to go back to that place of pain, poverty and silence, yet they feel that they have no right to belong in the new place without taking those less fortunate with them. Such themes are echoed by Lawler's (1999) work on narratives of upward mobility for women in which 'the fantasy of "getting out and getting away" may be achieved only at the price of entering another set of social relations, in which the assumed pathology of their (working-class women's) history and their desires is brought home to them more intensely' (p19).

Therefore, we need to understand upward mobility as having a deeply defensive aspect. The discourses through which to read upward mobility present it as a freeing, a success. This discourse, transported into the popular narratives of a women's magazine, was what provided a vehicle for the fantasy of moving away from pain and silence and provided a material means for doing so – earning money as an au pair. In the same way, the promise of new homes, bodies and minds in contemporary television seems to offer routes for getting from one place (an overweight, stupid, pathologically stuck self) to another (the slim, clever, rationally adaptive self). Thus, defences and desires (which, of course, can also be defensive) work through popular narratives, formal discourses.

CHANGING PLACES

But what of those girls and women for whom education cannot offer a fantasy of liberatory path toward bourgeois identity; those constituted as unambiguous failures in the educational race to new standards and achievements; those working-class subjects unaccounted for by the blinding educational discourse of girls' success at boys' expense in contemporary educational debates on gender (Epstein *et al.*, 1998; Ali *et al.*, 2004; Francis and Skelton, 2005)? How are these girls and young women to negotiate a fantasy of upward mobility, to stake out an identity as bourgeois and consuming subject, to live up to the new neo-liberal fictions of female success?

We will refer to one example from Walkerdine *et al.*'s (2001) study of transition to womanhood in 1990s Britain. We focus on one young woman whose family bought their council house during the period of the Conservative government under Margaret Thatcher, which introduced a 'right to buy' scheme, under which working-class people could become homeowners.

Lisa's family lived in a Victorian house in a socially mixed area of London, the house having been bought by the council to add to their housing stock at some point. The family bought the house under the right to buy scheme and meticulously did it up in the current fashionable style of restoration, with the aid of books on Victorian decor from the public library. During the housing boom of the 1980s, they sold the house and moved to the North of England, to the small town where Lisa's maternal grandmother had grown up, where the houses were much cheaper. With the proceeds of the sale of the council house, they were able to buy a cottage in a village setting, which they set about extending and renovating, also setting up a franchise of the watch and clock repair business that Lisa's father had worked for in the extension. The cottage had some considerable land on which Lisa kept a horse.

We explore Lisa's narratives of her subjectivity, taken from interviews and video diaries made by her at the ages of 16 and 18. In particular, we look at the way in which she understands herself, as a subject, as a young child in a council house in London and the way she transforms herself from failing schoolgirl to a young, middle-class country businesswoman in the North.

Lisa's struggle to reinvent herself relates to the study of pariahs and parvenus by the sociologist, Zygmunt Bauman (2001), who makes a particular case that modernity is the moment of the parvenu. What Bauman makes clear, though, is that the self-invention involves a journey, a material and imagined transformation of status. This is certainly what Lisa and her family undergo, but it is also what the apparently classless self-invention involves. Lisa's family sought to remake themselves as middle-class country people by the purchase and subsequent sale of their council house and the move north. What we consider is how Lisa understands her old childhood subjectivity as a working-class girl in a council house, her difficult relationship to schooling, and how she understands and fantasizes her new subjectivity and remaking herself, which demands a complete negation of her Other self. She engages in powerful and pleasurable fantasies about the kind of woman she wants to become. Held inside these fantasies, though, is a painful Other, that which she fears that she is and wants not to be.

Lisa had performed poorly in school in London, and had struggled greatly with the transition to her new school when her family moved to the North when she was aged nine. During the interview when Lisa was 16, it emerged that she had barely passed her GCSEs, achieving only one D. After completing a work experience placement as a carer with the 'elderly' (of which she said, 'I hated that job. I could never do it'), and having rejected the 'persistent' advice of her careers teacher to go into tech, Lisa's career options were extremely bleak: nursery nurse, undertaking or hairdressing. Facing these avenues, Lisa's father encouraged her to go into business with him at 16 and made her his legal business partner at 17. By her interview at 18, however, much of this is submerged beneath a seemingly seamless fiction of middle-class success – a complex relation to bourgeois identity Lisa struggles to carve out for herself through her narrative.

Lisa presents to the camera in her video diary a model of an English countrywoman. She describes herself as an established businesswoman, as owning a horse and a car, and having much more money than her old school friends, who, she repeatedly says, are 'going nowhere'. It is as though, for the world, the remake has been a success.

Yet, in the interview, she gives a narrative of depression, eating disorders and unhappiness set against the relentless story of becoming a horse-riding, middle-class, country lady and career woman. Everything in the old life is presented as Other. At one point, she talks about her father growing up in a council house and that she now looks down on people who live in council houses. Yet it was not just her father, of course, who grew up in a council house, but she also until the age of eight. Why does she 'forget' this part of her own history? Perhaps it is too difficult to bear the fact that she now 'looks down' on that part of herself who lived in a council house, who did poorly in school, who was marked out to become a nursery nurse.

She presents the village where she lives as populated with lords and ladies, and full of friendly locals, who hail her as she passes on her horse. She reads the magazine *Horse and Hound*, a conservative and upper-class country magazine favoured by the hunting, shooting and fishing set. She presents herself as totally immersed in the community and describes how she, like the locals in the nearby small town, crosses over the road so as not to walk directly in front of the local Indian restaurant to show the Asian owners that they are not welcome. Yet, this is a young woman who grew up until the age of eight in a multicultural, inner-city setting, and who, by her own admission at interview, knew all about Indian festivals, like Divali, and Indian deities. It is as though Lisa wants to be more local than the locals (an idea that Bauman works with) and to do so, she must take another subject position that risks negating her past.

The past has, therefore, to be reworked. As with the women in 'Didn't She Do Well?' and those interviewed by Lawler (1999), the present is lived in relation to the shame of the past and the fear of exposure and ridicule. Only one small window to this past emerges while discussing her identity as a 'business partner':

> It's a great showpiece now when you're talking to your friends – I had great fun telling my careers teacher, 'cos he thought I'd been up to, you know, not a lot – so he said – 'You should go to tech and do this course' – and er I felt like going back to him and saying 'Well I'm a partner in a business, thriving business, thank you'... I've seen him in the car. I thought 'Should I hit him – or should I swerve and just miss him?'

In this revenge fantasy, Lisa plays out the satisfaction of telling her careers teacher she has become somebody and also of running him down with her car. We see that it is directly against the pain and humiliation of the educational discourse of working-class failure that she is attempting to create herself as a career woman with certain tastes and style, what we can term a whole aesthetics of herself, to remake herself in the image of the country, middle-class, career woman:

> I want the business to grow and I want to say – I think the main point is that making a name for myself, because you know as – you know, you're getting more money round here – you've got big cars and you've got bigger houses and people are starting to take a note of you, yeah – and I think that sort of the most important thing to me is my status.

> I've got lots of suits – a lot of business suits. When I'm out with my friends I like to be the person that turns the heads rather than my friends.

She works with her father, training to be a horologist (the term she uses rather than a watch and clock repairer). She likes to wear business suits, fantasizes a 90-year-old billionaire with a heart defect as her 'ideal man', never having children, living in a stylish and uncomfortable house and driving a Mercedes:

> I love looking the part, and I can't wait to drive the Mercedes ... I'll look the part when I step outside the Merc.

Lisa performs this aesthetic, this commodification of herself through the complex manifestations of signs, discourses, practices and narratives that constitute her immersion in this life, yet everything that is not present in this performance contains that other narrative, the narrative of being Other, now pushed into the place opposite to the position she now holds. Her world, her self is marked as follows:

Country
Middle class
Conservative
Adult
White
Successful
and away from
The city
Working class
Childish
Black
Educational failure

Little by little in the interview, a story emerges, however, in which she is rejected for being overweight ('you're fat, you know, oh go away!'); is rejected for being a Londoner ('they would say 'she's a Londoner, keep her out'); is depressed ('I literally nearly had a nervous breakdown'); is not eating ('I lost so much weight and I thought this is great you know, I can do this again like yeah – and that's when I just started going around with just like a packet of crisps for the whole day and I was feeling dizzy and sick and I thought, no, this isn't right'); is feeling that she had no childhood; is tired of trying to succeed; and longs to be accepted, respectable and respected. So the narrative of the parvenu, the mimetic narrative which aims to produce as reality that identity which she fantasizes being ('I'll probably have a very sort of flashy, sort of snobby lifestyle'), is a narrative which displaces and avoids the rejection and failure which accompanies the narrative of Otherness, the narrative condemned to psychopathology because illness (depression and eating disorders) is the only way in which it can be spoken. Only the relentless pursuit of this new narrative identity and the 'success' implied within it can quieten the other insistent narrative in order to attempt the impossible task, as Bauman says, the complete displacement of what one was.

Lisa wants to be a businesswoman, which is not the same identity as a villager – she wants to have a particular position – one of high status and a lifestyle that demands money and high levels of consumption. The creation of a desirable work identity is crucial for her, as for all the young women in the study. But cut off from an educational route to respectability, Lisa's identity as businesswoman exists as a complex site of bourgeois fantasy staked in opposition to the shame of educational failure. The business suits, flash cars and stylish home are a means to create in fantasy the possibility of an Other space, an Other life, a life in which failures, depression and eating disorders do not exist because this is the life of wealth and success. Thus, it is the fantasy of being that Other, the desire to be that Other, which is absolutely central for us to understand. It is how that desire positions her in the practice of working, of upward mobility, and produces the practices of self-management through which she can be inscribed in those identities to which she aspires. And always this desire must be set against its Other, that which it defends against, the other positions – not only that which she has left behind in London, and her struggle with school and failure, but also what it would mean not to have money and wealth. These other positions are to some extent medicalized and psychologized and presented in the form of illness: depression and eating disorders, the available ways for articulating and living the impossibility of success, of arrival, of being a unitary subject.

As Gonick (2001) says, to 'become somebody', the task of neo-liberalism, is an impossible task, revealing 'the delusionary character of self-determining, individualistic and autonomous ideas of subjectivity' (p204). What the examples reveal is the problem of contradiction between positions, possible identities, identifications and the shaky move between them. Bauman (2001) calls this 'ambivalence', that is, the discursive place where there is a slip or sliding, ambiguity between classifications. It is this, not this. He argues that, discursively, this is a problem for narrative organization in that it is difficult to hold something as existing within opposing narratives and discourses. He argues further that the single and simple discursive classification is what makes possible the fiction of the rational unitary and autonomous subject – I am this. Therefore, the failure to classify, that he calls ambivalence, is experienced as great pain and anxiety for the subject because it is lived as a failure to become the desired singular subjectivity, the subjectivity that one can consume oneself into being, the subject for which happiness is apparently possible. The goal of happiness is invested in the endless becoming of the unitary subject through turning oneself into a commodity and thereby owning the means to consume. It is a pleasure endlessly displaced and postponed, glimpsed in snatches of holidays, cars and clothes as though it were life. It contains failure inside it as an inevitability. The working-class woman embodies this failure to consume appropriately and the failure to reconcile with the feminine as bourgeois sign. She must be exiled, crushed, made-over in regulatory processes in which psychology is constantly called upon to intercede with the self. This gives us a glimpse of how class is both lived and elided within the present and allows us to understand the discourses and narratives that inform the upwardly mobile, neo-liberal subject. We see also the necessity to work with the complex intersection of narratives and discourses, particularly Other and occluded narratives, through which gendered and classed subjectivity within the present might be understood.

REFERENCES

Aapola, S, Gonick, M and Harris, A (2005) *Young femininity: girlhood, power and social change*. London: Palgrave.

Adkins, L (1995) *Gendered work: sexuality, family and the labour market*. Buckingham: Open University Press.

Ali, S, Benjamin, S, and Mauthner, M (2004) *The politics of gender and education: critical perspectives*. London: Palgrave.

Bauman, Z (2001) Pariahs and parvenus, in Beilharz, P (ed) *The Bauman reader*. Oxford: Blackwell.

Belotti, E (1975) *Little girls*. London: Writers and Readers Publishing Co-op.

Butler, J (1990) *Gender trouble: feminism and the subversion of identity*. New York: Routledge.

Butler, J (1993) *Bodies that matter: on the discursive limits of 'sex'*. New York: Routledge.

Cohen, P and Ainley, P (2000) 'In the country of the blind?: youth studies and cultural studies in Britain. *Journal of Youth Studies*, 3: 79–95.

Connell, R (1987) *Gender and power*. Cambridge: Polity Press.

Davies, B (1989) *Frogs and snails and feminist tails*. Sydney: Allen & Unwin.

Douglas, JWB (1964) *The home and the school*. Glasgow: McGibbon & Kee.

du Gay, P (1996) *Consumption and identity at work*. London: Sage.

Epstein, D, Elwod, J, Hey, V and Maw, J (eds) (1998) *Failing boys? issues in gender and achievement*. Buckingham: Open University Press.

Erwin, L (1996) Having it all in the nineties: the work and family aspirations of women undergraduates, in Galaway, B and Hudson, J (eds) *Youth in transition, perspectives on research and policy*. Toronto: Thompson Educational Publishing.

Foster, V (2000) Is female educational 'success' destabilizing the male learner-citizen?, in Arnot, M and Dillabough, J (eds) *Challenging democracy: international perspectives on gender, education and citizenship*. London: Routledge/Falmer.

Francis, B (2000) *Boys, girls and achievement.* London: Routledge.

Francis, B and Skelton, C (2005) *Reassessing gender and achievement: questioning contemporary key debates.* London: Routledge.

Gee, J (1999) New people in new worlds: networks, the new capitalism and schools, in Cope, B and Kalantzis, M (eds) *Multiliteracies: literacy learning and the design of social futures.* London: Routledge.

Giddens, A (1991) *Modernity and self-identity: self and society in the late modern age* Oxford: Polity Press.

Giddens, A (1994) *Beyond left and right.* Oxford: Polity Press.

Gillies, V (2005) Raising the 'meritocracy': parenting and the individualization of social class. *Sociology,* 39: 835–53.

Gilligan, C (1982) *In a different voice.* Harvard: Harvard University Press.

Gonick, M (2001) Between the door of the unknown and the book of old plots: ambivalence, femininity and identifactory practices. Unpublished PhD thesis, Ontario Institute for Studies in Education.

Gorz, A (1982) *Farewell to the working class.* London: Pluto.

Halsey, AH, Heath, AF and Ridge, JM (1980) *Origins and destinations: family, class and education in modern Britain.* Oxford: Clarendon Press.

Henriques, J Hollway, W, Urwin, C, Venn, C and Walkerdine, V (1984) *Changing the subject: psychology, social regulation and subjectivity.* London: Methuen.

Lawler, S (1999) 'Getting out and getting away': women's narratives of class mobility. *Feminist Review,* 63: 3–23.

MacInnes, M (1998) *The end of masculinity.* Buckingham: Open University Press.

McRobbie, A (2001) Sweet smell of success? New ways of being young women. Unpublished keynote address at A New Girl Order? Young Women and the Future of Feminist Inquiry Conference, London, 12–14 November.

McRobbie, A (2004) Notes on postfeminism and popular culture: Bridget Jones and the new gender regime, in Harris A (ed) *All about the girl: culture, power and identity.* London: Routledge.

Pateman, C (1988) *The sexual contract.* Cambridge: Polity Press.

Pheterson, G (1993) Historical and material determinants of psychodynamic development, in Adleman, J and Enguidanos, G (eds) *Racism in the lives of women.* New York: Haworth Press.

Pilcher, J and Whelehan, I (2004) *50 key concepts in gender studies.* London: Sage.

Reay, D (1998) Rethinking social class: qualitative perspectives on class and gender. *Sociology,* 32: 259–75.

Reay, D (2001) The paradox of contemporary femininities in education: combining fluidity with fixity, in Francis, B and Skelton, C (eds) *Investigating gender: contemporary perspectives in education.* Buckingham: Open University Press.

Ringrose, J. (forthcoming, 2007) Successful girls?; Complicating post-feminist, neo-liberal discourses of educational achievement and gender equality. *Gender and Education,* 32.

Rose, N (1999) *Governing the soul* (2nd edn). London: Free Association Books.

Skeggs, B (1997) *Formations of class and gender.* London: Sage.

Spender, D (1982) *Invisible Women: the schooling scandal.* London: Writers and Readers.

Walkerdine, V (1991) Film: *Did't she do well?* (Working Pictures).

Walkerdine, V (1991) *Schoolgirl fictions.* London: Verso.

Walkerdine, V (1996). Working class women: psychological and social aspects of survival, in Wilkinson S (ed) *Feminist social psychologies: international perspectives.* Buckingham: Open University Press.

Walkerdine, V (1997) *Daddy's girl: young girls and popular culture.* London: Macmillan.

Walkerdine, V (2002) Psychology, post modernity and neo-liberalism. Keynote address at the Politics of Psychological Knowledge Conference, Free University of Berlin.

Walkerdine, V, Lucey, H and Melody, J (2001) *Growing up girl: psychosocial explorations of gender and class.* London: Palgrave.

Whitehead, S (2002) *Men and masculinities.* Cambridge: Polity Press.

NOTES

1. Valerie is grateful to Taylor and Francis for permission to reproduce some of the arguments and discussion which first appeared in her article, 'Reclassifying upward mobility: femininity and the neo-liberal subject', published in the journal *Gender and Education*, 25: 237–48.

2. For examples of such British TV shows that tend to pathologize working-class women and mothers as 'reproducing' the 'cycle of deprivation', through poor diet and socialization environments, see 'Honey, we're killing the kids' (BBC3) and 'You are what you eat' (C4) (Gillies, 2005). Although we do not have space to explore these in greater detail, a host of other UK and US makeover shows, like '10 years Younger' (C4) 'Extreme make-over' (ABC), 'What not to wear' (BBC), 'Ladette to lady' (ITVl) and 'Australian princess' (ITV2), focus variously on transforming objects of failed (often working-class) femininity into appropriately bourgeois feminine subjects.

4

'Education Feminism(s)', Gender Theory and Social Thought: Illuminating Moments and Critical Impasses

Jo-Anne Dillabough

In recent decades, feminism and gender theory have made major contributions both to the development of educational theory and to broader social theory. The focus of this chapter is to celebrate as well as to assess the achievements of what has been, and remains, an extraordinarily powerful and influential cumulative body of work. In recognition of this fact, the account sets the scope of 'education feminism(s)' upon a broad canvas, by offering a critical consideration of some key moments, across time, in its complex and creative engagement with important cognate strands of modern social theory. This rich and mutually productive interface offers an important perspective both for understanding and for judging the wide-reaching impact of feminist research from the mid-twentieth century onward. Such work has been continuously important in establishing productive and challenging links between gender theory, education feminism(s)[1] and social theory as it has developed within other traditions.

Concentrating upon recent theoretical work in the 'West', principally within British and North American settings, the chapter particularly considers the significance of the ubiquitous 'cultural turn' for recent theoretical debates about gender. The value of such a strategy is that it conveniently highlights the relation between emergent stances in critical educational theories and post-structural accounts, and those enduringly important materialist positions developed by feminist accounts of cultural reproduction in earlier years. In this way, the strength of feminist research is revealed in its simultaneous capacity both for intellectual flexibility and for deep theoretical coherence. We should therefore begin with a brief historical account of the achievements of feminist research in the field of education.

A BRIEF HISTORY OF THE 'SEX/GENDER' DEBATE: FROM SEX ROLE SOCIALIZATION TO QUESTIONS ABOUT 'IDENTITY' AND 'THE SUBJECT'

In the early years of gender research in education (1970-80), sex-role theory was dominant (see Deem, 1980; Wolpe, 1988).[2] The key emphasis here was that social relationships in schools were strongly bound to biological differences between the sexes, which were modeled on practical gender role expectations derived from eighteenth- and nineteenth- century accounts of citizenship.[3] Feminist critiques of schooling during this period were therefore directed toward the socializing role of education, particularly in the school, in shaping male and female behavior to conform to gender distinctions derived from biological essentialisms. Central to feminist critiques of early sex-role theory was the notion of gender as conformity to prescribed gender roles or a set of normative socialization rules for men and women (Connell, 2000). Early feminist critiques of sex-role theory therefore pointed the way toward an 'uncoupling' of the concept of *gender* from normative definitions of sex.[4] These distinctions further clarified the importance of viewing *gender* as a relational social construct which was ultimately more flexible than previously understood within sex-role theory and *sex* as a highly deterministic concept deriving from the biological sciences.

Challenges to sex-role theorizing emerged on many theoretical fronts, drawing particularly on critiques of patriarchal language used in schools and textbooks (Spender, 1980; 1987); demands for equal representation of girls and women in school subjects and in the education professions (see Acker, 1987, for discussion of this issue); the notion of the maternal teacher and relational, women-centered schooling approaches (Noddings, 1987; Brown and Gilligan, 1992); and neo-Marxist feminist critiques of state education highlighting education as a hegemonic institutional force reproducing economic patriarchy and the public/private split (MacDonald, 1980; Arnot, 2002). By the mid-1980s, equality feminism – the liberal notion of women as free and equal in the state – had become arguably the most dominant gender theory of education and therefore central to mainstream education analyses (Arnot, 1981). However, though the liberal feminist tradition continued to play a major role in increasing middle-class women's demands for access to the workplace, it left substantially unchallenged 'structural barriers to access [for minority ethnic and economically disadvantaged girls and women] and the roots of liberalism in male epistemologies of knowledge' (Dillabough and Arnot, 2001: 31; see also Weiler, 1991 (our addition)).

As a response to emerging critiques of liberalism and positivist epistemologies in social thought more generally (see Alcoff and Potter, 1994), many feminist sociologists of education challenged liberal feminist approaches by developing a theoretical framework through which to examine the structural and institutional role of education in reproducing unequal gender relations. For this, they drew successively upon second-wave feminist ideals and late Durkheimian concepts of the holistic society (see MacDonald, 1980) or upon neo-Marxist and Gramscian concerns with 'conflict, consciousness and social change' (Dillabough and Arnot, 2001: 31). Central to this feminist materialist critique was an understanding of education as an 'ideological state apparatus' (see Althusser and Gramsci) which not only represented a key site of social and cultural reproduction but also supported a male-dominated system of 'ideological hegemony' which all 'citizens' apparently internalized and ultimately consented to (see Althusser, 1968).

In this context, both British feminist sociologists and education feminists, some of whom were indirectly linked to anthropological, sociological, linguistic and hermeneutic traditions (e.g. Bourdieu, Bernstein, Levi-Strauss) sought to broaden the scope of gender theory in education. This developing approach – broadly described as *feminist reproduction theory* – highlighted larger, macroquestions of structure and their role in shaping gender relations as a historically grounded set of gender relations and codes (see Arnot, 1982; Connell, 1987). It is often argued that feminist reproduction theory is especially indebted to the intellectual projects of Durkheim and Gramsci. Although this may be so for earlier versions of reproduction theory, later versions were also linked to the work of feminist theorists, who wished to distance themselves from functionalist accounts of gender inequality, and move instead toward more culturally oriented neo-Marxist thinkers, such as Bourdieu, Bernstein, and Althusser. The theoretical premises of accounts influenced by these strands of thought – whether primarily structuralist or functionalist – indicated schools as sites where both the possibilities for, and limits of, the democratization of gender relations, were present. This meant that earlier liberal preoccupations with sex differences in education were forced to give ground to macroconcerns about the relation between gender and social structure, and to the legacy of a long history of critical feminist interventions in the state and women's position within it.[5]

The educational project of gender equality gained momentum alongside wider developments in social theory. Debates in social thought which disturbed equality of opportunity discourses thus began to gain greater visibility as part of larger social theory debates. These movements pointed toward a reconfiguration of gender theories of education in a more culturally oriented direction. What emerged was a set of key ideas about how culture, discourse and identity might be seen as intersecting in part with larger macroquestions about women's and men's social positioning in state education. Feminist theory and cultural theory were brought closer than they had ever been in the past, leading to the emergence of number of important new concerns, including critiques of the self-esteem industry, of the deterministic nature of Marxist accounts of educational patriarchy, of the absence of a feminist dialogue on difference and particularity, and of the emergent 'uncoupling of sex and gender' (Dietz, 2003). Toward the end of the late twentieth century (1980s), then, a proliferation of different research paradigms were challenging dominant education feminism(s), accompanied methodologically by a corresponding rise in microlevel, local and interpretive research forms. A deepening gap had opened, as Shain and Ozga (2001: 115) suggested, between 'structural and interpretive approaches' – a gap that education feminism(s) struggled, at this juncture, to resolve.

BECOMING A GENDER THEORIST IN EDUCATION IN THE TWENTY-FIRST CENTURY

Toward the end of the 1980s and in the early 1990s, new approaches to gender theory in education began to emerge. These were linked to a burgeoning interest by feminist researchers in the UK and the USA in critical education studies (see Arnot and Whitty, 1982), and more generally to the powerful impact of French theory on educational debates.

This helped to stimulate a surge of interest in interdisciplinary gender studies in education, moving away from the perceived limitations of formalistic models of theoretical positivism in the social sciences. Tensions emerging from this challenge were most evident at the height of 'contentious' political challenges to modernist feminist approaches (see Benhabib *et al.*, 1996; see also Frances, 1999) in the late 1980s. Today, interdisciplinarity is a well-established theoretical approach in the study of gender in education. Consequently, the simple exposure to more diverse theoretical approaches, alongside the rise in postmodern Continental and cultural approaches, has meant that the theoretical reach of education feminism(s) is both wider and more powerful than in previous theoretical periods, more often representing what Dietz (2003) refers to as an 'inventive combination' of critical feminist approaches.[6,7]

Second, a closer relationship between 'education feminism(s)', identity politics and theoretical expansion has taken hold in the field over the last two decades. This relationship has emerged largely as a consequence of larger political wars within gender studies, which have coincided with forms of modernization and the rise of particular social movements. One theoretical and epistemological outcome of this is that a heightened emphasis has been placed upon the politics of experience and recognition (see Fraser, 1997) within educational feminist thought and related theoretical paradigms (see Brah and Minhas, 1985; Deitz, 2003). While women's experience has always been high on the feminist agenda, its remit and coverage has widened considerably. Women's experiences of education and the diverse ways in which gender has been conceptualized have been at the centre of a multitude of identity-oriented research/theory paradigms over the last two decades. This focus on the intersection of identity and experience has led to a proliferation of feminist educational theories tied to particular local identities and cultural issues of exclusion in place of those posited upon a more universal notion of a singular feminist collective. In dissolving the categories of sex and gender, particularity and difference instead became central concepts for gender theorists in education (see Dietz, 2003: 408; see also Epstein *et al.*, 1998).[8] Diversity feminism and queer theory in education are two notable expressions of this theoretical shift.

Third, despite such substantial developments in the practice of 'theory making', education feminism has continued to operate with a relatively close set of theoretical presuppositions by comparison with gender studies. The reasons for this are primarily historical. Education, as a developing field of study, is in the process of accumulating the theoretical and disciplinary weight enjoyed by feminist sociology or philosophy. In short, education is still in the process of building an intellectual history which is specific to itself. At the same time, schools have benefited directly from education feminism's unique historical trajectory. This is largely because its political aims were explicitly directed toward education. The direct political commitments of feminist educators toward schooling meant that their impact on levels of social change in relation to agency, pedagogy, policy and equal opportunity was profound (London Feminist Salon Collective, 2004).

Having sketched a brief historical background, we should now turn to look more closely at contemporary ideological/theoretical currents in gender theories of education and seek to identify that which each has to offer to the study of gender and education. These currents are not exhaustive nor do they cover the substantive range of debates in the field. From among the many possible starting points for such a discussion, I will concentrate principally upon those trends, chiefly emanating from theoretical work in the 'West', and particularly within British and North American settings, which may be seen as having achieved what Kuhn (1962) would have called paradigmatic legitimacy in the field.

Power as discursive and discourse(s) of power: the rise of cultural and continental theory (and the 'eroding foundations'[9]) in the study of gender and education

E.P. Thompson's seminal notion that 'class itself is not a thing, it is a happening'[10] dovetailed nicely with the ideas of feminist post-structuralists and cultural theorists that forms of gender power, 'gender regimes' or the nature of gendered discourses are not located – as they had been configured in the earlier Althusserian or Gramscian movement – in one stratified institutional or patriarchal form. Rather, according to Thompson, such power formations could be seen as deeply *cultural* and relational in form. Thompson's concerns with culture as a relation (rather than as a straightforward objectifiable structure) resonates, to give a prime example, with Judith Butler's (1990, 2004) post-structuralist understanding of power. Here, power is seen as circulating through culturally and historically derived language forms to regulate, rather than determine, gender relations. Once gender was conceptualized in this more culturally fluid way, it could be seen as anti-essential in form and regulated by historically evolving micropractices of power. In place of an emphasis upon the mere reproduction of material and ideological relations in the state, gendered discourses of power were seen to offer far more subtle explanations of gender inequality in schools. Power could be seen as more complex, discursive and covert in form, and therefore capable of being located in multiple sites. The direct links between gender, class and inequality were no longer as clear as they had once seemed (see Bonnell and Hunt, 1999; Francis, 1999; Dillabough and Arnot, 2001; Francis and Skelton, 2001).[11] New work sought radically to disrupt normative and largely structural accounts of gender inequality (particularly Marxist feminism) and to expose the manner in which gender was drawn upon in education as a set of binary codes which shaped school knowledge and curriculum (see Walkerdine, 1986; Davies, 1989; Butler, 1990).

Influenced by the field of linguistics, Bronwyn Davies' (1989, see also Francis, 1997) now seminal work – *Frogs and Snails and Feminist Tales* – is often seen as one of the early influential works affecting 'third-wave' developments of gender theory in education. Rather than looking at gendered structures or biological gender distinctions, Davies' work concentrated upon young children's culturally constructed discourses of gender. For Davies, it was necessary to 'deconstruct' traditional understandings of gender in order to expose their metanormative origins.[12] From this view, education – as a set of institutional language events/games (see Derrida, 1974) – could be seen to regulate, rather than to determine, gender inequality.

Coined first by Jacques Derrida (1974; 1981) and drawn upon substantially by feminist Foucauldians and other post-structuralists in education, deconstruction is the method used to critique the gendered meta-narratives of modernity, such as the category 'women' (see Butler, 1990; 2004). Feminist deconstruction is typically defined as a feminist method of reading power relations which takes as its central task the uncovering of the role of gendered language 'in signifying a particular dominance and undoing any polarities of such language' (Johnson, 1981) in institutional sites.[13] The necessity for a deconstructive reading is based upon the Derridian assumption that an uncritical reading of texts or the idea that a text holds only one meaning ignores the principle that language/texts manifest multiple meaning, which even their 'author or the reader may not have understood or intended' (Johnson, 1981). In short, deconstruction feminism argued for 'dismantling gender's inhibiting polarities of male and female altogether. This perspective rejected any notion of an a priori female subject grounded in a pre-sexed body, any concept of women as the foundation of a feminist politics, or any conception of sexual difference that instantiates the feminine or a presumptive sexuality as the privileged locus or ethics of existence' (Dietz, 2003: 40].[14] Deconstruction has been attractive to many gender theorists in education as a way of critiquing the ways in which gender – as a powerful language formation, system of thought and category of analysis – has been drawn upon by schools, teachers, students and policy makers (Yates, 2000; Pillow, 2004) in reconstituting a broad range of social inequalities (see Haywood and Mac an Ghaill, 1997).

Theorizing identity as power and the power of identity: the making and 'multiplying'[15] of the female subject in education

In responding to multifaceted critiques of the sex/gender distinction in educational thought, another element of the cultural turn in gender theory has been an emerging critique of singular or binary notions of gender identity as they have been expressed through schooling (see Haywood and Mac an Ghaill, 1997; Dillabough, 2001). This critique resonated, if often in unrecognized ways, with feminist critiques of the sex/gender distinction during the second-wave period, which had begun to generate theoretical conceptions of gender as a social construction. Such was the intellectual climate in which post-structuralist analysis of the making of identities in discourse and related critques of identity began to move to the centre of educational debates (see Connell, 2000; Francis, 2002). These critiques can be seen to have emerged from multiple strands of feminist thought, of which three possessed particularly important paradigmatic status during the third-wave period.

The first and perhaps most visible strand stemmed from French critiques of female identity which extended to many parts of the 'Western' world. These critiques suggested that gender theorists should concern themselves with the ways in which discourses of gender in education are used to 'characterize, permeate and constitute' (Foucault, 1980) gender subjectivities rather than determine them.[16] Drawing primarily upon Foucault and the work of Judith Butler, many post-structuralist feminists used this critique to expose the difficulty in identifying 'girls' as a distinct category of analysis (see McLeod, 2002). There is, in this case, no singular 'boy' or 'girl' (see Arnot and Dillabough, 1999) that can be associated with a set of characteristic traits or socialized gender roles. For gender theorists, a need therefore emerged to address the ways in which gender identity had become normalized as a form of 'deviancy' in educational contexts of asymmetrical power. The key argument used to explain the social construction of female deviancy was that the liberal humanist tradition reproduced normative ideas about female and male normalcy rather than challenged them. Once the normal 'girl' or 'boy' was defined through educational discourses of achievement and success, it was essential to define its mirror opposite, that is, the deviant 'male' or 'female' (or the underachieving male or female). One of the key theoretical issues raised in ensuing debates was the sometimes problematic conflation of particular notions of gender identity with corresponding accounts of equality and access (liberal equality discourses, discourses of apparent freedom, economic discourses of patriarchy and the 'working-class girl'). These conflations were criticized by feminist Foucauldians as reproducing the very platform they had sought to eradicate in schools and ultimately the need, to borrow from Judith Butler (1990), to 'trouble gender'. Schooling, as a complex gendered process, rather than an ideologically oriented social institution, could be seen as shaping, regulating and reconstituting (rather than determining) identities in relation to time, place and space (see also Massey, 1995). Education, as a site for the cultivation of female equality, was challenged.

Many theorists within this strand of education feminism were concerned with the processes of male and female youth subject formation (as a fluid, dynamic and sometimes fragmented process) as against the question of subjection to power as a passive subject. Work on subject formation in gender theory (and its application to education) falls into two broadly based camps. On the one hand, there are those theorists interested in charting the development of girls' subjectivities, particularly in relation to the experience of marginalization. These researchers tend to focus on the cultural processes underlying subject formation, most notably, immediate local context, psychodynamic operations (see Walkerdine and Lucey, 1989; Luttrell, 2002), gender, class and race relations, and the role played by the family and the gendered state in this process. On the other hand, contemporary issues of social change (such as heightened forms of individualization, risk and globalization) also figure in understandings of subject and subject formation (Beck, 1999; Kenway and Bullen, 2001; Harris, 2004). For example, Harris (2004) and Bettie (2004) demonstrate how issues of youth subject formation are deeply influenced by highly individualized gendered discourses of power under the dynamics of social change (e.g. globalization). This work is designed to explore the relationship between youth subject formation from a post-structuralist perspective and the late modern accounts of individualization – the uncoupling of gender identity from more traditional roles and forms of socialization for young men and women – given by Ulrich Beck (1999) and Lois McNay (2000). Taken as a whole, this work could be seen as forming the basis of what Harris (2004) has named 'girl studies' in education.

A second critique of normative accounts of gender identity emerged from diversity and difference feminists, who argued that the forms of inequality or post-colonial oppression reported by feminist educational researchers were typically concerned with the intersection of class or gender rather than racialization and ethnicity as gender issues. Indeed, 'education feminists' interested in race and ethnicity raised questions about the links between colonialism, culture and gender exclusion (Lopez, 2003) and have played a central role in shaping the 'identity crisis' (see Deitz, 2003) in gender theory. Reviewing the seminal works of education feminism, Carby (1982), Brah and Minhas (1985), and others (e.g. Fuller, 1985) argued that they were not only insufficiently attentive to the relationship between culture, ethnicity and race but were also deeply heterosexist in form (Mirza, 1997; Deitz, 2003). A number of gender theorists in education therefore took up the question of cultural identity, cultural location, and/or the intersections of race, gender and class as educational questions which confronted the 'politics of location' in gender research (see Callender and Wright, 2000; Mirza and Reay, 2000). Broadly speaking, this work covers a range of theoretical positions such as anti-racist feminist theory, postcolonial feminist perspectives (Brah, 1996), women's standpoint (Collins, 1991), voice theory, youth subcultural theory (Nayak, 2003),[17] and the conjunction of race, gender and sexuality studies in education.

More recent work in this area focuses upon the intersection of globalization, race, gender, identity, and school exclusion. This work, while epistemologically diverse, exhibits two key tendencies. First, it focuses on the relationship between racialization and gender with a particular emphasis on youth exclusion as it is produced under the dynamics of global reform (see Calander and Wright, 2000; Dolby, 2001; Pattman and Chege, 2003). In a related way, it also focuses upon the relationship between critiques of race, migration and identity and their relationship to educational studies of gender and achievement (Archer and Francis, 2005).

Secondly, this theoretical turn centres upon the links between locality, culture and context (see Brah *et al.*, 2004). Within this genre of research, local elements of gender (as it pertains to globalization) begin to account for issues such as difference and particularity. They also foreground the 'local' as central to understanding gendered subject formation and youth exclusion, and as an element of microculture which is lost in dominant macroforms of structural argumentation but which is nevertheless linked to the dynamics of global change. Geography and social change are central to such theorizations, as are the links between microlevel, youth cultural formations and macrolevel, global formations (see Kenway and Bullen, 2001; Reay and Lucey, 2000, 2003). Consequently, schools could no longer be seen as singularly or straightforwardly responsible for gender inequality. Instead, peer relations and culture, individualization, racialization, geographical sites undergoing global transformations, the internationalization of state education, citizenship, migration and diasporic identity all played a part (see also Massey, 1999; Tuhiwai-Smith, 1999; Nayak, 2003; Dillabough, *et al.*, 2005).

A third field which has grown rapidly in the wake of the rise of 'identity studies' in education is the area of sexuality. The central premise of this work is that sexuality – as a gendered discourse embedded in schools – serves as an organizing principle of educational life. Terms describing the school system as premised on 'compulsory heterosexuality',[18] 'heteronormativity, and male hegemony' have been at the centre of this work (see Epstein, 1997; Rasmussen and Harwood, 2003). Work in this large and still growing body of work concentrates upon the notions of compulsory heterosexuality, multiple masculinities and femininities, and queer theory in relation to schooling practices.

While the cultural turn in gender theory and education is an important theoretical break with an earlier dominance of structuralism and formalist thinking, the parameters of what might broadly be understood as the post-structuralist project are rendered problematical by the ubiquity of an emphasis which sometimes understands culture and discourse as comprehending anything and everything. This has made any defence of more precise sociological definitions of gendered discourse and its relationship to structure/materialism increasingly difficult. The discursive/deconstructive turn has, in its nature, entailed a substantial move away from the relation of gender to class structures, theories of stratification, and the social distribution of educational opportunity. This has meant that substantive sociological questions have in part been marginalized in gender theory, to be replaced by a preoccupation with various elements of discourse, culture and identity/self. While this work has involved a profoundly sophisticated shift in gender theorizing, some might argue that the price has been high – the loss of key social issues concerning social exclusion, social agency and social inequality (see Dillabough, 2001; London Feminist Salon Collective, 2004). This seems a particularly pertinent concern given the current, transnational, neo-liberal, educational agenda wherein issues of stratification are playing a substantial material role in shaping the life chances of diverse young men and women. It is for this reason that such issues are slowly re-emerging in scholarly debate.

Coded symbolic power, cultural reproduction and 'masculine domination'[19]

Despite the dramatic rise of post-structuralist and culturalist approaches, it has been impossible to ignore the sustaining features of feminist reproduction theory and its continuing hold over the field of gender and education. This has been expressed in a recent revival in a materialist form of cultural sociology and its application to gender and education. Much of this work extends outward from both the earlier and more recent theoretical formulations of Pierre Bourdieu on symbolic power, and to a lesser extent from Bernsteinian sociology. In the contemporary moment, reproduction accounts have been strongly influenced by the later work of Pierre Bourdieu, *Masculine Domination* (1998), and related feminist followers (see, for example, McNay, 2000; McLeod, 2002; Reay, 2004; Skeggs and Adkins, 2005).

The efforts of feminist sociologists in education have been reflected in many of Bourdieu's ideas concerning masculine/symbolic domination. This work has typically, although not exclusively, combined the insights of cultural sociologists on the left with more pragmatic feminist concerns about gender inequalities in schools and society. Feminist sociologists have therefore been most centrally concerned with what Bourdieu has referred to as the 'constancy of structure' in gender relations – an observation about the ways in which social relations and our 'categories of understanding' about sex and gender produce a constant gendered division of labour – if with shifting elements – which is embodied in the consciousness of political subjects and enacted through class relations in education over time. Such theorists have also examined the ways in which education reproduces symbolic forms of masculinized privilege which are seen by Bourdieu as essentially ensured through the exercise of social and cultural ideas and practices in education. In making a commitment to the study of domination as an educational practice, then, the key empirical question which has increasingly set a familiar but renewed research agenda (see Reay, 2004, for an excellent review of Bourdieu's notion of habitus) for contemporary education feminists is as follows: 'to what degree does education function as a cultural system which deploys symbolic and historically inherited forms of masculine domination and privilege and thus continues to shape the social conditions and opportunities for girls and boys in schools?'

Bourdieu's work, *Masculine Domination*, has focused upon a number of key advances made by feminist and gender theorists in education. First, against the grain of feminist post-structuralism, his notion of gendered discourse links power to both micro-and macrostructures of domination in education. In this theoretical paradigm, discourse is contingent upon experience and materiality in fundamental ways. At the same time, Bourdieu's work does not disavow class and social relations in shaping the idiomatic character of the discourse. In this way, for example, masculine discourse cannot be seen as a straightforwardly measurable, objective form of inequality or merely as a form of social regulation. Rather, it is manifested and naturalized in social and cultural space – as habitus – and often embodied as normal and legitimate. To engage in masculine domination in education is therefore not simply to oppress women and girls as a liberal and objectifiable practice or as a simple expression of discourse. Instead, masculine domination is embodied in language, texts, knowledge, policies, human practices and notions of that which constitutes the legitimate political subject. It is also realised through human experience, and relies upon such experience for its expression.

Secondly, in contrast to strong Marxist accounts of inequality which concerned themselves only with class, Bourdieu's position does not view patriarchy or symbolic domination as a singular system of economic oppression. It posits instead a symbolic form of cultural domination that is dialectically shaped over time through both the 'cultural arbitrary'[20] and the contested nature of social reality, shifting gender relations and changing and restructured political economies. This comprehensive account of gender inequality reflects education feminists' attempts to move beyond purely economic accounts of gender inequality in schools toward a more socio-cultural understanding of gender inequality (see Reay, 2004).

Thirdly, in emphasizing a relationship between culture and the economy, Bourdieu remained committed, in part, to a labor theory of the state whereby the sexual division of labor – as part of an accumulated cultural history – might be seen to play a framing role in the cultural production of gender inequality through education (e.g. single-sex schooling, gendered differentiation of school subjects). Culture cannot therefore be eclipsed at the expense of structure in any analysis of masculine domination in schools. This emphasis on structure in understanding the cultural production of masculine domination exposes education's part in the sexual division of labor (in the maintenance of symbolic capital) and its gendered expression through habitus. In this way, Bourdieu recognizes the fictions generated about gender identity through the material practices of cultural production. In such a model, identity, culture and social structure are intimately entwined, and questions of cultural and economic stratification remain centre stage. Perhaps it is this powerful connection between identity, culture and the state that serves as one example of an important theoretical bridge between earlier materialist approaches to the study of gender and education and the larger question of culture and the 'cultural turn' in social thought.

CONCLUSION

Based upon the above review of trends and concepts in gender theory in education, it might be argued that the future of the field remains unpredictable. It is increasingly difficult to define the boundaries of the field or to assess its lasting impact in education. As I have argued, this is largely due to the proliferation of theoretical positions and cutting-edge debates in social thought and their impact on what was previously known as 'education feminism' but might now more accurately be named gender theory in education. Over the last 30 years, we have moved from a focus upon gender socialization theories toward what many identify as a cultural turn concerned with Continental interests in identity and discourse. This particular move should in no way be seen as linear nor should all aspects of structuralism be seen as standing outside these various 'turns', for structuralism is implicated, paradoxically, in each of the intellectual currents that have flowed across the twentieth century.

What we have learned over the last decade is that the proliferation of gender theory has led to further democratization in the study of gender education. At the same time, certain traces of the past have been retained and recently revived in gender theory, largely due to the re-emerging importance of class and social stratification under the dynamics of globalization and neo-liberal shifts in transnational educational contexts. This widening of theoretical remit reaffirms the need for fields like education to unify more closely with the social sciences in responding to the urgent social issues of our times, as well as the need to expand the epistemological premises of theoretical debate in the field. It also reaffirms the requirement for the construction of an 'intellectual-cultural-material' (see Fay, 1996) climate for continuing to pursue interesting and relevant theoretical work in the study of gender and education.

One of the main lessons of this review has been to point to the diversity in feminist thought in education, and to call into question a field still too narrowly defined, and which may not yet be seen as robust enough to respond to all of challenges currently facing it. I am therefore advocating a dialectical way of viewing gender theory in which differences between positions are not conceptualized as absolute or oppositional, but rather as complementary. The tensions which have been created through 'competing' theoretical paradigms in gender theory 'originally thought to have exhausted the possibilities can then be replaced with a wider viewpoint which recognizes the worth in the original positions but which goes beyond them' (Fay, 1996: 224).

REFERENCES

Acker, S (1987) Feminist theory and education and the study of gender and education. *International Review of Education*, 33: 419–35.
Alcoff, L and Potter, E (1994) *Feminist epistemologies*. New York: Routledge.
Althusser, L (1968) Ideology and ideological state apparatuses: notes toward an investigation, in Brewster, B (trans.) *Lenin and philosophy and other essays*. London: New Left Books.

Archer, L and Francis, B (2005) 'They never go off the rails like other ethnic groups': teachers' constructions of British Chinese pupils' gender identities and approaches to learning. *British Journal of Sociology of Education*, 26: 165–82.

Arnot, M (1981) Culture and political economy: dual perspectives in the sociology of women's education. *Educational Analysis*, 3: 97–116.

Arnot, M (1982) Male hegemony, social class and women's education. *Journal of Education*, 164: 64–89.

Arnot, M (2002) Sociological understandings of contemporary gender transformations in schooling in the UK, in Arnot, M *Reproducing gender: essays on educational theory and feminist politics* (175–99). New York: RoutledgeFalmer.

Arnot, M and Dillabough, J (1999) Feminist politics and democratic values in education, *Curriculum Inquiry*, 29: 159–89.

Arnot, M and Dillabough, J (eds) (2000) *Challenging democracy: international perspectives on gender, education and citizenship*. London: RoutledgeFalmer.

Arnot, M and Whitty, G (1982) From reproduction to transformation: recent radical perspectives on the curriculum from the USA. *British Journal of Sociology of Education*, 3: 93–103.

Baert, P (2000) *Social theory in the twentieth century*. Cambridge: Polity Press.

Beck, U (1999) *The risk society*. London: Sage.

Bettie, J (2003) *Women without class: girls, race and identity*. Berkeley, CA: University of California Press.

Benhabib, S, Butler, J, Cornell, D and Fraser, N (1996) *Feminist contentions: a philosophical exchange*. London: Routledge.

Benhabib, S (1997) Feminism and postmodernism: an uneasy alliance. in Benhabib, S, Butler, J, Cornell, D and Fraser, N (eds) *Feminist contentions: a philosophical exchange*. Routledge:New York.

Bonnell, VE and Hunt, L (eds) (1999) *Beyond the cultural turn: new directions in the study of society and culture*. Berkeley, CA: University of California Press.

Bourdieu, P (1998) *Masculine domination*. Stanford, CA: Stanford University Press.

Brah, A (1996) *Cartographies of diaspora: contesting identities*. London: Routledge.

Brah, A and Minhas, R (1985) Structural racism or cultural difference: schooling for Asian girls, in Weiner G (ed) *Just a bunch of girls: feminist approaches to schooling*. Milton Keynes: Open University Press.

Brah, A, Hickman, H and Mac an Ghaill, M (eds) (1999) *Global futures: migration, environment and globalization*. London: Macmillan.

Brah, A, Hickman, M and Mac an Ghaill, M (2004) *Thinking identities: ethnicity, racism, and culture*. London: Palgrave Macmillan.

Brown, LM and Gilligan, C (1992) *Meeting at the crossroads: women's psychology and girls' development*. Cambridge, MA: Harvard University Press.

Butler, J (1990) *Gender trouble: feminism and the subversion of identity*. New York: Routledge.

Butler, J (2004) *Undoing gender*. New York: RoutledgeFalmer.

Callender, C and Wright, C (2000) Discipline and democracy: race, gender, school sanctions and control, in Arnot, M and Dillabough, J (eds) *Challenging democracy: international perspectives on gender, education and citizenship*. New York: RoutledgeFalmer.

Carby, H (1982) Schooling in Babylon, in Centre for Contemporary Cultural Studies (ed) *The empire strikes back: race and racism in 70s Britain*. London: Hutchinson.

Collins, PH (1991) *Black feminist thought: knowledge, consciousness, and the politics of empowerment*. Boston: Unwin Hyman (reprint, New York: Routledge).

Connell, RW (1987) *Gender and power*. Cambridge: Polity Press.

Connell, RW (2000) Masculinities and globalization, in Connell, RW *The men and the boys* (39–56). Cambridge: Polity Press.

Davies, B (1989) *Frogs, snails and feminist tales: preschool children and gender*. Sydney: Allen & Unwin.

Deem, R (1980) Women and schooling, in Deem, R (ed) *Schooling for women's work*. London: Routledge and Kegan Paul.

Deitz, M (2003) Current controversies in feminist theory. *Annual Review of Political Science*, 6: 399–431.

Derrida, J (1974) *Of grammatology*. Baltimore, MD: Johns Hopkins University Press.

Derrida, J (1981) *Dessemination*. Johnson, B (trans and notes) Chicago: University of Chicago Press.

Dillabough, J (2001) Gender equity in education: modernist traditions and emerging contemporary themes, in Francis, B & Skelton, C (eds) *Investigating gender: perspectives in education* (11–26). Milton Keynes: Open University Press.

Dillabough, J and Arnot, M (2001) Feminist sociology of education: dynamics, debates and directions, in Demaine, J (ed) *Sociology of education today* (30–48). New York: Palgrave.

Dillabough, J, Wang, E and Kennelly, J (2005) 'Ginas,' 'thugs,' and 'gangstas': young people's struggles to 'become somebody' in working-class urban Canada. *Journal of Curriculum Theorizing,* 21: 83–108.

Dolby, N (2001) *Constructing race: youth, identity and popular culture in South Africa.* Albany, NY: State University of New York Press.

Epstein, D (1997) Boyz' own story: masculinities and sexualities in schools. *Gender and Education,* 9: 105–16.

Epstein, D, Elwood, J, Hey, V and Maw, J (eds) (1998) *Failing boys?: issues in gender and achievement.* Philadelphia: Open University Press.

Fay, B (1996) *Contemporary philosophy of social science: a multicultural approach.* Cambridge, MA: Blackwell.

Foucault, M (1980) *Power/knowledge: selected interviews and other writings, 1972–1977.* Gordon, C (ed), Gordon, C *et al.* (trans) New York: Pantheon.

Francis, B (1997) Power plays: children's construction of gender and power in role plays. *Gender and Education,* 9: 179–92.

Francis, B (1999) Modernist reductionism or post-structural relativism: can we move on? An evaluation of the arguments in relation to feminist educational research. *Gender and Education,* 11: 381–93.

Francis, B (2002) Relativism, realism, and feminism: an analysis of some theoretical tensions in research on gender identity. *Journal of Gender Studies.* 11: 39–54.

Francis, B and Skelton, C (eds) (2001) *Investigating gender.* Buckingham: Open University Press.

Fraser, N (1997) Heterosexism, misrecognition, and capitalism: a response to Judith Butler. *Social Text,* 15: 279–89.

Fuller, M (1985) Unit 27: Inequality: Gender Race and Class, Mcare, The New Politics of Race and Gender. www.education.ed.ac.uk/ceres/Resource/AEfiles/AE2.htm - 27k.

Harris, A (2004) *Future girl: young women in the 21st* century. New York: Routledge.

Johnson, B (1981) *The critical difference.* Baltimore, MD: Johns Hopkins University Press.

Kehily, M J (2002) *Sexuality, gender, and schooling.* London: Routledge.

Kenway, J and Bullen, E (2001) *Consuming children: education, entertainment, advertising.* Philadelphia: Open University Press.

Kuhn, T (1962) *The structure of scientific revolutions.* Chicago: Chicago University Press.

London Feminist Salon Collective (2004) The problematization of agency in post-modern theory: as feminist educational researchers where do we go from here? *Gender and Education,* 16: 25–34.

Lopez, N (2003) *Hopeful girls, troubled boys: race and gender disparity in urban education.* New York: Routledge.

Lovell, T (2002) Thinking feminism with and against Bourdieu. *Feminist Theory,* 1: 11–32.

Luttrell, W (1997) *Schoolsmart and motherwise: working-class women's identity and schooling.* New York: Routledge.

Luttrell, W (2002) *Pregnant bodies, fertile minds.* New York: RoutledgeFalmer.

Mac an Ghaill, M (1994) *The making of men: masculinities, sexualities and schooling.* Buckingham: Open University Press.

Mac an Ghiall, M and Haywood, C (1997) Materialism and deconstructivism: education and the epistemology of identity. *Cambridge Journal of Education,* 27: 261–72.

MacDonald, M (1980) Schooling and the reproduction of class and gender relations, in. Barton, L, Meighan, R and Walker, S (eds) *Schooling, ideology and the curriculum.* Barcombe: Falmer Press.

Massey, D (1995) *Spatial divisions of labour.* London: Macmillan Press.

Massey, D (1999) Imagining globalization: power-geometries of time-space, in Brah, A, Hickman, I and Mac an Ghaill, M (eds) *Global futures: migration, environment and globalization.* Basingstoke and London: Macmillan.

McLeod, J (2002) Working out intimacy: young people and friendship in an age of reflexivity. *Discourse,* 23: 211–36.

McNay, L (2000) *Gender and agency: reconfiguring the subject in feminist social theory.* Cambridge: Polity.

McRobbie, A (1978) Working class girls and the culture of feminity, in Women's Studies Group, Centre for Contemporary Cultural Studies, University of Birmingham (ed) *Women take issue: aspects of women's subordination.* London: Hutchinson.

Mirza, H (1992) *Young, female and black.* London: Routledge.

Mirza, H (ed) (1997) *Black British feminism: a reader.* London: Routledge.

Mirza, H and Reay, D (2000) Redefining citizenship: Black women educators and the 'third space', in Arnot M and Dillabough, J (eds) *Challenging democracy: international perspectives on gender, education and citizenship.* London: RoutledgeFalmer.

Mottier, V (2002) Masculine domination: gender and power in Bourdieu's writings. *Feminist Theory,* 3: 345–59.

Nayak, A (2003) *Race, place and globalization: youth cultures in a changing world.* London: Berg.

Noddings, N (1987) *Caring: a feminine approach to ethics and moral education.* Berkeley, CA: University of California Press.

Pattman, R and Chege, F (2003) *Finding our voices: gendered and sexual identities and HIV/AIDS in education.* Nairobi: UNICEF Eastern and Southern Africa.

Pillow, W (2004) *Unfit subjects: educational policy and the teen mother.* New York: RoutledgeFalmer.

Rasmussen, M and Harwood, V (2003) Performativity, youth and injurious speech. *Teaching Education,* 14(1): 25–36.

Reay, D (2004) 'It's all becoming a habitus': beyond the habitual use of habitus in educational research. *British Journal of Sociology of Education,* 14: 431–44.

Reay, D and Lucey, H (2000) 'I don't really like it here but I don't want to be anywhere else': children and inner city council estates. *Antipode,* 32: 410–28.

Reay, D and Lucey, H (2003) The limits of "choice": children and inner city schooling. *Sociology,* 37: 121–42.

Shain, F and Ozga, J (2001) Identity crisis? Sociology of education. *British Journal of Sociology of Education,* 22: 109–20.

Skeggs, B and Adkins, L (2005) *Feminism after Bourdieu.* London: Blackwell.

Spender, D (1980) *Man made language.* London: Routledge and Kegan Paul.

Spender, D (1987) Education: the patriarchal paradigm and the response to feminism, in Arnot, M and Weiner, G (eds) *Gender and the politics of schooling.* London: Hutchinson.

Stone, L (ed) (1994) *The education feminism reader.* New York: Routledge.

Tuhiwai-Smith, L (1999) *Decolonizing methodologies: research and indigenous peoples.* London: Zed Books.

Walkerdine, V (1986) Post-structural theory and everyday social practices, in Wilkinson, S (ed) *Feminist social psychology.* Milton Keynes: Open University Press.

Walkerdine, V and Lucey, H (1989) *Democracy in the kitchen.* London: Virago.

Weiler, K (1991) Freire and a feminist pedagogy of difference. *Harvard Educational Review,* 61: 449–74.

Willis, P (1977) *Learning to labour.* Farnborough: Saxon House.

Wolpe, AM (1988) Experiences as an analytic framework: does it account for girls' education?, in Cole, M (ed) *Bowles and Gintis revisited: correspondence and contradiction in educational theory.* New York: Falmer Press.

Yates, L (2000) The 'facts of the case': gender equity for boys as a public policy issue, in Lesko, N (ed) *Masculinities at school* (305–22). Thousand Oaks, CA: Sage.

NOTES

1. This term was coined by Lynda Stone (1994) in her edited collection entitled, *Education Feminisms.* In the words of Alwood and Wadia (2002), *Feminism has taken many forms over time and place and according to social, political and cultural contexts. It is neither fixed nor homogeneous, and it is cut through by and division around class, ethnicity, sexuality and ideology* (p213).

2. This excellent article by Kathleen Weiler (1991) describes the limits of liberal feminism and the importance of feminist reproduction theory in education, championed largely by Madeleine Arnot (formerly known as MacDonald).

3. Connell, 2000: 7.

4. Deitz, 2003: 401.

5. Feminist engagements with reproduction theory have been revived in recent years in response to a perceived over-emphasis on feminist post-structuralism and 'voice approaches' (see also Lovell, McNay, Skeggs, Mottier) in educational research with their limited attention to the question of materiality.

6. For excellent examples of interdisciplinary feminist sociological approaches, see McNay (2000), Lovell (2002), and Mottier (2002).

7. Even structuralist approaches to the study of gender and education now often share a strong commitment to interdisciplinarity. From an epistemological standpoint, there are many diverse and sometimes contradictory premises underlying this work; however, breadth in epistemological reach seems to have greater importance than the potentially contradictory elements of the approach itself.

8. Heida Mirza's (1992), *Young, Black and female*, is a distinct articulation of this theoretical shift, as is Christine Callender's and Cecile Wright's study of Black masculinity and femininity in schools. Wendy Luttrell's (1997) work with African-American women attending adult literacy program in the USA is another excellent example of this kind of theoretical work in gender and education.

9. This phrase was borrowed from Patrick Baert's (2000) excellent book, *Social theory in the twentieth century*.

10. E.P. Thompson, *The making of the English working class* (1991, 2nd edn).

11. While particular forms of structuralism remained dominant in the mid-to late twentieth century, other approaches were also operating, such as phenomenology, albeit with much less force. As Foucault himself commented when discussing the force of structuralism in post-war France: 'The problem of language appeared and it was clear that phenomenology was no match for structural analysis in accounting for the effects of meaning that could be produced by a structure of the linguistic type, in which the subject (in the phenomenological sense) did not intervene to confer meaning. And quite naturally, with the phenomenological spouse finding herself disqualified by her inability to address language, structuralism became the new bride' (Foucault, 1980). As Foucault goes on to state: 'I have never been a Freudian, I have never been a Marxist, and I have never been a structuralist' (p114).

12. Key examples of research embracing this tradition are Epstein's (1997) research on the role of schooling in shaping cultural understandings of sexuality, masculinity and gender; Mac an Ghaill's (1994) research on the making of multiple masculinities; Wanda Pillow's (2004) assessment of educational policy as a form of discourse regulating the lives of teen mothers; and Kehily's (2002) work on the role of sex education as a form of discourse shaping male and female friendships and forms of masculinity and femininity.

13. As Johnson (1981) clarifies, 'if anything is destroyed in a deconstructive reading, it is not the text, but the claim to unequivocal domination of one mode of signifying over another. A deconstructive reading analyzes the specificity of the text's critical difference from itself'.

14. Education feminists located in the new colonies (e.g. Australia) were more heavily influenced by these traditions. A focus upon these traditions shifted the emphasis from the macroimpact of social forces to nuanced questions about the impact of the local cultural context of education.

15. See Dietz (2003) on 'multiplying the subject'. I have borrowed this phrase from her work.

16. Foucault (1980) writes: 'I would say that we are forced to produce the truth of power that our society demands, of which it has need, in order to function; we must speak the truth; we are constrained or condemned to confess or discover the truth. … In the end, we are judged, condemned, classified, determined in our undertakings, destined to a certain mode of living or dying, as a function of the true discourses which are the bearers of the specific effects of power' (p32).

17. The now seminal work of Willis (1977) and McRobbie (1978), as ethnographies of youth culture were exemplary attempts at highlighting the importance of the local and the particular, even if race in this earlier stage of youth cultural studies was not centre stage.

18. The term 'compulsory heterosexuality' was coined by Adrienne Rich in 1980.

19. This section has been adapted from the article entitled 'Class, culture and the predicaments of masculine domination: encountering Pierre Bourdieu', published in the *British Journal of the Sociology of Education*, 25: 489–506.

20. This term refers to the ways in which elements of both cultural life and cultural reproduction are unpredictable, or function outside the domain of logic.

5

Gender and Methodology

Catherine Marshall and
Michelle D. Young

INTRODUCTION: THE NEED FOR ASSERTIVE METHODOLOGIES

> Today women are talking to each other, recovering an oral culture, telling our life stories, reading aloud to each other the books that have moved and healed us, analyzing the language that has lied about us, reading our own words aloud to each other.
>   (Adrienne Rich, 1995: 13, on the political revolutions inspired by activist and methodologically innovative gender research.)

This chapter, in describing methodological insights developed in gender research, asserts the need to view gender[1] research as revolution. This chapter identifies how doing research on gender issues delves into sensitive areas of identity and sexuality, identifies white male hegemony, and makes creative methodological leaps. We begin by showing that researching gender should incorporate feminist stances, making the point that feminist approaches offer methodological insights especially on the focus of the research, the relationship with the researched, and the necessity of values-stances for research. We then review methodological concerns that ensue and we emphasize the need for assertive methodologies. Finally, we note accomplishments, yet continuing challenges for researchers who persevere, knowing that the simple step of doing feminist research is a political act and one that can make a difference in education.

Feminist research in education: pushing at boundaries

Feminist research in education, like feminist research in other fields, has laid bare the ways the traditions in academies; in theory, research, and methodology;

and in the politics of knowledge have historically excluded women's issues and perspectives (Smith, 1987). As a result, researchers use both feminism and social science to 'talk back … in a spirited critique' (Devault, 1999: 27), to push boundaries in support of gender equity in education.

Question reframing research

Although feminist research has provided the foundation for some of the most significant understandings and changes regarding gender equity in education, not all research on gender issues is feminist. Moreover, in mainstream scholarship, gender research (feminist or not), which 'has as its goal equality, equity, and empowerment, has not gained legitimacy' (Mak, 1996: ix). Most acceptable are projects that describe gender differences, such as boys' and girls' access to and use of computer terminals or girls' and boys' performance in math and English. This type of research, while drawing attention to a number of important differentials, has in many cases served to reinforce traditional and firmly entrenched ideas about gender differences – usually framing differences as resulting from innate characteristics (see, for example, Gurian's (2001) research on how girls and boys learn differently). Even with questions broadened to an exploration of the consequences of differences, scholars' analyses rarely question traditional assumptions about the patterns and why they exist.

Less supported and utilized questions and methodologies are those that frame differences and patterns as the effects of the social construction of gender. Such research demonstrates how constructions invent assumptions, such as the conflation of leadership with 'male' behaviors, and use tools, such as femininity and masculinity, to reinforce certain behaviors, encouraging adolescent girls to worry over their weight more than their calculus and encouraging boys to be more interested in sports than theater. Research on schools' contributions to these constructions moves beyond effects on students to reveal the societal contributions to gendered hierarchies and power dynamics in employment, families, religions, schools, businesses, and politics. Studies of this ilk locate research questions beyond the classroom in larger arenas, allowing an examination of how institutions provide legitimacy to patriarchy and reify oppressive gender relations. Within this more critical framework, the differences between males and females and the way they are treated or provided access to resources and opportunities are considered to be the result of complex social, political and cultural forces.

Researchers operating out of such critical frameworks, such as Marshall (1997), Stromquist (1997), Pateman (1985) and Connell (1987), often develop research agendas aimed at empowerment from repressive and oppressive structures. Feminist scholars rethink traditional approaches to research topics, how they pose research questions, and how they frame their research. For example, Pillow (1997) examined traditional policy assumptions about teen pregnancy. Her research asked, 'what/who is silenced in the naming of teen pregnancy as a policy problem and how does this silencing affect intervention programs?' (p135). Similarly, Young (2003) examined how policy discourse on the school administrators' career pipeline was being defined as a serious crisis. By shifting the focus of the crisis discourse, she revealed that analyses failed to consider seriously the role of gender in the shortage, relegating it to the category of 'non-issue'. Such feminist reframing is often necessary to uproot limited and androcentric gender biases. Such revolutionary research reframing and designs, however, gain little acknowledgement from those in positions of power (in academia, in government, and in social interactions). They are ignored in part because they contradict common-sense beliefs about essential gender differences, because they embed explanations within critiques of cultural and societal gender relations, and because their analyses often emphasize the continuous pattern of inequity in which males are privileged, attaining more resources, positions of power and wealth no matter what their educational or social accomplishments. Indeed, such critical feminist reframing uncomfortably uncovers 'the ideological messages and educational practices that reproduce male and female identities' (Stromquist, 1997: 38), and the complex mixes of class, race, gender, sexuality, and school experiences.

Constructing research questions and political strategies for equity

To support equity, methodology used to investigate gender issues must involve assertive question shifting, redefinitions of issues, sharp attention to the power of dominant values, and vigilant monitoring of how questions are asked and how research is used. Having equity as a goal of research contributes to the rigor of feminist-critical research. Researchers hold themselves to a higher level of ethical responsibility for conducting valuable and trustworthy inquiry. Research conducted in Australia, the USA, and 'developing countries' provides examples of such rigorous, equity-focused research.

Scholars, femocrats (feminists in leadership positions), and activists in Australia participated in a series of policy-research panels developed to expand policy questions. Panel participants reframed mainstream research and policy agendas to incorporate the social construction of gender, including masculinity and ethnicity. Further, they pushed for research and program designs that addressed the ways gender and education intertwined with wider issues such as the status of women in leadership, career choices, pay equity, the justice system, health, transportation, domestic violence, homelessness, and so on (Yates, 1993; Marshall, 2000). In one example, a study showing a high percentage of schoolchildren experiencing some form of sexual harassment, with an assertive media-savvy dissemination, demanded national attention. Australia passed the comprehensive National Policy for the Education of Girls in Australian Schools in 1987. Later, in Australia and elsewhere, research methodologies and shifting research questions revealed the interrelatedness of health, self-image, aspiration, support, and educational opportunity. The research and advocacy on the effects of sexual harassment, mentioned above; research on body image and eating disorders affecting young girls; and the recognition that the dropout problem and teen pregnancy are interrelated, all required a shifting of research questions from a traditional focus on school effects to a critical view of the impact that wider context and social forces had on schools and the children within them.

However, the lack of legitimacy of most research on gender issues has made it difficult for some to have their findings acknowledged, appreciated and acted upon by public officials. It is likely that this condition moved feminist researchers to monitor and, in some cases, exploit value shifts in society. For example, researchers, attuned to value shifts, such as the 'backlash' in broader society and the 'boy turn' in gender research, reinforced their efforts to monitor gender effects. Thus, when Australia's politicians used research on how pressures on boys increased dropouts and suicides, femocrats understood the time was right to insert other gender equity issues into the public arena, such as women's educational accomplishments long term, in relation to their wages and careers (Marshall, 2000).

A different example of linking feminist research to dominant values/policy in order to achieve feminist goals was the push for passage of Title IX in the USA. Title IX built upon research on sex differences, but momentum for the bill's passage came from coupling sex discrimination with the dominant values of the equal and civil rights movement (Fishel and Pottker, 1977). Despite weak implementation, Title IX's effects prevail, due less to the research and more to its logic in relation to the liberal equal rights/civil rights tradition, and, perhaps, from the highly visible accomplishments of female Olympic athletes.

Indeed, researchers have become much smarter about when and how to package and present their research. For example, it is understood that research designs with questions and methodologies that bundle equal opportunity with the economies of developing countries are most likely to get UNESCO, governmental and foundation support. Moreover, research designed to tie the level of education of mothers to healthier birth rates, health of children, and even to economic development, has led, in some countries to more educational opportunities for girls and women. Framing methodological approaches to bundle together such factors is an example of question reframing and issue shifting, affixing dominant values upon feminist research. Feminist researchers, then, to affect change in education, must find ways to tune their designs to their political context, even while they are challenging dominant values in those contexts.

FEMINIST FRAMEWORKS AND METHODOLOGICAL STANCES

It is impossible to identify definitively a clear point of origin for any theory (Derrida, 1988) or to agree on its meaning. Often, feminists resist the notion that there are essentials of feminist theory and methodology (DeVault, 1999). Nevertheless, there are important underlying beliefs that drive feminist scholarship and key characteristics that signify their practice.[2] We now discuss several of the beliefs and distinctive characteristics of these theoretical frameworks and methodological stances.

Feminist frameworks

Whether the theoretical roots of research come from liberal feminism, critical feminism, post-structuralist feminism or post-feminism, theories lay the groundwork for choices of methodological approaches. Moreover, just as different feminist frameworks affect methodological approaches, they also affect the policy implications for education. Liberal feminisms that focus on unequal opportunity and sexism, for example, frame research questions in the immediate school environment, such as identifying the paucity of illustrations and problems that show competent women and girls in math and science texts, and the research on teachers' differential attention to boys and girls in classroom interaction.

A different framing is used to focus specifically on 'women's ways' of valuing, knowing, making meaning, living, and working. This framework focuses solely on women, who had been previously left out of researching and theorizing, and develops new theories of relationship and ethics (Gilligan, 1982; Belenkey *et al.*, 1986). Research questions that take on a 'women's ways' of framing, explore educational practices that build upon androcentric assumptions (e.g. competitive versus collaborative learning).

Still another framing of feminist research is provided by critical feminists. These scholars frame research focusing on power and patriarchy to 'out' hegemony, showing power sources that maintain control over the generation, legitimation, and interpretation of research, in ways that advance the interests of dominant groups, usually white males. Research designs, then, focus on arenas of power and dominance, such as boards of trustees, courts, and legislators, and also on powerful policy artefacts, such as curriculum guidelines, and on unobtrusive policies in practice, such as the understandings of deference to male voices in faculty meetings. Weis' (1997) analysis of major education reform reports ignoring gender and Laible's (1995) identification of school board members' narrow definitions of sexual harassment are examples of critical framings.

Researching the heretofore excluded

Early feminist critiques of theory and methodology point to the omission and distortion of women's experiences in the work of traditional research as well as the tendency to universalize the male experience. Beyond presenting the notion that research samples must include women and girls before drawing conclusions about health, leadership, and moral reasoning, feminist research has moved to another stance: studying women in their own right in order to develop versions of reality that more accurately reflect their experiences. Methods emphasized identification, trust, empathy, and nonexploitative relationships, with intent 'to provide for women explanations of social phenomena that they want and need' (Harding, 1987: 8). This has produced radical re-examinations of assumptions, and reconstructions of previously accepted interpretations across a broad range of disciplines.

ELICITING THE PERSONAL AND ISSUES OF SEX, SEXUALITY, AND THE PRIVATE SPHERE

Feminist researchers see gender in an ever-expanding range of topics – topics that were previously considered not important, too personal, or nonacademic in education and health have been particularly important to the feminist project (Olesen, 2000). Thus, research on girls and women, 'women's issues', 'women's work,' 'the private sphere', and the wide context of the personal, the political, and the economic have become topics worthy of incorporation for research and theory. For example, Reay's (1998) research on the impact of social class on the involvement of mothers in their children's education and Chase's (1995) study of the inhibiting structures with which many female superintendents struggle would have been given little if any attention in the past. These, along with examinations of the double and triple shift of 'women's work' and of the complexity of adolescent girls' identity negotiations, have ushered in important shifts in thinking for researchers and the consumers of research.

Understanding gender as a social construction

In many social science studies, gender is a primary category used for analysis. In feminist research, gender analysis is the basis for critique of social and political relations and systems (Harstock, 1974; Harding, 1987; Smith, 1987; Reinharz, 1992). Some feminist researchers, however, say that focusing on gender provides more visibility and power to what is essentially a social construction, that gender is a construction created within cultural and historical discursive practices.

Fuss (1989) cautions that any discussion of women as a group is open to criticisms of essentialism and universalism. Still, Kristeva (1980) and Irigaray (1980) argue that doing away with the concept of women would diminish efforts to change the way that gendered social norms are unequally constructed. Since women as a group still live in uneven and oppressed conditions and are thought of in most societies as a collective, we must use gender and categories like 'women' for strategic purposes.

Beyond essentialist labels and sexist epistemologies[3]

To this day, the legacy of white male hegemony tyrannizes many forms of knowledge, knowers, and approaches to knowing. This, of course, 'has implications for the social structures of education, laboratories, journals, learned societies, funding agencies – indeed for social life in general' (Harding, 1987: 7). The power to define 'good' methodologies, 'good' research questions, and 'correct' interpretations and modes of dissemination is also the power to control, making clear why critical feminist research, with a 'sensitivity to the power of discourse and textual bases of ruling as they organize everyday life' (Naples, 2003: 198), is essential.

Viewing knowledge and knowing in this way has led to feminist methodologies that veer from the traditional. It has also enabled farther-reaching discussions regarding epistemology to emerge. For example, Collins' (1990) work (and that of many other feminists of color) emphasized the danger of using excessively idealist definitions of women, which relied on ideological rather than culturally embedded criteria. Interrupting common misrepresentations of women from non-majority groups, Zinn (1982), for example, argued against depictions of Hispanic women as resigned, quiet, simple women, dependent on macho men. Researchers have also debunked myths and destabilized research with regard to lesbians (Butler, 1990; Hall, 1991; Weston, 1991), women with disabilities (Asch and Fine, 1992; Gill, 1997), and women in non-Western industrialized societies (Alexander and Mohanty, 1997).

Beyond 'add women and stir'

Scholars have gone well beyond simply documenting women's realities (which is in and of itself an important accomplishment). Rather, feminist research has worked to expand narrow understandings, to deconstruct distorted assumptions about women, to valorize activities such as teaching that are commonly associated with women, and to 'expose' the important contributions made by women, their perspectives, and their work. Far beyond the 'add women and stir' response, feminist researchers have enriched the research field epistemologically, ontologically, and methodologically.

FEMINIST METHOD

Rich discussions around feminism and methodology gained momentum during the 1980s with Harding's (1987) edited anthology that illustrated a variety of feminist methods. Although there is no real consensus regarding what counts as feminist methodology (Oakley, 1981; Ramazanoglu, 1989; Gorelick, 1991; Gelsthorpe, 1992; Atkinson and Hammersley, 1994; DeVault, 1999), we address feminist method as a fairly broad category including any approach that uses or develops feminist insights.[4]

According to DeVault (1999), Cook and Fonow (1986) and Reinharz (1992) provided important compilations of research exemplifying feminist approaches to research. These included adaptations of survey and experimental methods (Eichler, 1988), interview research (Oakley, 1981), inductive fieldwork (Reinharz, 1983), Marxist and ethnomethodological approaches (Smith, 1987; Stanley and Wise, 1993), phenomenology (Leveque-Lopman, 1988), action/participatory research (Mies, 1983; Maguire, 1987), oral history (Personal Narratives Group, 1989; Gluck and Patai, 1991), and others. More recent additions to the list include feminist versions of experimental ethnography (*Inscriptions,* 1988), and methods based on post-structuralist insights (Game, 1991; Lather, 1991). Thus, a range of research tools and processes have been used to undertake feminist research. One attraction of this pluralism is the lack of a research hierarchy within a community of scholars who are dedicated to issues of equity (Reinharz, 1992). Yet, there are certain practices that tend to characterize feminist research.

Qualitative and/or quantitative feminist research

Although more closely aligned philosophically with qualitative research, feminist scholars use both quantitative and qualitative research methods in their work. Some qualitative feminist researchers openly claim that qualitative methods are more feminist than quantitative (Kasper, 1994). For example, DeVault (1999) asserts that qualitative methods 'give voice' to women respondents, allow women to help determine the direction and focus of the research, and emphasize particularity over generalization. Further, Oppong (1982) and Harding (1987) worry that quantitative research, particularly survey techniques, can reinforce assumptions about gender and culture through item construction.

However, a number of feminist scholars criticize the tendency to associate feminism so strongly with qualitative over quantitative approaches to research (e.g. Sprague and Zimmerman, 1993; Kelly et al., 1994; Maynard and Purvis, 1994). Spalter-Roth and Hartmann (1991), for example, point out that on policy issues, 'hard data' are often needed to convince those who work outside academe. Some argue that poorly constructed qualitative research can be detrimental. For example, Cannon et al. (1988) point out that small-scale qualitative research projects may be more likely to lead to the reproduction of race and class biases if findings are inappropriately generalized.

Relatively little has been written about feminist quantitative research methods. Feminist researchers who use quantitative methods are less likely to describe their actual methodology as feminist. Eichler (1988) points out ways to eliminate sexism in traditional research (e.g. instrument validation and norms to include women). Beyond this, feminist quantitative research can use feminist theory in the interpretation of the data (Risman, 1993). For example, in their evaluations of various policies for women, Spalter-Roth and Hartmann (1991) use a quantitative tool (cost-benefit analysis) with a feminist policy framework. They asked women-centered questions of the data, resisting the traditional idea that there is one public, and identifying the costs and benefits of certain policies for women and other groups. Similarly, Bruner and Grogan's (2005) national survey of women superintendents was a fairly traditional instrument. However, the authors employed feminist perspectives in their analysis. Some researchers reference or include secondary analyses of quantitative data to make a point or support a feminist argument. Smith (1994), for example, employs a feminist perspective to examine statistical studies, considering them tools of the dominant group used to manage the social structure.

For greatest impact, feminist researchers should be prepared as a group to conduct research by both qualitative and quantitative methods. As DeVault (1999) points out, this will require that feminist researchers let go of some of their prejudices, and focus on providing data and analyses that challenge hegemony and traditional notions of what it means to be a man or woman by expanding tools for understanding women and girls, their experiences, gender issues, oppression, and how to make this world more equitable.

Seeking equity and genuineness in method

For many feminists, the greatest dilemma in the research process is the imbalance of power. One type of power imbalance involves the different positionalities of the researcher and the researched. The hierarchies that are created from these differences can have powerful impacts on the research process, the data, the findings, and the people involved. A second type of imbalance occurs when researchers maintain all or most of the control over the design and carrying out of the research, and a third type of power imbalance derives from the researcher's paradigm and perspectives dominating the interpretations.

These imbalances are recognized by many (though not all) feminist researchers as problematic and have spurred many to challenge their own assumptions[5] and the way they do research (e.g. adopting more collaborative research approaches and developing egalitarian relationships and friendships during the research process). Such relationships not only increase participants' willingness to share but may reduce the exploitative nature of research (Wolf, 1996).

Collaborative research can dynamically alter the roles of people involved in research to achieve a more egalitarian and responsive relationship (Reinharz, 1992). For example, Laible (1995) worked to develop through dialog 'meaningful relationships' with her participants, who were racially, culturally, and economically different from herself (p7). According to Laible, this requires a sense of humility, respect, faith, and self-reflection on how the girls, teachers, and administrators in her study influenced her.

For some, collaborative research is seen as an avenue for contributing to the social and political struggles of oppressed groups (e.g. women, people of color, the working poor, the disabled). Participants collaborating in defining the research topic afford greater possibility that the results will be useful for those involved. Participatory action research has laid important groundwork in this area, especially in institutional and international research efforts (e.g. Smith, 1987).

Some feminist researchers who conduct collaborative research argue that certain likenesses between themselves and their research participants support the blurring of the self–Other binary and enhance the collaborative process, providing a means for identification and better understanding (Millman, 1986; Collins, 1990). However, others have cautioned that these links or likenesses are temporal and do not provide researchers with epistemological privilege (Sawicki, 1994). Indeed, questions of whether women's voices are authentically presented; whether knowledge is discovered, created, achieved, or constructed; whether dialog and collaboration can truly eliminate the power differential;

and whether and how much of the researcher's influence is acceptable are still contentious issues.[6]

When, through dialog, the researcher and participants together explore a phenomenon and generate a process of reflection and understanding, they reduce the risk of 'imperial translation' and form 'communities of friendly critical informants' for help in thinking through which voices and analyses to front and which ones to foreground (Fine, 1994: 80). Some scholars take collaboration a step further by making the writing process collaborative (Fine and Gordon, 1992). By self-consciously working the hyphen between self and Other they argue researchers will be better situated to dissect the boundaries of their relationships with their participants, to understand the politics involved in their work, and to seek ways of resisting or interrupting Othering.

Embracing subjectivity

Feminist research (Fonow and Cook, 1991; Smith, 1992; Denzin and Lincoln, 2000) calls into question standard models of research design, data collection, and evaluation (e.g. objectivity, validity, and reliability). Ladner (1987), for example, asks, 'why should anyone think it good to be "objective" (indifferent, disinterested, dispassionate, value neutral)' (p74).

Feminists are especially concerned about research authenticity and integrity; however, they do not define their concerns in traditional ways.[7] Thus, what a logicopositivist would consider a bias, a qualitative feminist researcher would see as a resource (Olesen, 2000). A self-reflexive understanding of one's identity is a necessary part of understanding the impact of one's presence and perspective on the research. The question, Is this objective truth?, in the hands of a feminist researcher, becomes, Is this faithful enough to some human construction that we feel safe in acting upon it? 'What is required … is sufficient reflexivity to uncover what may be deep-seated but poorly recognized views on issues central to the research and a full account of the researcher's views, thinking, and conduct' (Olesen, 2000: 165). Thus, 'sufficient reflexivity' constitutes both a strategy for reducing the problematics of feminist research and a factor to consider when evaluating feminist research. It requires acknowledgement and communication of one's primary subjective experience.

GENDER RESEARCH AS THEORY IN/FOR ACTION

Research alone, no matter what the methodology, cannot prevent backsliding or fix gender and education challenges unless it is action- and values-oriented, as it challenges hegemony with world-changing findings. Such research is not a passive, compliant, supported act; instead, it is theory in action, and it often requires creative and challenging methodologies.

Dynamic, creative, world-changing methodological approaches

Whether the research design is the avant-garde auto-ethnography or the survey, research for action is important. It can correct judicial doubting of memories of sexual abuse, of the injuries of sexual harassment in schools and on the job, or of the reality of damages in rape-without-bruises (MacKinnon, 1989; Naples, 2003). Dynamic, creative, world-changing methodological approaches, such as participatory action research, move beyond women-as-victim framing (Maguire, 2001), by putting women's voices, women's work, women's experiences, and women's interest at the center.

Empowerment-oriented methodological approaches have catalytic validity, when 'the research process, re-orients, focuses and energizes participants towards knowing reality, in order to transform it' (Lather, 1991: 68). Then researchers move beyond traditional beliefs about detached observation. Theirs is active and purposeful engagement. The 'British Girls and Occupational Choice' and the 'Girls in Science and Technology' projects, are good examples of action research. Though criticized as being too prescriptive (Chisholm, 1990), they exemplify advocacy-oriented methodology. Singh and Vithal's (2003) research on the needs of women faculties in post-apartheid South African is another good example of participative research. Their work was embedded with cultural, race, gender, and hierarchical complexities, requiring that they use methods that go beyond the boundaries of white, Western feminisms; move beyond old binaries of men/women and rural/urban; incorporate the insights of African feminisms; and make use of a collaborative design and questions that serve as political tools. One respondent said 'just filling out the questionnaire inspired me to try to do something' (p14). Similarly, Christman *et al*.'s (1995) feminist journal-writing project highlighted the lived realities of five female elementary and middle-school principals, and became a catalyst for action, consciousness raising, and further research in the participants' schools.

Balancing credibility and creativity in methodologies with action orientation

Creative exploration and reframing of questions and analyses, and methodological experimentation open gender research to superscrutiny. Maintaining credibility for such research requires methodological/political skill in order to answer the anticipated attacks on the validity, objectivity, subjectivity, and data quality. It requires that feminist researchers implement research with strong designs (Maynard, 1994). Although, for some, this requirement might seem contradictory or too far in the camp of logical-positivism, we argue that rigor and researcher responsibility for ethical practice and trustworthy research are something all researchers should embrace, while understanding that their epistemological, ontological, and methodological frameworks will determine the meanings of these criteria. As Gelsthorpe (1992) noted, feminist researchers have not chosen between subjectivity and analytic rigor. Rather, they seek methods that enable both, or that, at the very least, do not deny subjectivity.

Accomplishments and political challenges

In the USA, the substantial increases of women's enrollment in business, agricultural and natural sciences, psychology, and physical sciences can be directly related to past research efforts to expose and change negative patterns. Similarly, more women have earned doctorates and professional degrees in dentistry, medicine, and law. Also, the training and professional development of teachers sometimes includes research on gender interactions in classrooms. Yet gender accomplishments remain uneven, and school advantages do not always constitute equitable accomplishments, since school achievements do not penetrate the gender divides in economic and political opportunities: the wage gap continues.

As the twenty-first century begins, all research funding and methodological approaches of gender and education issues in the USA are politicized, especially with the 'erosion of hard-won gains for women under the Bush administration' (Women's Law Center, 2004: 1). Data on women are being 'deleted, buried, altered, or otherwise gone missing from government websites and publications … funding cut, research findings distorted, important social differences masked, and critical committees and programs dismantled' (National Council for Research on Women, 2004: 1). Gender equity is omitted in the reporting in the major US educational equity reform legislation!

We see retrenchment from the academy's support of women's studies and, we are told, our research is biased, that everything about girls and women has already been studied and fixed. Vigilant monitoring of how gender-research questions and data are framed, collected, and reported (or silenced) requires activist researcher stances with feminist voices challenging academia, media, foundations, and government agencies to ask that gendered data be collected, and 'spun' reports debunked.

CONCLUSION

Gender research has inspired methodological exploration in areas of representation, ethics, and collaboration. With feminist framing, research requires redefinitions and question shifting, an activist values stance, and continuing vigilance against misuse and backsliding. Gender research designs must often transgress boundaries and locate gender and education issues beyond schools, encompassing their cultural, political, and economic contexts, and presenting uncomfortable challenges to dominant practice. Explorations in methodological approaches for gender research promise fertile agendas for scholars and for improving education.

REFERENCES

Alexander, MJ and Mohanty, CT (eds) (1997) *Feminist genealogies colonial legacies, democratic futures.* New York: Routledge.

Asch, A and Fine, M (1992) Beyond the pedestals: revisiting the lives of women with disabilities, in Fine, M (ed) *Disruptive voices: the possibilities of feminist research* (139–74). Ann Arbor, MI: University of Michigan Press.

Atkinson, P and Hammersley, M (1994) Ethnography and participant observation, in Denzin, NK and Lincoln, YS (eds) *The handbook of qualitative research* (248–61). Newbury Park, CA: Sage.

Belenky, M, Clinchy, B, Goldberger, N and Tarule, J (1986) *Women's ways of knowing.* New York: Basic Books.

Bloom, LB and Munro, P (1995) Conflicts of selves: nonunitary subjectivity in women administrators' life history narratives, in Hatch JA and Wisniewski, R (eds) *Life history and narrative.* London: Falmer Press.

Bruner, C and Grogan, M (2005) National study of women in the superintendency. Paper presented at the national meeting of the American Educational Research Association, Montreal, Canada.

Butler, J (1990) *Gender trouble: feminism and the subversion of identity.* New York: Routledge.

Cannon, L, Higginbotham, L and Leung, M (1988) Race and class bias in qualitative research on women. *Gender and Society,* 2: 449–62.

Chase, SE (1995) *Ambiguous empowerment – the work narratives of women school superintendents.* Amherst, MA: University of Massachusetts Press.

Chisholm, L (1990) Action research: some methodological and political considerations. *British Educational Research Journal,* 16: 249–57.

Christman, J, Hirshman, J, Holtz, A, Perry, H, Spelkoman, R and Williams, M (1995) Doing Eve's work: women principals write about their practice. *Anthropology and Education Quarterly,* 26: 213–27.

Collins, P (1990) *Black feminist thought: knowledge, consciousness, and the politics of empowerment.* Boston: Unwin Hyman.

Connell, RW (1987) *Gender and power.* Cambridge: Polity Press.

Cook, J and Fonow, M (1986) Knowledge and women's interests: issues of epistemology and methodology in feminist sociological research. *Sociological Inquiry,* 56: 2–29.

Denzin, NK and Lincoln, YS (2000) Introduction: the discipline and practice of qualitative research, in Denzin, NK and Lincoln, YS (eds) *The handbook of qualitative research* (1–29). Thousand Oaks, CA: Sage.

Derrida, J (1988) *The ear of the Other.* Kamuf, P (trans). Lincoln, NE: University of Nebraska Press.

DeVault, M (1999) *Liberating method: feminism and social research.* Philadelphia, PA: Temple University Press.

Eichler, M (1988) *Nonsexist research methods: a practical guide.* Boston: Unwin Hyman.

Fine, M (1994) Working the hyphens: reinventing self and Other in qualitative research, in Denzin, NK and Lincoln, YS (eds) *The handbook of qualitative research* (70–82). Newbury Park, CA: Sage.

Fine, M and Gordon, SM (1992) Feminist transformation of/despite psychology, in Fine, M (ed) *Disruptive voices* (1–26). Ann Arbor, MI: University of Michigan Press.

Fishel, A and Pottker, J (1977) *National politics and sex discrimination in education.* Lexington, MA: Lexington Books, D.C. Heath.

Fonow, M and Cook, J (1991) *Beyond methodology: feminist scholarship as lived research.* Bloomington, IN: Indiana University Press.

Freire, P (1972) *Pedagogy of the oppressed.* New York: Continuum.

Fuss, D (1989) *Essentially speaking: feminism, nature and difference.* New York: Routledge.

Game, A (1991) *Undoing the social: towards a deconstructive sociology.* Toronto: University of Toronto Press.

Gelsthorpe, L (1992) Response to Martyn Hammersley's paper 'On feminist methodology'. *Sociology,* 26: 213–18.

Gill, CJ (1997) The last sisters: health issues of women with disabilities, in Ruzek, SB, V. Olesen and Clarke, A (eds) *Women's health: complexities and differences* (96–112). Columbus, OH: Ohio State University Press.

Gilligan, C (1982) *In a different voice.* Cambridge, MA: Harvard University Press.

Gluck, S and Patai, D (1991) *Women's words: the feminist practice of oral history.* New York: Routledge.

Gorelick, S (1989) The changer and the changed: methodological reflections on studying Jewish feminists, in Jaggar A and Bordo S (eds) *Gender/body/knowledge: feminist reconstructions of being and knowing* (336–58). New Brunswick, NJ: Rutgers University Press.

Gorelick, S (1991) Contradictions of feminist methodology. *Gender and Society*, 5: 459–77.

Gurian, M (2001) *Boys and girls learn differently: a guide for teachers and parents.* San Francisco, CA: Jossey-Bass.

Hall, S (1991) Ethnicity, identity and difference. *Radical America*, 3: 9–22.

Harding, S (1987) Introduction: is there a feminist method?, in Harding, S (ed) *Feminism and methodology.* Bloomington, IN: Indiana University Press. pp 1–14.

Harstock, N (1974) Political change: two perspectives on power, *Quest: A Feminist Quarterly*, 1(1). Reprinted in *Building feminist theory: essays from Quest* (3–19). New York: Longman, 1981.

Hawkesworth, M (1994) Policy studies within a feminist frame. *Policy Sciences,* 27: 97–118.

Inscriptions (1988) *Special issue. Feminism and the critique of colonial discourse, Inscriptions*, 3 and 4.

Irigaray, L (1980) Approaches to semiotics, in Marks, E and de Courtivron, I (eds) *New French feminisms: an anthology.* Amherst, MA: University of Massachusetts Press.

Kasper, A (1994) A feminist, qualitative methodology: a study of women with breast cancer. *Qualitative Sociology,* 17: 263–81.

Kelly, L, Burton, S and Regan, L (1994) Researching women's lives or studying women's oppression: what constitutes feminist research?, in Maynard, M and Purvis, J (eds) *Researching women's lives from a feminist perspective* (27–48). London: Taylor & Francis.

Kristeva, J (1980) *Desire in language: a semiotic approach to literature and art.* Gora, T, Jardine, A and Roudiez, LS (trans). New York: Columbia University Press.

Ladner, J (1987) Tomorrow's tomorrow: the Black woman, in Harding, S (ed) *Feminism and methodology* (74–83). Bloomington, IN: Indiana University Press.

Laible, J (1995, April) Crossing borders: the use of self-reflexivity and collaboration by a Gringa as she speaks for others in Texas/Mexico border schools. Paper presented at the annual meeting of the American Educational Research Association, San Francisco, CA.

Lather, P (1991) *Getting smart: feminist research and pedagogy with/in the postmodern.* New York: Routledge.

Leveque-Lopman, L (1988) *Claiming reality: phenomenology and women's experience.* Totawa, NJ: Rowan and Littlefield.

MacKinnon, CA (1989) *Toward a feminist theory of the state.* Cambridge, MA: Harvard University Press.

Maguire, P (1987) *Doing participatory research: a feminist approach.* Amherst, MA: Center for International Education.

Maguire, P (2001) Uneven ground: feminisms and action research, in Reason, P and Bradbury, H (eds) *Handbook of action research: participative inquiry and practice* (59–69). Thousand Oaks, CA: Sage.

Mak, GCL (ed) (1996) 'Preface', *Women, education, and development in Asia* (ix–xi). New York: Garland Publishing.

Marshall, C (1997) *Feminist critical policy analysis.* London: Falmer Press.

Marshall, C (2000) Policy as discourse: negotiating gender equity. *Journal of Education Policy*, 5: 125–56.

Maynard, M (1994) Methods, practice and epistemology: the debate about feminism and research, in Maynard, M and Purvis, J (eds) *Researching women's lives from a feminist perspective* (27–48). London: Taylor & Francis.

Maynard, M and Purvis, J (eds) (1994) *Researching women's lives from a feminist perspective.* London: Taylor & Francis.

Mies, M (1983) Towards a methodology for feminist research, in Bowles, G and Klein, R (eds) *Theories of women's studies* (117–39). London: Routledge.

Millman, M (1986) *Such a pretty face: being fat in America.* Berkeley, CA: Berkeley Publishing Co.

Mohanty, C (1991) Cartographies of struggle: Third World women and the politics of feminism, in Mohanty, C, Russo, A and Torres, L (eds) *Third World women and the politics of feminism* (1–47). Bloomington, IN: Indiana University Press.

Naples, NA (2003) *Feminism and method – ethnography, discourse analysis, and activist research.* New York: Routledge.

National Council for Research on Women (2004) *Missing: information about women's lives.* New York: Author.

National Women's Law Center (2004) Slip-sliding away: the erosion of hard-won gains for women under the Bush administration and an agenda for moving forward. Washington, DC: National Women's Law Center. www.nwlc.org/pdf/AdminRecordOnWomen2004.pdf.

Oakley, A (1981) Interviewing women, in Roberts, H (ed) *Doing feminist research* (30–61). New York: Routledge.

Olesen, V (2000) Feminisms and qualitative research into the millennium, in Denzin, NK and Lincoln, YS (eds) *Handbook of qualitative research* (215–55). Thousand Oaks, CA: Sage.

Oppong, C (1982) Family structure and women's reproductive and productive roles, and in Anker, R, Buvinic, M and Youssef, N (eds) *Women's roles and population trends in the Third World* (135–50). London: Croom Helm.

Pateman, C (1985) Introduction, in Godenow, J and Pateman, C (eds) *Women, social science and public policy.* Wincester, MA: Northeastern University Press.

Personal Narratives Group (1989) *Interpreting women's lives: feminist theory and personal narratives.* Bloomington, IN: Indiana University Press.

Pillow, W (1997) Decentering silences/troubling irony: teen pregnancy's challenge to policy analysis, in Marshall, C (ed) *Feminist critical policy analysis* (135–52). London: Falmer Press.

Ramazanoglu, C (1989) Improving on sociology: the problems of taking a feminist standpoint. *Sociology,* 23: 427–42.

Reason, P (1994) Three approaches to participative inquiry, in Denzin, NK and Lincoln, YS (eds) *Handbook of qualitative research* (324–39). Thousand Oaks, CA: Sage.

Reay, D (1998) The fallacy of easy access. *Women's Studies International Forum,* 18: 205–13.

Reinharz, S (1983) Experiential analysis: a contribution to feminist research, in Bowles, G and Klein, R (eds) *Theories of women's studies* (162–91). London: Routledge.

Reinharz, S (with Davidman, L) (1992) *Feminist methods in social research.* New York: Oxford University Press.

Rich, A (1995) *On lies, secrets, and silence.* New York: Norton.

Risman, B (1993) Methodological implications of feminist scholarship. *American Sociologist,* 24: 15–25.

Sawicki, J (1994) Foucault, feminism and questions of identity, in Gutting, G (ed) *The Cambridge companion to Foucault.* Cambridge: Cambridge University Press.

Singh, S and Vithal, R (2003) Feminism's courtship with survey: dangerous liaisons or close encounters of a feminist kind? *Education Bulletin,* 1: no. 1.

Smith, DE (1987) *The everyday world as problematic: a feminist sociology.* Toronto: University of Toronto Press.

Smith, DE (1992) Sociology from women's experience: a reaffirmation. *Sociological Theory,* 10: 88–98.

Smith, M (1994) Enhancing the quality of survey data on violence against women: a feminist approach. *Gender and Society,* 8: 109–27.

Spalter-Roth, R and Hartmann, H (1991) Science and politics and the dual vision of feminist policy research: the example of family and medical leave, in Hude, J and Essex, M (eds) *Parental leave and child care: setting a research and policy agenda* (41–65). Philadelphia: Temple University Press.

Sprague, J and Zimmerman, M (1993) Overcoming dualisms: a feminist agenda for sociological methodology, in England, P (ed) *Theory on gender/feminism on theory* (25–80). New York: Aldine.

Stage, F (1997) Reframing research, informing policy: another view of women in the mathematics/science pipeline, in Marshall, C (ed) *Feminist critical policy analysis II: a perspective from post-secondary education* (99–121). London: Falmer Press.

Stanley, L and Wise, S (1993) *Breaking out again: feminist ontology and epistemology.* (new edn). New York: Routledge.

Stromquist, NP (1997) State policies and gender equity: comparative perspectives, in Bank, J and Hall, P (eds) *Gender, equity, and schooling: policy and practice.* New York: Garland.

Weis, L (1997) Gender and the reports: the case of the missing piece, in Marshall, C (ed) *Feminist critical policy analysis* (73–90). London: Falmer Press.

Weston, K (1991) *Families we chose: lesbians gays, kinship*. New York: Columbia University.

Wolf, D (1996) Situating feminist dilemmas in fieldwork, in Wolf, D (ed) *Feminist dilemmas in fieldwork* (1–55). Boulder, Co: Westview Press.

Yates, L (1993) Feminism and Australian state policy. Some questions for the 1990s, in Arnot, M and Weiler, K (eds) *Feminism and social justice in education: international perspectives*. London: Falmer Press.

Young, MD (2000) Considering (irreconcilable?) contradictions in cross-group feminist research. *International Journal of Qualitative Studies in Education,* 13: 558–88.

Young, MD (2003) The leadership crisis: gender and the shortage of school administrators, in Young, MD and Skrla, L (eds) *Reconsidering feminist research in educational leadership*. Albany, NY: State University of New York Press.

Zinn, M (1982) Mexican-American women in the social sciences. *Signs,* 8: 259–72.

NOTES

1. For the purpose of this chapter, we use 'gender' as an umbrella term for both sex and gender.

2. In the end, what counts as feminist research really depends on the perspective of the persons framing the research questions and methodological approaches as well as on the intentions of the consumer of that research. A simplistic comparison of girls' and boys' vocational education can be used by regimes, whether in the USA or Afghanistan, to declare 'success' when success might mean channeling girls and boys into sex-stereotyped work. But when the framing is feminist, the research asks how gendered constructions affect the topic being studied, with intentional ferreting out of any oppressive patterns, and the methodology demonstrates respect for respondent's meaning making. The consumer target includes those who need insights for reducing oppressive structures, in organizations, families, and policies. Without such feminist intentions, research can actually be used to reify and expand oppressive regimes.

3. Epistemology is the study knowledge, particularly what can be known, who can be a knower and how reality can be known.

4. Who can qualify as a feminist researcher? Some feminists, like Millman (1986), argue that male sociologists have a serious handicap when researching women because they cannot take the role of their female subjects, while others argue that it is one's perspective, not one's sex, that determines whether research is feminist. Yes, some men can do research and many women scholars do not.

5. Mohanty (1991) challenges feminist scholars to examine critically their understandings and their potential misunderstandings of participants' actions as well as the linkages between the power of their own location and their ability to define the Other.

6. Although many see collaboration and relationship building as important strategies for lessening the problems of cross-group feminist research, others believe that practices such as these are exploitative and can create fraudulent relationships – where participants are initially given the impressions of true friendship but later find that their relationship with the researcher was based on convenience (Young, 2000).

7. For example, demands for traditional presentation of findings, reliability, and validity would ruin the postmodern recognition that one's gendered self-identity is a continuous nonunitary construction, full of contradictions, resistances and fragmentation in women's lives. Yet that very recognition was essential to the depth of understandings in, for example, Bloom and Munro's (1995) life-history narratives of women in the male-dominated career of school administration.

6

Out of the Ruins: Feminist Pedagogy in Recovery

Gaby Weiner

Asked what effect a more sophisticated musical education would have had on his talent, [Irving] Berlin replied, 'Ruin it'. (Weatherby, 2005)

[T]eaching is a question of justice not a search for truth.... As such, the transgressive force of teaching does not lie so much in matters of content as in the way pedagogy can hold open the temporality of questioning so as to resist being characterized as a transaction that can be concluded, either with the giving of grades or the granting of degrees. (Readings, 1996: 19)

The second of the above quotations comes from a book entitled *The University in Ruins,* which, among other things, argues that universities have lost their role as investigators and producers of nation-state cultures. The term 'ruins' in the title of his book is used by Readings to describe the collapse of the nineteenth-century version of the university, which has been replaced by the contemporary university mired in a discourse of excellence that serves the needs of the global corporate state. However, St Pierre and Pillow (2000) suggest that 'ruin' can also be used as a metaphor for humanism's regimes of truth 'that have failed us', and Weiler (2005) applies it to the collapse of confidence in the Enlightenment narrative of rationality, progress, and moral vigour, leading to the uncertainties illuminated by the 'posts', that is, post-structuralism, postmodernism, post-colonialism, and even post-feminism.

This chapter draws on the ideas of things 'falling apart' and 'coming together' as a general framework for feminist pedagogy. The intention is to determine whether feminist pedagogy exists and what it might look like, and also like

Ropers-Huilman (1998: xix), to examine the 'social forces that continually shape its discourses, practices and interpretations'. Deconstruction rather than prescription will thus be the aim. The era may be characterized as in ruins in relation, for example, to progressive educational history or policy, belief in definitive solutions to society ills, or moral certainty. It is an era of scepticism and cynicism in relation to claims of ideology and state governance. Feminism has both suffered and profited from this situation. Particularly, feminism as a form of progressive politics has become unsustainable as a coherent force, as we shall see later. Moreover, third-wave feminism has sought to explain why this has happened. However, as Lather (personal communication, 10 February 2005) argues, terms no longer understood as fulfilling their initial promise do not become useless. Rather, 'their very failures become provisional grounds and new uses are derived'. The position from which I propose to discuss feminist pedagogy is as a productive concept with a ruined history from which we have much to learn.

The first part of the chapter provides a brief overview of feminism as a social phenomenon with a dynamic and complex history, yet highly contested and fragmented at present even if most feminists agree that the political project of improving the lot of women remains important. Challenges to feminism have come from different directions: from post-colonial theorists, who have illuminated the colonial vantage point of much Western feminist theorizing; from post-structural and postmodern theorists, who critique the aim in feminism as merely adding women to the male Enlightenment project; from so-called postfeminism, which argues that feminism has lost its pertinence; and, of course, from the old enemy, traditional, male patriarchal forces and the wish to protect male power. The chapter provides three brief examples of the ruination or undoing of feminism and the implication this might have for the notion of feminist pedagogy. The following questions are posed: what forms of pedagogy are available, possible, and potentially productive in this ruined post-feminist and postmodern world? How might the academic insights of third-wave feminism be applicable to the more concrete worlds of first- and second-wave feminist classrooms or lecture theatres? This discussion is followed by an exploration of the arguments for and against the realization of feminist pedagogy, with particular criticism of one-size-fits-all prescriptions. The chapter concludes with some sense of moving beyond the fragments of ruin to something worthwhile and feasible.

The arguments offered in the paper draw on international literature on feminism, gender and education, yet are also shaped by the author's early experience as a primary teacher, and for the last 25 years or so, as researcher of gender issues in education, mainly in the UK, but also for six years in Sweden and Europe more generally. The perspectives offered are thus largely informed by Anglophone and European dimensions, which should be treated with caution at the very least in relation to other cultural settings and social conditions.

FALLING APART AND COMING TOGETHER: STORIES OF FEMINISM

As a social phenomenon, feminism has been subject to different interpretations. It emerged in different forms, with different titles and meanings, at different times. In the UK, it was variously referred to as 'the woman question' (in the nineteenth century); as sex differences and sex roles (in the 1950s and 1960s); as the feminist, women's, or women's liberation movement (in the 1960s and 1970s); and as equal opportunities, gender, social justice, and social inclusion, respectively (from the 1980s onward). It was termed 'jämställdhet' in Sweden from the 1970s onward, and 'womanism' by North American black feminists in the 1980s. Feminism also emerged in different forms within Europe after 1945 as a consequence of the impact of war on different European nation states.

In order to provide an indication of the ruined state of feminism at the start of the twenty-first century, as well as of its dynamism, positionality, and cultural and historical embeddedness, I briefly, in this section, explore three discourses:

1. Waves between waves, relating to debates between second- and third-wave feminism that have in many ways churned up the field.
2. Critiques of white feminism by black feminists representing the insertion of 'the Other' into previous naive feminist discourses of universal sisterhood and consensuality.
3. European feminism(s), which show clearly the impact of national histories and traumas on the forms of feminism that are practised.

Waves between waves

Conventionally, we have come to understand feminist history in three stages or waves. Nineteenth- and early twentieth-century feminism concentrated on opening up the access of woman as a category (and not a class) to political, economic and social aspects of public and private life from which they had been hitherto excluded. The fight was mainly, though not exclusively, a bourgeois one, although it led in a number of countries to important gains for other groups, for example, in terms of voting rights and access to education and welfare. Second-wave feminism, which emerged in the 1960s and 1970s, continued the struggle to extend access and benefits but also fought for a broader agenda that concentrated on factors specifically affecting women: for example, reproduction, sexuality, domestic labour, violence in the home, and paid working conditions. However, the concept of 'woman', which was so unifying at the beginning of the wave, proved feminism's main difficulty, as it sought to preserve women's shared interests yet acknowledge and struggle for the rights of difference, as for various racialized and ethnic groups. Third-wave feminism emerged from these contestations from the 1990s onward, drawing in also a new generation of gender scholars (mainly women but some men), who, while having benefited from the efforts of their mothers or grandmothers, identified their own viewpoints and struggles.

Third-wave feminism is primarily claimed as the feminism of a new generation 'that responds to the political, economic, technological and cultural circumstances that are unique to the current era' (Kinser, 2004: 124). It rejects earlier conceptions of feminism as embodying a more or less coherent set of values and ideas, and argues also for a more rounded conception of agency that incorporates how women have acted autonomously and politically in the past despite crippling social sanctions (McNay, 2000). Separation of academic and activist or practical feminism has been a recurring dilemma.

> The appropriation of feminism by the academy has a long tradition in the discipline's history and has resulted in an antagonism by those on the streets to the intellectualizing, rather than activating, of feminist discourse (not that the two are necessarily different). (Gillis, et al., 2004: 3).

Third-wave feminism thus seems more attached to the academy than previous waves, partly due to the widening of access to university education (and teaching) for women; partly to the relatively safe and privileged space of the university, which makes theorizing possible; and partly to the presence of a willing (female) student audience for consumption of new ideas and theories, if not an enthusiasm to engage in political action.

The idea of 'recovery' has been proposed to insert a sense of continuity and cohesion between the feminist waves. Following Zalewski (2000), 'recovery' can be understood in several different ways: as a layering by the newer feminism over of the old ones so that they are buried and mainly lost – and thus to be 'recovered' – or as the creation of stronger and stronger layers or linked threads surrounding and connecting feminist theories and practices, which draw strength from and 'recover' each other; or in terms of recovery as if from an illness, suggesting a return to more conventional ways of thinking (Zalewski, 2000). Thus, recovery can imply the dangers of annihilation of certain feminist discourses, or the inevitable dialectic of different feminisms, or feminism at worst as a malign, and at best an irrelevant, force, that has no place in present intellectual and political debates. So there clearly is and continues to be dissension (or waves) particularly between second- and third-wave theorizing, even though, for many activists across the world, the issues of second-wave feminism remain a persuasive call to action.

Black feminist critiques

The attempt to unify second-wave feminism was fractured primarily by its positioning, however benign, as a totalizing and excluding elite. From the 1970s onward the most widespread feminist perspective was that of white, Western feminism, which, nevertheless, aspired to represent women across class and racial divisions. In so doing, it became a target of criticism, especially from the concurrent black feminist movement, which argued that the eradication of inequalities based on supposed racial factors was an essential component of an inclusive feminism. For example, Amos and Parmar (1984) argued that racism (in addition to sexism) *must* be a concern of white feminists if they are not, themselves, to reproduce racism. This includes:

1. taking the specificities of black women's experiences into account when theorizing women's oppression;
2. not presenting black women in the form of stereotypes, and through the lens of white, Western cultural values;
3. not relegating black women and their experiences to the margins of women's movements (adapted from Räthzel, 2001).

However, this call to extend sisterhood across racialized borders has been difficult achieve. For example, disappointed by the absence of a feminist position in Chicana nationalism, Chicana women in the USA in the 1970s looked unsuccessfully to white feminism for support.

> Long term coalitions never developed due to the inability of most white women to recognize the class and race biases inherent in the structures of their own organizations. Furthermore, they replicated, in another realm, the same kind of privileging of one kind of oppression over another that had bothered Chicanas in relation to Chicanos. Insisting on the primacy of gender oppression, white feminists disregarded the class- and race-based oppressions suffered by the Chicana. (Moya, 1997: 143)

The problem became defined in terms of the power (in this case of white, Western women) to define discursively the field of feminism (and its academic subject, women's studies) and thus render anyone outside the field as the 'Other'. One attempt to resolve this problem for black feminism points to the value of a more autonomous position. Thus, in a landmark collection on black British feminism published in 1997, Mirza highlights the importance of identity, agency and a 'place called home'.

> In this context [the desire for a 'place'], then, black feminism as a spontaneous yet conscious coalition is a meaningful act of identification. In this 'place called home' named black feminism, we as racialized and gendered subjects can collectively mark our presence in the world where black women have so long been denied the privilege to speak; to have a 'valid' identity of our own, a space to 'name' ourselves ... we, as black British women invoke our agency; we speak of our difference, our uniqueness, our 'otherness'. (Mirza, 1997: 4)

However, this identification of a 'place called home' underlines yet again the impossibility of second-wave feminism's early dream of all-embracing solidarity between sisters.

European feminist movements

An important site of feminism and its claims to a material base is its situated specificity; geographically, historically and culturally. European feminism provides a good example of this. European feminism re-emerged in the post-World War II settlement and its concretization and expansion in what we now know as the European Union (EU). For example, Kaplan (1992) notes that when feminists mobilized after 1945, picking up the threads of previous feminist activity was most difficult for countries closely associated with fascist regimes and ideologies, such as Germany and Italy, than for those with a less fractured history of democratic development, such as the UK, the USA and Sweden. Moreover, different national histories generated distinctive preoccupations. For example, Italian feminists were particularly hostile to feminist calls for separatism, because, under fascism, women were 'allowed' a separate if narrow and confined space in public life.

Significantly, feminist movements were associated in Europe with left-wing or politically progressive ideas, in particular those arising from the student political movements of the 1960s. Yet, feminists swiftly created their own spaces, signalling 'an interest in a cause which was to take them far from the socialist mainstream into new modes of thought and action' (Lovenduski, 1986: 72). Although many national feminist movements in Western liberal democracies were influenced by the North American feminism, stronger and weaker forms emerged, due to specific cultures and politics of the countries in which they were located. Thus, in the 1970s, more energetic and influential movements emerged in the UK, the Netherlands, Finland, Denmark and Norway; less so in West Germany, France, Sweden and Belgium (Lovenduski, 1986). Feminism in the Nordic countries (especially Sweden) was viewed as lacking a 'radical' edge, mainly because gender change was assiduously pursued by state governments in their preference for women over migrant workers to make up deficiencies in the Nordic labor market (Lundh, 1994). In the newly emergent democracies of Spain and Portugal, feminism came later and developed more slowly, although both had distinctive movements by the end of the 1970s (Lovenduski, 1986).

Meanwhile, in countries within the Eastern European communist bloc (until 1989), there was little evidence of autonomous feminist movements. Indeed, the political party structure which controlled avenues to political power, and which set the conditions in which political activism could take place obstructed such a possibility. Moreover, while sex equality was a founding principle in communist states, women having greater access to education and paid employment, this did not result in women's greater participation in economic or political spheres (Lovenduski, 1986).

More recently, European feminism has shifted away from a focus on national policy making toward investigating the new Europe, as equated with the EU, and in particular, whom it includes and excludes. As Walby (1999) shows, EU gender policies had a significant impact on national governments, although this varied depending on the previous gains made by organized feminism. Feminists were generally critical of the EU; for example, they criticized it for marginalizing working-class women (Brine, 1999) and denying access to black women and ethnic minorities

(Einhorn and Gregory, 1998). A more positive stance has been taken by Braidotti (2004), who argues for a post-nationalist sense of European identity and flexible citizenship. She draws on the feminist politics of location as a method and strategy which was developed and theorized by feminists to account for consciousness raising. Essentialism is thus avoided in her envisioning of 'a radical restructuring of European identity as post-nationalistic... concretely translated into a set of "flexible forms of citizenship" that would allow for all "others"... to acquire legal status in what would otherwise deserve the label of "Fortress Europe"' (Braidotti, 2004: 133, 137–8). Particularly useful is Braidotti's concept of imaginary – a vision of what is to be.

> My question therefore becomes: how do you develop such a new European imaginary? I think that such a notion is a project, not a given; nonetheless, this does not make it Utopian in the sense of over-idealistic. It is even the contrary: it is a virtual social reality which can be actualized by a joint endeavour on the part of active, conscious and desiring citizens. (Braidotti, 2004: 139–40)

Thus, we have seen in these three discourses of feminism that ideological disagreements between feminists exist but also that they may be seen as productive and indicative of a live intellectual force. Thus, however ruined, present-day feminism remains a powerful discursive and epistemological influence.

CONCEPTULIZATIONS OF FEMINIST PEDAGOGY

It has been feminist teachers who have been most articulate in arguing for pedagogic interventions in sexist (and racist) practices in the academy and in schooling. Significantly, interest in feminist pedagogy arose initially not from theoretical debates within feminism or in education or teaching, but rather from practical concerns of feminist schoolteachers and university lecturers wishing to address gender and other equality issues in their classrooms. Such work emerged from a growing discontent with the patriarchy of schooling and the absence of gender as a category of interest or analysis in most pedagogic theory, even those that claimed to be progressive and critical (Luke and Gore, 1992).

Here, as elsewhere, motivation to do feminist work arose from the failure of academic disciplines and theoretical frameworks to institute gender as a central and organising concept. Influenced by Paulo Freire's noted text *The Pedagogy of the Oppressed* (1972), feminist and anti-racist educators developed parallel 'critical' pedagogies to support and challenge Freire's vision. More recently, educators influenced by post-structuralism and post-colonialism have considered pedagogy both in terms of desire (Britzman, 1998) and in deconstructing the workings of white, Western privilege and cultural assumptions in the classroom. As Weiler (2005) notes, such developments have raised questions about power, representation, authority, and performance, and, indeed, about the whole enterprise of pedagogy. In general, however, feminist pedagogy has focused on the following:

- *Classroom methods,* particularly in relation to the role and authority of the teacher, the role of (student) experience, and the challenge of questions of difference. An alternative educational experience to that conventionally offered is envisioned, which seeks to encourage students to engage in some form of political or activist work, such as feminism (Weiler, 1991).
- *Individual experience* of both teacher and student, as a key influence in affective as well as intellectual educational domains. 'Conscious-raising' was a term used within second-wave feminism to denote the importance of personal narrative to the accumulation of knowledge about women. Thus, personal experience was legitimated as an appropriate arena of intellectual enquiry. Most feminist educators, Culley and Portuges claim (1985: 2), *understand that knowledge is not neutral, that the teacher and students alike bring 'texts' of their own to the classroom which shape the transactions within it.*
- *Increased equality in power relations,* which is seen to arise from feminist teachers' commitment to reflection on their practice, in particular, in exploring how it relates to the encouragement of critical thinking in students and the living out of particular values in practice. Lewis (1990: 469) identifies the psychological, social, and sexual dynamics of the classroom, where female as well as male students need to be encouraged to 'develop a critical understanding' aimed at conscious transformation.
- *Transformative power,* Lewis (1990) further argues, is a key element of feminist pedagogy in that it enables greater consciousness and understanding of the gendered context of classroom practice and therefore of the possibility of changing society through changing practice.

Following on from this earlier work, Webb *et al.* (2002) identify in their overview of the field, six general 'principles' that are usually present in conceptualizations of feminist pedagogy:

1. reformation of the professor–student relationship, that is, blurring of roles;
2. empowerment, that is, enabling at least some power to be shared;
3. building community, that is, collaborative learning through relationships and dialogue;
4. privileging the individual voice, that is, extending the right to have a voice;
5. respect for diversity of personal experience, that is, affirmation of personal experience as a central component of learning;
6. challenging traditional views, that is, revealing the social and political origins of theory, research, and teaching.

Interestingly, few empirical studies have been carried out on the effectiveness of feminist pedagogy. Exceptions are Thomsen *et al.* (1995), who found that in classes organized around feminist pedagogy, students, especially female students, are more likely to self-identify as feminists and become active on women's issues; Stake and Rose (1994), who suggest that these tendencies remain over an extended period; and Bargad and Hyde (1991), who note evidence of increased feminist consciousness in other classes where gender is discussed. However, feminist pedagogy also has its detractors and resisters. For example, Markowitz (2005) found that general resistance to feminist pedagogy is threefold:

1. denial of social facts that contradict students' worldview;
2. students' focus on the teacher as an object of animosity, as in male-hating;
3. refusal to consider alternative explanations of social organization and functioning.

IS FEMINIST PEDAGOGY POSSIBLE?

If the six principles of Webb *et al.* (2002) given above can be said to be a summary of the discursive nature of the field, and given recent studies (also above) on both its effectiveness and the resistance it faces, what can we say about the possibilities of feminist pedagogy? First, the fragmented nature of feminism, as outlined earlier in this chapter, suggests that pedagogy needs to be pluralized, since one pedagogy cannot speak for (or represent) all feminisms. Second, some of the defining features of feminist pedagogy have attracted substantial criticism, as we shall see below.

Conceptualization of feminism

A criticism of feminist pedagogy is that while generally drawing on practical situations located in time and place, the strategies used are then reported in ways that presume that others will share similar understandings and situations to the extent of replicating or applying strategy and analysis. Moreover, notions of feminist pedagogy rest on modernist, progressivist views of transformative projects (Heald, 1997), where feminist teachers are invested with (unacknowledged) power to assert their particular reading of the world, and to decide what is best for their students (Heald, 1997; Patai, 2001). In this sense, feminist pedagogy may be regarded as derived from second-wave thinking, and therefore vulnerable to the general criticisms made by third-wavers of representing a universally agreed feminist position or consensual feminist set of strategies. On the other hand, feminist pedagogy necessarily demands practical decisions, and second-wave feminism's strength is/was its engagement with practical action. Indeed, however realized, feminist pedagogy at least offers an alternative to more conventional modes of doing and performing, in its promotion, for example, of inclusiveness, non-hierarchy, and redistributed power relations. There is, arguably, little to help practitioners in the work of Butler (1999) and other third-wavers who deny foundational claims and definitions, and are better at taking things apart than putting them together.

Applying rhetoric to practice

One of the most difficult tasks of teachers is to translate their ambitions into practice. Formalized lesson plans or course guidelines might offer the promise of 'systematic implementation', but apart from the most hardened program-learning theorists, teaching and learning are generally seen as human activities that defy reproduction, systematization, or prediction. Organizing a class to include the six principles as outlined above is probably impossible on a regular basis, in terms of the practicalities of planning, carrying out, and realization. It comes as no surprise that the examples of feminist pedagogy given in the literature tend to be oriented toward addressing specific equity issues rather than to more general, run-of-the-mill teaching situations.

Moral tone

Taylor (1993) raises the important question of how teachers can create critical or feminist consciousness or ways of knowing, without implying ideological correctness or clashing with the complex desires and subjectivities of female and male students. She argues that feminist practitioners have not only to recognize and, to an extent, support students' resistance to feminism, but also to understand their involvement in the pedagogic process as a complex interplay of subjectivities in which femininities and masculinities are chosen or constructed; adopted or rejected. In particular, self-righteousness and high moral tone on the part of the teacher are likely to detract from the overall enterprise, while being 'cool' and engaging with responses derived from the student group in context, may achieve a more productive outcome.

Experience

As we have seen above, central to the task of feminist pedagogy is the concept of 'experience' in the sense that its appropriation in the classroom is seen in terms both of extending inclusiveness, democracy, and participation in the pedagogic process, and of utilizing the authenticity of personal experience as a counter to impersonal, academic forms of knowledge. Accordingly, the unfolding of experience promises insights and perspectives absent elsewhere. Scott, however, challenges this kind of thinking in arguing that while experience serves as a way of talking about what has happened, and establishing difference and similarity of viewpoint, it cannot be seen as incontestable or 'real'. At its point of revelation, she says, 'experience is at once always already an interpretation and something that needs to be interpreted' (Scott, 1991: 777, 797). Its conscious articulation is already second-hand, of something already passed, and therefore cannot be anything other than interpretive. Thus, when, as teachers, we seek to include individual experience, what we get is not authentic and 'real' but performed, constructed and shaped for the audience at a particular moment for a particular purpose.

Similarly, Lather argues that we need to understand identification with the self as a social rather than authentic, personal process. 'The goal is … a shift from a romantic view of the self as unchanging, authentic essence to a concept of the "self" as a conjunction of diverse social practices produced and positioned socially, without an underlying essence' (Lather, 1991: 82). Teachers and researchers, as well as, students, therefore need constantly to think against themselves as they 'struggle towards ways of knowing which can move us beyond ourselves' (Lather, 1991: 83).

Empowerment

As we have seen, 'empowerment' is a central concept for pedagogies that consciously seek to challenge predominant power relations and orthodoxies. Ellsworth (1992) argues, however, that the forms of empowerment suggested by 'critical pedagogies' (including feminist pedagogy, though she does not mention it by name) are, in practice, 'repressive myths that perpetuate relations of domination'. On the basis of her experience of working with pedagogies focusing on anti-racism, she points to their potentially crushing failure:

> I mean that when participants in our class attempted to put into practice prescriptions offered in the literature concerning empowerment, student voice, and dialogue, we produced results that were not only unhelpful, but actually exacerbated the very conditions we were trying to work against, including Euro-centrism, racism, sexism, classism, and 'banking education'. (Ellsworth, 1992: 91)

Ellsworth found that despite the intentions of herself, her colleagues and the students who enrolled on her courses, the form of dialogue employed in the class remained the sole responsibility of the teachers – as enforcers of the rules of reason in the classroom. Ellsworth argues that while critical pedagogies suggest the redistribution, sharing and giving away of power, this in fact does not happen. Instead, 'empowerment' treats the symptoms while leaving the disease unnamed and untouched. Thus, since oppressive classroom discourses of reason and logic remain in the main untouched and undisturbed, the proposal to give away or redistribute power becomes merely a rhetorical and idealized impossibility.

One-size-fits-all

The history of feminism has taught us, above all, that prescriptions of action taken from one place are unlikely to work in another, even if worked examples mean that we can learn from what has gone on before. Certainly, it is important that we know our history if mistakes are not to be repeated and bad experiences replicated. The intention of the analysis of feminism briefly outlined in this chapter is that readers become better able to understand the enterprise that has been called feminist pedagogy and their responses to it. However, as I hope I have also shown, the one-size-fits-all principle that certain features *constitute* feminist pedagogy is also untenable. Indeed, my own and others' attempts to work with them has tended more often than not to end in failure, as in the case of Ellsworth reported above. Indeed, sometimes such pedagogies might make the situation worse by implying erroneously that issues of equity are being dealt with. A better alternative, I suggest, is the development of a set of *dispositions* to feminist pedagogy, more in tune with feminist uncertainties and partialities of the present period. This will be the task of the next and final section of the chapter.

FEMINIST PEDAGOGY IN RECOVERY

Given that we have rejected the approach to feminist pedagogy that relies on the presentation of principles or characteristics that should be followed, does this mean that feminist pedagogy is no longer a viable consideration or ambition? My response is that, following Braidotti (2004), we should conceive of feminist pedagogy as an aspiration and imaginary, and develop dispositions which bring us closer to that imaginary. These dispositions resemble what Bourdieu terms 'habitus', that is, a means by which individuals produce action that is both predictable, arising out of specific social and cultural contexts, and unpredictable due to the variety of circumstances that confront them. This happens 'in such a way that one cannot move simply and mechanically from knowledge of the conditions of production to knowledge of the products' (Bourdieu, 1993: 87). For feminist teachers, therefore, dispositions will be premised on certain assumptions based on their positioning epistemologically, ideologically, discursively, geographically, and temporally. For me, at this present time, they include the following.

First, we need to be explicit about *the form of feminism* we aspire to, and how we understand feminist recovery, whether as linked to, or separate from, one or more feminist waves. We need to be aware of whose voice 'our' feminism speaks, the ideological baggage that we have accrued, and then consider how this may be represented in our teaching. Second, as teachers, we *cannot give away power* – we have it bodily, intellectually, and institutionally. Rather, we have to learn to use it productively in such a way as to challenge and deconstruct common-sense assumptions and uncritical judgements in our students and ourselves. Third, it is essential that we work with the *situatedness* of our students, which is not to say that we erase intellectual and demanding ideas. Rather, we have to do the hard work of introducing and translating difficult concepts and ideas so that they will be comprehensible and indeed interesting to them at this particular moment. Fourth, we must expect and even invite *resistance*, for it is only through resistance that we can see that we have succeeded in puncturing complacency and taken-for-grantedness. Finally, if our pedagogy is to make a difference, if it is to be transgressive, it *will make trouble for us*. We should expect students, for example, to question assignments or confront the authorities on campus or in the staff room, or challenge professional judgements – all of which are likely to affect the way we ourselves might be viewed by our peers and employers.

Where does this leave feminist pedagogy? I suggest that it remains a risky business; but, released from its previous associations with method and virtue, it is now more of a pragmatic imaginary somewhere teetering on the ruins of feminism yet strengthened by feminism's continuing dynamism. No more and no less.

REFERENCES

Amos, V and Parmar, P (1984) Challenging imperial feminism. *Feminist Review*, 17: 3–18.
Bargad, A and Hyde, JS (1991) Women's studies: a study of feminist identity development in women. *Psychology of Women Quarterly*, 15: 181–201.
Bourdieu, P (1993) The field of cultural production or the economic world reversed. *Poetics*, 12: 311–356.
Braidotti, R (2004) Gender and power in a post-nationalist European Union. *NORA*, 12: 130–42.
Brine, J (1999) *Undereducating women: globalizing inequality*. Buckingham: Open University Press.

Britzman, DP (1998) *Lost subjects, contested objects: toward a psychoanalytic inquiry of learning.* Albany, NY: State University of New York Press.

Butler, J (1999) *Gender trouble: feminism and the subversion of identity.* New York: Routledge.

Culley, M and Portuges, C (1985) Introduction. In Culley, M and Portuges, C (eds) *Gendered subjects: the dynamics of feminist teaching* (1–7). Boston: Routledge & Kegan Paul.

Einhorn, B and Gregory, J (1998) Introduction. Special issue: *The idea of Europe. European Journal of Women's Studies,* 5: 293–6.

Ellsworth, E (1992) Why doesn't this feel empowering? Working through the repressive myths of critical pedagogy, in Luke, C and Gore, J (eds) *Feminisms and critical pedagogy* (90–119). London: Routledge.

Freire, P (1972) *The pedagogy of the oppressed.* London: Penguin.

Gillis, G Howie, G and Munford, R (2004) *Third wave feminism: a critical exploration.* Basingstoke: Palgrave/Macmillan.

Heald, S (1997) Events without witness: living/teaching difference within the paternalist university. *Curriculum Studies,* 1: 39–48.

Kaplan, G (1992) *Contemporary Western European feminism.* London: Allen & Unwin.

Kinser, AE (2004) Negotiating spaces for/through third-wave feminism. *NWSA Journal,* 16: 124–53.

Lather, P (1991) *Getting smart: feminist research and pedagogy with/in the postmodern.* New York: Routledge.

Lewis, M (1992) Interrupting patriarchy: politics, resistance and transformation in the feminist classroom. *Harvard Educational Review,* 60: 467–88.

Lovenduski, J (1986) *Women and European politics: contemporary feminism and public policy.* Brighton: Harvester Press.

Luke, C and Gore, J (1992) Introduction. In Luke,C and Gore, J (eds) *Feminisms and critical pedagogy* (1–14). London: Routledge.

Lundh, C (1994) Invandrarna I den svenska modellen – hot eller reserve? Fackligt program på 1960-talet [Immigrants in the Swedish model – threat or reserve? Trade Union programmes of the 1960s]. *Arbetarhistoria,* 18: 70, 23–36.

McNay, L (2000) *Gender and agency: reconfiguring the subject in feminist and social theory.* Cambridge: Polity Press.

Markowitz, L (2005) Unmasking moral dichotomies: can feminist pedagogy overcome student resistance? *Gender and Education,* 17: 39–55.

Mirza, HS (1997) Introduction: mapping a genealogy of Black British feminism, in Mirza, HS (ed) *Black British feminism: a reader* (1–30). London: Routledge.

Moya, PM (1997) Postmodernism, 'realism', and the politics of identity, in Jacqui, M Alexander MJ and Mohanty, CT *Feminist genealogies, colonial legacies, democratic futures.* New York: Routledge.

Patai, D (2001) Rhetoric and reality in women's studies. *Gender Issues,* Spring: 21–60.

Räthzel, N (2001) Feminism and differences – feminisms and divisions?, in Nationella sekretariatet för genusforskning (ed) *Svensk genusforskning i världen. Globala perspektiv i svensk genusforskning och svensk. Genusforskning i ett globalt perspektiv [Swedish gender research in the world: global perspectives in Swedish gender research]* (25–50). Göteborg: Nationella sekretariatet för genusforskning.

Readings, B (1996).*The university in ruins.* Cambridge, MA: Harvard University Press.

Ropers-Huilman, B (1998) *Feminist teaching in theory and practice: situating power and knowledge in poststructural classrooms.* New York: Teachers College.

Scott, JW (1991) The evidence of experience. *Critical Inquiry,* Summer: 773–97.

Stake, J and Rose, S (1994) The long term impact of women's studies on students' personal lives and political activism. *Psychology of Women's Quarterly,* 18: 403–12.

St Pierre, E and Pillow, WS (2000) Introduction: inquiry among the ruins, in St Pierre, E and Pillow, WS (eds) *Working the ruins: feminist poststructural theory and methods in education.* (1–24). New York: Routledge.

Taylor, S (1993) Transforming the texts: towards a feminist classroom practice, in Christian, L (ed) *Texts of desire: girls, popular fiction and education.* London: Falmer Press.

Thomsen, CJ, Basu, AM and Reinitz, MT (1995) Effects of women's studies courses on students' personal lives and political activism. *Psychology of Women Quarterly*, 19: 419–26.

Walby, S (1999) The new regulatory state: the social powers of the European Union. *British Journal of Sociology*, 50: 118–40.

Weatherby, WJ (2005) From the archives. *Guardian Review*, 5 February, p24.

Webb, LM, Allen, MW and Walker, KL (2002) Feminist pedagogy: identifying principles. *Academic Education Quarterly*, 6: 67–72.

Weiler, K (1991) Freire and feminist pedagogy of difference. *Harvard Educational Review*, 61: 449–74.

Weiler, K (2005) Pedagogy in the ruins. Unpublished lecture, University of Washington, 13 January.

Zalewski, M (2000) *Feminism after postmodernism: theorising through practice*. London: Routledge.

7

Gender, Education and Development[1]

Elaine Unterhalter

In 2003, UNESCO estimated that girls and women, worldwide, comprised two-thirds of the one billion people with little or no education (UNESCO, 2004). Poverty, global inequality and gender discrimination scar the political, economic and social landscape of too much of the world and powerfully shape the academic, activist and policy literature on gender, education and development. This chapter first outlines some changing features of gender inequalities in access to schooling in developing countries as measured by official statistics and then contrasts the ways in which different disciplinary assumptions about gender and development have engaged with the picture this presents and the policy challenges in this field.

EXPANDING GENDER EQUALITY IN ACCESS TO EDUCATION

From the beginning of the twentieth century, nationalist movements in Asia, Africa and Latin America fostered aims to expand education. Post-war decolonization saw new governments establishing mass systems of schooling linked to projects of national development. These expanded the limited provision of the colonial era when education had been largely for élites and was only sporadically available to the rest of the population in under-resourced schools (Carnoy and Samoff, 1990). But expansion of access to education was not uniform. Regional and social inequalities, magnified by gender, were reflected in who did and did not enrol in school. Table 7.1 shows the growth of enrolment in primary and secondary school by gender in different parts of the world since the 1960s.

Table 7.1   Girls' (and boys') primary gross enrolment ratios in selected years 1965–2000

	1965 GER	1975 GER	1985 GER	1995 GER	2000 NER
Arab states	41 (71)	56 (86)	70 (91)	77 (93)	86 (97)
East Asia and Pacific	83 (116)	107 (120)	110 (124)	115 (122)	109 (110)
Latin America and Caribbean	80 (82)	97 (99)	105 (108)	104 (107)	102 (102)
North America and W.Europe	102 (104)	100 (100)	99 (101)	100 (102)	87 (104)
South Asia	50 (88)	58 (92)	72 (100)	81 (103)	76 (89)
Sub-Saharan Africa	37 (56)	55 (73)	67 (82)	64 (77)	56 (61)

Sources: World Bank, 2002; UNESCO, 1995: 33; UNESCO, 2003: 234–5. GER: gross enrolment rations; NER: net enrolment rate.

Table 7.2   Primary net enrolment ratios (NER) for girls (and boys) c.1980–2000 in 11 African countries

	1980	1988	1995	2000
Angola	67 (74)	56 (59)*	35 (32)	28 (32)**
Botswana	83 (70)	100 (95)	83 (79)	81 (78)
Ethiopia	...	22 (31)	21 (35)	38 (50)
Kenya	89 (92)	74 (74)*	86 (87)	67 (66)***
Mozambique	34 (39)	41 (49)	34 (45)	50 (58)
Malawi	38 (48)	53 (56)	100 (98)	81 (81)**
Senegal	30 (44)	40 (54)*	48 (60)	59 (66)
Tanzania	...	49 (48)	48 (47)	50 (49)
Uganda	35 (43)	50 (57)	52 (58)	100...
Zambia	73 (81)	79 (82)	74 (76)	65 (67)
Zimbabwe	...	100 (100)	...	81 (81)

*1990 figures.
**2001 figures.
***2003 figures.
Sources: World Bank, 2002; UNESCO, 1995, 2005; Unterhalter *et al.*, 2005e.

Although the proportion of girls and boys in primary school has risen in every region the gender gap, evident in all regions (except North America, Western Europe, Latin America and the Caribbean) in the 1960s had only been eradicated in 2000 in East Asia, persisting, despite some narrowing, in all other regions. Girls' and boys' gross enrolment ratios (GER) in Africa fell over the 1990s, with a much more dramatic fall for girls. There was a considerable slowing of the rate of improvement in countries affected by the restrictions on public sector growth demanded by imposed structural adjustment programs.

Table 7.2 shows a slowing rate of increase in net enrolment rate (NER) from the mid-1980s in many African countries, with particulary harsh effects for girls.

In South and East Asia, this trend was not so pronounced, but in a number of countries, such as Pakistan and Laos, gender inequalities in enrolment persisted (see Table 7.3).

There are considerable difficulties in relying only, as these tables do, on official figures of enrolment and attendance to analyze these trends (Unterhalter *et al.*, 2005).

The problems of the faltering of the post-war aspirations to ensure all children an adequate education were addressed with increasing rigor in a series of international conferences from 1990 that considered the challenge of gender inequality in education primarily in terms of schooling. The challenge for activists and analysts since 1990 has partly been to hold government and intergovernment organizations to account for these promises, and partly to defend and advance the vision of the Beijing Declaration (1995), which conceived gender equality in education as a larger demand than just girls' access to school.

MAPPING THE ANALYTIC FIELD

The literature on gender, education and development has been shaped by, and helped shape responses to, global inequality in education as sketched above. Table 7.5 summarizes heuristically four approaches to thinking and action concerning gender education, development and equality since approximately 1970. (For a fuller discussion of some of the theoretical issues raised and more extensive referencing, see Unterhalter, 2003a; 2005a;b.) While, in practice, there are considerable overlaps between the four approaches, I have separated them analytically to highlight some of their key differences.

The WID (women in development) approach stresses expansion of schooling for girls and women to secure efficient economic growth or good governance. Here gender is understood descriptively in terms of biological categories. WID generates clear policy directives on including women, for example employing more women teachers to reassure parents regarding girls' safety at school. Partly because of its clarity, but partly also because it evades the difficult question of power, WID has had most influence on the policies of governments, intergovernment organizations and non-governmental organizations (NGOs).

The GAD (gender and development) approach considers gender as a process, part of complex and changing social relations. Influential for more than 20 years among women's organizations concerned with development, GAD has only slowly made an impact on the thinking of some governments and education NGOs. Because GAD is alert to nuance in the reproduction and transformation of gendered relations, it is less easily translatable into simple policy demands. However, GAD approaches have had some impact on education practice, particularly with regard to how teachers view work in a gendered classroom, how women's organizations link education demands within wider demands for empowerment, and the ways in which gender equality advocates work in institutions.

Post-structuralist approaches question the stability of definitions of gender, paying particular attention to the fluidity of gendered identification and shifting forms of action. Some writers look at how discourses – that is, particular formations of ideas regarding what is natural, or how things should be – are spoken in policies and practices concerning gender in schools. For example, a discourse assuming that gendered behaviour is natural speaks through policies which assume a deficit

Table 7.5 Four approaches to gender, education and development

Framework	Linked theories	Understandings of gender	Understandings of development	Understandings of education	Understandings of equality
WID (from 1970s To the present)	Modernization; Human capital theory	Gender = women, girls	Growth, efficiency, good governance, social cohesion	Schooling	Equality of resources; sometimes termed parity.
GAD (from 1098s present)	Structuralism Marxism	Constructed social relations, power	Challenging inequity and oppression	Conscientization	Redistribution of power; sometimes termed equity.
Post-structuralism (from 1990s to the present)	Post-colonial theory	Shifting and performed identities	Struggling with the past in the present to shape multifaceted identities and new narratives	Deconstructive	Stress on difference
Human development (from 1990s to the present)	The capability approach	Inequality and capability denial	Development as freedom	A basic capability	Equality of rights and capabilities

GAD: gender and development approach
WID: women in development approach

in girls' capacity to do science and maths. This approach has not influenced government or international policies directly, but post-structuralism has influenced academic critique and pointed to the need to affirm subordinated identities in the development of curriculum.

The last framework is concerned with human development and human rights in development. In some ways, this is a metatheory, working at a higher level of abstraction, and suggesting not concrete policies or forms of practice, but a framework in which these can be developed ethically.

BRINGING GIRLS AND WOMEN INTO SCHOOL: THE DOMINANCE OF WID

WID, with its stress on bringing women into political, economic and cultural development, and hence girls and women into school, has links to aspects of liberal feminism in the global north. It stresses the importance of including women in development planning to improve efficiency, but not necessarily challenging the multiple sources of women's subordination.

WID research in education has been the most widely published and had the most influence on policy. The collection edited by King and Hill in 1993 for the World Bank is a key instance. This stressed counting girls and women, particularly the rates at which they enrolled in school and completed a period of study, and how this correlated with increases in gross domestic product (GDP) per capita and decreases in fertility and infant mortality. The major analytic concern was how to overcome the barriers to access and realize the *social* benefits of girls in school (King and Hill, 1993). Very precise calculations were offered of how much a year of schooling for a girl could offer her community in terms of increased income or productivity in farming (Quisumbing, 1996; Dollar and Gatti, 1999). Questions of exploitation, subordination and social division were generally not considered. The slogan, if you educate a woman, you educate the nation, nicely captures the thinking which underpins this approach, suggesting that the education of women is for others, not for women themselves. The benefits of women's education are to be realized in the household, often the site of the harshest discrimination.

A great deal of the empirical work using this framework has been carried out by government ministries, including census departments. Large-scale surveys have looked at how household relations affect decisions about sending girls to school and keeping them there (Alderman *et al.*, 1996; Hadden *et al.*, 1996). Analysis has concentrated on quantifying the benefits of girls' and women's schooling in terms of reduced fertility and improved uptake of immunization (Subbarao and Raney, 1995; Klasen, 1999). Much of this work has been undertaken by multilateral organisations that employ international research teams, frequently led by economists who draw on local research assistance.

Some work mixes qualitative and quantitative data to look at gender in relation to achievement at school (Nath and Chowdhury, 2001). In the Caribbean, this work has looked at the reasons that boys drop out of school (Kutnick *et al*., 1997). While the qualitative research provides some insight into social relations difficult to discern in the quantitative work, the assumptions that underpin it are the same.

Quantitative work on gender, access, retention and achievement tends not to deal with other dimensions of inequality, particularly race, ethnicity, caste and disability. While some acknowledgement is made of differences between rural and urban girls (Hadden and London, 1996), there is little engagement with the complexity of social division. This resonates with the way writers in the WID framework interpret equality, generally in terms of equal numbers of resources, such as places in school for girls and boys, male and female teachers employed, or equal numbers of images in textbooks of men and women (Obura, 1991). Thus, little attention is given to gendered processes of learning, the conditions in which women teachers work, the way their work is regarded by their societies, or the meanings children make and take from the images they see in textbooks.

Policies associated with WID have concentrated on improving access through giving girls stipends or abolishing school fees, allocating to girls food for education, developing the infrastructure of training or accommodation to ensure more women teachers are employed, digging latrines and providing water. Some associated practice has entailed mobilizing teachers and communities to encourage girls to enter schools and ensure they pass examinations. WID practice has been less concerned with the content of what girls learn, how they learn, or whether gender inequalities face them after their years in school. Generally, WID analysts comment on the content of schooling when it has a bearing on access, but not more generally. For example, a study in Kenya of how to encourage parents to send daughters to secondary school concentrated on the fact that the availability of science teaching was an inducement for their enrolment (as this was seen as linked to employability), but failed to comment on the intrinsic benefits of learning science (Herz *et al*., 1991).

The WID framework cannot comprehend more complex aspects of gender equality and inequality in school. However, the simple WID policy and practice message, and the research that supports this despite – or possibly because of – its lack of analytic complexity, has galvanized huge programs by government and intergovernment organizations, mobilised additional funding, and led to some important legal changes. Despite the many drawbacks of the WID failure to look for gender equality beyond the school gate, the policy achievements of the last two decades associated with the framework must be acknowledged.

THE GENDERED POWER STRUCTURES OF SCHOOL AND SOCIETY: DRAWING ON GAD IN EDUCATION

GAD emerged as a critique of WID in the late 1980s, highlighting the significance of gendered power structures of inequality in a range of contexts. GAD theorists noted how inequality needed to be challenged politically and could not merely be ameliorated by a process of inclusion, welfare, or the belief in the greater efficiency of projects or programmes that included women. GAD grew partly out of poor rural and urban women's experiences of organization, debates about feminism in the Third World, and feminist critiques in development studies (Kabeer, 1994; DAWN, 1995). There was some resonance in this work with the approach of socialist feminists in Western Europe. Radical feminism, with its trenchant critique of the politics of the family, was less significant politically in developing countries.

GAD focused on the sexual division of labor inside and outside the household, and on changing gendered structures of power. GAD paid relatively little attention to issues concerning formal schooling. Partly because education is so centrally concerned with the state, which provides an ambiguous partner for transforming gendered social relations, the writings of key GAD theorists tended not to deal with formal education.

A central element in GAD analysis was the distinction of practical gender needs and strategic gender interests. Practical gender needs are immediate day-to-day requirements like food, water and shelter. Strategic gender interests entail challenging the deeply entrenched forms of gender discrimination in the legal system, sexual violence in the family, the lack of political representation, and discrimination in the workplace (Kabeer, 1994; Molyneux, 1998). Although there was considerable debate on the link between gender needs and interests, GAD programs focused on both levels as a means to bring about changes for greater equality. Very little writing on gender, education and development engaged with the debate about needs and interests. Seeing education as a need or an interest entailing elements of rights or capabilities generated very different approaches to policy (Unterhalter, 2005c).

GAD writers also engaged in the debate about empowerment which had emerged in feminist movements that stressed the importance of enhancing agency among the poorest (Rowlands, 1997). However, initial attempts to give empowerment conceptual coherence suffered from a number of difficulties. These included the problem of how to specify the relationship of agency and empowerment to social context and theories of justice. In addition, there was a problem with changing meanings of empowerment, as the language of choice and agency came to be associated with agendas of privatization and global restructuring, very different from those of the women's movement (Yuval-Davis, 1994; Rai, 2001).

Kabeer provides an approach to overcoming some of these difficulties, suggesting three dimensions of empowerment, which each indicate engagement with particular social structures and constitute a different meaning of choice from that promoted by advocates of the free market. Empowerment entails, firstly, access to resources; secondly, agency in decision making and negotiating power; and, thirdly, achievements of outcomes of value. Kabeer argues that an adequate assessment of empowerment requires triangulation of measurement of all three dimensions (Kabeer, 1999). While this rigorous framework can be criticized for the rather sharp distinction between resources and agency, on the one hand, and agency and outcomes, on the other hand, a distinction that is often difficult to discern empirically, the approach does illuminate some interesting critiques of the simple WID stress on equality of resources. Mapping Kabeer's framework onto the field of education in order to explore questions of empowerment, one would need to assess resources such as access to schooling up to a certain level. Access includes retention, that is, the capacity to retain access, and achievement, that is, capacity to gain knowledge resources from schooling. Women's agency would need to be examined; for example, their participation in decision making about education, in households, schools education ministries, or village education councils. Achievements that flow from education are not just narrowly defined notions of reading and writing up to a certain level, but also more complex notions of well-being (Unterhalter, 2005d). Janet Raynor has explored this empirically in Bangladesh, showing how the dimension of resources is much more easily fulfilled than that of agency or outcomes (Raynor, 2005).

In contrast to the WID interpretation of equality based on equality of resources, GAD theorists consider equality in terms of the removal of the structures that shape gender inequality: discriminatory laws, labor market practices, management regimes in institutions, the exclusion of women from decision making in public and private settings, and inequitable processes in the distribution of time, money, schooling and consideration. The process of remedy is sometimes seen as empowerment but is also sometimes conceptualized as equity, an approach to instituting fairness. This might entail inequalities in resources, as in affirmative action programs. Thus, equality is an ideal of equal power, participation and distribution, but the process of achieving it might sometimes look inequitable because historical and contextual issues cannot be excluded from analysis.

The literature using a GAD framework to look at education has yielded some illuminating studies of gendered relations in schools and households and the way these affected decisions about which children went to and remained in school (Vavrus, 2003; Colclough *et al.*, 2004). Analyses of the gendered politics of community involvement in education indicate how ambiguous decentralization policies are in societies where there are severe constraints on women's participation in decision making (Subrahmanian, 2005). A number of studies have highlighted high levels of gender-based violence in school (Mirembe and Davies, 2001; Leach *et al.*, 2003). GAD work has also shown the gendered politics of policy, highlighting the forms of alliance feminist organizations have made with the state over education (Stromquist, 2000), and the dynamics of relations with international donors (Sato, 1997; Swainson, 2000).

In contrast to the prevalence of economists in research associated with WID, writers working on education within a GAD framework drew on history, sociology, anthropology, politics and development studies. Generally, GAD research has not been conducted on commissions from large multilateral organizations, but represents small-scale projects, often by academics living in developing countries.

There are some interesting contrasts between the GAD work on education and that of feminist scholars in high-income countries where gender and education were given political and theoretical coherence largely by teachers in schools and teacher education institutions who were directly involved in the women's movement. A number of these later moved on to work in higher education and education ministries, continuing to research in schools. Thus, political and academic work was organic with practice. For them, the liberal feminism, so influential on WID, had very little resonance. Much more influential were theorists who could help analyze the persistence of gender, class and race/ethnic inequality, despite universal access and high levels of achievement by girls. Thus, Bernstein's work on class, Bourdieu's work on habitus, Foucault's analysis of power, concerns with the simultaneous exclusions and inclusions of citizenship, a number of feminist post-structuralist accounts regarding the negotiations of meaning, and feminist analysis of embodiment were the most generative of theoretical and political insight. In contrast to writings in gender, education and development, this literature has been more theoretically engaged with debates in sociology, cultural studies and women's studies, and has emerged from classroom practice.

The work of theorists using GAD in education has not generated the simple 'what works' messages associated with WID. GAD influence on policy and practice can be seen at two levels. Firstly, GAD thinkers have developed critiques of policy making that look at the gendered processes of decision making. Gender mainstreaming seeks to legitimate gender equality as a fundamental value that is reflected in development choices and institutional practices for a society as a whole, to drive gender equality from central, key ministries, and to facilitate the presence of women as decision makers (UNDP, 2002: 7). Gender budgeting seeks to identify how a departmental budget is spent and which elements can be seen to yield specific benefits to women and girls (Budlender and Hewitt, 2002). Some evaluative work on gender mainstreaming and gender budgeting has been published, showing some of the uneven processes involved (Razavi and Miller, 1995; Derbyshire, 1998), but empirical studies of gender mainstreaming and gender budgeting in education have yet to be undertaken.

The achievement of GAD analysts and activists has been to highlight how complex and important institutional and social change is. They have generated key demands to involve women in changing gendered structures of power that bear on education, a demand which resonates with that of the global women's movement.

PROBLEMATIZING UNIVERSAL CATEGORIES: THE CHALLENGE OF POST-STRUCTURALISM

WID and GAD emerged out of development politics and practice, but the post-structuralist challenge to the universalizing categories they employed came primarily from highly educated critics located in universities. Post-structuralists critiqued development practice and the methodologies associated with thinking about the Third World. Commentaries highlighted problems in the universalization of a notion of 'Third World woman' and 'development' and the power relations masked and perpetuated by development assistance rhetoric (Mohanty, 1988; Marchand and Parpart, 1995; Spivak, 1999). Some writers saw schooling as a space that disrupts and diminishes the power of women's local or indigenous knowledges (Kolawole, 1997; Tuhiwai Smith, 1999). A key question posed by writers drawing on this framework, but largely absent from most WID and GAD discussions on gender, education and development, concerns issues of methodology and the power entailed in the 'colonial gaze', the process by which research participants 'become gendered', in accordance with certain ascribed meanings of the term and the silencing and erasure of women from many conventional sources for data collection.

Post-structuralist thinkers have raised critical questions about identity and shown how the meaning of gender entails fluid and shifting processes of identification. For these writers, the process of education is partly a process of recognizing this fluidity and critiquing the processes of 'othering' and marginalization of non-mainstream identities. Thus, in this framework, equality is not the major concern, as the key political and theoretical objective is the recognition of difference (Mannathoko, 1999).

There has been relatively little work using a post-structuralist approach to look at gender and education in development settings, in contrast to the rich literature on this theme in the global north. However, the complexity of the HIV/AIDs epidemic has generated work that considers the gendered and sexualized identities of learners and teachers (Pattman and Chege, 2003) and ways in which meanings associated with school spaces can subvert concerns with gender equality (Kent, 2004). The fluid identities of educated women in Africa and India have also been documented (Narayan, 1997; Stambach, 2000).

While the influence of post-structuralists on government and NGO policies has not been large, the analysis they make of the importance of identities has had resonance with political mobilization around subordinated identities, such as gay and lesbian identities in South Africa or Dalit identities in India. These mobilizations entail the development of learning materials for use outside formal schooling. Generally, post-structuralist writers on gender, education and development have been employed in higher education, either working in or closely connected with Western European and North American institutions. It is here that their influence has been most pronounced in course content and in the focus of what is published.

EQUALITY OF WHAT IN EDUCATION?
RIGHTS AND CAPABILITIES

WID, GAD and post-structuralism all pose the question of gender equality in terms of relations and resources. Questions concerning the reasons for equality and how this links with views of justice are generally implicit, rather than explicit. By contrast writing on rights and capabilities asks foundational questions regarding why gender equality is important and what conceptions of the person and the just society it derives from.

Amartya Sen's capability approach has been influential in a number of UN organizations in helping to frame policy regarding gender equality in education. The capability approach considers that the evaluation of equality, as in education provision, needs to be based on an understanding of human capabilities; that is, the valued freedoms of every individual (Sen, 1999). This contrasts sharply with the human capital approach, influential in WID analysis, which stresses that the evaluation of education provision is about some aggregated benefit to present or future society. While human capital theory has little to say about injustices and inequality in the household, the workplace or the state, the capability approach is centrally concerned with these, but supports its critique not by outlining the structures of inequality (as GAD does), but by positing a strategy based on an ethical notion of valuing freedoms and affirming rights as ethical obligations of each person to others.

Sen has outlined how he sees the significance of education as a key capability that is intrinsically and instrumentally valuable to individuals (Sen, 1999). The concern of the capability approach with analyzing the process of converting resources into valued outcomes and with the multidimensionality of development has been a key influence on UNDP's *Human Development Reports*. Partly because of this, research using the approach is highly interdisciplinary.

The capabilities approach is not without important critics, particularly with regard to its failure to take account of injustices of recognition, not just distribution (Fraser, 1997); its inability to engage with dimensions of group-based social mobilization for democratization and gender equality (Stewart, 2005); and its tendency to universalize that may not take sufficient account of particular contexts (Uyan, 2005).

To some extent, empirical and conceptual work shows how issues of recognition and social context can enrich the approach. Alkire (2002) details how evaluations of women's literacy can be enhanced by drawing on the approach, and similar nuance emerges when considering how the approach might be utilized in considering policy to overcome gender violence in the context of HIV in South Africa (Unterhalter, 2003b), women's access to higher education (Walker, 2006), and the understanding of equality in the context of disability (Terzi, 2005).

This work highlights the obligations of governments to establish and sustain the conditions for every individual, irrespective of gender, ethnicity, race or regional location, to achieve valued outcomes. These may entail ensuring that each person acquires a certain level of educational attainment, but they undoubtedly entail ensuring the freedoms that allow valued outcomes to be articulated and achieved (Gasper, 2004; Unterhalter, 2005d). Thus, for example, failing to ensure that sexual violence in, and on the way to, school is identified and eradicated would be a failure to ensure freedom for valued outcomes. While GAD writers have tended to describe the structures that generate these problems, the capability approach contains an ethical injunction with regard to formulating policy for change.

The capability approach attempts to overcome some of the difficulties with the universalism in the concept of rights by highlighting the importance of securing the conditions for individuals articulating valued freedoms. The stress on securing conditions for social justice and the intrinsic value of education sets this approach apart from WID, with its stress on practical strategies; GAD, with its focus on disempowering structures; and post-structuralism, with its emphasis on identities. However, the approach cannot of itself comprehend the complex gendered relations in education settings and requires operationalization in conjunction with social science.

CONCLUSION

One of the Millennium Development Goals set by the UN in 2000 was equal numbers of boys and girls in school by 2005. This has not been realized, despite a range of WID-inspired policies and research. Gender activists have used the failure to achieve gender parity in schooling by 2005 as an opportunity to revisit some of the assumptions of the WID approach. This chapter has sketched some of the research and policy problems they must overcome, including the challenge of improving measurement that goes beyond the GEEI, if, in the coming decade, the comprehensive vision of gender, education and development of the Beijing Declaration of 1995 is to be realized.

REFERENCES

Alderman, H, Orazem, P and Paterno, E (1996) School quality, school cost, and the public/private choices of low-income households in Pakistan. *Impact evaluation of education reform,* Working Paper no. 2, World Bank Development Research Group. Washington, DC: World Bank.

Alkire, S (2002) *Valuing freedom. Sen's capability approach and poverty reduction.* Oxford: Oxford University Press.

Budlender, D. and Hewitt, G (2002) *Gender budgets make more cents: country studies and good practice.* London: Commonwealth Secretariat.

Carnoy, M and Samoff, J (1990) *Education and social transition in the Third World.* Princeton, NJ: Princeton University Press.

Colclough, C, Al Samarrai, S, Rose, P and Tembon, M (2004) *Achieving schooling for all in Africa: costs, commitment and gender.* Aldershot: Ashgate.

DAWN, (Development Alternatives with Women for a New Era) (1995) Rethinking social development: DAWN's vision. *World Development,* 23: 2001–4.

Derbyshire, H (1998) *Mainstreaming gender equality in project implementation,* London: Department for International Development.

Dollar, D and Gatti, R (1999) *Gender inequality, income and growth: are good times good for women?* World Bank Policy Research Report on Gender and Development. Working Paper series 1. Washington, DC: World Bank.

Filmer, D and Pritchett, L. (1999) The effect of household wealth on educational attainment: evidence from 35 countries. *Population and Development Review,* 25: 85–120.

Fraser, N (1997) *Justice interruptus. Critical reflections on the 'postsocialist' condition.* New York: Routledge.

Gasper, D (2004) *The ethics of development.* Edinburgh: Edinburgh University Press.

Goetz, AM (ed) (1997) *Getting institutions right for women in development.* London: Zed.

Hadden, K and London, B (1996) Educating girls in the Third World: the demographic, basic needs and economic benefits. *International Journal of Comparative Sociology,* 37: 31–46.

Herz, B and Sperling, G (2004) *What works in girls' education.* New York: Council on Foreign Relations.

Herz, B, Subbarao, K and Habib, M (1991) *Letting girls learn: promising approaches in primary and secondary education.* World Bank Discussion Paper no. 133. Washington, DC: World Bank.

Kabeer, N (1994) *Reversed realities.* London: Verso.

Kabeer, N (1999) Resources, agency, achievements: reflections on the measurement of women's empowerment. *Development and Change,.* 30: 435–64.

Kent, A (2004) Living life on the edge: examining space and sexualities within a township high school in greater Durban in the context of the HIV epidemic. *Transformation,* 54: 59–75.

King, EM and Hill, MA (eds) (1993) *Women's education in developing countries: barriers, benefits and policies.* Washington, DC: World Bank.

Klasen, S (1999) Does gender inequality reduce growth and development? Evidence from cross-country regressions. Policy Research Report on Gender and Development Working Paper no. 7. Washington, DC: World Bank.

Kolawole, MEM (1997) *Womanism and African consciousness.* Trenton, NJ: Trentham Books.

Kutnick, P, Jules, V and Layne, A (1997) *Gender and school achievement in the Caribbean.* London: Department for International Development (Education Research Serial no. 21).

Leach, F, Fiscian, V and Kadzamira, E (2003) *An investigative study of the abuse of girls in African schools.* London: DFID.

Mannathoko, C (1999) Theoretical perspectives on gender in education: the case of Eastern and Southern Africa. *International Review of Education,* 45 (nos. 5/6): 445–60.

Marchand, M and Parpart, J (eds) (1995) *Feminism, postmodernism, development.* London: Routledge.

Mirembe, R and Davies, L (2001) Is schooling a risk? Gender, power relations and school culture in Uganda. *Gender and Education,* 13: 401–16.

Mohanty, C (1988) Under Western eyes: feminist scholarship and colonial discourse. *Feminist Review,* 30: 65–88.

Molyneux, M (1998) Analysing women's movements, in Jackson, C and Pearson, R (eds) *Feminist visions of development. Gender analysis and policy* (65–88). London: Routledge.

Narayan, U (1997) *Dislocating cultures. Third World feminism and the politics of knowledge.* New York: Routledge.

Nath, SR and Chowdhury, AMR (eds) (2001) *A question of quality: state of primary education in Bangladesh.* Vol II. *Achievement of competencies.* Dhaka: Campaign for Popular Education and University Press Limited.

Obura, A (1991) *Changing images: the portrayal of girls and women in Kenyan textbooks.* Nairobi: African Centre for Technology Studies.

Pattman, R and Chege, F (2003) *Finding our voices: gendered and sexual identities and HIV/AIDS in education.* Nairobi: UNICEF.

Quisumbing, A (1996) Male–female differences in agricultural productivity: methodological issues and empirical evidence. *World Development,* 24: 1579–95.

Rai, S (2001) *Gender and the political economy of development.* Cambridge: Polity Press.

Raynor, J (2005) Resources, agency and outcomes: girls talk about education in Bangladesh. Unpublished paper presented to research seminar, Institute of Education, University of London.

Razavi, S and Miller, C (1995) *From WID to GAD. Conceptual shift in the women and development discourse.* Geneva:United Nations Research Institute for Social Development.

Rowlands, J (1997) *Questioning empowerment. Working with women in Honduras.* Oxford: Oxfam.

Sato, Y (1997) Development assistance in poverty and WID: experience of Japan. *International Co-operation Study,*13–2: 9–24. Japan International Cooperation Agency.

Sen, A (1999) *Development as freedom.* Oxford: Oxford University Press.

Spivak, G (1999) *A critique of postcolonial reason.* London: Harvard University Press.

Stambach, A (2000) *Lessons from Mount Kilamanjaro.* New York: Routledge.

Stewart, F (2005) Groups and capabilities. *Journal of Human Development,* 6:165–204.

Stromquist, N (2000) Voice, harmony and fugue in global feminism. *Gender and Education,* 12: 419–34.

Subbarao, K and Raney, L (1995) Social gains from female education. *Economic Development and Cultural Change,* 44: 105–28.

Subrahmanian, R (2005) Education exclusion and the development state, in Chopra, R and Jeffrey, P (eds) *Education regimes in contemporary India.* Delhi: Sage.

Swainson, N (2000) Knowledge and power: the design and implementation of gender policies in education in Malawi, Tanzania and Zimbabwe. *International Journal of Educational Development,* 20: 49–64.

Terzi, L (2005) A capability perspective on impairment, disability and special needs: towards social justice in education. *Theory and Research in Education,* 3: 197–224.

Tuhiwai Smith, L (1999) *Decolonizing methodologies: research and indigenous peoples* London: Zed Books.

UNDP (2002) *Gender mainstreaming. Learning and development pack.* New York: UNDP (www.sdnp.undp.org/gender/) (accessed June 2005).

UNESCO (1995) *World education report 1995.* Oxford: Oxford University Press.

UNESCO (2003) *Gender and education for all: the leap to equality.* Paris: UNESCO Publishing.

UNESCO Statistics Division (2005a) UNESCO statistics (http://unstats.un.org/unsd/demographic/products/indwm/ww2005/tab4a.htm) (accessed June 2005).

UNESCO (2005) *EFA Global Monitoring Report.* Paris: UNESCO.

Unterhalter, E (2003a) Gender, education and development: competing perspectives, in Lazaro Lorente, L M and Martinez Usarralde, MJ (eds) *Studies in Comparative Education* (*Estudios de Educación Comparada*) (277–300). Valencia: Martin Impresores.

Unterhalter, E (2003b) The capabilities approach and gendered education: an examination of South African complexities. *Theory and Research in Education,*1: 7–22.

Unterhalter, E (2005a) Gender equality and education in South Africa: measurements, scores and strategies, in Chisholm, L and September, J (eds) *Gender equity in South African education 1994–2004. Conference proceedings.* Cape Town: HSRC Press.

Unterhalter, E (2005b) Fragmented frameworks: researching women, gender, education and development, in Aikman, S and Unterhalter, E (eds) *Beyond access: transforming policy and practice for gender equality in education* (15–36). Oxford: Oxfam Publishing.

Unterhalter, E (2005c) Needs, rights and capabilities: the political foundations of the demand for gender equality in education. Paper presented at 5th Capabilities Conference, Paris.

Unterhalter, E (2005d) Global inequality, capabilities, social justice: the millennium development goal for gender equity in education. *International Journal of Education and Development,* 26: 111–22.

Unterhalter, E, Kioko-Echessa and E Pattman, R (2005e) Scaling up. *Developing an approach to measuring progress on girls' education in Commonwealth countries in Africa.* London: Commonwealth Secretariat.

Unterhalter, E, Challender, C and Rajagopalan, R (2005) Measuring gender equality in education, in Aikman, S and Unterhalter, E (eds) *Beyond access: transforming policy and practice for gender equality in education* (60–82). Oxford: Oxfam Publishing.

Uyan, P (2005) Reconsidering the capabilities list: what does her story tell? Paper presented at the 5th International Conference on the Capability Approach, UNESCO, Paris.

Vavrus, F (2003) *Desire and decline: schooling and crisis in Tanzania.* New York: Peter Lang.

Walker, M (2006) *Higher education pedagogies.* Maidenhead: Open University Press.

World Bank (2002) Genderstats webpage (http://devdata.worldbank.org/genderstats/home.asp) (accessed June 2005).

Yuval-Davis, N (1994) Women, ethnicity and empowerment. *Feminism and Psychology, Shifting identities shifting racisms*, 4:179–98.

NOTE

1 This paper draws on work conducted by the Beyond Access: Gender, Education and Development partnership between Oxfam, DFID and Institute of Education, University of London. My thanks to all colleagues who worked on the project, and to Joe Crawford, Rosa Crawford and Belou Charlaff for research assistance with this paper.

8

Gender and Movement in Social Policy

Meg Maguire

INTRODUCTION

A short chapter cannot possibly cover all the complexities of gender policy and its processes and outcomes, for, as Francis and Skelton (2005: 37) note, 'policy on gender is not uniform in content or focus across countries in the Western world'. There is already a considerable amount of work that looks critically and comparatively at education policy and reform in general terms (Lewin, 2001; Zajda, 2005). There is also a substantial body of work that concentrates on gender policy in different national contexts (Kenway, 1990; Datnow, 1998; O'Connor *et al.*, 1999; Erskine and Wilson, 1999; Salisbury and Riddell, 2000). Therefore, in this chapter, I want to explore gender policy from a critical policy analysis perspective rather than concentrating on the specificities of policy texts and policy outcomes, important though these are.

My case is that policy is sometimes the unexplained 'Other'. In much work that focuses on policy texts, policy implementation and outcomes, there is sometimes an absence, an unexplored problematic, where policy is taken as a 'given' and not seen as part of the problem. Sometimes policy analysis takes a single-focus approach. That is, it fails to recognize the ways in which contrasting sets of policies coexist and that they sometimes complement as well as contradict or displace one another. In what follows, I want to explore gender policy in a way that highlights some of these policy questions. Most of my examples, but not all, will be drawn from the British setting, as this is the context with which I am most familiar.

Table 7.3 Primary NER for girls (and boys) *c.* 1980–2000 in 10 Asian countries

	1980	1988	1995	2000
Bangladesh	48 (69)	57 (67)	…	88 (87)
Cambodia	…	61 (73)*	90 (100)	81 (88)
China	…	97 (100)	98 (98)	93 (92)
India	…	…	…	76 (91)
Indonesia	83 (93)	98 (100)	94 (97)	91 (92)
Laos	…	58 (67)*	66 (74)	78 (85)
Nepal	34 (79)	43 (84)	…	66 (75)
Pakistan	…	…	…	57 (76)
Sir Lanka	…	100 (100)	…	100 (100)**
Vietnam	…	87 (94)*	…	92 (98)

* 1990 figure.
** 1998 figure.
Sources: World Bank, 2002; UNESCO, 1995: 118–21;UNESCO, 2005, Unterhalter & McCowan, 2005.

Table 7.4 Changes in GEEI in 1990–2000 in selected African, Asian and Latin American countries

	GEEI % c.1993	GEEI% c.2003	Percentage increase/decrease	%increase needed to reach GEEI of 95%
Mauritius	89	81	−9	17.28
Botswana	73	78	7	21.79
Ghana	34	39	15	143.59
Mozambique	20	20	0	375.00
Cameroon	33	15	−55	533.33
Singapore	100	100	0	0
Japan	100	100	0	0
Azerbaijan	84	84	0	13.09
Laos	20	26	30	265.39
Pakistan	23	20	−13	375.00
Chile	86	97	13	0
Cuba	88	94	7	1.06
Venezuela	70	86	23	10.46
Nicaragua	33	46	39	106.52
Guatemala	26	39	50	143.58

Source: Unterhalter *et al.*, 2005.
GEEI: gender equality in education index.

To try to chart a somewhat more nuanced picture, I have developed the gender equality in education index (GEEI). This is a weighted measure of the extent to which countries are able to secure gender equality in primary and secondary schooling and ensure lives with good health and adequate incomes to women. A GEEI of 95% indicates adequate provision in all these areas. Table 7.4 shows changes in GEEI in Africa, Asia and Latin America since 1990 and shows the huge level of improvement needed over the next 10 years to reach an adequate index of 95%. The countries in Table 7.4 for each region are those with the two highest GEEI, the two lowest and the GEEI closest to the median for that region (For fuller tables and discussion, see Unterhalter *et al.*, 2005.)

In this chapter, I start by outlining some of the complexities involved in critical policy analysis. The chapter then explores some of the ways in which different constructions of gender, a contested and shifting discourse, has affected policy in education. Finally, the chapter considers the implications of these discussions for gender policy and policy work more broadly.

A CRITICAL APPROACH TO POLICY

There was a time when policy making was more of a taken-for-granted event that was often viewed as a 'democratic consensual process' rather than a political endeavour (Olssen *et al.*, 2004: 2). In the last 25 years or so, policy analysis and policy debate have received more critical attention. Policy making and policy implementation are now more generally regarded as highly charged and contested political processes, even if this is not always reflected in policy accounts (Ozga, 2000). A critical approach recognizes that what counts as policy and what drives a specific policy agenda is shaped by social changes and transformations in the wider economic, political, cultural and social settings.

These changes and transformations are not all of a piece. They conflict with and contradict one another, and they do not always influence policy outcomes in a straightforward manner. For example, changes that occur in the civil setting because of wider social movements that oppose the status quo, such as the civil rights movements in the USA in the 1960s, can sometimes eventually influence the policy process of the nation state (Anyon, 2005). Frequently, policy outcomes are diluted responses that become adopted after much contestation and struggle. Transnational shifts in the political-economic setting, for example, neo-liberalism, individualism and changes in modes of production, such as the advent of techno-logical developments (Castells, 1999), will also influence the policy terrain. Political and economic discourses may be evoked as inevitable and irrevocable by bureaucrats and politicians. These claims are then used to justify and rationalize specific public policy interventions. The alleged need to raise educational achieve-ment in a competitive international knowledge economy is a prime example of transnational policy discourse (Francis and Skelton, 2005: 1).

Processes of change and influence shift over time; they can become reversed, marginalized, and discounted or incorporated. They sometimes become dominant and sedimented into policy and practice. In this way, some policy positions become naturalized and normalized. In this shifting, complex and contested process, what 'counts' in policy terms, at one point, might well become 'rejected' at another moment in time:

> The meaning and significance of policy at any particular historical juncture is something that must be rendered intelligible through a process of interrogation, by ascertaining the way that discursive contexts inherent within the social and historical process manifest themselves in and through textual production, formulation and articulation. (Olssen *et al.*, 2004: 4)

There are conceptual and practical dangers in ignoring policy work. As Ball (1997) has explained, some educational research has written policy out of the context. Ball (1997: 265) claims that sometimes research focuses on classrooms and teachers as if they were 'unaffected or unconstrained' by mandated policy requirements. For example, in a setting where teachers and schools are pressured to raise their attainment year on year, some gendered issues might take a back seat, not because of sexism but because of the pressure of performance demands. In the current setting, policies are always seen as solutions but never become recognized as part of the problem (Ball, 1997: 265). This policy-blind or policy-neutral approach displaces any consideration of the complex and sometimes unintended impacts that aspects of policy can have in educational settings, as elsewhere. This approach to policy analysis contains within itself a normalizing approach whereby policy becomes naturalized, under-researched and taken as a given. In contrast, Ball believes that policy studies need to take a reflexive stance; one that recognizes that policies can create problems and generate new contexts for action/practice.

Another danger lies in a single-focus approach to policy. While some policy analysis concentrates on the way in which one element of policy making affects practice, in reality, many policies are in play simultaneously. 'When we focus on one policy we may conveniently forget that other policies are in circulation and that the enactment of one may inhibit or contradict or influence the possibility of the enactment of others' (Ball, 1997: 265). Policies that focus only on enhancing effective management may displace any consideration of gender regimes and hierarchies in schools. Equally, policy accounts that deal only with gender may displace other compelling policy influences. Related to this issue of policy circulation, Ball (1994) has argued that policies have first-and second-order effects. First-order policy effects are changes in practice or structure that can be seen across the system. For example, the focus on performance and league tables are first-order effects of policy changes in education. Second-order effects are the impact of first-order effects in terms of access, opportunity and social justice. It is here that gendered impacts will be evident even if the policy itself appears to be gender blind.

Critical policy analysis highlights the role of agency, although this is struggled over and contested. Bowe *et al.* (1992: 22) have argued that 'Practitioners do not confront policy texts as naïve readers, they come with histories, with experience, with values and purposes of their own ... policy writers cannot control the meanings of their texts'. Therefore, what happens in practice will be mediated by the values, ethics, professional and personal commitments of those who work in educational settings. In a school, if there is a critical mass of workers who prioritize social justice issues, there may be more scope for innovative gender work, even if the dominant policy discourse seems to suggest otherwise. In cases like this, individuals in educational institutions will find themselves caught up in sets of dilemmas (Berlak and Berlak, 1981) where they will try to bring off socially just practice in contradictory policy settings.

Institutional norms and values will also play a part in mediating the way that policy is realized. For example, many institutes of higher education have equality and diversity units that 'speak' to their legal commitments in these areas. However, practices and norms-in-circulation may not support change very much on the ground if they are deemed to be too costly, such as adequate levels of child-care provision, or if they challenge the status quo, or by ensuring that differences are reflected in all parts and levels of the workforce (Acker and Feurverger, 1997).

There are other critical policy issues that sometimes go unrecognized in policy work. Policies morph and shift over time; they are struggled over, resisted, contested; sometimes they just peter out. Sometimes policies simply do not work. There are other problems, too, with policy work. Claims are sometimes made about the impact of policy after a short period has lapsed (Power, 1992). Some policy changes take a long time to bed down and take effect. For example, the still controversial findings from Headstart and High/Scope in the USA suggest long-term direct and indirect benefits of early intervention (Whitty, 2000). In educational settings, policies can be produced at different levels, at national or local state level (the local education authority in England) and sometimes at individual school level. This distinction is sometimes not addressed in policy analysis.

CONTEXTUALIZING POLICY

Ball (1997) has argued that policy construction has sometimes been conducted in isolation from broader social changes. Indeed, one of his examples concerning this neglect of changes elsewhere relates to the 'more general impact and influence of feminist and postmodern theories' (Ball, 1997: 68). Ball (1997: 269) claims that any policy analysis that fails to take into account the 'ways in which education is embedded in a set of more general economic and political changes' limits the possibilities for interpretation and decontextualizes the policy process. This has also been argued forcefully by Power (1992: 498). Her case is that sometimes policy analysis becomes reduced to tracking policy 'formulation and implementation'. She believes that policy explorations of this type can work to disguise the wider role of schooling and its significance for social reproduction more generally. Power illustrated her argument in relation to the insertion of market forces in UK education provision through the Education Reform Act 1988. Her point was that the distribution of education in a competitive market setting had always occurred, and was not simply a consequence of a specific piece of education policy making. 'Education is constructed along market principles simply because of its constitution within, and relationship to, a capitalist mode of production' (Power, 1992: 498). In terms of gender policy, the relationship between economic production and social reproduction is a powerful constraint. As Blackmore (1997: 451) has argued, 'equity is not a factor in the market'.

Policy analysis also has to take account of the complexity of value shifts in the broader social setting. Shifts away from a concern with the common good or public interest (Galbraith, 1970) toward what, in the UK, has been termed the post-welfarist society, where private interests look set to dominate (Tomlinson, 2000), have had a complex but distinctive impact on some aspects of policy making. For example, in the UK educational market, the first-order policy effect is that 'choosing' privileges some (individual families) who are better placed to access 'good' schools. However, in a competitive education market where examination performance drives provision, choice and reputation, some children and students might become seen as 'easier to teach' and more desirable to recruit to the school. The second-order policy effect is that some institutions are able to cherry-pick and they do the 'choosing'. In the UK setting, where research suggests that girls do better than boys, some schools may work hard to recruit this constituency, not for reasons of equity but to enhance their league table position (Ball and Gewirtz, 1997). Indeed, evidence of 'choosing' in UK schools and post-compulsory settings (Ball and Gewirtz, 1997; Ball *et al.*, 2000) shows that girls are targeted for recruitment by some institutions.

Other broad shifts in the political and economic sphere have affected educational policy making. Economic imperatives and a discourse of educational crisis have resulted in managerialism, marketization and a concentration on performance. But while there may be some convergence in terms of policy attention, there are distinctive policy outcomes in different national settings. For example, one aspect of international concern about achievement concentrates on the 'gender gap'. As Francis and Skelton (2005) argue, there has been a focus in Australia on social justice and gender issues (although differently interpreted at particular moments in time), while the USA and Canada have concentrated on equity 'and this is particularly in relation to charting and addressing differences between ethnic groups' (Francis and Skelton, 2005: 41). In the UK, the approach has been to focus on the need to raise standards and the policy imperative of social inclusion. Jones points out that 'disability, gender and race have become essential to thinking about reform' in the UK (Jones, 2003: 7). The dilemma is that these intentions might not always be well resourced, and other, more dominant policy pressures and policy enactments to meet performance targets might dilute and distort any policy impact based on inclusion rather than social justice.

One of the fundamental dilemmas in policy analysis is that in much of what is written, 'the meaning of policy is taken for granted and it is not difficult to find the term policy being used to describe very different "things"' at different points in the same study (Ball, 2006: 44). Borrowing from Ball, I am taking policy to be both 'things', as in texts and practices, but also processes that derive from discourses. In this chapter, my focus is with situating and problematizing policy as process, 'thing' and discourse. The same dilemma also relates to the substantive focus of this chapter; that is, the way in which gender as a discourse has been differently approached and differently articulated at different times.

DISCURSIVE TURNS IN (EDUCATIONAL) GENDER THEORY

It is not possible here to do justice to the complexities involved in theorizing gender (but see Dillabough, 2001; Alsop *et al.*, 2002; Arnot, 2002; Evans, 2003). However, it is necessary to highlight some distinctions and 'moves' in gender theory that (sometimes) have had outcomes in specific policy formulations. For example, in the UK post-war setting, education research tended to concentrate on social-class outcomes rather than what went on inside schools (Whitty, 2000). This period could be characterized as taking a gender-blind approach to policy, although, in practice, the gendered story was somewhat different. Women and men were ascribed different roles and responsibilities, and while these had overlapped somewhat during the war years (1939–45), after the war 'normal services were resumed'. In consequence, gendered roles were constructed in traditional binary terms. This approach permeated policy and practices in social, cultural, economic and political terms. Gender might not have been an overt strand of policy making, but in terms of policy-in-action, the expectation was of traditionally gendered aspirations and outcomes. While this approach was contested to a degree, particularly by some of the single-sex independent girls schools (Delamont, 1996), the status quo was deeply steeped in a traditional, gendered regime.

One of the most powerful changes that affected discourses of gender in the UK was the change in patterns of women's employment, particularly within the domains of the welfare state in the period immediately after World War II. As Arnot *et al.* (1999: 58) argue: 'Many of the new jobs resembled the kinds of work that women had previously been expected to carry out either at home or on a voluntary basis'. The post-war expansion of the UK welfare state produced increased demands for labor in a range of areas, such as social services, health, education and welfare. The 1950s and 1960s were periods of growth in the UK, with low unemployment rates and labor shortages, and more women were desperately needed in the labor market. It was an expansionist time when women's aspirations and expectations accelerated. These changes were reflected in emerging demands for equal pay and a call for a reduction in the discrimination that women faced in the workplace. In this period, gender was no longer neutral (even if it ever had been), nor was policy gender-blind, but neither was it sensitive or responsive to the contradictions faced by many women who entered the labor market 'between their roles in the public world of work and the privacy of the family' (Arnot *et al.*, 1999: 64). Gender was on the agenda but only in terms of 'manpower' issues in the labor market. Education policy reflected the social reality that the majority of girls and women would work before and during marriage. But policy and provision still reflected an essentialized binary perspective in its construction of gendered issues, as in relation to boy's subjects and male occupations and girls' subjects and female occupations (Weiner, 1985).

Two key trajectories in education policy typified the 1950s and early 1960s and had implications for the way in which gender was approached. The first was a 'liberal' and 'meritocratic' approach. This approach argued that since compulsory education had now been extended to all children in the UK, and that since extended educational opportunities were available for all those who could benefit from them, what made a difference was merit. Thus, women could advance in educational and career terms, if they were 'able' to do so. They could attend universities and they could enter the traditional (male-dominated) professions. What was left unspoken was the destinies (and identities) of the girls and women who were deemed 'less able'. The second approach to gender construction was a related discourse of individualism. In a period of equality of opportunity, 'able' individuals could advance. Thus, any more critical gender discourses were silenced and marginalized by these dominant liberal and individualized approaches and gender discourses.

In the mid-to late 1960s and throughout the 1970s, these liberal approaches to gender issues started to become more overtly contested. With the advent of second-wave feminism, the fact of being female or male was now recognized as having a significant part to play in social reproduction. During the 1970s and 1980s, there was a focus on gendered issues in a way that still seemed to locate gender in a binary position, although the focus was on the oppression of women. To a certain extent in educational settings, gendered accounts that contrasted boys with girls, men with women, became part of the policy orthodoxy. Education policy started to concentrate on offering girls access to the same curriculum as boys (Kenway and Willis, 1992). The focus was on changing sex-role socialization and gender-related legislation.

This policy approach sometimes worked to marginalize and displace other aspects of identification, as it contained within itself a tendency to essentialize the experiences and behaviours of all women and all men. During this period, one of the most significant critiques of feminist discourses was produced by Black feminists (hooks, 1982; Love, 1984; Amos and Parmar, 1987; Carby, 1987), who highlighted the failure 'to recognize the key question of difference – that black and minority girls' experiences and family life are distinct from the white cultural narrative' (Dillabough, 2001: 19). What this perspective also exposed was the 'Eurocentrism and racist elements' of some earlier forms of feminist thinking (Dillabough, 2001: 19). In consequence, theories of gender have subsequently taken a 'cultural turn'.

This has meant that, more recently, work in the area of gender theory has expanded and diversified to include postmodernist/post-structuralist work. Gendered identities and identifications and shifts in social theory have produced a complexity of accounts that highlight fluidity as well as diversities within differences. Factors of class, as well as race, sex and differences such as age, faith and sexuality, are involved in identity construction, and this complexity has been reflected in much of the related research (Datnow, 1998; Epstein *et al.*, 1998; Erskine and Wilson, 1999; Walkerdine *et al.*, 2001; Archer, 2003). Simultaneously, feminist research has continued to demonstrate the 'enduring stability of the gender order in girl's and women's working lives, despite transformations in contemporary gender relations' (Dillabough, 2001: 24).

In terms of gender theories, there has been a conceptual struggle, conducted over the last 50 years or so, in which gendered impacts were either overtly disregarded, positioned as *the* reason for continued social and material inequalities, or seen as part of an interrelated combination of factors that have influenced patterns and forms of social reproduction. Differences within difference have been recognized, and identity and cultural studies have expanded to incorporate situated and contextualized gender theorization. The theoretical situation is now rich, complex and multifaceted:

> If class stratification and gender once stood at the center of the project of feminist reproduction theorists, they now need to be seen as necessary but no longer sufficient conceptual tools for the new theoretical landscape we inhabit today. (Dillabough, 2003: 379)

The problem, of course, is that education policy making and education policy-inaction is often caught up in and limited by conceptual lags and gaps. Discourses of 'merit', liberalism and individualism still influence the policy process. It took some time for the concerns of second-wave feminists to 'reach' the attention of education policy makers. It took even longer for any policy effects to be seen in practice. Currently, educational policy making still seems to be significantly influenced by an essentializing and binary construction of gendered reproduction in education; that is, a focus on comparing and contrasting what it is that girls achieve (and achievement is the only game in town) with the performance of boys (Francis and Skelton, 2005). Recent developments in gender theory have, it seems, had very little impact in terms of dominant strands in educational policy making, in the UK at least, and older discourses are still in circulation.

POLICY AND GENDER ISSUES IN THE UK SETTING

In this part of the chapter, I pull together the ways in which gender has affected educational policy making, and I want to provide a brief account and overview of the forms that this has taken over time. My argument is that there are sets of discontinuities between gender as a discourse and the field of academic enquiry; between policy makers' interests and concerns and the broader policy landscape. These three elements articulate in complex ways and produce outcomes, in practice, that may not bear much resemblance to theorizations or even policy intentions. This is because the multidimensionality of the change/education/policy matrix is frequently not recognized or acknowledged. In what follows, I want to explore three main gender policy 'moments' that reveal these disarticulations; that is, the second-wave feminist movements of the late 1960s onward; the educational attempt to 'fix the girls'; and the current 'what about the boys?' approach (Eyre *et al.*, 2004). These three periods or moments are presented as a heuristic device through which to consider policy-theory-contextual disarticulations. In practice, they persist and overlap and interweave in complex ways.

By the late 1960s and into the 1970s, 'the stirrings of feminist consciousness about their lives were articulated locally, nationally and internationally through writings and through groups of women getting together to organize themselves informally' (Arnot *et al.*, 1999: 63). This movement of second-wave feminism was characterized by women organizing to make changes for themselves on behalf of themselves. Pressure was put on the state to demand equal pay for equal work, equal opportunities, and contraception and termination rights on demand, as well as improved nursery provision. The UK government's responses to these claims were 'somewhat lukewarm' (Arnot *et al.*, 1999: 63). However, the pressure for change did eventually result in some legislation (the Equal Pay Act of 1970 that was eventually implemented in 1975, and the Sex Discrimination Act of 1975).

While little was done directly in terms of education policy and practice, the growth and reach of feminism meant that its debates were reflected more widely, even if they were sometimes ridiculed in the popular press. Young women growing up in the 1960s and 1970s witnessed a challenge to the status quo of traditional gendered regimes in their social worlds. They saw their own mothers 'working and struggling with "family" relationships in highly constrained circumstances' (Arnot *et al.*, 1999: 65). Feminism and the second-wave women's movement addressed these issues. Social and cultural changes were reflected in developments such as the Women's Press, feminist magazines like *Spare Rib*, and women's pages in national broadsheets. They were spurred on by technological-pharmaceutical advances in birth control. The women's liberation movement was visible and active in most northern hemisphere nations. This 'moment' of second-wave feminism highlighted patriarchal power relations. Gender theory and enquiry focused on equal rights for women. Feminist work did acknowledge differences between women as well as different perspectives within feminisms, although these subtleties were less often reflected in policy (Weiner, 1994). Policy makers were brought to focus on these issues by dint of the hard work and campaigning of activist feminists and their supporters, locally and nationally. In terms of the broader policy landscape, the engine for change was the need for an educated labor force that drew increasingly on women's paid labor.

By the late 1970s and into the 1980s, these raised expectations and changes in value positions were reflected in the work of those feminists who struggled to create change and reform through education. This move reflected a growing awareness that schools were recognized 'both as an important site for the reproduction of gender relations and as a site for intervention and change' (Aveling, 2002: 267). Teachers in the UK, particularly those in metropolitan local education authorities (LEAs), were encouraged to develop anti-sexist strategies and were urged to produce girl-friendly curriculum materials (Myers, 1987). Again, much of the impetus for these changes came initially from outside the formal education policy networks. However, much educational gender research, by academics as well as teachers' researching their own practice, was situated in feminist discourses and feminist theory (Mahony, 1985; Mahony and Jones, 1989). During this period, gender work was interpreted as working with and for girls. The broader policy landscape (at least in some LEAs) was enabling to some degree, of this form of gender work.

At the level of the local state, some of the more egalitarian LEAs took a committed approach to equal opportunities, and centres were set up to promote anti-sexist work – although it has to be said that many schools found it easier to be girl-friendly than anti-sexist (Weiner, 1985). In some schools, the focus was on ensuring that girls were portrayed in non-stereotypical ways in texts and curriculum materials, and on ensuring that they were offered equal access to the curriculum. However, even in LEAs with a high-profile commitment to egalitarianism and equality, in-school developments were sometimes partial and patchy, and they frequently depended on the commitments of key individuals (Delamont, 1990; Myers, 2000). Eyre *et al.* (2004) have described this period as a time for 'fixing the girls'.

In this second 'moment', discourses of educational gender theory and enquiry were still largely characterized by essentializing perspectives, at least in the policy environment. The thrust was with offering a wider curriculum to girls in school and ensuring their equality of access to the curriculum. Many investigations explored girls' perceptions, experiences and outcomes in what were stereotypically male subjects such as mathematics, science and engineering. Educational policy makers with responsibility for curriculum development took up these sorts of issues, mainly at a local level. At the national policy level, there was no educational response until the advent of the National Curriculum (1988), which made all subjects compulsory up until the end of formal schooling; an example of where first-order policy making urged to facilitate comparison and control had some second-order outcomes that affected gender equality concerns.

In terms of the broader policy landscape, while equal opportunities had started to permeate the policy environment to some extent, contrasting discourses of economism, markets and managerialism were being evoked as the 'best' way to deliver welfare provision such as education and health. During this second 'moment', policy discontinuities that challenged equality discourses were being produced in the broader policy landscape that threatened the gains that had been made in the previous period. Simultaneously, the gains that had been made by feminist activists in the previous decade were also being challenged on many fronts, as excluding, essentializing and no longer necessary. Girls were now succeeding in schooling, and their problems were 'fixed'; that is, they were now performing 'better' than boys. In contrast, a 'crisis in masculinity' needed to be addressed.

In the third policy 'moment', a shift away from girls toward boys started to influence policy and practice at national, local and school level. The 'crisis' of masculinity was taken seriously in policy terms by policy makers and influenced the broader policy landscape far more profoundly than any concerns about girls' and young women's progress in educational terms had ever done. This was achieved in a particular discursive form in the UK context. Under New Labour, those concerned about social exclusion pointed to the disproportionate number of boys and young men who were socially, economically and educationally excluded. This 'crisis' had implications across the welfare state. Youth workers, social workers, employment officials, and those involved with the Youth Justice system, as well as educational policy makers, were alerted to the 'crisis':

> There is a pressing urgency about doing something about the problem of boys. In school, at home and on the streets, many boys are violent, damaging to others and to themselves and systematically underachieving, academically. (Salisbury and Jackson, 1996: 14)

Caught up in this extract are some of the 'older' tensions of gender work such as a tendency toward essentialism. In relation to the 'systematic underachievement' of boys, questions need to be asked about which boys, which subjects, and which age/stage (Epstein *et al.*, 1998; Francis and Skelton 2005). Indeed, the whole matter of 'underachievement' needs critical exploration; is this in contrast to (some) girls, over time, or is the current concern of 'underachievement' in males being utilised to accrue additional resources in financially lean times? Although there is not enough space to deal adequately with these contradictory matters (but see Francis and Skelton, 2005), it does seem that girls are out-performing boys in public examinations at 16. Boys are not doing as well as girls in certain subjects, and girls have caught up with and are outstripping boys at 18 in the UK.

Reay (2001: 152) believes that 'the contemporary concern with "a crisis of masculinity" has successfully eluded in-depth scrutiny of what is happening to girls and women'. As she argues, post-structuralist gender theories have highlighted the existence of multiple femininities. She adds, 'the seduction of binaries such as male: female, boy: girl often prevents us from seeing the full range of diversity and differentiation existing within one gender as well as between categories of male and female' (Reay, 2001: 163). This *seduction of binaries* seems to have been part of much gender policy work in the UK for a considerable period. The 'what about the boys approach?' fits well into a broader policy landscape of concerns with attainment, target setting and standards – into the problems-oriented approach. A whole panoply of strategies have been deployed to assuage the 'crisis of masculinity', even though, as Skelton (2001: 165) has warned, this focus (in policy and practice) might contain within itself many contradictions and produce unwanted and counter-productive (second-order) outcomes. She suggests, for example, that single-sexed groups might reinforce sex stereotyping, that 'boy-friendly' approaches might take resources away from girls, and that a repeated policy concern with 'failing boys' might produce a self-fulfilling prophecy effect.

In this third 'moment', gendered theorization has become more fluid, complex and inclusive, yet this more nuanced and sophisticated approach has not reached the attention of policy makers. In the UK, at least, there seems to be a reach-back into older discourses, Reay's seductive binaries. Gender theory complexity and the requirement for sensitive and democratic policies in educational settings will be difficult to establish in a policy climate that does not acknowledge these shifts in direction.

DISCUSSION

In terms of the process of policy making, the complexities and subtleties of the policy matrix can produce a daunting spectacle for those charged with devising policies to deal with 'problems'. These 'problems', are generally identified and defined as such by the media, politicians and powerful groups in society. The powerless are located as part of the 'problem', and their views are frequently sidelined or not considered at all. And very often, these 'problems' require a quick fix. In consequence, gender-binary approaches offer a convenient way forward for policy work. Exploring what can be done to ameliorate the 'problems' presented by one group (a group generally not positioned in any complex and multidimensional way) makes targeting resources and monitoring the impacts an easier proposition. In this way, policy becomes a top-down bureaucratic activity. Power is held by those who shape the nature of the policy 'problem' and the policy response, and (frequently) by those who then evaluate the policy outcome. The perspectives of those who have policy 'done' to them, rarely figure in the policy-development agenda.

In a policy climate where politicians urgently seek 'answers' to perceived/socially-constructed problems, the search is on for rapid policy responses that signal energetic attention and immediate responses. It is sometimes forgotten that politicians and bureaucrats who are charged with producing responses to social problems will themselves be judged in terms of how frequently they are able to do this. As administrations change and personnel change their roles, the micropolitics of their work setting will demand that they show their mettle and take a proactive policy lead. There is a need to demonstrate active governance, and this is an approach that can also make for 'bad' policy work.

A large amount of work has explored gender policy work in various nation states (O'Connor et al., 1999; Erskine and Wilson, 1999). What is evident from these studies, and others, is that in Canada and in Australia, for example, there has been more success at bringing about gender reforms through state policy work than in the UK. The Australian government has, for instance, 'actively intervened in the education of girls' (Francis and Skelton, 2005: 39) by feminist approaches. However, until very recently, there has been a close relationship between the academy and the educational state in Australia, with senior academics taking up government posts and responsibilities (Lingard, 2003). In Australia, Yates (1993) has explored how feminist analyses have been taken up by the state and the various ways in which some issues are tackled while others are sidelined. Francis and Skelton (2005: 39) conclude that 'such was the strength of a feminist presence in

Australian policy-making that the term "femocrats" was coined to denote those workers employed because of their feminist politics'. In other nations, such as the USA, the reform and change agenda is worked more through legislative challenge, using the constitution, to argue for social justice and equal rights. State policies are differently constructed and enacted because of different histories, cultures and systems of power relations.

Educational gender policy has frequently been couched in terms of binary positions, and more complex approaches to identity and identifications have not yet figured in gender policy work. In the UK, for example, the context in practice (in education, health and welfare) can be a little more complex. For example, the 'crisis' of school-aged teenage mothers in the UK continues to focus on girls and young women rather than a more inclusive approach that understands social constructions of sexualities/sexual relationships. In policy terms, boys and men, it seems, are frequently left out of this particular policy agenda. In contemporary mainstream educational policy work, the converse is true. Boys are the focus of the raising attainment discourse – the dominant strand in education policy work. Girls are 'successful', so the needs of some particular girls, for example working-class girls, figure much less, if at all, in education policy directives (Walkerdine *et al.*, 2001). These one-dimensional decontextualized policy approaches to gendered attainment may mask the role played by the material conditions of the social world.

Francis and Skelton have claimed that educational researchers and practitioners working to promote change have often produced innovative educational policies and practices in the area of gender. They have argued that current developments in theorizing gender 'will inform the next cycle of interventionist strategies in schools' (Francis and Skelton, 2001: 195). In contrast, Yates' (1999) analyses of the interplay between theory, policy and practice in Australia suggest that sophisticated theoretical work may produce even less effective policy. Stromquist (2005: 136) has argued that there are tensions between 'endorsing a flexible identity and proposing rights'. She is concerned that in a theoretical concern with complexity, we may be led away from the need to 'fight poverty, injustice and insecurity faced by millions of women and powerfully visible in national and global statistics' (2005: 136). She claims that there is a distinction to be drawn between philosophical discourses of equality and equality as a political goal – that theorization is not the same as action.

In this chapter, my focus has been on movement in policy and policy analysis as much as, if not more than, on the substantive issue of gender. This is because I believe that it is important to 'recover' the complexities of policy work if we are to understand why gendered issues get taken up, or not, and why some contexts are more enabling than others of socially just outcomes. What will also be needed will be a more subtle, nuanced and democratic approach to a critical social policy that recognizes the need to tackle poverty and disadvantage more broadly. Without this approach, movements in gender theory, even if they become reflected in education policy and practice, are not likely to make much of a difference by themselves.

REFERENCES

Acker, S and Feurverger, G (1997) Doing good and feeling bad: the work of women university teachers. *Cambridge Journal of Education*, 26: 401–22.

Alsop, R, Fitzsimons, A and Lennon, K (with a guest chapter on psychoanalysis by Minsky, R) (2002) *Theorizing gender*. Cambridge: Polity/Blackwell.

Amos, V and Parmar, P (1987) Resistances and responses: the experiences of black girls in Britain, in Arnot M and Weiner G (eds) *Gender and the politics of schooling*, (211–22). London: Unwin Hyman.

Anyon, J (2005) *Radical possibilities: public policy, urban education and a new social movement*. New York: Routledge.

Archer, L (2003) *Race, masculinity and schooling: Muslim boys and education*. Maidenhead: Open University Press.

Arnot, M (2002) *Reproducing gender*. London: Routledge/Falmer.

Arnot, M, David, M and Weiner, G (1999) *Closing the gender gap, postwar education and social change*. Cambridge: Polity.

Aveling, N (2002) 'Having it all' and the discourse of equal opportunity: reflections on choices and changing perceptions. *Gender and Education*, 14: 265–80.

Ball, SJ (1994) *Educational reform: a critical and post-structural approach*. Buckingham: Open University Press.

Ball, SJ (1997) Policy sociology and critical social research: a personal review of recent education policy and policy research. *British Educational Research Journal*, 23: 257–74.

Ball, SJ (2006) *Education policy and social class*. London: Routledge.

Ball, SJ and Gewirtz, S (1997) Girls in the education market: choice, competition and complexity. *Gender and Education*, 9: 207–22.

Ball, SJ, Maguire, M and Macrae, S (2000) *Choice, pathways and transitions post-16*. London: RoutledgeFalmer.

Berlak, A and Berlak, H (1981) *Dilemmas of schooling: teaching and social change*. London: Methuen.

Blackmore, J (1997) 'Level playing field?': feminist observations on global/local articulations of the re-gendering and restructuring of educational work. *International Review of Education*, 43: 438–61.

Bowe, R, Ball, SJ and Gold, A (1992) *Reforming education and changing schools: case studies in policy sociology*. London: Routledge.

Carby, HV (1987) Black feminism and the boundaries of sisterhood, in Arnot M and Weiner G (eds) *Gender and the politics of schooling* (64–75). London: Unwin Hyman.

Castells, M (1999) *Critical education in the new information age*. Lanham, MD: Rowman and Littlefield.

Crozier, G and Reay, D (2005) (eds) *Activating participation: parents and teachers working towards partnership*. Stoke on Trent: Trentham Books.

Datnow, A (1998) *The gender politics of educational change*. London: Falmer Press.

Delamont, S (1990) *Sex roles and the school* (2nd edn). London: Routledge.

Delamont, S (1996) *A women's place in education: historical and sociological perspectives on gender and education*. Aldershot: Avebury.

Dillabough, J (2001) Gender theory and research in education: modernist traditions and emerging contemporary themes, in Francis B and Skelton C (eds) *Investigating gender. Contemporary perspectives in education* (11–26). Buckingham: Open University Press.

Dillabough, J (2003) Gender, education and society: the limits and possibilities of feminist reproduction theory. *Sociology of Education*, 76: 376–9.

Epstein, D, Elwood, J, Hey, V and Maw, J (1998) (eds) *Failing boys? Issues in gender and achievement*. Buckingham: Open University Press.

Erskine, S and Wilson, M (eds) (1999) *Gender issues in international education: beyond policy and practice*. New York: Falmer Press.

Evans, M (2003) *Gender and social theory*. Buckingham: Open University Press.

Eyre, L, Lovell, TA and Smith, CC (2004) Gender equity policy and education: reporting on/from Canada, in Ali S, Benjamin, S and Mauthner, ML (eds) *The politics of gender and education. Critical perspectives* (67–86). Basingstoke: Palgrave Macmillan.

Francis, B and Skelton, C (2005) *Reassessing gender and achievement. Questioning contemporary key debates.* London: Routledge.

Galbraith, JK (1970) The affluent society (2nd edn). Harmondsworth: Penguin.

hooks, b (1982) *Ain't I a woman?: black women and feminism.* London: Pluto.

Jones, K (2003) *Education in Britain 1944 to the present.* Cambridge: Polity.

Kenway, J (1990) *Gender and education policy: a call for new directions.* Geelong: Deakin University Press.

Kenway, J and Willis, S (1998) *Answering back: girls, boys and feminism in schools.* London: Routledge.

Lewin, B (2001) *Reforming education. From origins to outcomes.* London: RoutledgeFalmer.

Lingard, B (2003) Where to in gender policy in education after recuperative masculinity politics? *International Journal of Inclusive Education,* 7: 33–56.

Love, DM (ed) (1984) *A salute to historic black women.* Chicago: Empack Birmingham.

Mahony, P (1985) *Schools for the boys: coeducation reassessed.* London: Hutchinson.

Mahony, P and Jones, C (1989) (eds) *Learning our lines: sexuality and social control in education.* London: Women's Press.

Myers, K (1987) *Genderwatch: self-assessment schedules for use in schools.* London: SCDC Publications.

Myers, K (2000) (ed) *Whatever happened to equal opportunities in schools?: gender equality initiatives in education.* Buckingham: Open University Press.

O'Connor, JS, Shola Orloff, A and Shaver, S (1999) *States, markets, families: gender, liberalism and social policy in Australia, Canada, Great Britain and the United States.* Cambridge: Cambridge University Press.

Olssen, M Codd, J and O'Neill, AM (2004) *Education policy. Globalization, citizenship and democracy.* London: Sage.

Ozga, J (2000) *Policy research in educational settings: contested terrain.* Buckingham: Open University Press.

Power, S (1992) Researching the impact of education policy: difficulties and discontinuities. *Journal of Education Policy,* 7: 493–500.

Reay, D (2001) The paradox of contemporary femininities in education: combining fluidity with fixity, in Francis, B and Skelton, C (eds) *Investigating gender. Contemporary perspectives in education* (152–63). Buckingham: Open University Press.

Salisbury, J and Jackson, D (1996) *Challenging macho values: practical ways of working with adolescent boys.* London: Falmer Press.

Salisbury, J and Riddell, S (eds) (2000) *Gender, policy and educational change: shifting agendas in the UK and Europe.* London: Routledge.

Skelton, C (2001) Typical boys? Theorising masculinity in educational settings, in Francis, B and Skelton, C (eds) *Investigating gender. Contemporary perspectives in education* (164–76). Buckingham: Open University Press.

Skelton, C and Francis, B (2001) Endnotes: gender, school policies and practices, in Francis, B and Skelton, C (eds) *Investigating gender. Contemporary perspectives in education* (189–95). Buckingham: Open University Press.

Stromquist, N (2005) Voice, harmony and fugue in global feminism, in Skelton, C and Francis, B (ed) A *feminist critique of education. 15 years of gender education* (124–39). London: Routledge.

Tomlinson, S (2000) *Education in a post-welfare society.* Buckingham: Open University Press.

Walkerdine, V, Lucey, H and Melody, J (2001) *Growing up girl. Psychosocial explorations of gender and class.* Basingstoke: Palgrave.

Weiner, G (ed) (1985) *Just a bunch of girls: feminist approaches to schooling.* Milton Keynes: Open University Press.

Weiner, G (1994) *Feminisms in education: an introduction.* Buckingham: Open University Press.

Whitty, G (2000) *Making sense of education policy*. London: Paul Chapman.

Yates, L (1993) What happens when feminism is an agenda of the state? Feminist theory and the case of education policy in Australia. *Discourse*, 14: 17–29.

Yates, L (1999) Feminism's fandango with the state revisited. *Women's Studies International Forum*, 22: 555–62.

Zajda, J (ed) (2005) *International handbook on globalisation, education and policy research*. Dordrecht: Springer.

Gender and the Educational Sectors

INTRODUCTION

The chapters in this section consider how gender informs the educational experiences of pupils and students at different stages in their learning careers. It is salutary to note that gender differences and stereotypes found by researchers studying the early years of children's school lives are perpetuated and reinforced as they progress through educational systems and institutions. Glenda MacNaughton begins her chapter on gender in the early years by reminding readers of the predominant understanding used to address inequities in schooling; that is, sex-role socialization. She does this in order to alert us to how limited strategies based on this perspective are in tackling deeply embedded ideas about gender held by very young children and their educators. MacNaughton draws on two recent research projects on gender-fair pedagogies to provide examples of children's constructions of gender and practical, interventionist advice for educators.

In Chapters 10 and 11 the elementary (primary) and secondary sectors come under scrutiny. Authors of both chapters point out how the 'problems of boys' have come to dominate the gender equity agenda in recent years. Furthermore, Christine Skelton (Chapter 10) and Kevin G. Davison and Frank Blye W. (Chapter 11) raise concerns as to how popularist approaches being advocated by Western governments, which are supposed to ameliorate boys' motivations and achievement, fly in the face of recognized good practice. What strategies centred on essentialist notions of 'boyness' do is ignore the plurality of masculinities (and indeed femininities) that exist, and, by so doing, exclude, through processes of marginalization and alienation, the majority of school populations.

Carole Leathwood urges readers to recognize the breadth and complexity of what is referred to here as the 'post-secondary' sector. In her chapter, she uses further education colleges in the UK as the main point of reference but draws attention to comparable patterns across other countries. One of the themes of particular concern in this sector is young women's take-up and involvement in 'traditional' vocational subjects, and the need to 'break the silence' around how some ('female') areas are valued less than those associated with conventionally male jobs.

In Chapter 13, Sara Delamont begins by showing how women are relative 'newcomers' to higher education. She focuses on five aspects of higher education in order to demonstrate the various sites of struggle over which women have strived for access, recognition and influence. Sara Delamont outlines the differing goals for women at different points in history – the first goal was to gain entry to higher education; for a later generation, it was to ensure that cultural, political and social mores did not drive them out of the universities; and more recently, women have directly confronted the taken-for-granted (that is, the masculine) nature of academic disciplines.

Diana Leonard's chapter sets out the complex and diverse arguments surrounding the politics and practices of single-sex education. She traces the historical debates of mixed versus single-sex education, concluding that, at least, the current concerns over single-sex schooling for boys has put the issue back on the political agenda.

9

Constructing Gender in Early-Years Education

Glenda MacNaughton

Boys and girls don't want to play with the opposite sex. They say, 'I don't want to play with her 'cos she is a girl'. We talk about this with the children. We say that, 'We are all friends, you don't have to play with someone you don't like. It doesn't mean because she/he is a girl/boy that you cannot be friends'. But, it doesn't seem to make a difference.

    Tania, early childhood teacher. Transcript D24: Teaching and Learning for Equity (TALE) project

Gender and its effects in the lives of young children often puzzle early childhood teachers. Sometimes, puzzlement arises from the presence of gender as a factor in children's ways of being, doing, thinking and feeling on a daily basis. At other times, teachers such as Tania in the extract above are puzzled by the persistence of many children's traditionally gendered ways in the face of teachers' and parents' non-sexist hopes, desires and actions.

Two broad theories of gender have dominated research and policy on gender in the early years: sex-role socialization theory, which posits gender as socially learnt; and relational (or feminist post-structuralist) theory, which posits gender as socially constructed. This chapter shows each broad gender theory in action and identifies the challenges and possibilities each theory offers staff who wish to develop classrooms that all children feel are 'fair'. The chapter uses data from two recent research projects on gender-fair pedagogies: the Teaching and Learning for Equity (TALE) research project (2002–03), which documented 39 teachers' beliefs, pedagogies and challenges in early childhood classrooms in Victoria, Australia; and Including Young Children's Voices: Early Years Gender Policy

(IYCV) (2004) – a mixed-method consultation between 12 early childhood educators and 99 preschool children about gender policy in children's services in South Australia.

SEX-ROLE SOCIALIZATION THEORY AND EARLY-CHILDHOOD PEDAGOGIES

Sex-role socialization and feminist post-structuralism have been discussed elsewhere in the book (see Chapters 1 and 4 in this volume), but it is worth reflecting on these here in order to illustrate their impact on early-years children.

For 50 years, researchers have examined the puzzle of gender in the lives of young minority world children extensively. Much of this research has embodied sex-role socialization theory, which divides gender into two opposing social categories – masculine and feminine (which are linked seamlessly with the two equivalent biological categories of sex – male and female). From this perspective, children's task in the early years is to learn the social roles appropriate to their sex, although they can also learn to be non-sexist.

Sex-role socialization researchers have produced indisputable evidence that very young children know about gender and acquire gendered ways of being and thinking; and they explain gender development as a combination of individual learning and wider social and cultural factors. These researchers identify four key agents in sex-role socialization: family, peer group, media and school (or early childhood setting); and they argue that children learn how to behave in ways appropriate to their sex role or category through observation, imitation and modelling.

Sex-role socialization theory has generated research data about minority world children that is now seen as classic. These data show that in the absence of external cultural gender markers (e.g. clothing or hair), it is extremely difficult to distinguish between boys and girls under two years of age (Maccoby and Jacklin, 1974; Honig, 1983; Browne and France, 1986). However, by three years of age, most children exhibit gender differences in their desires, preferences, behaviors and feelings (Honig, 1983; Browne and France, 1986). From three years of age, most children construct ways of being that increasingly express traditional gender stereotypes; and they play, think, and react in traditionally gender-stereotyped ways in early years education (e.g. Silva, 1980; Meade, 1982; Rickwood and Bussey, 1983; Smith and Grimwood, 1983). Since the 1970s, extensive sex-role socialization research on minority world children has demonstrated that young children's play, play patterns, play styles and use of play materials in early years education is gender-stereotyped (e.g. Flerx *et al.*, 1976; Wangman and Wagner, 1977; Holman and Williamson, 1979; Beeson and Williams, 1982; Dunn and Morgan, 1987; Thomas, 1986; Logan, 1988; Fishbein and Imai, 1993). Such research has also shown that preschool children often actively create and maintain gender stereotypes in their own behaviors and in their peers' behavior. When children agree with a gender stereotype, they often change their behavior to match it (Eccles *et al.*, 1998); and by five years of age, children are often biased firmly against the other gender (Powlishta *et al.*, 1994; Molnar Ziontas, 1996). Recent research has shown that gender affects young children's preference for particular musical instruments (Harrison and O'Neill, 2003); and sex-role socialization theory continues to influence early childhood educators and researchers, not least through the journal *Sex Roles*.

Sex-role socialization theorists argue that children think and act in sexist (or non-sexist) ways because this expresses the traditional, stereotyped sex roles they learn; and these traditional sex roles limit children's experiences and produce gender inequity in early education. For instance, girls gravitate to 'homemaking' activities, such as playing with dolls or cooking because of the traditional sex roles they learn; and an equivalent argument applies to boys. From that perspective, educators wishing to create gender equity must reteach (or resocialize) children to be non-sexist, by modelling non-sexist behaviour and by offering children a non-sexist curriculum. Yana, a TALE participant, is a contemporary Australian early childhood teacher who adheres to this perspective. She tries to create gender equity through three strategies – use non-sexist language, offer non-sexist resources and encourage non-sexist play:

> Avoid saying, 'policeman' or 'policewoman', say 'police officer'.
> Provide posters and pictures of both genders doing all jobs so that children do not develop stereotypes.
> Encourage children to play in all areas.
> (D22 TALE Transcript)

Yana's three strategies were favoured by 91% (35 of 39) of TALE participants, even though they knew that they were ineffective. Most TALE participants shared Yana's experiences of children's resisting 'sex-role re-socialization'; and in the 1980s and early 1990s, children's resistance to Yana's three strategies was documented extensively by researchers, who found that children's stereotyped play reduced for only a short time (Flerx *et al.*, 1976; De Lisi and Johns, 1984; Ayers and Ayers, 1989; Butterworth, 1991). Other studies indicate that teachers may have to intervene actively, deliberately and intensively over several months to shift gender stereotyping in early-childhood programs (Swadener, 1988). When TALE participants were asked how they responded to the failure of their strategies, they were either unsure (10), silent (15) or reiterated their existing, but failing strategies (13).

Sex-role socialization theories emerged in the 1970s and continue to influence early-childhood curriculum texts and teachers' pedagogies. However, they have been criticized for their simplistic understandings of gender and its effects in young children's lives and for their failure to produce gender-fair classrooms (e.g. MacNaughton, 1999; 2000; 2001). These failings have led several educational researchers to explore whether the ideas associated with feminist post-structuralism can explain children's resistance to anti-sexist curriculum and can suggest more effective ways to create gender-fair classrooms (e.g. MacNaughton, 2000; Campbell, 2001; Smith, 2003).

RELATIONAL THEORIES OF GENDER AND POWER

Feminist post-structuralists pose three challenges to sex-role socialization researchers' view that gender consists of roles that children can take up or change at will (e.g. Connell, 1987; Davies, 1993). First, they argue that children *construct* their gender, rather than merely absorbing it through observing 'model' non-sexist behavior; and that, as active constructors, children may well resist non-sexist messages in an early childhood classroom. Second, feminist post-structuralists argue that genders are not distinct categories (whether social or biological), but are, instead, relational and interdependent (e.g. Davies, 1989; Walkerdine and Lucey, 1989; Alloway, 1995; Walkerdine, 1997). Genders are relational because being a girl is related to and defined by girls' relationships with boys; and vice versa. Genders are interdependent because ways of being masculine and feminine form a continuum, rather than distinct categories, with some ways to be masculine overlapping some ways to be feminine. However – and this is their third point – traditional ways to be masculine or feminine are more powerful than those that challenge traditions because they are more pleasurable (Weedon, 1997). Consequently, to ask children to change from being sexist to being non-sexist is an intensely emotional request, because it requires children to 'give up' ways of being that are pleasurable. Such a request involves more that merely learning a new gender role. For instance, to ask a four-year-old girl who has learnt to love playing with dolls suddenly to see such play as 'sexist' and 'limiting' is to ask her to see something that is pleasurable as suddenly not pleasurable; and to ask her to find playing with trucks as pleasurable as playing with dolls is just bewildering.

In the following statements by children in the IYCV consultation, gender is linked clearly with pleasure. What you 'like' and 'love', or what feels 'nice' or 'good' and 'fun' depends on your gender:

Boy: Boys love climbing up trees and finding lizards. [LGK¹23]

Boy: [Boys like] tractors, they go fishing and catch lizards. [TGK215]

Girl: Boys like each other. [TGK13]

Girl: Girls like smelling roses and flowers too. [LGK35]

Boy: Girls just think about dolls. [TGK16]

Girl: It feels good, 'cause you dress up. [TGK14]

Girl: (On being a girl) It's nice. They be nice, not chasing the boys, not kissing the boys. Making paintings and doing the right stuff. [SGK3 6]

Boys commented not only on what boys liked but also on how they differed from girls in this respect; girls made equivalent comments:

Boy: Well, boys like to drink juice and cordial.
Teacher: Do you think girls like to drink juice and cordial?
Boy: Uh-uh (indicating no). They like to drink … I don't know. [GVK4c]
Girl: Girls like to play Barbie dolls and cats.
Teacher: Can boys play Barbie dolls?
Girl: Nup, 'cause they're not girls.
Teacher: Can girls play robots?
Girl: No, 'cause they're not boys, they're girls. [TGK34]

Teacher: Would girls like motorbikes?
Girl: No.
Teacher: Why wouldn't they like that motorbike?
Girl: Because it might be too fast.
Teacher: Don't you think girls like fast things?
Girl: No, I don't.
Teacher: Why do boys like fast things?
Girl: Because they like to be with other boys. They like to get on one and boys like to be with other boys. [GVK3d]

Girl: If you are a girl you can't fight because it's not nice … it's not nice for boys. [ERK6]

Girl: It's really fun and you can play with play dough or you can have a Barbie lunch box or you can have a play with Barbies or you can play with the doll's house. You can have a Barbie bag or you can have a fairy room or a butterfly room. [LGK66]

Boy: [Boys] like to knock buildings down … because that's much fun for boys [but] they need to build them own towers to knock down buildings. [GVK4c]

From a feminist post-structuralist perspective, pleasures derive from the links between power and discourses; and the most powerful gender discourses in young children's lives are those that define the normal ways to be girls and boys, women and men. These discourses often express stereotyped, mutually exclusive relationships between genders: a girl is not a boy and so she does not act, think or feel as a boy does; and vice versa. Children adopt these discourses because they find pleasure in 'getting it right' and 'being normal' for their specific culture, time and place. For instance, in contemporary Australian society, having a Barbie lunch box appears as a normal way to be a girl more persistently than fighting, so girls are more likely to have a Barbie lunch box than to fight, because it is pleasurable for them to 'get it right'.

The statements (above) by the children in the IYCV consultations 'prove' that boys and girls do not play together because they are different. On girls and boys playing together, one boy said:

> *Boy:*   It won't be fun. Because. I don't want to. Because. It's not fun. Because. We want to play by ourselves and we like shooting the girls, because I love guns. [SGK11]

Another boy was even clearer that boys and girls playing together is inappropriate:

> *Teacher:*   So what can girls and boys play together?
> *Boy:*   Nothing. [SGK19]

Children in the IYCV consultation were clear that gender differences made it hard – even, at times, unsafe – to play together:

> *Girl:*   Boys and girls can have fun together when they play safe … talk and talk and talk together … maybe climbing together, but not fun to fall down. [ERK 6]

> *Boy:*   You can learn with the girls and play with them if you have a friend that's a girl – but you can't fight with them. [SGK10]

> *Girl:*   [Girls and boys should learn …] No kicking. No pinching other people's snack. No throwing sand. No snatching. No climbing when other people on these 'cos maybe you will hurt yourself. No hitting. No smacking. No hitting when somebody is being nice to you. [SGK13]

Some children were prepared to consider boys and girls playing and learning together as a theoretical possibility. For example:

> *Girl:*   Yeah … boys and girls maybe can do the slide. Boys and girls can wait turn to slide. [ERK10]

> *Boy:*   They should know what we should know and girls should know what we should know. [ERK 3]

However, other children made it clear that collaborative play between boys and girls does not happen automatically, but must be 'learnt':

> *Girl:*   They could play on the swings … learn to be good together. [ERK11]

> *Girl:*   We learn to be friends … We can learn sharing. We can push on the swings, not really high, not just a little bit … just …only a big bit of a little bit. [ERK2]

> *Girl:*   The boys should learn the same things as we girls. If (the teacher) says, 'Climb the tree', we should all learn to climb the tree. The boys shouldn't fight. [GVK4a]

Other children believed that collaborative play between boys and girls depends on keeping to traditional gender roles, such as boys being 'kings' and girls being 'princesses':

Boy: I would do good things like having fun … When we play together … William, Thomas and the two Williams and they like playing with me … we play … play good games like princess and king games. I was the king and princess was C … you know the wooden house outside? That's where I play princesses. I rescued the princess … because she was lovely … I was the king that transformed into the guard. I was the strongest guard with heaps of muscles. I was strong because I was the king. [ERK3]

In the IYCV consultations, boys and girls regulated their own and other children's gender by actively maintaining clear, gendered role divisions. In the following episode, the boy wants to play in the home corner, but is constrained by how the girls position him and by his belief that games need to be for girls or for boys:

Boy: I like playing in the sandpit, it's fun, you make sandcastles. In the home corner there is babies there, we play baby games.
Teacher: What else do you play?
Boy: We play mum and dad.
Teacher: Who are you in the game?
Boy: I'm the dad.
Teacher: Can you be the mum?
Boy: No. I'm a boy. The girls say 'You are the dad'.
Teacher: Would you like to play the mum?
Boy: Yes, but the girls won't let me play mum. I like drawing, because you can draw stuff and the climbing. I like the doll's house.
Teacher: What do you play at the doll's house?
Boy: Girl game.
Teacher: What's a girl game?
Boy: I don't know.
Teacher: Can you play boy games at the doll's house?
Boy: No, because it's a girl game. [TGK19]

Another boy was clear that in the home corner, girls were the 'boss':

Teacher: What's something you never want to play?
Boy: Home corner.
Teacher: Why?
Boy: It's for girls, mums and girls, mum cooks at home. When mum is in the bath, dad cooks toast and coffee. Daddy takes the bins out and feeds the cat. Mum is the boss of the kids and dad is the boss of the family.
Teacher: Can a girl be boss in the blocks?
Boy: No. [TGK34]

Gendered power relations were most apparent when children said what makes pre-school feel unfair and unsafe. Several girls (25%) talked directly about being teased or harassed at kindergarten by boys. Harassment ranged from boys pushing the girls too high on the swing, to boys punching and smacking girls and throwing sand in their eyes. For instance:

Girl: Sometimes, it is unfair and on the swing the boys push too high and you can fall off the swing … you can make it fair if you can't fall off there. [ERK7]

Girl: When no boys tease … sometimes they tease me … when no one follows me around … when J punches me and I ask him to stop it … if he listens to me, that is good. If girls listen to boys and boys listen to girls, then it would be a nice day. [ERK7]

> *Girl:* Some boys put sand in my eyes. Sometimes I don't want to play with the boys and girls; sometimes I want to play by myself. [LG48]

> *Girl:* When someone pushes you over, it's not fun. ... Someone ... somebody pushes me over. [ERK5]

> *Girl:* Not always fair. ... Like people hurting me and it hurts me. It hurts my feelings. Like they try to chase and try to smack me and I don't like it because it hurts my feelings very badly. [SGK7]

One girl found boys' violent and harassing behaviour puzzling and unsettling:

> *Teacher:* Is it always fair for you at kindy?
> *Girl:* No. Because, other boys smack me. I don't know why. I cry. The teacher gets you an ice pack. It's sore. The boy gets in trouble because he smacked the girls. [SGK13]

Children also felt that kindergarten was unfair when other children teased them, and in each instance, teasing was linked with gender. For example:

> *Girl:* Sometimes the boys tease girls and the girls say, 'Stop. I don't like you being silly at me' ... Girls can say, 'I don't like it when you tease me' and then go and get the teacher ... Sometimes the girls tease boys. [ERK7]

> *Girl:* Actually, I don't like playing dress ups, 'cause the boys come along and say, 'You look so gay in that'. [TGK34]

However, not every girl felt intimidated by the boys, and some girls actively demanded fairness. For example:

> *Girl:* Boys can play with anything they want. Girls can play with anything at kindy, like in the sandpit. At the puppet theatre, boys play nasty. I heard two persons – boys – say to girls they can't play there. The girls said, 'Well you have to share'. [TGK20]

Gender-safe and gender-fair

For feminist post-structuralists, gender is not simply a role. Instead, gender is a complex and dynamic set of ideas, actions and feelings about what it means to be a boy or a girl in a specific place, culture and time (see MacNaughton, 2001). These dynamic identities can explain why some children resist non-sexist pedagogies; and it is in and through these complex, dynamic gendered identities that children try to create safe and fair relationships. An emerging tradition of research is showing that preschool children can tell adults much about their daily lives – including what gender pedagogies work for them and what do not – that can improve our knowledge of what children feel is gender-safe and gender-fair (e.g. Campbell, 2001; MacNaughton, 2001a,b,c; Smith, 2003).

As we saw, girls and boys in the IYCV consultation rejected the idea that they should play together; and girls complained frequently of harassment and violence by the boys. In such circumstances, children may like clear distinctions between genders because they identify who is safe and fair to play with and who is not; and the teacher's task is creating gender-safe and gender-fair classrooms, rather than making children reverse their choices around gender. Why should a girl want to play with boys when they harass, hit and tease her? Children in the IYCV consultation identified three things that made their classroom feel gender-safe and gender fair: teacher support, counter-harassment strategies and explicit rules. First, nearly 25% (7) of the girls saw the teacher as someone to call upon for help to make things safe and/or fair:

Girl: … girls can say, 'I don't like it when you tease me' and then go and get the teacher. … Sometimes the girls tease the boys. [ERK7]

Girl: I'm not fighting … I just talking to teacher if people fighting. [ERK10]

Girl: If someone says they don't want to play, then go ask the teachers. The teachers say, 'Someone wants to play. So let them play and be so kind to them'. [LGK63]

Girl: Sometimes it's not safe when someone hurts you. When someone hurts you, your friend gets the teacher to help you. [SGK9]

Girl: You got to go and tell your teachers. That's right – when they kick you, or hurt you or bite you or punch you. [SGK6]

The boys also recognized the teacher's authority and power to make things safer:

Boy: Yes, because if you're scared you can tell the teachers. [LGK57]

Boy: If they keep doing it … [hurting somebody] … tell the teacher. [SGK8]

Second, several girls felt safer because they had been taught strategies to counter harassment. Those girls tried to stop harassment and some felt that they had the power to do this:

Girl: Sometimes boys tease girls and the girls say, 'Stop. I don't like you being silly at me.' [ERK7]

Girl: When people fighting … I say, 'Stop, no fighting.' [ERK10]

Girl: Boys can play with anything they want. Girls can play with anything at kindy, like in the sandpit. At the puppet theatre, boys play nasty. I heard two persons – boys – say to girls they can't play there. The girls said, 'Well you have to share'. [TGK20]

Girl: When you hit you say, 'Stop'. You don't like it. [SGK12]

Third, children felt that gender relations were fairest when there were explicit rules (e.g. 'line-up and wait your turn', 'no fighting', 'no hitting') that every child knew:

Girl: The girls and boys are friends. We have to wear a hat or go on the verandah ... boys and girls can go on the verandah. [ERK2]

Girl: Everybody has to line up and when it's your turn you can have the next turn. [ERK8]

Boy: No fighting. By saying 'Stop!'. Play safely. [SGK8]

Boy: I like to play Batman. It's got fighting in it, so I can't play it at kindy. [ERK1]

Boy: Because you are not allowed to go over the gate and run away and you're not allowed to punch people in the face. [LGK76]

Boy: If we share. [GVK4b]

Boy: No hitting. [LGK56]

Girl: You say good words, not mean words. [GV4c]

Children in the IYCV consultation did not always want, or were able, to solve problems for themselves. Rather, they wanted the teacher to create and police broad gender rules that support each child's safety and fairness for all. Clearly, this requires teachers to do more than just encourage role-reversal and use non-sexist language and images in their curriculum. To tackle the gendered power relations that the children produce and experience, teachers must intervene actively in children's play and relationships, prescribing what is fair and what is not and enforcing those prescriptions. Further, teachers may need to engage with disagreement and dissent about what is safe and fair. What feels safe and fair for one child may not feel the same for another. This dissent is likely to be suffused with issues of gender, power and pleasure. One IYCV boy said, 'Yes, it's fair for me, but not for girls' [SGK10]; and another said that kindergarten was fair for him because 'nobody hurts me' and because he 'kill girls and girls and girls everyday – because it's fair for me' [SGK11]. One IYCV boy became quite excited by the discussion about fairness at his kindergarten. In his view, it is hard to make things gender-fair:

Teacher: Is it fair at kindy?
Boy: Number one – boys and girls can go on anything together. It is fair at this kindy? They thinks that's fair in the cars and the doll's house because the home corner is close. It's hard to make it fair. My heart is beating fast. These questions are a little bit hard.

Teacher: Do you want to stop now?
Boy: Yes, but just one thing. In the sandpit, the girls don't let the boys play with the girls. That's not fair. The girls don't like the boys playing with them. [TGK18]

Future research could explore what happens when teachers intervene in this way. How do specific children respond? What are the gendered power effects of teachers' active policing of gender relations? Constructing gender-safe and gender-fair early-childhood settings brings promise, challenge and a new puzzle: How do we manage dissent in ways that produce safer and fairer lives for girls and boys in early-childhood settings? This is surely a contemporary puzzle worth tackling with some urgency.

REFERENCES

Alloway, N (1995) *Foundation stones: the construction of gender in early childhood.* Melbourne: Curriculum Corporation.

Ayers, M and Ayers, M (1989) Effects of traditional and reversed sex-typed characters and family relationships on children's gender role perceptions. Paper presents at the International Conference on Early Childhood Education and Development, Hong Kong, August.

Beeson, B and Williams, A (1982) Sex stereotyping of young children's play. ED287566. Education Resources Information Center.

Browne, N and France, P (1986) *Untying the apron strings: anti-sexist provision for the under fives.* Milton Keynes: Open University Press.

Butterworth, D (1991) Gender equity in early childhood: the state of play. *Australian Journal of Early Childhood,* 10: 48–52.

Campbell, S (2001) A social justice disposition in young children. Unpublished doctoral dissertation. University of Melbourne, Melbourne.

Connell, RW (1987) *Gender and power.* Sydney: Allen and Unwin.

Davies, B (1989) *Frogs and snails and feminist tales.* Sydney: Allen and Unwin.

Davis, B (1993) *Shards of glass: children reading and writing beyond gendered identities.* Sydney: Allen and Unwin.

De Lisi, R and Johns, M (1984) The effects of books and gender constancy development on kindergarten children's sex-role attitudes. *Journal of Applied Developmental Psychology,* 5: 173–84.

Dunn, S and Morgan, V (1987) Nursery and infant school play patterns: sex related differences. *British Educational Research Journal,* 13: 281–91.

Eccles, JS, Wigfield, A and Schiefele, U (1998). Motivation to succeed, in Eisenberg, N (ed) *Handbook of child psychology: social, emotional and personality development* (1017–95). New York: Wiley.

Fishbein, H and Imai, S (1993) Preschoolers select playmates on the basis of gender and race. *Journal of Applied Developmental Psychology,* 14: 303–16.

Flerx, V, Fidler, D and Rogers, R (1976) Sex role stereotypes: developmental aspects and early intervention. *Child Development,* 47: 998–1007.

Harrison, A and O'Neill, S (2003). Preferences and children's use of gender-stereotyped knowledge about musical instruments: making judgments about other children's preferences. *Sex Roles: A Journal of Research,* Oct.

Holman, J and Williamson, A (1979) Sex labelling: adult perceptions of the child. *Australian Journal of Early Childhood,* 4: 41.

Honig, A (1983) Sex role socialisation in early childhood. *Young Children,* September: 67–70.

Jordon, E (1995) Fighting boys and fantasy play: the construction of masculinity in the early years. *Gender and Education,* 7: 69–86.

Logan, L (1988) Gender, family composition and sex role stereotyping by young children. ED290564. Education Resources Information Center.

Maccoby, EE and Jacklin, CN (1974) *The psychology of sex differences*. Stanford, CA: Stanford University Press.

Maccoby, EE and Jacklin, CN (1980) Sex differences in aggression: a rejoinder and reprise. *Child Development,* 51: 964–80.

MacNaughton, G (1999) Promoting gender equity for young children in the South and South East Asian region. *International Journal of Early Years Education*, 1: 315–22.

MacNaughton, G (2000) *Rethinking gender in early childhood education*. Sydney: Allen and Unwin.

MacNaughton, G (2001) The gender factor, in Dau, E (ed) *The anti-bias approach in early childhood*. Frenchs Forest: Longman.

MacNaughton, G (2001a) Dolls for equity: foregrounding children's voices in learning respect and unlearning unfairness. *New Zealand Council for Educational Research Early Childhood Folio,* 5: 27–30.

MacNaughton, G (2001b) Silences and subtexts in immigrant and non-immigrant's children's understandings of diversity. *Childhood Education,* 78: 30–6.

MacNaughton, G (2001c) 'Blushes and birthday parties': telling silences in young children's constructions of 'race'. *Journal for Australian Research in Early Childhood Education*, 8: 41–51.

Meade, A (1982) Don't take that dress off James! *Australian Journal of Early Childhood,* 7: 37–42.

Molner Ziontas, L (1996) Young children's attitudes regarding ethnicity and disability. Unpublished PhD. University of North Texas.

Powlishta, K, Serbin, L and Doyle, A (1994) Gender, ethnic and body-type biases: the generality of prejudice in childhood. *Developmental Psychology*, 30: 526–38.

Rickwook, D and Bussey, K (1983) Sex differences in gender schema processing. *Australian Journal of Early Childhood,* 8: 40–1.

Ruble, DN and Martin, CL (1998). Gender development. In Eisenberg, N (ed) *Handbook of child psychology: social, emotional and personality development*. New York: Wiley.

Silva, P (1980) Experiences, activities and the preschool child: a report from the Dunedin multidisciplinary study. *Australian Journal of Early Childhood*, 5: 13–8.

Smith, A and Grimwood, S (1983) Sex role stereotyping and children's concepts of teachers and principals. *Australian Journal of Early Childhood,* 8: 23–8.

Smith, K (2003) Reconceptualising observation in the early childhood curriculum. Unpublished doctoral dissertation, University of Melbourne, Melbourne.

Swadener, EB (1988) Implementation of education that is multicultural in early childhood settings: A case study of two day-care programs. *Urban Review,* 20: 8–27.

Thomas, G (1986) Assessing nursery attitudes and behaviour, in Browne, N and France, P (eds) *Untying the apron strings: anti-sexist provision for the under fives* (104–20). Milton Keynes: Open University Press.

Walkerdine, V and Lucey, H (1989) *Democracy in the Kitchen*. London: Virago.

Walkerdine, V (1997) *Daddy's girl: young girls and popular culture*. Basingstoke: Palgrave.

Wangman, N and Wagner, S (1977) *Choices: learning about sex roles*. Minneapolis, MN: Jenny Publishing Co.

Weedon, C (1997) *Feminist practice and post-structuralist theory* (2nd edn). London: Basil Blackwell.

10

Boys and Girls in the Elementary School

Christine Skelton

The use of the words 'boys and girls', rather than 'gender', in the chapter title is to draw attention to how recent education policy has focused on, and emphasized differences between, the two sexes. In fact, there was a great temptation to call the chapter 'Boys *Versus* Girls in the Elementary/Primary School' in order to highlight the extent to which current educational policy, research and literature in many Western countries are premised on the idea that elementary schools are a 'utopia' for girls but a 'battleground' for boys (see, for example, Biddulph, 1998). This simplistic juxtaposition of 'girls' success' equals 'boys' failure' is a by-product of the greater emphasis on assessment and achievement of pupils in public examinations (as evidenced in the Education Reform Act 1988 in the UK and No Child Left Behind Act 2002 in the USA). These public examinations have indicated that boys in elementary schools are not doing as well as girls, especially in literacy, and, in seeking for reasons for this, some researchers have identified the 'feminization' of this sector as a root cause. Here, 'feminization' is narrowly interpreted as meaning that a majority of teaching staff are females and therefore 'have not been trained in how boys and girls learn differently' (Gurian, 2002: 126) and 'have no empathy with [boy's] boisterous energy' (Neall, 2002: xviii). Furthermore, such writers claim that when 'boys find themselves in a world of learning that is not associated with a masculine figure in their formative years ... the activities it involves – principally reading and writing – are devalued in their eyes' (Bleach, 1998: 10). Such popularist (and antifeminist) declarations fail both pupils and teachers in that they do not accurately reflect the complex and nuanced factors that contribute to the shaping of gendered learning identities in the primary school. The intention in this chapter is to offer a broader overview of the research literature in order to show how and where 'gender' affects boys' and girls' learning experiences in elementary schooling in the west.[1] The discussion will be organized into two overarching themes that inevitably overlap but are used here to reflect where current theoretical/methodological and policy energies are directed. These two themes are (i) gender, schooling and achievement; and (ii) gendered learning identities.

Before exploring these areas, however, a few words are needed to place this chapter into a theoretical context. It is written from a feminist, social constructionist perspective, and, as a consequence, the writings of those who adopt biological explanations for differences between boys and girls, such as those promulgated by Biddulph (1998), Kindlon and Thompson (1999), and Gurian (2002), are judged to be naive and one-dimensional (for discussion, see Francis and Skelton, 2005). At the same time, social constructionist feminists do not all see 'gender' in precisely similar ways, for, as Biklen and Pollard (2001: 724) state, 'How gender issues get named relates both to the field the researchers are in and to the kind of feminist theory the authors hold'. (See also Chapters 1 and 3 in this volume.) The position adopted here is that gender is a system of relations where masculinity is privileged, but both masculinity and femininity are intersected by other variables such as 'race', ethnicity, religion, social class and sexuality. Therefore, power relations are of key importance.

GENDER, SCHOOLING AND ACHIEVEMENT

Research into gender in elementary schools has, historically, been subject to certain 'trends in fashion' and, in the same way that people hang onto certain dress styles long after they are considered outmoded, some researchers retain allegiance to particular theoretical perspectives although ideas have moved on. So, the centrality of sex-difference theories (popular in the 1970s and early 1980s) in explaining that boys and girls are 'naturally' different or are socialized into masculine and feminine ways of being through powerful gendered practices and expectations embedded within the institutions of family, school and media (Best, 1983; Whyte, 1983) are still around today (Bauer, 2000; Frawley, 2005) (see also Chapter 9 in this volume). What is implicit in sex-difference approaches is that there are fundamental biological and/or cognitive and/or emotional differences between boys and girls. The question that underpins these approaches is, 'to what extent [do] some of the traits, aptitudes, and abilities girls have differ in important ways from the ones possessed by boys?' (Biklen and Pollard, 2001: 725).

The idea that differences in academic achievement and motivation for schooling between boys and girls aged 5–11 years are the result of biological differences can be found within debates on boys' underachievement. For example, Biddulph (1998: 33) states that boys get into trouble in elementary school for not listening when, in fact, 'young boys tend to have growing spurts that affect their ear canals' (the question here has to be, and don't girls?). Similarly, Gurian (2002) advocates physiological explanations and understandings in arguing that 'girls' brains mature earlier than boys' (p19), and lists 10 areas where this influences learning, including highly debatable assertions, such as 'girls are better at self-managing boredom', and 'girls do not generally need to move around as much while learning' (pp46–47). Others argue that it is socialization processes that define boys' characters and abilities, and that these are not welcomed by schools. According to Pollack (1998), schools fail boys on four counts (by not noticing the problems boys are having in reading and writing; by being 'poorly versed in the specific social and emotional needs of our sons' (p232); by always classifying their behaviour as a discipline problem rather than attempting to 'probe behind the misconduct to discover their genuine emotional needs' (p232); and by not developing curriculum materials which appeal to boys' interests). Lucinda Neall (2002) agrees with such sentiments, and her book sets out to list ways in which teachers 'can value boys for who they are and get to like the rumbustious qualities many of them have; [also], we can learn skills that bring out the best in boys at school' (pxx). Neall's suggested strategies for teachers to *bring out the best in boys* are common to those classified as 'men's rights' perspectives. Indeed, the recommend strategies to address these gender differences are strikingly similar, whether the belief is that they are 'natural' or a result of socialization:

- raise their self-esteem by respecting them, showing that their opinion is valued, praising their achievements, reminding them of their successes, and giving them particular responsibilities (Noble and Bradford, 2000; Neall, 2002);
- encourage boys' 'natural' characteristics through competitive sports and classroom activities (Sax, 2005a), ensuring there is space for boys to move around to facilitate their learning (Gurian, 2002);
- respond to boys' needs and interests in the curriculum by, for example, providing single-sex teaching; incorporating 'action-orientated' reading material; and, bringing men into the classroom to act as role models (Biddulph, 1998; Thompson and Barker, 2000).

There is not the space here to set out the vigorous and persuasive challenges that have been brought to bear on these 'biological/naturalistic' explanations of, and recommendations on, boys and schooling (for these, see Lingard *et al.*, 2003; Francis and Skelton, 2005). The point is that proponents of 'natural' differences base their recommendations for 'how to educate boys' on the idea that these biological truths are incontrovertible and unchangeable – teachers just have to learn to deal with them. Apart from the fact that there is little agreement among scientists about such 'truths' (Halpern, 1992), these biological/naturalistic explanations of boys' underachievement and lack of motivation in schooling marginalize and minimize the situation of girls in school. Another body of work, based on socialization theories, is also premised on differences between boys and girls, but these are created not by inherent characteristics but through interactions with family, media, schools and peer group. Strategies to address such socialized differences are located within 'equity' or 'equal opportunities' frameworks.

It was 'equal opportunities' initiatives, based on liberal, feminist notions of ensuring that girls and boys have equal access to the curriculum and resources, that, in the 1970s and 1980s, were incorporated into the daily work of primary schools. The recommended strategies for promoting equal opportunities fell into four broad categories: [1] organization and management; [2] teaching resources and assessment; [3] staffing structures; [4] teacher attitudes (Delamont, 1980). Three of these continue to feature in guidance provided today with discussions about 'staffing structures' having moved away from the need to encourage more women teachers into leadership positions to one of increasing the numbers of male teachers in elementary schools. Before we go on to discuss these three areas, readers should note that one of the weaknesses of an 'equal opportunities' approach is that it tends both to be 'race blind' and to lack any recognition of 'social class'; furthermore, such schemes fail to engage with differences within the two genders, such as those created by age or wealth, for example.

Organization and management

Common and taken-for-granted procedures, such as having separate colored record cards, cloakrooms and playgrounds for boys and girls are now, we assume, a thing of the past. Rather ironically, given the earlier discussion about strategies advocated to address boys' underachievement, equal opportunities policies in the 1980s, recommended that teachers should not encourage competition between girls and boys in general knowledge quizzes, or set 'races' to complete work, tidy up or line up at the door (Hough, 1985). However, there continues to be a debate about segregating boys and girls for teaching purposes.

There is a long history of debate over single-sex teaching, and this, which was once a province of deliberations on equal opportunities in the secondary/high school, has now entered discussions on primary/elementary education. There is little current agreement on how effective this is for boys and girls. Historically, it was generally agreed by those undertaking research into secondary schooling that girls performed better academically when they were not being distracted by the behaviour of, or harassment by, boys (Mahony, 1985). However, it was found that social class was a significant factor here in that it was middle-class girls who were most likely to attend single-sex schools, and thus, their 'cultural capital' provided them with an advantage (Smithers and Robinson, 1995). The more recent refocus on single-sex teaching has come about because of the concern about boys' under-achievement and perhaps what we should note is that the arguments for and against single-sex classes for girls are not the same as those for boys. In the case of girls, it is whether they are enabled to work more effectively away from boys who are busy demeaning them and the 'non-macho' boys (Jackson, 2002). For boys, the argument for single-sex teaching tends to be twofold. On the one hand, rather than 'boy-only' classes being about developing (non-stereotypical) learning styles and approaches, they are seen as providing an opportunity for teachers to tap into traditionally masculine stereotyped interests and behaviours to promote learning. For example, it has been observed how teachers in an English class chose material designed to appeal to boys' interests (e.g. war, guns, surfing magazines) and also developed 'hands-on' approaches (making models, turning tasks into games), which they saw to be 'typical' of boys' approaches to learning (Martino and Meyenn, 2002). A second argument is that the 'hard wiring' of boys' and girls' brains demands that different teaching and learning styles (Sax, 2005b). What the research does tell us is that teachers rarely change their pedagogical style when working with single-sex, as opposed to mixed-sex, classes (see Francis and Skelton, 2005, for wider discussion of these issues).

Teaching resources and assessment

In second-wave feminism, analysis of textbooks for images of masculinity and femininity employed a 'content-analysis' approach; that is, books were examined in terms of how many representations of men/boys there were in relation to women/girls, what roles they were portrayed in, and the terminology used to speak about males and females. This approach demonstrated that women had been rendered insignificant or invisible in many reading scheme, maths and science books (Skelton, 1997). With the 'gender problem' of the twenty-first century being that of boys and schooling, it is perhaps no surprise to discover that there is a concern about the portrayal of males in school textbooks. A study by Evans and Davies (2000) of elementary school reading textbooks found that males continue to be depicted in a stereotypical way; that is, as aggressive, competitive and argumentative. This is not to say that females are represented in a non-stereotypical way, as research by Gooden and Gooden (2001) has shown that, although there has been progress in terms of the numbers of women represented as the main character in children's picture books, they continue to be portrayed in a stereotypical manner.

The emphasis and importance given to formal assessment in countries adopting a market-led approach to education has meant that significant attention has been given to gender dimensions (Hoff Sommers, 2000; Myhill, 2002; Connolly, 2004; Warrington *et al.*, 2006). This is because the marketization of education has forced schools to compete with each other, the 'best schools' being judged by government agencies to be those that get the maximum number of pupils the highest grades in public examinations. The UK goverment publishes 'league tables' of school success rates in these examinations to help parents 'choose' (*sic*) which ones they want to send their children to. When these first appeared (1994 for secondary schools; 1996 for primary schools), it became apparent that boys were not doing as well as girls across the board. Hence, the problem of 'boys' underachievement' was born, and attention was focused on all aspects of their schooling, including and especially the means by which boys and girls are tested and assessed. There are a number of ways in which 'gender-fair' assessment has been adjudged (Gipps and Murphy, 1994). Most notably, these include the extent to which boys/girls might feel alienated from the content of the test and/or how familiar they are with the test materials – for example, in the UK, in 1999, 11-year-old boys' reading scores increased by 14 percentage points in national (Key Stage 2) tests. There was some debate in the press as to whether this huge increase was due to the fact that the reading test was split into three different passages about spiders – thus responding to boys' 'interest' in spiders and their need for 'bite-sized' portions of text (as opposed to lengthier pieces) (Downes, 1999; Hackett, 1999). (For a detailed discussion of implementing 'gender fair' practices in the primary classroom, see Skelton and Francis, 2003.)

Integral to assessment processes and procedures are teacher attitudes and expectations.

Teacher attitudes

The importance of teacher attitudes in shaping the learning experiences of pupils has been evident from second-wave feminism through to today. A majority of elementary teachers are aware of how and where gender stereotypes can appear in the classroom (Rensenbrink, 2001; Gray and Leith, 2004). That is, teachers are aware that boys are more likely to dominate their time through behavioral issues or requiring assistance with their work (Sadker, 2000), and that they need to be careful about making gendered assumptions about pupils (Rensenbrink, 2001). Of course, this is somewhat ironic given that, in the current climate, teachers are encouraged to focus more on boys and their perceived needs! For the most part, guidelines for 'good practice' continue to appear that are not based on 'boy-centred' practices; rather, they exhort teachers to examine their own classroom behavior by being sensitive to the ways they provide feedback (e.g. ensuring they provide positive constructive feedback to girls, and not just boys); paying attention to how much time they give to boys; monitoring their language by using degendered terms (e.g. 'fire officer' not 'fireman'); and avoiding clichés such as 'girls don't fight' (see Frawley, 2005, as an example of an article on equity strategies).

As indicated at the beginning of this section, my argument is that while 'equity' or 'equal opportunity' practices are important and teachers need to ensure they are built into the daily rules and routines of the elementary school day, they are not in themselves enough to make any real impact on the learning identities of young children. Glenda MacNaughton (1998) offers the example of Fay, an early childhood educator who subscribed to liberal feminist notions of 'equal opportunities'. Her beliefs that boys and girls should be treated equally was further reinforced by her early-childhood training whereby emphasis is placed on developmental theories – where by all children are enabled to reach their full potential through 'free choice'. Fay wanted the boys and girls in her class to have equal access to the block play (traditionally, a boy-dominated area) and the home corner (traditionally occupied by girls). Over the course of several months, she removed the barriers between the block-play and home-corner sections, renamed these as 'the dramatic play area', and then re-presented this as the 'imagination area' in which combinations of home-corner and block-play materials were interchanged. All of these attempts failed to encourage pupils to act in non-stereotyped ways, and boys continued to use the large blocks and cars. What MacNaughton argues from this is that it is not enough to present children with alternatives without disrupting their pre-existing narratives (because of their investment in 'gender dualism' as a key part of their identities – see Chapter 9 in this volume for discussion). Following on from Davies's (1989) work on young children's 'category maintenance', whereby their reaction to feminist fairytales was to resist alternative constructions of the 'beautiful princess' and 'brave prince' because it did not 'fit' their notions of what a 'real princess/prince' is, MacNaughton calls for a 'taking apart' of teachers' gendered preconceptions, as well as pupils', beliefs and practices (see also MacNaughton, 2000).

Furthermore, equal opportunities/equity approaches fail to engage in the variables that help shape identities. Children are not just gendered beings, but also have an ethnicity, a social class, a culture and so forth. Age is also a factor; after all, how accurate is it to assume that the attitudes and behaviours of a 13-year-old boy are applicable to those of a five-year-old boy? And, again, pupils' experiences of bullying or racial/sexual harassment contribute to constructions of identity (Connolly, 1998; Reay, 2003). Thus, teachers require a more thorough understanding of how gender interacts with other identity variables to recognize their own, and their pupils' attitudes, expectations and beliefs in order to adopt strategies that critically engage with these. It is opportune at this point to turn to look at the second broad area of gender research, which is that concerned with gendered learning identities.

GENDERED LEARNING IDENTITIES

The last section ended with a discussion of teacher attitudes, and so it is appropriate to continue this discussion to illustrate how research based on 'difference and diversity' theoretical approaches provides greater insights and opportunities for critically engaging with young children's gendered frameworks.

Carla Rensenbrink's (2001) study of three feminist elementary teachers found that, even with their knowledge of feminism, they would still produce behaviors that resulted in boys receiving different educational experiences than girls. This finding shows how, even with teachers who are ostensibly committed to promoting equity, gendered assumptions and expectations are deeply embedded in the psyche. Thus, it is not too surprising to read of research which tells us that teachers continue to see girls as succeeding through their quiet diligence and hard work, while boys are more 'naturally clever' and this is only inhibited by their laziness. Indeed, it is fair to say that this is probably *the* most frequently cited finding of studies of both elementary and high schools (Francis, 1998; Sadker, 2000; Jones and Myhill, 2004). For example, Maynard's (2002: 67) research into boys and literacy in a primary school showed how teachers talked of the 'untapped potential' of underachieving boys, while academically able girls in Renold's (2001: 580) study were spoken of as 'bossy' or 'overconfident'.

Such presumptions about the abilities of girls and boys can have implications for assessment. In one study involving 48 elementary school teachers' assessment of their pupils in mathematics, it was discovered that they tended to hold stereotyped assumptions about the abilities of their pupils, but that this was mediated by the student's performance level. That is, boys of average and low performance were seen as having more developmental resources in maths than girls, but this was not true of high-achieving boys and girls (Tiedemann, 2002). As Jones and Myhill (2004) argue, concepts of 'achievement' and 'underachievement' are highly gendered:

> Teachers know what underachievement looks like: it looks like a boy who is bright, but bored ... The consequence is that underachievement in girls is often overlooked or rendered invisible. Underachievement is concerned with potential not lack of ability, while high and low achievement are concerned with performance. It becomes a matter of concern if teachers perceive boys as the vessel of potential and of latent ability, while the high achievements of girls are seen to be about performance, not ability. (p531)

Furthermore, in this study and one undertaken by Gray and Leith (2004) on teachers' perceptions of gender, it was found that age of pupils was of significant importance. Here older children were judged by their teachers to be reacting differently from their younger peers. For example, Jones and Myhill (2004) found that younger boys were thought to be underachieving by teachers because of their lack of confidence (among other things), but 'confidence' was not seen to be a contributory factor for older underachieving boys. For older boys, the problem was seen to be laziness; again, this was not seen to be an issue for younger underachieving boys. Gray and Leith (2004: 10) discovered that teachers thought that 'stereotypical behaviours [were] significantly more evident in older children's play'. In contrast, gender divisions were more observable in mixed-sex working groups of younger children.

Of course, teachers' pre-existing and gendered attitudes and perceptions are just one element that influences constructions of identity. How pupils position themselves in relation to curriculum subjects, and classroom teaching and learning processes have been topics of a number of studies. In the UK context, Lucey *et al.* (2003) looked at children's performance in the national numeracy strategy. They point out how, in the numeracy hour, a competitive and performative learner style is demanded of pupils. However, they discovered that the girls' (and boys') ways of interacting in the maths classroom were traditionally familiar, with some boys pushing themselves forward to answer questions while the girls tended to take a back seat. The researchers warned teachers to 'be wary of letting whole class sessions become a public arena for confident children, predominantly boys, to demonstrate their autonomy and creativity, and in which less confident children dread being exposed' (p55). Instead, they advocate group discussions to take the focus away from individual performance.

At the same time, recent research on high achieving pupils indicates more similarities than differences between boys and girls. Renold and Allan's (2004) study of primary school girls' femininities found that constructions of achievement among the successful girls differed but that these were comparable to those found among high-achieving boys. For example, one girl, Shamilla, constructed herself as an 'effortless achiever', that is, not being seen to work too hard or push herself forward in the class, as some boys do (Swain, 2002). Another, Nyla, felt that her lack of popularity with her peers was because of her cleverness, in the same way that many clever boys risk being labelled 'boffs', 'swots' and 'geeks'. Finally, Libby manages to carry off what some boys do, which is to be popular and clever (see Mac an Ghaill's (1994) 'real Englishmen', or Skelton's (2001) 'Star footballers'). However, as Renold and Allan (2004) make clear, these constructions of high achievement remain contextualized by gendered frames; so Shamilla responded 'modestly' to public peer recognition of her success, Nyla was quite isolated from the other girls and seen as 'moody' and 'man-like', while Libby positioned herself as a 'normal girl' (rather than a 'girly girl'), but this did leave her displays of confidence open to accusations of 'bossiness', 'arrogance' and 'selfishness'.

Obviously, pupils' constructions of their identities do not take place only in relation to teachers and the official curriculum but also in the social spaces of the playground and classroom. It is here that sexuality (including 'romance relationships'), homophobia, harassment and bullying have been subject to scrutiny by researchers and considered in relation to social class and ethnicity. Connolly (1998), in his study of a multicultural primary school, describes how a group of five-and six-year-old Black boys placed a great deal of emphasis on girlfriends in forging their identities. This created conflict with white boys in terms of who 'owned' the girls. In a later article, he describes how he observed what started out as a pleasurable game of 'kiss chase' turned into something far more disturbing for one girl, who, after being 'caught', found her captor unwilling to let her go:

> and she began to struggle. At this point he swung her around and tipped her over onto the grass where he manoeuvred himself so that he lay on top of her, pinning her arms to the ground. The boy then appeared to simulate sex by thrusting his pelvis up and down and the girl quickly became increasingly distressed. The boy saw me walking towards them and jumped up and ran off. (Connolly, 2003: 121).

Boys, too, are subjected to homophobic bullying in the primary school playground, being called 'sissy', 'faggot', 'poofter', 'gayboy', and 'queer' (Thorne, 1993; Redman, 1996; Epstein, 1998). There are various reasons (or 'excuses') that are given for bullying behavior to start, and Reay (2003) found that one of these is boys' hard work at school. In her research with Dylan Wiliam (Reay and Wiliam, 1999), Reay found clear links between the SATs[2] (national public tests) and bullying, whereby successful boys would be subject to physical assaults in the classroom and playground by other boys; indeed, she noted that bullying in primary schools was on the increase.

However, as is also implied above, there is a fine line between romance relations and sexual harassment as has been implied in several studies of primary schools (Thorne, 1993; Hatcher, 1994; Redman, 1996; Connolly, 1998; Skelton, 2001;). In a detailed and rare study of 10-11-year-old boys and girls, Emma Renold (2005) shows that sexual identities are a fundamental part of children's daily school lives. She argues that (adults/teachers) need to be careful not to dismiss the significance of these developing sexual identities and to note the differing ways in which boys and girls 'do' sexuality, but which, ultimately, are all subject to the heterosexual male gaze (see Skeggs, 1991; Skelton, 2002). What she, together with other researchers adopting 'difference and diversity' theoretical approaches (that is, those informed by post-structuralism), argues for are strategies that disrupt and intervene in children's traditional gender-stereotyped attitudes and behaviors (for practical strategies, see MacNaughton, 2000; Skelton and Francis, 2003; Francis and Skelton, 2005).

CONCLUSIONS

This chapter has outlined the various gender issues in elementary schooling that have occupied the attention of researchers in recent years. In keeping with other contributors to this book, I have indicated how key differences in theories held about how, why and where gender differentiation occurs influences what strategies are needed to redress inequities.

What the research discussed in this chapter has shown is how gender intersects with a number of variables to structure and influence children's gendered learning and social identities. These studies, are for the most part, located within social justice theoretical frameworks and, also, importantly, are concerned with power relations and inequalities. In contrast, many of the strategies that are recommended under the banner of 'equal opportunities' and, the dominant perspective of boys' underachievement (See Chapter 26 in this volume) fail to critique power relations or see these as a crucial factor in determining inequitable schooling experiences. It has been argued here that literature and research exclusively on 'boys' underachievement' are frequently couched within essentialist understandings of gender and, worryingly, recommend ways of dealing with boys that will marginalize girls, effectively turning the clock back several years. Furthermore, we can only hope that in all Western countries research funders concerned with 'pupil achievement' keep in mind that 'lifelong learning' identities are about more than passing tests.

REFERENCES

Bauer, K (2000) Promoting gender equity in schools. *Contemporary Education,* 71: 22–6.

Best, R (1983) *We've all got scars: what boys and girls learn in elementary school.* Bloomington, IN: Indiana University Press.

Biddulph, S (1998) *Raising boys.* London: Thorsons.

Biklen, S and Pollard, D (2001) Feminist perspectives on gender in classrooms, in Richardson, V (ed) *Handbook of research on teaching* (723–46). Washington, DC: American Educational Research Association.

Bleach, K (ed) (1998) *Raising boys' achievement in schools*. Stoke-on-Trent: Trentham Books.

Connolly, P (1998) *Racism, gender identities and young children*. London: Routledge.

Connolly, P (2003) Gendered and gendering spaces: playgrounds in the early years, in Skelton, C and Francis, B (eds) *Boys and girls in the primary classroom*. Buckingham: Open University Press.

Connolly, P (2004) *Boys and schooling in the early years*. London: RoutledgeFalmer.

Davies, B (1989) *Frogs and snails and feminist tales*. London: Allen and Unwin.

Davies, L (2004) *Education and conflict*. London: RoutledgeFalmer.

Delamont, S (1980) *Sex roles and the school*. London: Methuen.

Downes, P (1999) 1999 reading test more boy-friendly. *Times Educational Supplement,* 15 Oct, p24.

Dunne, M, Humphreys, S and Leach, F (2006) Gender violence in schools in the developing world. *Gender and Education,* 18: 75–98.

Epstein, D (1998) Stranger in the mirror: gender, ethnicity, sexuality and nation in schooling. Paper presented at Multiple Marginalities: Gender Citizenship and Nationality in Education Conference. Nordic-Baltic Research Symposium (NORFA) in Helsinki: August.

Evans, L and Davies, K (2000) No sissy boys here: a content analysis of the representation of masculinity in elementary school reading textbooks. *Sex Roles,* 42 (3–4): 255–70.

Francis, B (1998) *Power plays*. Stoke-on-Trent: Trentham.

Francis, B and Skelton, C (2005) *Reassessing gender and achievement*. London: RoutledgeFalmer.

Frawley, T (2005) Gender bias in the classroom: current controversies and implications for teachers. *Childhood Education,* Summer. www.findarticles.com/p/articles/mi_qa3614/is_200707/ai_n14683848/ (accessed 24 July 2005).

Gipps, C and Murphy, P (1994) *A fair test?* Buckingham: Open University Press.

Gooden, A and Gooden, M (2001) Gender representation in notable children's picture books: 1995–1999. *Sex Roles,* 45(1–2): 89–101.

Gray, C and Leith, H (2004) Perpetuating gender stereotypes in the classroom: a teacher perspective. *Educational Studies,* 30: 3–17.

Gurian, M (2002) *Boys and girls learn differently!* San Francisco, CA: Jossey Bass.

Hackett, G (1999) Did spider tests raise boys scores? *Times Educational Supplement,* 15 Oct, pp1–2.

Halpern, D (1992) *Sex differences in cognitive abilities,* (2nd edn). Hillsdale, NJ: Lawrence Erlbaum.

Hatcher, R (1995) Boyfriends, girlfriends: gender and 'race' in children's cultures. *International Play Journal,* 3: 187–97.

Hoff Sommers, C (2000) *The war against boys (how misguided feminism is harming our young men)*. New York: Simon & Schuster.

Hough, J (1985) Developing individuals rather than boys and girls. *School Organization,* 5: 17–25.

Jackson, C (2002) Can single-sex classes in co-educational schools enhance the learning experiences of girls and/or boys? an exploration of pupils' perceptions. *British Educational Research Journal,* 28: 37–48.

Jones, S and Myhill, D (2004) Seeing things differently: teachers' constructions of underachievement. *Gender and Education,* 16: 531–46.

Kindlon, D and Thompson, M (1999) *Raising Cain*. London: Michael Joseph.

Lingard, B, Martino, W, Mills, M and Bahr, M (2003) *Addressing the educational needs of boys*. Canberra: Department of Education, Science and Training (www.dest.gov.au/schools/publications/2002/boyseducation/index.htm).

Lucey, H, Brown, M, Denvir, H, Askew, M and Rhodes, V (2003) Girls and boys in the primary maths classroom, in Skelton, C and Francis, B (eds) *Boys and girls in the primary classroom*. Maidenhead: McGraw-Hill.

Mac an Ghaill, M (1994) *The making of men: masculinities, sexualities and schooling*. Buckingham: Open University Press.

MacNaughton, G (1998) Improving our gender equity 'tools': a case for discourse analysis, in Yelland, N (ed) *Gender in early childhood*. London: Routledge.

MacNaughton, G (2000) *Rethinking gender in early childhood education.* London: Paul Chapman.

Mahony, P (1985) *Schools for the boys?* London: Hutchinson.

Martino, W and Meyenn, B (2002) 'War, guns and cool, tough things': interrogating single-sex classes as a strategy for engaging boys in English. *Cambridge Journal of Education,* 32: 303–24.

Maynard, T (2002) *Exploring the boys and literacy issue.* London: Routledge/Falmer.

Myhill, D (2002) Bad boys and good girls? patterns of interaction and response in whole class teaching. *British Educational Research Journal,* 28: 339–52.

National Center For Education Statistics (2001) *Educational achievement and Black-White inequality.* Statistical Analysis Report, July 2001.

Neall, L (2002) *Bringing out the best in boys.* Gloucester: Hawthorn Press.

Noble, C and Bradford, W (2000) *Getting it right for boys ... and girls.* London: Routledge.

Pollack, W (1998) *Real boys.* New York: Owl Books.

Pourzand, N (1999) Female education and citizenship in Afghanistan: a turbulent relationship, in Yuval-Davis, N and Werbner, P (eds) *Women, citizenship and difference.* London: Zed Books.

Reay, D (2003) Troubling, troubled and troublesome? Working with boys in the primary classroom, in Skelton, C and Francis, B (eds) *Boys and girls in the primary classroom.* Maidenhead: McGraw-Hill/Open University Press.

Reay, D and Wiliam, D (1999) 'I'll be a nothing': structure, agency and the construction of identity through assessment. *British Educational Research Journal,* 25: 343–54.

Redman, P (1996) Curtis loves Ranjit: heterosexual masculinities, schooling and pupils' sexual cultures. *Educational Review,* 48: 175–82.

Renold, E (2001) 'Square-girls', femininity and the negotation of academic success in the primary school. *British Educational Research Journal,* 27: 577–88.

Renold, E (2005) *Girls, boys and junior sexualities.* London: RoutledgeFalmer.

Renold, E and Allan, A (2004) Bright and beautiful: high-achieving girls and the negotiation of young 'girlie' femininities'. Paper presented at British Educational Research Association Annual Conference, 16–18 September, UMIST, Manchester, UK.

Rensenbrink, CW (2001) *All in our places: feminist challenges in elementary school classrooms.* Lanham, MD: Rowman and Littlefield.

Sadker, D (2000) Gender equity: still knocking at the classroom door. *Equity and Excellence in Education,* 33: 80–3.

Sax, L (2005a) *Why gender matters.* New York: Doubleday.

Sax, L (2005b) The promise and peril of a single-sex *public* education. *Education Week,* 2 March (www.edweek.org/ew/articles/2005/03/02/25sax.h24).

Skeggs, B (1991) Challenging masculinity and using sexuality. *British Journal of Sociology of Education,* 12: 127–39.

Skelton, C (1997) Women and education, in Robinson, V and Richardson, D (eds) *Introducing women's studies* (2nd edn). London: Macmillan.

Skelton, C (2001) *Schooling the boys: masculinities and primary education.* Buckingham: Open University Press.

Skelton, C (2002) Constructing dominant masculinity and negotiating the 'male gaze'. *International Journal of Inclusive Education,* 6: 17–31.

Skelton, C and Francis, B (2003) *Boys and girls in the primary classroom.* Maidenhead: Open University Press/McGraw-Hill.

Smithers, A and Robinson, P (1995) *Co-educational and single-sex schooling.* Manchester: CEER, University of Manchester.

Stambach, A (2000) *Lessons from Mount Kilimanjaro: schooling, community and gender in East Africa.* London: Routledge.

Swain, J (2002) The resources and strategies boys use to establish status in a junior school without competitive sport. *Discourse,* 23: 91–107.

Thompson, M and Barker, T (2000) *Speaking of boys.* New York: Ballantine.

Thorne, B (1993) *Gender play: girls and boys in school*. Buckingham: Open University Press.

Tiedemann, J (2002) Teachers' gender stereotypes as determinants of teacher perceptions in elementary school mathematics. *Educational Studies in Mathematics*, 50: 49–62.

Warrington, M, Younger, M and Bearne, E (2006) *Raising boys' achievement in primary schools: towards a holistic approach*. Maidenhead: Open University Press/McGraw-Hill.

Whyte, J (1983) *Beyond the Wendy house: sex role stereotyping in primary schools*. York: Longman.

NOTES

1. It should be noted that this chapter concentrates on the research and literature on boys and girls in primary schools in Western society because it is impossible to do justice to the global situation regarding primary schooling in just one chapter. This is not, however, a failure to recognize that the circumstances for girls and boys in the West is very different to that in developing countries. Whereas contemporary concern in Australia, North America, the UK and much of Europe is with boys' underachievement, in many countries the major obstacle is obtaining a basic education for girls (Pourzand, 1999; Davies, 2004) and to ensure that, when they are in school, they are not subjected to physical and sexual abuse by (male) teachers (Stambach, 2000; Dunne *et al.*, 2006).

2. Standard Assessment Tasks (SATS) take place in England at ages 7, 11, 14 and 16.

11

Masculinities and Femininities and Secondary Schooling: The Case for a Gender Analysis in the Postmodern Condition

Kevin G. Davison and Blye W. Frank

INTRODUCTION

Secondary schools are locations where students spend a great deal of time not only learning, but also navigating gendered identities.[1] 'People grow between the ages of 11 and 18. These "tweenage" years are distinctive in the making of masculinities and femininities, since not only does the body change, but body meanings and the image repertoire of bodies become, in contradictory ways, "available"' (Corrigan, 1991: 206). Secondary students often struggle with the contradictions and demands of gender. However much we would like to think the social world is separate from the educational world, these struggles with gender are not disconnected from students' everyday schooling routines. The social obligations and restrictions on how gender is practised by individual students often conflict with the institutional discourses of public schooling.

By accounting for the plurality of gender performances by students, we open up greater possibilities to retheorize how the social details of student bodies affect pedagogical practices and learning. There is a great need to analyze critically the breadth of gendered practices in school, and to acknowledge the long history of systematically resisting a gender analysis.

In the twenty-first-century postmodern condition of multiple subjectivities, new communications technologies and mass media infiltration, the reluctance to consider gender is more than an oversight. It is a political and ideological choice to hold on to modernist approaches to gender and education despite the fact that that modernist ways of understanding gender can no longer accommodate some of the social and gendered realities of contemporary students.

This chapter will aim to address how lived practices of gender continue to rub against the grain of discourses of secondary schooling. A critical examination of gender performances in schools, taking into account the complex ways that gender intersects the lives of students, may enable a shift away from understanding gender as a threat to education, and instead, offer an opportunity to re-examine how secondary educators might incorporate a gender analysis as a pedagogical tool to address the academic and social needs of students. Our hope is that this examination of the various moments where the seemingly tidy category of gender breaks down and often frustrates the project of secondary education, can offer some insight into what is at stake in the opposition to a gender analysis.

DIFFERENCE AND GENDER

Because the history and design of public education includes a high degree of social regulation, differences continue to remain problematic in schools. 'Like and like go together. Likeness is liking, whatever they say about opposites' (Winterson, 2004: 15). As Winterson suggests, difference, by definition, is, more often than not, seen as an anomaly, while similarity suffers less suspicion. Even attempts to acknowledge difference in educational contexts, for example, inclusive education reforms and the resulting pedagogical adjustments, are grounded in the recognition of difference *from* the dominant population. That is, difference is defined as *not like* the 'norm', regardless of whether it is a different, race, sex, gender, sexuality or ability. This creates an 'Othering' effect in which the non-dominant category becomes the repository of the fear and distaste of those in the dominant group (Butler, 1991; Fuss, 1995). More often than not, differences are viewed uncritically through 'common-sense' under-theorizing and, as a result, 'definitions of femininity and masculinity [...] are implicitly assumed to be ahistorical, unitary, universal, and unchanging categories' (Mac an Ghaill, 1994: 8). By uncritically engaging in dominant discourses, students regulate their own behavior to construct a sense of identity that seems to 'make sense' because of its similarity to other social and gendered performances. This process of replicating dominant discourses and incorporating them into one's individual understanding of the world is what Foucault referred to as 'discourses of the self' (1980). However, in regulating dominant discourses that are tied to 'common-sense' understandings, students play a role in making the power relations and inequities invisible, and perpetuate difference-based inequities through the institutional structures which they inhabit.

> Discourse in institutional life can be viewed as a means for the naturalization and disguise of power relations that are tied to inequalities in the social production and distribution of symbolic and material resources. This means that dominant discourses in contemporary cultures tend to represent those social formations and power relations that are the products of history, social formation, and culture … as if they were the product of organic, biological, and essential necessity (Luke, 1995: 12)

Thus, the naturalization of inequities is learned, replicated and supported by discourses that are historical products, but are assumed to be 'common-sense' prescriptions for living. 'It is precisely such historically long-established positions that inform our phenomenology of gender, our sense of the masculine and feminine. The unconscious mapping of these positions continues to saturate our affective experience of excitement and anxiety about difference' (Benjamin, 1998: 62). Because the discourses of the self are assumed to be 'common sense', it can be difficult to engage critically with inequities that seem 'natural', and it can become uncomfortable when individual experiences of gender do not resemble dominant gender expectations. Thus, because of the assumption of the 'naturalness' of particular expressions of masculinity and femininity, the resistance to critically examining gender is often a reaction to the perceived assumption that such an analysis is unfair or harmful to boys and men because of its feminist critique of power and privilege (Walkerdine, 1989).

Feminists have long argued that gender difference is not a simple difference. Butler insists that '"men" and "women" are political categories, and not natural facts' (1990: 115). Masculinity and femininity are defined by, and against, one another in a way that promotes inequity among women and men. Yeatman explains that 'the very necessity of feminism arises from the material existence of a patriarchal ideological binary and hierarchical ordering of the terms male (masculine, men) and female (feminine, women)' (1994: 49). Understanding gender difference in this way explicitly points to how gender privileges men over women, and in so doing, creates a shift from seeing difference as something that needs to be simply acknowledged, to an obligation to identify how the way we understand differences is responsible for inequity, especially in schools.

By the time they enter secondary school, young women and young men are well aware of gender differences and acutely understand the social rewards and punishments for performing gender in very specific ways (Lesko, 1988). Students have a complex psychic and social investment in gender, and schools assist students in this sorting process by supporting those who conform to the hierarchy of gender ideals (Kenway, 1995). School 'microcultures of management, teachers and students are key infrastructural mechanisms through which masculinities and femininities are mediated and lived out' (Mac an Ghaill, 1994: 4). By not employing a critical gender analysis to the daily social and educational interactions, schools assist in the 'normalization' of inequitable gender relations.

Students who do not, or cannot, conform to the social demands of rigid definitions of masculinity and femininity are often socially terrorized, ostracized, isolated, abused, and alienated, and under such conditions end up dreading their participation in obligatory schooling (Rofes, 1995; Davison, 1996, 2000a). Research on gender, sexuality, bullying and harassment in schools regularly recounts students' struggles against being identified by others as different (see for example, Frank, 1987, 1990; Larkin, 1994; Hazler, 1996; Epstein and Johnson, 1998; Davison, 2004; Sullivan, *et al.*, 2003). Difference only becomes problematic when defined by those within the dominant social group. Most schools support gender ideals through 'a normalizing gaze, a surveillance that makes it possible to qualify, to classify and to punish' (Foucault cited in Rainbow, 1984: 197). When acts of violence, harassment or bullying arise they are usually addressed as individual acts of aggression or discrimination, and not as a product of systematic gender inequity and intolerance of difference. In refusing to address gender harassment as systemic, schools and teachers often collude with students who attempt to police the dominant gender order. Most teachers, educational administrators, and policy makers are products of the same educational system as contemporary students, and, in the journey from student to educator or administrator, they have gainfully navigated schooling in such a way that they, too, have produced discourses of the self that are in line with dominant educational and gender discourses. Without a gender analysis, teachers and administrators, therefore, may be more likely to perpetuate inequities in pedagogy and curriculum design and content that seem to them simply 'naturally' embedded in 'common-sense' differences between women and men.

Feminist critiques do not see the social consequences of gender in school simply as a disruptive side issue, but rather as a symptom of institutionalized education. Educational administrators and policy makers often dismiss or ignore a more complex analysis of gender in favour of an analysis that does not hold the institution accountable (Frank, *et al.*, 2003). Furthermore, feminist critical gender analyses are often perceived to be a threat to the privilege of men and boys, and therefore are rejected outright. We would like to use the example of the current 'panics' about boys and schooling to illustrate how the resistance to a gender analysis of schooling has fuelled a bubbling backlash against feminism. In rejecting a gender analysis, this backlash has failed to address many of the critical social and educational concerns in contemporary schools and continues to support and replicate greater inequities.

Backlash/resistance

This chapter is not able to recount in full the long history of feminist educators who have fought for gender-based change over the last century; however, it is necessary to sketch briefly the context that has led to contemporary anti-feminist backlash. The second-wave women's movement, which occurred at the same time that there was a large growth in public education and educational reform in Europe, North

America, and Australia, set the stage for addressing issues of educational inequities of girls and women. Since the 1960s, feminists have attempted to raise awareness of how gendered expectations were disadvantaging young women in sciences and maths, which were traditionally regarded as more 'masculine' subjects.[2]

Feminists struggled for many years to convince educators of how young women were being short-changed by sexist assumptions about the abilities of women and girls. It was often difficult to convince young women that succeeding in science and maths need not be a social stigma in the face of 'common-sense' discourses about women, femininity, and education. Arguments that fewer girls and women in science and maths fuelled educational and employment inequities were continually resisted or mocked in favour of a gender order that advantaged men and boys. Yet, over several decades, against great resistance, more 'traditional' beliefs regarding femininity were renegotiated to the extent that the gap between girls and boys in science and maths was reduced. Achieving this goal did not radically turn the tables on gender to favour women and girls, but it did provide opportunities for more women and girls where previously little opportunity existed.

Those who resisted this reform felt that such gains for women implied a zero-sum game that would result in disadvantages to men and boys, and a seed was planted for future backlash. If it is assumed that attention to gender inequities implies working within a fixed zero-sum game, the best strategy for either gender would be to make the best of the inequities that have befallen you while ensuring that the other binary does not obtain any advantages at your expense. Therefore, the assumption that gender can allocate only a limited amount of privileges reduces the strategies within a fixed system. But if the zero-sum game is demystified and we are able to rearticulate gender as not a binary, but as a plurality of performances with the potential for equity and equi-valued consequences, the inequities embedded in the differences become more apparent and a gender analysis becomes less threatening. The resistance to a critical gender analysis, and anti-feminist backlash politics, arise not only from the history of educational reform addressing inequities for young women, but also from a contemporary and popular shift in educational priorities to address young men and underachievement in schools.

In the late 1980s and 1990s, there was a growth in critical masculinity and schooling scholarship. This work was influenced by the feminist tradition of addressing gendered power and privilege, and accounting for those on the margins, both men and women. Research by such scholars as Connell (1987; 1995), Mac an Ghaill (1994), Martino (1994; 2000), Kenway and Willis (1998), Frank (1987; 1990; 1993), Gilbert and Gilbert (1998), and Davison (1996; 2000a;b) added to the feminist critique and critically examined the lives of boys and young men in schools. Whether examining bullying, sport, homophobia or academic achievement, much of this literature aimed to investigate the everyday gendered practices of boys and young men in schools, while at the same time acknowledging that young men and masculinities are not unified categories.

The application of feminist theory to the lives of young men and the critical analysis of masculinity called into question some of the 'common-sense' discourses that inform masculinity, and in so doing opened up a place for some young men to challenge the ways masculinity can be harmful to both young men and young women in school (Skelton, 1998; Kehler *et al.*, 2005). In our own research (Frank 1990, 1994; Davison, 1996, 2003), we have found that young men in secondary schools have welcomed the opportunity to examine critically their gendered practices, and they often remark upon the paucity of opportunities to engage with feminist critiques of masculinity.

By the mid- to late-1990s, there was a rise of scholarship which pointed to a concern for boys' emotional needs in schools and attempted to address the perceived academic underachievement of boys as a group (see, for example Kindlon and Thompson, 1999; Pollock, 1999; Chapter 26 in this volume). This research did not rely on feminist scholarship or theory and offered no critique of gender, difference, sexuality, power, or privilege. Because of the lack of complexity and the reliance on a 'common-sense' approach, and because it catered to those who resisted feminist critiques of masculinities, this scholarship had wide appeal and added to a growing 'panic' about 'the boys' and schooling (Frank *et al.*, 2003).

Unfortunately, however, as this scholarship avoided or resisted an analysis catering to the complexity of gender and schooling, the 'panic' that was created to address boys' needs in schools offered only 'quick-fix' solutions that encouraged a greater privileging of *some* boys at the expense of the majority of other boys and girls. For example, to encourage more boys to read, it is often suggested that the curriculum, assumed to favour girls' reading interests and styles, be changed so that boys' interests and alternative literacies are addressed (Simpson, 1996; see also Chapter 26 in this volume). But in such a solution there is rarely an acknowledgement of how more 'masculine'[3] books and alternative literacy practices, such as video games, are able both to measure comprehension and vocabulary acquisition, and to prepare boys for a workplace that is likely to involve diverse literacy practices not limited to 'masculine' interests alone (Hall and Coles, 2001). Some of this research came out of a sociology of education perspective, some research examined peer group cultures, such as the classic ethnography on masculinities and schooling by Willis (1977), while other research focused on personal narratives, discourse analysis, and psychoanalytic examinations of gender in school (see Walkerdine, 1989; Redman, 1996; Frosh *et al.*, 2003; Pattman *et al.*, 2005). When facing the demands of the need for a mobile labour market and the economic realities of globalization:

> The 21st-century citizen will work in media-, text-, and symbol-saturated environments. For the unemployed, underemployed, and employed alike, a great deal of service and information-based work, consumption, and leisure depends on their capacities to construct, control, and manipulate texts and symbols. It should not be surprising, then, that many of the new social conflicts are about representation and subjectivity. (Luke, 1995: 6)

Despite the shift in global economies and shifting subjectivities, the suggestion to cater to boys' interests to counter low academic achievement in literacy and language arts fails boys even as it attempts to privilege them.

Contemporary concerns for boys and schooling seldom consider the plurality of differences among boys. The fear is always that 'boys', as a unified group, are suffering academically. The lack of attention to the specific boys who are not doing well in school, in favour of a blanket concern for boys as a whole, reflects a desire arising from an anti-feminist backlash to ensure that the academic and educational gaze is shifted from the girls to the boys without engaging in the very specific ways that some boys retain privilege while other boys and young women continue to be marginalized (Epstein, 1998; Skelton, 1998; Frank and Davison, 2001 and Chapter 26 in this volume).

When the critical masculinities scholarship is taken into account and the differences among boys are considered, the advantages and privileges of masculinities, as well as the resistance to feminist analyses, become more apparent. While there are indeed *some* boys and young men who struggle with literacy, there does not appear to be any evidence that boys *as a group* are being disadvantaged, and that these struggles with literacy issues in school have serious effects for their employment opportunities. The advantages and disadvantages for future employment and social 'success' often lie in the degree to which one is able to invoke hegemonic masculinity over others. Even marginalized boys struggle to obtain the gender privileges that they are denied when alienated from the gender ideal (Frank, *et al.*, 2003).

We acknowledge that claims of an anti-feminist backlash is a political assessment of how some scholars have chosen to examine the lives young women and young men in school. Yet this position is more than personal ideological bias.[4] Rather, it arises out of a concern to identify how secondary school students navigate the multiple contradictions and inequities they encounter in school that are difficult to account for without critically examining gender. Instead of ignoring gender as a pre-destined and unproblematic reality, we believe that when a 'contradiction is impossible to resolve except by a lie, then we know that it is really a door' (Weil, 1970).

Therefore, in addressing masculinities and femininities in secondary schools, we feel it is necessary to take into account the postmodern condition in order to point to the importance of acknowledging the complexities of gender in the lives of students. We believe that folding the postmodern across a feminist gender analysis of schooling will point to the flaws of modernist conceptions of gender and create spaces for new theories that can better accommodate the many ways gender shapes those in school.

GENDER AND THE POSTMODERN

> ... fragmentation is a way of living with differences without turning them into opposites, not trying to assimilate them out of insecurity. (Trinh, 1992: 156)

Fragmentation, as Trinh explains, is a critical element to postmodern theory. Since the Enlightenment, scholars and scientists have struggled to produce theories that explain phenomena and help to sort meaning in tidy, contained, categories. The reduction of complex concepts into simple binary opposites is one way that categories can be contained. Yet, as Halberstam notes: 'The human potential for precise classifications has been demonstrated in multiple arenas; why then do we settle for a paucity of classifications when it comes to gender?' (1998: 27). To understand masculine as 'not feminine' not only positions two social constructions as opposites, but also serves to narrow the definition to that of clear-cut difference. For example, 'psychological research, from its early animal psychology formulations to cognitivist computer-simulated models, has tended to emphasize individual difference rather than cultural heterogeneity and hybridity' (Luke, 1995: 6). Our history of ignoring the complexity of gender differences has led us to rely on simplified theories of gender categories that we have, over time, come to believe are 'natural' and therefore unavailable for critique. 'Indeed, theory is no longer theoretical when it loses sight of its own conditional nature, takes no risk in speculation, and circulates as a form of administrative inquisition' (Trinh, 1989: 42).

Postmodernism is not the opposite of modernism, nor does it assume that modernist ways of knowing are historically irrelevant. Rather, postmodernism builds on, and grows out of, the imperfections and slippages of modernist thought. 'Despite our desperate, eternal attempt to separate, contain and mend, categories always leak' (Trinh, 1989: 94). Postmodernism is curious about such leakages and attempts to begin enquiry where previous theories can no longer hold. By pointing to the limits of particular theory, postmodernism undercuts and fractures the foundations of our knowing and encourages new theories that do not rely on our habitual ways of understanding the world.

Postmodernism is sceptical of 'the assumption that people have singular, essential social identities or fixed cultural, social class, or gendered characteristics. It assumes that subjectivities are strategically constructed and contested through textual practices and that they are crafted in the dynamics of everyday life' (Luke, 1995: 14). This approach allows both individual human agency, as well as hope that social change is possible. Acknowledging that change is both possible and an ordinary component of all living organisms, compels us to interrogate identities with a more sophisticated academic gaze. As Hall explains:

> identities are never unified and, in late modern times, increasingly fragmented and fractured; never singular but multiply constructed across different, often intersecting and antagonistic, discourses, practices and positions. They are subject to a radical historicization, and are constantly in the process of change and transformation. (1996: 4)

Inevitably, those who resist the messiness of postmodern analyses tend to do so because the fracturing, equi-valued meanings, and multiple subjectivities do not allow for an obvious place to begin enquiry or theory – and that is precisely the point. 'Postmodernism [...] is willing to live with the pain of unrepresentability' (Jay, 1994, p583). It is the very act of refusing categorization that enables a shift in thinking about gender. 'If identity is ambivalent and fluid, then those solid categories that constitute identity will be destabilized as well. Therefore gone is the neatness of the distinctions between man/woman, Black/White, homosexual/heterosexual, and so on' (Khayatt, 1997: 132). It is this messiness that we find most useful in our own work on masculinities and schooling, and believe is critical to consider when examining gendered identities at the secondary school level. If we begin an analysis with the belief that gender is performative (Butler, 1990), gender 'becomes a verb, not a noun, a position to occupy rather than a fixed role' (McRae, 2005). If we see gender as something that you *do*, we can examine the different ways individual students actively occupy and take up particular gender performances that have social and educational consequences.

Since the 1960s, transgender people, drag queens, and, more recently drag kings, have demonstrated that gender need not be a rigidly defined or performed concept. As Halberstam has pointed out: 'imitation makes even the most stable of distinctions (i.e. gender) unstable' (1991: 443). The performativity of gender allows for the parodying of how so many people take gender so seriously. Zizek believes that it is the act of mimicking that gives the socially constructed and psychic understanding of gender 'legitimacy' or a sense of 'realness'. 'The only authenticity at our disposal is that of impersonation, of "taking our act (posture) seriously"' (Zizek, 2001: 34). Gender can feel more authentic because the rigidity of hegemonic 'common-sense' gender discourses is stripped away. Thus, 'what is lost in a loss of what we never possessed is the "essential appearance" which ruled our lives' (Zizek, 2001: 41). What has been 'lost' is the illusion of gender coherence that was our own creation.

Secondary students are usually quite adept at reading the postmodern around them and have developed a very different understanding of gender, sexuality and their bodies than have previous generations. Over the last decade, the issue of young women and eating disorders has become a more publicly visible socio-psychological disorder that has occupied educators and parents/guardians (Bordo, 1993; West, 1994; Abraham,1997). Recently, it has been documented that young men have also developed a kind of reverse anorexia where their distorted body image has to do with an unhappiness with the perceived muscularity of their body (Schneider and Agras, 1987; Pope, *et al.*, 2000) Tattooing, body piercing, and other body modifications have become popular with youth over the last decade, and such markings have acquired a high degree of cultural capital to young men and women today.

> Many people who regard modernization and postmodernization as a fall rather than an advance attempt to resist the march of history by recovering the body. When the body appears to be endangered, it becomes an obsession. This is one of the primary reasons that tattooing (as well as piercing and scarification) has become so widespread during this particular historical and cultural period. *Tattooing represents the attempt to mark the body at the very moment it is disappearing.* (Taylor, 1997: 127–9)

In refusing to engage in the way postmodernism shapes students as consumers, as gendered bodies with desires, and as citizens, we shut down an opportunity to take into account the way the social affects their regulated routine at school. McLaren believes that 'it is imperative that as educators for the postmodern age we begin to examine issues such as the feminization and masculinization of the body and the reification of the body politic' (1991: 165). As socially aware educators, we have to become more accountable to the gendered bodies in schools. As Yeatman explains:

if there is to be a vision of freedom which contests phallocentrism, it must admit the existence and significance of the particularity of embodied subjects. This means admitting the differences between differently embodied subjects. These differences are not reducible to a simple dimorphic sex difference, nor are they without socio-cultural mediation. [...] Such admission depends on providing the discursive space in which differently embodied subjects themselves can find their own voices regarding their differences as embodied subjects. (1994: 24)

This accountability, as Yeatman acknowledges, necessitates the creation of spaces in schools where various discourses can be examined and supported instead of resisted and actively repressed.

In breaking down the way gender has been traditionally understood as connected to biological sex, we are able to slip from the knot of what we assumed was the 'truth' of gender, to begin to see gender as a simulacrum – an endless repetition of a copy of a copy of a copy that has no original or 'natural' form. This is not so different from the philosopher who mistakes the philosophical frame for the truth – 'One thinks that one is tracing the outline of a thing's nature over and over again, and one is merely tracing round the frame through which we look at it' (Wittgenstein, 2002/1953: 41). Therefore, educators considering masculinities and femininities in secondary schools may do well to examine critically the institutional frame that has shaped our understanding of gender. By disrupting modernist notions of gender, and the anti-feminist backlash response, educators will be in a better position to support students in their learning and as they negotiate the social and intellectual world around them.

CONCLUSION

Every conclusion is but a new beginning, a fresh set of problems, frustrations and dilemmas. Hope allows us to deceive ourselves into thinking that life is parceled into discrete chunks – that our lives are stories with beginnings, middles and ends. That there IS narrative, linearity, and not chaos, chance and luck. (Byrne, 2002: 39)

Trinh argues that 'difference need not be suppressed in the name of theory' (1989: 43). Postmodernism may offer the tools for better understanding how gender differences shape the way students are able to access knowledge. For example, if a transgender student is displaced by binary-sexed changing rooms for physical education class, more modernist understandings of gender would not be able to accommodate the student's needs in a way that allows that student to participate fully in the learning environment. To refuse to consider the ways gender is multiple and not a simple rigid binary is 'symptomatic of an advanced case of hardening of the categories' (Haraway, 1997: 161). Fortunately, this prognosis is avoidable by considering that the categories we ourselves have constructed to make sense of our world are not static; they are continually changing, and that need not be a threat to educators or the education system if we take steps to create policy and curriculum better able to account for the way dominant performances of femininity and masculinity can place limits on how students can participate in their education. To offer a further example, if a young woman is continually bullied and harassed because she does not conform to the demands of 'acceptable' femininity, she will be less able to take up her studies than a non-harassed young woman. As educators, we have a responsibility to ensure that students feel safe and supported in schools, yet the refusal of schools and educators to acknowledge how hegemonic femininity and masculinity are implicated in social exclusion, bullying, harassment, violence, and low academic performance is tantamount to an act of abandoning students that are marginalized by the everyday inequity of gender discourses.

This chapter has attempted to illustrate how resistance to a critical examination of gender can work to perpetuate harm and hinder learning for all students. Taking up the various ways masculinities and femininities are multiple and ever-shifting, and troubling to our own performances, understandings, and comfortability regarding the plurality of gender in the postmodern, can demystify what we have come to believe are the 'truths' of gender. As Zizek explains: 'Contemporary experience again and again confronts us with situations in which we are compelled to take note of how our sense of reality and normal attitude toward it is grounded in a symbolic fiction' (2001: 219). Acknowledging that what we thought was stable is but a fiction can be disorienting for some, and can produce a longing for tidier modernist categories. Lyotard has written of the 'mourning and melancholy for the lost illusions of modernism' (1985: 33). However, as Haraway notes: 'Breakdown provokes a space of possibility precisely because things don't work smoothly anymore' (1999: 115). The moments and instances where gender seems to create friction in educational institutions may be the precise locations where enquiry is necessary. If, as Spivak suggests, 'Our lesson is to act in the fractures of identities in struggle' (1992: 803), then seeking cracks and fissures in our understanding and theorizing about gender and education may offer us an entry point to re-examine assumptions about gender and come closer to understanding the discourses that shape secondary students' lives. A step toward embracing gender plurality and resisting what appear to be 'common-sense' beliefs about gender can create an educational climate that is welcoming of difference and is better able to address some of the social and educational concerns in schools, from violence and bullying to homophobia and academic underachievement.

REFERENCES

Abraham, S (1997) *Eating disorders: the facts.* New York: Oxford University Press.
Benjamin, J (1998) *Shadow of the Other: intersubjectivity and gender in psychoanalysis.* New York: Routledge.
Bordo, S (1993) *Unbearable weight: feminism, Western culture, and the body.* Berkeley, CA: University of California Press.
Butler, J (1991) Imitation and gender insubordination, in Fuss, D (ed) *Inside/out: lesbian theories, gay theories.* (13–31). New York: Routledge.

Butler, J (1990) *Gender trouble: feminism and the subversion of the Other*. London: Routledge.

Byrne, D (2002) *The new sins*. London: Faber and Faber.

Connell, RW (1987) *Gender and power: society, the person, and sexual politics*. Stanford, CA: Stanford University Press.

Connell, RW (1995) *Masculinities*. Berkeley, CA: University of California Press.

Corrigan, PRD (1991) The making of the boy: meditations on what grammar school did with, to, and for my body, in Giroux, H (ed) *Postmodernism, feminism and cultural politics: redrawing educational boundaries* (196–216). Albany, NY: State University of New York Press.

Davison, KG (1996) Manly expectations: memories of masculinities in school. Unpublished master's thesis, Simon Fraser University, Burnaby, British Columbia, Canada.

Davison, KG (2000a) Masculinities, sexualities and the student body: 'sorting' gender identities in school, in James, CE (ed) *Experiencing difference* (44–52). Halifax: Fernwood Press.

Davison, KG (2000b) Boys' bodies in school: physical education. *Journal of Men's Studies*, 8: 255–66.

Davison, KG (2003) Body talk and masculinities: texting gender with/out the body. Unpublished doctoral dissertation, University of South Australia, Adelaide, Australia.

Davison, KG (2004) Texting gender and body as a distant/ced memory: an autobiographical account of bodies, masculinities and schooling. *Journal of Curriculum Theorizing*, 20: 129–49.

Epstein, D (1998) Real boys don't work: 'underachievement', masculinity, and the harassment of 'sissies', in Epstein, D, Elwood, J, Hey, V and Maw, J (eds) *Failing boys?: issues in gender and achievement* (96–108). Buckingham: Open University Press.

Epstein, D and Johnson, R (1998) *Schooling sexualities*. Birmingham: Open University Press.

Foucault, M (1980) *Power/knowledge: selected interviews and other writings 1972–1977*. Gordon, C (ed) New York: Pantheon Books.

Frank, B (1987) Hegemonic heterosexual masculinity. *Studies in Political Economy*, Autumn: 159–70.

Frank, B (1990) Everyday masculinities. Unpublished doctoral dissertation, Dalhousie University, Halifax, Nova Scotia, Canada.

Frank, B (1993) Straight/strait jackets for masculinity: educating for 'real men'. *Atlantis*, 18(1 and 2): 47–59.

Frank, B (1994) Queer selves/queer in schools: young men and sexualities, in Prentice, S (ed) *Sex in schools: Canadian education and sexual regulation* (44–59). Toronto: Our Schools/Our Selves Education Foundation.

Frank, B (1997) Masculinity meets postmodernism: theorizing the 'man made' man. *Canadian Folklore Canadien*, 19: 15–33.

Frank, B and Davison, K (2001) Masculinities and schooling: challenging present practices and 'panics'. *Exceptionality Education Canada*, 10 (1 and 2): 63–74.

Frank, B, Kehler, M, Lovell, T and Davison K (2003) A tangle of trouble: boys, masculinity and schooling, future directions, in Martino, W and Berrill, D (eds) *Educational Review*. Special Issue: *Masculinities and Schooling*, 55: 120–33.

Frank, B, Vibert, A, Davison, K, and Lovell, T (2003) Canadian boys and underachievement: no proof for panic, in Ali, S, Benjamin, S and Mauthner, M (eds) *The politics of gender and education: critical perspectives* (50–64). London: Palgrave/Macmillan.

Frosh, S, Phoenix, A, and Pattman, R (2003) Taking a stand: using psychoanalysis to explore the positioning of subjects in discourse. *British Journal of Social Psychology*, 42: 39–53.

Fuss, D (1995) *Identification papers*. New York: Routledge.

Gilbert, R and Gilbert, P (1998) *Masculinity goes to school*. London: Routledge.

Halberstam, J (1991) Automating gender: postmodern feminism in the age of the smart machine. *Feminist Studies*, 17: 439–59.

Halberstam, J (1998) *Female masculinity*. Durham, NC: Duke University Press.

Hall, C and Coles, M (2001) Boys, books and breaking boundaries: developing literacy in and out of school, in Martino, W and Meyenn, B (eds) *What about the boys?* (211–21). Open University Press: Buckingham.

Hall, S (1996) Who needs identity?, in Hall, S and du Gay, P (eds) *Questions of cultural identity* (1–17). Thousand Oaks, CA: Sage.

Haraway, D (1997). *Modist_witness@second_millennium.femaleMan©_meets_Oncomouse™: feminism and technoscience.* London: Routledge.

Haraway, D. (1999) *How like a leaf: An interview with Donna J. Haraway.* New York: Routledge.

Hazler, R (1996) *Breaking the cycle of violence: interventions for bullying and victimization.* Washington, DC: Accelerated Development.

Jay, M (1994) *Downcast eyes: the degeneration of vision in twentieth-century French thought.* Berkeley, CA: University of California Press.

Kehler, M, Davison, K and Frank, B (2005) Contradictions and tensions of the practice of masculinities in school: interrogating embodiment and 'good buddy talk', *Journal of Curriculum Theorizing,* 21: 59–72.

Kenway, J (1995) Masculinities in schools: under siege, on the defensive and under reconstruction. *Discourse: Studies in the Cultural Politics of Education,* 16: 59–79.

Kenway, J and Willis, S (1998) *Answering back: girls, boys and feminism in schools.* London: Routledge.

Khayatt, D (1997) Sex and the teacher: should we come out in class?, *Harvard Educational Review,* 67 1: 126–43.

Kindlon, D and Thompson, M (1999) *Raising Cain: protecting the emotional life of boys.* New York: Ballantine Books.

Larkin, J (1994) *Sexual harassment: high school girls speak out.* Toronto: Second Story Press.

Lesko, N (1988) *Symbolizing society: stories, rites and structure in a Catholic high School.* Philadelphia: Falmer Press.

Luke, A (1995) Text and discourse in education: an introduction to critical discourse analysis. *Review of Research in Education,* 21: 3–48.

Lyotard, J-F (1985) A conversation with Jean-François Lyotard. *Flash Art,* March: 33.

Mac an Ghaill, M (1994) *The making of men: masculinities, sexualities and schooling.* Birmingham: Open University Press.

Martino, W (1994) Masculinity and learning: exploring boys' underachievement and under-representation in subject English. *Interpretations,* special edition: *Boys in English,* 27: 22–57.

Martino, W (2000) Policing masculinities: investigating the role of homophobia and heteronormativity in the lives of adolescent school boys. *Journal of Men's Studies,* 8: 213–36.

McLaren, P (1991) Schooling the postmodern body: critical pedagogy and the politics of enfleshment, in Giroux, H. (ed) *Postmodernism, feminism and cultural politics: redrawing educational boundaries.* New York: State University of New York Press, 144–73.

McRae, S (2005) Coming apart at the seams: sex, text and the virtual body, web citation: www.usyd.edu.au/su/social/papers/mcrae.html (accessed 30 September 2005).

Pattman, R, Frosh, S and Phoenix, A (2005) Constructing and experiencing boyhoods in research in London. *Gender and Education,* 17: 555–61.

Pollock, W (1999) *Real boys: rescuing our sons from the myth of boyhood.* New York: Henry Holt.

Pope, HG, Phillips, KA and Olivardia, R (2000) *The Adonis complex: the secret crisis of male body obsession.* New York: Free Press.

Rainbow, P (ed) (1984) *Foucault reader.* New York: Pantheon Books.

Redman, P (1996) Curtis loves Ranjit: heterosexual masculinities, schooling and pupils' sexual cultures. *Educational Review,* 48: 175–82.

Rofes, E (1995) Making our schools safe for sissies, in Unks, G (ed) *The gay teen: education, practice and theory for lesbian gay and bisexual adolescents* (79–84). New York: Routledge.

Schneider, J and Agras, WS (1987) Bulimia in males: a matched comparison with females. *International Journal of Eating Disorders,* 6: 235–42.

Simpson, A (1996) Fictions and facts: an investigation of the reading practices of girls and boys. *English Education,* 28: 268–79.

Skelton, C (1998) Feminism and research into masculinities and schooling, *Gender and Education,* 10: 217–27.

Spivak, GC (1992) Identity bits/identity talk. *Critical Inquiry,* 18: 770–803.

Sullivan, K, Cleary, M, and Sullivan, G (2003) *Bullying in secondary schools: what it looks like, and how to manage it.* London: Paul Chapman/Sage.

Taylor, MC (1997) *Hiding*. Chicago: University of Chicago Press.
Trinh, MT (1989) *Woman native, Other: writing postcoloniality and feminism*. Bloomington, IN: Indiana University Press.
Trinh, MT (1992) *Framer framed*. London: Routledge.
Walkerdine, V (1989) *Counting girls out*. London: Virago.
Weil, S (1970) *First and last notebooks*. Rees, R (trans). London: Oxford University Press.
West, R (1994) *Eating disorders: anorexia nervosa and bulimia nervosa*. London: Office of Health Economics.
Willis, P (1977) *Learning to labor: how working class kids get working class jobs*. New York: Columbia University Press.
Winterson, J (2004) *Lighthousekeeping*. Toronto: Alfred A. Knopf.
Wittgenstein, L (2002/1953) *Philosophische Untersuchungen/Philosophical investigations* Anscombe, GEM (trans). Oxford: Blackwell.
Yeatman, A (1994) *Postmodern revisionings of the political*. London: Routledge.
Zizek, S (2001) *Enjoy your symptom!: Jacques Lacan in Hollywood and out*. New York: Routledge.

NOTES

1. Of course, raced, classed and sexual subject positions are also learned and navigated in schools, but this chapter will focus on masculinities and femininities.

2. Note how the subject areas absorb the gender bias. That is, subjects and disciplines cannot be gendered, but assumptions about how the people who succeed in such areas are gendered are transferred to the subject.

3. Again, note how objects become gendered almost by the contagious human touch alone.

4. We would like to acknowledge our understanding that bias is inevitable, and our solidarity with feminists in the belief that the personal is political. To examine individual lives of students in school is to engage in unavoidable political struggles.

12

Gender Equity in Post-Secondary Education

Carole Leathwood

The historical and contemporary contexts of the post-secondary education sector are characterized by gendered patterns of access, participation and outcomes. Such patterns, while globally evident, are differently configured in different geographical, socio-economic, cultural and historical contexts. While, for example, women students now outnumber men students in further education colleges in the UK, in Ethiopia, women constitute only 20% of students in technical, vocational education and training (Gonon *et al.*, 2001), and the main issue in many countries remains girls' access to *primary* schooling (EFA, 2005). This is not to argue, however, that gender inequalities in the UK post-secondary sector are not an issue, but rather that attention to the different formations and patterns of gender inequity in different local, national and international contexts, as mediated by 'race'/ethnicity, social class and other markers of difference, is important.

In many ways, to talk of the post-secondary *sector* of education suggests that it is a singular, unified and coherent segment of the field of education. In fact, it is considerably varied, encompassing a broad spectrum of educational participants, programs and institutions. In general, it refers to education beyond secondary schooling, although the term 'post-compulsory education' is more usually used in the UK to incorporate voluntary attendance at school or college beyond the school-leaving age (age 16), as well as post-school education. In the USA, the term tends to refer to post-high-school education, and includes community colleges and higher education institutions. Post-secondary education also encompasses vocational education and training, adult and community provision, lifelong learning, higher education, apprenticeships and work-based learning.

Given the breadth and complexity of the sector, the focus of this chapter is necessarily selective. I will concentrate on education and training provided predominantly by further, community, vocational and technical colleges, that is, non-higher-education, post-secondary provision. I will use further education (FE) colleges in the UK as my main point of reference, highlighting comparable patterns across other countries where possible. Global trends, in particular the increasing dominance of neo-liberalism and the growth of education and training markets, provide the wider context for developments in the sector (Lakes and Carter, 2004), and although the impact of such trends is contingent on local systems, processes and priorities, similar patterns can be identified across a number of countries.

In the UK, further and vocational education has always been the poor relation of the education system in terms of both financial resources and levels of prestige, despite catering for the vast majority of post-16-year-olds and adults in the education system. A similar lack of status and recognition has also been noted in Australia, where the sector has been referred to as 'the etcetera part of education' (Fooks, 1994; cited by Butler and Ferrier, 2000). The reasons, I suggest, are to do primarily with social class. While the majority of white, middle-class students attend the better-resourced school sixth forms, working-class and minority ethnic students are over-represented in FE colleges. These colleges now offer a range of academic and vocational courses for a wide range of students, but they have their roots in the provision of technical and craft education for working-class men, and they still tend to be seen as providing for those who are not academically inclined and/or have 'failed' in the school system.

Most mainstream work in this field has tended to ignore gender issues completely, and although there is a growing body of critical feminist literature on higher education, there still remains relatively little related to further and vocational education in the UK. Butler and Ferrier, in a review of literature on women and vocational education in Australia, conclude that there is an extensive body of relevant work, but that much remains hidden or inaccessible. They note, 'there are very many women who are the embodied holders of important local knowledges of a breadth of events, struggles and issues that may never be recorded as "literature"' (Butler and Ferrier, 2000: 5).

THE GENDER/ING OF FURTHER AND VOCATIONAL EDUCATION

Technical and vocational education has traditionally been a masculine arena, with men dominating the system as lecturers/instructors and students/trainees for much of its history. In contrast, adult and community education, often positioned as education 'for leisure', has traditionally been seen as a more feminine arena. The reasons for these gendered constructions of educational forms and arenas are multiple and draw on common themes in feminist theory, including the public/private dichotomy, associated and essentialized notions of sex and gender, and (differential, classed and racialized) constructions of masculinity and femininity. As will be seen, while there have certainly been some changes in the gendering of the sector both in the UK and elsewhere, gendered patterns remain stubbornly persistent.

The primary purpose of further and vocational education, both historically and in the contemporary arena, has been to meet the needs of the labor market through the supply of skilled/trained workers. Work on the sector has recognized class issues: 'the history of technical and further education in Britain is also a history of our class system' (Flint and Austin, 1994; p13), but gender has tended to be completely ignored. As Butler and Ferrier (2000) note, in relation to vocational education and training (VET) in Australia, a gendered construction of 'work' and the economy is evident in this emphasis on the needs of the labor market – ignoring the unpaid/domestic work so often done by women. Yet, although the history of FE is predominantly one of education for (some) men, working-class women have not been entirely ignored. Despite pervasive assumptions about women's 'natural' caring and domestic abilities, there is a history of educational provision designed to ensure that young (working-class) women learnt how to perform these duties 'properly', that is, in terms of middle-class values. Skeggs (1997) examined the history of caring courses to show how working-class young women were schooled in their domestic role as unpaid workers in the home and community. Women have, of course, always been integral to the labor market, and such courses were concerned to provide the labor to support men in their productive roles while also ensuring the 'proper' reproduction and nurturing of future generations of workers. The dominant gender paradigm was one of women's essential difference from men and of women's 'natural' and proper place being in the private domestic sphere – even where this was not their own home but the domestic sphere of the middle-classes where they went into service.

Assumptions about women's 'natural' roles and interests persisted. After World War II, a time when many women entered traditionally masculine areas of employment in the UK, FE was still concerned to offer classes to meet 'women's specialized interests', that is, those to do with home-making (Ministry of Education, 1947), while key national reports on education in the 1950s and 1960s persisted in identifying subject areas most suitable to girls and women. It was only in the late 1970s and 1980s that notions of gender equity began to enter overtly the discursive field of further and vocational education.

The participation of women students in the sector increased dramatically at this time. An analysis of student participation in one English region reported that in 1973, men outnumbered women in all areas of FE study, but, by 1993, this picture was reversed entirely (Wallis, 1996). However, a more detailed analysis of the 1993 statistics shows that, although women were now in the majority in broad areas such as science and agriculture, this was still highly gendered, with, for example, women in science studying nursery nursing. Furthermore, in Australia in the 1980s, women's skills and work still went largely unrecognized, with far fewer vocational education and training opportunities available for women than for men (Pocock, 1988). There was, however, an increase in provision for women students in FE in the UK at this time, and this was matched by some increase in the proportion of women staff (Deem, *et al.*, 2000). In the 1970s, men constituted 81% of lecturing staff, a figure that had reduced to 70% by the early 1990s (Hall, 1994).

Feminist research highlighted a range of issues facing women students at this time, including gendered subject segregation, sexist practices and curricula, the marginalization of women, and the reproduction of gender inequalities and power relations (see Cockburn, 1987; Weiner *et al.*, 1998). Pocock (1988; cited by Butler and Ferrier, 2000) reported that the college environment in Australia tended to be dominated by young men and was often a hostile space for women, with inappropriate posters and graffiti, sexual harassment and no child-care provision. Stanworth, in research in a UK FE college, argued that subtle practices continued to generate a sexual hierarchy of worth in the coeducational classroom. She observed gendered teacher expectations of young women and men students, a greater level of classroom attention demanded by and given to the men, and the sexual innuendo of a male teacher. She argued that in such a context, women learn to accept second place and that education 'tends to act as a vehicle for the reproduction of patterns of subordination and domination which characterize our society' (Stanworth, 1983: 14). Young women were not passive 'dupes' in this context: they recognised the sexual differentiation that took place but, argued Stanworth, did not have a theoretical framework within which to understand their experiences. Skegg's (1991) ethnographic study of young women taking caring courses in an FE college in England also highlighted the normalization of masculinity in education through the regulation of sexuality, while stressing the young women's agency in the ways in which they challenged masculinity (albeit within the confines of heterosexuality).

The 1980s were also characterized by significant levels of feminist activity in education in the UK (Weiner, 1994; Leonard, 1999; Leathwood, 2004), with anti-racist work and positive image campaigns around lesbian and gay issues also contributing to a climate of intense progressive educational and political activity in some colleges. Activities included liberal feminist initiatives focusing on equal opportunities, such as programs to encourage women to take science and technology subjects, as well as more radical initiatives concerned with, for example, challenging the construction of those subjects as masculine and ethnocentric. Campaigns were mounted to rid colleges of sexist curricula and images, policies on sexual harassment were drawn up, and women-only courses and activities were established. There were also attempts to 'mainstream' (although this was not the language used at the time) anti-sexist and anti-racist work to produce a more inclusive curriculum, inspired by second-wave feminist practices of consciousness-raising to provide students with the theoretical and political framework that Stanworth (1983) had identified as missing in her research. Although these activities made a difference to many women working and studying in colleges at that time, and equality issues were firmly placed on the agenda, this level of activity and challenge was not sustained. Some feminists have since problematized many of the approaches used, with, for example, Kenway *et al.* (1994: 194) arguing that many young women encouraged to take traditionally masculine subjects 'felt diminished or insulted because their different preferences for knowledge and work were implicitly downgraded'. The emergence of identity politics also led to some fragmentation of feminist and equality activity, but it was the rise of the New Right that was most significant in the gradual undermining of feminist work in education (Epstein, 1993; Leonard, 1999; Arnot, 2002).

Within the UK, the growing marketization of the FE sector was marked by increased competition, privatization, new managerialism and the 'cult of efficiency'. Cuts in public funding, intensified workloads, and a discourse of derision of teachers and lecturers, along with explicit attacks on feminist and other progressive campaigns, combined to undermine feminist work in colleges. Neoliberal economic restructuring has had a global impact and has served to mask inequalities, as Fenwick (2004a) noted in relation to Canada. Henry and Taylor (1993), writing about the Australian context, also note that equality has been reframed by discourses of economic rationalism, and refocused from notions of empowering disadvantaged groups to an emphasis on individual rights in a market economy. Yet, the market did bring some benefits for some women. For example, in the UK, mature women returners to education were identified as a key new market for colleges in the 1980s, and specific courses and facilities for women students were encouraged and supported.

Yet, the New Right backlash, accompanied by a new vocationalism, had a heavy impact on the FE sector. While elements of the new vocationalism in relation to schooling in the UK included reference to equal opportunities (Arnot, 2002), the college sector was largely dominated by narrow and highly gender-segregated training courses based on a human capital model, a process which Nicoll and Chappell (1998) also noted in Australia. The increasing emphasis on key skills for the workplace tends to be based on masculinist constructions of competence and workplace effectiveness (Blackmore, 1997), with women's skills continually undervalued (Fenwick, 2004a). Greater control of the curriculum to reflect market ideology was also in evidence in the UK, with assessment systems ensuring fewer opportunities for lecturers to subvert this (Kilminster, 1994). Of course, some women were able to benefit from the courses on offer, and feminist teaching staff continued to insert a feminist-inspired curriculum as far as possible, but, for many, such courses tended to reinforce and reconstruct the gendered, classed and racialied patterns of the labor market.

Today, women are in the majority in the FE sector in the UK, representing 61% of all students in 2003-04. And they are doing well, out-performing their male colleagues even in subjects previously regarded as masculine. There is, however, continued gender segmentation of the sector, with women students constituting 77% of those in adult and community education in 2003-04, but only 41% of those in work-based learning (LSC, 2005a). Those parts of the sector with the highest proportion of women students, and/or provision specifically aimed at addressing gender inequities, appear to be continually under-funded or at risk of funding reductions. Adult education in FE colleges in the UK, for example, recently suffered a severe funding cut, while Butler and Ferrier (2000) noted that adult and community education is Australia is also the most poorly resourced part of the VET sector. Such provision tends to be seen as marginal to the needs of the labor market and hence not a priority, reflecting the human capital rationale underpinning much post-secondary education. Lasonen (2001) notes that, in Ethiopia, women are underrepresented in technical and vocational training programmes, but 'nonformal' education provides a range of useful learning opportunities for women and other marginalized groups. However, this has lower levels of resourcing and prestige. Legislative changes in the USA in recent years also reduced support for women and girls in vocational education and training (NCWGE, 2001). Social class continues to play a significant role in access to educational opportunities, with Connole (2000) in Australia noting that material factors, such as low levels of income, poor transport and inadequate housing, continue to limit women's participation in VET. Furthermore, it is the most senior and/or most highly qualified, and full-time, rather than part-time, staff who are most likely to receive job-related training, with men receiving more hours training per week than women on average (DfES, 2004a). Women's significantly lower participation than that of men in on-the-job training is a global phenomenon (World Bank, 2003).

Subject segmentation also remains highly gendered across the world (see Gonon *et al.*, 2001). In the UK, most apprentices in child-care are women, while apprenticeships in construction, engineering, skilled trades and information technology are overwhelmingly taken by men (Miller *et al.*, 2004). Women achieve more National Vocational Qualifications than men, but these are mostly in hairdressing – that is, in traditional, and low-paid, women's work. In Botswana, too, hairdressing is the main training provision for women (Akoojee *et al.*, 2005), while, in Korea, training in construction is generally taboo for women (Pae and Lakes, 2004). Yet, while there are some indications that young women in the UK are more willing to consider non-traditional career options than in the past, broadly gendered patterns of career choice persist, with girls more likely to choose caring and artistic careers, and boys technical and scientific ones (Francis, 2000). The association of women with personal service and caring courses and men with technical areas remains.

There are also some indications that classroom cultures and practices remain not only highly gendered, but also, in some cases, hostile to women, although there is little contemporary feminist research of the kind that Stanworth (1983) and Skeggs (1997) undertook in the UK, or to match that of Pocock (1988) in Australia (Butler and Ferrier, 2000). There has, however, been work on the construction and normalization of masculinities within the context of the sexual cultures of FE (Haywood and Mac an Ghaill, 1997). A recent study on 'transforming learning cultures in FE' in the UK, while not specifically focusing on gender issues, is highlighting the persistence of classed and gendered learning cultures, values and identifications in vocational provision (Colley *et al.*, 2003), while Pae and Lakes

(2004) note the pressures and demands of particular (and classed) constructions of femininity on women in vocational education in Korea. In the UK, Dale *et al.* (2005) report a lack of support and encouragement for women wanting to enter non-traditional fields, a lack of women lecturers, and discrimination from employers. Evidence of bullying of young women in non-traditional areas in the UK (Miller *et al.*, 2005), and reluctance on the part of young women to work in these areas because of a culture of 'machismo, bullying and harassment' (EOC, 2004: 4), are matched in Australia, where women in non-traditional trades in VET all too often have to deal with unacceptable behaviour from employers, teaching staff and other students (Connole, 2000). Butler and Ferrier (2000: 6) note that, 'despite the efforts of the last decade and beyond, the culture and practices of VET remain masculinized, as do its structures and processes'. Indeed, resistance to change was identified both in the VET sector in Australia (ibid.) and among some employers in the UK (Miller *et al.*, 2005).

While the position of women staff in the sector has improved, gendered and racialized patterns remain. Women now represent 54% of full-time staff in FE colleges in the UK, and 70% of part-time staff (LSC, 2005b). Black staff, however, are still under-represented in lecturing (and management) posts (Maylor *et al.*, 2002).[1] The patterns of subject segregation identified for students are also replicated for staff. Women lecturers, for example, are far more likely to be in social care departments, and minority ethnic lecturers are disproportionately represented in basic skills and continuing education departments (ibid.). Administrative support work in colleges is done predominantly by women, with minority ethnic women more likely to be in such posts than in teaching or management (ibid.). Although in recent years (white) women have begun to make some inroads into middle-management positions (Deem *et al.*, 2000), men still hold three-quarters of all the principal/executive director posts in colleges, and black staff are still seriously under-represented in management posts (Maylor *et al.*, 2002). The new public sector management practices that have accompanied the growing marketization of the sector have opened up some opportunities for (mainly white) women staff in FE in the UK, particularly at middle-management level, but there has also been a move in the culture of FE management 'from a largely benign, liberal paternalism, to a more aggressive, competitive, instrumental style of managing' (Whitehead, 1997: 152). The management opportunities that have been opened up for women are therefore problematic, with Ozga and Walker (1999: 111) arguing that new managerialism 'co-opts women managers into using their "people and process" skills in improving economy and efficiency', but often at great cost to the women themselves. While there is evidence of women staff resisting new managerialism (Leonard, 1998), there are particular difficulties and costs in negotiating both feminist and/or feminine personal identities with FE manager and other staff identities in the contemporary context (Leathwood 2000; 2005), and in facilitating positive gender equity reform from such positions (Ozga, 2000). Yet in many countries, such as Ethiopia, women are still seriously under-represented in staff positions, including lecturer posts (Lasonen, 2001).

Differential gendered outcomes for students also remain. Despite women's overall achievements in education, a higher proportion of women than men of working age in the UK have no qualifications (14.9% of women compared to 12.4% of men) (DfES, 2004b), a finding that is paralleled in Australia (Butler and Ferrier, 2000). Furthermore, men working full-time earn, on average, more than equivalently qualified women working full-time at all qualification levels (DfES, 2004b), with the pay gap between full-time employed men and women in the UK now 19.5%. Young men who enter traditionally female areas of study and employment in France still gain better labor market positions than women entering the same fields (Couppie and Epiphane, 2001). Opportunities for social mobility for working-class young people have reduced in the last 20 years in the UK, and these outcomes are classed and racialized. For those young women who do succeed academically, the psycho-social costs can be high (Walkerdine *et al.*, 2001).

Despite this, the main gender equity concern remains the lower levels of achievement and participation of young men in post-16 education and training. Yet, as the above analysis indicates, in the gendering of further and vocational education, it is primarily women who lose out, although working-class and minority ethnic men are also disadvantaged by the classed assumptions of the sector as a whole and the consequent lower levels of prestige and funding than in other sectors of education.

Although there is some recognition in UK government circles that gender subject stratification is a problem, this is largely because a skill/ 'manpower' shortage has been identified in certain predominantly masculine industries such as construction, and hence women are sought to fill the human capital gap. Continued gender subject stratification, along with women's lower levels of pay, is constructed not as a consequence of social, cultural, and economic processes and structures, but as an outcome of girls' and women's choices. Such conceptualizations fail to acknowledge the ways in which these macrostructures and processes contribute to such gendered outcomes, nor the costs to women who choose to study and work in highly masculinist environments. The differential valuing and financial rewards of traditional women's areas of work, compared to those of men, are rarely questioned.

The notion of 'choice' is particularly problematic, not least because it is based on highly gendered constructions of 'economic man' as a rational, choice-making individual free of domestic responsibilities (Ferber and Nelson, 1993), but also because it locates the responsibility with individual girls and women, who are then positioned as making the 'wrong' choices – or 'irrational' ones when faced with evidence of the higher earning potential of traditionally masculine areas of work. And given women's resistance to entering such areas despite the number of programs which attempt to persuade them to do so, their choices can also be constructed as evidence of their 'natural' wants and desires, and hence of women's essential difference from men. While few in UK government circles would admit to holding such views, the lack of concern about persistent gender inequalities in further/vocational education and the labor market indicates, I suggest, a sense of gender essentialism and inevitability underpinning dominant policy discourses in this arena. Worryingly, Fenwick (2004b) reports a similar sense of inevitability about gendered patterns of work and domestic labor among young women in Canada. Such inevitability is, of course, convenient for a global (and local) economy both built upon and requiring continuing inequalities in paid and unpaid labour.

TOWARD GENDER EQUITY?

In many ways, the contemporary context is perhaps more hostile to feminist and gender reform work than it was, for example, in the UK in the 1980s, with neo-liberalism, individualism, choice discourses and the human capital model, along with a sense that gender inequality has been dealt with in the West, all serving to deny and/or disguise persistent inequalities and undermine feminist concerns and activities. Yet, feminism has a proud history of struggle against overwhelming odds – and now is not the time to quit.

Of course, there are positive developments. The considerable increase in women's participation in further and vocational education in the West is important, and global commitments to enhancing women's access to such provision in the rest of the world are in place.[2] New vocational education and training projects for women are regularly established across the world, and although the rationale is often primarily a human capital one reflecting the involvement of the World Bank, these programs have the potential to make a difference to women's lives and to their local communities. The construction of vocational areas as masculine or feminine is open to change – medicine, for example, has long been considered a masculine arena in the UK, but more women than men are now entering this field. There is also evidence that many young women will consider non-traditional careers (EOC, 2005) and that others resist traditional norms about 'appropriate' femininity and associated areas of study and work (see Cho, 2000). And despite accounts of the failure of feminist interventions in the 1980s, a powerful legacy of this work remains in the actions of individual teachers (Leonard, 1999). Feminist educational professionals continue to make a difference through a commitment to feminist pedagogies and curricula, and feminist networks continue to campaign and organize.[3]

Yet, there is still plenty to do, on both macro-and microlevels, in critiquing policy, challenging employers and developing educational practice. Continuing to question and confront the assumed inevitability of both neo-liberalism and persisting inequalities on a global level is crucial, as is the repeated assertion that gender is a social construct and hence open to change. Within the sector, there remains a need to provide students with an opportunity to engage with and construct theoretical and political frameworks that can help them to make sense of their gendered experiences – of the kind that Stanworth (1983) argued was required in FE in the UK 25 years ago. Fenwick (2004a: 148) insists that:

emancipatory vocational education is vital, beginning with a critical analysis of the effects of neo-liberal ideology and gendered structures on the workplace, examining the patterns creating increased insecurity and workloads, then helping people to take action to resist or transform it.

We also need to move away from assimilationist approaches that try to change women to fit into existing cultures, structures and practices (Kenway *et al.*, 1994; Yates, 1998; Butler and Ferrier, 2000; Eyre *et al.*, 2004), and focus on contesting masculinist educational and employment assumptions and contexts. Of course, good careers advice is important, but we also need to take account of issues of identity, pleasure, desire and investment (see Kenway *et al.*, 1994) in girl's and women's educational participation and employment preferences, and in our own educational and political activities. We constantly need to be asking 'which women' are succeeding, and continually draw attention to the structures, cultures and processes which keep other women, as well as some men, 'in their place' (Skeggs, 2004). Finally, we need to break the silence around the differential valuing of traditionally feminine subjects and areas of work – both paid and unpaid. Why should plumbing and construction be valued and paid so much more than work in the caring fields? By repeatedly asserting the importance of this work and the high level of skills involved, we not only challenge the patriarchal assumptions that underpin the economy and the labor market, but also ensure that we recognize and respect the work of women in traditionally feminine areas of employment, and the decisions of those who choose to enter these areas of study.

As Butler and Ferrier (2000) note, there is plenty of advice about what needs to be done to tackle gender and other inequities in the sector – the issue is the political will to act.

REFERENCES

Akoojee, S, Gewer, A and McGrath, S (2005) *Vocational education and training in Southern Africa: a comparative study.* Cape Town: HSRC Press.

Arnot, M (2002) *Reproducing gender? Essays on educational theory and feminist politics.* London: RoutledgeFalmer.

Blackmore, J (1997) The gendering of skill and vocationalism in twentieth-century Australian education, in Halsey, AH, Lauder, H, Brown, P and Stuart Wells, A (eds) *Education: culture, economy, society.* Oxford: Oxford University Press.

Butler, E and Ferrier, F (2000) *'Don't be too polite, girls!' Women, work and vocational education and training: a critical review of the literature.* Kensington Park, Australia: NCVER.

Cho, MK (2000) Bodily regulation and vocational schooling. *Gender and Education,* 12: 149–64.

Cockburn, C (1987) *Two-track training: sex inequalities in the youth training scheme.* London: Macmillan.

Colley, H, James, D, Tedder, M and Diment, K (2003) Learning as becoming in vocational education and training: class, gender and the role of vocational habitus. *Journal of Vocational Education and Training,* 55: 471–97.

Connole, H (2000) *Packaging training for gender equity.* Darlinghurst: TAFE NSW.

Couppie, T and Epiphane, D (2001) Closing the gender gap? Non-traditional curriculum choices and entry into working life. *Cereq Training and Employment,* 44(July–September): 1–4.

Dale, A, Jackson, N and Hill, N (2005) *Women in non-traditional training and employment*. Manchester: Equal Opportunities Commission.

Deem, R, Ozga, JT and Prichard, C (2000) Managing further education: is it still men's work too? *Journal of Further and Higher Education*, 24: 231–50.

DfES (2004a) *Education and training statistics for the United Kingdom*. London: TSO.

DfES (2004b) *The level of highest qualification held by young people and adults: England 2003*. National Statistics First Release, SRF 03/2004: Department for Education and Skills.

EFA (2005) *Education for all: the quality imperative*. UNESCO Publishing.

EOC (2004) *Apprenticeships Task Force meeting 8 December 2004: task force update on recent report (ATF/04/24B)*. Manchester: Equal Opportunities Commission.

EOC (2005) *Free to choose: tackling gender barriers to better jobs*. Manchester: Equal Opportunities Commission.

Epstein, D (1993) *Changing classroom cultures: anti-racism, politics and schools*. Stoke-on-Trent: Trentham Books.

Eyre, L, Lovell, TA and Smith, CA (2004) Gender equity policy and education: reporting on/from Canada, in Ali, S, Benjamin, S and Mauthner, M (eds) *The politics of gender and education: critical perspectives*. London: Palgrave Macmillan.

Fenwick, T (2004a) Gender and the new economy – enterprise discourses in Canada: implications for workplace learning and education, in Lakes, RD and Carter, PA (eds) *Globalizing education for work: comparative perspectives on gender and the new economy*. Mahwah, NJ: Lawrence Erlbaum Associates.

Fenwick, T (2004b) What happens to girls? Gender, work and learning in Canada's 'new economy'. *Gender and Education* 16: 169–85.

Ferber, MA and Nelson, JA (eds) (1993) *Beyond economic man: feminist theory and economics*. Chicago: University of Chicago Press.

Flint, C and Austin, M (eds) (1994) *Going further: essays in further education*. Blagdon: The Staff College and the Association for Colleges.

Francis, B (2000) *Boys, girls and achievement: addressing the classroom issues*. London: RoutledgeFalmer Press.

Gonon, P, Haefeli, K, Heikkinen, A and Ludwig, I (eds) (2001) *Gender perspectives on vocational education: historical, cultural and policy aspects*. Bern: Peter Lang.

Hall, V (1994) *Further education in the United Kingdom*. London: Collins.

Haywood, C and Mac an Ghaill, M (1997) 'A man in the making': sexual masculinities within changing training cultures. *Sociological Review*, 45: 576–90.

Henry, M and Taylor, S (1993) Gender equity and economic rationalism: an uneasy alliance, in Lingard, B, Knight, J and Porter, P (eds) *Schooling reform in hard times*. London: Falmer.

Kenway, J, Willis, S, Blackmore, J and Rennie, L (1994) Making 'hope practical' rather than 'despair convincing': feminist post-structuralism, gender reform and educational change. *British Journal of the Sociology of Education*, 15: 187–210.

Kilminster, S (1994) Changing working-class women's education: shifting ideologies. Paper presented at the Annual SCUTREA conference. Available on Education-line at www.leeds.ac.uk/educol.

Lakes, RD and Carter, PA (eds) (2004) *Globalizing education for work: comparative perspectives on gender and the new economy*. Mahwah, NJ: Lawrence Erlbaum Associates.

Lasonen, J (2001) Poverty and powerlessness in Ethiopia: shaping gender equity through technical, vocational education, and training, in Gonon, P, Haefeli, K, Heikkinen, A and Ludwig, I (eds) *Gender perspectives on vocational education: historical, cultural and policy aspects*. Bern: Peter Lang.

Leathwood, C (2000) Happy families? Pedagogy, management and parental discourses of control in the corporatised further education college. *Journal of Further and Higher Education*, 24: 163–82.

Leathwood, C (2004) Doing difference in different times: theory, politics and women-only spaces in education. *Women's Studies International Forum*, 27: 447–58.

Leathwood, C (2005) 'Treat me as a human being – don't look at me as a woman': femininities and professional identities in further education. *Gender and Education*, 17: 387–410.

Leonard, D (1999) Teachers, femocrats and academics: activism in London in the 1980s, in Myers, K (ed) *Whatever happened to equal opportunities?* Milton Keynes: Open University Press.

Leonard, P (1998) Gendering change? Management, masculinity and the dynamics of incorporation. *Gender and Education,* 10: 71–84.

LSC (2005a) *National statistics first release: further education, work-based learning for young people and adult and community learning – learner numbers in England – October 2004. ILR/SFR06.* Coventry: Learning and Skills Council.

LSC (2005b) *Staff statistics 2003-04,* London: www.lsc.gov.uk/National/Partners/Data/Statistics/StaffStatistics/StaffStatistics.htm (Accessed 15 June 2005).

Maylor, U, Dalgety, J, Leathwood, C and Archer, L (2002) *National survey of Black staff in further education: final report.* London: Institute for Policy Studies in Education, University of North London, for the Commission for Black Staff in Further Education.

Miller, L, Neathey, F, Pollard, E and Hill, D (2004) *Occupational segregation, gender gaps and skill gaps.* Manchester: Equal Opportunities Commission.

Miller, L, Pollard, E, Neathey, F, Hill, D and Ritchie, H (2005) *Gender segregation in apprenticeships.* Manchester: Equal Opportunities Commission.

Ministry of Education (1947) *The scope and content of its opportunities under the Education Act, 1944.* Ministry of Education Pamphlet no. 8: Further Education.

NCWGE (2001) *Invisible again: the impact of changes on federal funding on vocational programs for women and girls.* Washington, DC: National Coalition for Women and Girls in Education.

Nicoll, K and Chappell, C (1998) Policy effects: 'flexible learning' in higher education and the 'de-differentiation' of the vocational sector. *Studies in Continuing Education,* 20: 39–40.

Ozga, J (2000) *Policy research in educational settings: contested terrain.* Buckingham: Open University Press.

Ozga, J and Walker, L (1999) In the company of men, in Whitehead, S and Moodley, R (eds) *Transforming managers: gendering change in the public sector.* London: UCL Press.

Pae, HK and Lakes, RD (2004) Preparation for (in)equality: women in South Korean vocational education, in Lakes, RD and Carter, PA (eds) *Globalizing education for work: comparative perspectives in gender and the new economy.* Mahwah, NJ: Lawrence Erlbaum Associates.

Pocock, B (1988) *Demanding skill: women and technical education in Australia.* North Sydney: Allen and Unwin.

Skeggs, B (1991) Challenging masculinity and using sexuality. *British Journal of the Sociology of Education,* 12: 127–39.

Skeggs, B (1997) *Formations of class and gender.* London: Sage.

Skeggs, B (2004) *Class, self, culture.* London: Routledge.

Stanworth, M (1983) *Gender and schooling.* London: Hutchinson.

Walkerdine, V, Lucey, H and Melody, J (2001) *Growing up girl: psychosocial explorations of gender and class.* Basingstoke: Palgrave.

Wallis, J (1996) Women in further education: a case study. Paper presented at the 1996 Annual SCUTREA Conference 2-4 July (University of Leeds) (available on Education-line @www.leeds.ac.uk/educol).

Weiner, G (1994) *Feminisms in education: an introduction.* Buckingham: Open University Press.

Weiner, GW, Arnot, M and David, M (1998) Who benefits from schooling? Equality issues in Britain, in Mackinnon, A, Elgqvist-Saltzman, I and Prentice, A (eds) *Education into the 21st century.* London: Falmer Press.

Whitehead, S (1997) Men/managers and the shifting discourses of post-compulsory education. *Research in Post-Compulsory Education,* 1: 151–68.

World Bank (2003) *Lifelong learning in the global knowledge economy: challenges for developing countries.* Washington, DC: World Bank.

Yates, L (1998) Constructing and deconstructing 'girls' as a category of concern, in Mackinnon, A Elgqvist-Saltzman, I and Prentice, A (eds) *Education into the 21st century.* London: Falmer Press.

NOTES

1. The Commission for Black Staff in Further Education, which funded this research, used the term 'Black' to refer to members of *African, African-Caribbean, Asian and other visible minority ethnic communities who are oppressed by racism.*

2. E.g Gender equality in education is one of the goals of the Education For All programme endorsed by 164 governments at the World Education forum, Dakar, Senegal, April 2000.

3. E.g. Women in Adult and Vocational Education (WAVE) in Australia and the Gender and Education Association (GEA) in the UK.

13

Gender and Higher Education

Sara Delamont

Women are newcomers to higher education. Men had been students for over 800 years in Europe and 200 in the USA before women were admitted a century ago. The higher education of the Islamic and Chinese civilizations were also closed to women. This chapter focuses on the USA and the UK and on students, not staff (see Chapter 34 in this volume). It deals with students, in three eras (1840–1920, 1920–70, 1970–2000), focusing on architecture, organizational structures, curricula, pedagogy, and social conventions. Architecture is a shorthand for domestic arrangements, such as catering and heating, as well as the buildings and landscapes. These are five dimensions of change in the higher education of women.

BACKGROUND

For two centuries, industrial societies have seen the steady expansion of higher education. New institutions were founded, new subjects taught, research expanded, staff numbers increased, and undergraduate and postgraduate numbers grew and grew. For example, in Germany, the number of male students rose from 13,000 to 61,000 between 1870 and 1914 (Mazon, 2003). Expansion, to meet the needs of the labor market, has meant more men and then women attending universities. In 2006, some experience as a student is common to between half and two-thirds of the 19–25 age-group in industrialized countries, whereas, in 1905, only 5% of men, and a tiny percentage of women, had ever been students. Mary Hamilton, a student at Cambridge in this period, recalled:

> People used to say to me 'You are at College?' and stare, as though they quite expected to see horns and a tail peeping out from under my skirt (1944: p24).

The removal of financial barriers and explicit class barriers widened the intake from the lower social classes. Changing attitudes to race, ethnicity, and religion led to the removal of barriers against those who were not white Protestants. In England, for example, before 1872, only men prepared to attest to their belief in the tenets of the Anglican Church could go to Oxford and Cambridge, thus banning Jews, non-conformists and Catholics, Sikhs, Buddhists, Muslims and Hindus as well as atheists and agnostics.

Changes in the graduate labor market affected women's involvement in universities. In the nineteenth century, as the professions and the sciences (Rossiter, 1982) became all-graduate, entry requirements became formal and legally enshrined; their all-male status was confirmed. Feminists therefore campaigned simultaneously for the right to enter higher education and those occupations. Early female graduates had few opportunities but teaching, until, after 1870, the other professions slowly opened up to women, and the utility of a degree for women grew. Medicine is the best-known example (Blake, 1990), but dentistry, veterinary science, law, accountancy, and theology followed (Franz, 1965; Holcombe, 1983).

The changing women's movement radically affected women in higher education. There are three broad phases. From 1840 to 1920, women fought for basic civil rights: the vote; ownership of their own property; and access to academic schooling, higher education, and the professions. Women campaigned to learn the traditionally 'male' subjects closed to them, such as Latin and physics. From 1920 to 1970, there was a second wave of feminism, focused on issues affecting married women, mothers, and children, such as access to contraception (for respectable married women), improved health care, and what Lemons (1973) calls 'social' feminism. The Great Depression (1929–39) was tough on institutions that offered an academic education to women: when parental incomes were falling, the education of daughters was an easy thing on which to economize (Delamont, 2003a). First-wave feminism was deeply unfashionable, and viewed with suspicion: the spinster becomes a figure of scorn. Holtby (1934) offers a refutation of that discourse of derision. After the 1939–45 war, there were attacks on academic and professional education for women, and calls for better domestic training (Friedan, 1969; Wilson, 1980). Domesticity was lauded, the age of marriage low, and the birth rate in the middle classes high.

Third-wave feminism developed after 1970 with refocused campaigns to open up courses and professions still closed to women: most noticeably, the occupations of 'clergy, ministers and priests'. Because third-wave feminism appeared in the same era as the student protests and the anti-war movement, it showed itself in higher education as well as the labor market and public politics. Third-wave feminism produced a new scholarly field (women's studies) and fundamental intellectual challenges to the epistemology of many disciplines (see Minnich *et al.*, 1988; Lie and O'Leary, 1990; Tierney, 1993; Weiler, 2001; McLaughlin and Tierney, 2002; Gumport, 2003). One benefit of third-wave feminism is scholarship devoted to the history of women and higher education. Researchers have focused on both staff (Dyhouse, 1995) and students in higher education. There are histories of individual institutions, such as Girton College, Cambridge (Bradbrook, institutions, 1969) and Mills College in California (Keep, 1946); comparative histories, such as that by Horowitz (1984) on the architectural styles of the American women's colleges; biographies of pioneers, such as Carey Thomas (Finch, 1947), Catherine Beecher (Sklar, 1973), and Elizabeth Wordsworth, (Battiscombe, 1978); and studies of women in medicine and science (Rossiter, 1982, 1995; Abir-Aam and Outram, 1987; Cassell, 1998). From this rich literature, the five dimensions are explored in each of the three eras.

1840–1920

This is the era of double conformity (Delamont, 1978; 1989; 1993; 2003a). Middle – and upper–middle–class ladies gained access first to academic secondary schooling and afterward to higher education, and then succeeded in surviving and even flourishing there, by adopting a strategy of double conformity. This meant not only doing all the academic work the men did but also following all the regulations about behavior, dress, and deportment that were then normal for respectable upper–middle–class ladies. Women of color, and those from the working class and from poor homes had little or no access to higher education in this period, although some used other routes, such as being pupil-teachers (Widdowson, 1980) or adult education (Purvis, 1989), to gain some higher knowledge. For those ladies who did persuade their families to pay for higher education, the institutions bore little resemblance to today's. The students understood double conformity, and they wore the hats and gloves, accepted the chaperonage, and were cautious about innovatory activities such as bicycling and field hockey. They accepted conventions about social relationships, which kept them apart not only from men, but also from Roman Catholics, suffragists, women from the lower classes, and other potential contaminations (Delamont, 1989). When much of the medical profession, many clergy, and the newspapers were hostile to the idea of educating ladies (Burstyn, 1980), the students knew, as did their teachers, that their performance, mental and physical health, marriage prospects, fertility, and ladylikeness were all under surveillance. So the women learnt ancient Greek not only to pass exams, but also to show that they could, that the attempt would not give them brain fever or make them so unattractive to men that they would never marry, and that they could still make small talk to their mothers' visitors and do embroidery. Agnata Frances Ramsay Butler (Delamont, 2004a), who got the best classics degree result in Cambridge in 1887, and then married the Master of Trinity College, Cambridge, was a new type of marriageable lady (Delamont, 1989). Many graduates of this era chose heterosexual celibacy and the respectable life of the self-supporting career woman made possible by the opening up of professions (Vicinus, 1985).

The architecture of the pioneering institutions embodied their mission. In a comparative study of Mount Holyoke, Vassar, Wellesley, Smith, Radcliffe, Bryn Mawr and Barnard, Horowitz (1984) shows clearly how fundamental the architecture was to the success of getting wealthy parents to pay for a college education, and to establishing the respectability of the new revolutionary institutions. The buildings had to look impressive, provide a healthy environment, and embody respectability. The buildings designed for these colleges included libraries, laboratories, chapels, study bedrooms, and facilities for physical education and exercise. Three messages were conveyed by the architecture. First, these were places where university-level learning would be done across the whole of the male curriculum of the period. So they had laboratories, but not needlework rooms. The health of the young ladies would be safeguarded against the prevalent infectious diseases (study bedrooms generously spaced along corridors, well-ventilated dormitories, etc.) and there were facilities for the physical education that the feminist pioneers introduced to counter arguments that education made ladies ill, or even killed them. So colleges had cloisters or sheltered spaces for walking, swimming pools, playing fields, tennis courts, and gymnasia, and required the students to use them (see Atkinson, 1978; 1987). These spaces were *private*, so that outsiders, especially men, could not see the young ladies in their sports clothes: that is, without corsets in gym tunics, or playing field hockey with their skirts above their ankles. Chapels reinforced the message that female students would be good Christian women.

The organizational structures set up emphasized respectability. Adult women of impeccable class position and morality were appointed to supervise the daily lives of the female students, and to enforce the social conventions. The Great Bangor Scandal of 1892 (Evans, 1990; Delamont, 1996) is a perfect example of how important this was. In mixed universities, there were separate women's halls of residence with wardens, and the overall welfare of the women students was the job of a Dean of women. In the USA, Marian Talbot of Chicago (see Talbot, 1936; Rosenberg, 1982; Delamont, 1992, 2003b) is the most famous, but there were many other redoubtable women. Bashaw (1999) analyses legendary Deans of women at Southern universities, such as Katherine S. Bowersox, who served for 32 years at Berea College in Kentucky, or Agnes Ellen Harris of Alabama.

There were two basic patterns of curricula. Institutions founded and run by the most ambitious feminists, notably, Girton College, Cambridge (Delamont, 1989; 2004b), and Smith College (Boas, 1935; Thorp, 1956), insisted that young women must do the male curriculum, even if it was old-fashioned, poorly planned or lacked intellectual coherence. Hence Cross's (1965: 37) comment that Carey Thomas's aim for Bryn Mawr was to give women an academic programme 'as rigorous and impractical as that provided at Harvard'. Similarly, Riesman and Jencks (1968: 306) wrote that 'the feminists' insisted on an education 'at least as bad as that given men'. These were 'uncompromising' institutions. Other institutions, Newnham College, Cambridge, and Lady Margaret Hall, Oxford, for example, whose founders were in the vanguard of curricula change, were keen to link the higher education of women to the innovative, not the traditional, male curricula.

Historical records do not tell us much about the pedagogy of women's education in this period. In many places, women were taught separately, but by the same male lecturers as the men: Radcliffe, for example. We do not know whether the women were taught differently, although we know they were less well grounded in maths, Latin and Greek because they had not been to well-established academic schools. As the pioneer women were all volunteers who had chosen an unusual and socially excluding path, it is likely that they were more highly motivated than many of their male counterparts, and so probably worked more enthusiastically with fewer diversions and dissipations.

In this period, women students lived at home under the surveillance of their parents, in college buildings under the surveillance of respectable ladies, or in lodgings inspected to ensure that their physical and social features were appropriate. Institutions were divided about how much housework students had to do, from some where the female students had servants as they would at home, to those where they shared the housekeeping. In many, the more junior students did some housework for the seniors. In an era of coal fires, hot water delivered in large jugs, and waitress service at communal meals, there was a great deal of work for servants. Tamboukou (2000) deals with these spatial issues and their impact on the lives of women students. She stresses the high value women students in this era placed on privacy, on having a space, however spartan, in which productive work could be done, and emotions hidden. Tamboukou also explores how the educational pioneers valued travel, and the freedom of movement that their salaries brought them. The popularity of the bicycle (Atkinson, 1978; 1987), which gave local freedom, is one example; the use of holidays to explore different landscapes another.

In this period, a generation of women chose to be single and heterosexually celibate, and upheld that as a respectable, successful lifestyle, an alternative *chosen* instead of marriage. Respectable career women lived in all-women communities in nursing, settlement work, schools, the deaconate, and higher education (Vicinus, 1985). Many lived in close, intimate relationships with other women, which need to be understood in their historical context, which was pre-Freudian, and had a very different 'take' on friendships between people of the same sex and a much more strongly developed pattern of sex segregation. Smith-Rosenberg (1985) argues eloquently that 'the long-lived, intimate, loving friendships between two women' (p53) should not be seen from a post-Freudian 'individual psychosexual perspective' but in their historical 'cultural and social setting' (p54). After the 1914–18 war, this group, by then elderly, found that their whole ideological position and way of life was regarded not only as old-fashioned, but also as deeply sinister (Deegan, 1988).

1920–1970

After the 1914–18 war, women could, in the Anglophone countries, vote and enter the majority of the learned professions (Marlow, 1999). These achievements had been primarily the work of, and had benefited, single women. After the war, there were three challenges to the ideas and the routines of the pioneers. First, the majority of the women who went to university after 1918 were not interested in heterosexual celibacy as a life choice: they wanted to marry men (see, for example, Mitchison, 1975; 1979). There was an intellectual and an embodied revulsion against the heterosexual celibacy of the educational pioneers (Jeffreys, 1985). Inside the educational institutions, there was a rejection by the students of double conformity. Fass (1979) explores how the women at American universities rebelled against the prohibition of fashionable hairstyles (shingling), clothing (short skirts), smoking, drinking, and spending time unchaperoned with men. Parallel rebellions can be traced in the other Anglophone countries.

Women also faced economic difficulties: between the wars, the depression meant that employment opportunities for educated women shrank, and the very institutions themselves struggled to survive. Enrolments fell, students had to leave because of family difficulties, and expansion plans were shelved. There was hostility in many spheres to 'spinsters' who had 'taken' jobs from men, especially war veterans, who had dependants to support. This discourse was strong, for example, in teachers' unions (Oram, 1996) and is central to Sayers' novel (1972) *Gaudy Night*, set in the 1930s in an Oxford women's college. The criminal is an embittered widow, who sees the spinster dons as harpies that sucked the lifeblood of her late husband, because they could not get husbands of their own.

The 1939–45 war meant that the labor of women was again in demand, whether they were married or single (Summerfield, 1984). Some opportunities for women in higher education widened (in the UK, all-male medical schools took women students during the war, only to revert to being all-male after 1945). The war changed sexual mores further from the conventions of the feminist, double-conformity pioneers. After this war, women in higher education found the surviving restrictions the double-conformity regime placed on their movements and behavior intolerable. The women staffing higher education were viewed as 'out of touch', negative role models. Horowitz (1984: 293) summarizes:

> Women faculty and administrators felt betrayed. Only a few years earlier they had been objects of student admiration. Now they were cast in the role of upholders of the Victorian moral order that had lost its hold over the young. Faculty and administrators, in turn, looked askance at students.

These factors affected all five themes, architecture, organization, curricula, pedagogy, and social conventions. There is less research on this era than on the period before 1920. In the USA, the coming of mass car ownership meant that the single-sex women's colleges were no longer physically isolated from cities, other colleges, and men.

Horowitz contrasts the institutions founded in the first era with three different, newly founded women's colleges, Sarah Lawrence (1926), Bennington (1932), and Scripps (1927), which offered a clean canvas (p319). No parallel institutions for British women were built in the 1920–45 period, and after the war the expansion of higher education was overwhelmingly co-educational. Women students who lived at home experienced a variety of conditions, depending on the attitudes of their parents; those in university accommodation were as closely supervised as ever; and those in lodgings were under varying degrees of physical and social control. Servants began to vanish, and women students would no longer expect to have so much domestic support. Until the late 1960s, many institutions of higher education catered for women in a segregated or semi-segregated way. In the USA, the Seven Sisters (women's colleges to match the men's Ivy League) were single sex, as were many less famous colleges. Where women were admitted to institutions that were already established for men, careful arrangements were made to safeguard the reputations of the ladies: chaperones, curfews, dress codes, and so on. Parkes (2004) in the history of the women at Trinity College, Dublin, shows how those safeguards were still in place in the 1960s.

The organization of women's higher education was shaped by the ideological climate after 1920. Concerns about 'unnatural' lesbians exercising undue influence on impressionable female students were expressed in fiction and by pundits (Jefferys, 1985). Where authority positions had been mainly held by spinsters, now men, widows, and married women were seen as better 'balanced' and more suitable to exercise control over women's higher education. However, as Dyhouse (1995) shows, most higher education institutions also had marriage bars, refused to appoint married women, and dismissed female staff who married.

The undergraduate curricula available to women between 1920 and 1970 were not gendered. However, it was almost impossible for women to find funding to continue into postgraduate scientific research (Rossiter, 1982; Dyhouse, 1995), and this meant there were few women science professors in the USA or the UK. The gender labelling of subjects was beginning to shift. Classics, which had been the highest status and the most masculine subject area, was replaced by sciences, especially physics and engineering, as the archetypically 'male' subject areas. By the 1960s, classics was no longer a male preserve: the sciences were the 'hardest', had the highest status, and were the most masculine. (Thomas,1990). Pedagogy in this period is under researched. The majority of women students after 1920 had an academic secondary education (unlike their predecessors in the nineteenth century), and they did not arrive in higher education severely disadvantaged compared to men, except perhaps in the sciences, since girls' schools were unlikely to have well equipped laboratories.

1970–2000

As far as the architecture is concerned, the big changes for women students since 1970 are the removal of supervision and the changed expectations about hygiene and privacy. Many female students live in privately rented accommodation without any university inspection of its physical or social nature: the days of the landlady are gone, and self-discipline rather than chaperonage is normal. Both private landlords and universities increasingly provide private bathrooms rather than shared ones, and facilities for doing laundry: both unheard of in the earlier periods. The scene set in the communal bathrooms in *Miss Pym Disposes* (Tey, 1947) is unimaginable today. The level of heating expected and the provision of refrigerators have also changed student accommodation. Self-catering and the abolition of formal meals served by waiting staff in favour of cafeterias with self-service food have changed the consumption patterns of students. In the UK, the age of majority has been lowered, so students are legally adults, and universities are not *in loco parentis*. Sexual activity or non-activity is seen as a personal matter (except for those from strict religious backgrounds). Parents do not expect universities to police the sexual conduct of female students.

The big change in organizational structures is co-education. Many single-sex, higher-education institutions, such as schools of nursing, teacher-training colleges, and women's universities, founded in the 1870–1920 era, survived the period 1920–70, only to be abolished by amalgamation or co-education in the era of the third wave. The single-sex women's colleges nearly all went co-educational (for example, Vassar and Girton College, Cambridge). Nursing became a mixed occupation with co-educational training courses, and single-sex, teacher-training colleges founded in the nineteenth century were merged into co-educational institutions (Fletcher, 1984). Even where single-sex institutions survive, and few do, the students expect to see men regularly both academically and socially. So where a young lady at Vassar in 1920 had all her classes with only women, and in term time her social life was mainly lived in that isolated town with other women students, Vassar, by 2000, was mixed, the social and academic life was co-educational, and the town was no longer isolated because of car ownership. Research on student life, such as that by Moffat (1990) and Holland and Eisenstadt (1990), reveals a very different social and intellectual world from that of the two previous eras.

This era has seen feminist scholarship spread in branded women's studies courses and programs, and mainstreamed into most arts and social science disciplines, although enthusiasm for feminist political movements has largely gone after a brief flourish in the 1980s. Although there are large numbers of women in higher education all over the world, the research on them is much sparser than that on school pupils. In the USA and the UK, there are relatively few published studies of women's experiences in higher education. Holland and Eisenhart (1990) report data from the early 1980s, and urgently need replications, in the USA and other industrialized countries. Holland and Eisenhart studied women undergraduates at two American universities, one traditionally African-American, one historically white. What they found was a similar peer culture, obsessed with heterosexual dating and courtship that 'absorbed a great deal of students' time and energy' (p85). Women's status on campus, unless they made a very brave decision to ignore the norms of the peer culture, was determined by the peer status of the men they dated. As one woman was told, 'You may be able to do calculus but I am dating a football player' (p104). The research found no engagement with the academic work, and when followed up four years later, most students had abandoned any 'career' path in favour of getting any job that fitted their social arrangements, such as marriage. Robbins' (2004) study of sororities produced similar conclusions.

As far as curricula are concerned, the period since 1970 has seen many women move into the professional schools (law, dentistry, medicine, and pharmacy) and stay for postgraduate work. All capitalist countries have difficulty in recruiting and retaining women in science and technology, and most have commissioned research on 'the leaky pipeline', followed by initiatives to encourage more women into those areas (Rees, 2001). Pedagogy is a related area, in that several authors have reported that it is the pedagogical culture of science and engineering that repels women, especially the competitive elements (Tobias, 1995), which are central to the way it is taught.

CONCLUSIONS

In the period 1840–2000, therefore, there has been a double shift in the core experience of women students. Up to 1920, women students were kept physically separate from men by strong formal and informal arrangements, while campaigning to learn the same subjects taught to the same standards. Since 1950, the formal and informal barriers between men and women have been falling rapidly, especially with the coming of mass co-education in higher education and the removal of adult surveillance of the social behavior of students, but, for students in humanities and social sciences, there has been a proliferation of curriculum options, some of which mean that women study different subfields of disciplines from men. A woman student studying history in 1920 would have done exactly the same courses as a man. Today, she could choose options in feminist historiography and women's history, and de facto be studying a different history syllabus from a man who did not.

There has been a complex relationship between feminist theorizing and campaigning and the structures and cultures of higher education since the 1840s. Gaining entry to higher education was a goal for first-wave feminism, rather than posing a challenge to intellectual regimes of the institutions. Staying inside the institutions was the major task for the women of second-wave feminism, given the impact of Freudianism, fascism, and the end of feminist heterosexual celibacy in the period 1918–68. Then, after 1968, when third-wave feminism broke, came major intellectual challenges to the nature of academic disciplines, coinciding with an ethos favouring co-educational higher education, which has led to the end of single-sex institutions in British and American higher education.

REFERENCES

Abir-Aam, PG and Outram, D (eds) (1987) *Uneasy careers and intimate lives.* London: Rutgers University Press.
Atkinson, PA (1978) Fitness, feminism and schooling, in Delamont, S and Duffin, L (eds) *The nineteenth century woman.* London: Croom Helm.
Atkinson, PA (1987) The feminist physique, in Mangan, J A and Park, RJ (eds) *From fair sex to feminism.* London: Frank Cass.

Blake, C (1990) *The charge of the parasols.* London: Virago.

Bashaw, CT (1999) *Stalwart women.* New York: Teachers College Press.

Battiscombe, G (1978) *Reluctant pioneer.* London: Constable.

Boas, LS (1935) *Women's education begins.* Norton, MA: Wheaton College Press.

Bradbrook, M (1969) *That infidel place.* London: Chatto and Windus.

Burstyn, J (1980) *Victorian education and the ideal of womanhood.* London: Croom Helm.

Cassell, J (1998) *The woman in the surgeon's body.* Cambridge, MA: Harvard University Press.

Deegan, MJ (1988) *Jane Addams and the men of the Chicago School.* New Brunswick, NJ: Rutgers University Press.

Delamont, S (1978) The contradictions in ladies education, in Delamont, S and Duffin, L (eds) *The nineteenth century woman.* London: Croom Helm.

Delamont, S (1989) *Knowledgable women.* London: Routledge.

Delamont, S (1993) Distant dangers and forgotten standards. *Women's History Review,* 2: 233–52.

Delamont, S (ed) (1996) *A woman's place in education.* Aldershot: Ashgate.

Delamont, S (2003) Planning enlightenment and dignity: the girls' schools 1918–1958, in Walford, G (ed) *British private schools* (57–76) London: Woburn Press.

Delamont, S (2003b) *Feminist sociology.* London: Sage.

Delamont, S (2004a) Agnata Frances Ramsay Butler. *Oxford dictionary of national biography.* Oxford: Oxford University Press.

Delamont, S (2004b) Emily Davies. *Oxford dictionary of national biography.* Oxford: Oxford University Press.

Dyhouse, C (1995) *No distinction of sex?* London: UCL Press.

Evans, GW (1990) *Education and female emancipation.* Cardiff: University of Wales Press.

Fass, P (1979) *The damned and the beautiful.* Oxford: Oxford University Press.

Finch, E (1947) *Carey Thomas of Bryn Mawr.* New York: Harper.

Fletcher, S (1984) *Women first.* London: Athlone.

Franz, N (1965) *English women enter the professions.* Cincinnati, OH: privately printed.

Friedan, B (1963) *The feminine mystique.* Harmondsworth: Penguin.

Gumport, P (2003) *Academic pathfinders.* Westport, CT: Greenwood Press.

Hamilton, MA (1944) *Newnham.* London: Faber.

Holcombe, L (1983) *Victorian ladies at work.* Newton Abbott: David and Charles.

Holtby, W (1934) *Women and a changing civilisation.* London: Bodley Head.

Holland, DC and Eisenhart, MA (1990) *Educated in romance.* Chicago: Chicago University Press.

Horowitz, HL (1984) *Alma Mater.* New York: Knopf.

Jefferys, S (1985) *The Spinster and her enemies.* London: Pandora.

Keep, R (1946) *Fourscore and ten years.* San Francisco, CA: Mills College.

Lemons, JS (1973) *The woman citizen.* Urbana, IL: University of Illinois Press.

Lie, SS and O'Leary, E (1990) (eds) *Storming the tower.* New Brunswick, NJ: Nichols.

Lie, SS, Malik, L and Harris, D (eds) *The gender gap in higher education.* London: Kogan Page.

Marlow, J (ed) (1999) *Women and the Great War.* London: Virago.

Mazon, P (2003) *Gender and the modern research university.* Stanford, CA: Stanford University Press.

McLaughlin, O and Tierney, W G (2002) *Naming silenced lives.* New York: Routledge.

Minnich, E O'Barr, J and Rosenfeld, R (1988) (eds) *Reconstructing the academy.* Chicago: University of Chicago Press.

Mitchison, N (1975) *All change here.* London: Bodley Head.

Mitchison, N (1979) *You may well ask.* London: Gollancz.

Moffat, N (1990) *Coming of age in New Jersey.* New Brunswick, NJ: Rutgers University Press.

Oram, A (1996) *Women teachers and feminist politics.* Manchester: Manchester University Press.

Parkes, SM (2004) (ed) *A danger to the men?* Dublin: Lilliput Press.

Purvis, J (1989) *Hard lessons.* Cambridge: Polity.

Rees, TL (2001) Mainstreaming gender equality in science in the European Union. *Gender and Education,* 13: 243–60.

Riesman, D and Jencks, C (1968) *The academic revolution*. New York: Doubleday.

Robbins, A (2004) *Pledged: the secret life of sororities*. New York: Hyperion.

Rosenberg, R (1982) *Beyond separate spheres*. New Haven, CT: Yale University Press.

Rossiter, M (1982) *Women scientists in America: struggles and strategies to 1940*. Baltimore, MD: Johns Hopkins University Press.

Rossiter, M (1995) *Women scientists in America: 1940–1970*. Baltimore, MD: Johns Hopkins University Press.

Sayers, DL (1972) *Gaudy night*. London: Fontana.

Sklar, KK (1973) *Catherine Beecher*. New Haven, CT: Yale University Press.

Smith-Rosenberg, C (1985) The female world of love and ritual, in Smith-Rosenberg, C *Disorderly conduct*. (53–76) London: Oxford University Press.

Summerfield, P (1984) *Women workers in the Second World War*. London: Routledge.

Talbot, M (1936) *More than lore*. Chicago: University of Chicago Press.

Tamboukou, M (2000) Of other spaces: women's colleges at the turn of the century. *Gender, Place and Culture* 7: 247–63.

Tey, J (1947) *Miss Pym disposes*. Glasgow: Fontana.

Thorp, MF (1956) *Neilson of Smith*. New York: Oxford University Press.

Tierney, W (1993) Tenure and academic freedom in the academy, in Cooper JE and Stevens, DD (eds) *Tenure in the sacred grove*. New York: State University of New York Press.

Thomas, K (1990) *Gender and subject in higher education*. Buckingham: Open University Press.

Tobias, S (1995) *They're not dumb, they're different*. Tucson, AZ: Research Corporation.

Vicinus, M (1985) *Independent women*. London: Virago.

Weiler, K (2001) (ed) *Feminist engagements*. London: Routledge.

Widdowson, F (1980) *Going up into the next class*. London: Hutchinson.

Wilson, E (1980) *Only halfway to Paradise*. London: Tavistock.

14

Single-Sex Schooling

Diana Leonard

Many countries have had various combinations and sequences of single- and mixed-gender schooling,[1] and from the USA to Japan to Pakistan, it remains a topic of abiding interest.[2] The UK, or more specifically English and Northern Irish education, is interesting in having a long history of single-sex education for all age groups, whereas, in the USA, secondary schooling has been largely co-educational, with, until the 1970s, many prominent single-sex colleges. There have been extensive debates everywhere around the relative merits of single-sex and co-educational education at all levels, although it is generally accepted for earlier ages, and the topic certainly arouses strong emotions. This chapter will try to address what there is to be learned from past experience, and for reasons of space and clarity, it will concentrate mainly on secondary schooling, and hence mainly on the UK.

CHANGES OVER TIME

With the introduction of education for the masses in nineteenth-century Britain, many of the schools established were single sex. However, where the numbers of pupils were small (as in schools run in a single room by one teacher, providing basic education as well as childcare; or in rural areas), schools might be mixed. In larger buildings, girls and infants, and boys often entered through separate entrances and had some separate (notably cloakroom) facilities. Some lessons were mixed but others segregated. Thus, although the terms 'mixed' and 'co-education' tend to be used interchangeably, mixed-sex schools, in fact, existed well before an ideology developed that promoted educating boys and girls together (Weinberg, 1979; Brehony, 1984). Elementary/primary schooling (for 5–10-year-olds) started moving to co-education in the UK in the 1920s, though there were still single-sex primaries in some parts of the country, including London, until the 1960s.

In the first half of the nineteenth-century, it was largely boys who were sent to school among the middle and upper classes. Girls usually received a limited education at home, from governesses, alongside younger brothers and sisters. Some boys went to local, day grammar schools – some of which had started as foundations for both sexes but moved to being for boys only. Others went to private boarding schools, an élite of which formed the Public Schools, which fostered appropriate sorts of (hegemonic, classed, and Christian) masculinity. Girls' instruction was mainly in 'accomplishments' to make them marriageable. It was therefore a key plank in first-wave feminists' struggles, from the 1870s, to provide schools for girls comparable to those already existing for boys. There was a continuing concern among the upper classes to seclude girls until they 'came out' and were introduced into society, and shortly thereafter married; and also to provide respectability for women students. So Oxford and Cambridge colleges and some teacher-training colleges were established for women only and continued so until the late 1960s. However, from the late nineteenth century and into the early twentieth century, there were concerns that single-sex, especially residential, establishments – boarding schools and colleges – could lead boys and girls to homosexuality (Faraday, 1989).

'Progressive' educators started to establish new co-educational secondary schools, including boarding schools, from the 1890s (Brice, 1980). These were attempted utopian communities, and were educationally successful. Later arguments followed that co-education was a more socially desirable mode even after puberty; and the influential writings of Dale (1969, 1971, 1974) were particularly influential in stressing its merits. Dale argued that educating boys alongside girls encouraged boys' achievement because girls' greater industriousness was communicated to them, and competition with girls spurred boys on. Co-education was also better overall because (he said) boys and girls have to learn to live together and the sooner they started to do so, the better.

Widespread co-education in state secondary education in Britain came mainly with the amalgamation of selective (academic grammar and vocational secondary modern) schools into large 'comprehensives' in the late 1960s and 1970s – as a largely unconsidered consequence of this process (Sutherland, 1985). Northern Ireland, however, continued to have largely selective and single-sex schools. For the rest, the change was swift and widespread. There are now virtually no single-sex state secondary schools in either Scotland or Wales, while England moved from an overwhelmingly single-sex private/independent sector, and 44% of all state secondary schools single-sex in 1965;[3] to only 29% of independent schools and a mere 12% of state secondary schools single-sex in 2004 (DfES, 2005). Single-sex state schools in England are nowadays still more likely to be selective (74% of the remaining grammar schools are single sex as against 9% of comprehensives); they have more children who get free school meals (a mark of poverty) and higher proportions of minority ethnic pupils than co-educational schools (30% against 13%). Where a district has several single-sex schools, the trend is to have more single-sex girls' schools, leading to there being proportionately more boys than girls in co-educational schools.

Overall, single-sex schools continue to be largely the preserve of the middle and upper classes - the independent (private and public) schools and the academically selective (grammar) schools – and they are also tied to concerns for religious education (and sexual morality and control) across the class structure. Catholic and Anglican schools, whether fee-paying or state-funded, remain quite substantially single-sex (as also in the USA and, of course, Northern Ireland), and Muslim parents in the West now also often want single-sex education for their daughters.

Many schools for pupils with special educational needs have also been, and some still are, sex segregated, and those that are not segregated are heavily boy dominated. In addition, most vocational training for 14–19-year-olds, including apprenticeships, was single-sex until the Sex Discrimination Act of 1975, and the Youth Training Scheme that followed and the current New Apprenticeship scheme have remained de facto largely single sex (Ferri *et al.*, 2003).

The prevalence of single-sex schooling has thus changed over time in the UK and varies by geographical area. Among current adults, at least some of those born in or before the 1940s experienced single-sex primary schools, and most went to single-sex secondary schools. Subsequently, most individuals will have been to mixed primary schools, but many born in the 1950s still went to single-sex secondary schools. The bulk of people born in the 1970s went to comprehensive schools, most but not all of which were co-educational; but among the middle classes, children often attended academically selective and/or private schools, some of which had religious affiliations, and a sizeable proportion of these continue to be single-sex. Many upper-class, public schools are also essentially single-sex, even if they have admitted some girls to their sixth forms (aged 16–18) or across the age range.

Putting it another way, single-sex schools have tended to differ from mixed-sex schools not simply in sex composition but also in being often fee-paying and/or academically selective. Hence, there have been difficulties in saying much about the effects of single-sex composition separately from the effects of pupils' socially privileged backgrounds, the differences in ability at age 11 of the children they recruit, and the schools' ethos and social standing. We need very large studies to control for these variables and to test some of the suggested consequences of the type of school itself (Leonard and Sullivan, 2005).

THE DEBATES AROUND SINGLE- AND MIXED-SEX EDUCATION

The progressive school movement and Dale both suggested that co-education could overcome the gender antagonisms of the nineteenth century. Dale talked about co-education promoting 'optimal adjustment to life', which, for him, involved men being leaders and women being carers but with more recognition of the contribution of both sexes, and with happier, more egalitarian marriages. He presented evidence from surveys he conducted which showed that boys and girls in mixed schools had more positive and friendly attitudes to one another than graduates of single-sex schools. Much of this evidence was based on selected open-ended responses, which were not representative. But a similar refrain about the importance of education in promoting and maintaining the stability of family life can be found throughout the government reports during and after World War II (Wolpe, 1977). It also underlies discussions of what sorts of women should be teachers (attractive ones who will go on to get married, and some older, married or widowed women who can support headmasters as surrogate mothers in caring for girls).

Consequently, although there have been many protests at school mergers over the years from women teachers and their organizations – who feared for their jobs and promotion in co-educational schools, and who argued the importance of girls' education and the need for successful women teachers to boost girls' aspirations (Dyhouse, 1985) – co-education has been surprisingly little challenged. By the 1960s, attention was overwhelmingly on social class inequalities in education, and the justification for non-selective (comprehensive) schools was that they would improve the opportunities and achievements of (all) children from working-class families, regardless of their gender.

However, although it was soon recognized, and was a cause for concern, that class inequalities continued inside comprehensive schools (produced, for instance, by streaming by ability), it was *not* recognized that gender inequalities might continue in co-education. It was thought that when boys and girls were educated together, any remaining girls' educational disadvantages would be resolved. Girls would then have access to the same facilities as boys, and any remaining differences, as for instance, in the vocational subjects they studied or the subjects they chose to take for examinations, were seen as 'chosen', and not major problems, because they were appropriate for the different future lives of men and women.

These presumptions were sharply contested by the women's movement in the 1970s and it was also then loudly (re)asserted that single-sex education was actually better for girls. Many of the women active in the movement had been to single-sex schools, initially it seemed these schools were better at producing high-achieving, self-assured, politically active women. Dale's work was reread, and he was reprimanded for having emphasized that boys did better academically in mixed-sex schools while sweeping under the carpet the fact that girls did not do as well in them. Feminists argued that girls got better academic results in single-sex schools, and they stressed the more pleasant and supportive learning environment where girls did not have to cope with boys. Dale Spender's influential early work (Spender and Sarah, 1980; Spender, 1982) presented anecdotal and small-scale observational and survey evidence that girls got more teacher time and attention, better access to resources – more hands-on time on the computers – and a more 'girl-friendly' experience in girls-only schools. She and others (e.g. Stanworth, 1983) believed that both the curriculum content and the pedagogic style in girls' schools helped to raise girls' self-esteem. Girls were said merely to 'get by' in mixed-sex schools (Shaw, 1976).

In addition, a school inspectors' report (DES, 1975) and a book by an Equal Opportunities Commission official (Byrne, 1978) both demonstrated that there was still curricular segregation for several subjects between boys and girls in mixed primary schools, and that while it had been thought that girls were not doing physics at secondary level because of the lack of laboratories in girls-only schools, in fact, both girls and boys made *more* sex-stereotyped choices when they were brought together in mixed-sex schools, despite the facilities. Boys, too, were less likely to take history or languages at A-level in mixed-sex situations than they were in single-sex boys' schools. That is to say, in this respect at least, co-education in fact increases differentiation between the sexes. To consolidate their gender identity, the sexes demarcate themselves from each other: in each other's presence, they defend their designated but also hard-won gender identities. When girls were asked to rank themselves and to say where the teacher placed them in terms of their skills and abilities in a particular subject in a mixed-sex classroom, they ranked themselves much lower and were more out of kilter with the teachers' perceptions of them than in a single-sex situation (Stanworth, 1983).

If anything was to be done about the low numbers of women in the science and engineering professions (a continuing concern of the government) or to get more women into skilled manual trades, it was argued that we needed not only a number of positively encouraging initiatives, but also to reconsider single-sex schooling. It might seem that being with boys in secondary school would toughen girls and make them used to a mixed-sex environment, so they would stick it out through university and into a science career. But the opposite seemed to be the case: girls who did physics in single-sex classrooms up to 16 were more likely to stay the course, at least to the end of a university degree (Thomas, 1990).

Subsequently, there have been various engagements with the feminist case. First, it was argued that, in fact, academic results were not better in single-sex schools if class and type of school and ability at age 11 were taken into account (Bone, 1983; Steedman 1983; ILEA, 1985).[4] High-achieving feminists had mainly experienced single-sex education because they had been to grammar or independent schools, and it was their type of school rather than its being single-sex, that had resulted in their success.

But the topic would not die, and there remains a significant voice in favor of single-sex schooling, especially for girls (Elwood and Gipps, 1998; Francis *et al.*, 2003). There has also been a lot of subsequent, apparently conflicting, research evidence (some of it funded by organizations representing the opposing sides), which will be disentangled in the next section.

A second critique of the 1970s feminist position involved noting some of the unpleasant aspects of all female environments: the ways in which girls may inflict various forms of unpleasantness on each other, a factor which was exacerbated in single-sex situations. To this was added a concern as to what would happen to the schooling of boys if we had single-sex schooling for girls, since all-male environments are seen as hypermasculine and unwelcome (e.g. Arnot, 1983, 1984).

As a result, parents are now often ambivalent and unsure which school to choose for a particular child (West and Hunter, 1993; Ball and Gewirtz, 1997; Jackson and Bisset, 2005). Single-sex secondary schooling is said to be good for girls, and parents of girls often cite the 'research evidence' about girls doing better in single-sex schools. They also find the élite overtones and the history of academic rigor and standards of girls' schools attractive. On the other hand, co-education is said to be better academically and more humanizing for boys; and there is a continuing belief in the 'intrinsic rightness' of co-education for both sexes.

This has given a new lease of life to girls' schools, and some now see single-sexedness as a unique selling point, given an increased stress on parental choice and a marketized education system. As a consequence, since co-educational schools want to continue to encourage girls to apply to them – especially since girls nowadays, overall, get better public examination results and so raise the school's standing in comparison to its neighbors, and because girls' presence conveys a positive work ethic and sense of discipline in a school – some mixed-sex schools are now fronting girls doing technology at their open evenings and stressing the attention they give to girls' interests such as art, music, and dance. They probably also include some continuing single-sex, out-of-school activities and classes for girls.

But there has also been a more general and government-supported panic during the 1990s in the UK (and elsewhere) about boys' 'underachievement' and the 'gender gap' in academic achievement – notably, boys' relatively poor performance in reading and English (Epstein *et al.*, 1998). This has also led to a renewed interest in single-sex teaching, but this time for boys and within co-educational schools.

The British birth cohort surveys of 1948, 1958, and 1970 had documented the changing relative educational achievements of men and women long before 'failing boys' became a political issue, with women born in 1958 cohort 'overtaking' men in terms of highest qualifications and in the proportion staying in education beyond the compulsory school-leaving age (Makepeace *et al.*, 2003). But increased testing in schools and the publication of individual schools' results has focused attention and shifted the gender debate from issues of social justice to those of performance (Arnot and Miles, 2005). Researchers have tried to stress the complexity of this issue and how difficult it is to disentangle what has been causing the changes (Arnot *et al.*, 1999). But it is often assumed that (all) girls are now doing well and that attention should shift to (all) boys. Boys are said to have been disadvantaged in some way in co-educational situations – including by teaching styles that have been feminized, by more resources having been put into girls, by boys' own 'laddish' behaviour, and by assertive girls 'putting boys off trying' in class. Boys are seen to need extra attention and encouragement, and perhaps the absence of girls may help. This is an interesting development, given past evidence that boys fare(d) better academically, suffered less bullying, and could display more emotional sensitivity in mixed schools (Askew and Ross, 1988).

THE EFFECTS OF SINGLE-SEX ENVIRONMENTS ON EDUCATIONAL PROGRESS: CONFLICTING RESEARCH EVIDENCE

Deeply held opinions on mixed- and single-sex schooling may continue, but we lack rigorous research evidence to inform the debate. Much of the available data is based on small-scale, synchronous studies, or is anecdotal, or does not control for relevant differences between types of school. It is nonetheless useful to try to separate out various elements.

Academic attainment[5]

One of the most contentious debates has been on academic attainment. As noted, feminist arguments in the 1970s advancing single-sex schools were countered by a stress on the cross-cutting effects of pupils' social class backgrounds and the differences between schools. But we need also to break 'attainment' down into (at least) subject choice (whether the type of school makes a difference to widening students willingness to take 'gender-atypical' subjects), examination results, and rates of staying on at school and continuing into further and higher education. We also need to consider whether the impact of single-sex and co-education schooling is the same for boys as for girls.

Subject choices

The 1970s recognition that both boys and girls make (rather) more sex-stereotyped choices when they are in mixed-sex schools has been followed up in recent work by, among others, Bell (1989) and Spielhofer *et al.* (2002) looking at differences in the science subjects currently on offer in single-sex and co-educational schools. They found that both girls and boys at single-sex schools were more likely to choose separate science subjects than their counterparts at co-educational schools.

Other recent work has, however, looked not at actual choices but rather at subject *preferences*, and here also the results generally confirm a greater polarization along traditional gender lines in co-educational schools Moreover, younger pupils (aged 11–12) in single-sex schools seem even more interested in gender-atypical choices than older ones (aged 15–16) (Stables, 1990). However, Francis and colleagues (2003) found that girls at both single-sex and co-educational schools had similar preferences, with art and English the most popular subjects, and science, modern languages and maths least popular, and no greater preference for science in single-sex girls' schools. They therefore suggest there has been a blurring of traditional boundaries at both types of school.

Examination results at 16

There have been a number of careful studies showing single-sex education to have a significant positive overall effect on girls' attainment and also to benefit both boys and girls with lower abilities, but not boys with average or higher abilities, (Thomas *et al.*, 1994; Ofsted, 1996; Feinstein and Symons, 1999; Spielhofer *et al.*, 2002).[6] Some of these studies have shown a positive effect of single-sex schooling for girls, and a negative effect for boys; others no effect for boys. But the effects are relatively small, and other authors would put a different spin on things and stress rather that 'the performance of a school in terms of examination results has much less to do with whether it is single-sex or not than with other factors' (Robinson and Smithers, 1999: 31) – including (in the case of independent schools) whether it is famous and distinguished or a smaller, less sought after one.

The pattern of outcomes between single-sex and co-education also varies when differentiated by subject. There are no clear trends supporting either single-sex schools or co-education for either sex for English;[7] but some studies in the UK show clear advantages for girls in maths in single-sex schools and to some extent in science. However, boys seem to do better in science in single-sex schools, especially grammar schools (see Daly, 1996; Jackson, 2002; Spielhofer *et al.*, 2002[8]).

The likelihood of pupils staying in education after the age of 16 or 18 and of having gender-atypical career aspirations

We know next to nothing about the longer-term effects of single-sex schooling on boys, but there does appear to be a sustained effect on the career aspirations of girls continuing beyond their school years. Girls from mixed schools make more traditional career choices (Lee and Marks, 1990), so in this respect also co-education appears to increase differentiation between the sexes.

The educational experience of boys and girls in single-and mixed-sex schools

Education is, of course, concerned not only with passing the right examinations, and it is important to assess students' subjective experiences and whether schooling increases their general sense of well-being and agency. It would also be interesting to know whether there have been any changes in the experience of single-sex schooling: is it now seen more or less positively than in the past?

Classroom experience

Many of the famous studies of pupils' cultures in particular schools make little comment on whether they were conducted in single-sex or co-educational schools and the effects this had. Many readers would have to think hard to recall what types of schools were studied in much classic research – partly because many authors have focused on one gender, and boys and girls tend to separate out into same-sex friendship groups in mixed-sex schools anyway. The same lack of qualification applies to much of the more recent work on ethnic minority, working-class, and homosexual boys and girls in school.

There seems, however, no reason to doubt that the same situation commented upon in the 1970s – that in mixed schools teachers give more time and attention to boys, have higher expectations of boys and skew the (new National) Curriculum in the direction of boys' interests to keep their attention, and that boys hog the most valued resources – continues today. Equally, research from the 1980s (Mahony, 1985; Jones and Mahony, 1989) showing how boys' behaviors routinely police what girls are allowed to do in the classroom, and how girls (and putatively gay boys) are continually subjected to gendered put-downs, endless low-level harassment, including sexual harassment, and sometimes attacks by other boys, has been reconfirmed in more recent studies (for instance, Mac an Ghaill, 1994; Epstein *et al.*, 2003). The 'distraction' provided by the presence of the opposite sex in co-education is not just a question of romantic interest.[9]

Important caveats have of course been entered about the quality of experience in single-sex schools too (Keise, 1992). There is a proportionately greater incidence of violent behavior and homosexual bullying in single-sex boys' than in co-educational schools (Mac an Ghaill, 2000; Watkins *et al.*, in press), while a greater dissatisfaction by girls with their bodies and an increase in eating disorders has been noted in all girls' schools in Australia (Mensinger, 2001). But we do not know whether other problems – such as truancy, non-violent misconduct in school, and criminal activity outside school – also vary according to whether boys and girls are attending single-or mixed-sex schools.

Single-sex classes in co-educational schools

Sport has continued to be taught in largely single-sex groupings in the UK, and there is support for pupils' preferences for single-sex sex education, at least for girls. However, it was innovatory (and hotly contested) in the 1970s and 1980s to provide girl-only groupings in co-educational primary and secondary schools so as to allow a more girl-friendly curriculum, access to resources and some respite from harassment. The effectiveness of these activities was relatively little evaluated, partly because of the rapid pulling of the plug on Equal Opportunities under the later Thatcher and Major governments, the impact of the 1988 Education Act, and Labour's failure to support the Local Education Authorities that were promoting them (Myers, 2000).

1990s and 2000s initiatives to provide single-sex classes for boys (including suggestions of separate classes for Afro-Caribbean boys) have been more ad hoc but equally politically driven. They may talk of differences in boys' *and girls'* interests and 'learning styles', etc., but they are in fact not much concerned with girls, since they do not see girls as (having) a problem. Their aim is to try to improve boys' achievement levels – to bring them up to the girls/to narrow the gap – by encouraging forms of masculinity that are less anti-learning, and to improve boys' behavior.[10] They are sometimes associated with 'men's movement'-type concerns to shift the focus and resources 'back' to boys, and pushed by educational consultants with biologically essentialist understandings. But more significantly, they have the support of a press that plays on sex antagonisms and seems prepared wilfully to misinterpret research so as to support single-sex education.

Given this public interest, Warrington and Younger have carried out key research on these initiatives in the UK.[11] They started by looking at several individual primary and secondary schools that were 'giving single-sex classes a whirl'

(Warrington and Younger, 2001; 2003), and this led to a four-year government-funded intervention research project, Raising Boys' Achievement (Young *et al.*, 2005). However, the evidence on these initiatives is not yet robust and does not provide justification for or against extending them.[12] We need experimental studies, with more systematic preparation for the initiative, and studies where they are continued for some time, and where it is possible to separate this from other initiatives (Arnot *et al.*, 1998).

Currently, both boys and girls may appreciate some single-sex classes in co-educational schools - though Jackson's work (2002) finds that girls are largely in favor while boys are much more ambivalent. But it seems likely, as strongly confirmed by a comparable large study in Australia (Lingard *et al.*, 2002; Martino *et al.*, 2005), that it is improved pedagogy in single-sex classes for boys that is producing the effects, not single-sexedness itself. In such classes, teachers tend to adapt their teaching styles to the perceived learning styles of boys (whereas they continue much as before with girls) and use quick-paced, short-term tasks, while also encouraging greater emotional openness and particularly challenging boys' stereotypical views of the 'feminine nature' of language-based subjects. However, there are warnings that such single-sex grouping can homogenize 'all boys' (and girls) and that stereotypical boys' behaviour could be reinforced if teaching were to focus on the areas where boys are already strong and ignore their areas of weakness. Teachers may also find all-girl classes less 'challenging' (which may equate to 'less interesting'), and groups of low-ability boys may be particularly difficult to manage and control.[13]

Effects of type of schooling on later life

We still have no research on whether the longer-term positive consequences of co-education proposed by Dale back in the 1960s have actually come to pass. Are men who have attended mixed schools more likely to marry and to be more egalitarian husbands? Are they less likely to be homosexual? Are women from mixed-school backgrounds more emotionally stable, more likely to have children, and better able to work and to succeed in mixed occupational settings – and so to be better paid (since occupations dominated by women are lower paid)? Who is more likely to have better mental health in later life, to be more active in community affairs, or to engage in criminal behavior?

We have only a few, very short, 'long-term' studies of the effects of co-education. Robinson and Smithers (1999), for instance, did a retrospective study with university students from both single-sex and co-educational state and private schools. But they found no clear patterns of attitude to single-sex or co-educational schools according to the type of school the students themselves had attended. There was a common preference for a co-educational sixth form (age 16–18), which was said to make adjustment to (co-educational) higher education easier, and, overall, the students said they were less likely to send their children to single-sex schools. But, unfortunately, these future children were not differentiated by sex, nor did the study look at possible differences in students' views of gender equity issues. However, a comparable study of alumni in the USA found that 'men who attended boys' schools exhibited more interest in English, reading, and history than did men who attended co-ed schools' (Norfleet and Richards, 2003: 142).

We remain, as so often, with far more questions than answers.

CONCLUSION

It is a cause for regret that the restructuring of British schools from the late 1960s was not organized in such a way as to enable quasi-experiments in different locations on 'what works' in respect of single-sex schooling/co-education. However, the concern with boys and new initiatives to support single-sex groupings to raise boys' achievement have at least kept gender on the agenda. With pressure from interested parties, we may be able to (re)stress the need for teacher 'training' to provide appropriate threshold knowledge about gender so that teachers' skills include not treating 'boys' and 'girls' as undifferentiated groups, assumed to perform in gender stereotyped ways. Rather, teachers should be enabled to explore with their pupils, in a mixture of single-and mixed-sex situations, the forms of gender itself: to value diversity and to reflect critically 'on the constraints and limitations imposed by a particular gender order which defines the masculine in opposition to the feminine' and the homosexual (Martino *et al.*, 2005: 238).

REFERENCES

AAUW (American Association of University Women) (1998) *Separated by sex: a critical look at single-sex education for girls.* Washington, DC: AAUW Educational Foundation.

AAUW (American Association of University Women) (2001) *Hostile hallways: bullying, teasing, and sexual harassment in school.* Washington, DC: AAUW Educational Foundation.

Albisetti, JC (2000) Un-learned lessons from the New World? English views of American co-education and women's colleges, c.1865–1910. *History of Education*, 29: 473–89.

Arnot, M (1983) A cloud over co-education: an analysis of forms of transmission of class and gender relations, in Walker, S and Barton, L (eds) *Gender, class and education.* Lewes: Falmer.

Arnot, M (1984) How shall we educate our sons?, in Deem, R (ed) *Co-education reconsidered.* Milton Keynes: Open University Press.

Arnot, M, Gray, J, James, M, Ruddock, J and Duveen, G (1998) *Review of recent research on gender and educational performance.* London: HMSO.

Arnot, M, David, M and Weiner, G (1999) *Closing the gender gap: postwar education and social change.* Cambridge: Polity Press.

Arnot, M and Mills, P (2005) A reconstruction of the gender agenda: the contradictory gender dimensions in New Labour's educational and economic policy. *Oxford Review of Education* 31: 173–89.

Askew, S and Ross, C (1988) *Boys don't cry: boys and sexism in education,* Milton Keynes: Open University Press.

Ball, S and Gewirtz, S (1997) Girls in the education market: choice, competition and complexity. *Gender and Education,* 9: 207–22.

Bell, J (1989) A comparison of science performance and uptake by fifteen-year-old boys and girls in co-educational and single-sex schools – APU survey findings. *Educational Studies,* 15: 193–203.

Bemmelen, S van and Vliet, M van (1985) *Co-education versus single-sex schooling: a comparison between Western and Third World perspectives*. The Hague: CESO.

Bone, A (1983) *Girls and girl-only schools: a review of the evidence*. Manchester: Equal Opportunities Commission.

Brehony, KJ (1984) Co-education: perspectives and debates in the early twentieth century, in Deem, R (ed) *Co-education reconsidered*. Milton Keynes: Open University Press.

Brice, I (1980) The early coeducation movement in English secondary education, *Melbourne Studies in Education*, 134–77.

Byrne, E (1978) *Women and education*. London: Tavistock.

Dale, RR (1969) *Mixed or single-sex school? Vol. 1: a research study in pupil–teacher relationships*. London: Routledge and Kegan Paul.

Dale, RR (1971) *Mixed or single-sex school? Vol. II: some social aspects*. London: Routledge and Kegan Paul.

Dale, RR (1974) *Mixed or single-sex school? Vol. III: attainment, attitudes and overview*. London: Routledge and Kegan Paul.

Datnow, A and Hubbard, L (eds) (2002) *Gender in policy and practice: perspectives on single-sex and co-educational schooling*, London: Routledge Falmer.

DES (Department of Education and Science) (1975) *Curricular differences for boys and girls*. London: HMSO.

DfES (Department for Education and Skills) (2005) Single sex education. Unpublished topic paper.

Dyhouse, C (1985) Feminism and the debate over coeducational/single-sex schooling: some historical perspectives, in Purvis, J (ed) *The education of girls and women*. Leicester: History of Education Society.

Elwood, J and Gipps, C (1998) *Review of recent research on the achievement of girls in single-sex schools*. London: Institute of Education for the Association of Maintained Girls' Schools.

Epstein, D, Elwood, J, Hey, V and Maw, J (eds) *Failing boys?* Buckingham: Open University Press.

Epstein, D, Hewitt, R, Leonard, D, Mauthner, M and Watkins, C (2003) Avoiding the issue: homophobia, school policies and identities in secondary schools; in Vincent C, (ed) *Social justice, education and identity*. London: RoutledgeFalmer.

Faraday, A (1989) Lessoning lesbians: girls' schools, co-education and anti-lesbianism between the wars; in Jones, C and Mahony, P (eds) *Learning our lines*. London: Women's Press.

Feinstein, L and Symons, J (1999). Attainment in secondary school. *Oxford Economic Papers,* 51: 300–21.

Ferri, E, Bynner, J and Wadsworth, M (eds) (2003) *Changing Britain, changing lives: three generations at the turn of the century*. London: Institute of Education, Bedford Way Papers.

Francis, B, Hutchings, M, Archer, L and Melling, L (2003) Subject choice and occupational aspirations among pupils at girls' schools. *Pedagogy, Culture and Society*, 11: 425–42.

Gill, J (1988) *Which way to school? A review of the evidence on the single sex versus co-education debate and an annotated bibliography of the research*. Canberra: Commonwealth Schools Commission.

Hannan, D, Smyth, E, McCullagh, J, O'Leary, R and Mahon, D (1996) *Co-education and gender equality – exam performance, stress and personal development*. Dublin: Oak Tree Press.

Harker, R (2000) Achievement, gender and the single-sex/co-ed debate. *British Journal of Sociology of Education*, 21: 203–18.

Herr, K and Arms, E (2004) Accountability and single-sex schools: a collision of reform agendas. *American Educational Research Journal*, 41: 527–55.

ILEA (1985) *Report of the work of the working party on single-sex and co-education*. London: Inner London Education Authority.

Jackson, C (2002) Can single-sex classes in co-educational schools enhance the learning experiences of girls and/or boys? An exploration of pupils' perceptions. *British Educational Research Journal*, 28: 37–48.

Jackson, C and Bisset, M (2005) Gender and school choice: factors influencing parents when choosing single-sex or co-educational independent schools for their children. *Cambridge Journal of Education*, 35: 195–211.

Jones, C and Mahony, P (eds) (1989) *Learning our lines: sexuality and social control in education*. London: Women's Press.

Keise, C (1992) *Sugar and spice? Bullying in single sex schools.* Stoke-on-Trent: Trentham.

Kruse, A-M (1992) 'We have learnt not to just sit back, twiddle our thumbs and let them take over'. Single-sex settings and the development of a pedagogy for girls and a pedagogy for boys in Danish schools. *Gender and Education*, 4: 81–103.

Kruse, A-M (1995) Single-sex settings: pedagogies for girls and boys in Danish schools, in Murphy, P and Gipps, C (eds) *Equity in the classroom: towards effective pedagogy for girls and boys.* London: Falmer.

Lasser, C (1987) *Educating men and women together: co-education in a changing world.* Oberlin College.

Lee, V and Marks, H (1990) Sustained effects of single-sex secondary school experience on attitudes, behaviours and values in college. *Journal of Educational Psychology*, 82.

Leonard, D and Sullivan, A (2005) Single and mixed sex schooling: life course consequences. Paper presented to the BERA annual conference, University of Glamorgan.

Lingard, B. *et al.* (2002) *Addressing the educational needs of boys.* Canberra: Department of Education, Science and Training.

Mac an Ghaill, M. (1994) *The making of men: masculinites, sexualities and schooling.* Buckingham: Open University Press.

Mac an Ghaill, M (2000) Rethinking (male) gendered sexualities in education: what about the British heteros? *Journal of Men's Studies*, 8: 195–212.

Mahony, P (1985) *Schools for the boys? Co-education reassessed.* London: Hutchinson.

Makepeace, G, Joshi, H, Woods, L and Galinda-Rueda, F (2003) From school to the labour market, in Ferri, E, Bynner, J and Wadsworth, M (eds) *Changing Britain: changing lives.* London: Institute of Education.

Marsh, W, Smith, I, Marsh, M and Owens, L (1988) The transition form single-sex to co-educational high schools: effects on multiple dimensions of self-concept and on academic achievement. *American Educational Research Journal*, 25.

Martino, W (2000) Policing masculinities: investigating the role of homophobia and heteronormativity in the lives of adolescent schools boys. *Journal of Men's Studies*, 8: 213–36.

Martino, W, Mills M, and Lingard, B (2005) Interrogating single-sex classes as a strategy for addressing boy's educational and social needs. *Oxford Review of Education*, 31: 237–54.

Mensinger, J (2001) Conflicting gender role prescriptions and disordered eating in single-sex and coeducational school environments. *Gender and Education*, 13: 417–29.

Mills, M (1996) 'Homophobia kills': a disruptive moment in the educational politics of legitimation, *British Journal of Sociology of Education*, 17: 315–26.

Mills, M (2000) Issues in implementing boys' programmes in schools: male teachers and empowerment, *Gender and Education*, 12: 221–38.

Morrell, R (1997) Single-sex schools: do they have a place in a future South African education system? Mimeo: Gender Equity Task Team background report.

Myers, K (ed) (2000) *Whatever happened to equal opportunities in schools? Gender equality initiatives in education.* Buckingham: Open University Press.

Norfleet, J and Richards, H (2003) Escaping stereotypes: educational attitudes of male alumni of single-sex and co-ed schools. *Psychology of Men and Masculinity*, 4: 136–48.

Ofsted/EOC (1996) *The gender divide: performance differences between boys and girls at school.* London: HMSO.

Riordan, C (1990) *Girls and boys in school: together or separate?* New York: Teachers College Press.

Robinson, P and Smithers, A (1999) Should the sexes be separated for secondary education – comparisons of single-sex and co-educational schools? *Research Papers in Education*, 14: 23–49.

Salomne, RC (2003) *Same, different, equal: rethinking single-sex schooling.* New Haven, CT: Yale University Press.

Shaw, J (1976) Finishing school: some implications of sex-segregated education, in Barker, DL and Allen, S (eds) *Sexual divisions and society: process and change.* London: Tavistock.

Smithers, A and Robinson, P (1997) *Co-educational and single-sex schooling revisited.* Brunel: Centre for Education and Employment Research.

Spender, D (1982). *Invisible women: the schooling scandal.* London: Writers and Readers Publishing Cooperative.

Spender, D and Sarah, E (eds) (1980) *Learning to lose: sexism and education.* London: Women's Press.

Spielhofer, T, O'Donnell, L, Benton, T, Schagen, S and Schagen, I (2002) *The impact of school size and single-sex education on performance.* LGA Research Report 33. Slough: NFER.

Stables, A (1990) Differences between pupils from mixed and single-sex schools in their enjoyment of school subjects and their attitudes to science and to school. *Educational Review,* 42: 221–9.

Stanworth, M (1983) *Gender and schooling: a study of sexual divisions in the classroom.* London: Hutchinson in association with the Explorations in Feminism Collective.

Steedman, J (1983) *Examination results in mixed and single-sex schools: findings from the National Child Development Study.* Manchester: EOC.

Stein, N (1999) *Classrooms and courtrooms: facing sexual harassment in K–12 schools.* New York: Teachers College Press.

Sukhnandan, L Lee, B and Kelleher, S (2000) *An investigation into gender differences in achievement: phase 2: schools and classroom strategies.* London: NFER.

Sutherland, M (1985) Whatever happened about co-education? *British Journal of Educational Studies,* 33: 155–63.

Thomas, K (1990) *Gender and subject in higher education.* Buckingham: Open University Press.

Thomas, S, Pan, D and Goldstein, H (1994) *Report on the analysis of 1992 examination results: AMA project on putting examination results in context.* London: Association of Metropolitan Authorities.

Tyack, DB and Hansot, E (1991) *Learning together: a history of coeducation in American schools.* New Haven, CT: Yale University Press.

van de Gaer, E, Pustjens, H, van Damme, J and de Munter, A (2004) Effects of single-sex versus co-educational classes and schools on gender differences in progress in language and mathematics achievement. *British Journal of Sociology of Education.* 25: 307–22.

Walker, J (1998) *Louts and legends.* Sydney: Allen and Unwin.

Warrington, M and Younger, M (2001) Single-sex classes and equal opportunities for girls and boys: perspectives through time from a mixed comprehensive school in England. *Oxford Review of Education,* 27: 339–56.

Warrington, M and Younger, M (2003) 'We decided to give it a twirl': single-sex teaching in English comprehensive schools. *Gender and Education,* 15: 339–50.

Watkins, C, Mauthner, M, Hewitt, R, Epstein, D and Leonard, D (in press) School violence, school differences and schools discourses. *British Educational Research Journal.*

West, A and Hunter, J (1993) Parents' view on mixed and single-sex secondary schools. *British Educational Research Journal,* 19.

Weinberg, A (1979) Analysis of the persistence of single-sex secondary school in the English education system. PhD thesis, University of Sussex.

Willis, P (1997) *Learning to labour.* Farnborough: Saxon House.

Wolpe, A-M (1977) *Some processes in sexist education.* London: WRRC Publications.

Woodward, L, Fergusson, D and Horwood, L (1999) Effects of single-sex and co-educational secondary schooling on children's academic achievement. *Australian Journal of Education,* 43: 142–56.

Younger, M and Warrington, M with Gray, J, Rudduck, J, McLellan, R, Bearne, E, Keshner, R and Bricheno, P (2005) *Raising boys' achievement.* Research Report 636. London: Department for Education and Skills.

NOTES

1. The common expression continues to be single or mixed sex, rather than gender and I will keep to this designation.

2. See, for example, studies on USA and Canada (Lasser, 1987, Riordan, 1990; Tyack and Hansot,1990; AAUW, 1998; Albisetti, 2000; Salomne, 2003; Datnow and Hubbard, 2002); on Australia (Gill 1988; Lingard *et al.*, 2002); on South Africa (Morrell, 1997); and on low-to medium-income countries (Bemmelen and Van Vliet, 1985).

3. In fact, the 1965 figures are for England and Wales. The two were disaggregated in 1970.

4. On the USA, see Marsh *et al.* (1988).

5. This section draws on DfES (2005).

6. Conversely, studies in New Zealand did not find girls did better in single-sex schools, while boys did seem to do better in single-sex than in co-educational schools (Woodward *et al.*, 1999; Harker, 2000).

7. Better results were found for girls in English by Spielhofer *et al.* (2002) in England, but not by Hannan *et al.* (1996) in the Republic of Ireland, nor by Harker (2000) in New Zealand.

8. See also Hannan *et al.* (1996) in Ireland and van de Gaer *et al.* (2004) in the Netherlands, but rather different findings by Harker (2000) in New Zealand.

9. On the USA, see Stein (1999), AAUW (2001); on Australia, see Walker (1988), Mills (1996), Martino (2000).

10. Other reasons given for such initiatives are to sort out imbalances in the numbers of boys and girls in year groups and sets; to show that dividing by gender may be the best way to help one sex without disadvantaging the other; or to influence boys and girls to have less stereotypical attitudes to subjects and to make wider choices.

11. See also Sukhnandan *et al.* (2000); and Jackson (2002). On Denmark, See Kruse (1992; 1995).

12. However, van der Gaer *et al.* (2004) in the Netherlands found that boys did better in Dutch in co-educational classes.

13. Also reported for the USA in Herr and Arms (2004).

Gender and School Subjects

INTRODUCTION

In this section, authors examine past and present research in a range of school subjects. In almost every case, they point out historical shifts that have occurred in the study of gender and school subjects. In many of these fields, early research worked within static notions of gender and identity, and focused on making girls fit into male-defined notions of success and achievement in school. From work that accepted dichotomous positioning of girls and boys, research has shifted more recently to work that examines the construction of gendered selves within discourses that often privilege existing gender positions in political, social and economic structures. Current researchers also explore the importance of geopolitical location, local knowledge and practice, which are necessary for understanding the negotiation of gendered selves within different school subjects and fields of study. The authors in this section note that research in gender and school subjects is inherently political; much of it documents the changes that need to be made to address inadequacies and inequalities in schools and disciplines.

In Chapter 15, Jo Boaler and Tesha Sengupta-Irving point out that some of the prior work on gender and mathematics has contributed to a discourse about girls' and women's inadequacies in the field of mathematics. They argue for an approach to studying gender and mathematics that is situated, relational and focused on the interactions between people and environments that promote or inhibit inequality. In Chapter 16, Angela Calabrese Barton and Nancy Brickhouse argue that rather than focusing on standard achievement in school-related activities and assessments, educators need to encourage engagement in science that leads to a new kind of participation and identity in a community of science learners. They also demonstrate the importance of defining engagement within the local geopolitical context in which the learning and teaching of science occur.

In their chapter on 'Gender and Literacy', Bronwyn Davies and Sue Saltmarsh explore how 'gender hierarchies and power relations are re/produced and negotiated through literacy practices', which, in turn, 'map onto, and are implicated in producing, neo-liberal economic discourses in distinctly gendered terms'. As children construct themselves and others, and are constructed as gendered through text, they also produce and reproduce current economic frameworks and agendas.

In Chapter 18, Bagele Chilisa argues that Western frameworks of study have limited our understanding of the need for local knowledge and practice in sex education. Using a case study of a sex education program in schools in Botswana, she demonstrates that current approaches tend to reinforce traditional notions of masculinity, control femininity and ignore local traditions and practices. Chapter 19, by Jannette Elwood, presents a continuum that represents different but interrelated understandings of learning, mind, assessment and gender. In Stage 1 of the continuum, learning, mind and gender are fixed and based within the individual; in Stage 2, learning, mind, gender and assessment are described as more complex, socially constructed and mediated concepts; and in Stage 3, learning, mind, gender and assessment are seen as historically, culturally and socially generated within particular contexts.

In Chapter 20, Tuula Gordon focuses on citizenship as a 'multidimensional' concept that addresses political, legal and social positions, and incorporates rights related to class, ethnicity, culture and sexuality. She argues that citizenship education must provide students with agency, the sense of being able to make decisions and carry them out. In Chapter 21, Linda M. von Hoene also calls for change in foreign language instruction. While research in foreign language acquisition has shifted to an examination of the 'impact of language learning processes on the construction of a gendered subject', foreign language instruction continues to encourage 'a colonialist and assimilationalist relationship to the foreign culture' that reinforces gender norms.

Finally, in her chapter on 'Gender and Technology', Jo Sanders provides a thorough review of prior research in social influences on computer attitudes, experience and use; patterns of classroom instruction and curriculum; and interventions to address gender inequities in participation and achievement in computer science and information technology. She points out that the field needs continued work on effective evaluation of intervention programs and on the role of race, ethnicity and class on technology participation and achievement.

15

Nature, Neglect and Nuance: Changing Accounts of Sex, Gender and Mathematics

Jo Boaler and Tesha Sengupta-Irving

INTRODUCTION

There is a popular idea, held by members of the public and supported by media in a number of countries, that girls are not as good as boys in mathematics and science. This outdated perception has a significant effect on the gender relations it claims to report, and it is one reason we argue that gender and mathematics remains a critical field in education. It is both curious and troubling to note that few researchers study or consider gender and mathematics as an academic field in the twenty-first century, despite the careful paths laid down by our predecessors in the academy. Part of the reason for the lack of attention is the increased performance of girls, who now achieve at the same or higher levels than boys in a number of countries. But we will argue in this chapter that girls and women are systematically discouraged from entering mathematical and scientific fields, and that research can provide important insights into the sources of such inequities. Controversially, perhaps, we will also argue that one of the sources of girls' discouragement over the years has been the research produced on gender and mathematics, some of which has inadvertently positioned girls in ways that are counter-productive to their advancement. In reviewing research, writing and societal views on the issue of gender and mathematics, we will consider different achievement and participation patterns in mathematics and gender in the 2000s, the different lenses that have been used to consider gender and mathematics, and newer, more productive ways in which gender may be understood and analyzed.

GENDER AND MATHEMATICS: PARTICIPATION AND PERFORMANCE PATTERNS IN THE TWENTY-FIRST CENTURY

When Larry Summers, president of Harvard University, speculated that 'innate differences' (Bombardieri, 2005: 1) between men and women caused fewer women to succeed in science and mathematics and that such differences affected school performance and participation beyond school, he sparked a media frenzy in the USA. Dramatically, the issue of gender and mathematics took center stage as journalists rushed to cover the story, drawing from wide-ranging sources to support or refute Summers' claim. Most journalists began their investigations of the genetic question by asking – is he right? Are girls behind in mathematics and science? Further, are performance differences in school the reason for women's low participation at higher levels? These issues are important to consider, and we precede our review of gender research with some answers to these questions, drawing upon data from two countries: the USA and the UK. Despite the limiting quality of such a small number of well-resourced cases, they do show interesting and different patterns of gender equity that are helpful in considering issues for students from a wider group of countries. Hanna's (1996) edited collection gives a broader look at issues of gender and mathematics in a wider range of countries across the world.

In considering whether girls perform at significantly lower levels than boys in mathematics, the USA provides an interesting case in point, as some tests show gender differences while others do not. Janet Hyde, Elizabeth Fennema and Susan Lamon (1990) produced a meta-analysis of gender differences in the 1990s, and even at that time – over 10 years ago – they found a minimal difference. They drew from over 100 studies involving 3 million subjects and derived an effect size of +0.15 standard deviations. Hyde and colleagues argued that gender differences are too small to be recognized as meaningful, and concluded that they have been overplayed and glamorized in the media, contributing to a discourse of difference that has itself created differences in the achievement of girls and boys.

The small performance differences between girls and boys that continue in the USA are manifested on the Scholastic Assessment Test (SAT) (Rosser, 1992) and the Advanced Placement (AP) examinations (Coley, 2001). These two assessments fuel a continued discourse concerning the inadequacy of women and girls in mathematics. Interestingly, the UK, a country with similar resources spent on education, shows a different pattern of results that has shifted dramatically over time. In England, almost all students take a mathematics examination at age 16, the General Certificate of Secondary Education (GCSE) in mathematics. As mathematics is compulsory to age 16, equal numbers of boys and girls take this examination. In the 1970s, boys used to pass the mathematics GCSE examination (then called the 'O level') in higher numbers and attain more of the highest grades; in the 1990s, girls and boys passed the exam in equal numbers, but boys achieved more of the highest grades. By the 2000s, girls were passing the exam at higher rates than boys and attaining more of the highest grades. In 2003/04, for example, 51% of the A–C grades went to girls ($n = 318,300$) (DfES, 2004). At ages 16–18, students who choose to stay in education may select a small number of subjects in which to specialize (usually three). The mathematics A-level course is comparable to the AP courses in the USA, but it includes higher-level work. At the end of that course, students also take a terminal examination. At A level, the participation of girls drops dramatically; although girls attained 51% of the top GCSE grades in 2004, they made up only 37% of the A-level cohort. Despite this, their achievement was strong, and the results on the examination in 2003/04 showed that they attained slightly better results than boys: 96% of boys passed the examination and 39% attained the highest grade of A, compared with 97% of girls who passed the examination, 41% attaining the highest grade. In England, girls now outperform boys in all subjects, including mathematics and physics, to GCSE and A level, and they now attain more of the highest grades in demanding high-level examinations.

But while the relative performance of the girls in England is higher than the USA, the participation of girls is lower. For example, in 2004 only 37% of the A-level cohort in England was female compared to 48% of the AP calculus cohort in the USA. In the USA in 2000, 48% of mathematics undergraduate degrees went to women (Statistical Research Center, 2003), and 48% of the AP cohort were women; in England, the proportion of women undergraduate students was 39% (DTI, 2005) and 37% of A-level students were women. The similarity in participation rates at school and university levels suggests a direct link between the two, lower participation at university reflecting choices made in school. In both countries, the proportion of women who are represented at higher levels is much smaller. In the USA in 1990, 18% of mathematics PhDs went to women (Chipman, 1996), and in 2000 the figure was 27% (Herzig, 2004a). Women's presence in occupations and professions that are mathematical and scientific is also extremely low. In 2000, in the USA for example, 9% of engineers were women. Herzig (2004b) has produced systematic evidence of the ways in which the climate of university mathematics departments may deter the participation of women and minority students.

In summary, data from these two countries show two patterns that are important and probably generalizable. The first is the positive achievement of girls and women, something that is being replicated across the globe in countries in which girls have equal access to education. Japan, Sweden and Iceland are other examples of countries in which girls outperform boys in mathematics. These examples should be sufficient to dispel any lasting ideas about the genetic superiority of boys. That girls are able to achieve such results within societies that maintain sexist images and ideas about genetic disadvantage shows the capability and resilience of girls. The second pattern that emerges from the data and that pertains in other countries (see also Bosch and Trigueros, 1996; Grevholm, 1996; Spitaleri,

1996) is the relatively low participation of girls and women in the mathematical sciences, which becomes more severe as the level increases (Herzig, 2004b).

These data come from two well-resourced countries, and the patterns of achievement and participation shown are higher than for many other countries, particularly those with less resources and/or more overtly sexist regimes. Yet, even these two countries show some clear issues that need attention, specifically the under-representation of women even when they are achieving at high levels. We started this section questioning whether there are important performance differences at secondary school that may explain women's low participation at post-graduate and professional levels. Data from neither England nor the USA support this explanation, as university participation is almost equal in the USA and in England, and where it is not, girls are opting out of mathematics *despite* their advanced performance in secondary school. The low participation of girls and women at high levels of mathematics and related fields is an important issue, and one that probably begins in school, despite the high achievement of girls, and becomes more accentuated as levels increase. This phenomenon requires sophisticated understandings of the issues facing girls and women in mathematics classrooms (see, for example, Herzig, 2004a,b; Mendick, 2005a,b) and more complex analyses than are generally offered in the media (Leder, 1996). In contributing to such analyses, we will spend some time reviewing recent and important work on gender and mathematics.

REVIEWING RESEARCH ON GENDER AND MATHEMATICS

Our review of research falls into six areas separated by the location of researchers' attention as well as the different methods and lenses employed by equity researchers. In considering these different lenses, we will make some points about the usefulness of the lenses themselves in relation to opportunities for equity.

Genetic differences

Research that has investigated genetic differences in mathematics performance has come at two distinct times. In the 1980s, Benbow and Stanley (1980) reported that boys achieved at half a standard deviation higher than girls in populations of students selected from among the top 2–3% of students (1980: 1262). The authors controversially claimed that the differences they found reflected superior mathematical ability among boys. This claim has subsequently been widely discredited, but the original report, which appeared in *Science* magazine, caused considerable damage. Eccles and Jacobs (1985) found that the Benbow and Stanley report significantly lowered mothers' expectations of their daughters' potential with mathematics.

A more recent line of research that may shed light on the question of innate differences comes from advances in brain-imaging technology. O'Hara (2005) summarized the emerging research on brain patterns and reported that the most consistent result from studies of memory shows females to have a better 'working memory'. In tests of visual-spatial abilities, males have been found to be faster navigators, but performances on tests have been equal. In the area of language, researchers have found differential patterns of brain processing but no performance differences between women and men. In the area of mathematics, the most relevant to our review, there have been a limited number of imaging studies, and, to date, gender differences have not been considered. In summary, O'Hara concluded, that brain imaging is a new field with no clear results. Where studies have been conducted, they have tended to show some differential processing in the brains of men and women with no impact on performance. Another researcher working in this field, Louann Brizendine, argues that because girls develop language skills faster than boys, boys gravitate toward toys that require minimal verbal interaction, such as building blocks and train sets and that help them in their mathematical development. 'These cognitive gaps between boys and girls close during high school, Brizendine said. But here's the problem. By high school boys have spent years reinforcing and strengthening their skills in math and science and girls in language arts' (Ryan, 2005: 7). Thus, brain research may explain the few mathematical differences that exist, not by showing any mathematical inferiority of girls but by different developmental stages that support certain types of activity over others.

Studies of brain processing do not support the idea that girls and women are genetically inferior to boys and men in their mathematical potential, yet this idea is one that appeals to many. The strength and breadth of this belief are independent of evidence and vastly out of proportion to any data that have ever been produced. Such ideas are harmful, they concern the intellectual potential of young people and they have contributed to the gender differences that prevail in society, men continuing to dominate mathematical and scientific fields.

Affect and attitude: girls will be girls

A large and important body of research in gender and mathematics has focused upon the affective and attitudinal beliefs of girls that affect their participation in mathematics. Researchers have studied the differences between boys and girls in categories such as anxiety, fear of success, confidence, self-concept, motivation and perceptions of the usefulness of mathematics (Leder, 1982; Hart, 1989; Ethington, 1992; Seegers and Boekaarts, 1996). The findings from such work suggest that girls differentially experience and engage in mathematics classes. For example, Hart (1989) found that boys interacted more with their teachers publicly (and therefore receive more positive public evaluation) than girls did, despite their confidence levels in the subject. Ethington (1992) found that the achievement of boys in mathematics classes was influenced more by prior achievement and value for the subject than girls, who were influenced more by their perceptions of the difficulty of the subject and the idea that it is a subject where males dominate.

One of the most important methodological contributions that came from this area of research was the Fennema-Sherman Attitude Scale, developed in 1976, which characterizes students' attitudes to mathematics. There is evidence, from this and related studies, that girls have lower self-images in mathematics as well as belief that mathematics is more suited to males. Such ideas, fueled by media reports (Jacobs and Eccles, 1985) are likely to suppress the participation of women and girls in mathematical fields. Attitudinal studies have provided valuable insights into the reasons for the relatively low participation of women and girls in mathematics. The legacy of such research lies in the various intervention programs that promote the participation of girls in mathematics and science in schools today. Indeed, these programs and their accompanying research studies illustrate the powerful potential for increased performance and participation of girls in mathematics through a deliberate focus on their individual needs (Fennema, *et al.*, 1981; Koontz, 1997). An additional, less fortunate outcome of such work is the perpetuation of ideas about female inadequacy. Tendencies, such as lack of confidence, anxiety and failure attributions, were generally presented as properties of girls, rather than as responses co-produced by particular working environments. Thus, proposed interventions aimed to change the girls so that they became less anxious and more confident - *essentially* more masculine. In such programs, the responsibility for change was laid at the feet of the girls, and problems with mathematical pedagogy and practice, and with the broader social system, were not addressed.

An example of research that positions the 'problem' within girls comes from Carol Dweck (1986), who has produced a number of influential analyses in which she concludes that girls, particularly those she terms 'bright' girls, have maladaptive motivational patterns that include avoiding high-risk learning situations and preferring situations in which they are sure to succeed. She claims that students with maladaptive patterns seek situations that will lead to correct answers, rather than those that are challenging and provide opportunity for learning. Dweck offers 'maladaptive' tendencies as a reason for the lower mathematical performance of some girls, particularly at advanced levels, but she treats these motivational patterns as inherent characteristics of girls that exist outside the settings in which girls are taught. This seems to be a fundamental flaw, as motivations must surely be highly situated. If we were to consider the tendencies Dweck noticed among 'bright girls', outside their setting, we might conclude that the tendencies were indeed 'maladaptive' in the sense that they were unproductive. But if we consider the system in which students were learning, we may view the tendencies of girls as highly adaptive. The majority of 'bright' girls are taught mathematics in high-ability groups in which the attainment of correct answers, at a fast pace, is what is valued (Boaler, 1997b). In such an environment, choosing to seek situations that will lead to correct answers, seems sensible and highly *adaptive*. The notion of adaptivity – central to theories of natural selection – rests upon environmental responsiveness, and the idea that 'girls' have maladaptive tendencies contravenes that basic premise. A different analysis would consider the constraints and affordances (Gibson, 1986;

Greeno and MMAP, 1998) provided by the environments in which girls work that lead to such responses.

The difference between the two approaches we have mentioned – one that considers the girls as maladaptive and the other that focuses on the teaching environments which produce such tendencies – is that the first would lead to recommendations to change the girls. The second interpretation would lead to recommendations to change the teaching environments in which students are working – environments that produce motivational patterns that are unproductive for learning.

Another characteristic of the area of research that we have termed 'girls will be girls' is its reliance on a distinct dichotomizing of boys and girls. Within much of the research, achievement and participatory patterns were explained through comparisons with boys. Thus, girls' achievements in mathematics became their *under*achievement in mathematics, without challenge, just as their adaptivity became their *mal*adaptivity. At the same time, boys' achievements, participation and behaviors were implicitly positioned as 'normative' and the benchmark against which girls were understood. In emphasizing comparative analyses within the field, researchers were actively distracted from focusing on girls' perspectives and responses as legitimate measures of their learning experiences as well as the educational practices that more and less inadvertently produced gender inequities. As a result, this area of research did not consider questions such as: what do girls bring to mathematics? What can they tell us about their experiences, which might provide greater insight into inequities? These are the types of questions – questions that outright reject a 'normative' male benchmark – that have rarely been asked.

Women's ways of knowing

Probably the most famous and influential example of work that rejected male benchmarks came from Carol Gilligan (1982), who showed through her work on moral judgments among women how seemingly normative benchmarks replicate and narrate a sexist notion that human development is modeled by male development. Her work, termed 'difference feminism' (DeBare, 2004: 199), and that of her successors paved the way for more research by, with and for women.

Belenky, *et al.* (1986) developed the educational implications of Gilligan's work by proposing 'stages' of knowing from a longitudinal interview study of women across multiple sites of formal education. In their analysis, the authors proposed a five-stage model of the ways women come to 'know', offering a progression from uncritical to critical ways of knowing. The authors suggest that a system of 'connected knowing' better represents women, while a system of 'separate knowing' better represents men. Elements under the rubric of 'separate knowing' include logic, rigor, abstraction and deduction, while 'connected knowing' reflects intuition, creativity, hypothesizing and induction (Becker, p167). Becker (1995) and Boaler (1997a) explored these notions in mathematics education, and Becker suggested that mathematics classes that reinforce connected knowing would, for example, 'share the process of solving problems with students, not just the finished product of proof' (p169), and that more emphasis would be placed on finding different ways to solve problems. This argument is supported by research that shows that girls often prefer cooperative and discussion-based learning environments, rather than individualized or competitive environments (Fennema and Leder, 1990; Boaler, 2002a,b).

Sexism and sex stereotyping

A fourth area of important research in gender and mathematics concerns teaching environments and curricular materials. This area of research explores the possibility that sex stereotyping in textbooks or sex-based discrimination by teachers affects the performance and participation of girls and women in mathematics (Forbes, 1996; Niederdrenk-Felgner, 1996). In this way, the 'problem' that requires intervention is no longer the girls but the textbooks and teacher–student interactions that girls are exposed to in their mathematics classes. There have been several important outcomes from this line of inquiry, including greater attention to gender representations in instructional materials (Burton, 1990), greater interest in the benefits of single-sex schooling (Marjoram, 1994; DeBare, 2004), and heightened awareness of teacher beliefs and bias in classroom interactions (Becker, 1981; Walden and Walkerdine, 1985; Hart, 1989; Walkerdine, 1989; Leach, 1994). The increased access girls now have to mathematics in classrooms is probably due to research that increased the awareness of teachers about gendered interactions in classrooms in the 1980s and later years (Spender, 1982).

Typical findings in this area of research showed that sex differences prevailed in the interactions of students and teachers that generally favored boys, boys receiving more attention, reinforcement and positive feedback from mathematics teachers (Becker, 1981). This work moved from the survey data that characterized affect studies, to quantitative data on student–teacher interactions and qualitative observations of environments. As researchers became more aware of the factors that could influence girls' participation and achievement, intervention areas moved from the student to the teacher and the teaching environments, as evidenced by the nature and quality of their interactions. Whereas moving the analytic home from girls to teachers unburdened the girls, it was equally clear that the 'blame' could not be laid on the teachers alone. As Hart (1989) remarked, 'Any explanation that focuses on the teacher alone or on the student alone is too simplistic' (Hart, 1989: 257).

A feminist mathematics

A different perspective on gender and mathematics research considers the nature of the discipline and the ways that mathematics, the subject, may be gendered. Such research takes up Johnston's proposition that:

Perhaps we don't take seriously enough the voices that say, again and again, 'but it doesn't make sense', and 'what's the point?' Perhaps what they are saying simply is true. Perhaps mathematics, their mathematics, secondary-school mathematics, doesn't make sense. Perhaps the fault is in the mathematics, and not the teaching, not the learning, not the people. (Johnston, 1995: 226)

This body of work begins with a basic premise: mathematics is a system of knowledge, a product of human thought, discovery and practice. In this way, understanding that mathematics is an informal, subjective exploration of the natural world is honest to its history. Yet, mathematics in schools belies this truth and presents a formalized, 'objective', and discrete system of skills and rules that is largely void of the context that gave rise to it. Feminist scholars suggest that a transformation of mathematics from its organic roots to a more synthetic rendering has detrimental implications because it purposely obscures power, privilege and the gendered nature of the discipline to its teachers and learners alike.

Scholars in this field of research generally advocate a feminist conception of the discipline. Leone Burton, for example, asks, 'If the body of knowledge known as mathematics can be shown to have been derived in a manner which excluded non-Europeans and their mathematical knowledge, why not conjecture that the perceived male-ness of mathematics is equally an artifact of its production and its producers?' (Burton, 1995: 213). As an alternative, positioning mathematics within a feminist epistemology enriches the discipline while also enabling historically marginalized communities, such as women, to feel that they, too, have the power to author and own it.

Heather Mendick has produced a related line of work in exploring the tensions faced by young women who study mathematics. Mendick found strongly gendered perceptions of mathematics that influenced young women's decisions to continue in the discipline. Through narrative analysis, Mendick (1995a,b) explores how women and men author their femininity and masculinity vis-à-vis the discipline, and she concludes, 'These discourses are oppositional and gendered; they inscribe mathematics as masculine, and so it is more difficult for girls and women to feel talented at and comfortable with mathematics and so to choose it and to do well at it' (1995a: 27–8). Although Mendick does not delve into the pedagogical roots of such perceptions, Marijolijn Witte offers this possibility:

The emphasis on knowledge-transmission creates a system of mathematics education in which students are taught to mimic experts. Children learn knowledge which is not necessarily useful to them in their (personal, or local) situations, or for solving their own problems. They are under the control of the teacher or the school textbook, outside authorities in matters which they feel are also their own. (1995: 238)

Supporters of feminist epistemologies argue that they could serve to open the discipline to a greater range of communities as well as further the discipline by releasing it from narrowly prescribed paths.

Although Burton perceives little support for challenging the notion of 'objectivity' in mathematics, the work of feminist science writers, such as Donna Haraway and Sandra Harding, add support to the idea that we can offer richer accounts of the world by employing critical feminist stances. One of the outcomes of such work would be 'humane, responsive, negotiable and creative' (Burton, 1995: 222) mathematics taught to students in schools. Helen Longino, a philosopher, offers an alternative to the notion of feminist epistemology, while still employing feminist principles. Longino suggests a contrast between two positions, those of 'feminist science' and of 'doing science as a feminist'. Rather than offering a different version of the discipline, she argues that researchers should approach the many activities that 'constitute science practice with a feminist sensibility' (1987: 475). Longino lists six virtues: empirical adequacy, novelty, ontological heterogeneity, complexity of relationship, applicability to current human needs, and diffusion of power. She argues that feminist epistemology should be understood as practice rather than content, and that it should shape the ways people approach their work in science and, we would argue, mathematics. Such approaches may of course lead to the positive changes in the disciplines that feminist mathematicians and scientists support.

No differences

A sixth body of work that considers gender in mathematics and science emanates from sociologists and others outside education. In recent years, an interesting counter-argument has been offered by researchers who dispute the idea of innate differences and suggest that gender differences have been overstated, exaggerated and grandized. Books such as *Same Difference: How Gender Myths are Hurting Our Relationships, Our Children and Our Jobs* (Barnett and Rivers, 2005) and *Deceptive Distinctions: Sex, Gender and the Social Order* (Epstein, 1988) argue against the *existence* of gender differences, saying that the act of focusing upon gender is harmful and dichotomizing, creating the very gender differences that researchers hope to eradicate. In their chapter on mathematics, Barnett and Rivers (2005) rely on meta-analyses that amalgamate the achievement scores of boys and girls on many different tests. The three meta-analyses they show lead them to the conclusion that 'math scores are roughly equivalent'. But while the 'dichotomous' argument carries the danger of essentialism and stereotyping, the counter-argument, that gender differences do not exist, runs a different risk – that of overlooking the harsh inequalities that pervail in many places and that cause unequal achievement and participation. The experiences of girls in mathematics classes in England provide a good case in point, as it was the work of feminist scholars in the 1970s and 1980s, responding to small achievement differences, that probably enhanced the experiences of girls in mathematics classes. If researchers had overlooked the subtle differences between the sexes, these important achievements may not have been made.

DISCUSSION AND CONCLUSION:
GENDER AS A COMPLEX INTERACTION

Perhaps the only conclusion that can be drawn from such a review of the field is that researchers need to consider many different factors that influence the performance and participation of girls and boys. Issues such as underconfidence, sexism in teaching environments, subject distortions, and different cognitive preferences may all play a part in low performance and participation. Of course, it is difficult for researchers to conduct studies that consider all variables, but the neglect of such critical variables as teaching environments should make researchers exercise considerable caution when drawing conclusions about the causes of differences. When Boaler conducted a study of two schools in England with different teaching approaches, she found that one school produced gender differences and one did not (1997a; 2002a,b). Further, the gender differences seemed to come about through a preference for a different learning approach that girls displayed in traditional classrooms. Boaler points out that one conclusion could be that the girls at Amber Hill, a school employing a traditional approach, preferred certain ways of working, and that these were not supported by the procedural approach of their school. She notes that this interpretation has some validity, but it also has potential dangers, as it locates the preferences that emerged *within the girls*. A different consideration of the data highlights the fact that gender responses were produced only within one of the two environments, suggesting that the underachievement and disaffection of girls from Amber Hill was a co-production, the mathematics environments playing a central role. Indeed, the vastly different responses and achievements of girls within the two different school environments would support the idea that environments, rather than institutionalized categories, such as gender or culture, may be a more productive site for the location of equity analyses. This positioning acknowledges the contributions of girls and pays attention to any preferences or approaches they bring, but the focus is on the environments and the ways they may promote or inhibit equity.

Relational analyses that locate gender as a response that emerges between people and environments may seem obvious and noncontroversial, but they differ from traditional equity analyses in many ways. Our preference for a situated, relational conception of gender and culture derives partly from a quest for ecological validity but also from the implications that such conceptions carry for action and change, and for the responsibility they place upon educational organizations for making change. We have a long history of equity research that has drawn conclusions about groups of people and publicized these, at some cost. In suggesting that girls were lacking whether through genetic inferiority, 'learned-helplessness' or 'maladaptive tendencies', researchers also suggested that girls needed to change, diverting the focus from other places, such as the classroom environment or subject, that may be more productively changed. Equity researchers, in particular, bear an enormous responsibility to consider the ways they are interpreting and framing their data, because of the 'mythologies' (Fennema, 1981: 384) of inadequacy that may be constructed. The prevailing notion that girls are innately inferior to boys in mathematics is certainly a stumbling block in our efforts to provide girls with equal access to advanced mathematical fields. But such notions have a long societal history and have proved to be resilient. Michele Cohen (1999) gives an important historical perspective on the tendency of some people to consider women and girls as inherently inferior. She analyzed the recent furor in the UK that has been prompted by national examination data showing that girls are now ahead of boys in all subjects, including mathematics and science (DfES, 2004). In doing so, she points out that female underachievement has always been partially accepted as a corollary of being female, whereas the idea of male underachievement has prompted recent, widespread investigations into the *external* culprits:

> Boys' achievement has been attributed to something within – the nature of their intellect – but their failure has been attributed to something external – a pedagogy, methods, texts, teachers. The full significance of this becomes clear when the subject of the discourse is girls, for in their case it is their failure which is attributed to something within – usually the nature of their intellect – and their success to something external: methods, teachers or particular conditions. (Cohen, 1999: 20)

Varenne and McDermott (1999) advocate a refocusing of the equity lens away from individuals and categories of people, and onto the systems which co-produce difference. The refocusing that they suggest involves departing from the essentialism of categories evident in claims that girls are 'maladaptive' or conceptually lacking, and committing resources to careful explorations of the circumstances that produce differences between groups. As with many such social constructs (e.g. race, ethnicity, class), gender has been used to order our world and categorically simplify it. Distinguishing masculine from feminine has, at times, served to propagate theories of inequality and inferiority rather than illuminate how context and practice create, indeed co-produce, gender inequality. In this chapter, the study of gender is taken up, not as validation of a culturally produced hierarchical social order, but rather to challenge such ordering and question its place in an emerging tradition of educational research and practice. Under this rubric of research, gender is not a tool of essentialism (as it has been used in the past) but rather an analytic lens through which to understand *gender as response* and develop equitable educational practices and learning environments to reduce the inequities they produce. We have reached an important point in history, characterized by widespread awareness of the need to make mathematics and science more equitable. We argue that an important part of the endeavor will involve displacing long-held myths concerning women's inferiority, and performing complex analyses of gender interactions in mathematics and beyond.

REFERENCES

Barnett, R and Rivers, C (2005) *Same difference: how gender myths are hurting our relationships, our children and our jobs.* New York: Basic Books.

Becker, J (1981) Differential treatment of females and males in mathematics class. *Journal for Research in Mathematics Education,* 12: 40–53.

Becker, J (1995) Women's ways of knowing in mathematics, in Rogers, P Kaiser, G (eds) *Equity in mathematics education: influences of feminism and culture* (163–74). London: Falmer Press.

Belenky, MF, Clinchy, BM, Golderberger, NR and Tarule, JM (1986) *Women's ways of knowing.* New York: Basic Books.

Benbow, CP and Stanley, JC (1980) Sex differences in mathematical ability: fact or artifact? *Science,* 210: 1262–4.

Boaler, J (1997a) *Experiencing school mathematics: teaching styles, sex and setting.* Buckingham: Open University Press.

Boaler, J (1997b) When even the winners are losers: evaluating the experiences of 'top set' students. *Journal of Curriculum Studies,* 29: 165–82.

Boaler, J (2002a) *Experiencing school mathematics: traditional and reform approaches to teaching and their impact on student learning* (rev expanded edn). Mahwah, NJ: Lawrence Erlbaum Associates.

Boaler, J (2002b) Paying the price for 'sugar and spice': shifting the analytical lens in equity research. *Mathematical Thinking and Learning,* 4(2 and 3): 127–44.

Bombardieri, M (2005) Summers' remarks on women draw fire. *Boston Globe,* 17 January 2005.

Bosch, C and Trigueros, M (1996) Gender and mathematics in Mexico, in Hanna, G (ed) *Towards gender equity in mathematics education: an ICMI study* (39–48). Dordrecht: Kluwer Academic Press.

Burton, L (ed) (1990) *Gender and mathematics: an international perspective.* London: Cassell.

Burton, L (1995) Moving towards a feminist epistemology of mathematics, in Rogers, P and Kaiser, G (eds) *Equity in mathematics education: influences of feminism and culture,* (209–25). London: Falmer Press.

Chipman, S (1996) Female participation in the study of mathematics: the US situation, in Hanna, G (ed) *Towards gender equity in mathematics education: an ICMI study.* Dordrecht: Kluwer Academic Press.

Cohen, M (1999) 'A habit of healthy idleness: boys' underachievement in historical perspective, in Epstein, D, Elwood, J and Hey, V (eds) *Failing boys? Issues in gender and achievement.* Buckingham: Open University Press.

Coley, R (2001) *Differences in the gender gap: comparisons across racial/ethnic groups in education and work.* Princeton, NJ: Policy Report of Educational Testing Service.

DeBare, I (2004) *Where girls come first: the rise, fall and surprising revival of girls' schools.* New York: Penguin.

Department for Education and Skills (2004) *GCSE and equivalent results for young people in England, 2003/04* (provisional). London: DfES.

Department for Education and Skills (2005) *GCE/VCE A/AS examination results for young people in England, 2003/04* (revised). London: DfES.

Department of Trade and Industry (DTI) (2005) Data on women's participation in mathematics and sciences. www.dti.gov.uk.

Dweck, CS (1986) Motivational processes affecting learning. *American Psychologist,* Special issue: *Psychological science and education,* 41: 1040–8.

Ethington, C (1992). Gender differences in a psychological model of mathematics achievement. *Journal for Research in Mathematics Education,* 23: 166–81.

Epstein, CF (1988) *Deceptive distinctions: sex, gender and the social order.* New York: Russell Sage Foundation.

Fennema, E (1981) Women and mathematics: does research matter? *Journal for Research in Mathematics Education,* 12: 380–5.

Fennema, E, Wolleat, P, Pedro, J and Becker, A (1981) Increasing women's participation in mathematics: an intervention study. *Journal for Research in Mathematics Education,* 12: 107–13.

Fennema, E and Leder, G (eds) (1990) *Mathematics and gender.* New York: Teachers College Press.

Forbes, S (1996) Curriculum and assessment: hitting girls twice? in Hanna, G (ed) *Towards gender equity in mathematics education: an ICMI study* (71–92). Dordrecht: Kluwer Academic Press.

Gibson, JJ (1986) *The ecological approach to visual perception.* Hillsdale, NJ: Lawrence Erlbaum.

Gilligan, C (1982) *In a different voice: psychological theory and women's development.* Cambridge, MA: Harvard University Press.

Greeno, JG, and MMAP (1998) The situativity of knowing, learning and research. *American Psychologist,* 53: 5–26.

Grevholm, B (1996) Women's participation in mathematics education in Sweden, in Hanna, G (ed) *Towards gender equity in mathematics education: an ICMI study* (111–24). Dordrecht: Kluwer Academic Press.

Hanna, G (ed) (1996) *Towards gender equity in mathematics education an ICMI study* (111–24). Dordrecht: Kluwer Academic Press.

Hart, L (1989) Classroom processes, sex of student, and confidence in learning mathematics. *Journal for Research in Mathematics Education*, 20: 242–60.

Herzig, A (2004a) Slaughtering this beautiful mathematics: graduate women choosing and leaving mathematics. *Gender and Education*, 16: 379–95.

Herzig, A (2004b) Becoming mathematicians: women and students of color choosing and leaving doctoral mathematics. *Review of Educational Research*, 74: 171–214.

Hyde, JS Fennema, E and Lamon, S (1990) Gender differences in mathematics performance: a meta-analysis. *Psychological Bulletin*, 107: 139–55.

Jacobs, J and Eccles, J (1985) Gender differences in math ability: the impact of media reports on parents. *Educational Researcher*, March: 20–5.

Johnston, B (1995) Mathematics: an abstracted discourse, in Rogers, P and Kaiser, G (eds) *Equity in mathematics education: influences of feminism and culture* (226–34). London: Falmer Press.

Koontz, T (1997) Know thyself: the evolution of an intervention gender-equity program, in Trentacosta, J and Kenney, M (eds) *Multicultural and gender equity in the mathematics classroom: the gift of diversity 1997 yearbook*. Washington, DC: National Council of Teachers of Mathematics.

Leach, L (1994). Sexism in the classroom: a self quiz for teachers, *Science Scope*, 17: 54–9.

Leder, G (1982) Mathematics achievement and fear of success. *Journal for Research in Mathematics Education*, 13: 124–35.

Leder, G (1996) Gender equity: a reappraisal, in Hanna, G (ed) *Towards gender equity in mathematics education: an ICMI study* (39–48). Dordrecht: Kluwer Academic Press.

Longino, H (1987) Can there be a feminist science? *Hypatia*, 2: 51–64.

Marjoram, T (1994) Are/should boys and girls in mathematics be taught together? *Gifted Education International*, 9: 152–3.

Mendick, H (2005a) A beautiful myth? The gendering of being/doing 'good at maths'. *Gender and Education*, 17: 203–19.

Mendick, H (2005b) Mathematical stories: why do more boys than girls choose to study mathematics at AS-level in England? *British Journal of Sociology of Education*, 26: 235–51.

Niederdrenk-Felgner, C (1996) Gender and mathematics education: a German view, in Hanna, G (ed) *Towards gender equity in mathematics education: an ICMI study* (179–96). Dordrecht: Kluwer Academic Press.

O'Hara, R (2005) *Gender in math, science, and engineering: Stanford researchers discuss new and important evidence*, 4 February, Stanford University (www.stanford.edu/group/IRWG/NewsAnd Events/Forum.html).

Rosser, P (1992) *The SAT gender gap: ETS responds*. Report: Center for Women Policy Studies.

Ryan, J (2005) Brains of men and women only part of story in science. *San Francisco Chronicle*, 3 March, B1.

Seegers, G and Boekaerts, M (1996) Gender-related differences in self-referenced cognitions in relation to mathematics. *Journal for Research in Mathematics Education*, 27: 215–40.

Spender, D (1982) *Invisible women: the schooling scandal*. London: Women's Press.

Spitaleri, RM (1996) Women's know-how and authority: Italian women and mathematics, in Hanna, G (ed) *Towards gender equity in mathematics education: an ICMI study* (205–14). Dordrecht: Kluwer Academic Press.

Statistical Research Center Report (2003) Physics trends. *National Center for Education Statistics, Digest of Education Statistics*.

Varenne, H and McDermott, R (1999) *Successful failure: the school America builds*. Boulder, CO: Westview Press.

Walden, R and Walkerdine, V (1985) *Girls and mathematics: from primary to secondary schooling*. London: University of London Institute of Education.

Walkerdine, V (1989) *Counting girls out*. London: Virago.

Witte, M (1995) Constraints on girls' actions in mathematics education, in Rogers, P and Kaiser, G (eds) *Equity in mathematics education: influences of feminism and culture.* (235–44). London: Falmer Press.

16

Engaging Girls in Science

Angela Calabrese Barton and
Nancy Brickhouse

INTRODUCTION: FEMINIST PATHWAYS IN SCIENCE EDUCATION

At its core, feminism has a dual nature: it is a theory of power relations between women and men, and it is a political movement seeking social justice (Weedon, 1999; Stromquist, 2000). Most researchers in gender and science education have drawn, at least to some extent, upon both of these critical dimensions of feminism. For example, Kenway and Gough (1998) categorize the research in gender and science education into three overlapping themes:

1. studies of girls' underrepresentation in school science and of those interventions intended to increase their participation in formal science experiences;
2. studies and interventions focused on increasing women's participation in tertiary-level science studies and science-related areas of employment;
3. studies which 'deconstruct' the multiple meanings and instantiations of gender and science and its implications for the design of instruction.

This suggests that most efforts to understand girls' participation in science are coupled with clear efforts to right these wrongs. Yet, while these three areas of gender scholarship in science education reinforce the dual nature of feminism as a theory about power relations between men and women and as a movement seeking justice, they also highlight the different nature of these goals.

As *a theory of power relations between men and women*, feminism in science education has worked to uncover sociocultural structures that frame women's experiences. For example, researchers have documented and explained the differences between girls and boys in terms of participation, attitudes, achievement, career trajectories, and learning strategies (e.g. Kahle *et al.*, 1993; Weinburg, 1995; Meece and Jones, 1996; Chambers and Andre, 1997; Baker, 2002; Jones, Howe and Rua, 2000; National Science Foundation, 2003). These issues have changed over time, with earlier studies focusing more on documenting differences between males and females and later studies focusing greater attention on how enactments of gender are mediated by context, including ethnicities, language, family, and socioeconomics (Brickhouse *et al.*, 2000).

As *a movement seeking social justice*, feminism has focused on both needs and rights. Underpinning much of the gender and science education literature has been attention to how understandings of gender and science might lead to pedagogical and curricular interventions that would right the wrongs caused by unequal relations of power between men and women in science and science-learning environments (Calabrese Barton, 1998). Here the research has been more varied, with foci on classroom environment concerns, such as single-sex schooling and coeducation (Baker, 2002; Parker and Rennie, 2002); pedagogical approaches, such as 'female-friendly science' (Rosser, 1997); instructional and curricular design (Mayberry, 1998; Roychoudhury *et al.*, 1995); mentoring, role models, and other equity initiatives (Packard and Hudgings, 2002; Packard, 2003); and teacher expectations and representations of science in the classroom (Gilbert, 2001; Letts, 2001).

While the dualistic nature of feminist work demonstrates clear differences in the focus of gender research in science education, two important commonalities are noted. First, those studies of feminism as a social movement reflect *historical shifts*, with earlier investigations focusing more on how to help girls 'fit' the standard paradigm, and later studies focusing on how the learning environment, instantiations of science, and success in science ought to shift to reflect broader circles of life experiences and worldviews.

Second, gender, as a construct, has gone undertheorized with respect to geopolitical location. In other words, while the examples offered above point to how investigations into gender and science in theory and movement have played out *over time* in science education, they give little insight into how geopolitical *location* matters in how gender is understood and described. Indeed, the vast majority of the literature focused on gender and science education concentrates on Western and industrialized nations. Feminism, as a movement seeking social justice, should explore the variety of ways in which strategies for improving girls' engagement in science must be contextualized by geopolitical location. For example, what opportunities do girls in developing countries have to learn science? What material and cultural resources shape the nature of girls' education in the sciences? How does multinational capitalism shape class relations and material resources in ways that influence school science? What kind of science education is best able to help girls and women improve their lives and the lives of those around them? How might answers to these questions vary in southern India, urban Thailand, or the rural USA?

The purpose of our chapter on gender and science is, therefore, twofold. First, we argue that girls' success in science is better understood through the lens of 'engagement', rather than through the more traditional lenses of 'achievement' or 'careers'. Second, drawing from global perspectives, we complicate our stance by examining engagement from the perspectives of 'feminism as a theory of relation between men and women' and 'feminism as movement toward social justice'. Specifically, in terms of feminism as a theory of power relations between men and women, we look at the tension set up by acknowledging the importance of understanding the commonalities of girls' engagement in science as well as the ways in which girls' engagement in science is embedded in more localized, sociopolitical structures. In terms of gender as a movement for justice, we examine the tension set up by those forms of engagement that are easily recognized by others as 'scientific' and those that may not be. We conclude by asking in what ways an engagement lens might offer a new agenda for science education.

ENGAGEMENT IN SCIENCE

We take our cues for understanding girls' engagement in science from feminist investigations into science and from situative perspectives on learning. Recent feminist science studies argue for an embodied understanding of science (Squier and Littlefield, 2004). These descriptions of an embodied science suggest that scientific practice is as much about the world being studied as it is about the language, symbols and systems we have created to study that world. Science involves not only how one comes to understand the natural world and how that knowledge/practice is situated historically, but also the continuous re-creation of scientific practices and ideas within the systems that support them (Herzig, 2004). In other words, scientific knowledge does not transcend the material world in order to explain it in some acultural manner. Instead, science, like all forms of knowledge, is embedded in the cultural and material resources that produce it.

Similarly, learning science is about not just what learners know, but also how what they know is part of a larger system of activity, feeling, value, and performance (Brickhouse, 2001). Situated theories of learning offer a range of perspectives informed by psychology, sociology, and anthropology on the nature of learning. Taken as a whole, these theories show us how learning is a process in which outcomes and goals are shaped by learners as well as by other historical, political, social, cultural, and physical factors. They challenge conventional explanations about learning as a process by which a learner internalizes knowledge, or where knowledge is 'discovered' by the learner, or 'transmitted' from one person to another. These explanations suggest that knowledge and learning are cerebral only, leaving the nature and context of the learner and his/her world unexplored – 'learning as internalization is too easily construed as an unproblematic process of absorbing the given, as a matter of transmission or assimilation' (Lave and Wenger, 1991: 47).

As these perspectives suggest, we see learning science as an *embodied* activity. Learning science involves not only learning content but also learning how to participate in scientific or science-related communities. In other words, we believe that the question of learning itself is better framed as a question about engagement. Engagement suggests an embodied activity where the process and outcomes are reflected in one's changing participation in socio/cognitive activity. Attention is paid not only to the knowledge, skills, or ways of thinking girls acquire and learn to use, but also to the identities that girls generate or accept within science (and science-related) communities, how these identities are dynamic and locally situated, their reasons for particular forms of engagement, and the relationship they perceive these roles have to the practice of science.

'The work of identity is ongoing' (Wenger, 1998: 154). As girls engage in scientific practices and are seen by others as engaging in scientific practices, identity changes. Understanding that identity has a trajectory is critical because it is what connects the past and the present with the future. Not all forms of engagement with science lead girls to gaining access to science and science-related communities. When girls are left merely to practice doing what they already know how to do (say, follow laboratory procedures), or are left to engage in forms of school science that seem irrelevant to scientific practices in any community outside school (such as memorizing vocabulary words), it seems unlikely that the trajectory of their identities will be toward fuller participation in science. Even well-intended pedagogical approaches that connect science to girls' interests and support girls in developing deep content understandings, but do nothing to cultivate new interests and practices, may ultimately limit girls' options in forming an identity with a trajectory toward new forms of participation in science and science-related communities. For example, Carlone (2004) argues that even when girls develop deep understandings of the content of physics, their opportunities for advancement in the subject are limited unless they take up a science identity that can be recognized and accessed by others.

Yet, as some feminists point out, such theories of learning are not without their limitations (Eisenhart and Finkel, 1998). While we find a situated approach to learning a powerful break from the more deterministic approaches, as feminists, we also believe it is important to keep situated perspectives 'in check' by reminding ourselves of how all situations – and those individuals, cultures, discourses, and histories which make up those situations – are framed by issues of power. Eisenhart and Finkel (1998) point out that power, not just history, is reproduced in situated activity, and both play an important role in who gains entry and how they engage in science within a community of practice. For this reason, our understanding of engagement must be filtered through a critical examination of those qualities of social activity that set up systems of oppression and domination.

How does a perspective on engagement help us to better understand gender and science?

Although men have often held the most lucrative and highly valued positions in science, women *have* engaged in science-related practices across the globe in ways that should be acknowledged and valued. Governmental agencies, such as the US National Science Foundation, the National Research Council Canada, and the African-Caribbean Network for Science and Technology in the UK, keep track of women's participation in science by counting academic degrees. While this is important information to have to know how well women are advancing in high-status science areas, it may present a distorted image of women as marginalized in science overall, when in fact, their marginalization should be understood as far more domain specific. For example, women have dominated the nursing profession for centuries. In recent years in the USA, more women than men have entered medical school, and pediatrics more specifically (AMA, 2004). Women have always been involved in making decisions about the health and nutrition of themselves and their families. Some of women's involvement with the health profession has been explicitly feminist in terms of teaching the medical profession to listen to women's concerns and experiences, and on insisting that medical research on new drugs and procedures take into account the biological differences of men and women (Boston Women's Health Group Collective, 1976). Other areas of science in which women have had an effect is agriculture and environmentalism. Women make environmental decisions based on ecological models (Kempton *et al.*, 1997). In countries such as India, women have been involved in agricultural practices and in activism related to preservation of local forests (Shiva, 1989). Women can be found in numerous science-related communities that often have marginal status, such as environmental action groups (Eisenhart and Finkel, 1998). Women have engaged in science as teachers.

Feminism, as a movement for social justice, points to the need for more and better engagement in science by women and girls. We want them to be more influential at the highest levels of science where they can more effectively affect the direction of scientific research. We want them to have access to those areas of science that remain elusive, such as computer science, mechanical engineering, and physics. We want them to be more effective in working with the health-care system to obtain the kind of medical care that is best for them and their families. And we want them even more involved in global efforts to preserve our natural resources so that we are all working toward a sustainable future.

We want to understand both the ways in which women have engaged in science and girls' engagement in science in equally comprehensive ways. It may well be that many girls are not captivated by the idea of a frictionless, massless pulley (although some are). Their interests in the life sciences may be due to their rather obvious relationship to everyday human needs and experiences. We need to pay attention to the ways in which girls prefer to engage in science while also cultivating interests that may not come so easily. For example, we know that girls and boys both spend many hours in front of computers. However, the nature of their engagement is often quite different between girls and boys (Cassell and Jenkins, 1998). Girls often engage in computing in ways that further their social agendas. Hence, they spend lots of time in chat rooms, and on instant messaging and other computing practices that connect them to other people. While we can value this activity in and of itself, we cannot be satisfied with it. To gain access to the kinds of computing practices that are valued in the computing industry, they must also learn how computers work and how they can be manipulated to do what girls want them to do. If we take learning to be changes in practices that provide access to new communities, we must learn ways of simultaneously recognizing and building on existing interests and competencies, while also building bridges to those forms of scientific practice that provide girls with new opportunities and forms of engagement.

School science certainly ought to be a place for learning new forms of participation in science. However, it seems to us that the problem with school science is that what is learned in school often does not provide real competence in science. The kind of science that is enacted in school is not much like any science-related community that exists outside school. However, school does serve a gatekeeping function. It is difficult to excel at the highest levels of science without considerable academic success in science, simply because academic degrees are the credentials that provide societal recognition of scientific competence. What do we make of achievement data suggesting that girls in developed countries are often doing quite well in science, when there are still large disparities in the numbers of girls who choose to take school science beyond the compulsory years? For example, in physics, computer science, and engineering, the rates of participation by American girls remain very low (NSF, 2003).

Standard forms of achievement neglect to take into account how achievement and actual engagement in science differ. For example, in countries where achievement gaps have narrowed and even closed, engagement in science, overall, is still shown to be unequal in the sense that while girls may be succeeding on measures of standard success, they are not necessarily strongly identifying with science or participating in science careers. For example, results from the ROSE (Relevance of Science Education) survey show that in several of the developing countries included in the survey, such as Uganda, the Philippines, and Ghana, boys and girls express strongly positive attitudes about the value of science and technology for society as well as for their own desires to be scientists (Sjoberg, 2004). In other countries, such as Finland and Japan, countries that scored the highest on PISA (Programme for International Student Assessment) achievement tests, girls expressed the least positive views regarding the value of science and technology for society as well as for their own desires to be scientists.

Furthermore, success in the science trajectory, particularly in high school and college, may have less to do with academic competence than with how one responds to a highly competitive environment that was designed by and for white males. In the USA, Seymour and Hewitt (1997) found that women (undergraduates) were more likely than equally achieving men to leave the sciences. Seymour and Hewitt (1997: 258–60) describe it as follows:

> We posit that entry to freshman science, mathematics, or engineering suddenly makes explicit and then heightens, what is actually a long-standing divergence in the socialization experiences of young men and women.... It occurs when a relatively small number of inexperienced young women are encouraged ... to venture into an institutionalized .... teaching and learning system which has evolved over a long time period as an approved way to induct young men into the adult fraternities of science, mathematics and engineering. Most young white men seem able to recognize and respond to the unwritten rules of this adult male social system. The rules are familiar because they are consistent with, and are an extension of, traditional male norms that were established by parents, and which have been reinforced by male adults and peers throughout their formal education, sports, and social life.

These results suggest that achievement in conventional terms, such as test scores or school grades, may not be a good indicator of whether girls or boys have taken up identities that are likely to lead to further participation in science in ways that will lead to improvements in society.

It seems important to us, therefore, to understand why it is that achievement does not necessarily lead to access to high-status science. If one wants to understand why it is that access to many areas of science continues to be a struggle, one must look beyond achievement and examine more broadly how gendered identities are constructed and how they interact with an educational system that serves an important gatekeeping function.

Although women's access to high-status science in Western countries has been the subject of considerable study and debate, we know far less about how women gain access to other kinds of scientific practices that are not tracked by elite organizations such as the National Science Foundation. For example, we know that adults use ecological models to make environmental decisions, but we do not know how women who do this effectively actually constructed these models. We know that some women (but not enough) read and effectively critique science in making decisions about the health of their babies (Lottero-Perdue, 2005). For example, Lottero-Perdue (2005) found that women in a nursing mothers organization critiqued medical texts that conflicted with their beliefs by examining funding sources and how such sources may be influenced by profit motives. However, this study also showed that these women rarely questioned scientific texts with which they agreed. What this literature as a whole suggests is that considerably more study is needed of how science is utilized in local contexts in ways that are empowering and effective and of the variety of ways such competence might be developed. These dual concerns for engagement in science that acknowledges the ways in which girls and women have engaged in science *and* argues for more and better forms of engagement in science can be examined through the experiences of Shagufta, a primary school teacher in urban Pakistan.

EXAMINING ENGAGEMENT FROM A FEMINIST PERSPECTIVE

Shagufta's story

Shagufta,[1] a primary school science teacher in a charity school serving the very poor in Lahore, Pakistan, is not typical of her country in many respects. Her route to becoming a science teacher was marked by numerous obstacles. She grew up in a high-poverty community and had to struggle against social and economic oppression to complete high school and then attend teacher-training school. Since she attended government-run schools, she had little access to high-status science courses and expectations were that her formal schooling would end at the secondary level. Further by completing high school and teacher training, Shagufta was criticized by community members and some family members as being 'unmarriable' and a danger to her community. Some even suggested that her late evening hours were not spent in school but as a 'woman of the night'. Yet, Shagufta worked hard to build alliances among family members, such as her father and grandmother, who had some familial and community influence in order to help her complete school.

Shagufta also sought out a teaching position in a high-poverty community, despite its low pay and status, because she believed in the importance of working to create new opportunities for other children from backgrounds similar to her own. Shagufta was realistic about how much she could help these children improve their prospects. From her own experiences, she knew that poor children in her country are pushed by economic structures into the labor market by the time they are 12 to help with family expenses. She also knew that the national curriculum in her country's schools focused on gearing students to pass national exams, and failed to take into account either how or why most of her students might not be in school long enough to take the exams. Further, she believed that the curricular expectations held at both the national and local levels neglected to embrace the teaching of subjects in ways that could be useful for children in their lives – in ways that could help them to live healthier lives or in ways that could help them to navigate the complex social and political structures which frame life in poverty in Pakistan.

Finally, Shagufta viewed the purposes of science education as both access to school knowledge and experiences that make further education possible, and access to scientific ideas and ways of thinking that might help girls and their families to live healthier lives. Shagufta believed that she should educate her students in science issues that relate directly to their health and well-being. For example, because of high child mortality rates resulting from water-borne diseases, Shagufta believed it was important to teach about the polluted, open-irrigation system in her community – a source of water that many children play in and drink from, but that also spreads disease. In addition to the power of science in daily decision making, Shagufta wanted to help her students understand the power that science can play in the community. She believed, for example, that open-irrigation systems were not a viable way of life, and that unless community members had the understanding they needed to speak up about the issue, these systems would continue to exist as the primary method of water irrigation. Shagufta believed that children needed to know that just because they belong to a caste in which education is viewed as a less powerful road to improved economic and social conditions than joining the labor market young, they need not give up on the prospect of using education to change their lives. Shagufta herself came from a poor family, but through her own persistence and willingness to be ostracized by her community, she was able to complete high school and become a science teacher, a position that made her somewhat economically powerful and independent within her community.

Shagufta's story raises two parallel tensions for us. First, her story illustrates how one's construction of a gendered identity within local and global frames controls access to opportunities to engage in science. Living as female in a society marked by patriarchal mores limited Shagufta's opportunities to participate in school science. However, her story also shows that she used her particular position as a determined daughter in a family willing to take social risks to find alternate routes into science. Second, Shagufta's story allows us to explore how one's choice – or need – to engage in science is related to access to power. We take up each of these tensions below, relating how both dimensions of engagement are critical yet not always complementary.

Feminism as a critique of power relations: understanding girls' engagement in science through gender as a unifying theme and a local construct

In this section we delve into the first tension set up by understanding girls' engagement through the lens of gender as a unifying theme and also as a local construct. Throughout this chapter, we describe research in science education in terms of gender, yet we also refer to the needs, experiences, and rights of women and girls. We should perhaps describe how we think about the category 'women' and 'girls', since this is a much debated matter within feminism.

Second-wave feminism has been criticized for overgeneralizing the experiences of white, middle-class women to *all* women across the globe. This met with objections from women of color, in both Western countries and developing countries, who argued that the experiences of white middle-class women were not their experiences (Nicholson, 1998), and from queer theorists, who claimed that a unitary meaning of 'woman' marginalizes certain practices and reinforces the binary of 'woman' in opposition to 'man' (Butler, 1990). While some feminists have argued that gender must be understood to have an infinite number of meanings, others have argued that feminists must be able to generalize if they are to have any kind of theory at all (Nicholson, 1998). We agree with Fraser and Nicholson (1990) that we should not simply assume either a common meaning for gender across contexts *or* a multiplicity of meanings with no overlap. Rather, we need to understand better where common experiences do and do not exist and how these experiences and our understandings of them are tied to diverse contexts (Nicholson, 1990).

Feminist researchers in developed countries argue for the use of 'gender' as the key analytic category in an effort to thwart attempts to naturalize differences between men and women (i.e. Scantlebury and Baker, in press). For example, in developed countries, the focus on 'gender' has led to studies focused on the relationship between gender and science and studies of ethnicity (Griffard and Wandersee, 1999); gay, lesbian, bisexual and transculture (Letts, 2001; Snyder and Broadway, 2004); and urban studies (Brickhouse, 2001). However, researchers in developing countries argue for the use of the category 'women' to focus attention on the link between women and lack of economic and social power in systems where the oppression of women is exceptionally great (Stromquist, 2000). In developing countries, the focus on 'women' and science has led to studies that document differential access with respect to political structure, predominant social mores, and economics (Scantlebury and Baker, in press). This makes sense: by and large, girls in developed countries have achieved greater access to science opportunities, and social structures have been put in place to help reduce structural inequities that work against women, yet differences in engagement in science still remain across girls from differing backgrounds. In developing countries, feminists still fight for the right for girls to attend school, to have schools located within commutable distances, or to have science (or any outside-the-home career) as viable options for women.

These two approaches set up an important tension that, if taken seriously, helps to elucidate both micro-and macrolevel structures of oppression that frame girls' experiences in science globally. The developed countries' focus on the diversity of gendered experiences has led to the depoliticization of women's experiences, yet its attention to embodied experiences opens up new ways of thinking about the complexity of relationships between sex, gender, ethnicity and science engagement. The developing countries' focus on woman can lead to the essentialization of women's experiences, yet serves to remind us of how macrostructures (such as the political state) frame interpretations of gender and access to science.

Engagement in science and feminism as a movement for social justice: understanding girls' engagement in science through authentic engagement and access to power

Returning to Shagufta's story, we see how her experiences with gender, science, and schooling illustrate a set of complex, but often contradictory concerns. Her story challenges current definitions of what it means to be successful in science, or of how or why young girls living in poverty in a developing country might be encouraged to engage in science. Her story involves a pressing blend of 'needing to achieve in easily recognized ways' for access and status issues of primary importance, given her sociocultural location, and 'needing to expand what science learning/engagement ought to look like' in order to help change the conditions that ultimately frame access, opportunity and status. Finally, her story shows us how science engagement for girls is deeply contextual and responsive to local, national, and global conditions. Had Shagufta grown up privileged in Pakistan, or even poor in the USA or another First World country, her story and beliefs about science would probably be different. In short, Shagufta's story foregrounds the importance of engaging in science in order to access the traditional power structures that mediate advancement in the sciences as well as the need to locate other modes for engaging girls in science that challenge the power dynamics that frame daily living.

Shagufta's story, therefore, reveals an important tension that emerges when we examine girls' and women's success in science through the lens of engagement: the tension between achieving in conventional, easily recognized ways and participating in ways that may have less status, but could help improve the living conditions of those around them. The first side of this tension highlights the important role that gatekeeping functions, such as access to rigorous science classes or high stakes tests, play in girls' opportunities to engage in science at powerful and formal levels.

The other side of the tension, challenging the standard direction, illustrates how using such a narrow focus is detrimental to seeking increased engagement in science by all girls across the globe. 'Other' modes of engagement that are not captured on standardized measures – from participation in an after-school technology club to learning about health hazards in the community – offer girls opportunities to engage in science in ways that foster the development of scientific identities, teach them about the content and practice of science, and give them credibility (power) within local communities, whether that be among their peers, their neighbors, or others. These other forms of engagement can sometimes be viewed as trajectories of success, because it is in these other places where girls may engage in science in ways that teach them new scientific understandings, foster new identities, and offer new forms of authorship/position.

However, we can also view these other forms of engagement as crucial 'entry points' into the standard science trajectory. If girls gain a sense of being scientific in an after-school club, it may be the momentum they need to propel them into high-level science courses or science careers. Girls should not be looked at as either in an inbound trajectory toward full participation in a scientific community or as a non-participant, but, rather, as moving within the gray spaces that occupy the (porous) boundaries of science and science-related communities (Wenger, 1998). Some may occupy other trajectories that lead to peripheral participation in science or trajectories that link communities of practice (Wenger, 1998).

Therefore, we need further understanding of how nonstandard opportunities to engage in science foster the ways in which girls learn to identify with and in science, and to feel capable of using science, as both a tool and context, for bringing about local change. What we are trying to capture in this tension is the idea that access to powerful scientific careers is partly determined by gatekeeping devices, and thus access on these standard terms ought to remain of high importance. However, access to science at any level – be it at the level of powerful science careers or family health care – is also mediated by opportunities to engage in science in authentic terms. Opportunities to gain power can strongly influence how one is able to engage authentically in science (or to help others do so), and authentic engagement opens up multiple entry points for identifying with and practicing in science. While we will never really know for sure whether Shagufta would have succeeded as a science teacher had she not had multiple points of entry into science, that is, a desire to make change in her community; an identity as someone who was competent, scientific, and strong; and consistent paternal support, we surmise that it was more than grades that allowed her to succeed. After all, her opportunities after high school were limited. However, she created circumstances to allow her to pursue her desire to be a science teacher.

A NEW AGENDA

In this chapter, we have discussed the importance of using the lens of engagement to describe girls' opportunities to learn and to succeed in science. We used two themes to help us flesh out our stance on engagement. First, that feminism is both a theory of gender relations and a movement seeking social justice. Second, that science and gender are both unifying themes and local embodiments that influence access both to power and to authentic science experiences. Both lenses are important for framing how, when, and why girls choose to – and are allowed to – *engage* in science. Engagement in science is a right that all girls should have. It is also a practice that is deeply grounded in the social practices and norms of the contexts in which girls live.

We believe that this approach opens up new questions about gender and science because it posits that helping girls meet the current norms for success in science is as important as asking how success ought to be understood (and measured). Girls' opportunities to engage in science are mediated by local contexts, and national and international narratives. Understanding how girls' experiences in science differ from boys must be positioned as emergent from normalized gendered practices and structures, and situationally relevant circumstances. Approaches to 'solving' the gender and science dilemma must be equally diverse.

As we attend to the needs of girls worldwide, it seems critical to attend to the local context and refrain from imposing Western standards in ways that do not fit local needs. Our understandings of gender will be enriched by a closer examination of the lives of women and girls in science across the globe. As feminists in the USA, we need to understand how the politics of our own country shape the nature of engagement of girls and women in science across the globe as well as our efforts to understand and define girls' engagement. We should never assume that effective interventions for girls in science in the developed world would have similar effects in the developing world. We should also never assume that how we measure success in the developed world is the only way of determining a girl's access to science. Limited understandings close doors to science for girls globally.

At the same time as we Western feminists need to be modest in what we claim to understand about girls and women in contexts very different from our own, we also need to give much greater attention to the needs of girls and women in places where access to science appears to be at least limited. The politics of feminism require building coalitions with those who are most knowledgeable and directly affected by the local conditions we seek to improve. Creating new ways of communicating with feminists across the globe, including feminists in academia, nongovernmental organization, the political state (at local, national and international levels), and the market place, will add complexity to how we describe, identify, or act upon the challenges and solutions to girls and science.

As we move toward a different global order, considerations of how girls' opportunities to succeed in science are mediated by national and international narratives around gender, science, and success and local instantiations of those narratives must remain challenged. We assert that by being ever mindful of how 'engagement' in science, as a reflection of our changing participation in science-related communities, frames access to science trajectories, we will create new opportunities and a new discourse for understanding the challenges girls face in gaining the knowledge, skills, or ways of thinking they need to engage in science on its own terms as well as to support emerging or new identities within science (and science-related) communities.

REFERENCES

American Medical Association (AMA) (2004) *Physician characteristics and distribution in the US*. Washington, DC: American Medical Association.

Baker, D (2002) Good intentions: an experiment in middle school single-sex science and mathematics classrooms with high minority enrollment. *Journal of Women and Minorities in Science and Engineering*, 8: 1–23.

Boston Women's Health Group Collective (1976) *Our bodies ourselves*. New York: Simon and Schuster.

Brickhouse, N (2001) Embodying science: a feminist perspective on learning. *Journal of Research in Science Teaching*, 38: 282–95.

Brickhouse, NW, Lowery, P and Schultz, K (2000) What kind of a girl does science? The construction of school science identities. *Journal of Research in Science Teaching*, 37: 441–58.

Butler, J (1990) *Gender trouble: feminism and the subversion of identity*. New York: Routledge.

Calabrese Barton, A (1998) *Feminist science education*. New York: Teachers College Press.

Carlone, H (2004) The cultural production of science in reform-based physics: girls' access, participation, and resistance. *Journal of Research in Science Teaching*, 41: 392–411.

Cassell, J and Jenkins, H (1998) *From Barbie to Mortal Kombat: gender and computer games*. Cambridge, MA: MIT Press.

Chambers, S and Andre, T (1997) Gender, prior knowledge, interest, and experience in electricity and conceptual change text manipulations in learning about direct current. *Journal of Research in Science Teaching*, 34: 107–25.

Eisenhart, MA and Finkel, E (1998) *Women's science: learning and succeeding from the margins.* Chicago, IL: University of Chicago Press.

Fraser, N and Nicholson, L (1990) Social criticism without philosophy: an encounter between feminism and postmodernism, in Nicholson, L (ed) *Feminism/postmodernism* (pp19–38) New York: Routledge.

Gilbert, J (2001) Science and its 'other': looking underneath 'woman' and 'science' for new directions in research on gender and science education. *Gender and Education,* 13: 291–305.

Griffard, P and Wandersee, J (1999) Challenges to meaningful learning in African-American females at an urban science high school. *International Journal of Science Education,* 21: 611–32.

Herzig, R (2004) On performance, productivity, and vocabularies of motive in recent studies of science. *Feminist Theory,* 5: 127–47.

Jones, MG, Howe, A and Rua, M (2000) Gender differences in students' experiences, interests, and attitudes toward science and scientists. *Science Education,* 84: 180–92.

Kahle, J, Parker, SH, Rennie, LJ and Riley, D (1993) Gender differences in science education: building a model. *Educational Psychologist,* 28: 379–404.

Kempton, W, Boster, JA and Hartley, J (1997) *Environmental values in American culture.* Boston, MA: MIT Press.

Kenway, J and Gough, A (1998) Gender and science education in schools: a review with 'attitude'. *Studies in Science Education,* 31: 1–30.

Lave, J and Wenger, E (1991) Situated learning: legitimate peripheral participation. Cambridge: Cambridge University Press.

Letts, WJ (2001) When science is strangely alluring: interrogating the masculinist and heteronormative nature of primary school science. *Gender and Education,* 13: 261–74.

Lottero-Perdue, PS (2005) Critical analysis of science-related texts in a breastfeeding information, support, and advocacy community of practice. Unpublished doctoral dissertation, University of Delaware.

Mayberry, M (1998) Reproductive and resistant pedagogies: the comparative roles of collaborative learning and feminist pedagogy in science education. *Journal of Research in Science Teaching,* 35: 443–59.

Meece, J and Jones, G (1996). Girls in mathematics and science: constructivism as a feminist perspective. *High School Journal,* 79: 242–9.

National Science Foundation (NSF) (2003) *Gender differences in the careers of academic scientists and engineers: a literature review.* Washington, DC: National Science Foundation.

Nicholson, L (1998) Gender, in Jaggar, AM and Young IM (eds) *A companion to feminist philosophy.* Malden, MA: Blackwell.

Packard, B (2003) Science career related possible selves of adolescent girls: a longitudinal study. *Journal of Career Development,* 29: 251–63.

Packard, B and Hudgings, D (2002) Physics careers web site: expanding college women's perceptions of physicists' lives and work. *Journal of College Science Teaching,* 32: 164–70.

Parker, L and Rennie, L (2002) Teachers' implementation of gender-inclusive instructional strategies in single-sex and mixed-sex science classrooms. *International Journal of Science Education,* 24: 881–97.

Rosser, S (1997) *Reengineering female friendly science.* New York: Teachers College Press.

Roychoudhury, A, Tippins, D and Nichols, S (1995) Gender-inclusive science teaching: a feminist constructive perspective. *Journal of Research in Science Teaching,* 32: 897–930.

Scantlebury, K and Baker, D (in press) Gender issues in science education research: remembering where the difference lies, in Abell, S and Lederman, N (eds) *Handbook of research in science teaching.* Lawrence Erlbaum Associates.

Seymour, E and Hewitt, N (1997) *Talking about leaving: why undergraduates leave the sciences.* Boulder, CO: Westview Press.

Shiva, V (1989) *Staying alive: women ecology and development.* London: Zed Books.

Sjoberg, SJ (2004) Science education: the voice of the learners. Paper presented at the conference on Increasing Human Resources for Science and Technology in Europe, Brussels, April 2004. http://folk.uio.no/sveinsj.

Snyder, V and Broadway, F (2004) Queering high school biology textbooks. *Journal of Research in Science Teaching*, 41: 617–36.

Squier, S and Littlefield, M (2004) Feminist theory and/of science. *Feminist Theory*, 5: 123–9.

Stromquist, N (2000) Voice, harmony, and fugue in global feminism. *Gender and Education*, 12: 419–33.

Upadhayay, B, Calabrese Barton, A and Zahur, R (2005) Teaching science in a poor school in urban Pakistan: tensions in the life history of a female elementary teacher. *Science Education*. Published online 30 June 2005.

Weedon, C (1999) *Feminism, theory and the politics of difference.* Malden, MA: Blackwell.

Weinburg, M (1995) Gender differences in student attitudes toward science: a meta-analysis of the literature from 1970 to 1991. *Journal of Research in Science Teaching*, 43: 387–98.

Wenger, E (1998) *Communities of practice: learning, meaning, and identity.* Cambridge: Cambridge University Press.

NOTE

1. A pseudonym. For a more detailed examination of Shagufta's story, see Upadhyay *et al.* (2005).

17

Gender and Literacy

Bronwyn Davies and Sue Saltmarsh

This chapter considers how the intersecting discourses of gender and literacy construct subjectivities in relation to the current neoliberal social and economic order. We discuss the formation of gendered and literate subjectivities, and gender/literacy debates in the context of neoliberal education reforms. We draw on Certeau's (1984) concept of the scriptural economy to illustrate how the economic order is implicated in literate practices, and how these, in turn, shape constructions of gender and literacy in school and home settings. We argue that gender inequity is exacerbated by the incorporation of economically driven ideologies into notions of what it means to be a gendered literate social subject.

THE DISCURSIVE CONSTRUCTION OF GENDERED LITERATE SUBJECTS

While literacy practices are often assumed to be liberatory, particularly in relation to populations who have been systematically disenfranchised (Freire, 1970) or nations that have not yet become part of the global economy, what we want to consider here is how literacy practices produce students as particular types of social subjects in ways which reproduce the binary gender order. Educational discursive practices, like the discursive practices of other disciplines (see Henriques *et al.*, 1984), are understood here as constitutive – producing students as simultaneously both gendered *and* literate. Because these constitutive processes are embedded within the routine practices of schooling, they are not always readily apparent, so that teachers' attempts to liberate children from what they perceive as limitations of class, poverty, ethnicity or gender may actually be undermined through literacy practices (Bjerrum Nielsen and Davies, 1997; Davies and Corson, 1997; Davies *et al.*, 2001; Phoenix, 2001; Alloway *et al.*, 2003).

The binary gender order is normalized and naturalized through discourses and practices of literacy in ways that are not necessarily easy to detect. Analyses of children's readers (Baker and Freebody, 1989; Jackson and Gee, 2005) show how literacy texts are implicated in shaping the subjectivities of young readers, and Davies' (1989; 1993) analyses of children's engagement with texts and storylines shows how gendered subjectivities are tacitly produced in texts and reproduced in students' play, and reading and writing activities. This production and reproduction is intrinsic to 'teaching-as-usual', which, in its apparent naturalness and normality, is not readily available to the reflexive, analytic gaze of either teachers or students (Davies and Hunt, 1994; Kamler *et al.*, 1994; Davies *et al.*, 2004).

This is not to suggest that individuals are unable to recognize and resist the (often prescriptive) gendered subject positions associated with literacy learning, but rather that they must negotiate their gendered subjectivities in relation to the subject positions made available to them in particular historic and discursive locations (Davies, 2000a). This may involve developing an awareness of the constitutive effect of inequitable discourses, and taking steps to change those discourses (Davies, 1990, 1997, 2000b; Francis and Skelton, 2005). A necessary step in opening the possibility of such agency for teachers and students in this context of literacy and gender is the careful examination of literacy and gender discourses at work (Francis, 2000).

In contemporary Western societies, intelligibility as a desirable social subject relies heavily on successfully accomplishing standards of literacy deemed appropriate within the gender order. This has become all the more important in the context of global education reforms, in which economic participation has become equated with notions of citizenship and social inclusion (Marginson, 1997). In the interests of shaping students up as workers, literacy (together with numeracy) has been promoted by successive governments internationally as a 'basic skill' to which all other measures of academic success and personal achievement must remain subordinate. Intelligibility, and indeed viability, as a social subject within this global context, require that literacy practices are presented as gender neutral. We will argue here that they are not.

NEO-LIBERAL REFORMS AND THE QUESTION OF BOYS' DISADVANTAGE

Neo-liberal education reforms are the subject of an extensive international literature that raises persistent concerns about the implications of educational provision according to market models (see, for example, Codd, 1993; Marginson, 1996; Ball, Bowe and Gewirtz, 1997; Whitty, *et al.*, 1998; Gillborn and Youdell, 2000; Apple, 2001; Tomlinson, 2001; Davies, 2005). Within such models, education and the knowledges and skills it imparts are recast as products, the purchase of which enables consumers to obtain 'positional advantage' (Hirsch, 1977; Marginson, 1995) in competition with others. Under the rhetorical guise of choice, flexibility, excellence, efficiency and accountability, advocates of market reforms argue that consumer demand for quality education is the best means of ensuring improvements in educational standards, as schools compete to deliver quality educational products and services which place them advantageously in the education market.

Within this context, literacy is presented as a desirable, albeit neutral, generic skill, around which an array of reforms such as national testing, standardization of curricula, reliance on evidence-based practice, increased reporting, and so on have been implemented. Cast as strategies for addressing consumer demand for educational excellence and practitioner accountability (rather than as addressing disparities of participation and outcomes), these technologies are intended to push teachers and students alike to attempt to generate higher levels of achievement for all students with the aim of fitting them to be appropriate workers in the neo-liberal economy (Davies, 2003). The increased focus on individuality, however, means that illiteracy or poor literacy attainment is construed as a consequence of individual deficit associated with notions of 'ability'[1] and/or with 'troubled' family and social backgrounds. Individual schools, in turn, whose students perform poorly, are construed as failing to provide the standards of excellence, efficiency and accountability required by the education market.

Under neo-liberalism, concerns about disparities of access, opportunity, participation and outcomes are displaced by discourses of individual merit and the supposed benefits of marketized educational provision. The impact of these discourses on gender/literacy debates has seen a shift away from concerns about girls' disadvantage in educational and in post-school options for higher education and employment (see Teese *et al.*, 1995; Collins *et al.*, 2000a,b). Turning instead to claims that boys' needs in education have been overlooked in favour of girls, the 'what about the boys?' lobby advocates redirecting funds and services toward specifically addressing the perceived 'natural' needs and interests of boys in schools (West, 2002), who are supposedly disadvantaged by an alleged 'feminization' of schooling. Equity funds have been redirected to boys' education, and to boys' literacy education in particular (Gilbert and Gilbert, 1998; Francis and Skelton, 2005), and inequitable incentives have been introduced with the specific aim of attracting men, in preference to women, to the teaching profession.

What we want to take up here, then, is how the acquisition of literacy (and related economic benefits) function in the current neo-liberal climate as gendered indicators of differential access to power. That some middle-class girls have outstripped some boys (Gilbert and Gilbert, 1998) does not, despite the moral panic surrounding boys' education, undo the inequitable structures and practices that favour men. Globally, low levels of literacy and poverty remain the province of 'poor women and women of colour' (Butler, 2004: 6), while the free, autonomous, competitive individual who is successful within neo-liberal economies is arguably white, middle class and male. Indeed, our search of the gender/literacy literature suggests a heightening of gender differences associated with literacy accomplishment, such that the desirable subject of educational discourse is increasingly one whose gender performativity and literate practices are aligned to (and indeed, reproduce) normative versions of the idealized gendered economic subject.

THE SCRIPTURAL ECONOMY: THE BLANK PAGE ON WHICH THE ECONOMIC SUBJECT IS WRITTEN

Introducing the term 'scriptural economy', Michel de Certeau (1984) directly links literate practices, or the deciphering and production of written scripts, with the economy. In doing so he reconfigures language and identity in terms of production. Certeau links the development of scriptural/writing practices to social changes that emerged in the sixteenth and seventeenth centuries, arguing that for the past three centuries in Western cultures, 'learning to write has been the very definition of entering into a capitalist and conquering society' (Certeau, 1984: 136). Through the elements of the blank page, the constructed text, and the production of meaning through which change is effected, Certeau argues, subjects are constituted according to the capitalist terms of modern Western societies.

The blank page is understood by Certeau as 'a space of its own [that] delimits a place of production for the subject' (Certeau, 1984: 134). Simultaneously, a site of isolation and distance from the world, *and* a site of mastery and autonomy over the production of text, the blank page is a means by which particular subject positions are made available. Through the blank space of the page, the scriptural subject is constituted within a particular set of discursive understandings and possibilities: 'In front of his blank page, every child is already put in the position of the industrialist, the urban planner, or the Cartesian philosopher – the position of having to manage a space that is his own and distinct from all others and in which he can exercise his own will' (Certeau, 1984: 134).

Through his choice of images and of pronouns here Certeau tacitly enters into the construction of the writing subject as masculine. The active subject who asserts his will on the blank fabric of the social world and who accomplishes himself as able to make a difference is readily mapped onto the masculine subject and onto neo-liberalism and the market economy. For the idealized (masculine) subject, the construction of text occurs in/on the space of the blank page (Certeau, 1984), and can be understood in terms of productive activity through which the components and structures of language are deployed to produce, rather than interpret, exterior realities, and to produce, rather than interpret, the individual masculine writing subject. While Certeau's interest here, it may be argued, is in showing how the economic (rather than the gendered) social subject is produced through the subject positions made available/taken up in conjunction with textual practices, his argument (with its tacit masculine subject) enables us to explore the production of the economic subject through literate practices *as a gendered production*. Extension of his argument to include the gendered nature of the literacy discourses and textual practices through which economic subjects are (in part) produced offers new possibilities for understanding the significance of gender and literacy discourses in relation to disparities of access, participation and outcomes in the broader social order. Thus, we might reread the gender/literacy literature with a view to understanding how gender hierarchies and power relations are re/produced and negotiated through literacy practices, as well as how these processes map onto, and are implicated in producing, neoliberal economic discourses in distinctly gendered terms.

Certeau argues that *the* '"meaning" ("sens") of scriptural play, the production of a system, a space of formalization, refers to the reality from which it has been distinguished *in order to change it*' (1984: 135, original emphasis). The manipulation of exteriority through scriptural practices involves both subjection and constitutive capacity, and these together are crucial to expansionist capitalist agendas:

> The island of the page is a transitional place in which an industrial inversion is made: what comes in is something 'received,' what comes out is a 'product.' The things that go in are the indexes of a certain 'passivity' of the subject with respect to a tradition; those that come out, the marks of his power of fabricating objects. The scriptural enterprise transforms or retains within itself what it receives from its outside and creates internally the instruments for an appropriation of the external space. It stocks up what it sifts out and gives itself the means to expand. Combining the power of *accumulating* the past and that of making the alterity of the universe *conform* to its models, it is capitalist and conquering. (Certeau, 1984: 135, original emphasis)

Certeau's argument has a number of implications for studies of gender and literacy, which have a long (albeit varied) tradition of voicing concerns about the ways in which girls, in particular, experience the effects of educational disadvantage in numerous aspects of social life within and beyond schooling. If, as Certeau suggests, scriptural practices are a discursive means by which subjects are produced primarily as economic subjects, then gender debates within literacy studies might usefully be reread in order to consider how the intersections between gender and literacy are implicated in patterns of dominance in the economic order. In the following section, we want to consider how economic discourses are inserted into discourses of gender and literacy in ways which make those economic discourses appear natural and desirable, such that gender/literacy debates facilitate a reconfiguration of gendered subject positions and power relations that are more readily aligned with current economic agendas.

GENDER IN/DIFFERENCES: GENDERED LITERACY PRACTICES AND THE ECONOMIC ORDER

We want to consider here the extent to which the gender order, which inevitably shapes the social and economic landscape out of which education policy emerges, is in turn shaped in literacy classrooms, parent–child interactions, and peer relations in ways which reflect and reinscribe the hidden gender dimensions of neoliberal discourse. For boys, becoming an appropriate/d gendered literate subject is a necessary component of becoming an economic subject, a point that is apparent to even young boys, as noted by Gilbert and Gilbert (1998: 135–36), whose interviews with primary school-age boys found that most 'were quite accepting of and even committed to the notion that school meant doing work and that that was important. When asked about this they invariably pointed out that you needed to do the work for pragmatic reasons – the need to prepare for high school and careers'. Thus, despite the tensions that masculine performativities produce in relation to literacy learning (Martino, 1995), even boys who are resistant to literacy practices are nonetheless aware of the discursive associations of education and economy.

Yet boys may (and, indeed, often do) choose not to conform to the discursive and relational demands placed on them in the processes of becoming and performing themselves as 'scriptural subjects'. They may resist producing themselves as what they perceive as obedient feminine subjects (Davies *et al.*, 2001), and may invest considerable effort in maintaining dominant positions in the social order of classrooms and playgrounds. Thus, while standardized testing may make boys appear less competent, it may also fail to reveal their literacy competencies. Further, it inevitably occludes relations of power and access to power within the gendered economic order, leading to suggestions that the neo-liberal emphasis on standardization and testing has more to do with the control of teachers following the undermining of trust in professional knowledge than with actual literacy and numeracy (Rose, 1999).

For educators concerned with gender equity, the imperative to cultivate students as economic, as well as literate, subjects presents a number of complexities, of which gender is a crucial dimension. Educators are faced with the paradox of calls for greater attention to the educational, emotional, and social needs of boys in schools and classrooms, despite ample evidence that the intersection of gender with factors such as social class, ethnicity, and geographical location is central in determining individual schooling success or failure (Gilbert and Gilbert, 1998; Francis and Skelton, 2005). Paradoxically, educators have been faced with the acknowledged need to find ways of engaging boys in the critical/deconstructive work of recognizing and reconfiguring the ways in which dominant versions of masculinity limit and constrain their educational choices, social relations, and learning outcomes (Davies, 1997).

The recent 'what about the boys?' campaign notwithstanding, a central concern of studies of gender/literacy is the extent to which girls' educational experiences and engagement with literate practices differ from the educational experiences of boys. Millard (1997) argues that boys and girls are discursively produced as 'differently literate' through gendered differences in interactions between teachers and students, through social relations between peers and the social organization of classrooms, and through the texts available to and taken up by students, as well as differences in writing practices, subject preferences, and academic achievements.

Differences in children's access to and location within gender discourses begin long before children enter formal schooling, however, and early childhood studies highlight the ways in which children are constructed, and construct themselves and others as gendered and literate social subjects from very early ages (Davies, 1989/2003; Francis, 1998; Davies and Kasama, 2004). Whether literacy instruction/ practices occur in the contexts of home and family, of popular culture, or of formalized early childhood settings, young children's literate practices are 'read' through discourses of gender, and the texts associated with literacy learning are an important component of their constitution as gendered subjects. For example, research from the 1970s onward (e.g. Baker and Freebody, 1989; Baker and Davies, 1993; Jackson and Gee, 2005) has shown how texts used in literacy instruction, and early childhood texts, construct the reading subject through gendered language, storylines, and visual images. This research documents an important means by which the construction of gendered subject positions and power relations occurs.

More recently some researchers (e.g. Marsh, 2000; 2003) argue that popular cultural texts can be usefully deployed to aid literacy learning. Incorporating popular cultural texts into literacy teaching and literacy activities is seen as a means of acknowledging and engaging with the texts and interests with which children are already familiar and from which they derive pleasure and produce meaning. Rather than reliance on the canonical 'high-culture' texts traditionally favoured in curricula, which, it is argued, fail to draw on children's cultural knowledge, the argument advanced by Dyson, Marsh, and numerous others (for an excellent overview, see Marsh, 2003) is that the popular texts enjoyed by children provide a rich resource for teaching and learning.

While such research acknowledges that popular culture texts are potentially problematic in their tacit reproduction of gender stereotypes, there is a growing tendency to view such texts as potential sites through which teachers can provide a space in which dominant narratives can be disrupted and alternative subject positions and gender identities explored (e.g. Kenway and Bullen, 2001). Notwithstanding the potential of popular texts to engage teachers and students in meaningful re/negotiations of their place in the gender order, it is important to recognize the commercial interests that are served by the successful generation of gendered desires in young consumers. While Marsh notes that the appeal of superhero and other popular figures is part of the 'consumerist universe' (Marsh, 2000: 210) that is already inhabited by children, we would argue that the pervasiveness of such texts in the lives of children raises important questions about how and in what ways popular texts are implicated in constituting the gendered social subjects that teachers encounter in the classroom. This is not to suggest eliminating popular texts as tools in literacy instruction, but rather to note the legitimation they accrue when used as curricular texts, and to mark the importance of interrogating the role of such texts in producing neo-liberal subjectivities and social relations which serve the economy in both implicit and explicit ways. We would argue that the remaking/reconfiguring of commercial texts into pedagogical texts reconfigures literacy teaching/learning (which is already, according to Certeau, a capitalist enterprise) as a transactional/commercial enterprise inexorably tied to industries and economies that education is obliged, through neo-liberal policies, to serve. In this way, the discourses of the market, which depend, in numerous ways, on maintaining gender binaries and hierarchies, become part of the fabric of what it means to be gendered and literate.

In a recent Australian study, Nichols (2002) analyzes how discourses of individualism, child-centred discourses, and discourses of developmentalism inform parents' constitution of their children as particular types of literate social subjects. Nichols' study demonstrates the significance of the concepts of individual choice and productivity that parents employ, so that, through the nuanced processes of categorization, subject positioning, and normalization elaborated in Nichols' study, it is possible to see how children (and their parents) are discursively produced as economic subjects.

Nichols suggests that the discourses of individualism drawn on by parents in the study involve categorizations organized around oppositional categories, and this, in turn, 'has effects on parents' understanding of their child's orientation to literacy' (Nichols, 2002: 130). For example, the description of some girls as 'indoor' types and their brothers as 'outdoor' types creates a distinction 'associated with literacy through a chain of associations linking reading and writing with particular locations and physical practices (e.g. indoors at a desk)' (Nichols, 2002: 130). Nichols argues that gender divides are maintained by attitudes to literacy activities that are understood as the product of individual preferences and characteristics, so that children's choices tend to be 'read' by parents in ways that reflect dominant discourses of gender differences, and then are mapped onto literacy practices in ways that validate or invalidate children's literacy-related preferences. For instance, whereas girls are perceived as having 'natural' or genuine interests in literacy-related activities, boys who engage in such activities may be perceived as merely copying the behavior of others, or as not genuinely interested. Nichols argues that girls are thus validated as literate subjects and boys are not: 'the discourse of individuality allows parents to mobilize notions of choice to validate and invalidate their children's actual behaviours' (Nichols, 2002: 132).

Notions of choice are naturalized as qualities or characteristics of particular categories of social subject and are woven into parents' support of girls' 'natural' qualities and orientations toward literate practices, and boys' choice to participate, or not, in literate practices. The act of choosing is thus reconfigured as a way of being – choosing to *do* literacy-related (or non-literacy related) activities is to *be* a particular natural kind of subject. Paradoxically, in light of Certeau's assertion of the 'scriptural enterprise' as 'capitalist and conquering', girls' veritable immersion in literacy activities by comparison to boys is naturalized and normalized – not so much as a *choice through which they act upon the world*, but rather as an innate disposition. Girls' literate practices are read as activities through which their gender appropriateness (hence their subordinate place in the economic order) is refined and expressed. Boys, on the other hand, are discursively validated as *choosers* and *doers* – so that their choosing and doing, rather than attending to the minutiae of literate skills and practices, is given discursive relevance, thus reflecting their dominant status in the broader economic order. Nichols adds that boys and girls are differentially positioned with respect to notions of creativity and imitation, such that boys' literacies and 'ways of learning' are understood in terms of creative 'production', whereas girls' literacies are constructed in terms of their roles as consumers or imitators of texts, and their 'ways of learning' as 'ways of working'. Such positionings establish boys, rather than girls, in terms of the creative entrepreneurial subjects required by neo-liberal economies.

The differences accomplished through parents' understandings of gender differences, and through popular culture are also reflected in children's writing. Kanaris (1999), for example, analyzes Australian primary school children's narrative accounts of a school excursion, in which girls' patterns of language use, narrative styles, and construction of agency differ considerably from that of boys. Kanaris argues that while girls generally write longer, more complex texts than boys, their texts position them as passive observers or recipients, rather than as the active, autonomous 'doers' at the centre of events and experiences:

> These children's writings reveal their different perceptions and a strongly gendered view of reality, where society's stereotypical notions of boys as doers in a world of action and girls as recipients, even in their own stories, are produced and reproduced and through which boys and girls take up and constantly reaffirm their positions as gendered individuals.
>
> (Kanaris, 1999: 264)

Recalling Certeau's claim that writing functions as a space through which writers act upon the world, Kanaris's findings show how the textual and metaphoric spaces available to and taken up by girls are marked by observation and elaboration, whereas the spaces available to and taken up by boys are marked by boys' recognition of themselves in terms of their capacity for and entitlement to autonomous, productive action on the world. Thus, girls' writing illustrates their recognition of their function in providing descriptive backdrops and elaborated spaces upon which masculine production is enacted. Kanaris notes that despite girls' development of more sophisticated literacy skills than boys, in the world beyond the classroom greater value is placed on the kinds of literacies developed by boys. Kanaris specifically links her argument to the world of work, arguing that girls' efforts at perfecting literacy skills, such as narrative writing, is insufficiently valued in workplaces, compared to the higher value placed on the kinds of literacy skills (with relation to technology use, for example) developed by boys, through which masculinities are secured, rather than threatened:

> As long as girls' achievements in literacy are devalued, girls will continue to be disadvantaged in the real world of work. They will continue … polishing and perfecting a skill which is relatively useless to them in later, post-school life, while boys get on with positioning themselves as noisy, attention-seeking active 'actors' in their own narratives, developing the skills which *will* be valuable to them post-school. (Kanaris, 1999: 266)

Of particular interest here is the extent to which children incorporate their readings of their location in a gender order, *which positions them as particular types of economic subjects,* into the day-to-day routinized reading, writing, and speaking practices through which they accomplish themselves as gendered literate subjects.

Speaking and listening are another means by which gendered learning in schools is facilitated, forming a crucial component of the social relations and discursive practices through which the accomplishment of appropriate gendered/ literate subjectivities are accomplished. Yet, just as the gender dimensions of reading and writing may not be readily discernible to teachers and students, studies of classroom talk (see Alloway and Gilbert, 1997; Bjerrum Nielsen and Davies, 1997; Gilbert, 2003) show how gendered aspects of speaking and listening are normalized in routine classroom practices. Indeed, the gendered aspects of oracy in classrooms are implicated in the production of the gendered economic order, and include the speaking positions available to/taken up by students, the gender-inflected differences in teacher–student interactions, and the role of speaking and listening practices in structuring classroom organization and social relations. Gilbert (2003) makes this link specific, highlighting the important, yet unrecognized work of girls in facilitating classroom learning and peer interaction, and noting the failure of contemporary workplaces to acknowledge the value of such skills:

> In classroom situations, these valuable social conversational skills may often go unnoticed – and, in fact, may not even be recognised skills …. The gendered – and perhaps hidden – dimension to these skills needs to be carefully considered. At a time where changing work cultures and the casualisation of labour emphasise the value of interpersonal communicative skills and competence, we do boys a serious disservice by not emphasising the importance of becoming proficient in these domains. (Gilbert, 2003: 191–2)

While Gilbert acknowledges the need to interrogate gendered aspects of speaking and listening practices in classrooms, she stops short of calling for recognition of the value that girls' skills should have in the world beyond the classroom. The importance of enhancing employability through cultivating these skills is instead posed as a need to offer boys the conversational abilities and aptitudes predominately demonstrated by girls in contemporary classrooms, despite masculine domination of labor market contexts. Reconfiguring communicative skills as marketable attributes necessary to boys' success exemplifies how girls' potential advantages are recast in terms of boys' disadvantage. Increasingly seen as advantageous to enterprise culture, 'soft' skills (empathy, sensitivity, altruism, etc.) are thus actively encouraged and promoted by schools eager to be seen as providing educational practices that are understood as crucial to the future success of businesses (Meadmore and McWilliam, 2001). These differences – treating girls' skills as invisible attributes, while, for boys, those same skills are treated as needing to be acquired to enhance their repertoire of marketable skills – 'highlight the significant link between the discourses of social and economic organization and the gendered acquisition of agency and subjection' (Meadmore and McWilliam, 2001).

We have endeavoured here to show how gender/literacy discourses both shape, and are shaped by, broader discourses of economic participation. The pervasive operation of market discourses in literacy education, we would argue, functions as a legitimating force by which even very young students are shaped to recognize themselves as social subjects whose accomplishment of appropriate gendered literate identities is contingent on their subjection to and alignment with the demands of consumerist societies. The interweaving of economic discourses into literacy teaching and learning, and into the gendered social relations through which literate selves are achieved, is an insidious means by which both literacy and gender reform – as two of the key means by which more equitable educational access, opportunities, and outcomes might be achieved – are conscripted into the neo-liberal project of reconfiguring education according to gendered market models.

REFERENCES

Alloway, N and Gilbert, P (1997) Poststructuralist theory and classroom talk, in Davies, B and Corson, D (eds) *Encyclopedia of language and education,* vol 3: *Oral discourse and education* (53–62). Dordrecht: Kluwer Academic Publishers.

Alloway, N, Gilbert, P, Gilbert, R and Henderson, R (2003) Boys performing English. *Gender and Education,* 15: 351–64.

Apple, M (2001) *Educating the 'right' way: markets, standards, God and inequality.* New York: RoutledgeFalmer.

Baker, C and Davies, B (1993) Literacy and gender in early childhood, in Luke, A and Gilbert, P (eds) *Literacy in contexts: Australian perspectives and issues.* St Leonard's: Allen and Unwin.

Baker, C and Freebody, P (1989) *Children's first schoolbooks.* Oxford: Basil Blackwell.

Ball, S, Bowe, R and Gewirtz, S (1997) Circuits of schooling: a sociological exploration of parental choice of school in social class contexts, in Halsey, A, Lauder, H, Brown, P and Stuart Wells, A (eds) *Education: culture, economy, society.* Oxford: Oxford University Press.

Bird, L and Drewery, W (2000) *Human development in Aotearoa: a journey through life.* Sydney: McGraw-Hill.

Bjerrum Nielsen, H and Davies, B (1997) The construction of gendered identity through classroom talk, in Davies, B and Corson, D (eds) *Oral discourse and education,* vol 3. *Encyclopedia of language and education* (125–35). Dordrecht: Kluwer.

Butler, J (2004) *Undoing gender.* New York: Routledge.

Certeau, M (1984) *The practice of everyday life.* Berkeley, CA: University of California Press.

Codd, J (1993) Neo-liberal education policy and the ideology of choice. *Educational Philosophy and Theory,* 25: 31–48.

Collins, C, Kenway, J and McLeod, J (2000a) *Factors influencing the educational performance of males and females at school and their initial destinations after leaving school.* Department of Education, Training and Youth Affairs. Canberra: AGPS.

Collins, C, Kenway, J and McLeod, J (2000b) Gender debates we still have to have. *Australian Educational Researcher,* 27: 37–48.

Davies, B (1989/2003) *Frogs and snails and feminist tales. Preschool children and gender.* Sydney: Allen and Unwin [2nd edn 2003, Hampton Press].

Davies, B (1990) Agency as a form of discursive practice. A classroom scene observed. *British Journal of Sociology of Education,* 11: 341–61.

Davies, B (1997) Critical literacy in pratice: language lessons for and about boys. *Interpretations.* Special edition: *Critical Literacies,* 30: 36–57.

Davies, B (2000a) *(In)scribing body/landscape relations.* Walnut Creek, CA: AltaMira Press.

Davies, B (2000b) The concept of agency. A feminist poststructuralist analysis, in *A body of writing 1989–1999.* Walnut Creek, CA: AltaMira Press.

Davies, B (1993/2003) *Shards of glass: children reading and writing beyond gendered identities,* rev edn. Cresskill, NJ: Hampton Press.

Davies, B and Corson, D (eds) (1997) Oral discourse and education, in *Encyclopedia of language and education,* vol 3 Dordrech: Kluwer.

Davies, B and Hunt, R (1994) Classroom competencies and marginal positionings. *British Journal of Sociology of Education,* 15: 389–408.

Davies, B and Kasama, H (2004) G*ender in Japanese preschools. Frogs and snails and feminist tales in Japan.* Cresskill, NJ: Hampton Press.

Davies, B, Dormer, S, Gannon, S, Laws, C, Lenz-Taguchi, H, McCann, H and Rocco, S (2001) Becoming schoolgirls: the ambivalent project of subjectification. G*ender and Education,*13: 167–82.

Davies, B, Browne, J, Gannon, S, Honan, E, Laws, C, Mueller-Rockstroh, B and Bendix Petersen, E (2004) The ambivalent practices of reflexivity. *Qualitative Inquiry,* 10: 360–90.

Francis, B (1998) *Power plays: primary school children's constructions of gender, power and adult work.* Stoke-on-Trent: Trentham Books.

Francis, B (2000) *Boys, girls and achievement: addressing the classroom issues.* London: RoutledgeFalmer.

Francis, B and Skelton, C (2005) *Reassessing gender and achievement.* London: Routledge.

Freire, P (1970) *Pedagogy of the oppressed.* New York: Continuum.

Gilbert, P (2003) Gender, talk and silence: speaking and listening in the classroom, in Bull, G and Anstey, M (eds) *The literacy lexicon* (2nd edn). French's Forest: Prentice-Hall.

Gilbert, R and Gilbert, P (1998) *Masculinity goes to school.* St Leonard's: Allen and Unwin.

Gillborn, D and Youdell, D (2000) *Rationing education: policy, practice, reform and equity.* Buckingham: Open University Press.

Henriques, J, Hollway, W and Urwin, C (1984) *Changing the subject. Psychology, social regulation and subjectivity.* London: Routledge. [2nd edn, 1998].

Hirsch, F (1977) *Social limits to growth.* London: Routledge and Kegan Paul.

Jackson, S and Gee, S (2005) 'Look Janet', 'No you look John': constructions of gender in early school reader illustrations across 50 years. *Gender and Education,* 17: 115–28.

Kamler, B, Maclean, R, Reid, J and Simpson, A (1994) *Shaping up nicely: the formation of schoolgirls and schoolboys in the first month of school: a report to the Gender Equity and Curriculum Reform Project, Department of Employment, Education and Training.* Canberra: Australian Government Publishing Service.

Kanaris, A (1999) Gendered journeys: children's writing and the construction of gender. *Language and Education,* 13: 254–68.

Kenway, J and Bullen, E (2001) *Consuming children: education, entertainment, advertising.* Buckingham: Open University Press.

Marginson, S (1995) Markets in education: a theoretical note. *Australian Journal of Education,* 39: 294–312.

Marginson, S (1996) Marketisation in Australian schooling. *Oxford Studies in Comparative Education,* 6: 111–27.

Marginson, S (1997) *Educating Australia: government, economy and citizen since 1960.* Cambridge: Cambridge University Press.

Marsh, J (2000) 'But I want to fly too!': girls and superhero play in the infant classroom. *Gender and Education,* 12: 209–20.

Marsh, J (2003) Early childhood literacy and popular culture, in Hall, N, Larson, J and Marsh, J (eds) *Handbook of early childhood literacy,* (112–25) London: Sage.

Martino, W (1995) Gendered learning practices: exploring the costs of hegemonic masculinity for girls and boys in schools, in Ministerial Council for Education, Employment, Training and Youth Affairs (MCEETYA) (1995) *Proceedings for the Promoting Gender Equity Conference* (343–64). Canberra: Department of Education and Training.

Meadmore, D and McWilliam, E (2001) The corporate curriculum: schools as sites of new knowledge production. *Australian Educational Researcher,* 28: 31–45.

Millard, E (1997) *Differently literate: boys, girls and the schooling of literacy.* London: FalmerPress.

Nichols, S (2002) Parents' construction of their children as gendered, literate subjects: a critical discourse analysis. *Journal of Early Childhood Literacy,* 2: 123–44.

Phoenix, A (2001) Racialization and gendering in the (re)production of educational inequalities, in Francis, B and Skelton, C (eds) *Investigating gender. Contemporary perspectives in education*. Buckingham: Open University Press.

Rose, N (1999) *Powers of freedom*. Cambridge: Cambridge University Press.

Teese, R, Davies, M, Charlton, M and Polesel, J (1995) *Who wins at school? Boys and girls in Australian secondary education*. Department of Education Policy and Management, University of Melbourne: JS McMillan.

Tomlinson, S (2001) *Education in a post-welfare society*. Buckingham: Open University Press.

West, P (2002) *What IS the matter with boys? Showing boys the way towards manhood*. Marrickville: Choice Books.

Whitty, G, Power, S and Halpin, D (1998) *Devolution and choice in education: the school, the state and the market*. Buckingham: Open University Press.

NOTE

1. For an excellent critique of discourses of 'ability', see Gillborn and Youdell, 2000; Bird and Drewary, 2000.

18

'Sex' Education: Subjugated Discourses and Adolescents' Voices

Bagele Chilisa

The teaching of sex education remains one of the biggest challenges for governments, educational institutions, teachers and policy makers in Sub-Saharan Africa. The word 'sex' as used in ordinary language is ambiguous, referring to both the biological category of being male or female and the act of engaging in sexual activities. Sexual activities, behaviors and attitudes to sex are informed by a gender system. Gender is a social construction that ascribes roles, behaviors and attitudes on the basis of sex. A sex/gender system is thus implicated in the marking of biological sex with socially constructed gender meaning of what it means to be a woman or a man. The word 'sex' will therefore be used to embrace the whole concept of sexuality. Sexuality is perceived as the social construction of a biological drive (Gupta, 2002), derived and sustained through a hierarchical sex/gender system (Collins, 1990). In this context, sex education includes legitimized knowledge and discourses on sexual behaviors, practices, attitudes and the asymmetrical power relations between boys/men and girls/women that are transmitted through the formal and the informal school curriculum as well as the subsequent resistant discourses that operate in the schools.

In view of this broad conceptualization of the meaning of sex education, some countries, for instance, New Zealand, have changed the name 'sex education' in their official curriculum to 'sexuality education' (Allen, 2004) while in Britain and the USA, the name 'sex education' is still predominantly used (Epstein and

Johnson, 1998; Kehily, 2002; Fine, 2003). In most countries in Sub-Saharan Africa, the preferred name is 'family life education' or 'life skills education'. This chapter maps the theoretical approaches that have been used to explain, analyze and interpret the nature and function of sex education. A case study of sex education in Botswana is used to illustrate contemporary trends, theories and discourses in 'sex education'.

Sex education is closely tied to sexuality and gender inequalities. The methods, strategies and tools of analysis and the theoretical landscape thus have a lot in common with gender studies and women studies. The most common theoretical perspectives in the study of sex education are as follows:

- conservative theoretical frameworks;
- liberal theoretical frameworks;
- Western feminist theories and perspectives;
- Third World feminist theories and perspectives;
- African feminist theories and perspectives;
- race-based theoretical perspectives;
- historical perspectives;
- discourses based on power and knowledge.

Lees (1993) identifies three political stances that inform the nature and teaching of sex education, namely, the conservative, liberal and feminist stances. She sees the conservative stance as concerned with morality and imagined ideals of family life and thus presenting an unchanging and naturalized 'social-gender order'. The most conservative proponents of this theoretical stance call for the elimination of sex education in the school and reliance on the family to dictate sexually appropriate values, norms and behaviors.

In contrast to the conservative stance, the liberal framework advocates the provision of appropriate information to adolescents so as to empower them to make appropriate choices. Fine (2003) argues that most sex education programs that take this stance tend to portray males as potential predators and females as victims. Intervention sex education programs that adopt this theoretical framework include 'abstinence-only' and 'abstinence-based' programs. Abstinence-only programs present abstinence as the only option for adolescents. Abstinence-based programs offer information about safer sex techniques in the event that adolescents do not choose abstinence (Weis and Carbonell-Medina, 2003).

Lees (1993) regards the third stance, namely, the feminist framework, as potentially the most progressive. This stance interrogates the sex-gender inequalities embedded in the social norms, traditions, common-sense assumptions, linguistic constructions, architectural buildings in the school, classroom sitting arrangements, textbooks, the formal and informal curriculum, and the pedagogy of difference that privilege boys. Writing from a culturally and geographical Western position, Lees (1993) fails to distinguish between other feminisms, namely, Third World and African feminisms. Third World feminists, including African feminists, problematize Western feminism's universalization of patriarchy and the representation of Third World women as a monolithic 'Other', ignorant and lacking agency

(Mohanty, 1991). Amadiume (1987) argues, for example, that colonialism and cultural imperialism changed the somewhat flexible gender system, which did not totally marginalize women, into a more entrenched patriarchal system. Third World and African feminisms call for the decolonization and deconstruction of Western theoretical frameworks, methods and categories of analysis. Echoing a similar view, Leclerc-Madla (2004: 6) notes that African scholars who try to write about sexuality are 'hampered by limited and inappropriate vocabulary that is the product of Victorian sexology'. They call for Afro-centric conceptual frameworks for understanding sexuality.

Western feminist research in sex education contributed to several discourses, among them the 'discourse of desire' and the 'discourse of erotics'. Feminist literature (Lees, 1994; Fine, 2003) revealed that there is a missing discourse of desire that positively acknowledges and incorporates young women's sexual desire in sex education program. There is now an emerging discourse of erotics (Allen, 2004) which acknowledges that all young people, whatever their gender and sexual identity, are sexual objects and have a right to experience sexual pleasure and desire. African feminists (Ntseane, 2005; Ntseane and Preece, 2005) note the presence of a discourse of sex as pleasure in traditional sex education that takes place in the home, family and community. They identify other discourses in traditional sex education among eight ethnic groups in Botswana, portraying sex as follows:

1. procreation;
2. exchange;
3. social interaction;
4. religion/spirituality;
5. cleansing and healing;
6. family property;
7. control and oppression.

These discourses vary depending on the ethnic group. Literature on family sex education in Western scholarship is almost non-existent. Although sex education from a conservative perspective should take place in the family, it is not clearly documented what its nature should be. What is also important to note is that traditional sex education in Botswana serves multiple purposes, in contrast to the West, where it is predominantly perceived as 'a tool for curbing rising rates of sexual transmitted infection, promiscuity, sexual deviance and unintended pregnancy' (Allen, 2004: 154).

Kehily (2002) has argued that theoretical frameworks as outlined by Lees (1993, 1994) tend to highlight the delivery of sex education at the expense of considering the ways in which this knowledge is received. She brings into the discussion power relations between teachers and students and the specific ways in which these power relations mediate classroom interactions and shape the context of sex education. In the USA, for example, what emerges from the contested power relations is a standard sex education curriculum in public school classrooms, characterized by:

1. the authorized suppression of a discourse of desire;
2. the promotion of female victimization;
3. the explicit privileging of married heterosexuality over other practices of sexuality (Fine 2003: 38).

There are also 'race-based' theoretical frameworks. Caldwell *et al.* (1989) have, for instance, argued that there is a distinct African sexuality that is inferior to Eurasian sexuality. In their contrast of Eurasian and African sexuality, Caldwell *et al.* (1989) argue that the major difference between the two is in the African female sexuality, which, unlike the Eurasian sexuality which is taken as the universal norm is blatantly free. According to Caldwell *et al.* (1989), African sexuality allows free sexual activity with no moral values attached and a female sexuality that is 'blatantly free'. Those in support of a permissive and 'blatantly free female sexuality' blame the spread of HIV/AIDS on the lack of restraint of girls/women, a violent sexual culture, the silence on sex, and sexuality informed by tradition and a culture that is resistant to modernization and development change. The thinking of Caldwell *et al.* (1989) is not new. Nineteenth-century literature consistently portrayed African women 'as possessing animal like sexual instincts that lead them to even copulate with apes' (Gilman, 1985, cited in Collins, 1990).

Other frameworks combine historical analysis with discourses of power and knowledge. Foucault (1978: 3) notes that at the beginning of the seventeenth century, in the West, 'sexual practices had little need for secrecy', and describes it as a period 'when bodies made displays of themselves'. A similar view is expressed about precolonial Sub-Saharan Africa. Ahlberg (1994) observes that among the Kikuyu in Kenya, there were many occasions where sexuality was publicly addressed. Today, in most Western countries, the state intervenes through legislation (for example, on marriage, rape, pregnancy, abortion and prostitution) to regulate gendered sexualities and to prescribe a national sexuality that schools adopt (Epstein and Johnson, 1998).

In Africa, the advance of Christianity, colonialism, and imperialism in the eighteenth century undermined the forms of sexual socialization and education that existed, and dismantled the forms of youth organization that played a key role in the socialization process (Delius and Glaser, 2002: 37). In most countries in Africa, the state assumes a borrowed Western sexuality that is informed by Christianity and regulated through statutes and laws borrowed from the West during the colonial period. In Botswana, the Roman Dutch law, Penal Code 0801: Section 164, inherited from Britain (a former colonial master) states: *Sexual practices against the order of nature are forbidden.* There is little evidence to suggest that homosexuality was forbidden in precolonial Africa. Among the Azande of Sudan, for instance, 'unmarried warriors were expected to take boy wives' (Leclerc-Madla 2004: 4) younger than them.

I start with sex education in pre-colonial Africa to trace historical trends in sex education in Sub-Saharan Africa, and to claim back and open space for African sexualities marginalized, stigmatized and dismissed as irrelevant. This, I believe, also opens a space for the integration of knowledge systems on sex education and sexuality with privileged and universalized Western sexualities.

PUBERTY MARKED SEX EDUCATION: A DISCOURSE OF EROTICS IN SUB-SAHARAN AFRICA?

Contemporary sex education programs in most countries in the world are marked by the invisibility of desire and pleasure in the curriculum (Fine, 2003; Allen, 2004). Allen proposes that sex education programs should acknowledge desire and pleasure and incorporate the embodied practicalities of these experiences. The presence of such discourses, it is argued, would involve the right to knowledge about the body as related to sexual response and pleasure, and may include the logistics of bodily engagement in sexual activity. An analysis of sex education in initiation in selected African countries suggests that desires and pleasures were acknowledged and celebrated.

Initiation ceremonies and rituals to mark the rite of passage from adolescence to manhood were central to the teaching of sex education in Sub-Saharan Africa. African communities recognized the power and centrality of sexuality in human experience and were 'aware of strong passions, which swayed pubescent hearts and minds' (Delius and Glaser, 2002: 31). Most societies established limited forms of sexual release by teaching the initiates non-penetrative sex. This practice, known as *hlobonga* among the Zulus, *amaqhisa* among the Xhosa in South Africa, *Kujuma* among the Swati of Swaziland and *ngwiko* among the Kikuyu in Kenya, was mainly for the purpose of achieving sexual satisfaction without penetration. Sexual discipline was taught by presenting the initiates with concrete situations where boys and girls were allowed to spend nights together. Taboos were invoked to maintain good sexual conduct. Among the Kikuyu, for instance, it was believed that breaking the sexual taboos could affect the health of the mother, father and siblings, and even cause death (Ahlberg, 1994). In addition to taboos and prohibitions, family, group and peer pressure was exerted to discourage breach of sexual conduct. Boys and girls going through the initiation ceremony monitored each other's relationships. These safe sex practices prevented premarital pregnancy while at the same time allowing adolescents to explore their bodies and experience pleasure.

CONTROL OF FEMALE SEXUALITY

In spite of the presence of desire, pleasure and erotics in traditional sex education, sex education still remained the vehicle through which men regulated and controlled female sexuality.

I will present here forms and practices that regulated female sexuality in traditional sex education in selected African societies to illustrate discourses of control of female sexuality. Among these were *go baya lotlhokwa* (engage a young woman for marriage) or *go opa mpa* (to strike the womb). This practice involved engagement with a girl who was still very young or reserving an unborn baby girl in an identified family for marriage. In some communities, the young girl would, before marriage, go through a process called *go ruta ngwana mokwata* (acquainting the child with the man's back). The practice involved the girl sleeping with the prospective husband before she even reached puberty. These practices violated the girl's right to choose a partner and encouraged marriage built on a hierarchy of age. Other practices include *Nkadzana/sebare* among the Bakalanga and the Nguni-speaking of southern Africa, and *Mantsala* among the Tswana-speaking in Botswana. *Nkadzana/sebare* describes the relationship of a married man and the younger sisters of his wife (Fidzani *et al.*, 2000). The young girls and their brother-in-law are traditionally allowed to be romantic toward each other, and, depending on the man and the situation, this relationship can become sexual. What is also obvious is that the girl, as in the practice of *go baya lotlhokwa,* is also placed in an unequal relationship of power based on age. These practices all marked the tendency of young girls to be introduced to sex by elderly men. *Mantsala* (playful sex) prepared girls to expect requests for sexual favours from sons of mothers' brothers, and mothers' brothers (Ntseane, 2005). Ntseane terms this 'sex as pleasure' and argues that, in playful sex, young women and men learnt different strategies for enjoying sex while at the same time preventing conception. She notes, however, that even in encounters of sexual pleasure, men ultimately decided when they wanted sex and how they wanted it.

THE NATIONAL SEXUAL CULTURE AND CONTEMPORARY SEX EDUCATION

Sex education program assume, carry and sell the national prescribed sexuality (Epstein and Johnson, 1998). In the West, schools are the sites where adolescent sexual culture and the national sexual culture prescribed by the school curriculum clash. In contrast, in Third World countries, that is in most of the former colonies with Western sexual culture, this culture clashes with adolescent culture informed by traditional sex education and adolescents' lived experiences.

The teaching of sex education in Sub-Saharan Africa today occupies a historical space between the past, where adolescents were taught the multiple functions of sex and to explore their bodies and experience pleasure – the present, informed by Christianity and Western concepts of sexuality – and an idealized future sex education, proposed by scholars, that recognizes young people's sexual desires and accommodates local knowledge systems of sex education and sexuality. What is evident in this historical space is the clash of cultures and the explosion of student discourses predominantly crafted by boys as they try to rehash traditional discourses that sought to control female sexuality. To illustrate contemporary issues in the teaching of sex education, I will examine the teaching of sex education in community junior secondary schools (CJSS) in Botswana and will argue that sex education is situated in the larger education framework that continues to universalize Western sexuality.

Three themes can be identified in the teaching of sex education in CJSS. The first theme is located within a repressive sex education ideology. The second theme draws on the construction of a 'raced' and gendered sex education. In this theme, I utilize interview and observation notes from a study on HIV/AIDS and sexuality in CJSS to argue that the school is implicated in the construction of a 'raced' and gendered sex education that further entrenches the oppression of girls by boys. In the last theme, I problematize the assumed neutrality of sex education. Here I show how students challenge teachers to personalize knowledge on sexuality.

Sex education in community junior secondary schools (CJSS) in Botswana

In the CJSS, sex education comes under the umbrella of life skills education. Topics in life skills education appear mainly in science, moral education, religious education, and guidance and counselling syllabi. Topics covered are personal moral issues, children's rights, child abuse and sexual abuse, sexual behaviour, reproduction, family life education and family planning, teenage pregnancy, abortion, population growth and sexually transmitted disease. I begin with the teaching of sex education through the hidden curriculum and present a case study of a school where sex education messages are, in addition to the formal curriculum, transmitted through the hidden curriculum.

The hidden curriculum: a repressive sex education
The teaching of sex education occurs through the formal as well as the informal school system. In some schools, teachers engage students in discourses concerning sexuality, and socio-cultural issues by using school regulations and magazines as a medium of communication. The school described here is located in an urban area. It has a population of about 1000 students aged 13–18 years. The school head believes in abstinence before marriage. In some of the classrooms, the school rules were on noticeboards, and one of them read *no sexual relations*. In this school, teachers, parents and students produce a magazine entitled *Tsaya Tsia* (Beware). The aim of the magazine is *to warn students on the temptation to indulge in sex*. Students write anonymous stories about their experiences of relationships at home and at school. Students' stories include abuse by family members; fear of sexual harassment by schoolmates, uncles, cousins, other family members and the public in general; temptation to indulge in sexual relationships; and fears and suspicions of being HIV/AIDS positive. Teachers respond to each story, giving advice to the students on possible solutions to their problems. The following are selected stories from *Tsaya Tsia*, vol 2.

Loves sex

Student: I have heard about AIDS and understand a lot about it, but the problem is I really love sex. What can I do to prevent myself from loving girls?

Response: The best medicine is abstinence. It is a very difficult thing, but if you are determined to save your life you can do it. As long as you are willing then you will abstain. Let not you emotion overcome your life.

Faced with temptation

Student: I always see a girl in the school for whom I have appetite. I love that girl but I don't want to engage in sex with her. Every time I see her I feel like I am falling in love with her. The most important thing is that I really understand about HIV/AIDS but I love that girl very much. Please what can I do?

Response: Firstly, you must learn to control your feelings, you shouldn't let your feelings control you. At your age, you are too young to fall in love. The temptation is that if you fall in love you will possibly have sex, therefore increasing your chances of contracting some STDs including HIV/AIDS. The best thing you can do for yourself is to abstain because with abstinence, you can be sure that you cannot contract HIV.

Abstinence is reiterated throughout the stories in the magazines and in some cases reinforced through the following biblical verses: Gen. 2:18 *The Lord God said, it is not good for the man to be alone. I will make a helper suitable for him*; Heb.13. 4: *Marriage should be honoured by all and the marriage bed kept pure, for God will judge the adulterers and all the sexually immoral*; Gal. 5:19 *The acts of the sinful are obvious, sexual immorality, impurity and debauchery.*

Sex education, as taught through the informal curriculum, is organized around moral values informed by Western religion. There is only one 'truth' in a subject matter that includes diverse student experiences, and that 'truth' is abstinence until marriage. This absolute truth is reinforced by readings from the Bible that both students and teachers regard as objective and rational. Students are thus taught to repress any other sexual urges, feelings and desires that they have. The education policy reinforces this approach by forbidding the distribution of condoms in the schools. Teachers and policy makers ignore the complex web of social and cultural practices, such as *mantsala* (playful sex) and *go ruta ngwana mokwata* (to acquaint the child with the man's back), which involve collective decisions between families and among community members and incorporate an individual's self-identity within the family or the community. Some of the verses are gendered; for example, Gen. 2.18 cited above, teaches students that the subordination of girls and therefore women is natural. A woman was created to be a helper and therefore an appendage of man and exist only in relation to man. The informal curriculum thus creates a gendered and sexual repressive culture. Thus, Western religion further entrenches the oppressive realities of patriarchy.

Students, however, challenge, rework and construct their own knowledge systems and sexualities. In negotiating a body of knowledge on sex education, boys use forms of control such as verbal abuse, insults, physical violence, and intimidation to dominate class discussion and to construct a body of knowledge that valorizes boys' sexuality. What follows is an elaboration of sex education as taught through topics in science, moral and religious education, and guidance, and counselling. I present excerpts based on notes from a qualitative study of four CJSS on gender sexuality and HIV/AIDS (Chilisa *et al.*, 2005). In the study, classroom observations and interviews of teachers teaching science, moral education, religious education, and guidance and counselling were done to find out how life skills education is taught.

The construction of a gendered sex education
Schools socialize boys and girls along a gendered division of roles and reinforce these gendered roles through selected texts in the formal and the informal curriculum (Chilisa, 2002). The gendered division of roles are the building blocks for valorizing boys' sexuality and controlling girls' sexuality to serve the interests of boys and men. Observations revealed that a gendered division of space physically distancing boys from girls characterizes Botswana classrooms. There is a common pattern, with boys more likely to sit at the back and on the sides of the classroom. This physical separation is sustained through traditional ideologies that define men/boys, as being in authority and superior to women/girls. So guarded are the boys' and girls' spaces that mixed-sex group work is problematic. In Setswana culture, men who associate with women are supposed to be weaklings (*ke bo pheramesesing*). Roles, expectations and attitudes of boys and girls to each other are also gendered. The majority of the boys felt that the reproductive role, more specifically, childbearing, requires women to perform light duties that will not harm their reproductive organs. Girls' duties in the schools included general cleaning, such as sweeping and polishing, while boys mowed grass and lifted desks.

Boys' disruptive behavior, such as inconsiderate remarks, insults, jeering and laughing when girls made mistakes or when the topic under discussion made reference to women, hampered girls' participation in class. Girls report that in the science classes, when the topic is reproduction, boys have a tendency to laugh when they see pictures of naked women. The boys get very excited and go around to the girls in class asking them to explain what they see in the pictures, as a way of embarrassing the girls.

Consequently, boys dominate discourses on sex education and construct local narratives on sex to their advantage. They invoke religion, language, proverbs and biological attributes to legitimize male power and dominance. In a number of classes observed, discussions by teachers and students reproduced stereotypes about oppositional attributes that society ascribes to boys and girls. Interviews with religious education teachers revealed that messages conveyed in this subject included the justification of a gender order that places boys first in the social hierarchy. Boys use verses in the Bible relating to male leadership to justify a hierarchical division of roles between boys and girls. Women and girls' subordinate role is justified on the ground that women in the Bible are portrayed as short-tempered and easily tempted. An interview of a moral education teacher revealed the following:

Teacher: Mostly, they disagree on topics that concern females and males. For example, we had a topic that was on morality and religion, and then I asked them about the fact that all religious leaders are males. I was enquiring from them whether that shows a factor of fairness or inequality. The boys said that the females should be at home. The reason being that if God wanted females to be leaders, He could have made the first woman to be a leader. The first person was a man, Adam. The woman was made from the rib of Adam. Even Jesus was a male. So, we ought to follow the trend. The girls are saying we can change from that. Again, the people who wrote the Bible are males, so they would portray Jesus as a male and not female.

Interviewer: This idea of males as leaders, where do you think it came from?

Teacher: I feel it comes from home. They even mentioned the Setswana proverb that says, 'Ga di nke di etelelwa ke manamagadi pele.' (Men are born leaders.) Again they argue that the reason why woman cannot lead is because they like bragging and are short-tempered and are easily tempted. They gave an example of Eve, who was the first to be tempted and influenced by the Devil, to do evil. They also gave example of Delilah, who tempted Samson. The girls would at the same time disagree. One of them said she was hurt by what the boys were saying and said that women were meant to help men make decisions and not men to make decisions alone.

Interestingly, we learn that the girls contested the assumption of the superiority of males, which the boys invoked using the Bible. Because of their verbal space advantage, the boys were more likely to relate the local constructed views on sex in the classroom and to challenge their teachers. Teachers confirmed that myths about sex and HIV/AIDS among the students were widespread. They revealed that their attempts to teach life skills education were negated by what students learnt from their peers outside the classroom, at home and in the community. Students learnt from peers myths about how to prevent pregnancy, how to cure HIV/AIDS and how to abort pregnancy. They learnt myths that justified indulgence in sexual relationships. A conversation with a teacher revealed this verbal dominance of boys on sex education topics. The teacher noted the following:

Teacher: There was this boy who said that someone told him that if he had sex with a girl standing up, she would not fall pregnant, or the girl drinking water immediately after sex or jumping up and down. This it was said, would bring the sperms down and one would not fall pregnant. They say these ideas come from their friends both in school and outside. It will seem that from outside the school and the classroom they only get the positive side of indulging in sex. They are told things like if one does not engage in sex he or she will suffer from some kind of disease, he or she will not be normal. So sex as discussed outside school is against what we teach in school. Thus there is a need to teach those outside, the society needs to be taught on issues like abortion and HIV/AIDS. For example, one was told that if you want to commit abortion, just boil five thebe coins and drink water from this. Alternatively one can boil matchsticks and the solution from this will help commit abortion.

The stories on sex are an indication of student and adolescence resistance against a standard and universal norm on sexual practices. They form a reservoir of knowledge on sexual practices from which students and adolescents who are vulnerable or find themselves in difficult situations draw. The teacher's reflection on students' stories demonstrates the arrogance of the education system in claiming the right to discredit and exclude all that is not in the school syllabi.

There is an implicit message from the teacher that only those certified by the school system have the right to teach sex education.

Local constructed narratives on sex are not only heard through the boys' voices but also have a tendency to pressurize girls to indulge in sex. Some of the narratives circulating in the school were as follows:

1. 'You will not bear a child if you are a virgin for too long.' The discourse of sex as pro-creation is rehashed.
2. 'Virginity makes you sick especially your back. Sleeping with a virgin helps.' The narra-tives rehash the teaching of sex as healing.
3. 'Condoms have worms.' It comes from the general public resistance to the use of con-doms. There is a belief that condoms are a Western strategy 'to wipe Africans from the face of the earth'. (see Ntseane and Preece, 2005 for discussion)

The teachers also participate in marginalizing girls' sexuality by making refer-ences and giving examples that appeal to boys' experiences and their sexualities. Teachers revealed that there were demonstrations on the use of a male condom where volunteers were mostly boys. A teacher had this to say:

> *Teacher (male):* With reproductive health, we taught the use of contraceptives, like the con-dom, the pill, and sterilization. There were some demonstrations by the teacher. At times the students (mostly boys) volunteer to demonstrate. We did not have the apparatus. We used the broomstick [laughing]. And I told them that the condom is not inserted on the broomstick. It is inserted on the male organ. We used the male condom. We did not have the female condom.

Problematizing the neutral teacher in sex education

Also of interest were the ways students and teachers constructed their relation-ships with each other and with the subject matter on sex education. Teachers reported that students challenge them to relate the topics they taught to their per-sonal experiences. The teachers preferred to take a neutral position on the sub-ject matter and taught it as an objective truth. Teachers were asked whether students asked sexuality-related questions that they felt were embarrassing. They had this to say:

> *Teacher 2 (female teacher):* I wouldn't say they are embarrassing. But they like saying 'you'. I always discourage them from using the word. I remember one student wanted to know if I have ever used a female condom, and how it feels. I told them that I have never used it and that they should not become personal when we talk about these things.

> *Teacher 3 (male teacher):* Sometimes they do. For example, I remember there was a child at one point when we were discussing abstinence and withdrawal. The student was saying from experience he knows that withdrawal is impossible. And I was supposed to make a comment on that.

It is clear from the interview transcripts that teachers divorce themselves from the subject matter and make claims of neutrality on the subject. The students challenge this neutral position and demand subject matter where personal sexual experiences are implicated. Most teachers reported that they were not comfortable in teaching topics related to sexuality.

SUMMARY AND CONCLUSIONS

A wide range of theoretical perspectives written from a Western perspective inform the teaching of sex education. There is very little demonstration of the application of these theoretical perspectives to schools in Asia, Africa or the Third World in general. The literature predominantly discusses sex education in the school and does not shed light on adolescent sex education in the family. In contrast, sex education in some countries in Sub-Saharan Africa coexists with traditional sex education. Adolescent sex education thus borrows and clashes with the two sex education types.

Texts from schools in Botswana show that sex education as taught through the informal and formal curriculum is constructed around Western values. This dismisses African values on sexuality as inappropriate and legitimizes a sex education organized around Western religion. It is a body of knowledge that is 'raced' and gendered and promotes a repressive sexual ideology. One form of oppression is nested in the lack of diversity in options that are available to the students as they try to cope with adolescent sexual urges.

The body of knowledge that finally emerges as school sexual culture is a mediated text that is predominantly crafted by boys. Boys take advantage of the gendered texts in the Bible, cultural texts such as proverbs and cultural practices to valorize their masculinities and to create controlled femininities for the girls that are relational and inferior to boys' masculinities. The gender-biased sex knowledge is exacerbated by the teachers' didactic approach. Often the teachers take a neutral stand toward the already gendered texts. Boys use their verbal advantage to challenge and intimidate the teachers in order to demonstrate their authority in the subject. The teachers' vulnerability and discomfort with teaching sexuality gives the boys an opportunity to mediate the texts to their advantage.

The texts are testimony to the need for a sex education that is inclusive of girls' and boys' voices, is sensitive and responsive to the local realities of the students, and respects and accommodates local knowledge systems. There is a need for a sex education that is inclusive of multiple ways of knowing, more specifically, those historically silenced local knowledge systems and practices. Students need to be encouraged to interrogate the controlling discourses based on gender, 'race' or ethnicity in sex education. In place of the current teaching approach that treats the subject as an objective body of knowledge, there is a need for a participatory pedagogy that problematizes the body of knowledge that informs sexual behaviour. This perspective is also echoed by Allen (2004), who calls for discourse of erotics in sex education.

REFERENCES

Ahlberg, B (1994) Is there distinct African sexuality? A critical response to Caldwell. *Africa* 64: 220–39.

Allen, L (2004) Beyond the birds and bees: constituting a discourse of erotics in sexuality education. *Gender and Education*, 16: 151–67.

Amadiume, I (1987) *Male daughters, female husbands; gender and sex in an African society.* London: Zed Books.

Caldwell, JC, Caldwell, P and Quiggin, P (1989) The social context of HIV/AIDS in Sub-Saharan Africa. *Population and Development Review*, 15: 125–33.

Chilisa, B (2002) National policies on pregnancy in the education system in Sub-Saharan Africa: a case of Botswana. *Gender and Education,* 14: 21–35.

Chilisa, B, Dube-Shomanah, M, Tsheko, N and Bontshetse, M (2005) *Gender HIV/AIDS and life skills education in community junior secondary schools in Botswana.* Nairobi: UNICEF.

Collins, P (1990) *Black feminist thought.* London: Hammersmith.

Delius, P and Glaser, C (2002) Sexual practices in Southern Africa. A historical perspective. *African Studies*, 61: 27–54.

Epstein, D and Johnson, R (1998) *Schooling sexualities.* Buckingham: Open University Press.

Fine, M (2003) Sexuality, schooling and adolescent females: the missing discourse of desire, in Fine, M and Weis, L (eds) *Silenced voices and extraordinary conversations.* Amsterdam: Teachers College Press.

Fidzani, NH (2000) *HIV/AIDS in the North East District: situation and response analysis.* Gaborone: UNDP.

Foucault, M (1978) *The history of sexuality.* New York: Vantage Books.

Gupta, GR (2000) Gender, sexuality and HIV/AIDS: the what, the why. Plenary Address, XIIIth International AIDS Conference, Durban, South Africa.

Kehily, MJ (2002) *Sexuality, gender and schooling: shifting agendas in social learning.* London: RoutledgeFalmer.

Leclerc-Madla, S (2004) Field of sexuality studies: what is it? *Sexuality in Africa*, 1: 4–7.

Lees, S (1993) *Sugar and spice sexuality and adolescent girls.* Harmondsworth: Penguin.

Lees, S (1994) Talking about sex in sex education. *Gender and Education*, 6: 281–92.

Mohanty, C (1991) Under Western eyes: feminist scholarship and colonial discourses, in Mohanty, C, Russo, A and Torres, L (eds) *Third World women and the politics of feminism.* Bloomington, IN: Indiana University Press.

Ntseane, P (2005) Cultural dimensions of sexuality: empowerment challenges for HIV/AIDS prevention in Botswana. UNESCO Special Issue on HIV/AIDS.

Ntseane, PG and Preece, J (2005) Why HIV/AIDS prevention strategies fail in Botswana: considering discourse of sexuality. *Development Southern Africa*, 22: 347–63.

Weis, L and Carbonell-Medina, D (2003) Learning to speak out in an abstinence-based sex education group: gender race work in an urban magnet school, in Fine, M and Weis, L (eds) *Silenced voices and extraordinary conversations.* Amsterdam: Teachers College Press.

19

Gender Issues in Testing and Assessment

Jannette Elwood

INTRODUCTION

Key areas of debate in the field of assessment and testing concern a 'paradigm shift' in how we view students' learning and how this learning should be assessed. These debates stem from research suggesting that more formative approaches to assessment will improve students' learning (Black and Wiliam, 1998, 2005; Shepard, 2000; Hargreaves *et al.*, 2002; CERI, 2005), and arguing that good, formative assessment (assessment done in classrooms, by teachers, with and for students' learning) will enhance student attainment and develop teachers' own assessment and pedagogical practice. However, these debates have generally ignored the social contexts of classrooms where formative assessment takes place and, to an even greater degree, have ignored the interaction of these different modes of assessment practice with gender and thus how they affect boys' and girls' performances.

While the 'assessment for learning' agenda gathers pace (Black and Wiliam, 2005), those of us concerned with the social consequences of assessment practices and who recognize that any form of assessment regime will have repercussions for boys' or girls' achievements, see very little attention given to the multiple contexts in which assessment for learning takes place. Moreover, the redefinition of the learner and the model of learning associated with formative assessment practices has major implications for teacher–student relationships, which are affected and mediated by gender and stereotypical perceptions of what boys and girls can achieve.

The aim of this chapter, therefore, is twofold: to consider research in relation to gender issues and testing and assessment, but also to offer new insights into

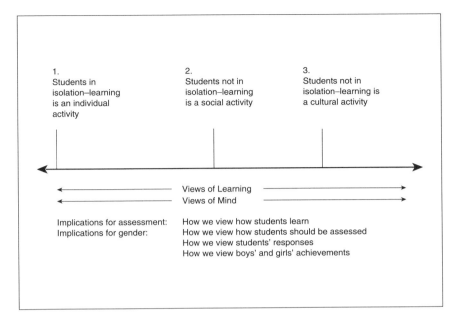

Figure 19.1   Continuum of views of learning, mind, assessment and gender

the very complex relationship between learning, mind, and assessment that demands a different way of looking at gender and its role in understanding achievement. Understanding this relationship is fundamental if we wish to comprehend fully boys' and girls' achievements in school.

As a framework for the ideas discussed in the chapter, I present a continuum (Fig. 19.1) along which differing views of learning, mind, assessment and gender are represented. As we move along from left to right, the ways in which we look at the four concepts (learning, mind, assessment and gender) shift considerably. Thus, in changing how we view mind and how we understand how students learn, we see there are major implications for how students should be assessed, how we view responses to assessment tasks and how we view gender in relation to these.

LINKING ASSESSMENT AND MODELS OF LEARNING

Very little research within the field of assessment concerns itself with the social consequences of assessment practice and policy (Broadfoot, 1996). Furthermore, many researchers in the field of assessment and testing more generally fail to articulate the model(s) of learning that support the assessment or testing system they promote. For example, the considerable growth of research in the field of computer-adaptive assessment rarely articulates the underpinning model of the learner or learning (Bennett *et al.*, 2003). Most of the research in this area continues to be on the development of the computer technology, the logistics of large-scale computer testing, and the way in which the student experience of the subject and of being tested will change (Baird, 2002). One cannot review systems of testing and assessment without acknowledging their relationship to the model of learning and of the learner underpinning the assessment or test. Moreover, this relationship between the model of assessment and testing, and that of the learner and learning demands a consideration of gender in all its complexities. This is because an understanding of how gender mediates learning, achievement, and teachers' and students' experiences of assessment and testing is crucial to an understanding of the performances observed.

Theories of learning are many and are often contested, and the prominence of certain theories changes over time and in different contexts (Murphy, 1999). McDermott (1999: 16) argues that 'learning traditionally gets measured on the assumption that it is a possession of individuals that can be found inside their heads [but] learning is not in heads but in the relations between people'. He goes on to suggest that learning is in the conditions that bring people together and points of contact that allow particular pieces of information to take on relevance; without these points of contact, without the system of relevancies, there is no learning. In relation to theories of learning, there are connected theories of mind, which, according to Murphy (1999), fall into two categories: symbolic cognition or processing (Bruner, 1999, Fordor, 2000) and situated cognition (Lave and Wenger, 1991). A symbolic processing view of mind is concerned with an individual's internal mental processing as the way to understand learning. The learner is seen as separate from the environment, and mind is symbolically represented as somewhere where learning can be stored and retrieved when required (like a computer). A situated view of mind is concerned with the interaction of human knowledge and the environment, the two being seen as inseparable. In this view of mind, learning is integral with the social world. Murphy (1999: ix) goes on to argue that these are by no means the only two approaches to mind that exist, but that 'the tension between these two "families" of theories is giving rise to a great deal of productive thinking about learners, learning and assessment', from which considerations of gender can also develop.

One could further argue that these two categories of mind can also be considered as a local model of mind (mind in the head, intrinsic to the learner) and a non-local model of mind (mind outside the head, mind between individuals). The non-local model of mind extends the situated cognition model, as it suggests that nothing about mind or learning is located within the individual. Thus, if we can understand how learning happens at all, it does not take place in the head but between individuals. A non-local view of mind goes further to suggest that the learner and the teacher are entangled, that learning cannot be viewed in isolation, but only in relationship between the learner and the teacher (or other).

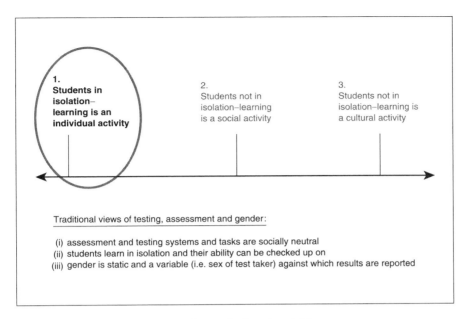

Figure 19.2   Assessment and testing as isolated activities

TESTING AND ASSESSMENT: AS ISOLATED ACTIVITIES

Stage 1 on the continuum (Fig. 19.2) positions learning, mind, and gender as things that are fixed and isolated within the individual. Assessment is seen as something done to an individual to measure this fixed learning, and gender is a category against which the measurement of this learning can be reported. Here assessment and testing are located within the traditional psychometric model of testing (Goldstein, 1996a). This is a powerful model, as it is underpins much of the world's testing systems and testing industry (Lemann, 2000) and influences the conduct of almost all forms of quantitative assessment (Goldstein, 1996a). The psychometric model of testing and assessment has underlying assumptions about the existence of psychological attributes and that observed responses to test items can provide evidence about the state or value of these attributes (often ability is classified as such an attribute). This model also assumes that tests and assessments are activities that take place in isolation from the classroom, the teacher and other learners. Furthermore, this model advocates the use of summative assessments that are carried out *on* students under test conditions at the end of a course or period of learning, and that these tests or examinations are independently checking up on a student's ability, what students can do *on their own*.

The model of learning underpinning such testing practices sees learning as an individual activity that takes place in isolation and via transmission; it is a one-way process that goes from teacher to student. This view of learning is consistent with behaviourist psychology, which emphasizes a stimulus-response theory of learning:

> The test item is the stimulus and the answer the response, and a learner has to be 'conditioned' to produce the appropriate response to any given stimulus. Because the response is the only observable, attention is not paid to any model of the thinking process of the pupil which might intervene between stimulus and response. (Black, 1999: 120)

Furthermore, this model of testing and its associated theory of learning assumes that mind is located (and isolated) within the student (the local or symbolic view of mind). Thus learning is seen as being *stored* within the student. When given a test, students *retrieve* the information they need to answer the items on the test, and the test is checking up on the *stored* knowledge. Furthermore, assessment tasks are seen as neutral, and the testing system itself has no influence on the performances observed. So, students responding to test items are isolated from social influences and are thus separately analyzable through the test items used.

This traditional view of assessment and testing also assumes a traditional view of gender. Within this perspective, gender is seen as the same as sex group (male and female), and is a static variable against which differences in test data can be reported (Goldstein, 1996b). The publication of sex-group differences is only one variable among many by which test data can be reported. For example, in the UK, differential performance data by males and females in public examinations and national curriculum tests are reported annually as a matter of course (JCGQ, 2004). This type of data, alongside research evidence from studies of large-scale international assessment programs (OECD, 2000; 2004) and research evidence from other studies focusing on sex differences in performance on tests (Willingham and Cole, 1997), show distinct patterns of performance between males and females, which are seen across different subjects, different ages and different testing situations. Some of these patterns of male and female performance in large-scale tests are outlined next.

International tests of achievement

In international tests of achievement, distinct patterns of performance for males and females across the subjects of English (or native language), maths and science have been identified. In the assessment of English, females consistently outperformed males in all main aspects of the subject, especially in reading and writing, across all assessment systems (NEAP, 2000; OECD, 2000, 2004). The gaps in performance between males and females are established early in primary school and continue to grow until females outperform males to a significant degree by the end of compulsory schooling. In maths, many international and cross-national surveys (Martin *et al.*, 1999; OECD, 2000, 2004) show that, on average, males and females in the earlier stages of schooling perform similarly in maths, but, as age increases, males generally outperform females, and by age 15/16, males achieve better performances in virtually all aspects of mathematics tested.

In science, evidence from large-scale assessment programs at both cross-national and international level show that males perform better than females in science, but that the gaps in science are the smallest across the three subject areas (Martin *et al.*, 1999; NEAP, 2000; OECD, 2004).

National assessments

At more local levels, performance patterns of males and females paint a similar picture. Thus, on more syllabus-based examinations, females tend to perform better than males across a range of subjects and leave school better qualified than their male counterparts (JCGQ, 2004). For example, in the UK, on large-scale assessment programs at ages 16 (GCSE) and 18 (GCE A level)[1], females are reported to have performed better than males across a range of subjects and at both stages of schooling. In the USA, recent studies show that females outperform males on state and national tests. They are also more likely to perform better on school-based measures of attainment, stay on at school longer and successfully graduate (Alperstein, 2005).

From sex group differences to gender differences

There are two aspects to the publication of results by sex group and the gendered discourse that surrounds them that are of interest in any consideration of gender and achievement.

First, published data on male and female achievement have improved over several years to the extent that we now have extensive datasets across various levels of testing and schooling that provide information on how males and females achieve on tests and examinations. Research in the field of gender and assessment and testing has greatly benefited from this data, especially as much of it is disaggregated at a number of levels – the examination as a whole, the examination or test paper, the test item, and the mode of assessment. Thus, we are better informed as to how males and females perform on various types of tests and assessments. These data have certainly enhanced our knowledge of differential performance, as we can monitor the results of different groups across a range of tests and assessments, and pursue questions of fairness and equity at a macrolevel.

Second, the routine publication of results by sex group has, however, brought associated gendered discourses that position boys and girls as opposites, and as competitors. Consequently, more popular interpretations of male and female patterns of performance have created debates about the underachievement of boys and the overachievement of girls. Thus, we have an annual circus of comparisons of boys' and girls' performances on examinations and associated gendered discourses that have created new gendered stereotypes (Elwood, 2005). In these discourses, boys are positioned as problematic, troublesome, and lacking, and their underachievement is seen as extrinsic to boys themselves (Epstein *et al.*, 1998). Girls, on the other hand, are positioned as a valuable commodity in the

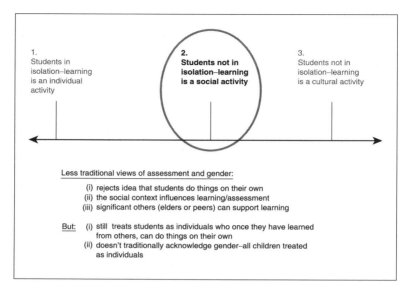

Figure 19.3   Assessment and testing as social activities

qualifications market place and their overachievement is seen as the result of the whole curriculum and examination system being feminized in their favour:

> Girls are doing better than boys in exams, but that does not mean they are brighter … . What has happened is that exams have been feminised – and so has the country. (Pirie, 2002: 1)

This traditional view of learning and assessment that considers gender as a static variable is reductionist and no longer helpful in understanding the complexities around gender and performance on tests and assessments. If we believe that learning does not take place in isolation and that examinations are not socially neutral, and if we observe that not all boys are underachieving and not all girls are overachieving, we are forced to look further along the continuum to different considerations of the learner, the mind, and assessment to help us understand gender differences in performance.

TESTING AND ASSESSMENT AS SOCIAL ACTIVITIES

Stage 2 on the continuum (Fig. 19.3) positions learning, mind, gender and assessment as complex concepts and activities that are socially generated and mediated. If we understand assessment and testing as social activities, we reject the idea that students do things on their own (in isolation from their teacher and others) and that tests check up on what individuals know. Furthermore, gender is viewed less in terms of sex-group differences and more as a socially positioned concept that influences students' experiences of school. Moreover, there is an acknowledgement that gender interacts with assessment activities and structures, and that this interaction is manifested in the differences in perform-ance observed (Elwood and Murphy, 2002; Francis *et al.*, 2003; Read *et al.*, 2004; Elwood, 2005); the social context and the gendered nature of learning, classrooms and schools influence assessment outcomes.

Here the view of learning and of the learner that underpins the model of assessment and testing is one of learners as active participants in their learning, and where learning from and with others is key:

> Human learning presupposes a specific social nature and a process by which children grow in to the intellectual life of those around them. (Vygotsky, 1978: 88)

This view of learning falls within social constructivist theories of learning (von Glaserfield, 1987), in which attention is focused on the need for 'models of mental processes to be involved when anyone responds to new information or to new prob-lems' (Black, 1999: 120), and in which instruction is seen 'not as direct transfer of knowledge but as an intervention in an ongoing knowledge construction process' (Gipps, 1999: 372). Thus, in social constructivist learning theories, students learn by 'actively making sense of new knowledge, making meaning from it and mapping it into their existing knowledge map or schema' (*ibid.*: 72). Even though social con-structivists argue that learning is a social activity and that learners construct their own meaning, a symbolic view of cognition still prevails and mind is still located 'in the head' (Cobb, 1999: 135). Thus, learning and meaning are co-constructed but eventu-ally this learning gets located back within the individual. Furthermore, formative or summative assessments are still measuring something that is the property of the indi-vidual. Learning is still about the internalization of external knowledge, and what the student can do alone after learning through social interaction (Vygotsky, 1978).

Researchers who advocate the benefits of formative assessment invoke social constructivist theories of learning to support arguments about assessment being something that should be done for and with the student rather than something that is done to them (Sadler, 1998; Gipps, 1999; Rust *et al.*, 2005). Here assessment is seen as the best way in which to seek clarification of students' existing knowledge and understanding and to enable them to acquire new knowledge and understand-ing based on this (Black, 1999). New forms of summative assessment and tests (especially in the UK) now tend to reflect these shifting views of learning and achievement, and aim to bring examinations closer to classroom learning and students' experiences (Elwood, 1995). The introduction of performance assess-ments in the USA reflected similar considerations (Gipps, 1999). Thus, examina-tion and test items reflect a more social emphasis on learning and knowing and broader definitions of achievement. Consequently, there has been a growth in the use of different assessment techniques (both formative and summative) in an attempt to articulate different achievements by boys and girls and to enable them to show their learning through different assessment activities and processes.

A view of assessment and learning from a social constructivist position sees *all* assessment tests and tasks as socially constructed, value-laden and highly problematic. Research into gender and performance from this perspective argues that tests and assessments themselves are contributing to the differences in performance observed (e.g. Stobart *et al.*, 1992a,b; Willingham and Cole, 1997; Murphy and Elwood, 1998; Elwood, 2001; Elwood and Murphy, 2002). In understanding differential performance, we need to look at the actual tests themselves. The choices made as to which assessment technique is used (multiple-choice tests, coursework portfolios, performance assessments, mode of response and styles of examination) and the assessment techniques themselves all have a role to play in the creation of the gender differences observed.

Gendered consequences of choice of assessment technique

In the UK, two key research studies (Stobart *et al.*, 1992b, Elwood and Comber, 1996) considered the impact of assessment and examining techniques on gender differences in performance. The critical focus of both these studies was how the social nature of public examinations shapes the experiences of students and teachers, their perceptions of subjects, the ways in which knowledge and understanding are assessed, and how these factors contribute to the differences observed.

Several factors in the design of examination systems and the assessment techniques used to assess students were identified as contributing significantly to gender differences in performance. For example, one key factor was the operational structure of examination systems at age 16. GCSE examination syllabuses in the UK are structured into different levels, or tiers of entry; each tier has a restricted set of grades that define the maximum and minimum achievement possible. For example, GCSE mathematics has three tiers of entry: foundation tier (grades D–G), intermediate tier (grades B–F) and higher tier (grades A*–C). Students are permitted to enter for one tier only at any one time, and any candidate not achieving the lowest restricted grade on any tier is unclassified.

Research found that one of the social consequences of the use of tiering is that gender significantly interacts with teachers' judgments on entry decisions; teachers use other considerations, not solely students' prior achievements, to allocate them to tiers (Stobart *et al.*, 1992b; Elwood and Murphy, 2002). For example, in GCSE maths, more boys than girls are entered for the foundation tier with maximum grade D, more girls are entered for the intermediate tier with maximum grade B, and more boys are entered for the higher tier with maximum grade A*. Disaffection among students (notably boys) seems to be increased in the foundation tier with the limited range of grades available. The intermediate tier acts as a safety net where less confident students (notably girls) are entered if anxious about failure. More confident students (notably boys) are entered for the higher tier and perform well.

Thus, teachers' decisions about which tier to enter students are based on affective factors (perceived ability, and confidence or anxiety within subjects) as well as cognitive factors, and this seems unintentionally to limit the achievements of some boys and some girls (Murphy and Elwood, 1998). Thus, even before students sit the examination, decisions are made about the limits of boys' and girls' achievements. Although supported as a valid way of assessing students that enables them to show their learning to good effect, the legacy of such systems is that boys and girls have differential access to either the full curriculum in certain subjects and/or the full range of grades available within the examination.

Therefore, the interaction of gender and assessment technique suggests that not all boys and not all girls are equally and fairly affected by all types of testing and assessment. The research outlined above and other similar work has mainly concerned itself with large-scale summative assessment (Gipps and Murphy, 1994; Willingham and Cole, 1997). Any such attention to gender and its interaction with formative assessment tasks and practices is rare (Murphy, 1995) as are any perspectives that consider problematic issues in classroom assessment reform. Indeed, Hargreaves *et al.* (2002) seem to be lone voices in cautiously reminding us that not all classroom-based assessments are 'humanistic and benign in their implications for supporting student learning and development' (2002: 70).

The assessment for learning movement promotes a view of learning within a social arena but tends to ignore gender. Proponents of this type of assessment tend to treat boys and girls as individuals and look only to within the individual to consider learning and achievement (Gipps, 1999; Black *et al.*, 2003). As yet, there are few considerations of the position of gender in the changed teacher–student relationship necessary for success in this assessment practice, or of the social contexts of classrooms in which this type of assessment takes place. From our knowledge of the interaction of gender and teachers' decision making around tiered examination systems, it is possible to argue that when teachers turn from the role of coach of students (for summative assessment) to that of judge of students (for formative assessment), gender significantly influences their evaluation of boys' and girls' achievements and successes.

This view of learning, mind, assessment and gender is still problematic for those of us seeking to understand fully the complex interactions of gender with classroom-based assessment tasks and the practice of assessment in general. We are thus pushed further along the continuum as we observe that classrooms have cultural contexts; that teacher–student relationships are gendered, complex and problematic; and that such relationships and interactions have major implications for how we assess boys and girls. When classrooms are viewed as cultural settings in which students participate, we can no longer omit from our evaluation of students' achievements what they bring to the classroom setting as a consequence of their participation in a myriad of other cultural contexts.

TESTING AND ASSESSMENT AS CULTURAL ACTIVITIES

Stage 3 on the continuum (Fig. 19.4) positions learning, mind, gender and assessment as things that are culturally generated and mediated. Here we recognize the

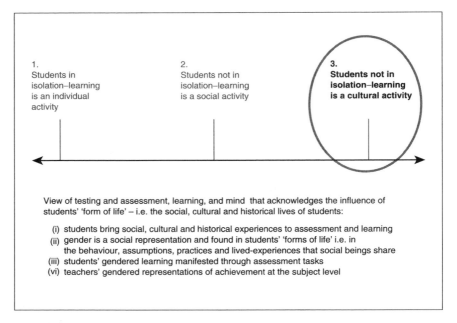

Figure 19.4   Assessment and testing as cultural activities

essential relationship and interaction between learning; the assessment of that learning; the social, cultural and historical lives of students and teachers; and the economic and political contexts in which assessment operates (Sutherland, 1996; Leathwood, 2005). Students and teachers bring social, cultural and historical experiences to assessment situations (Murphy and Ivinson, 2004), and to understand students' performances on assessment tasks we need to look into students' histories, into their 'forms of life' (McGinn, 1997) and not into their heads. It is by looking into their forms of life that we can start to understand their learning and why they respond to tasks in different and gendered ways.

The model of learning at this stage is one underpinned by socio-cultural perspectives on learning. Socio-cultural theorists consider a view of learning that takes account of the socially constituted nature of individuals; they cannot be considered in isolation from their social and historical contexts (Rogoff, 2003; Murphy and Ivinson, 2004). Bruner and Haste (1987) further suggest that through

> social life, the child acquires a framework for interpreting experience and learns how to negotiate meaning in a manner congruent with the requirements of the culture. Making sense is a social process; it is an activity that is always situated in a cultural and historical perspective. (1987: 1)

Aligned with a socio-cultural view of learning, there is a different view of mind. In this model, mind is considered situated between individuals 'in social action' (Cobb, 1999: 135). Wertsch (1991: 6) describes a socio-cultural approach to mind as one that 'creates an account of human mental processes that recognizes the essential relationship between these processes and their cultural, historical and institutional settings'. Thus, mind is not local to the individual but situated in the cultural setting and within cultural relationships, and resides between individuals' interactions and reactions. A non-local view of mind suggests further that the learner and the teacher are entangled, and that learning (ability or achievement) is the product of the relationship between the teacher, the student and the test paper or assessment task.

The theoretical underpinning of a non-local view of mind comes also from considerations of Wittgenstein's philosophy, in relation to how he viewed meaning, understanding, and especially *form of life* (Bloor, 1983; McGinn, 1997; Grayling, 2001). Further, there is an analogue to this view of mind within quantum theory, which has entanglement at its heart (Herbert, 1985; Moore, 2001; Pinkerton, 2002; Morrison, 2005).

Grayling (2001) offers us an interpretation of Wittgenstein's 'forms of life'. He describes it as the

> Underlying consensus of linguistic and non-linguistic behaviour, assumptions, practices, traditions and natural propensities which humans as social beings share with one another and which is therefore presupposed in the language they use. (2001: 97)

Form of life is the frame of reference we learn to work within when trained (or educated) in the language of our community. Thus, meaning, knowledge and understanding reside within communities (however defined) and can be understood only within this cultural context. Gender, in this respect, is intricate to form of life. Girls and boys experience different, gendered forms of life and learn through a gendered mediating of the wider communities to which they belong (social, subject and gender).

The analogue of a non-local view of mind in quantum theory allows us to talk about entanglement, influence, and action and reaction. Entanglement is defined as follows:

> When two systems of which we know the states by their respective representation, enter into a temporary physical interaction due to known forces between them and when after a time of mutual influence the systems separate again, then they can no longer be described as before, viz. by endowing each of them with a representative of its own. (Schrödinger, 1935, in Aczel, 2003: 70)

If we take the analogy that teachers and students are like quantum systems, then once in interaction, they can no longer be separately described or analyzed. They become part of an indivisible whole; neither teacher nor student is separate, and the product of learning (ability) is not separately analyzable. If we bring gender into this situation, we can see that as with 'form of life', gender becomes something that is absolutely entangled with the interactions of students and teachers – gender becomes part of the indivisible whole of the teacher, the student, the assessment task and the ability represented in the response.

Thus, we can articulate gender, in a very profound way, as a fluid, social representation – a set of ideas, social norms, conventions and associations within society that has definition within our community (Ivinson and Murphy, 2003) rather than something that is fixed and static. Boys and girls create and are created by their different forms of life, their entangled, social interactions with teachers and others, and the gendered appropriation of subject knowledge, thought processes and lived-experiences. Viewing learning, mind and gender in this way has profound implications for assessment practice and how we understand assessment outcomes.

Gender differences in styles and approaches to the study of English

In using socio-cultural approaches to understand assessment data and the social representation of gender, Murphy and Ivinson (2004) argue that, within teachers' practice, there are strong, gendered messages indirectly presented to students about what constitutes valued subject knowledge and knowledge that is equated with success. Boys and girls interact with these messages very differently by the way in which they respond to assessment tasks. To illustrate these points further, Elwood (1998) considered teachers' evaluations of the differences in boys' and girls' expression in writing and choices of writing styles in advanced level English. These considerations highlighted interesting notions of what teachers valued as 'good English writing' at this stage of schooling. Teachers articulated an ideal style of writing that again showed gender as a mediating factor:

> I think the boy's approach is much more effective at A level, far more effective. He will write you a side-and-a-half where others are writing four of five pages ... it is like a knife through butter – almost notes but not quite, a very sparse style of writing. I have never seen a girl do that, never. (female English teacher, quoted in Elwood, 1998: 177).

> He combines a flair for literature with an analytical instinct, whereas she emphasizes more but is less analytical and I would argue ... that's what distinguishes the very best [students] from the rest. (male English teacher, quoted in Elwood, 1998: 177)

These statements illustrate that certain styles of expression are expected and associated with success in this particular subject. Moreover, similar work suggests that such gendered expectations carry on into third-level study and within academic literacies more generally (Lillis, 2001; Francis *et al.*, 2003; Read *et al.*, 2004, 2005). Teachers give out messages, either knowingly or unknowingly, to students about what type of achievement aligns with success. Often the non-explicit nature of these messages means that some students (either boys or girls) either can or cannot meet teachers' criteria for success. Thus, how teachers view success in the community of the subject, with its conventions, forms, practices and cultural settings, significantly influences their judgments of boys' and girls' abilities. These definitions of success are entangled with teachers' and students' forms of life; it is only by looking into these forms of life that we begin to obtain a more humble understanding of gender and attainment.

CONCLUSION

This chapter has attempted to explore the very complex relationship between assessment, learning, mind, and gender. To support this exploration, I offered the reader a continuum as a framework along which to understand the differing notions of these fundamental and interrelated concepts and activities. In moving along the continuum in an attempt to get a more holistic and humble understanding of gender and achievement, I suggested the rejection of the traditional view of learning as something done in isolation, of mind as something that is located in the head, of gender as a static variable and the traditional psychometric view of assessment which sees it as checking up on what students know. Such a position, I have argued, gives us a very limited and distorted view of how boys and girls learn and how they achieve. Thus, to understand fully the highly complex relationship between gender and achievement, I have advocated the position along the far end of the continuum that views learning as a cultural activity, mind as between individuals, gender as a fluid, social representation, and assessment and testing as cultural activities that can describe students learning only in relationship to their teachers and their form of life. It is this position that offers a more humble approach to what we can actually say about boys' and girls' achievements in schools. The way in which we view learning, mind, gender and assessment at this position, has, I would argue, the most radical implications yet considered for how we evaluate students' learning. This is the true 'paradigm shift' in our thinking about these issues; boys' and girls' forms of life in relationship and entanglement with their teachers' must be part of our evaluations of their response to assessment tasks and tests. Such a perspective will considerably change how we view their learning, how we understand how learning takes place, and what we are actually doing when we attempt to capture and *measure* boys' and girls' achievements.

REFERENCES

Aczel, A (2003) *Entanglement: the greatest mystery in physics*. Chichester: Wiley.
Alperstein, JF (2005) Commentary on girls and boys, test scores and more. *Teachers College Record*, 16 May. www.tcrecord.org ID number 11874 (accessed 15 June 2005).
Barid, J (2002) Challenges of computerized assessment. Paper presented to the 27th Annual Conference of the International Association for Educational Assessment, Brazil, May 2001.
Bennett, R, Jenkins, F, Persky, H and Weiss, A (2003) Assessing complex problem-solving performances. *Assessment in Education*, 10: 347–60.
Black, P (1999) Assessment, learning theories and testing systems, in Murphy, P (ed) *Learners, learning and assessment* (118–34). London: Paul Chapman.

Black, P and Wiliam, D (1998) Assessment and classroom learning. *Assessment in Education*, 5: 7–71.

Black, P and Wiliam, D (2005) Lessons from around the world: how policies, politics and cultures constrain and afford assessment practices. *Curriculum Journal*, 16: 249–61.

Black, P, Harrison, C, Lee, C, Marshall, B and Wiliam, D (2003) *Assessment for learning: putting it into practice*. Buckingham: Open University Press.

Bloor, D (1983) *Wittgenstein: a social theory of knowledge*. New York: Columbia University Press.

Broadfoot, P (1996) *Education, assessment and society*. Milton Keynes: Open University Press.

Bruner, J (1999) Culture, mind and education, in Moon, B and Murphy, P (eds) *Curriculum in context*. (148–78). London: Paul Chapman.

Bruner, J and Haste, H (1987) *Making sense: the child's construction of the world*. New York: Routledge.

Centre for Educational Research and Innovation (CERI) (2005) *Formative assessment – improving learning in secondary classrooms*. Paris: OECD.

Cobb, P (1999) Where is the mind?, in Murphy, P (ed) *Learners, learning and assessment*. London: (135–50). Paul Chapman.

Elwood, J (1995) Undermining gender stereotypes: examination and coursework performance in the UK at 16. *Assessment in Education*, 2: 283–303.

Elwood, J (1998) Gender and performance in the GCE A level: gender-equity and the 'gold standard'. PhD dissertation, University of London, Institute of Education.

Elwood, J (2001) Examination techniques: issues of validity and effects on pupils' performance, in Scott, D (ed) *Curriculum and assessment*. (83–104). Westport, CT: Ablex.

Elwood, J (2005) Gender and achievement – what have exams got to do with it?, *Oxford Review of Education*, 31: 373–93.

Elwood, J and Comber, C (1996) *Gender differences in examinations at 18+: final report*. London: Institute of Education for the Nuffield Foundation.

Elwood, J and Murphy, P (2002) Tests, tiers and achievement: gender and performance at 16 and 14 in England. *European Journal of Education*, 37: 395–416.

Epstein, D, Elwood, J, Hey, V and Maw, J (eds) (1998) *Failing boys? Issues in gender and achievement*. Buckingham: Open University Press.

Fordor, J (2000) *The mind doesn't work that way: the scope and limits of computational psychology*. Cambridge, MA: MIT Press.

Francis, B, Robson, J, Read, B and Melling, L (2003) Lecturers' perceptions of gender and undergraduate writing style. *British Journal of Sociology of Education*, 24: 357–73.

Gipps, C (1999) Socio-cultural aspects of assessment. *Review of Research in Education*, 24: 355–92.

Gipps, C and Murphy, P (1994) *A fair test? Assessment, achievement and equity*. Buckingham: Open University Press.

Goldstein, H (1996a) Statistical and psychometric models for assessment, in Goldstein, H and Toby, L (eds) *Assessment: problems, developments and statistical issues*. (41–56). Chichester: Wiley.

Goldstein, H (1996b) Group differences and bias in assessment, in Goldstein, H and Lewis, T (eds) *Assessment: problems, developments and statistical issues* (85–94). Chichester: Wiley.

Grayling, AC (2001) *Wittgenstein: a very short introduction*. Oxford: Oxford Paperbacks.

Hargreaves, A Earl, L and Schmidt, M (2002) Perspectives on alternative assessment reform. *American Educational Research Journal*, 39: 69–95.

Herbert, N (1985) *Quantum reality: beyond the new physics*. New York: Anchor Press.

Ivinson, G and Murphy, P (2003) Boys don't write romance: the construction of knowledge and social gender identities in English classrooms. *Pedagogy, Culture and Society*, 11: 89–111.

Joint Council for General Qualifications (JCGQ) (2004) *National provisional GCSE full course results June 2004 (all UK candidates)*. www.jcgq.org.uk/exam-result-data/gcse-statsistics-summer.2004.pdf (accessed on 13 February 2005).

Lave, J and Wenger, E (1991) *Situated learning: legitimate peripheral participation*. Cambridge: Cambridge University Press.

Leathwood, C (2005) Assessment policy and practice in higher education: purpose standards and equity. *Assessment and Evaluation in Higher Education*, 30: 307–24.

Lemann, N (2000) *The big test: the secret history of the American meritocracy*. New York: Farrar, Straus and Giroux.

Lillis, TM (2001) *Student writing: access, regulation and desire*. London: Routledge.

Martin, MO, Mullis, IVS, Gonzales, EJ, Gregory, KD, Smith, TA, Chrostowski, SJ, Garden, RA and O'Connor KM (1999) *TIMSS 1999 International Science Report: findings from the IEA's repeat of the Third International Mathematics and Science Study at the Eighth Grade*. Boston, MA: Boston College.

McDermott, RP (1999) On becoming labelled – the story of Adam, in Murphy, P (ed) *Learners, learning and assessment* (1–21). London: Paul Chapman.

McGinn, M (1997) *Wittgenstein and the philosophical investigations*. London: Routledge.

Moore, F (2001) Rethinking measurement in psychology and education: a quantum perspective. Doctor of Education dissertation, Queen's University Belfast, Northern Ireland.

Morrison, H (2005) Personal communication.

Murphy, P (1995) Sources of inequity: understanding students' responses to assessment. *Assessment in Education*, 2: 249–70.

Murphy, P (ed) (1999) *Learners, learning and assessment*. London: Paul Chapman.

Murphy, P and Elwood, J (1998) Gendered experiences, choices and achievement: exploring the links. *International Journal of Inclusive Education* 2: 85–118.

Murphy, P and Ivinson, G (2004) Gender differences in educational achievement: a socio-cultural analysis, in Olssen, M (ed) *Culture and learning: access and opportunity in the curriculum*. Greenwich, CT: Information Age Publishing.

National Assessment of Educational Progress (NEAP) (2000) *Trends in academic progress: three decades of student performance*. Washington, DC: National Centre for Educational Statistics.

Organisation for Economic and Co-operation and Development (OECD) (2000) *Knowledge and skills for life: first results from PISA 2000*. Paris: OECD.

Organisation for Economic and Co-operation and Development (OECD) (2004) *Learning for tomorrow's world – first results from PISA 2003*. Paris: OECD.

Pinkerton, M (2002) Quantification, standards and the elusive search for transparency in monitoring school performance. Doctor of Education dissertation, Queen's University of Belfast, Northern Ireland.

Pirie, M (2001) How exams are fixed in favour of girls. *The Spectator*, 20 January.

Read, B, Francis, B and Robson, J (2004) Re-viewing undergraduate writing: tutors' perceptions of essay qualities according to gender. *Research in Post-Compulsory Education*, 9: 217–38.

Read, B, Francis, B and Robosn, J (2005) Gender , 'bias', assessment and feedback: analysing the written assessment of undergraduate history essays. *Assessment and Evaluation in Higher Education*, 30: 241–60.

Rogoff, B (2003) *The cultural nature of human development*. Oxford: Oxford University Press.

Rust, C O'Donovan, B and Price, M (2005) A social constructivist assessment process model: how the research literature shows us this could be the best practice. *Assessment and Evaluation in Higher Education*, 30: 231–40.

Sadler, R (1998) Formative assessment: revisiting the territory. *Assessment in Education*, 5: 77–84.

Shepard, L (2000) The role of assessment in a learning culture. *Educational Researcher*, 29: 4–14.

Stobart, G, Elwood, J and Quinlan, M (1992a) Gender bias in examinations: how equal are the opportunities? *British Educational Research Journal*, 18: 261–76.

Stobart, G, White, J, Elwood, J, Hayden, M and Mason, K (1992b) *Differential performance in GCSE maths and English – final report*. London: SEAC.

Sutherland, G (1996) Assessment: some historical perspectives, in Goldstein, H and Toby, L (eds) *Assessment: problems, developments and statistical issues*. (9–20). Chichester: Wiley.

von Glaserfield, E (1987) Learning as a constructive activity, in Janvier, C (ed) *Problems in the representation in the teaching and learning of mathematics*. (3–18) Hillsdale, NJ: Erlbaum.

von Glaserfield, E (1989) Cognition, construction of knowledge and teaching. *Synthese*, 80: 121–40.

Vygotsky, L (1978) *Mind in society.* London: Harvard University Press.

Wertsch, J (1991) *Voices of the mind: a sociocultural approach to mediated action.* Cambridge, MA: Harvard University Press.

Wilder, GZ and Powell, K (1989) *Sex differences in test performance: a survey of the literature.* New York: College Board Publications.

Willingham, WW and Cole NS (eds) (1997) *Gender and fair assessment.* Mahwah, NJ: Laurence Erlbaum.

NOTE

1. The General Certificate of Secondary Education (GCSE) is the main examination taken by 16-year-olds in England, Wales and Northern Ireland at the end of compulsory schooling. Passing grades are A*–G; the benchmark for higher performances is A*–C, and the proportion of students obtaining five or more GCSEs at grades A*–C is used as an indicator of accountability for schools. The General Certificate of Education (GCE) A level is the main examination taken by 18-year-olds in England, Wales and Northern Ireland. Passing grades are A–E, and results in these examinations are used (primarily) for entrance to university. Results in these examinations are also used to evaluate schools.

20

Gender and Citizenship

Tuula Gordon

INTRODUCTION

The history of the formation of liberal democratic nation states is linked to the formation of citizens – citizenship refers to membership of such a state. Generally, children are assigned citizenship at birth. This membership confers rights, duties and responsibilities, although some of these rights are related to age, so that, for example, the right to vote is available to those citizens who are deemed adults. In this context, children and young people are often thought to be in the process of becoming, as citizens-to-be. However, children do have all the rights of a citizen unless otherwise stated (such as regarding age of consent or consumption of alcohol). Thus, school students should be able to exercise agency over their own circumstances, albeit with consideration of the rights of others.

Iris Marion Young (1995) has argued that the claim for human rights of liberty and equality has been crucial for feminism. But, for women, this has also meant that they are 'positioned in and as a contradiction' (1995: 1) in liberal democratic states. The idea of group representation poses difficulties, because it encompasses an assumption of common interests. Therefore, it is difficult to take into account diverse dimensions of difference when gender is emphasized, for example, social class or ethnicity may be silenced. Education and schooling have been considered important arenas for addressing inequalities, and women have campaigned for the access of girls and women (cf. Berkovitch, 1999).

T.H. Marshall (1963) suggested that in order to alleviate inequities related to wealth, citizenship should be thought of as multidimensional in welfare societies. Political citizenship refers to the right to participate in democratic processes such as elections. Legal citizenship refers to equity in law. Finally, social citizenship refers to processes and practices that aim to ensure that people are able to exercise equal political and legal citizenship. Thus, social welfare provisions were considered necessary in order to facilitate equity. Marshall was particularly concerned with social class, and his theorization did not take gender into account (cf. Jones, 1990).

Initially, citizenship was reserved for white men with property. In practice, it was exclusionary, and only gradually did more groups, including women, acquire citizenship rights. Yet, it is argued that the model of a citizen is still male. Wendy Sarvasy (1992) has suggested that citizenship as concept and practice would have different content, if single mothers were the model of a citizen. Barbara Hobson (1997) has also argued that welfare policies in relation to single mothers provide an excellent litmus test when analyzing inclusiveness of welfare policies. Moreover, other dimensions of difference are also implicated in exclusionary practices – such as social class, ethnicity, culture, embodiment and sexuality.

A powerful statement about intertwining of categories of difference was attributed in 1851 to Sojourner Truth, an emancipated slave. She intervened in the proceedings in a women's convention in Ohio, and her talk was recorded:

> That man over there says that women need to be helped into carriages, and lifted over ditches, and to have the best place everywhere. Nobody ever helps me into carriages, or over mud-puddles, or gives me any best place! And ain't I a woman? Look at me! Look at my arm! I have ploughed and planted, and gathered into barns, and no man could head me! And ain't I a woman? I could work as much and eat as much as a man when I could get it – and bear the lash as well! And ain't I a woman? I have borne thirteen children, and seen most all sold off to slavery, and when I cried out with my mother's grief, none but Jesus heard me! And ain't I a woman? (www.fordham.edu/halsall/mod/sojtruth-woman.html)

Although the acuracy of the record is not certain, her speech clearly made a powerful impact:

> One of the most unique and interesting speeches of the Convention was made by Sojourner Truth, an emancipated slave. It is impossible to transfer it to paper, or convey any adequate idea of the effect it produced upon the audience. *Anti-Slavery Bugle,* Salem, Ohio, 1851 June 21 (www.kyphilom.com/www/truth.html)

Truth was an advocate of both women's rights and the rights of blacks. She noted that among black people there were women, and among women there were black women. This was an evocative multidimensional approach to the question of rights.

EDUCATION AND CITIZENSHIP

Education and citizenship are connected in many ways. Education was initially available only to privileged boys. The significance of education has been evident to those outside the education systems, and self-education, either individually or collectively, has been practised by many. For example, historically, Richard Johnson (1976) has discussed the notion of 'really useful knowledge' generated by working-class collective educational practices. More recently, Heidi Safia Mirza (1997) has analyzed the informal educational practices of Afro-Caribbean women in the UK. Adult education has expanded, and it is an important avenue for many (cf. Mirza and Reay, 2000; Hughes, 2002). Recent social changes in education have further complicated questions about citizenship. Nation states are becoming more diversified. Such diversity has been a characteristic of countries such as the USA and the UK for a long time, but, increasingly, many European countries have encountered questions related to nationality and ethnicity as well as settlement of immigrants and refugees. All citizens of EU countries should be able to benefit from welfare provisions in whatever other EU country they are in. Nevertheless, as Sandra Ponzanesi (2002) has noted, countries such as Germany, the UK, France and Italy have diverse policies on immigration.

Citizenship debates are currently connected to questions about globalization and the crossing of borders between nation states. It is suggested that nation states are losing their significance, but it is also argued they are still a vibrant feature of the political, social and cultural organization. Such debates pose different theories about the relationship between nationality and citizenship and about the significance of nations and nationality. I consider these debates and propose that citizenship is still significant in the organization of rights and responsibilities, and argue that questions about citizenship need to be addressed in the context of theorizing social justice.

Production of appropriate citizens in the context of the nation state is a crucial task given to the education system. In this process, citizenship and nationality overlap and are not easy to disentangle from each other. Further, while citizenship is about rights, duties and responsibilities, in the context of everyday practices at school, the duties and responsibilities of school students are emphasized more than their rights. In our ethnographic comparative and cross-cultural research in secondary schools in the UK and in Finland, we found that students are treated as if citizens-to-be, in the process of becoming (Gordon *et al.*, 2000). As suggested earlier, although children and young people are not able to exercise all citizenship rights, such as voting in elections, they are nevertheless entitled to all those rights that are not connected to age. Yet, for example, use of voice and mobility in space of school students are curtailed in ways that many of them find difficult at times, and at some points almost intolerable. Such control practices are often gendered, so that in the everyday practices of the school, the movement of boys, as well as their use of voice, is considered more acceptable by teachers, although, in principle, a great majority of teachers would advocate equality. There are generally taken for granted cultural assumptions that masculinities are more associated with exercise of agency while femininities are more associated with self-control.

Central issues addressed in citizenship education include political rights, particularly universal suffrage. Students are typically also taught various age-related rights, such as when they will be able to vote, obtain a driving licence and have access to social services such as housing. This teaching of entitlement is not sufficient to ensure a sense of agency among young people. Seyla Benhabib (2002) suggests that abstract debates on social justice usually differentiate between universalism and multiculturalism. In universalism, there is an idea that the general status of being a human being is more central than particular characteristics of individual people. Multiculturalism draws attention to differentiation between groups of people. Benhabib argues that cultures should not be seen as clearly defined wholes. She suggests that flexible citizenship develops in the context of institutional power sharing, and is compatible with 'deliberative democracy' and pluralism.

MULTIPLE DIMENSIONS OF CITIZENSHIP

There are vibrant debates about gender and citizenship, and the search for feminist approaches to citizenship is ongoing (cf. Voet, 1998). In schools, cross-national political, social and cultural developments and processes of globalization raise ever new issues about entitlements related to citizenship (cf. Osler and Vincent, 2002). At the same time, concerns are expressed about the need to control access to citizenship of different categories of people. The plight of the poor and dispossessed is an issue that raises the question of duties and responsibilities of those who have more access to economic, social and cultural resources.

T.H. Marshall's (1963) theory of political, legal and social citizenship has been both criticized and extended. The rights of lesbian and gay people are addressed through the concept of 'sexual citizenship' (Richardson, 2000). Opportunities to cross borders are discussed through the concepts 'cosmopolitan citizenship' (Stevenson, 2003) and 'world citizenship' (Westwood and Phizacklea, 2000). Local ways of exercising rights, duties and responsibilities are addressed in debates on 'urban citizenship' (Beauregard and Bounds, 2000). Moreover, there is a call for the development of 'post-national citizenship' (Sassen, 2002).

Cross-national political, social and cultural developments and processes of economic globalization raise ever new issues about entitlements related to citizenship (cf. Osler and Vincent, 2002). Because there are concerns about global and transnational movement of people from countries outside the European Union, there are new ways in which policies related to immigration and refugees are discussed. While borders within the European Union have become more flexible, other international movement is restricted. It is suggested that the borders of Europe are becoming increasingly impermeable to immigrants and refugees from other continents. Stricter immigration policies have also been instituted, as for example, by the USA. For some people, movement is a privilege exercised with relative ease, while for others movement is a necessity characterized by obstacles. Although there have been problems, such as the illegal status of many domestic employees, globalization works in contradictory ways, providing both limitations as well opportunities, as, for example, Miriam Henry (2001) suggests. Access to education is an important resource of entitlement in the emergent cross-cultural, global world.

For those people who have not experienced difficulties in moving across borders, the idea of citizenship does not necessarily seem important. For example, it is possible to consider the situation of a young Finnish woman Jatta, in our study on transitions (Gordon and Lahelma, 2003). By her early twenties, Jatta had resided and worked in several countries. Jatta did not consider nationality or citizenship as significant concepts, issues or practices in her life. She had worked in multinational settings and expressed her lack of interest in thinking about her location in terms of nation states:

Tuula: OK – what do you think about yourself in relation to citizenship and such matters? You are a Finnish citizen, aren't you?

Jatta: Yes [pause]. No, no, but – it's a bit terrible to say, but it's not – I think it's because I don't really think about it much, because in the kind of work that I do, you get there, you get to a place where there are about fifteen different nationalities.

Jatta operates in a place where citizenship seems to be of little relevance. Yet her work in such an international context is facilitated by the existence of the European Union, because she is located in a member state. Border crossing is relatively easy for Jatta, and hence there are few challenges to her sense of being nowhere and yet being located and having a experience of belonging – albeit in a context that is subsidiary to a nation state. Jatta's work is also located in a transnational space. She suggests that in such a place 'how people act' and 'what they do' is more important than their nationality or the citizenship that is assigned to people in their passports.

So, in today's educational contexts, dimensions such as (hetero)sexism, racism and classism, and other intersecting dimensions of differentiation must be analyzed and challenged in multiple ways (cf. Ali, 2003; Archer and Francis, 2005) and in multiple contexts. Fauza Ahmad (2001) notes that the participation of young British South Asian Muslim women in higher education is increasing. These young women are faced with a range of contradictions when they negotiate their cultural, religious and personal locations. A range of concepts is needed when analysing such trends. While the main focus here is on compulsory schooling – primary and secondary education – it is also important to analyze citizenship in places such as day nurseries and pre-schools (cf. Lappalainen, 2003) and adult education (cf. Hughes, 2002), as well as in the context of more informal education.

SCHOOLING AND EDUCATION

Transnationalism and globalization place increasing challenges on education in general and compulsory schooling in particular. Schools are key places where inclusive citizenship can be constructed, practised and fostered. Such citizenship is centrally concerned with rights. Young people often find that duties and responsibilities are emphasized more then their rights. But children and young people are citizens with rights here and now, even though they are often thought of as *future* citizens.

In schools, the framework within which school students are located is most often clearly inscribed. Typically, guidelines provided to school students, such as school timetables and school rules, guide them to established time–space paths which frame the pattern of their school day; these documents usually determine where they are supposed to be at any given time. A place that a student has to be in during a particular lesson is a place that is not accessible at another point in time (Gordon *et al.*, 2000).

In the classroom, the movement of students is – most typically – to come to a halt, and they are expected to settle in their place, and their bodies are to be still while their minds are expected to be active in tasks related to learning. They should acquire skills that are deemed necessary for educated, enlightened citizens capable of understanding their rights, duties and responsibilities, and able to exercise them. However, duties and responsibilities are subject to greater emphasis in the present, and rights are more associated with the future.

Our interviews with school students addressed use of voice and space. It was evident that some young women found the position of immobility and silence as enabling learning to take place (Gordon, 2006). But many of them would also express frustration about silence and immobility. One young woman described the practice of sitting still in lessons in the following way: 'Your arse goes numb, you get all sweaty' (interview, T.G.).

There are tensions between ways in which multiple dimensions of diversity can be taken into account. For example, in the USA, particularly in states such as California, diversity of students is emphasized. Schools keep records of the ethnic composition of students, and usually visitors are informed about these. There are attempts to address differentiation, and the aim is to construct inclusive within-school policies. Differentiation in the Californian context (as in many others) takes place more between schools than within them. In multiethnic state schools that are characterised by diversity, the proportion of white students is often low, to the extent that terms such as 'white flight' have been coined.

In a court case addressing ethnicity and culture in Britain, a Muslim schoolgirl was alleged to have had her rights violated when the school did not allow her to wear a body-concealing gown (the jilbab). The school was not ordered to allow her to wear the robe, but in court it was suggested that her human rights should be considered. It was argued that the school is 'an extension of the state', and therefore it is required to 'justify the limitation on her freedom created by the school's uniform code and the way in which it was enforced'. The school suggested that its uniform policy was a result of widespread consultation, and called for more guidance to schools in how to comply with human-rights law (Lyall, 2005).

Dimensions of citizenship education

In his study of the history of citizenship education, Derek Heater (2004) notes that education for citizenship was already flourishing in Greece by the eighth century BC. The purpose was to teach how people should act in the capacity of citizens and how to exercise allegiance to the abstract idea of the state. Current challenges to citizenship education, he suggests, are the consideration of the European dimension, as well as the idea of world citizenship. It is to be hoped that such concerns will be reflected in ways in which citizenship education is currently developed. It is questionable whether such practices are prevalent in schools at the moment, based on a review of research in schools in UK and in Finland, as well as school visits in California and in Vancouver, Canada. However, practices of inclusion can be observed too.

There are different patterns in ways in which equality and social justice are promoted. In the UK, the emphasis has been more on multiculturalism, in California on cultural diversity, and in Canada on a mosaic pattern. There are some difficulties in enacting the Californian and British aims, because differentiation between schools is connected to patterns of wealth reflected in housing. Therefore, a school in Oakland, California, may indeed encompass considerable cultural diversity, but white students tend to be absent. Such differentiation is also typical in many urban regions in the UK. The range of ethnicities in Vancouver included 'white' Canadians, so, in that sense, diversity was more comprehensive. However, the espousal of the 'mosaic' pattern meant that school had no deliberate policy of production of commonalities in the context of differences. The 'mosaic' ideal was interpreted in such a way that there was no explicit aim to support cross-national or cross-cultural collaboration. The current 'no child left behind' policy in the USA is also premised on the idea of being skilled and coping, and solving problems. The child that does not have sufficient skills and does not fit into the category of 'all' is particularly disadvantaged in this context, as Thomas S. Popkewitz and Sverker Lindblad (2004) suggest.

The idea of the mosaic pattern has gained some popularity elsewhere too. However, here it is useful to note Benhabib's (2004) criticism of the idea that cultures have distinct borders and that such distinctions serve to maintain inequitable differentiation. The mosaic pattern is also connected to challenges that globalization presents to education and schooling. It is feared that local cultures give way to transnational trends and that diversity of cultures constricts. But globalization is not merely a negative process concerned with the movement of capital and poorly paid migrant labor. The contradictions provide spaces for constructing alternative, critical practices too.

There are connections between schooling and the nation state (cf. Arnot and Dillabough, 2000). Nevertheless, some alternative conceptions that do not take nationality for granted were also observed. For example, in a London school, the students were discussing the relationship between being English and being British. There was a suggestion that Britishness is more associated with diversity than Englishness. In Finland, music teaching included world music and discussion absout the cultural contexts in which such music was typically produced (Gordon and Holland, 2003).

In a comparison of 'civic education' in 24 countries, Steiner-Khamsi *et al.* (2002) found more similarities than differences between the models. They propose that there was a discrepancy between theories of citizenship and practices of civic education. It is suggested that such a phenomenon of 'educational transfer' is partly explained by the existence of transfer of civic education packages that are translated into national languages and adopted as teaching materials. This is, however, a partial explanation. It is important that teaching should encourage students to construct meaningful knowledge. Emphasizing political knowledge implies the importance of the study of politics and government. Nevertheless such a study can be developed in a manner that encourages students to participate actively in their own environment, with awareness of its global context too, as Osler and Vincent (2002) emphasize.

Inclusive citizenship education must be based on theorization about gender as well as other social, cultural, economic, sexual and embodied dimensions of difference. Citizenship is historically linked with the idea of an abstract individual who is capable of exercising universal rights. Such a notion of citizenship is based on a taken-for-granted model of a hegemonic maleness. But in this situation, women have had to enter a space which is not inclusive.

Michelle Cohen (1996) proposes that although girls have had access to education for some time, the idea of a learner is still associated with maleness and masculinity. The idea of learning citizenship and conceptions of femininity are argued to be in some conflict still. Victoria Foster (1996) has argued that the space of learning is associated with masculinity to the extent that a girl who actively asserts herself in a space of learning is entering a transpositional space which is still associated with maleness. As Jane Kenway and her colleagues (1998) suggest, a girl who talks in class is adopting a speaking position that is in some conflict with notions of femininity, and hence she is likely to be considered to be 'answering back'. Valerie Hey (1997) noticed that girls wrote a lot of notes to each other in the classroom, in order to avoid being criticized for talking too much. Yet, as bell hooks (1989) argues, 'talking back' is necessary if girls are to develop and use an active voice.

Feminist analyses are important in order to develop democratic perspectives and social justice in education and schooling. International perspectives are needed in order to understand commonalities and similarities in ways in which gender relations are produced and maintained, and ways in which they are intertwined with social, cultural differences. How these differences are embodied and spatialised is significant too. Challenging inequalities is crucial on a global scale and reflects the education for all (UNESCO) policy ratified by all countries.

Practices of citizenship education

In school practices, there is a great deal of emphasis on preparing students for future adult citizenship. Children and young people have access to all the rights that have not been legally established otherwise for their own protection. This idea of general entitlement of all citizens regardless of age is not always expressed explicitly to school students. Most typically, citizenship education tends to mean that school students are taught about representative democracy and about parliamentary politics. They learn about the operation of various institutions in society, and often also about the history of political rights. Such teaching and learning can be rather mechanical, and young people may not be encouraged to think about their rights here and now.

When we have asked 18-year-old Finnish school students to talk about citizenship, they may have found it difficult do deal with such an abstract concept. Citizenship was likely to be thought of in terms of politics and the parliamentary system and was most often expressed as the right – and duty – to vote.

Tero: I haven't voted once (laughs). This is really embarrassing, yeah, but the second time I was – I don't remember where I was – it was something, I mean no, I have voted, I did vote in the presidential elections.
(…)
Tuula: Why do you think it's embarrassing?
Tero: You mean not voting?
Tuula: Yes.
Tero: Well, isn't it a bit like a citizenship duty – I don't know.

Katri expresses similar sentiments that emphasize responsibility, but she extends her point beyond the sphere of representative politics:

Katri: Well, I think it's more like having a responsibility, sort of, I mean about your own behavior in public places and – otherwise too. Yeah, responsibility is freedom.

Another young woman expresses more negative views on citizenship. Her background is multicultural, and she has dual citizenship. When I ask her to discuss what comes to mind about citizenship, she responds:

Noora: Citizenship? Well, mostly bureaucracy.

Several young people presented critical views about the concept of citizenship, and did not invest commitment to it, or consider citizenship particularly enabling, as the following quotation demonstrates. Yet citizenship was one way of expressing differentiation between nation states.

Krista: I don't think that a citizen of some other country is less important than a Finn.
Heli: Yes. It's not like – I'm Finnish, yeah great, I'm Finnish [laughs]. (…) Of course one is proud about one's own – I mean sort of – not exactly proud – it is that a bit.
Krista: It's nicer to be here than in Afghanistan or Pakistan, being a Finnish woman.

Krista and Heli begin by expressing inclusive views, and present gender and rights of women, as important. In order to underline that difference, they cite two countries where the position of women is particularly subservient. Moreover, both Afghanistan and Pakistan have been in the news in negative contexts of instability, trouble and strife. It is notable that Krista and Heli do not compare themselves to men in Finland. It would be more difficult to reproduce the notion of a 'strong Nordic woman' if that was the comparison point (cf. Lahelma and Öhrn, 2003).

In her study on suffragettes, Wendy Parkins (2000, p63) has suggested that there was a significant difference in the strategies of the movement when women did not only act to become citizens or act as if citizens, but changed their practices and actually 'acted citizenship'. Acting citizenship therefore refers to practices that are exercised by people in their lives. In transposing her analysis to schooling, it can be suggested that students are often represented as future citizens, who learn about the rights that they will have when they reach the age of an adult. Yet children and young people are citizens here and now, and ought to be able to act citizenship at school. If we envision such active citizenship, everyday lives in schools would change, and all participants would be able to make a greater contribution.

Many of the tensions in everyday life at school centre on time–space paths. They provide an easy way of demonstrating resistance, by not turning up in the right place at the right time. Students often sought inventive ways of diversifying their use of time and space. For example, in a London school in our ethnographic research, children had discovered a small gap in the fence and left the school grounds unobserved through it. In Helsinki schools, students were not supposed to leave school grounds except during the dinner breaks. However, students regularly went to nearby shops, and smokers found accessible corners in the vicinity of the school. During lessons, time was often negotiated (Gordon *et al.*, 2000). 'Having a voice' is a metaphor that has been used to refer to active participation (Fine, 1992). This means that pedagogic practices should allow and enable students to speak about issues that are important to them. However, in everyday practice in schools, teachers often feel that there is little time for discussions.

The use of voice, time and space is gender differentiated. Often boys have more opportunities in exercising agency and have more control over their embodiment and location in spatial relations.

Studies also demonstrate difficulties that boys may experience at school. Although the model of a learned citizen tends to be associated with maleness, tasks to be performed in everyday life at school are often considered feminine, because they entail embodied passivity, such as sitting still, listening and writing (cf. Connell, 1989; Mac an Ghaill, 1994). The idea that students can be more flexible about gendered behavior benefits both girls and boys (Francis, 2000).

AGENCY

The idea of developing and using a voice, as well as the idea of acting citizenship, is associated with the need to exercise agency. It is necessary for girls to construct a position of a speaking 'I', if they are to be successful in schooling. This speaking 'I' is not equally accessible to all male students either, as masculinities are hierarchically organized. Sense of agency is important in the establishment of an idea of the self that is associated with a successful citizen. Such a sense of the self need not necessarily be individualistic. The concept of the 'individual' and its connection to citizenship have been criticized because of the limitations of both these concepts in terms of extending rights to all social and cultural groups. The notion of abstract individuals removes people from the social and cultural connections and their embodied and spatial locations. Independence becomes the main desired characteristic of such an individual. Men are more typically thought of as individual citizens, whereas women are more likely to be perceived in connection with others.

Valerie Walkerdine and colleagues (2001) have explored anxieties experienced by (particularly working-class) girls when pursuing their educational careers (cf. Shaw, 1995). Dutiful insertion of oneself into authority relations can also be beneficial for girls, as Bronwyn Davies and her colleagues argue (2001). Based on memory work from their own school days, they suggested that making themselves as subservient in authority relations provided an opportunity to achieve in education. Subsequently, this enabled them to construct academic careers. Although enforced silence is likely to be painful muteness, as a choice, silence can be protective for young girls.

Agency is a complex concept, and, similarly, practices referred to in relation to agency are also difficult to define. In order to act on one's circumstances a sense of agency is crucial. Therefore, an important aspect of schooling and of adult education in both formal and informal contexts is to promote this sense of agency and the idea that there are opportunities for exercising agency. All school students should have the opportunity to address their circumstances, to explore their emotions, and to consider ways in which they can exercise more agency.

Considering the challenge posed to education on a global level is important, because there is a call for cheap female labor in the context of neo-conservative and neo-liberal politics. Especially, the domain of domestic work is growing. Citizenship rights of immigrant and transnational workers are an important concern (Westwood and Phizacklea, 2000). It is a challenge for educational systems to promote the citizenship rights of all those participating in educational institutions. Refugees may be stateless, and many school students may be living transnational lives in transnational families (Orellana *et al.*, 2001; Thorne *et al.,* 2003).

All these issues point to the need to consider agency both in theory and practice. A crucial task for education is to cultivate a sense of being able to make decisions and being able to carry them out – without forgetting consideration for others. Individual agency is located in collective contexts that include both micro- and macroprocesses. Assertiveness is particularly important to those groups that are less likely to be located in positions of power. Yet, such assertiveness needs to take into account the opportunities for other people's agency in ways that enhance equity and social justice.

CONCLUSIONS

The exercise of citizenship requires the notion of the 'I' – perceiving oneself as a person who can enact. But that perception should be located in a more collective context, because the success of 'I' without recourse to 'we' is likely to be curtailed. Citizenship education needs to go beyond citing rights and naming them; the promotion of the exercise of such rights is crucial too. This means that at the everyday level of the school, pedagogies and teaching methods need to be examined and updated. The everyday organization of the schools – including spatiality and temporality and the ways in which time–space paths are instituted – also needs to be examined. There is a challenge to determine what is necessary and useful knowledge for everybody, while also considering special needs. The idea that educational practices are collective and collaborative can boost individual agency while not losing sight of the contexts in which people operate.

REFERENCES

Aapola, S, Gonick, M and Harris, A (2004) *Young femininity: girlhood, power and social change*. Houndmills: Palgrave.

Ahmad, F (2001) Modern traditions? British Muslim women and academic achievement. *Gender and Education*, 13: 137–52.

Ali, S (2003) 'To be a girl': culture and class in schools. *Gender and Education*, 15: 269–83.

Archer, L and Francis, B (2005) 'They never go off the rails like other ethnic groups': teachers' constructions of British Chinese pupils' gender identities and approaches to teaching. *British Journal of Sociology of Education*, 26: 165–82.

Arnot, M and Dillabough, J-A (eds) (2000) *Challenging democracy: international perspectives on gender, education and citizenship*. London: RoutledgeFalmer.

Beauregard, R and Bounds, A (2000) Urban citizenship, in Isin, EF (ed) *Democracy, citizenship and the global city*. London: Routledge.

Benhabib, S (2002) *The claims of culture and equality, and diversity in the global era*. Princeton, NJ: Princeton University Press.

Benhabib, S (2004) *The rights of others: aliens, residents and citizens*. Cambridge: Cambridge University Press.

Berkovitch, N (1999) *From motherhood to citizenship: women's rights and international organizations*. Baltimore, MD: Johns Hopkins University Press.

Cameron, D (1995) *Verbal hygiene*. London: Routledge.

Cohen, M (1996) Is there a space for the achieving girl?, in Murphy, PF and Gipps, CV (eds) *Equity in the classroom*. London: Falmer Press.

Connell, RW (1989) Cool guys, swots and wimps: the interplay of masculinity and education. *Oxford Review of Education*, 15: 291–303.

Davies, B, Dormer, S, Gannon, S, Laws, C, Rocco, S, Lenz Taguchi, H and McCann, H (2001) Becoming school girls: the ambivalent project of subjectification. *Gender and Education*, 13: 167–82.

Fine, M (1992) *Disruptive voices: the possibilities of feminist research*. Ann Arbor, MI: University of Michigan Press.

Foster, V (1996) Space invaders: desire and threat in the schooling of girls. *Discourse: studies in the cultural economics of learning*, 17: 43–63.

Francis, B (2000) *Boys, girls and achievement*. London: RoutledgeFalmer.

Gordon, T and Lahelma, E (2003) From ethnography to life history: tracing transitions of school students. *International Journal of Social Research Methodology*, 6: 245–54.

Gordon, T, Lahelma, E, Hynninen, P, Metso, T, Palmu, T and Tolonen, T (1999) Learning the routines: professionalisation of newcomers in secondary school. *International Journal of Qualitative Studies of Education*, 12: 689–706.

Gordon, T, Holland, J and Lahelma, E (2000a) *Making spaces: citizenship and difference in schools.* London: PalgraveMacmillan.

Gordon, T, Holland, J and Lahelma, E (2000b) From pupil to citizen: a gendered route, in Arnot, M and Dillabough, J-A (eds) (2000) *Challenging democracy: international perspectives on gender, education and citizenship.* London: RoutledgeFalmer.

Heater, D (2004) *A history of education for citizenship.* London: RoutledgeFalmer.

Henry, M (2001) Globalisation and the politics of accountability: issues and dilemmas for gender equity in education. *Gender and Education*, 13: 87–100.

Hey, V (1997) *The company she keeps. An ethnography of girls' friendships.* Buckingham: Open University Press.

hooks, b (1989) *Talking back: thinking feminist, thinking black.* Boston, MA: South End Press.

Hudson, B (1997) Social control; in Maguire, M, Morgan, R and Reiner, R (eds) *The Oxford handbook of criminology* (2nd ed). Oxford: Oxford University Press.

Hughes, C (2002) Beyond the poststructuralist–modern impasse: the woman returner as 'exile' or 'nomad', *Gender and Education*, 14: 411–24.

Johnson, R (1976) Educational policy and social control in early Victorian England. *Past and Present*, 49: 96–119.

Kenway, J and Willis, S (with Blackmore, J and Rennie, L) (1998) *Answering back.* London: Routledge.

Lahelma, E and Öhrn, E (2003) 'Strong Nordic women' in the making? Gender policies and classroom practices, in Beach, D, Gordon, T and Lahelma, E (ed) *Democratic education: ethnographic challenges.* London: Tufnell Press.

Lappalainen, S (2003) Celebrating internationality: constructions of nationality at preschool, in Beach, D, Gordon, T and Lahelma, E (ed) *Democratic education: ethnographic challenges.* London: Tufnell Press.

Lyall, S (2005) Muslim student in Britain wins religious right case. *San Francisco Chronicle*, 3 March, A5.

Mac an Ghaill, M (1994) *The making of men.* Buckingham: Open University Press.

Marshall, TH (1963) *Sociology at crossroads*, London: Heinemann.

Mirza, HS (1997) Black women in education: a collective movement for social change, in Mirza, HS (ed) *Black British feminism: a reader.* London: Routledge.

Mirza, HS and Reay, D (2000) Redefining citizenship: Black women educators and 'the third space', in Arnot, M and Dillabough, J-A (eds) (2000) *Challenging democracy: international perspectives on gender, education and citizenship.* London: RoutledgeFalmer.

Orellana, FM, Thorne, B, Chee, A and Lam, WSE (2001) Transnational childhoods: the participation of children in processes of family migration. *Social Problems*, 48: 573–92.

Osler, A and Vincent, K (2002) *Citizenship and the challenge of global education.* Stoke: Trentham.

Parkins, W (2000) Protesting like a girl: embodiment, dissent and feminist agency. *Feminist Theory*, 1: 59–78.

Ponzanesi, S (2002) Diasporic subjects and migration in Europe, in Braidotti, R and Griffin, G (eds) *A reader in European women's studies.* London: Zed Books.

Popkewitz, TS and Lindblad, S (2004) Historicizing the future: educational reform, systems of reason, and the making of children who are the future citizens. *Journal of Educational Change*, 5: 229–47.

Richardson, D (2000) Claiming citizenship? Sexuality, citizenship and lesbian/feminist theory. *Sexualities*, 3: 255–72.

Sarvasy, W (1992) Beyond difference versus equality policy debate: postsuffrage feminism, citizenship, and the quest for a feminist welfare state. *Signs* 17: 329–62.

Sassen, S (2002) Towards post-national and denationalized citizenship, in Engin, IF and Turner, BS (eds) *Handbook of citizenship studies* (277–91). Princeton, NJ: Princeton University Press.

Scott, JW (1995) Universalism and the history of feminism. *Differences: A Journal of Feminist Cultural Studies,* 7: 1–14.

Shaw, J (1995) *Education, gender and anxiety.* London: Taylor and Francis.

Steiner-Khamsi, G, Torney-Purta, J and Schwille, J (eds) (2002) Introduction: issues and insights in cross-national analysis of qualitative studies, in *New paradigms and recurring paradoxes in education for citizenship: an international comparison* (1–36). Oxford: Elsevier.

Thorne, B (1993) *Gender play: girls and boys in school.* Buckingham: Open University Press.

Thorne, B, Orellana, FM, Lam, WS, E and Chee, A (2003) Raising children – and growing up – in transnational contexts: comparative perspectives on generation and gender, in Hondagneu-Sotelo, P (ed) *Gender and U.S. immigration: contemporary trends.* Berkeley, CA: University of California Press.

Voet, R (1998) *Feminism and citizenship.* London: Sage.

Walkerdine, V, Lucey, H and Melody, J (2001) *Growing up girl. Psychosocial explorations of gender and class.* Houndmills: Palgrave.

Weis, L and Fine, M (2004) *Citizenship and social justice.* New York: Routledge.

Westwood, S and Phizacklea, A (2000) *Trans-nationalism and the politics of belonging.* London: Routledge.

21

Gender and Modern Language Education

Linda M. von Hoene

The thematization of gender in the scholarship on modern language education is indebted to and must be read against broader changes that have taken place over the past three decades in feminist theory and women and gender studies.[1] Much like the history of feminism itself, research on foreign language education and gender has moved from a focus on gender as a stable and isolated characteristic of identity that affects how languages are learned to a poststructuralist emphasis on the language learner as a subject discursively constructed through language and characterized by multiple differences, including those of gender, race, ethnicity, and age, among others.

As will be discussed in this chapter, however, the manner in which gender has been taken up in the research on foreign language acquisition, in particular since the mid-1990s, has been far more progressive and critical than the approach to gender that has dominated the teaching of foreign languages in educational settings since the 1970s. Seen from the perspective of a critical, feminist pedagogy, the failure of foreign language instruction to attend to this gap has fundamental consequences for educational outcomes that go beyond the acquisition of language. As I will argue, the prevailing methods used to teach foreign languages implicitly encourage a colonialist and assimilationist relationship to the foreign culture that maintains rather than challenges a normatively gendered worldview.

This chapter will first examine the way in which gender has been explored in the research on foreign language acquisition over the past several decades, putting these developments in dialog with shifts that have occurred in feminist theory and gender studies. I will then examine the dominant methodologies in foreign language education since the 1970s and the implications of these practices for a critical relationship to gender and other aspects of identity.[2] The chapter employs feminist and poststructuralist theory to rethink the teaching and learning of foreign languages as a process of self-reflexive, cross-cultural travel predicated on the vigilant attentiveness to how we respond to difference. I will conclude by making suggestions on how post-secondary departments of modern languages can make changes in their approaches to language teaching and teacher training so as to serve the educational mission of the institutions they inhabit as well as the larger social good by becoming departments of cross-cultural difference.

HISTORY OF RESEARCH ON GENDER AND FOREIGN LANGUAGE EDUCATION

The impact of gender difference

Research on gender and foreign language education emerges against the backdrop of scholarship that began in the early to mid-1970s on women and language and feminist studies in the psychology of gender. The work of Lakoff (1975), and of the contributors to Thorne and Henley's (1975) volume, established what has now become a rich field of language and gender studies.[3] This early work on gender and language focused primarily on the differences between men and women in their styles of communication and explored such issues as the use of tag questions, turns at talk, length of time in holding the floor, interruptions, and information solicitation in demarcating women's speech as a product of women's place in a male-dominated social order. In foreign language education, the work of Gass and Varonis (1986) and Pica *et al.* (1991) explores similar questions about the impact of gender on conversational strategies used by native and nonnative speakers, although the cultural context out of which these differences might emerge was absent in their work. In paired conversations between nonnative speakers, Gass and Varonis (1986) determined that the patterns of negotiation of meaning that existed in same-sex versus opposite-sex interactions differed along gender lines: in mixed sex dyads, women provided more comprehensible input (such as information seeking or follow-up questions) and men more comprehensible output (information or responses to questions). In paired conversations between native speakers and nonnative speakers, Pica *et al.* (1991) determined that women negotiate meaning more actively with a female native-speaker interlocutor than with a male native-speaker interlocutor.

This strand of research on the impact of gender on the negotiation of meaning in classroom settings has continued, along with other approaches, through the 1990s to the present. For example, Meunier (1994) raises the question as to whether the 'genderlects' of the first language re-emerge in the language of the foreign language classroom. Like Meunier, Chavez (2000) explores gender as used in the discourse of the German classroom and corroborates much of the findings of other researchers, namely, that while men are more talkative in the classroom (Meunier, Sunderland), women tend to be engaged more substantively in learning the language. Building on the work of Campbell (1998), Chavez (2000) also finds that men are more anxious about learning foreign languages than women. These findings have implications for the classroom and the impact of gender – both that of the students and of the teacher – on second language acquisition.

While the work of Gass and Varonis (1986), Pica *et al.* (1991), Meunier (1994) and Chavez (2000) focuses on conversational strategies, a substantial body of research on the impact of gender on individual learners and the strategies they use in learning the foreign language began to appear in the late 1980s. Building on Politzer (1983), Oxford *et al.* (1988), Ehrman and Oxford (1989), Nyikos (1990), Bacon (1992), Bacon and Finneman (1992), Oxford (1993), and Green and Oxford (1995), Zoubir-Shaw and Oxford (1994) found that women and men differ in the learning strategies they use in acquiring a foreign language. Women, they maintain, employ more global, socially oriented strategies (for example, elicitation of input) than men, particularly in speaking and listening. Relying heavily on scholarship in the social psychology of gender as articulated by Maccoby and Jacklin (1974), Gilligan (1982), and Belenky *et al.* (1986), these foreign language researchers posited that female foreign language learners define themselves relationally and demonstrate behaviors predicated on cooperation and integration. Men, on the other hand, employed learning strategies that were less global and more analytic. Ehrman and Oxford (1989), for example, demonstrated that women have greater facility with those language-learning strategies that involve eliciting information, whereas Bacon (1992) found that women were interested in getting the gist of what they hear. Men, on the other hand, were focused more on the details.

This focus on the impact of gender on the choice of learning strategies use remains central to research on gender and foreign language education today, as can be evidenced by more recent articles on gender and learning strategies, such as those by Grace (2000) and Brantmeier (2003). Unlike the studies on learning strategies used in listening and speaking, however, both Brantmeier (2003) and Young and Oxford (1997) found that gender does not affect the choice of learning strategies used in reading.

Most of the work emanating from this strand of research on foreign language learning and gender differences asserts that, based on their socialization, women are generally more successful than men in foreign language learning (e.g. Nyikos, 1990), particularly in introductory courses. Though this work has certain shortcomings due to its lack of emphasis on other aspects of identity that may intersect with gender and, as will be discussed below, its inattention to the impact of language learning on gendered subjectivity, these studies should interest teachers and scholars of modern languages, as they raise the question of socialization and its impact on classroom behavior and learning styles. The recommendations made by these researchers are all sound practices to foster learning in any discipline. For example, instructors are encouraged to use a broad range of teaching styles to address differences that exist in the classroom and to provide students with opportunities to become familiar with a broad array of learning strategies that may enhance their success at language learning.

Poststructuralist approaches to gender and language learning

Starting in the early to mid-1990s, the research on gender in foreign language education begins to shift away from an exclusive focus on the impact of gender on the learning process to the impact of the language-learning process on the construction of the gendered subject. This shift results from the integration of poststructuralist, postcolonialist, psychoanalytic, and feminist theory into the research on gender and foreign language education by such scholars as Kramsch (1993), Kramsch and von Hoene (1995), von Hoene (1995), Pierce (1995), Sunderland (1995), Siegal (1996), von Hoene (1999), and Kramsch and von Hoene (2001). This strand of research on gender and foreign language learning views the subject or learner as constructed through language, discourse, and social relations of power. It also raises the question of how subjectivity may be potentially reconstructed through the cross-cultural encounter with difference.

Though not explicitly taking up the question of gender, Claire Kramsch's pioneering work, *Context and Culture in Language Teaching* (1993), was foundational in rethinking the impact of foreign language study on the learner. Informed by the work of the postcolonial theorist Bhabha (1994) and poststructuralist theorists such as Roland Barthes (1966), Kramsch maintained that a third, hybrid space is constructed between languages such that the learner does not move in a linear fashion from language 1 (L1) and culture 1 (C1) to language 2 (L2) and culture 2 (C2), but rather creates a hybrid identity between cultures, language 3 (L3) and culture 3 (C3). Kramsch's work productively called into question the goal of assimilation or full identification with an imagined native speaker (who was himself a fictive and exclusionary construct) as the goal of foreign language study, and underscored instead the value of this 'third' critical space between cultures.

Building on this work, Kramsch and von Hoene (1995) brought feminist theory to bear on the process of foreign language study. Using the writings of women of color and Third World women, which had radically transformed feminism's myopic focus on gender to the exclusion of other aspects of difference, Kramsch and von Hoene (1995) urged foreign language educators to focus explicitly on the manner in which students travel to other cultures and respond to difference. Invoking the work of the feminist theorists Gloria Anzaldúa (1987, 1990), bell hooks (1984, 1989), Maria Lugones (1990), and Trinh T. Minh-ha (1989), Kramsch and von Hoene (1995) called for the development of a 'multi-voiced consciousness' that would vigilantly tease out and be attentive to difference.

Following up on the work of Kramsch and von Hoene (1995), von Hoene (1995; 1999) employed feminist, psychoanalytic, and postcolonial theory to highlight how the application of these theoretical discourses to the training of teaching assistants could fundamentally transform the teaching of foreign languages. Drawing on psychoanalytic theory, in particular Lacan's mirror stage (1977) and Kristeva's (1980) 'subject-in-process', von Hoene (1995) contended that if foreign language study is to be conducted in a noncolonialist, feminist fashion, instructors must encourage students to examine their response to the foreign Other. Colonialist models would be reflected, for example, in the desire to identify with and assimilate into the Other or the desire to reject what is perceived to be the abject, foreign Other. The promotion of a postcolonial response to otherness, which is fundamental to the third space posited by Kramsch (1993) and Bhabha (1994), and the *mestiza* consciousness described by Anzaldúa (1987), provides an alternative model for living with difference. von Hoene (1999) suggests that departments of foreign languages and literatures reconstitute themselves as departments of cross-cultural difference where students can consciously examine their relationship to otherness. By so doing, foreign language departments would be contributing significantly to the broader mission of preparing students for democratic, civic engagement.

The question of how subjectivity in general and gendered subjectivity in particular are affected by the encounter with difference also runs through several other important works that were published in the mid-1990s by Jane Sunderland (1995), Bonny Norton Pierce (1995), Livia Polanyi (1995), and Meryl Siegal (1996). Bonnie Norton Pierce's work (1995) points to second language acquisition theory's failure to construct a model of language learning that can accommodate the interface between the individual learner and the social context. Critiquing Krashen (1982) for his limited definition of the individual and Schumann (1976) for the focus on acculturation without attention to the individual, Pierce (1995) suggests that we consider the notion of 'investment' as a more localized and context-specific way to investigate relations of power and their impact on a learner's motivation to engage with the foreign language. Drawing on Weedon's (1987) work on feminist poststructuralism in her study of immigrant women learning English in Canada, Pierce (1995), like Kramsch and von Hoene (1995), Sunderland (1995), and Siegal (1996), advocates a notion of the subject that is multiple, changing, and a site of discursive struggle.

The work of Jane Sunderland (1995; 2004) on the constitution of gendered subjectivity in the process of foreign language study contributes significantly to the poststructuralist approaches under discussion. Sunderland distinguishes herself by bringing to light the impact on both men and women of reconstituting gendered selves in the foreign language classroom. In her analysis of a seventh-grade German class, Sunderland (1995) examines an exchange that occurs between the teacher and the students when the teacher asks for boys to act out male parts in a dialog. Three girls eagerly volunteer by yelling, 'We're boys, miss!' Through analysis of the classroom dialog and conversations with the three girls, the teacher, and several boys in the class, Sunderland identifies the asymmetry that exists for boys and girls in taking on the role of the other sex in the foreign language classroom. For the boys to call out, 'We're girls, miss!' would be unthinkable, because they would be equating themselves with femininity, the devalued Other. For girls, who are identifying with the valued Other, this would not be the case.

Sunderland (2004) deepens her analysis of this phenomenon by suggesting that more may be at stake for men in speaking a foreign language because through this process they occupy the position of the Other and can therefore experience a much greater sense of vulnerability. Because the experience of being othered may not be unfamiliar to women or to other 'marked' groups, such as ethnic minorities and students with disabilities, for them, speaking a foreign language may be less destabilizing than it is for men. More research is needed in this area.

Much work on the poststructuralist construction of gendered identity through the study of foreign languages has been done in the field of Japanese language. The gender-specific differences in pitch level and certain morphologic and syntactic markers make this a very fruitful site of research. Siegal (1996), for example, examined the linguistic choices of white, Western women studying abroad and demonstrated that they consciously constructed an identity that shifted between identification and transgression of the expected female linguistic norms. A research study conducted by Ohara (2001), which consisted of recordings of students at different levels of fluency and interviews with some of the students, showed that language learners consciously choose to construct a hybrid, gendered relationship in learning Japanese rather than simply emulating normative, gendered behaviors. This is particularly striking given the presentation of gendered language in Japanese textbooks, which presents a more dichotomized view of gender distinctions than may in reality exist (Ohara et al., 2001).

The imprint of poststructuralist thought on foreign language education research is also evidenced in 'critical language awareness' approaches most closely associated with the work of Norman Fairclough (1992). This work draws on the work of Michel Foucault and Paolo Freire by emphasizing the construction of subjectivity through discourse and advocates the development of critical consciousness that will lead to the improvement of society. Ohara, et al. (2001) employ this approach to challenge the gender norms presented in a beginning Japanese course. They inject several new modules in the course that use advertisements from Japanese television to highlight the gendered stereotypes that exist in Japanese culture and use questionnaires to determine whether students gain knowledge and a critical stance to the stereotypes based on the new modules. While the goals of this approach are well intentioned, the failure of the authors to have the students take note of similar tendencies in US culture is unfortunate. In addition, the idea that US students should be rallied to judge sexism in Japan lacks the self-reflexive, contextually-based approach to moving between languages that is described above (and also discussed below), and that calls for vigilant scrutiny of how one travels to another culture in a noncolonialist fashion.

Gender and foreign language textbooks

Another fruitful area in the research on gender and foreign language education has been the examination and use of classroom materials. Indeed, the discussion that has emerged in this area reflects the overall shifts in the approach to gender and modern language education discussed thus far. One approach is to analyze textbooks in terms of how equitably they represent men and women in the readings, dialogs, and exercises (Graci, 1989). Sunderland *et al.* (2002) argue, however, that it is not so much the classroom materials themselves but what a person does with them that makes a difference. The mediation of teachers, and their ability to foster critical reading skills can enable students to become aware of how course materials construct gender. These critical reading skills are eminently transferable to other disciplines. More work should be done in this area to provide examples of how foreign language instructors can assist students in learning to read critically regardless of the text that is used.

One of the most provocative articles written on foreign language textbooks is that of Durham (1995) (also discussed in Pavlenko, 2004), who points out the dangers of projecting US stereotypes about sexism onto a foreign language textbook. Durham's article was written in response to the decision made by the Yale French department to discontinue the use of the textbook *French in Action* due to the gender stereotypes that many of the US students identified in the book. Durham, invoking a poststructuralist perspective, points to this projection of cultural norms and also to the lack of attentiveness on the part of the students to the self-reflexive linguistic clues given in the book that call into question these very stereotypes. Durham's critique anticipates Sunderland's in that both point to the necessity of putting the stereotypes into dialog with other, self-reflexive components of the book or of carefully scrutinizing them in the spirit of critical discourse awareness. Durham's focus on the need to read these images within the context of their meaning in French culture resonates with shifts toward a more transnational, postcolonial approach to gender that has evolved in feminism. Along these lines, students would need to be encouraged to read the text, not through the lens of US culture, but rather on its own terms.

Study abroad

The movement between cultures and the questioning of assumptions about how gender is constructed and experienced in the study of foreign languages has also been productively addressed in research on study-abroad programs. Polanyi (1995) and Talburt and Stewart (1999) bring to light the gender-specific and often negative experiences that women encounter as they become the foreign, often exoticized Other in study-abroad programs in Spain and Russia respectively.

Talburt and Stewart's work demonstrates that the manner in which we prepare students for study-abroad programs needs to take into account specific aspects of identity and their reception in the foreign culture. Polanyi (1995) conveys the results of research that she undertook with women students studying in Russia who kept journals to record their experiences. The findings are sobering: the experiences that the female students had in Russia were often so negative that they were precluded from participating in the target culture to the same degree as men. Both Polanyi (1995) and Talburt and Stewart (1999) show that even though women may leave the home university with more advanced language skills, the degree of improvement they experience abroad is less than that of their male counterparts. Other articles on the gendered experience in study-abroad programs (for example, Siegal, 1995) suggest that resistance to gendered linguistic norms may be possible for some women. More research on how to prepare students for study-abroad experience is needed.

INTERSECTION OF RESEARCH WITH EDUCATIONAL PRACTICES

Though the topic of gender continues to be addressed in productive ways in foreign language acquisition research, the impact of this work on classroom practices has not been realized substantially. The reason for this may be attributable to the theoretical approaches that have informed foreign language education over the past several decades.

Communicative competence

The emergence of communicative language teaching methods in the 1970s shifted the focus of language learning from linguistic structures to authentic, communicative tasks. Communicative teaching methods emerged from the work done on communicative competence by the critical theorist Habermas (1970), the linguist Hymes (1972), and the linguistic philosophers Austin (1962) and Searle (1969). These methods stress how to do things with words to accomplish communicative goals and fulfill communicative needs. In foreign language research, the name most closely related to communicative competence is Sandra Savignon (1972; 1983).

Though communicative language teaching has added much to the experience of language learning by enabling learners to communicate in a more authentic manner in the target culture, it has not promoted critical reflection on how we travel to other cultures and respond to difference. This failure to promote critical language awareness has an impact on how we understand and respond to the discursive construction of gender and other aspects of subjectivity in the process of studying a foreign language.

The emphasis on authenticity has fostered in many ways a culture of identification and mimesis (von Hoene, 1999). Students are expected to mimic the behavior of foreign language speakers as much as possible and, in a sense, to become the Other. This method has dealt only superficially with the complexity of difference that abounds in the foreign culture and focuses instead on executing tasks and accomplishing goals. The communicative method has done very little to foster a sense of reflection among learners and consciousness about the impact that the movement between two languages could have on subjects themselves.

As von Hoene (1999) notes, the concept of communicative competence as formulated by Jürgen Habermas (1970) implied a dialogically based, critical approach to communication. The translation of this theory into the practice of teaching foreign languages has taken on a degree of instrumentality that Habermas may have never intended. The notion of communicative competence in second language learning focuses primarily on using language to fulfill communicative tasks. Instead of teasing out and highlighting differences, the communicative method implicitly levels difference by imagining an ever increasing ability on the part of the learner to be folded into the discourse community of the target language.

The natural approach

The second method that has dominated the teaching of foreign languages over the past 20 years and is closely linked to the communicative method of teaching is the natural approach, most closely affiliated with Krashen (1982) and Krashen and Terrell (1983). In the natural approach, a high premium is placed on keeping the process of conscious monitoring of language use at a minimum. The goal is to lower what Krashen calls the 'affective filter', so that anxiety cannot impede learning, and to recreate a language-learning environment that resembles as much as possible that of first language learning. In addition to the critique that has been put forward by Pierce (1995), von Hoene (1999) sees in Krashen's equation of first and second language acquisition, and his emphasis on reducing conscious monitoring, a return to origins, an attempt to recreate learners, as a blank slates in order to interpellate them into the ideology of a new culture.

As Kramsch and von Hoene have discussed (2001), textbooks that are informed by the natural approach are less likely to have readings, exercises, or activities that engage critical reflection or promote cross-cultural awareness. Because the natural approach does not advocate critical reflection on how one crosses cultures, the engagement with the textbook that Sunderland (2002) identifies will be missing unless instructors construct pedagogical activities that would offer students this type of critique.

RECOMMENDATIONS AND FUTURE DIRECTIONS

Post-secondary departments of foreign languages often lament decreased enrollments. These discussions generally include an exchange about how to provide a rationale to students that will convince them that studying a foreign language will be of value. With increased globalization and the spread of English, foreign language departments may feel impending doom. However, one could also argue that now, more than ever, they are needed. Foreign language departments are ideally positioned to provide a crucible and training ground to rethink the way in which we interface with difference and travel to other cultures. It is along these lines that the following recommendations are made.

Teaching assistant education

Most foreign language teachers in higher education have been trained through M.A. or Ph.D. programs in departments of languages and literature. In the USA, most of these instructors have been exposed to many of the poststructuralist, feminist, psychoanalytic, and postcolonial discourses mentioned in this chapter through their study of literature and culture. However, given the split that exists between language teaching and the study of literature and culture, those discourses rarely are integrated substantively into the training of teaching assistants.

von Hoene (1999) provides research questions, themes, and suggested texts around which discrete modules for training teaching assistants could be created. For example, language program directors might consider bringing together foreign language learning and postcolonial and feminist theory and exploring these connections.

Similarly, teaching assistants should be introduced to critical discourse analysis (Fairclough, 1992) and formulate ways to apply this in the classroom. They might also be asked to read Butler's seminal work, *Gender Trouble* (1990), to explore the role of gender performance in the foreign language classroom. With Sunderland's (1995; 2004) work in mind, teaching assistants could conduct small research projects with students to understand more fully how identities are reconstituted through the study of a foreign language. In research seminars, teaching assistants might explore the relationship between language and subject formation. For example, what is the extent to which the interface with difference in the foreign language classroom will actually affect subjectivity? How rigid or malleable is subjectivity? Has its 'fluidity' been overstated in research on gender and foreign language study? What are the implications for both men and women?

Teaching assistants might also be asked to take a closer look at the relationship of masculinity and foreign language study. How can studies on language and masculinity (Johnson and Meinhof, 1997) be put in dialog with work that has already been done on gender and foreign language study? What research projects could teaching assistants undertake to obtain a more differentiated idea of language learning and the construction and revision of gendered subjectivity in the classroom?

The tendency to look at gender as an isolated aspect of identity still plagues many areas of research on gender. Teaching assistants might be asked to explore explicitly how gender can be rethought by instructors as always intersecting with other aspects of difference. Research projects might ask how the gendered experiences of foreign language students differ along the lines of ethnicity, age, physical ability, and fluency in other languages. These questions could also be examined against the framework of investment that Pierce (1995) has suggested for language study.

Though the research questions posed above could also simply be used to further research in gender and foreign language education, it seems imperative to forge a link between research and the training of those who will do much of the teaching of students in foreign language courses, so that the current gap that exists between research and teaching practice can be closed.

Classroom materials

Other recommendations for bridging the gap between the research on gender and foreign language and instructional practices might also involve a more proactive stance by the researchers themselves. For example, scholars involved with research on gender and foreign language acquisition could increase efforts to interact with textbook publishers. Researchers might consider collaborating with colleagues in the writing of textbooks so that the languages can be taught with a critical approach to difference. Because the textbook industry is aligned substantially with colonialist and masculinist views of travel to other cultures, researchers should make an attempt not only to invite publishers to display and sell their wares at conference book fairs but also to attend sessions and be introduced to the body of research on foreign language acquisition and the cross-cultural, cross-linguistic construction of identity.

Preparing students for study-abroad programs

As has been discussed, universities would be wise to implement a course, for students who wish to study abroad, on traveling both literally and figuratively to other cultures. This course would provide students with the opportunity to reflect on how differences along the lines of gender, race, physical ability, and other aspects of identity emerge in the target culture and how students can work with those differences to enhance their experience abroad.

REFERENCES

Anzaldúa, G (1987) *Borderlands/la frontera: the new mestiza*. San Francisco, CA: Spinsters/Aunt Lute.
Anzaldúa, G (ed) (1990) *Making face, making soul: hacienda caras*. San Francisco, CA: Aunt Lute.
Austin, JL (1962) *How to do things with words*. Cambridge, MA: Harvard University Press.
Bacon, SM (1992) The relationship between gender, comprehension, processing strategies, and cognitive and affective response in foreign language listening. *Modern Language Journal*, 76: 160–78.

Bacon, S and Finnemann, MD (1992) Sex-differences in self-reported beliefs about foreign-language learning and authentic oral and written input. *Language Learning: A Journal of Applied Linguistics,* 42: 471–95.

Barthes, R (1966) *Critique et vérité.* Paris: Editions du Seuil.

Belenky, MF, Clinchy, BM, Goldberger, NR and Tarulet, JM (1986) *Women's ways of knowing: the development of self, voice, and mind.* New York: Basic Books.

Bhabha, H (1994) *The location of culture.* London: Routledge.

Brantmeier, C (2003) The role of gender and strategy use in processing authentic written input at the intermediate level, *Hispania: A Journal Devoted to the Teaching of Spanish and Portuguese,* 86: 844–56.

Butler, J (1990) *Gender trouble: feminism and the subversion of identity.* New York: Routledge.

Campbell, CM (1998) Language anxiety in men and women: dealing with gender difference in the language classroom, in Young, DJ and Horwita, EK (eds), *Affect in foreign language and second language learning: a practical guide to creating a low-anxiety classroom atmosphere.* (191–215). Boston, MA: McGraw-Hill.

Chavez, M (2000) Teacher and student gender and peer group gender composition in German foreign language classroom discourse: an exploratory study. *Journal of Pragmatics: An Interdisciplinary Journal of Language Studies,* 32: 1019–58.

Durham, CA (1995) At the crossroads of gender and culture: where feminism and sexism interact. *Modern Language Journal,* 79: 153–65.

Ehrman, M and Oxford, R (1989) Effects of sex differences, career choice, and psychological type on adult language learning strategies. *Modern Language Journal,* 73: 1–13.

Fairclough, N (1992) *Critical language awareness.* London: Longman.

Gass, S and Varonis, EM (1986) Sex differences in NNS/NNS interactions, in Day, R (ed), *Talking to learn.* (327–51). Rowley, MA: Newbury House.

Gilligan, C (1982) *In a different voice: psychological theory and women's development.* Cambridge, MA: Harvard University Press.

Grace, CA (2000) Gender differences: vocabulary retention and access to translations for beginning language learners in CALL. *Modern Language Journal,* 84: 214–24.

Graci, J (1989) Are foreign language textbooks sexist? An exploration of modes of evaluation. *Foreign Language Annals,* 22: 477–86.

Green, JM and Oxford, R (1995) A closer look at learning strategies, L2 proficiency, and gender. *TESOL Quarterly,* 29: 261–97.

Habermas, J (1970) Toward a theory of communicative competence, in Dreitzel HP (ed) *Patterns of communicative behavior* (114–48). New York: Macmillan.

Hymes, D (1972) On communicative competence, in Pride, JP and Holmes, J (eds) *Sociolinguistics* (260–93). Harmondsworth: Penguin Books.

hooks, b (1984) *Feminist theory: from margin to center.* Boston, MA: South End.

hooks, b (1989) *Talking back: thinking feminist, thinking black.* Boston, MA: South End.

Johnson, S and Meinhof, UH (1997) *Language and masculinity.* Oxford: Blackwell.

Kramsch, C (1993) *Context and culture in language teaching.* Oxford: Oxford University Press.

Kramsch, C and von Hoene, L (1995) The dialogic emergence of difference: feminist explorations in foreign language learning and teaching, in Stanton, DC and Stewart, AJ (eds) *Feminisms in the academy* (330–57). Ann Arbor, MI: University of Michigan.

Kramsch, C and von Hoene, L (2001) Cross-cultural excursions: foreign language study and feminist discourses of travel, in Pavlenko, A, Blackledge, A, Piller, I and Dwyer, M (eds) *Multilingualism, second language learning, and gender.* (283–306). Berlin: Mouton de Gruyter.

Krashen, S (1982) *Principles and practices in second language acquisition.* Oxford: Pergamon.

Krashen, S and Terrell, T (1983) *The natural approach.* New York: Pergamon.

Kristeva, J (1980) *Desire in language.* New York: Columbia University Press.

Lacan, J (1977) The mirror stage as formative of the function of the I, in *Écrits* (1–7). London: Tavistock.

Lakoff, R (1975) *Language and women's place*. New York: Harper and Collins.

Lugones, M (1990) Playfulness, 'world'-traveling, and loving perception, in Anzaldúa, G (ed) *Making face, making soul: hacienda caras*. (390–402). San Francisco, CA: Aunt Lute.

Maccoby, E and Jacklin, CN (1974) *The psychology of sex differences*. Stanford, CA: Stanford University Press.

Meunier, LE (1994) Native genderlects and their relation to gender issues in second language class-rooms: the sex of our students as a sociolinguistic variable, in Klee, CA (ed) *Faces in a crowd: the individual learner in multisection courses* (47–77). Boston, MA: Heinle and Heinel.

Nyikos, M (1990) Sex-related differences in adult language learning: socialization and memory factors. *Modern Language Journal*, 74: 273–87.

Ohara, Y (2001) Finding one's voice in Japanese: a study of the pitch levels of L2 users, in Pavlenko, A, Blackledge, A, Piller, I and Dwyer, M (eds) *Multilingualism, Second language learning, and gender* (231–54). Berlin: Mouton de Gruyter.

Ohara, Y Saft, S and Crookes, G (2001) Toward a feminist critical pedagogy in a beginning Japanese-as-a-foreign-language class. *Japanese Language and Literature*, 35: 105–33.

Oxford, RL (1993) Gender differences in styles and strategies for language learning: what do they mean? Should we pay attention? in Alatis, JE (ed) Strategic interactions and language acquisition: theory, practice, and research (541–57). Georgetown University Round Table on Languages and Linguistics.

Oxford, R Nyikos, M and Ehrman, M (1988) *Vive la difference*? Reflections on sex differences in use of language learning strategies. *Foreign Language Annals*, 21: 321–9.

Pavlenko, A (2004) Gender and sexuality in foreign and second language education: critical and feminist approaches, in Norton, B and Toohey, K (eds) *Critical pedagogies and language learning*. (53–71). Cambridge: Cambridge University Press.

Pavlenko, A, Blackedge, A, Piller, I and Teutsch-Dwyer, M (2001) *Multilingualism, second language learning and gender*. Berlin: Mouton de Gruyter.

Pica, T, Holliday, L, Lewis, N, Berducci, D, and Newman, J (1991) Language learning through interaction: what role does gender play? *Studies in Second Language Acquisition*, 13: 343–76.

Pierce, BN (1995) Social identity, investment, and language learning. *TESOL Quarterly*, 29: 9–31.

Polanyi, L (1995) Language learning and living abroad: stories from the field, in Freed, BF (ed) *Second language acquisition in a study abroad context*, (271–91). Amsterdam: John Benjamins.

Politzer, RL (1983) Research notes: an exploratory study of self-reported language learning behaviors and their relationship to achievement. *Studies in Second Language Acquisition*, 6: 54–68.

Savignon, S (1972) *Communicative competence: an experiment in foreign language teaching*. Philadelphia: Center for Curriculum Development.

Savignon, S (1983) *Communicative competence: theory and classroom practice*. Reading, MA: Addison-Wesley.

Schumann, J (1976) Social distance as a factor in second language acquisition. *Language Learning*, 26: 135–43.

Searle, J (1969) *Speech acts*. Cambridge: Cambridge University Press.

Siegal, M (1995) Individual differences and study abroad: women learning Japanese in Japan, in Freed, BF (ed) *Second language acquisition in a study abroad context* (225–44). Amsterdam: John Benjamins.

Siegal, M (1996) The role of learner subjectivity in second language sociolinguistic competency: Western women learning Japanese. *Applied Linguistics*, 17: 356–82.

Sunderland, J (1995) 'We're boys, miss!' Finding gendered identities and looking for gendering of identities in the foreign language classroom, in Mills, S(ed) *Language and gender: interdisciplinary perspectives*. (160–78). London: Longman.

Sunderland, J (2004) Classroom interaction, gender, and foreign language learning, in Norton, B and Toohey, K (eds) *Critical pedagogies and language learning* (222–41). Cambridge: Cambridge University Press.

Sunderland, J, Cowley, M, Rahim, FA, Leontzakou, C and Shattuck, J (2002) From representation towards discursive practices: gender in the foreign language textbook revisited, in Litosseliti, L and Sunderland, J (eds) (223–55). *Gender identity and discourse analysis*. Amsterdam: John Benjamins.

Talburt, S and Stewart, MA (1999) What's the subject of study abroad?: race, gender, and 'living culture'. *Modern Language Journal,* 83: 163–75.

Thorne, B and Henley, N (1975) *Language and sex: difference and dominance.* Rowley, MA: Newbury House.

Trinh, T Minh-ha (1989) *Woman, native, Other: writing, postcoloniality and feminism.* Bloomington, IN: Indiana University Press.

von Hoene, LM (1995) Subjects-in-process: revisioning TA development through psychoanlaytic, feminist, and postcolonial theory. In Kramsch, C (ed) *Redefining the boundaries of language study* (39–57). Boston, MA: Heinle and Heinle.

von Hoene, LM (1999) Imagining otherwise: rethinking departments of foreign languages as departments of cross-cultural difference. *ADFL Bulletin,* 30: 26–9.

Weedon, C (1987) *Feminist practice and poststructuralist theory.* London: Blackwell.

Young, DJ and Oxford, RL (1997) A gender-related analysis of strategies used to process written input in the native language and a foreign language. *Applied Language Learning,* 8: 43–73.

Zoubir-Shaw, S and Oxford, RL (1994) Gender differences in language learning strategy use in university-level introductory French classes: a pilot study employing a strategy questionnaire, in Klee, CA (ed) *Faces in a crowd: the individual learner in multisection courses* (181–213). Boston, MA: Heinle & Heinle.

NOTES

I would like to thank the two anonymous reviewers of this chapter who provided helpful feedback.

1. Although this article will draw on research findings from second language acquisition and applied linguistics, its primary focus will be on the role of gender in *foreign* language learning that takes place in educational settings, that is, classrooms and study-abroad programs, rather than on the long-term experience of individuals acquiring a *second* language in a new cultural environment. For recent research on gender and second language acquisition, see Pavlenko *et al.*, (2001). 'Gender' in this chapter does not refer to grammatical gender.

2. While this chapter draws mainly on foreign language study and instructor preparation for teaching in post-secondary settings, the questions raised and conclusions drawn can be fruitfully applied to foreign language study and teacher training in K–12 education.

3. Both the field of feminist linguistics and the emerging research on gender and foreign language acquisition have their origins in the broader women's movement of the late 1960s and 1970s that revolutionized many facets of society, including education.

22

Gender and Technology: What the Research Tells Us[1]

Jo Sanders

In 1982, James Johnson, a freelance writer from New Jersey, published an article about inequalities in American society and its schools, optimistically entitled 'Can Computers Close the Educational Equity Gap?' (Johnson, 1982). His concern was caused, in large part, by women's low representation in the sciences. The new field of computer science (CS), though, held promise for women. In 1982, women earned a greater share of bachelor's degrees in CS than in engineering, physics, or chemistry. CS, unlike the other fields, did not have the centuries-old burden of male history, so perhaps women would be able to enter this new field more easily.

As it turned out, Johnson could not have been more wrong. Twenty years later, women have indeed made progress in engineering, physics, and chemistry. Computer science, however, has been another story. While women's representation in the other sciences rose steadily, their share of CS degrees in those years *dropped* by nearly a third. This trend is not limited to the USA. Women are significantly underrepresented in information and communication technologies (ICT) in most countries for which data are available, down to a level of 10% or less (Galpin, 2002; Huyer, 2003).

Technology therefore earns its place as an anomaly over the past generation or two: an area in which women's professional achievement has actually regressed, as contrasted with virtually all other areas of importance to women. In view of the growing role of technology in the world at the beginning of the twenty-first century – in education, communications, occupations, and entertainment, and as a tool for solving the world's problems – women's low and decreasing representation is a major worry.

As we examine the research on gender and technology, first a word on methodology. Several researchers have pointed out deficiencies in methods used to collect data on gender differences in computer-related behavior, resulting in inconsistent findings that may be more apparent than real (Bannert and Arbinger, 1996; Cooper and Stone, 1996). Statistically significant gender differences may not have any practical value, unstudied variables may influence students' computer-related behavior, and students' self-ratings may be especially problematic due to boys' frequently observed tendency to overestimate, and girls to underestimate, their abilities. In reviews of the literature on gender differences in computer-related behavior and attitudes, Kay (1992) and others have pointed out methodological and construct inconsistencies that reduce comparability of studies.

As a framework for the analysis that follows, Littleton and Hoyles (2002) posited three developmental stages with respect to gender and technology.

- Stage 1: noticing the gender imbalance at home, in school, and in attitudes;
- Stage 2: changing female participation in ICT activities through role models and collaborative groupings;
- Stage 3: challenging the dominant paradigm of ICT as culturally and historically male.

As will be seen, the majority of the research to date falls solidly into stage 1, with some in stage 2. There is very little in stage 3, although there is a good amount of published work that acknowledges the male paradigm. It is important to remember, however, that relevant research may exist in the related areas of science, mathematics, and engineering.

SOCIETAL INFLUENCES

Because gender bias pervades societies throughout the world, we can expect to find gender bias influencing girls' choices in many ways. Areas addressed in the literature on social influences on computing include parental influence, advertising, the role of race and class, and the male culture of computing.

Parents are one source of gender stereotypes with respect to computing. In Romania and Scotland, parents had more stereotyped computer attitudes than their children (Durndell et al., 1997). In the USA, parents, especially white and high-socioeconomic status (SES) parents, were found to give less computer-related support to girls than to boys (Kekelis et al., 2005). Shashaani found that parents' computer stereotypes in favor of males encouraged their sons' computer involvement and discouraged their daughters' (Shashaani, 1994).

Magazines have been reviewed by Knupfer (1998) as well as Sanders (1998) for gender stereotyping and found wanting. Knupfer also examined computer advertisements, the Internet, television and movies and found rampant gender stereotypes about people in technical roles.

Many reports exist that students of color are afforded lesser computer opportunities than white students (Maxwell, 2000; Goode *et al.*, 2006). Studies in the USA, Australia, Iran, and the UK were unanimous in correlating high parental SES, particularly higher parental educational achievement, with greater computer encouragement of girls (Shashaani, 1994; Attewell and Battle, 1999; Shashaani and Khalili, 2001).

There is a wealth of research on the male-dominated culture of computing. Thoughtful analyses of the hallmarks of the male-computing culture – invisibility, exclusion, condescension, hostility, an emphasis on speed and competitiveness, and other dynamics – have been published every decade since the 80s (MIT, 1983; Seymour and Hewitt, 1997; Gurer and Camp, 2002; Margolis and Fisher, 2002). Women students speak of 'the harassment of continually bumping into male egos' (Durndell *et al.*, 1990: 159). Several researchers have indicated that the violent language of technology may be invisible to males but can be a problem for females. Consider 'hard disc', 'hard drive', 'reboot', 'cold boot', 'hits', 'permanent fatal error', and so forth. Recreational or even educational software for children often includes title words such as 'attack' or 'war' (Cole *et al.*, 1994; Gurer and Camp, 1998; Linn, 1999).

Students at the high school and even younger levels in the USA, Canada, and New Zealand have negative notions of the computer culture and characterize computer enthusiasts as geeky, nerdy, social isolates who are adolescent, competitive, and exclusively focused on programming (Pearl *et al.*, 1990; Selby, 1997; Klawe and Leveson, 2001). These factors have also been widely noted at the post-secondary level. In short, Canada and Brusca conclude, 'it is not necessarily computers and technology per se that females avoid, but rather the competitive, male environment that surrounds the field' (Canada and Brusca, 1991: 47).

AGE, STAGE AND PIPELINE ISSUES

Gender issues in computing have been studied with children as young as three and findings are inconsistent, but most found gender differences in preschool children's attitudes and behavior. Most studies also found that gender differences in attitudes and behavior are relatively small at younger ages but increase as students become older (Whitley, 1997; Kirkpatrick and Cuban, 1998).

The researcher most associated with identifying the factors in the loss of females in computing from high school through careers is Tracy Camp, who suggests many causes for the 'leaky pipeline' (Camp, 1997; Gurer and Camp, 1998, 2002). One cause is lack of accurate information about ICT careers; closely related is the prevalence in many students' minds of negative stereotypes about computer workers. Sanders and Lubetkin (1991) remind us to include technician-level occupations in pipeline considerations, since most women are not college educated.

This entire chapter is, in a sense, an explanation for the 'leaky pipeline' for women in technology. However, several writers have offered additional reasons:

work/family balance problems (Pearl *et al.*, 1990), the use of freshman courses to weed out students (Bohonak, 1995), and inequitable financial support (Leveson, 1990). A particularly interesting theory by Charles and Bradley (2006) comes from the analysis of data from 21 countries: women's ICT representation tends to be relatively high in countries that score low as liberal egalitarian societies. They speculate that in countries where women have a freer choice of careers, gender stereotypes lead them to make stereotyped career choices, while government practices that encourage a more meritocratic approach may contribute to greater equality across fields of study.

EXPERIENCE, ATTITUDE AND USE PATTERNS

Experience

An overwhelming majority of studies have found that boys have greater computer experience than girls in many countries including the USA, Australia, Norway, Canada, England, Scotland, Israel, and Iran. Boys have an edge in home computer use, school computer use, computer course-taking, games, and in free-time exploratory use. Of these, games and free-time exploratory use are most frequently cited as the primary causes of boys' greater computer experience. Computer course-taking in high school in the USA was roughly equal until 1994; however, the latest data (for 2001) show that it is more unequal now, favoring boys, than at any time since such data were collected in 1982 (Snyder *et al.*, 2004). A few studies, however, have not found greater male computer experience.

Beyond overall experience patterns, several studies have had particularly interesting, although inconsistent, results. When first-year college students were randomly assigned to a writing course with required or optional computer use, Arch and Cummins (1989) found that females' computer use levels by the end of the course were higher in the computer-required condition than for females in the optional condition or for males in either condition, suggesting that requiring the use of computers may be beneficial. In another study, a large number of children in grades 4 to 10 were surveyed annually for three years. The more experienced the students, particularly the girls, became with computers, the less confidence they had in their computer skills (Krendl *et al.*, 1989). The authors conclude that experience alone will not close the computer gender gap. In most studies dealing with experience and attitudes, though, greater experience tended to result in improved attitudes.

In a well known effort to increase women's CS enrollment at Carnegie Mellon University, Margolis and Fisher (2002) observed that foreign women tended to have less computer experience than US women – sometimes none at all – but nevertheless persisted because of economic and pragmatic realities. Gurer and Camp (2002) have pointed out that when instructors in prerequisite courses for ICT majors in college discover that women have not had extensive computer experience, they erroneously infer the women's lack of ability or interest, presumably leading to differential treatment in class.

Attitudes

There has been more research on attitudes to computers, by far, than about any other topic, and perhaps more confusion as well. Published studies number literally in the hundreds, using dozens of home-grown as well as validated instruments. Definitions are not reliably consistent; even the term 'computer' means different things to preschoolers than postgraduate students. Volman and Eck (2001) have pointed out that gender differences in computer attitudes are both a cause and a consequence of gender differences in ICT participation and performance.

With some exceptions, studies in many countries find that boys have more positive feelings about the computer than girls – boys tend to like computers more and are more interested in them. Again with some exceptions, many studies find that the level of computer experience correlates with liking and interest. Typically, studies find that computer liking and interest decrease with age for both girls and boys but more strongly for girls (Lage, 1991; Whitley, 1997; Gurer and Camp, 2002).

By and large, studies find that females' comfort level and confidence with computers increase (and anxiety decreases) with experience. Several studies that examined the relationship of computer confidence to masculinity or femininity, as measured by the Bem Sex Role Inventory, agreed that positive computer attitudes correlated with high masculinity for both males and females, not with maleness *per se* (Brosnan, 1998a, b; Charlton, 1999). Some studies found that males' and females' confidence in their computer ability was equal, but most found females' confidence level significantly lower than that of males even when females were more successful than the males in the class (Selby, 1997; Shashaani, 1997; Gurer and Camp, 1998). Parental encouragement correlates with confidence for both girls and boys, but boys receive more of it (Shashaani, 1994; Shashaani and Khalili, 2001). There is also a healthy literature on computer anxiety, which finds computer anxiety higher in females than in males, at all ages and in many countries (Todman, 2000; King *et al.*, 2002).

The final computer attitude to be examined here is the self-efficacy, competence, skill, and aptitude cluster. The overall conclusion from the research is that females consistently underestimate their technology skills regardless of what their skills really are. Any discussion of females' computer competence must be filtered through Henwood's astute perception about the minority of women in university-level computing programs who see themselves, and are seen by men, as exceptional 'and therefore, by implication, different from the majority of women, who are thereby rendered incompetent and outsiders in technological culture. ... [T]he task of changing the outcomes of women's education in computer technologies is more complicated than simply teaching them how to use computers. … It is also necessary to change how the women (and the men around them) understand and talk about the presence and competence of women' (Henwood, 1999: 24–5).

Computer use patterns

Studies in this area have examined programming, Internet use, and computer software. Since the first female programmers of the ENIAC computer during World War II, programming has become a male enclave with high-school, college, and postgraduate programming enrollments primarily male. One barrier to female programming enrollment is the negative stereotype of the geeky computer nerd, discussed above. Another is that many females erroneously believe that CS is nothing but programming, an unpleasant prospect to them (Fisher *et al.*, 1997; Margolis and Fisher, 2002). Female underrepresentation in programming is still a cause for concern because there is a correlation between taking programming in high school and persistence in CS in college (Nelson *et al.*, 1991).

The Advanced Placement (AP) program in the USA gives college credit to students who pass advanced courses taken in high school. Female participation in the AP CS exams on programming languages has decreased substantially since their start in 1984 (Stumpf and Stanley, 1997). Recently, Sanders and Nelson (2004) showed that girls who achieved highly in mathematics were less likely than boys with similar scores to enroll in AP CS courses and received lower scores on the AP exams.

The Internet presents quite a different picture. In the USA, use of the Internet in 2001 (the most recent data available) was roughly equal by students of all ages in school, with a slight male advantage at younger ages and a slight female advantage beginning in high school (Snyder *et al.*, 2004). At home, Internet usage remained roughly equal until graduate school, when females had an advantage.

The very existence of software 'for girls' confirms that software is indeed for boys. Early on, it was clearly seen that software was designed by males for males. Software developed for girls has been based on common gender stereotypes: 'shopping, makeup, fashion, dating' (Rubin *et al.*, 1997: 1). Sexism in software occurs in characters, content, reward systems, and structure. There has been little recent research on gender and software. It is not clear whether this is because current educational software makes a gender analysis irrelevant or whether the topic has merely dropped out of fashion.

IN THE CLASSROOM

Several empirical studies reveal substantial gender stereotyping among students, which influences their peers. When British college students rated written descriptions of 'Stephen's' and 'Susan's' identical programming experience for their skill level, both sexes rated 'Stephen's 'programming ability higher than

Susan's' (Colley *et al.*, 1995). In several experiments with university students, when computers 'spoke' about male- or female-stereotypical topics in synthetic low- (male) or high-pitched (female) voices, college students of both sexes rated the 'female' computer more knowledgeable about feminine topics and the 'male' computer more knowledgeable about male topics. Students of both sexes found evaluation by the 'male' computer more credible, but they denied that gender played any role in their judgments (Nass *et al.*, 1997; Nass and Brave, 2005). Consistently, girls and boys believed males to be better at computing than females; just as consistently, boys were more likely to hold stronger stereotypes in this regard than girls (Shashaani, 1993; Durndell *et al.*, 1995).

The social context of computing makes a difference. Several studies have found that both sexes perform a computer task worse in public than in private when they expect it to be difficult (Robinson-Staveley and Cooper, 1990; Tsai, 2002). Another found that only girls perform worse in public (Cooper and Hall, 1986). A study of college students found that the presence of another person results in lower performance on a computer task among women with little previous computer experience than when alone, while for men another person's presence has the opposite effect. Males and females with extensive computer experience are unaffected (Robinson-Staveley and Cooper, 1990).

This research clearly raises the issue of stereotype threat, the anxiety felt in evaluative contexts (tests, public speaking, etc.) by people who identify with groups about which a negative stereotype exists because they are concerned they might confirm the stereotype about their group or themselves. The anxiety itself seems to decrease performance, a finding which appears to confirm the stereotype (Steele, 1997; Aronson, 2002). Several studies have confirmed the stereotype threat effect for females in math, in which females perform worse when their female identity is emphasized, and there has even been a study on knowledge of politics and civics, but none as yet in technology.

Pedagogy

Hundreds of papers and articles deal with pedagogical issues in gender and technology, but most of them simply describe programs without evaluating outcomes, or they repeat commonly accepted notions rather than contributing new knowledge. The assertion of a technique, no matter how frequent, or even a finding that girls like it, still leaves open the question of whether it is in fact better for their learning or persistence in technology. Very few studies on collaboration, for example, escape the assertion trap.

Much of the research comparing single-sex with mixed-sex educational environments is problematic. Girls (or girls' parents) who choose single-sex schools or classes may well have other characteristics, such as academic orientation, that might account more strongly for any differences found. Randomization would control for this, but no studies have as yet done so. Many do not specify the basis for condition assignment, thus limiting their value. In addition, many studies that contrast single-sex with coed settings have different and non-comparable teachers, curricula, or other circumstances, further limiting their value. Volman (1990) warns that some single-sex programs risk appealing to girls on the basis of gender stereotypes, much as we have seen software do. One issue in the area of pedagogy and technology is critical mass. Sanders (1985b) discovered that it is not the presence of boys at the computers that discourages girls' participation, but rather the absence of the girls' girlfriends. Probably the best recent study is by Cohoon (2001), who found that a critical mass of other women correlated more strongly than any other factor with women's retention in CS majors in Virginia (USA) universities. One of the factors credited for raising the female presence in Carnegie Mellon University's School of Computer Science was the critical mass provided by increasing numbers of women (Blum, 2001a). According to several theorists, when computer enrollment becomes more equalized by sex, the culture changes in ways that are positive for both men and women (Blum and Frieze, 2005). Support groups are an attempt to create a critical mass, although I found nothing on the effectiveness of support groups for women's learning or persistence in ICT.

Many studies confuse the related concepts of mentor and role model. A mentor is a trusted and known guide and adviser; a role model is a person looked upon as an example to follow, who may not be personally known. There are a few good studies on faculty as mentors. Cohoon (2001) determined that the time that CS faculty of either sex spent mentoring female students correlated with the students' retention in CS. She also found that CS faculty spent less time mentoring female students than biology faculty did; there is a higher percentage of female enrollment in biology (Cohoon, 2002). In a study of college freshmen at SUNY-Binghamton, New York, there was a correlation between female retention in math, science, and technology and the number of these courses taught by women. The correlation did not hold for women's retention in other courses nor for men (Robst *et al.*, 1996). Unlike mentoring, which has real evidence in its favor, no studies were found that documented a positive relationship between female enrollment and or retention in technology with a role-model intervention.

Curriculum

Criticism of the standard computer curriculum from the standpoint of females includes its exclusive focus on programming (Schofield, 1995), its emphasis on basic skills as opposed to problem solving (Goode *et al.*, 2006), and the fact that complex and more interesting projects are often reserved for advanced courses that come too late for most women (Linn, 2005). However, much of the research presumes female homogeneity, manifestly not the case, and does not establish a correlation between curriculum variations and persistence in technology. Two themes run through most of the work on curriculum improvement for girls or women in technology. First and most frequent, make curriculum relevant to real-world concerns, partly by making it cross-disciplinary. Second, use different curricular approaches and teaching methods to appeal to diverse learning styles. There is little clear evidence of the effectiveness of either approach, however.

Teachers and faculty

Several studies have documented teachers' sexist beliefs about their female students' computer abilities. In Canada, teachers explained gender differences in computing with stereotypes but denied that gender was a consideration in their explanations (Bryson and de Castell, 1998). A large sample of US high-school students of both sexes agreed that teachers, counselors, and parents all believed that computers were more appropriate for males than females (Shashaani, 1993). Cole *et al.* (1994) reported that teachers saw less need for technology in the future of their female students. In Japan and Costa Rica, teachers were seen to encourage males more than females (Makrakis, 1993; Huber and Scaglion, 1995). UK teachers and counselors recognized the existence of gender stereotypes in computing and expressed a commitment to equal opportunity, but saw the source of stereotypes as occurring exclusively outside school in parents, peers, and the media (Culley, 1998). These studies matter, of course, because teachers' expectations can become self-fulfilling prophecies.

Several researchers have observed that foreign-born CS instructors at the post-secondary level have cultural biases against females. In a survey of teachers in 20 countries, Reinen and Plomp (1993) found that most computer teachers were male and that most female computer teachers had less confidence in their own skills and knowledge. Cohoon (2001; 2002) reported that females' retention in CS is positively related to their professors' positive attitudes to women students and negatively related to their professors' belief that female students are not well suited to their major.

What seems to work to improve teachers' gender-related behavior is staff development that emphasizes no personal blame for universally learned gender stereotypes, attention to the WIIFM (what's in it for me?) rule, praise for progress whenever possible, and the need for teachers to be explicit with students about gender bias, because merely modeling exemplary behavior is often not sufficient to counteract the students' sexist notions (Sanders, 1996; 2005). Much more research is needed here, however.

INTERVENTIONS

The literature is full of publications on interventions at all educational levels. The National Science Foundation has published the most comprehensive source of information on interventions from 250 funded projects (McNees, 2003). When the AAUW Educational Foundation (2004) analyzed a decade of funded projects in the USA, they found that the majority of technology projects were for girls only, were extracurricular, and focused on attitudes rather than academics. Extracurricular projects were typically after-school, weekend, and summer programs with limited and voluntary participation, by definition not involving all girls or all teachers.

There are several common failings of research on interventions. First, virtually none of them present evaluation data (two exceptions are the Computer Mania Day program for middle-school girls, which found improved attitudes (Morrell *et al.*, 2004), and a summer institute program in which high-school girls said they were more likely to be involved with technology in the future (Volk and Holsey, 1997)). Second, evaluation of most of these programs would be problematic due to multiple simultaneous interventions. Third, none of them were conducted longitudinally, leaving their ultimate effectiveness unknown.

Nearly all references to teacher education with respect to gender and technology involve in-service education with classroom teachers. Variations run from short-term teacher training to training over one to two years. Margolis and Fisher (2002) described weeklong workshops for high-school AP computer teachers at Carnegie Mellon, but Sanders' (2002) evaluation data for that project found disappointing results, in that girls' enrollment increases were probably due to factors other than the gender equity intervention and the number of intervention strategies carried out by participating teachers.

Research on gender and technology in pre-service teacher education is nearly nonexistent (Sanders 1997; 2000). There is a web-based course on gender and technology for pre- and in-service teachers at the postsecondary and secondary levels (Sanders and Tescione, 2004), but this does not escape the problem of focusing on supplying gender-equity materials for teachers while paying no attention to demand, which may be far lower (Sanders, 1995).

Reinen and Plomp (1997) point out the importance of establishing gender-equity policy at the departmental level in elementary, middle and high schools to counteract girls' often lesser access to computers at home, but most papers on this topic concern the postsecondary (tertiary) level. At Carnegie Mellon, changes that occurred included the creation of new entry courses in the School of Computer Science to allow for differential initial knowledge levels, new cross-disciplinary courses, and accepting students with less computer experience than previously. In the web course mentioned above, suggested departmental changes include a climate survey among students, a recommendation that the best instructors teach the introductory courses, gender-equity education for faculty, and a new-student orientation that includes attention to gender equity issues (Sanders and Tescione, 2004).

CONCLUSIONS

What we need to know

This review of the research has raised some questions about gender and technology to which answers are needed.

- We know that parental influence on daughters' technology interests and behavior varies by SES and educational level, but does it vary by racial-ethnic group?

- There is a great deal of research on attitudes and on behavior, but what is the causative direction? Does attitude vary by student characteristics? If so, which characteristics are relevant?
- Does computer game playing in childhood lead to technology competence and careers in adulthood?
- Is stereotype threat a factor in females' computer technology behavior and performance?
- What is the relationship, if any, between role models, support groups, collaborative learning, or single-sex learning environments and females' academic achievement and persistence in technology? Do these vary by race ethnicity or other characteristics?
- Are there curricular approaches that correlate with persistence in technology? What curricular approaches are better for different groups of learners, and which characteristics are relevant in light of females' (and males') multiple learning styles?
- What approaches to staff development are most effective with different groups of teachers?

What we need to do

One rather glaring hole in this review is research on teachers from their point of view. What is it that makes teachers want to help close the computer gender gap? Could that motivation or skill set be more widely shared with their colleagues? Most developmental work originates in activists' belief in their ability to produce programs and materials that teachers will value and that will be effective in increasing female participation in technology. As this chapter should make clear, while we certainly do not know all the answers, we have enough of them to know that the lack of progress is not due to total ignorance. Good ideas, good practices, and good materials exist in easily accessible forms. What does not exist nearly as much is educators' desire to make use of them. It is time for gender equity researchers and advocates to focus on demand.

A great deal of the research on gender and technology represents wasted opportunities. For all the effort that has gone in to providing compensatory programs for girls and women in technology, we would know a great deal more than we do had the programs been conceptualized to permit effective evaluation. Closer cooperation between program developers and researchers would help, since each needs the other for optimal effectiveness. Equally helpful would be an understanding from governmental and private funding sources that short-term answers do not serve our long-term needs well. Longitudinal research is expensive but necessary, and funders must recognize that reality.

Most research in gender and technology has focused on female deficits: their lower experience levels, less positive attitudes, and failure to persist and perform well in educational programs, as compared with males. Research on gender and mathematics, science and engineering, further along than technology, repeatedly points to the value of including 'different' people – women, people of color, people with disabilities, and others – to expand the scope of the questions asked and paths followed. How do the technological disciplines change if they are approached from different points of view, with different desired outcomes, indeed, with different understandings of the disciplines themselves? We need to reimagine technology, to shift it from what it can do to what it can serve, and, in so doing, to free ourselves from the conceptual constraints posed by business as usual according to the male model.

Finally, because women are performing at a high level in technology careers, there is no question about women's capability in the field. The issue for education is therefore to remove the barriers that are interfering with girls' and women's access to technology and success in it. This review of the research identifies many ways that barriers have been removed, usually on a small scale, and suggests ways they might be removed on a wider scale in the future.

Myra Sadker, the late gender-equity advocate, used to say, 'If the cure for cancer is in the mind of a girl, we might never find it'. Myra died of cancer when she was only 54. The person who finds a cure will need a solid background in technology. What can we do, each and every one of us, to make it possible for that girl to find the cure some day?

REFERENCES

An annotated and searchable bibliography on gender and technology on about 700 sources, including keywords, can be found at www.umbc.edu/cwit/itgenderbib/
Please note that one keyword is 'research review'.

AAUW (American Association of University Women) Educational Foundation Commission on Technology, Gender, and Teacher Education (2004) *Under the microscope: a decade of gender equity projects in the sciences*. Washington, DC: Author.

Aronson, Joshua (2002) Stereotype threat: contending and coping with unnerving expectations, in Aronson, J (ed) *Improving academic achievement: impact of psychological factors on education* (281–301). San Diego, CA: Academic Press.

Attewell, Paul and Battle, Juan (1999) Home computers and school performance. *The Information Society*, 15: 1–10.

Bannert, Maria and Arbinger, Paul Roland (1996) Gender-related differences in exposure to and use of computers: results of a survey of secondary school students. *European Journal of Psychology of Education*, 11: 269–82.

Blum, Lenore (2001a) Transforming the culture of computing at Carnegie Mellon. *Computing Research News*, 13: 2–9.

Blum, Lenore and Frieze, Carol (2005) The evolving culture of computing: similarity is the difference. *Frontiers: A Journal of Women's Studies*, 26: 110 ff.

Bohonak, Noni McCullough (1995) Attracting and retaining women in graduate programs in computer science, in Rosser, SV (ed) *Teaching the majority: breaking the gender barrier in science, mathematics, and engineering* (169–80). New York: Teachers College Press.

Brosnan, Mark J (1998a) The impact of psychological gender, gender-related perceptions, significant others, and the introducer of technology upon computer anxiety in students. *Journal of Educational Computing Research*, 18: 63–78.

Brosnan, Mark J (1998b) The role of psychological gender in the computer-related attainments of primary school children (aged 6–11). *Computers and Education*, 30(3–4). 203–8.

Bryson, Mary and de Castell, Suzanne (1998) New technologies and the cultural ecology of primary schooling: imagining teachers as Luddites in/deed. *Educational Policy*, 12: 542–67.

Camp, Tracy (1997) The incredible shrinking pipeline. *Communications of the ACM*, 40: 103–10.

Canada, Katherine and Brusca, Frank (1991) The technological gender gap: evidence and recommendations for educators and computer-based instruction designers. *Educational Technology Research and Development*, 39: 43–51.

Charles, Maria and Bradley, Karen (2006) A matter of degrees: female underrepresentation in computer science programs cross-nationally, in Aspray, WC and McGrath, J (eds) *Women and information technology: research on the reasons for underrepresentation* (183–204). Cambridge, MA: MIT Press.

Charlton, John P (1999) Biological sex, sex-role identity, and the spectrum of computing orientations: a re-appraisal at the end of the 90s. *Journal of Educational Computing Research,* 21: 393–412.

Cohoon, J McGrath (2001) Toward improving female retention in the computer science major. *Communications of the ACM,* 44: 108–14.

Cohoon, J McGrath (2002) Women in CS and biology. Paper presented at the SIGCSE Technical Symposium on Computer Science Education, Northern Kentucky University.

Cole, Anne, Conlon, Tom, Jackson, Sylia and Welch, Dorothy (1994) Information technology and gender: problems and proposals. *Gender and Education,* 6: 77–85.

Colley, Ann, Hill, Fiona, Hill, Justin and Jones, Anna (1995) Gender effects in the stereotyping of those with different kinds of computing experience. *Journal of Educational Computing Research,* 12: 19–27.

Cooper, Joel and Hall, Joan (1986) Use with caution: the consequences of sex-biased software. Unpublished manuscript, Princeton University, Princeton, NJ.

Cooper, Joel and Stone, Jeff (1996) Gender, computer-assisted learning, and anxiety: with a little help from a friend. *Journal of Educational Computing Research,* 15: 67–91.

Culley, Lorraine (1998) Option choice and careers guidance: gender and computing in secondary schools. *British Journal of Guidance and Counseling,* 16: 73–82.

Durndell, Alan, Siann, Gerda and Glissov, Peter (1990) Gender differences and computing in course choice at entry into higher education. *British Educational Research Journal,* 16: 149–62.

Durndell, Alan, Glissov, Peter and Siann, Gerda (1995) Gender and computing: persisting differences. *Educational Research,* 37: 219–27.

Durndell, A, Cameron, C, Knox, A and Stocks, R (1997) Gender and computing: West and East Europe. *Computers in Human Behavior,* 13: 269–80.

Fisher, Allan, Margolis, Jane and Miller, Faye (1997) Undergraduate women in computer science: experience, motivation and culture. Paper presented at the SIGCSE Technical Symposium, San Jose, CA.

Galpin, Vashti (2002) Women in computing around the world. *SIGCSE Bulletin,* 34: 94–100.

Goode, Joanna, Estrella, Rachel and Margolis, Jane (2006) Lost in translation: Gender and high school computer science, in Aspray, WC, McGrath, J (ed) *Women and information technology: research on the reasons for under-representation* (89–114). Cambridge, MA: MIT Press.

Gurer, Denise and Camp, Tracy (1998) *Investigating the incredible shrinking pipeline for women in computer science* (Final report of NSF Project). Arlington, VA: National Science Foundation.

Gurer, Denise and Camp, Tracy (2002) An ACM-W literature review on women in computing. *ACM SIGCSE Bulletin,* 34: 121–7.

Henwood, Flis (1999) Exceptional women? Gender and technology in U.K. higher education. *IEEE Technology and Society Magazine,* 18: 21–7.

Huber, Brad R and Scaglion, Richard (1995) Gender differences in computer education: a Costa Rican case study. *Journal of Educational,* 13: 271–304.

Huyer, Sophia (2003) Gender, ICT, and education. Unpublished manuscript.

Johnson, James P (1982) Can computers close the educational equity gap? *Civil Rights Quarterly Perspectives,* 14: 20–5.

Kay, Robin H (1992) An analysis of methods used to examine gender differences in computer-related behavior. *Journal of Educational Computing Research,* 8: 277–90.

Kay, Robin H (1992) Understanding gender differences in computer attitudes, aptitude, and use: an invitation to build theory. *Journal of Research on Computing in Education,* 25: 159–71.

Kekelis, Linda S, Ancheta, Rebecca Wepsic and Heber Etta (2005) Hurdles in the pipeline: girls and technology careers. *Frontiers: A Journal of Women's Studies,* 26.

King, John, Bond, Trevor and Blandford, Sonya (2002) An investigation of computer anxiety by gender and grade. *Computers in Human Behavior,* 18: 69–84.

Kirkpatrick, Heather and Cuban, Larry (1998) Should be we worried? What the research says about gender differences in access, use, attitudes, and achievement with computers. *Education and Computing,* 38: 56–61.

Klawe, Maria and Leveson, Nancy (2001) Refreshing the nerds. *Communications of the ACM,* 44: 67 ff.

Knupfer, Nancy Nelson (1998) Gender divisions across technology advertisements and the WWW: implications for educational equity. *Theory into Practice,* 37: 54–63.

Krendl, Kathy A, Broihier, Mary C Fleetwood, Cynthia (1989) Children and computers: do sex-related differences persist? *Journal of Communication,* 39: 85–93.

Lage, Elisabeth (1991) Boys, girls, and microcomputing. *European Journal of Psychology of Women,* 6: 29–44.

Leveson, Nancy G (1990) Educational pipeline issues for women. Paper presented at the Computing Research Association, Snowbird.

Linn, Eleanor (1999) Gender equity and computer technology. *Equity Coalition,* 5: 14–17.

Linn, Marcia C (2005) Technology and gender equity: what works?, in Russo, NFC, Kenkel, C, Beth, M, Travis, CB and Vasquez, M (ed) *Women in science and technology.* New York: American Psychological Association.

Makrakis, Vasilios (1993) Gender and computing in schools in Japan: the 'we can, I can't' paradox. *Computers and Education,* 20: 191–8.

Margolis, Jane and Fisher, Allan (2002) *Unlocking the clubhouse: women in computing.* Cambridge, MA: MIT Press.

Maxwell, D Jackson (2000) Technology and inequality with the United States school systems. *Journal of Educational Thought,* 34: 43–57.

McNees, Pat (2003) *New formulas for America's workforce: girls in science and engineering.* Arlington, VA: National Science Foundation, NSF 03–207.

MIT Computer Science Female Graduate Students and Research Staff (1983) *Barriers to equality in academia: women in computer science at MIT.* Cambridge, MA: Laboratory for Computer Science, MIT.

Morrell, Claudia, Cotten, Sheila, Sparks, Alisha and Spurgas, Alyson (2004) *Computer mania day: an effective intervention for increasing youth's interest in technology.* Baltimore, MD: Center for Women and Information Technology, University of Maryland.

Nass, Clifford and Brave, Scott (2005) Gender stereotyping of voices: sex is everywhere, in Nass, C (ed) *Wired for speech: how voice activates and advances the human–computer relationship* (ch 3). Cambridge, MA: MIT Press.

Nass, Clifford, Moon, Youngme and Green, Nancy (1997) Are computers gender-neutral? Gender stereotypic responses to computers. *Journal of Applied Social Psychology,* 27: 864–76.

Nelson, Lori J, Weise, Gina M and Cooper, Joel (1991) Getting started with computers: experience, anxiety, and relational style. *Computers in Human Behavior,* 7: 185–202.

Pearl, Amy, Pollack, Martha E, Riskin, Eve, Thomas, Becky, Wolf, Elizabeth and Wu, Alice (1990) Becoming a computer scientist: a report by the ACM Committee on the status of women in computer science. *Communications of the ACM,* 33: 47–57.

Reinen, Ingeborg Janssen and Plomp, Tjeerd (1993) Some gender issues in educational computer use: results of an international comparative survey. *Computers and Education,* 20; 353–65.

Reinen, Ingeborg Janssen and Plomp, Tjeerd (1997) Information technology and gender equality: a contradiction in terms? *Computers and Education,* 28: 65–78.

Robinson-Staveley, Kris and Cooper, Joel (1990) Mere presence, gender, and reactions to computers: studying human–computer interaction in the social context. *Journal of Experimental Social Psychology,* 26: 168–83.

Robst, John, Russo, Dean and Keil, Jack (1996) Female role models: the effect of gender composition of faculty on student retention. Paper presented at the Association for Institutional Research, Albuquerque, New Mexico.

Rubin, Andee, Murray, Megan, O'Neil, Kim and Ashley, Juania (1997) What kind of educational computer games would girls like? Paper presented at the American Educational Research Association, Chicago.

Sanders, Jo (1995) How do we get educators to teach gender equity? Paper presented at the Is There a Pedagogy for Girls? conference, London.

Sanders, Jo (1996) What works to create change on an individual basis? Paper presented at the American Educational Research Association, New York City.

Sanders, Jo (1997) Teacher education and gender equity. *ERIC Digest,* 96.

Sanders, Jo (1998) The molehill and the mountain. *TIES: The Magazine of Design and Technology Education,* 1 (Sept).

Sanders, Jo (2000) Women in science and technology, and the role of public policy. Paper presented at the Association for Public Policy Analysis and Management, Seattle, Washington.

Sanders, Jo (2002) Snatching defeat from the jaws of victory: when good projects go bad. Girls and computer science. Paper presented at the American Educational Research Association, New Orleans.

Sanders, Jo (2005) Teaching teachers about gender equity in computing. Paper presented at the Crossing Cultures, Changing Lives: Integrating Research on Girls' Choices of IT Careers conference, Oxford, England.

Sanders, Jo and Lubetkin, Rebecca (1991) Preparing female students for technician careers: dealing with our own elitist biases. *Peabody Journal of Education*, 66: 113–26.

Sanders, Jo and Nelson, Sarah Cotton (2004) Closing gender gaps in science. *Educational Leadership*, 62: 74–7.

Sanders, Jo and Tescione, Susan T (2004) *Equity in the IT classroom*. www.josanders.com/portal/index.htm.

Sanders, Jo Shuchat (1985a) Here's how you can help girls take greater advantage of school computers. *American School Board Journal*, 12: 37–8.

Sanders, Jo Shuchat (1985b) Making the computer neuter. *The Computing Teacher*, 23–7.

Schofield, Janet Ward (1995) *Computers and classroom culture*. New York: Cambridge University Press.

Selby, Linda (1997) Increasing the participation of women in tertiary level computing courses: what works and why. Paper presented at the Australian Society for Computers in Learning in Tertiary Education, Perth.

Seymour, Elaine and Hewitt, Nancy M (1997) *Talking about leaving: why undergraduates leave the sciences*. Boulder, CO: Westview Press.

Shashaani, Lily (1993) Gender-based differences in attitudes toward computers. *Computers and Education*, 20: 169–81.

Shashaani, Lily (1994) Socioeconomic status, parents' sex-role stereotypes, and the gender gap in computing. *Journal of Research on Computing in Education*, 26: 433–51.

Shashaani, Lily (1997) Gender differences in computer attitudes and use among college students. *Journal of Educational Computing Research*, 16: 37–51.

Shashaani, Lily and Khalili, Ashmad (2001) Gender and computers: similarities and differences in Iranian college students' attitudes toward computers. *Computers and Education*, 37(3–4): 363–75.

Snyder, Thomas D, Tan, Alexandra G and Hoffman, Charlene M (2004) *Digest of education statistics 2003*. Washington, DC: US Department of Education, Institute of Education Sciences.

Steele, Claude M (1997) A threat in the air: how stereotypes shape intellectual identity and performance. *American Psychologist*, 52: 613–29.

Stumpf, Heinrich and Stanley, Julian C (1997) The gender gap in advanced placement computer science: participation and performance, 1984–1996. *College Board Review*, 181: 22–7.

Todman, John (2000) Gender differences in computer anxiety among university entrants since 1992. *Computers and Education*, 34: 27–35.

Tsai, Meng-Jung (2002) Do male students often perform better than female students when learning computers? A study of Taiwanese eighth graders' computer education through strategic and cooperative learning. *Journal of Education*, 26: 67–85.

Volk, Ken and Holsey, Lilla (1997) TAP: a gender equity program in high technology. *Technology Teacher*, 1: 10–13.

Volman, Monique and van Eck, Edith (2001) Gender equity and information technology in education: the second decade. *Review of Educational Research*, 71: 613–34.

Whitley, Bernard E Jr (1997) Gender differences in computer-related attitudes and behavior: a meta-analysis. *Computers in Human Behavior*, 13: 1–22.

NOTE

1. In view of space limitations here, a more extended analysis of the literature with complete citations and references can be found at www.josanders.com/resources.

Gender, Identity and Educational Sites

INTRODUCTION

The chapters in this section pay particular attention to the intersection of gender with other aspects of identity, including ethnicity, social class, dis/abilities and sexualities. All the authors in the section consider how identities are theorized and advocate a recognition of the multiplicity of discourses that individuals inhabit.

In Chapter 23, Janie Victoria Ward and Tracy L. Robinson-Wood draw our attention to a number of important points, including the fact that the achievement of Black children has increased steadily year on year. However, not only is the achievement of Black girls frequently overlooked and a focus given to the under-achievement of Black boys, but also male experiences in schooling are provided a privileged voice that ignores the difficulties of girls. Ward and Robinson-Wood put out a plea that strategies be developed that recognize the interplay of variables that make up schooling identities in order to improve Black students' educational opportunities and sense of belonging to the schools they attend.

In Chapter 24, Diane Reay argues that the preoccupation with gender, in terms of 'boys' underachievement', negates our knowledge and understanding of how education is inextricably interwoven with narratives of social class. By drawing on data from a project that focused on classroom interaction in one secondary school classroom, she illustrates how macro relationships between social class, gender and education are played out at the micro level for both working- and middle-class males and females.

Chapter 25 places the spotlight on a subject that runs through many of the chapters in this book – 'boys' underachievement'. Wayne Martino draws on the situation in Australia to illustrate how essentialist discourses on boys dominate political agendas and effectively removes attention from the power disparities that shape the educational opportunities of the majority of boys and all girls in schools. Australia is in the forefront of implementing programs that are ostensibly aimed at tackling 'the problems of boys' but which have been widely critiqued for their restrictive conceptions of masculinity. Martino makes the case for including student voices in the evaluation of these on the basis that hearing the views of an array of young people will cause the damaging and backward-moving rightist agendas which underpin these programs to be challenged.

The chapter by Carrie Paechter on femininities would make valuable reading for policy makers who have invested in the kinds of boys' programs discussed in Chapter 26. Here Paechter discusses the variety of ways in which girls construct femininities but also observes how risky it is for them to challenge or step out of those deemed 'acceptable' femininities. Similarly, in Chapter 27, D. James Mellor and Debbie Epstein use the same terminology of 'risk' in showing how discourses around sexuality are constructed along narrow lines, and that for pupils to be identified as anything 'other' than heterosexual generates dangerous sanctions. Chapter 28 provides further evidence of how the interrelationship of gender with other positions can exacerbate young people's marginalization within educational systems. Here, Michael L. Wehmeyer and Harilyn Rousso take up the theme of disabilities and focus exclusively on girls and young women. Their reason for so doing is that equity for females with disabilities is 'almost universally poorer than for others, including boys with disability'.

The final chapter in this section by Madeleine Arnot explores 'gender voices' in three quite different theoretical traditions: firstly, feminist epistemological concerns with the centrality of voice, language identity; secondly, the silenced (gendered) voices of young people; and, thirdly, how the concept of pupil voice has been used to bolster the commodification of education.

23

Room at the Table: Racial and Gendered Realities in the Schooling of Black Children

Janie Victoria Ward and Tracy L. Robinson-Wood

CONTEXTUAL CONSIDERATIONS

We are African-American women, psychologists, researchers, educators and academicians. Our racial, gendered, cultural and professional identities inform our scholarship. That scholarship focuses on the intersections of gender, race and class within educational contexts. While our analysis is sensitive to children across racial and ethnic diversity within the USA and the UK, in this work we emphasize the experiences of Black boys and girls in public schools.

Our focus is guided by a central observation. In comparison to their White and ethnic minority peers, disproportionate numbers of Black students in the USA and the UK attend schools where educational inequality is undeniably apparent. Lower standardized test scores and academic achievement levels, lower rates of graduation, and higher rates of disciplinary actions resulting in suspension, expulsion and social alienation from the school experience are indicative of these inequalities.

A review of the literature of Black schoolchildren in the USA and the UK reveals a deficit framing of students' experiences highlighting their growing academic marginality and failure in comparison to White students and other ethnic minority children. The pejorative public discourse that positions the problem of academic underachievement within Black children themselves more often than not fails to address essential ecological factors that affect the lives of these children, their parents, and the communities in which they live and work. Moreover, this discourse tends to obscure the very real educational advances that have been achieved by Black students and by school systems. There is an undeniable achievement gap that continues to persist between Black students and other children; however, the evidence suggests that it is not worsening in the USA and the UK. In the USA, the perception of declining academic performance between Black and other children reproduces a cultural stereotype that Blacks are intellectually inferior and has encouraged the development of policy initiatives such as the No Child Left Behind (NCLB) act. The purpose of this legislation was to level the playing field for all students by requiring schools to report results on annual standardized tests for each segment of the student population (Diaz *et al.*, 2006). By doing so, poorly performing groups of students and the institutions they attend are identified for the private and public scrutiny of parents, politicians and the professional educational community.

In the past few decades, researchers have focused attention on the convergence of gender, race, ethnicity and social class in children's educational experiences. Most of the literature has addressed the predicament of girls (read White girls) (Sadker and Sadker, 1994; AAUW, 1995; Weiner *et al.*, 1997), White boys (Pollack, 1998), and, more recently, Black boys (Mac an Ghall, 1994; Sewell, 1997, 2004; Ferguson, 2001). In Both the USA and the UK Black girls are underrepresented in this current race and gender focus (Mirza, 1992; Paul, 2003; Wright and Weekes, 2003; Evans-Winters, 2005). The presumption of Black girls' superior academic performance in comparison to Black boys is commonly accepted as truth.

It is critical that we pay attention to inequality in education for several reasons. Population shifts indicate growing numbers of non-White people in the USA and the UK. This has implications for demographic changes within the classroom. Few would argue that there are no benefits associated with receiving a quality education, such as lower rates of poverty, unemployment, crime, and incarceration. Increasing the levels of educational attainment of its citizens is one of the most important contributions a nation can make in building a strong citizenry.

THEORIZING RACE

Race, racial status and differences within and between racial groups have been a central concern to social scientists studying educational achievement. Efforts to theorize race have changed considerably over time. Historically, notions of race, based on biogenetic categories, were seen as deterministic and fixed. Over time, the biological basis of race has been refuted and replaced with a more generalized acceptance among scholars that race is a social construct. However, regarding race as only a social construction suggests that race itself is illusory, a notion which denies the lived experience of non-White people in relationship with themselves and one another. Omi and Winant (2004) argue that 'race is a fundamental principle of social organization and identity formation' (2004: 9) that is, and will remain, a feature of social reality across the globe. Race is neither an illusive, ideological concept, nor is it simply an objective condition. Race is contextual, historical, relational, and political – forever being reconstituted in the present.

In today's postmodern and post-colonial world, racism depends on neither overt acts of discrimination nor specific references to racialized language. Conceptions of race are more nebulous than ever before. Coded racial signifiers reproduce racialized images and racial myths that are deeply embedded in our collective psyches and shape self-perception and our interpersonal and institutional relationships with one another. Consider the unexamined assumptions and biases behind the terms used in school practice and research. For example, 'gifted' has become a proxy for the white middle-class. Conversely, 'special education' tends to be used as a stand-in for blackness (Ladson-Billings, 2004).

Music has been theorized as deeply central to the identities and politics of African people throughout the diaspora (Back, 1996). Due to the profound influence of popular culture, particularly Black music forms, such as reggae, rap, samba, Afro-pop, and hip hop, there is an emergence of a diasporic consciousness, the internalization of meanings of blackness that are being introjected into cultural identities of Black people across the globe.

Compared to their White counterparts, people of African descent have a lived experience that is shaped by racism in its multiple forms – interpersonal, institutional, and cultural (Jones, 1996). In a context where the reality of racism is denied and regarded as passé, individuals who experience racial oppression identify with others who are similarly situated. As long as race continues to be a primary aspect of social difference and a mechanism for the reproduction of inequality, people who perceive themselves as oppressed by their status in the racial hierarchy will hold tenaciously to the belief that race still matters, and that the shared experience of continued racial oppression connects Black people throughout the world.

RACE, GENDER AND CLASS IN EDUCATION

Fifty years after the success of *Brown v. the Board of Education* (the landmark federal court case that mandated the racial desegregation of US schools), racially segregated, educationally unequal schools persist. Schools in the USA are 41% non-White, the great majority of non-white students attending racially and often economically segregated institutions (Orfield, 2001). Today, approximately three-quarters of Black and Latino students attend majority-minority public schools due in large part to the racially isolated neighborhoods in which they live.

The nation's poverty rate is 12% (Robinson, 2005). Despite a growing Black and Latino middle class, the current poverty rate for African-Americans is 23%. For Latinos, who can be of any race, the poverty rate is 21%. Nearly 52% of Black US children live in communities where one in five people live in poverty (Annie E. Casey Foundation, 2003). The availability of school resources is linked to educational quality. Weaker education is generally provided to highly impoverished schools (Orfield and Lee, 2005). Achievement scores are correlated with a school's racial composition. Graduation rates at low-income, segregated schools tend to be low. Teachers in high-poverty schools tend to be less qualified, they teach in poor working conditions (e.g. inadequate facilities, less availability of textbooks and supplies, large, overcrowded classes, and fewer administrative supports), and they experience a turnover rate that is one-third higher than the rate for all teachers in all other schools (National Commission on Teaching and America's Future, 2003). These teachers are also more likely to perceive the school and classroom climate less positively (Hale-Benson, 1986; Kunjufu, 1988).

The early 1950s saw the first large wave of Afro-Caribbean immigration to the UK, and, much like in the USA, Black and other ethnic minority children often attend racially segregated schools in similarly segregated communities. In an interview with *The Guardian*, Ted Cantle, a member of the Community Cohesion Review Team, reported on the depth of physical segregation of housing estates found in inner-city areas. The Review Team's report, entitled *Whose Schools, Whose Rules,* provides a commentary on the failures of the UK educational system for Black and other ethnic minority pupils. The report highlights the extent of dual social systems in UK society, noting that many communities operate on the basis of a series of parallel lives with separate educational arrangements, churches, social networks, languages, and employment (Community Cohesion Review Team, 2002). In delineating the powerful forces working against Black students in racially separated schools, Lee Jasper, Senior Equalities Adviser to the Mayor of London, wrote that 'Racism, stereotyping low teacher expectation, underachievement, and exclusions form a formidable case pointing to the failure of the present education system' (Jasper, 2001: 6). Amplifying the inequities in British schools, Gillborn (2004) said, 'attempts to challenge racism in British education have a long and troubled ancestry' (p35). In the UK, the education of Black schoolchildren has been referred to as a silent catastrophe. Underachievement, high rates of truancy, conflicts with the law, and interpersonal conflicts between teachers and students were cited as school-related barriers to Black student success. As in to the USA, most of the majority-minority schools in the UK have a predominantly White teaching faculty. In London, for example, less than 3% of teachers are Black, yet Blacks constitute nearly 20% of London's student population.

In the study of Black student underachievement, the focus on race and schooling has too often concentrated on the experience of Black males and the interplay of masculinity within the context of schools. In comparison, the voices and experiences of Black schoolgirls have been largely ignored. Although Black girls and boys reside within the same communities and attend the same schools, a literature that privileges the challenges and experiences of one group (e.g. male) ultimately downplays the urgency to explicate Black schoolgirls' vulnerabilities and resiliencies.

ACHIEVEMENT DISPARITIES

The achievement gap is central to the discourse on race, gender, and class in education throughout the USA, and the UK. Defined in the USA as the average difference in performance on standardized and end-of-year tests across grade levels when comparing large numbers of students (Uhlenberg & Brown, 2002), the achievement gap has been readily documented. Since 1969, the National Assessment of Educational Progress (NAEP, 2004) has measured US students' achievement in several subjects, including reading and mathematics, for students in grades 4, 8, and 12 (refers to ages 9, 13, and 17 respectively). In reading, White students generally outperform all other students across race and ethnicity at all grade levels. Black, Latino, and Native American reading scores at grades 4 and 8 are very close, either differing slightly by at most four points or showing no difference in average scores (NCES, 2004).

Despite the gaps in scores, progress has been and continues to be made. For instance, at all three ages, Black students' average reading scores in 2004 were higher than in 1971. Subsequently, the gap between White and Black students in reading was smaller than in 1971 (NCES, 2005a). In mathematics, Asian/Pacific Islander (includes Chinese, Japanese, and Asian Indian) children have higher average scores than White, Black, Latino, and Native American students in grades 4, 8, and 12 (NCES, 2005b).

In the UK, disparities in education also exist, but they differ from those in the USA. Data were analyzed from the Department of Education and Employment (DfEE) and Local Education Authority (LEA) submissions to the Ethnic Minority Achievement Grant and material based on the Youth Cohort Study of England and Wales. Outcomes refer to the attainment of at least five higher grade (A*–C) GCSEs (General Certificate of Secondary Education). Although all groups have improved academically since the late 1980s-1990s, data suggest that in eight out of 10 LEAs, Indian students attained higher outcomes than their White counterparts. Since the introduction of the GCSE, White and Indian students are the only groups to have improved consistently. Afro-Caribbean and Pakistani boys and girls have not fared as well as White, Indian, and Bangladeshi students. Bangladeshi students improved at levels faster than Afro-Caribbean and Pakistani. In fact, the gap between Afro-Caribbean, Pakistani and White students is larger now than it was a decade ago (Gillborn and Mirza, 2000). Afro-Caribbean students are also less likely to attain five higher-grade GCSEs than White and Indian boys. However, very recent data from 2004 indicate that Afro-Caribbean students improved their GCSE performance, almost an extra 3% achieving five or more (A*–C) grades.

When the data are disaggregated by class and analyzed over time, Black students in 1988 were the most successful of the groups from manual backgrounds but fell behind other working-class peers in levels of attainment. It can be said that independent of class background, inequalities of attainment are evident for Black students (Gillborn and Mirza, 2000). Research shows that Black Caribbean pupils make a sound start in primary school, but their performance markedly declines at secondary level (Office for Standards in Education, 1999).

There are indicators of school performance that are gender related and which contribute to the current discourse that Black girls are experiencing greater educational success than are Black boys. In the USA, Black girls clearly outperform Black boys in reading at grades 4, 8, and 12. However, these data are consistent with the performance of other racial and ethnic groups. More specifically, all girls have higher average reading scores than boys of their same racial and ethnic group.

However, when we turn to the math scores, Black girls do not outperform Black boys at grades 4, 8, and 12. Black students, both boys and girls, do less well in math on standardized scores than all other students at every level. That large numbers of Black students are being educated in racially segregated, resource-poor, economically disadvantaged schools with higher percentages of uncertified or out-of-field teachers in math and science may explain Black students' poor math performance (Jerald, 2002; Orfield and Lee, 2005). Black students' lack of progress in math and science is cause for concern, given that the high-paying jobs of the twenty-first century require solid math and science skills. To say Black girls are doing better than Black boys in school is to overlook the advantage that all girls as a group have over boys in reading at every level. It also overlooks the very real disparities that exist as a function of race. This discourse artificially magnifies Black male students' problems in school while rendering invisible the effect of racism on Black schoolgirls.

Decades of research provide dramatic illustration of the many ways in which teachers unconsciously reinforce existing social hierarchies, traditional gender roles and racial stereotypes. Within the same school and classroom, schools respond to children of 'varying race-gender statuses in systematically different ways, reinforcing differentiation' (Grant, 1984: 98). While there may be no conscious attempt to treat Black youth in a different way from White youth, schools reinforce existing social structures through informal practices and formal teaching (Sanders, 2000: 182).

Teachers' perceptions of students are grounded in their own location of race, class, and gender categories. These social locations form the basis of teachers' interactions with pupils and inform the conditions of their work. Their cultural experiences and racialized/gendered knowledge (or lack of experiences and lack of knowledge) provide a framework from which teachers interpret, organize, and act upon information (Ferguson, 2001). Unexamined responses to difference, unconscious stereotyping, and self-fulfilling prophecies create a school climate that is not conducive to Black students' achievement and that weakens the rapport between teachers and Black students (Mac an Ghall, 1988; Bierda, 2000).

Often repeated in the literature on the educational experiences of Black children is their opposition to achievement due to fears of acting White (Fordham and Ogbu, 1986). Explanations linking black student underachievement to beliefs about anti-intellectualism among their families and their communities is potentially damaging to black students and their relationships with their peers and teachers. Fordham and Ogbu (1986) explore 'the burden of acting white' by describing Black students' resistance to an education that links social mobility and acceptance to Blacks' emulation of Whiteness." The wider social context in which Black students receive their educations affects their school performance. Steele's (1995; 1999) critical work on stereotype threat maintains that negative stereotypes of the intellectual abilities of African-Americans hinders their performance on standardized tests. The threat of being perceived as a negative stereotype or the fear of poor performance to confirm this stereotype is powerful enough to affect the intellectual and academic performance and identities of an entire group. Black students in testing situations can become deeply concerned (e.g. anxious) that their Blackness will be used to perpetuate stereotypes about their and other Black people's intellectual and academic inferiority.

BLACK BOYS

A unique convergence of factors contributes to the psychosocial stressors and academic underachievement of Black boys. In the context of schools, there is a disturbing parallel occurring between the reactions to Blacks boys in the USA and in the UK. Schools are sites in which Black males are subject to various forms of stigma centered on the persistence of racial and gender stereotyping (Noguera, 2002). In 2000-01, Black boys represented 8.6% of national public school enrollments, and yet they were 20% of the children classified as mentally retarded, 21% of those classified as emotionally disturbed and 12% of those with a specific learning disability, and 15% of those placed in special education (Smith, 2004). Black boys are also more likely than any other group to be suspended and expelled from school and to be missing from advanced placement and honors courses. Twice as many African-American boys are in special education as Black girls. According to Smith (2004), 'this fact rules out heredity and home environment as primary causes and highlights school factors' (p49). The process of labeling black males as less intelligent and prone to behavior problems begins at a young age (Noguera, 2002). Energetic and sometimes finding it harder to stay focused in elementary classrooms, younger black boys are seen as hyperactive (Hale-Benson, 1986; Kunjufu, 1988), hard to manage, and thus in need of teacher control. In her ethnographic study of Black elementary school boys, Ann Ferguson notes that as they become older, 'Black children are "adultified", and they are no longer seen as child like' (Ferguson, 2001). Denied the masculine dispensation constituting White males as being 'naturally naughty', Ferguson maintains that black boys are believed to be 'willfully bad' (Ferguson, 2001, p84). The focus on controlling the behavior of African-American males serves both to justify their persistent academic underachievement and provide an explanation for overlooking at other times Black boys' boisterous or aggressive behavior, as if this is the way they are naturally supposed to behave (Irvine, 1990). In response to these mixed and conflicting messages, some Black students question the purpose, goals, and objectives of school (Irvine, 1990). Others may reject the knowledge claims asserted within the classroom, disidentify with school, and turn instead to alternative knowledge sources situated within their communities (Sewell, 1997). Finally, others engage in externalizing (acting out) behaviors, which are associated with increased stigmatization and lead to further alienation from school.

Researchers in both the USA and the UK often cite a link between Black boys' school behavior and the performance of black masculinity (Majors and Bilson, 1992; Alexander, 1996; Sewell, 1997; Ferguson, 2001). Black masculinity in the USA and in the UK has been labeled 'a social identity in crisis' (Mirza, 1999: 139). Variously described as compensatory behavior evoked in response to powerlessness or seen as an attempt to empower black males by rendering them visible to those who would discount and marginalize them, the performance of black masculinity is seen as a response to black men's lack of power rooted in their social location (Alexander, 1996; Mirza, 1999).

Central to Sewell's (1997) study of black youth in the UK is what he calls the 'myth of the African-Caribbean challenge', which refers to the teacher's assumption of the inherent sexual proclivities of Afro-Caribbean boys, who are then seen as naturally aggressive and uninterested in education. The degree to which Black boys are attracted to and emulate the popular hip-hop culture and adopt specific masculinized behaviors and cultural aspects of speech performance, including choice of dress, Black English, and ways of communicating identity through bodily discourse and linguistic practices, serves to mark them as different, dangerous, and divorced from the business of school (Wright *et al.*, 1998; Archer and Yamashita, 2003). A nonconforming cultural repertoire exhibited by students may feel alien to teachers, who, in turn, focus on controlling the behavior of Black males. Frequently subjected to heightened scrutiny in and outside the school, teachers and administrators come down hard on Black boys' behavior, and with time the negative reactions of school personnel become normalized and culturally sanctioned. In a large-scale, multiracial study of nearly 25,000 students, Osborn (1997) found a correlation between school performance and self-esteem, both of which decline dramatically for black males over their years in high school. African-American boys were found to base their self-esteem largely on peers' perceptions and their athletic success (Osborn, 1997). It is clear from the literature on Black boys in school that they face a disproportionate number of obstacles to achieving social and academic success.

BLACK GIRLS

Focused attention to gender equity has, over the past 15 years, led to pronounced improvement in girls' education and the reduction of the gender gap in math and science. For example, by the year 2000, girls were as likely as boys to take math courses in high school, and they performed as well as did boys in those courses (NCES, 2004). Efforts to increase female representation in male-dominated college majors, such as engineering and the physical sciences, has met with success in many schools as well (Spain and Bianchi, 1996). However, to which group of girls do the data refer? African-American girls and Latinas continue to lag behind Asian and White girls and boys (Hanson, *et al.*, 2000). An analysis of racial group differences, particularly during adolescence, often depict the Black girl as faring better than her male counterpart (Ward, 2000). Black girls' higher high-school graduation rates and lower rates of expulsion, suspension, and referrals to special education are often cited as evidence of girls' academic strengths over those of Black boys.

There is increasing awareness of the myriad influence on girls' developing self-concept and the importance of integrating one's multiple identities (racial, gender, social class, and sexual orientation). For Black girls, obstacles to academic success are multiplied by the effects of colliding pressures and challenges, ranging from lack of access to resources to race, gender, and class biases.

Research on US schoolgirls reported in the ground-breaking research report from the American Association of University Women (AAUW) entitled, 'Shortchanging Girls, Shortchanging America' indicates a marked drop in self-esteem during early adolescence (Orenstein, 1994; Pipher, 1995). In comparison to their White counterparts, Black girls were better able to maintain high self-esteem over the course of their years in school. Despite their devalued racial and gender status, many Black girls convey a confidence and competence and are prepared to take on the challenges of adulthood (AAUW, 1995; Commonwealth Fund *Survey of Adolescent Girls*, 1997).

Early research from the 1980s revealed that Black girls received less positive feedback from teachers and were more likely to be praised for their social behavior than their academic skill (Grant, 1984). Interactions between teachers and Black girls are often brief, teachers being more likely to ask Black girls to assume nonacademic tasks and function as 'go-betweens,' 'rule enforcers,' and 'caregivers'. Grant also found Black girls more likely to be ignored by teachers than are other racial and groups (Grant, 1984). Irvine (1986) found that school can be particularly tough for preadolescent black girls in the junior-high-school years, as these girls become increasingly invisible to the teaching staff. These findings may account for the low opinions some Black girls may hold of their teachers and the lack of academic confidence observed among black girls reported in the AAUW report.

In the UK, Ali (2003) found similar results with Afro-Caribbean girls, who succeeded within schools while esteeming traditional cultural values and interpersonal relationships. Afro-Caribbean girls were also found to be proeducation but antischool. This position was regarded as being intimately tied to a healthy sense of girls' gendered and racial identities (Youdell, 2004). Referred to as 'resistance within accommodation', Mac an Ghaill (1988) stated that Afro-Caribbean schoolgirls exhibited strategies of institutional survival. Mirza (1992) noted that Afro-Caribbean girls prized education, finding creative and subversive ways to access higher education within the constraints of a 'racially and sexually divisive educational and economic system' (p202). Simultaneously, these girls empathized with the experiences of their Afro-Caribbean male school peers. She argues that Black females not only resist through accommodation but are deliberate and strategic in their methods to coexist within schools while transforming these environments for their own purposes. Acts of resistance within educational contexts included Asian girls who were united with Afro-Caribbean girls as 'Black sisters' (Bhatti, 2004).

RESISTANCE MATTERS

Fifteen years ago, we presented a theory of resistance (Robinson and Ward, 1991), initially developed for Black teenage girls. The purpose of the model was to provide Black adolescents with tools to push back against racism, sexism, and other forms of discrimination that pressed down on their lives. Two forms of resistance were identified, optimal and suboptimal. Optimal resistance reflects a sociopolitical awareness of oppressive forces and a parallel utilization of healthy strategies that can serve people well in their efforts to push back against various forms of oppression. Suboptimal or survival-oriented resistance refers to short-term dysfunctional adaptations to oppression. Although they often have immediate or short-term numbing/soothing effects, short-term adaptations do not serve Black students well in the long run. Choosing to resist by not 'doing school' in order to preserve one's reference group identity and sense of integrity within a racist system represents a suboptimal resistance strategy. Learning to design and put into place an effective resistance system is one way for Black students to sit at the table of educational opportunity and partake of its essential bounty.

At the beginning of this work, we stated that Black students, in comparison to their White and ethnic minority peers, struggle to achieve educational parity in schools. This observation is neither specific to the USA nor new. For many Black students, school environments feel dismissive, irrelevant, and culturally alien. In an effort to navigate these environments, Black children employ multiple strategies, some which are helpful and uplifting and others that do not serve the individual child and/or their communities well. Although racism is not gender specific (Back, 1996), strategies of resistance often appear to be organized by gender or the corollaries of masculinity and femininity (Wright et al., 1999). For example, the efforts of Black boys to resist negating school practices are too often coupled with a pathologizing language that becomes tied to masculinity.

Tony Sewell's study of Afro-Caribbean boys suggests that, while Black pupils do not reject the concept of education itself (e.g. they are not antieducation), they may reject the function of schooling and the attendant knowledge that schools offer. We argue that Black students' educational efficacy requires them to attain the necessary skills to shift from a suboptimal resistance orientation that is anti-school. Black students who optimally resist have identified and integrated into their behavioral, attitudinal, and affective repertoire strategies that allow them to achieve their educational goals despite barriers they encounter throughout their years in the education system. Resistance speaks to students' dispositions toward the power relations they observe and experience in school (Wright and Weekes, 2003), particularly the experiences of racialized and gendered discrimination perceived by Blacks. Researchers have identified a wide range of factors Black students resist, and the various resistance strategies undertaken by Black youth in schools. In their study of Black students' resistance to teacher authority and school sanctions, Wright and Weekes (2003) found that Afro-Caribbean students resist the 'mechanisms of control and knowledge production in schools' and they reject schooling when it is seen as not leading to their empowerment (p11). To this end, students were described as engaging in 'resistance within accommodation'; that is, the strategic employment of resistance behaviors in situations in which they may have looked as though they are complicit when in fact they were manipulating their environments to obtain desired ends. For example, Mirza (1992; 2004) found that Black girls and women initially opted for accessible careers that allowed them future entry into more lucrative and desired career choices. This 'backdoor' technique was strategically used by women to access coveted higher education and essential credentials less available to them via traditional routes. In her study of academically successful Black girls, Fordham (1993) found that Black girls used silence, not as a form of acquiescence but rather as an act of defiance. Silence was invoked as a critical rejection of the low expectations of Black students held by many school officials.

Cultural and racial socialization practices play a significant role in shaping Black girls' psychological stance. Studies of cultural and racial socialization practices in the USA show that African-American families hold particularly high expectations for their daughters and emphasize strong values, inner strength, self-reliance and perseverance (Ward, 1996; 2000). Although self-efficacy may be an asset in Black homes and neighborhoods, Black girls' efforts to negotiate their environments in a way that allows them to maintain their identities and agency is frequently considered a liability in school. Socially confident girls may be misread as having an 'attitude', particularly if they are unwilling to conform to rigidly gendered dimensions of acceptable and appropriate (middle-class, White) behavior (Ginsberg, 2002).

Strategies of resistance may be organized by gender; however, the need to resist the powerful and demeaning effects of racism in educational settings demands that both girls and boys be equally strategic and survivalist. Sewell's studies (1997; 2004) show that Afro-Caribbean boys adapt their knowledge of the racialized and gendered nature of schools to challenge the limitations, low expectations and faulty assumptions educators place on them. Unfortunately, Black boys' (even more than Black girls') efforts to resist negating school practices are frequently pathologized and used to justify exclusion and marginalization. And yet Black boys' strategies are surprisingly similar to the resistance strategies used successfully over the generations by African-American males and females as a chief means of social uplift and empowerment (Lee and Slaughter-Defoe, 2004).

More studies exploring the intersections of gender, race and ethnicity and schooling are needed, particularly those identifying strategies of resistance that improve black students' educational outcomes, shore up students' academic self-esteem, and cultivate a sense of attachment and belonging to the schools they attend.

REFERENCES

Alexander, C (1996) *The art of being Black: the creation of Black british youth identities.* Oxford: Clarendon Press.

Ali, S (2003) 'To be a girl': culture and class in schools. *Gender and education,* 15: 269–83.

American Association of University Women (AAUW) (1995) *How schools shortchange girls: the AAUW report. A study of major findings on girls and education.* New York: Marlowe.

Annie E Casey Foundation (2003) *Kids count: African American children state level measures of child well being from the 2000 census.* Annie E Casey Foundation.

Archer, L and Yamashita, H (2003) Theorizing inner-city masculinities: 'race', class, gender and education. *Gender and Education,* 15: 115–32.

Back, L (1996) *New ethnicities and urban culture: racisms and multiculture in young lives.* London: UCL Press.

Bhatti, G (2004) Good, bad and normal teachers: the experiences of south Asian children, in Ladson-Billings, G and Gillborn, D (eds.). *The RoutledgeFalmer reader in multicultural education.* (139–62). New York: RoutledgeFarmer.

Bierda, A (2000) The mythical African American male. *WEEA Digest,* November.

Commonwealth Fund (1997). *Survey of the health of adolescent girls.* New York: WEEA Equity Resource Center.

Community Cohesion Review Team (2002) Whose schools, whose rules. Briefing paper by the 1990 Trust for 1990 Trust Conference, 2002. London.

Diaz, CF, Pelletier, C M and Provenzo, EF Jr (2006). *Touch the future: teach.* Boston: Allyn and Bacon.

Evans-Winters, V (2005) *Teaching Black girls.* New York: Peter Lang.

Ferguson, AA (2001) *Bad boys: public schools in the making of black masculinity.* Ann Arbor, M: University of Michigan Press.

Fordham, S (1993) Those loud Black girls: (Black) women, silence, and gender 'passing' in the academy, in Seller, M and Weis, L (eds) *Beyond Black and White: new faces and voices in U.S. schools.* Albany, NY: State University of New York Press.

Fordham, S and Ogbu, J (1986) Black student success: coping with the burden of 'acting White.' *Urban Review,* 18: 175–206.

Gillborn, D (2004) Anti-racism: from policy to praxis, in Ladson-Billings, G and Gillborn, D (eds) *The RoutledgeFalmer reader in multicultural education.* New York: (35–48). RoutledgeFarmer.

Gillborn, D and Mirza, HS (2000) Educational inequality: mapping race, class, and gender. London: Office for Standards in Education.

Ginsberg, A (2002) Building on student knowledge: a new frame for gender equity in education that transcends the sameness/difference dichotomy. *Current Issues in Comparative Education,* 5: 24–37.

Grant, L (1984) Black females' 'place' in desegregated classrooms. *Sociology of Education,* 57: 98–111.

Hale-Benson, J (1986) *Black children: their roots, culture, and learning styles.* Baltimore, MD: Johns Hopkins University Press.

Hanson, K Smith, SJ and Kapur, A (2000) Does all mean all? Education for girls and Women, in Hoffman, N Hidalgo, N and Silber, E (eds) *Women's Studies Quarterly*, 28, (3 and 4): 249–86.

Irvine, J (1986) Teacher–student interactions: effects of student race, sex, and grade level. *Journal of Educational Psychology*, 78: 14–21.

Irvine, J (1990) *Black students and school failure.* New York: Praeger.

Jasper, L (2001) Black schools, white rules? *Black to Black*, November: 3–4.

Jerald, CD (2002) *All talk, no action: putting an end to out-of-field teaching.* Washington, DC: The Education Trust.

Jones, JM (1996) *Prejudice and racism.* New York: McGraw-Hill.

Kunjufu, J (1988) *To be popular or smart.* Chicago: African American Images.

Ladson-Billings, G (2004) 'Just what is critical race theory and what's it doing in a nice field like educa- tion?' in Ladson-Billings, G and Gillborn, D (eds) (49–67). *The RoutledgeFalmer reader in multicul- tural education.* New York: RoutledgeFarmer.

Lee, CD and Slaughter-Defoe, DT (2004) Historical and sociocultural influences on African American edu- cation, in Banks, JA and Banks, CAM (eds) *Handbook of research on multicultural education* (462–90). New York: Macmillan.

Mac an Ghall, M (1988) Young, gifted, and black: student–teacher relations in schooling of Black youth. Milton Keynes: Open University Press.

Mac an Ghall, M (1994) *The making of men: masculinities, sexualities, and schooling.* Buckingham: Open University Press.

Majors, R and Bilson, JM (1992) *Cool pose: the dilemmas of Black manhood in America.* New York: Lexington Books.

Mirza, H (1992) *Young, female and Black.* London: Routledge.

Mirza, H (1992) Black masculinities and schooling. *British Journal of the Sociology of Education*, 20: 137–48.

Mirza, HS (2004) Black women in education: a collective movement for social change, in Ladson-Billings, G and Gillborn, D (201–11). *The RoutledgeFalmer reader in multicultural education.* London: Routledge.

National Assessment of Educational Progress (NAEP) (2004) *The nation's report card: reading highlights 2003.* National Center for Education Statistics. Institute of Education Sciences, US Department of Education.

National Center for Educational Statistics (NCES) (2005a*) Long-term trend: the nation's report card. Trends in average reading scale scores by race/ethnicity: White–Black gap.* Institute of Education Sciences, US Department of Education.

National Center for Educational Statistics (NCES) (2005b) *Long-term trend: the nation's report card. Trends in average mathematics scale scores by gender.* Institute of Education Sciences, US Department of Education.

National Commission on Teaching and America's Future (2003) *No dream denied: a pledge to America's children.* Washington, DC: Author.

Noguera, PA (2002) The trouble with Black boys: the role and influence of environmental and cultural factors on the academic performance of African American males. *In Motion Magazine, 13 May.*

Office for Standards in Education (1999) *Raising the attainment of minority ethnic pupils. School and LEA responses.* London OFSTED.

Office of Juvenile Justice and Delinquency Prevention (1998) *Guiding principles for promising female programming.* Washington, DC: Office of Juvenile Justice and Delinquency Prevention.

Omi, M and Winant, H (2004) On the theoretical status of the concept of race, in Ladson-Billings, G and Gillborn, D (eds) *The RoutledgeFalmer reader in multicultural education* (7–15). New York: RoutledgeFarmer.

Orenstein, P (1994) *Schoolgirls: young women, self-esteem and the confidence gap.* New York: Doubleday.

Orfield, G (2001) Schools more separate: consequences of a decade of resegregation. The Civil Rights Project. Harvard University.

Orfield, G and Lee, C (2005) *Why segregation matters: poverty and educational inequality*. The Civil Rights Project. Harvard University.

Osborn, J (1997) Race and academic disidentification. *Journal of Educational Psychology*, 89: 728–35.

Paul, DG (2003) *Talkin' back: raising and educating resilient Black girls*. West Port, CT: Praeger.

Pipher, M (1995) *Reviving Ophelia: saving the selves of adolescent girls*. New York: GP Putnam.

Pollack, WS (1998) *Real boys*. New York: Holt.

Robinson, TL (2005) *The convergence of race, ethnicity, and gender: multiple identities in counseling*. Upper Saddle River, NJ: Merrill Prentice-Hall.

Robinson, TL and Ward, JV (1991) A belief in self far greater than any one's disbelief: cultivating resistance among African American girls, in Gilligan, C, Rogers, A and Tolman, D (eds) *Women, girls, and psychotherapy: reframing resistance*, New York: Haworth Press.

Sadker, M and Sadker, D (1994) *Failing at fairness: how America's schools cheat girls*. New York: Scribner.

Sanders, R (2000) Gender equity in the classroom: an arena for correspondence, in *Keeping gender on the chalkboard, Women's Studies Quarterly*, 28(3 and 4): 192–3.

Sewell, T (1997) *Black masculinities and schooling: how Black boys survive modern schooling*. Stoke on Trent: Trentham.

Sewell, T (2004) Loose cannons: exploding the myth of the black 'macho' lad, in Ladson-Billings, G and Gillborn, D (eds) *The RoutledgeFalmer reader in multicultural education* (103–16). New York: RoutledgeFarmer.

Smith, RA (2004) Saving Black boys: the elusive promises of public education. *The American Prospect*, 15: 2.

Spain, D and Bianchi, SM (1996) *Balancing act: mother, marriage and employment among American women*. New York: Russell Sage Foundation.

Steele, CM (1999) Thin ice: stereotype threat and Black college students. *Atlantic Monthly*, 248: 44–54.

Steele, CM and Aronson, J (1995) Stereotype threat and the intellectual test performance of African Americans. *Journal of Personality and Social Psychology*, 69: 797–811.

Uhlenberg, J and Brown, KM (2002) Racial gap in teachers' perceptions of the achievement gap. *Education and Urban Society*, 34: 493–530.

Ward, JV (1996) Raising resisters: the role of truth telling in the psychological development of African American girls, in Leadbeater, B and Way, N (eds) *Urban girls: resisting stereotypes, creating identities* (85–99). New York: New York University Press.

Ward, JV (2000) *The skin we're in: teaching our teens to be emotionally strong, socially smart and spiritually connected*. New York: Free Press.

Weekes, DC (1996) Discourses of blackness and the construction of Black femininity. Paper presented to the British Psychological Society, Annual Conference.

Weiner, G, Arnot, M and David, M (1997) Is the future female? Female success, male disadvantage, and changing gender patterns in education, in Halse, AH, Lauder, H, Brown, P and Wells, AS (eds) *Education: culture, economy, society* (620–30). Oxford: Oxford University Press.

Wright, C and Weekes, D (2003) Race and gender in the contestation and resistance of teacher authority and school sanctions: the case of African Caribbean pupils in England. *Comparative Education Review*, 47: 3–20.

Wright, C, Weekes, D, McGlaughlin, A and Webb, D (1998) Masculinised discourses within education and the construction of Black male identities. *British Journal of the Sociology of Education*, 19: 75–88.

Wright, C, Weekes, D and McGlaughlin, A (1999) Gender-blind racism in the experience of schooling and identity formation. *International Journal of Inclusive Education*, 3: 293–307.

Youdell, D (2004) Identity traps or how Black students fail: the interactions between biographical, sub-cultural and learner identities, in Ladson-Billings, G and Gillborn, D (eds) *The RoutledgeFalmer reader in multicultural education* (84–102). New York: RoutledgeFarmer.

24

Compounding Inequalities: Gender and Class in Education

Diane Reay

INTRODUCTION

At the beginning of the twenty-first century, the relationship between education and gender is a continuing concern in the UK. Ironically for feminists like myself, the current preoccupation with gender is primarily about the position of boys within schooling. There is alarm among our political élite that gendered patterns of educational inequality are being inverted as girls surge ahead of boys academically. Yet, high attainment is still, as always, a class-related phenomenon, even if that class attainment is cross-cut by gender (Walkerdine *et al.*, 2001). As Arnot, *et al.*, (1999: 156) point out, 'the national picture of female educational success masks the continuing significance of class inequalities in society'. To avoid such an elision, I want to offer an analysis that argues that relationships between gender and education do not make sense unless they are informed by social class. The story of gender in education is inextricably interwoven with narratives of social class that are all too often overlooked in the panic about boys' underachievement. Consequently, this chapter is about gendered class relationships to education and how they affect educational experiences and outcomes. I also want to raise a number of crucial questions about gender and social class in education. Do they compound or ameliorate each other? Can we even talk about gendered class processes as if they are in any sense coherent and unified? Or do we need to recognize a complex fluid messiness in which sometimes gender is more salient; at other times, class; and, at still others, both are overshadowed by issues of ethnicity, age, dis/ability or sexuality?

Contemporary class analysis in the UK, and, in particular, feminist work, through its focus on gendered and racialized class processes rather than class positioning (Mahony and Zmroczek, 1997; Skeggs, 1997; Anthias, 2001; Walkerdine *et al.*, 2001), addresses diversity within the traditional class groupings of upper, middle and working. Increasingly, the sociology of education is theorizing in terms of a plurality of middle and working classes (Savage *et al.*, 2001; Ball, 2003; Power *et al.*, 2003; Reay *et al.*, 2005). However, the recognition of Bourdieu's (1990) 'heterogeneity within homogeneity' does not dissolve the hierarchies, inequalities and exclusions arising from class relationships of power. Rather, the fragmentation of the traditional three-class structure calls for more sophisticated understandings of the complexities of class relationships to education. As Jane Thompson (2000) points out, difference, the new mantra within sociological theorising, and diversity, the new mantra in relation to British educational provision, are still always about inequalities. In this chapter, I illustrate, by drawing on empirical data, the powerful underlying continuities of social class in British education. There is also a recognition that social class today and, in particular, the ways in which it is mediated by gender, are very different from relations of social class and education 50, even 20, years ago.

GENDER AND CLASS IN ACADEMIC ACHIEVEMENT

There are still remnants of an earlier association of social class with masculinity that operates to marginalize what is happening to girls and women from different class backgrounds. The contemporary preoccupation with boys' academic underachievement in the UK (Epstein *et al.*, 1998, Skelton, 2001; Connolly, 2004; Francis and Skelton, 2005) has meant that the link between girls' relative academic success and social class background is often overlooked. As Jane Martin (2000: 35) points out, 'the debate on male underachievement may be another way of perpetuating the myth of female classlessness in education'.

Over the last two decades, femininity has moved from being equated with poor academic performance to a position at the beginning of the twenty-first century where it is now viewed as coterminous with high achievement. While research in the 1970s and 1980s found female students avoided displays of cleverness because they felt boys would then find them unattractive (Spender 1982; Lees, 1986), today many girls articulate a confidence in female educational abilities (Francis, 2000). Furthermore, disruptive 'failing boys'' behavior has given girls an unexpected window of opportunity through which some variants of femininities can be valorized over specific pathologized masculinities, particularly in the arena of educational achievement (Epstein *et al.*, 1998). However, what is frequently overlooked is that the achieving girls and the underachieving boys do not come from the same constituency. The girls who succeed are overwhelmingly middle class, and the boys who fail tend to be working class. Educational success remains central to the construction of middle-class, hegemonic masculinities (Lucey and Walkerdine, 1999), despite middle-class boys falling behind middle-class girls academically. What has changed is the gendered composition of middle-class academic success.

What has caused these shifts in relation to middle-class gendered achievement? Walkerdine, *et al.*,(2000) offer one explanation, arguing that, over the last 20 years, the possibility has opened up 'of making the feminine rational and the rational feminine' (p60). They assert that this has allowed middle-class girls to become rational subjects, taking up places in the professions once occupied by men. When attainment figures are scrutinized, it becomes clear that what is described as girls' high performance is mostly the high performance of girls in 'middle-class' schools (Walkerdine *et al.*, 2001). So we have reached a historical juncture at which middle-class girls, alongside their brothers, have become bearers of what was previously seen to be an exclusively male rationality. Yet, as Walkerdine *et al.* (2001) go on to argue, the entry of middle-class girls into masculine norms of rational academic excellence comes at a price. It is not achieved easily. Powerful associations of cleverness with asexuality (Willis, 1977) and unfemininity (Walkerdine, 1989) still abound. Middle-class girls are caught up in a delicate balancing act in relation to femininity and cleverness, in which being feminine cannot be allowed to interfere with academic success. The melding of middle class femininity with the rational bourgeois subject requires a huge psychic investment, in which femininity has to be struggled over and sexuality sometimes renounced. Indeed, academic success is produced out of the suppression of aspects of femininity and sexuality, a suppression which can generate intense identity crises and has led to an increase in eating disorders, such as anorexia and bulimia, primarily among middle-class teenage girls (Evans *et al.*, 2004).

THE RESEARCH STUDY

In the rest of the chapter, I illustrate how such macrorelationships between social class, gender and education are played out at the microlevel for both working- and middle-class males and females. I draw on data from an ESRC (Economic and Social Research Council) research project on teaching and learning (carried out in collaboration with Madeleine Arnot) that focus on classroom interaction in one secondary school classroom. My intention is to use students' words to illuminate how gendered class processes continue to exert a powerful effect on educational experiences in England.

The London-based research was carried out in Year 8 in Nelson Mandela, an inner-city, mixed comprehensive. Nelson Mandela was selected for having a high percentage of disengaged students. It serves a very mixed urban population, including many minority ethnic groups, mainly Turkish, Greek, Bengali, Black British, and Cantonese. Twenty-two per cent of students come from homes where English is a second language. Although largely working class, the school is located in an area which has become gentrified in recent years, and it recruits from middle-class professional families as well as from the unemployed and those with no tradition of further and higher education. However, it recruits two boys for every girl. Currently, 64% of the school population is male. A quarter of the students are eligible for free school meals, while over a fifth are on the register of special educational needs. In 2003, 41% of Year 11 students gained five grades A to C at GCSE (General Certificate of Secondary Education) (normally taken by students in their last year of compulsory schooling). This compared to a national average of just over 50%. The staff at Nelson Mandela are vocal in their commitment to the kinds of values which once typified the now defunct Inner London Education Authority (ILEA). This is reflected in discourses of equality and in a defence of a broad, humanistic curriculum. Teaching is still mainly mixed ability and there is no school uniform.

Our research task was to elicit students' voices and perspectives on their teaching and learning, and we did this through a mixed-methods approach which utilized questionnaires, and both focus and individual interviews. The focus-group interviews and individual interviews generated different perspectives on the same issues. The focus groups provided valuable insights into social processes and dynamics, while the individual interviews provided insights into particular students' understanding and experience of teaching and learning in the classroom. The two different types of interview, together with participant observation of lessons, allowed for a process of triangulation. We could look for reinforcement of findings as well as contradictory evidence across all three sources of data. Reports summarizing findings from the focus-group interviews were then fed back to both the teachers and students in the school.

CONFLICT AND COMPETITION IN THE CLASSROOM

What emerged most strongly was that, while the voices of the students were distinctly gendered, they were also powerfully differentiated by social class. There were as many occasions when commonalities of class perspective cut across and fractured gendered student voices, as when shared gender experiences resulted in very different perspectives among students of the same class background. The working-class boys' descriptions of classroom interaction are saturated with references to regulation. However, in contrast to their own regulation, the boys perceive the girls as the ones in the class receiving quality time from the teachers, what one boy, David, calls 'nice attention'. For the working-class boys in the class, the unfairness of teachers, and especially the preferential treatment given to the girls, is a constant theme.

Also evident is the competitive conflictual nature of the Mandela peer group culture. The data reveal a tutor group characterized by competing interests, low cohesion and fractious interaction:

Diane: *Do you think people in your class get on with one another?*
Bobbie: *No, wars all the time.*
George: *It's true you get little different groups.*
Jack: *Lots of them and they have different wars in the classroom. It's like fights all the time.*
Diane: *So these groups don't get on with each other?*
George: *No way.*
Bobbie: *No, they don't.*

In Mandela, despite its traditional egalitarian, mixed-ability ethos, class, ability and sex are powerful indices of stratification. The heterogeneity of the group was often reduced to a fractionalism in which differences among students in relation to learning requirements surfaced in competing needs and oppositional demands. In the excerpt below, the middle-class, white girls identify ability and sex as indicators for high levels of attention in the classroom, but they then go on to focus on the peer group rather than teaching and learning. Embedded in their account is the power and social control vested in the male peer group culture:

Katherine: *Some people are definitely seen as more important in our class.*
Fran: *But it depends on what they are seen as more important for. Some people seem more important because they have to be helped a lot with their learning. So they get helped a lot more and shown what to do better.*
Emma: *But also just in terms of class relationships people think they're more important if they are more popular.*
Jasmine: *Not the girls so much. It affects the boys more.*
Emma: *Yeah, definitely.*
Katherine: *If they're good at sport and stuff.*
Jasmine: *But not if they're clever.*
Emma: *Yeah, they're popular if they're like not really stupid and not really clever.*
Jasmine: *What makes them less popular is if they're really clever.*
Emma: *Yeah, you're not popular if you're a boy and you're seen as too clever.*
Fran: *Because they think they are like goody-goodies and they do everything the teacher asks them to do.*
Emma: *To be popular you have to be clever at different things.*

The male peer-group culture maintains its power despite the classroom context for the majority of boys in this class. We can see the power of local peer relations acting as a barrier to the transmission of official school knowledge. As Lois Weis (2004) found in relation to American working-class students, for working-class boys, and to a lesser extent, working-class girls, the differentiated school setting is facilitating the dominance of the informal, autonomous youth culture as the major source of community and belonging, displacing the school to a more marginal position in the formation of pedagogic identities. In Mandela, being clever in 'official', school-based ways is denigrated and, as Emma asserts, 'to be popular as a boy you have to be clever in different ways' that validate the 'local' rather than the 'official'. One consequence is that there are irresolvable issues around social inclusion within the peer group and high achievement for a majority of the boys, but particularly those from working-class families.

'A DIFFICULT FIT': SOCIAL EXCLUSIONS IN THE CLASSROOM

The sense that cleverness marginalizes students within the male peer group is reinforced by the identification, by all the focus groups, of the two most studious (and most middle-class) boys as the two students who are most regularly excluded. These boys experienced 'a difficult fit' between their cultural capital and interests and the pupil, peer-group culture. Lisa sums up the collective feeling of the rest of the class when she asserts, 'No one likes the geeks'. As the class tutor asserts, 'There's two or three middle-class boys who have sacrificed any kind of social standing in order just to get on with their work'. Yet, these two boys (one English, one African), together with two other high-ability boys (one working-class Asian, one middle-class, mixed race), of all the students in the tutor group, are the most comfortably positioned in relation to official school knowledge. They expected, and asserted that they received adequate attention and a reasonable amount of praise. They felt they were treated fairly by the teachers. In contrast to the rest of their peer group, they gave a strong sense that they were heard within the classroom context. Perhaps that was why they were the only group to treat the issue of teacher attention with equanimity rather than the passion it evoked in the other groups.

Paradoxically, it is the middle-class boys, who, in most clearly understanding the hierarchical rules underpinning school-based learning (Bernstein, 1990: 65), are least subject to their force. Their acceptance of, and willingness to work with, rather than contest the authority of the teacher translates into relatively flat hierarchical relations between teacher and taught. However, they, and to a lesser extent, the middle-class girls, benefit most from the classroom status quo. As Bernstein asserts, 'all education is intrinsically a moral activity which articulates the dominant ideologies of dominant groups' (1990: 66). There is less to contest for the middle-class children because they are served by a curriculum and system aligned with their capitals and interests. In contrast, the working-class groupings in the class have to confront cultural dissonance and a far harder task in order to relate comfortably to school-based knowledge. Unlike their middle-class counterparts, they have to deal with a 'difficult fit' between their capitals and interests and what schooling has to offer.

This 'difficult fit' emerges strongly in what the working-class children have to say about social inclusion in the classroom. Their narratives of student–teacher interaction configure a distanced, hierarchical pedagogic relationship:

David: Some teachers are a bit snobby, sort of. And some teachers act as if the child is stupid. Because they've got a posh accent. Like they talk without 'innits' and

> 'mans', like they talk proper English. And they say - that isn't the way you talk like putting you down. Like I think telling you a different way is sort of good, but I think the way they do it isn't good because they correct you and making you look stupid.
>
> Matthew: Those teachers look down on you.
> David: Yeah, like they think you're dumb.
> Matthew: We don't expect them to treat us like their own children. They're not. But we are still kids. I'd say to them, 'you've got kids. You treat them with love but you don't need to love us. All you need to do is treat us like humans'.

While the middle-ability, working-class boys are the most vocal and vociferous group in their opposition to official pedagogic discourses, the working-class girls' sense of alienation is just as raw and tangible. A potent sense of unfairness and unequal treatment infuses their attitudes to both seating and levels of teacher attention:

> Jenna: Yeah, our English teacher. He likes the three clever girls a lot because they are always answering questions. He never gives other people a chance to say——
> Sarah: If we put our hands up and we want to answer the question, the cleverest person, he will ask them, and we all know it's the right answer. And then he starts shouting at us saying that we are not answering.
> Alex: Yeah, and like, with them lot as well, if they ask to sit next to their friends they get to sit next to their friends.
> Sharmaine: And we're split up and made to sit with boys.
> Sarah: Yeah, but it's just them three particular girls, they get to always sit where they want to sit.

And

> Sharmaine: Sometimes we feel left out.
> Sarah: Because you know, teachers are not meant to have favourites.
> Sharmaine: You can have, but you can't show it, you know. That's unfair to the other people.
> Sarah: Because there's a whole class there and you want to pick that particular person, and you are nice to that one, and the rest you don't care about.
> Alex: But everyone has to be the same.
> Sharmaine: He needs to treat everyone equal.

But not all the female students felt overlooked and left out. Some middle-class girls took up powerful positions within the classroom context. Below we glimpse the arrogance of a group of white, middle-class girls and their contempt for their perceived lower-achieving, working-class peers:

> Emma: We aren't treated fairly by the teachers.
> Fran: No, because they sit us next to people who are stupid so that we can help them but it doesn't help us.
> Jasmine: They do it for their benefit not our benefit.
> Emma: And if they are going to waste like half our time that we could be learning, helping someone else, then we are just like, we might as well be the teacher then and not do anything.
> Katherine: We're not learning' cos we're helping other kids.
> Fran: And it's annoying having to help other people.
> Emma: Why should we help the dumb kids?

And:

> Megan: They should teach everyone like tell the whole class what they are doing and then
>   put us on a group table with some of the boys that are clever and then just come
>   over to us and tell us something else because we know that's easy.
> Emma: Like in primary school they put you in groups of cleverness.
> Megan: The red group, blue group, orange group or whatever. And each group would be
>   the cleverer one, the next cleverest and then the people who find it more difficult.
>   And that would be so much better.

When I asked the girls to select who would go into the top group, they chose themselves and the only four middle-class boys in the class. However, both SATS (Standard Attainment Tests) and test results from the end of the children's first year in secondary school showed that there were three working-class children, one girl and two boys, who had achieved more highly than a number of the middle-class students. However, these three had been summarily relegated to the middle group by these girls, who felt entitled to articulate their views on classroom organization and pedagogy, not only to me as a visiting researcher, but to their teacher.

In contrast to the middle-class students, both male and female, who for the most part felt valued and listened to within schooling, working-class boys and girls make explicit both their sense of not being heard and feelings of exclusion. The class tutor spells out an historical transition in which it becomes evident just how far Mandela has been forced by external policy changes to move from a position committed to equality and equal rights. In doing so, he spells out not only the consequences for teaching but also the consequences for a majority of the working-class students', both boys and girls, feelings of self-worth:

> I think teachers are becoming more and more aware that everything seems to follow
> on from testing, as it were, it seems to dictate so much of what we're doing and that
> wasn't the case when I first came here. There does seem a real preoccupation amongst
> senior managers in school, with raising achievement, which seems to me to be basically
> league tables, that we need 5 A–C from a higher percentage of children. And that is their
> definition of raising achievement, it seems. And now virtually everything in school seems
> to be secondary to that. So we spend a lot of time target setting and things which I think
> a lot of staff would say are of dubious value. It just isn't the way we've worked in the
> past, and it results in a lot of kids in my class, especially the ones who find the work
> difficult, feeling really exposed.

Explicit in this statement is the way in which the new regimes of testing and stan-dards operate as strategies of deficit and blame, exposing the learner to scrutiny and constant surveillance. Bernstein (1971) asserts that socialization within schooling can be 'deeply wounding' for working-class children, and below we catch sight of these 'wounds' and some students' strategies for dealing with them:

> I think Year 8 is a crucial year because that's when a lot of students come to a realisation
> about their learning identities. I think it's at that stage a lot of them tend to think that just
> trying hard isn't going to make me do well. And then they start to engage in all these other
> sort of strategies in order to maintain self-worth. That's suddenly why the peer group
> becomes so important, but at the same time it starts to sanction people more who appear

to try. Because when students realize that trying hard isn't going to make them do well some of them want to withdraw their effort and create a social situation where the cool thing to do is not to work and put all their efforts into that. (Year 8 tutor)

These narratives configure contradictory, opposing accounts in which working-class boys blame the girls for monopolizing positive teacher time and attention in the classroom, and both working-class boys and girls feel, to differing degrees, educationally excluded. The middle-class boys feel the most at home within official schooling despite their low status in the peer group, while the middle-class girls are able to take up powerful positions in the classroom, yet retain a strong sense they are being treated unfairly. All these competing, fractious, gendered class practices are taking place in a predominantly working-class classroom. In classrooms where the class balance is mainly middle class, I suggest that other, equally contradictory and confusing gendered class processes will be in play.

Gendered class processes are always fluid. They shift and change across different microlevel, local contexts, and can both compound and ameliorate each other. Yet, there remain troubling continuities. The workings of both class and gender continue to generate unacceptable inequalities in classroom positions vis-à-vis the teacher and peer group, and, as we can see in the students' accounts, a sense of belonging and recognition, despite dominant discursive claims of classlessness and the continuing concern with boys' underachievement, still appears to come most readily to middle-class boys.

CONCLUSION

Any understanding of gendered class relationships to education in the UK needs continually to keep in play the tensions between the intransigence of class – its refusal to fade away – and important transformations in gender relationships to education. The resounding educational success of girls spoken about in recent decades is primarily about middle-class girls, and it has set in motion a debate about a crisis of masculinity, not just in the UK but in many post-industrial societies (Kenway *et al.*, 1997; Walkerdine *et al.*, 2001; Weis, 2004). As Walkerdine *et al.* (2001) assert, classification operates in and through individuals, disrupting the smooth surface of discourses of classlessness. I have tried to illustrate some of the ways these *class*ificatory processes work by looking at the perceptions and positioning of both middle-and working-class students within schooling. According to these data, working-class girls, while not as alienated as working-class boys, feel similarly undervalued and overlooked. Furthermore, both the celebratory discourses of 'girl power' within education and the discursive laments about boys' underachievement need to be treated with caution. On a macrolevel, class differences between young women figure as largely as they did 30 years ago, while white, upper-middle-class boys are achieving just as highly as they ever did. On a microlevel, as seen through the lens of one secondary classroom, a sense of value and recognition in schooling remains both powerfully classed and gendered.

REFERENCES

Anthias, F (2001) The concept of 'social division' and theorising social stratification: looking at ethnicity and class. *Sociology*, 35: 835–54.

Arnot, M (1983) A cloud over coeducation: an analysis of the forms of transmission of class and gender relations, in Walker, S and Barton, L (eds) *Gender, class and education*. Basingstoke: Falmer Press.

Arnot, M David, M and Weiner, G (1999) *Closing the gender gap: postwar education and social change*. Cambridge: Polity Press.

Ball, SJ (2003) *Class strategies and the educational market: the middle classes and social advantage* London: RoutledgeFalmer.

Bernstein, B (1971) *Class, codes and control*. Vol I, *Theoretical studies toward a sociology of language*. London: Routledge and Kegan Paul.

Bernstein, B (1990) *The structuring of pedagogic discourse*. Vol IV, *Class, codes and control*. London: Routledge.

Bourdieu, P (1990) *The logic of practice*. Cambridge: Polity Press.

Connolly, P (2004) *Boys and schooling in the early years*. London: RoutledgeFalmer.

Epstein, D, Elwood, J, Hey, V and Maw, J (1998) *Failing boys? Issues in gender and achievement*. Buckingham: Open University Press.

Evans, J, Rich, E and Holroyd, R (2004) Disordered eating and disordered schooling: what schools do to middle class girls. *British Journal of Sociology of Education*, 25: 123–42.

Francis, B (2000) *Boys, girls and achievement: addressing the classroom issues*. London: RoutledgeFalmer.

Francis, B and Skelton, C (2005) *Reassessing gender and achievement*. London: Routledge.

Kenway, J, Willis, S, Blackmore, J and Rennie, L (1997) *Answering back: girls, boys and feminism in schools*. Sydney: Allen and Unwin.

Lees, S (1986) *Sugar and spice*. Harmondsworth: Penguin.

Lucey, H and Walkerdine, V (1999) Boys' underachievement: social class and changing masculinities, in Cox, T (ed) *Combating educational disadvantage* (37–52). London: Falmer.

Mahony, P and Zmroczek, C (1997) *Class matters*. London: Falmer Press.

Martin, J (2000) Gender, education and the new millennium, in Cole M (ed), *Education: equality and human rights*. London: RoutledgeFalmer.

Miller, J (1992) *More has meant women: the feminisation of schooling*. London: Tufnell Park Press with the Institute of Education.

Plummer, G (2000) *The failing working-class girl*. Stoke-on-Trent: Trentham Books.

Power, S, Edwards, T, Whitty, G and Wigfall, V (2003) *Education and the middle class*. Buckingham: Open University Press.

Reay, D, David, M and Ball, SJ (2005) *Degrees of choice: social class, race and gender in higher education*. Stoke-on-Trent: Trentham Books.

Savage, M, Bagnall, G and Longhurst, B (2001) Ordinary, ambivalent and defensive: class identities in the Northwest of England. *Sociology*, 35: 875–92.

Schostak, J (2000) Developing under-developing circumstances: the personal and social development of students and the process of schooling, in Altrichter, H and Elliott, J (eds) *Images of educational change* (37–52). Buckingham: Open University Press.

Skeggs, B (1997) *Formations of class and gender*. London: Sage.

Skelton, C (2001) *Schooling the boys*. Buckingham: Open University Press.

Spender, D (1982) *Invisible women: the schooling scandal*. London: Writers and Readers.

Tawney, RH (1931) *Equality*. London: Allen and Unwin.

Thompson, J (2000) *Women, class and education*. London: Routledge.

Tomlinson, S (2001) *Education in a post-welfare society*. Buckingham: Open University Press.

Walkerdine, V (1989) *Counting girls out*. London: Virago.

Walkerdine, V, Lucey, H and Melody, J (2000) Class, attainment and sexuality in late twentieth-century Britain, in Zmroczek, C and Mahony, P (eds) *Women and social class: international feminist perspectives* (51–68). London: UCL Press.

Walkerdine, V, Lucey, H and Melody, J (2001) *Growing up girl: gender and class in the twenty-first century*. London: Macmillan.

Weis, L (2004) *Class reunion: the remaking of the American white working class*. London: Routledge.

Willis, P (1977) *Learning to lose: how working class kids get working class jobs*. Farnborough: Saxon House.

25

The 'Right' Way to Educate Boys: Interrogating the Politics of Boys' Education in Australia

Wayne Martino

INTRODUCTION

The resurgence of the New Right has emerged in the form of a *moral panic* with regard to designating boys as the new disadvantaged in Australia, North America and the UK (see Epstein *et al.*, 1998; Foster *et al.*, 2001; Mahony; 2003; Mills, 2003; Martino and Berrill, 2003; Weaver-Hightower, 2005). While this chapter focuses specifically on manifestations of this phenomenon in the Australian context, it is important to foreground the extent to which such a recuperative masculinity politics (Lingard and Douglas, 1999) has fuelled the boys' education debates in other countries (Mahony, 1997; Titus, 2004). In fact, many of the key issues are similar in relation to addressing boys' underachievement in schools and revolve around advocating the need to counteract the feminization of boys and schooling through implementing a boy-friendly curriculum, introducing single-sex classes for boys and increasing the number of male teachers, particularly in elementary schools (see Martino, 2004; Martino *et al.*, 2004, 2005, Martino and Kelher, in press). The deployment of such strategies has often resulted in reinstating essentialized notions of masculinity and, hence, is grounded in a negation of the very significant ways in which hierarchical power relations affect the lives of boys and girls in schools (Frank, 1993; Archer and Yamashita, 2003; Kehler, 2004; Martino and Pallotta-Chiarolli, 2005).

Arnot and Miles (2005), for instance, illuminate how such a policy shift in the UK, driven by New Labour's educational and economic policy involving a focus on performativity in relation to boys' underachievement, has led to a (re)masculinization of schooling that has 'ignored the impact of the production of hierarchical masculinities and laddishness' (p173). In addition, they argue that such rightist agendas have masked the exclusion and disadvantages that continue to affect working-class girls in schools and, more broadly, I would argue, the influence of hierarchical power relations negotiated by girls around body image, appearance and differential cultural capital involving the performativity of femininities (Reay, 2001; Martino and Pallotta-Chiraolli, 2005). Similarly, in the USA, Titus (2004) documents the media-driven moral panic surrounding underachieving boys, which collapses into reasserting a form of biological essentialism as an explanatory framework that denies the intersectionality of race, social class and gender in young people's lives at school (see also Kumahsiro, 2002; Weaver-Hightower, 2005). There is further evidence in the research literature that such a rhetorical framing of boys' underachievement is also emerging in the Canadian context, where boys' failure is being linked to the increasing feminization of schooling and, hence, to the lack of male role models in elementary schools (see Kehler and Greig, 2005; Martino and Kehler, 2006). Recent developments in Australia highlight how the intensification of such issues, within the discursive limits of such rhetorical framing of the underachieving boy, has led to policy, government-funded research and educational initiatives that continue to essentialize and naturalize boys' masculinities. As will be demonstrated in this chapter, this has been supported by a neo-liberal and neo-conservative political agenda that has actively silenced and denied research literature and theoretical frameworks that draw on the social construction of gender (see also Gaskell and Taylor, 2003).

RECUPERATIVE MASCULINITY POLITICS IN THE AUSTRALIAN CONTEXT

The politics of boys' education in Australia has been and continues to be influenced by rightest beliefs, theories and proposals that support common sense and essentialist understandings of gender (Buckingham, 2005; see also Apple, 2001, for a detailed explication of conservative reform agendas). Within such a neo-liberal and neo-conservative context, certain government reports on boys' education set the terms of reference for recasting a gender-equity policy framework in which boys are ascribed a disadvantaged status (see Martino and Berrill, 2003, for a further critique of such a new Right agenda). They are often constituted in terms that resort to invoking a *naturalised* masculinity which needs to be restored and celebrated. Thus, such reports function as a powerful means for determining what is to count as official knowledge about boys and best practice for educating boys (see DEST, 2003). In this sense, the aim of this chapter to is draw attention to the discursive limits of these reports and the reception regimes they impose in terms of constituting both boys as particular sorts of normalized, gendered subjects and a reform agenda in schools that is committed to sustaining and reproducing rather than interrogating gender binaries and hierarchies (see Davies, 1993; Connell, 1995; Martino and Pallotta-Chiarolli, 2003; 2005). This analytic focus and critique is consistent with that advocated by Apple (2001), who argues that it is necessary to identify and to interrogate the 'conservative social movements that are having a powerful impact on debates over policy and practice in education and in the larger social arena' (p59) (see also Maddox, 2005).

Background

The Australian government has already spent millions of dollars on a parliamentary inquiry into boys' education (House of Representatives Standing Committee, 2002), which has been used to justify a further four million dollars to fund specific educational initiatives and programs for boys in schools. Stage one of this project, known as the Boys' Education Lighthouse Program, has been completed, and stage two is still in progress. Under this program, the Howard government has provided specific grants to individual schools to document successful practice in educating boys. In addition, the Australian government has recently announced that it will be committing a further 19.4 million dollars to what it terms a Success for Boys initiative, which will build on the Boys' Education Lighthouse Program. Significantly, it claims that this program has been 'successful', although the research has not been completed and, schools are yet to provide any evidence-based reports on or evaluation of 'best-practice' educational programs for boys (DEST, 2005). What has been released is a report on stage one of the Boys' Lighthouse Project, entitled, *Meeting the Challenge*.

In this chapter, I provide an analysis of the rightist agenda informing the guiding principles that are articulated in this report as determining the foundation for developing successful programs for addressing the educational and social needs of boys. Furthermore, I map the extent to which the discursive limits for framing success in boys' education, within the context of this report, are delimited by the terms and frames of reference established by the report on the parliamentary inquiry into the education of boys, *Boys: Getting it Right*. This latter report, it is argued, functions as a regime of truth for authorizing and legitimating certain knowledge claims about boys and their learning/social needs.

It is in this sense that the parliamentary inquiry report functions as an exemplary instance of recuperative masculinity politics (Lingard and Douglas, 1999) committed to setting the limits for constituting boys as particular sorts of gendered subjects. This needs to be understood in terms which resort to inscribing boys as essentially and innately different from girls in their approach to learning and relating to others. The effect of this, I argue, is to sustain a gender system, committed to a binary construction of masculinity and femininity as identity categories, that leaves unexamined the operations of masculine power. On the basis of these innate gender differences, certain pedagogical and curricular reforms are advocated, which involve adopting 'boy-friendly' strategies such as single-sex classes for boys, hands-on learning and male role models. In so doing, certain research-based literature about boys, schooling and masculinities, which calls into question the very legitimacy of such educational programs for boys or which authorizes knowledge about the social construction of masculinities and their deleterious effects is denied or refused (see Walker, 1988; Frank, 1993; Mac an Ghaill, 1994; Salisbury and Jackson, 1996; Epstein, 1997; Epstein *et al.*, 1998; Gilbert and Gilbert, 1998; Francis, 1999; Martino, 1999, 2000; Plummer, 1999; Mills, 2000; Skelton, 2000, 2001; Lingard *et al.*, 2002; Martino and Meyenn, 2002).

Boys: getting it right

The parliamentary inquiry into boys' education, as its title suggests, needs to be read carefully in terms of the 'truth claims' it purports to establish and the knowledge it authorizes about how best to address the educational needs of boys in schools. The aim of the inquiry, as stated in the executive summary of the report, was to 'evaluate evidence of boys' educational under-achievement and disengagement from learning, as well as strategies being used to address these issues' (pxv). Its claims and recommendations are produced in response to drawing selectively on evidence in the form of 231 written submissions and 235 witnesses who appeared before the committee. However, only certain submissions are cited to support the ideological standpoint on boys' education that has already gained currency in the popular media (see Buckingham, 2005), which represents boys as the 'new disadvantaged' whose educational and social needs are not being met in schools. As will be demonstrated, this is supposedly related to the fact that schools are apparently feminized domains that are not particularly 'boy-friendly' (see Lingard and Douglas, 1999; Lingard, 2003; Martino and Kehler, in press, 2005, for a critique of such backlash rhetoric).

The report draws on discourses of affirmative action in its rhetorical framing of the problems that boys are experiencing in schools (see Titus, 2004). For example, it states that the 'assumption in recent decades appears to have been that girls have urgent educational needs to be addressed and that boys will be all right' (pxvi). There is a sense conveyed throughout the report that a decided attempt has been made to deny the reality of boys' educational and social disadvantage in schools. Hence, the aim is to set the record straight and to provide evidence for many of the concerns about boys' education', which it claims are not being 'adequately addressed' within the current gender-equity framework policy document:

> Girls' education strategies and programs have, as a by-product of their original purpose, assisted girls through the social and economic changes of the last 20 years. In comparison, over this period, little was done to help boys understand and negotiate the same changes.

> The current gender equity framework is partly a continuation of the earlier approaches to
> address girls' needs. As such, it does not separately research and identify boys' needs, and
> at times it is couched in negative terms, even setting boys' needs in the context of what still
> needs to be achieved for girls. (pxviii)

The logic governing the report's direction from the outset is captured here – the
need for a 'new' gender-equity policy to outline a separate boys' education strategy. It states that while many teachers who contributed to the inquiry appear
eager to address boys' education as a part of their overall commitment to
improve the quality of schooling for all students, this does not appear to be the
case at the official institutional level of education departments and unions:

> It is difficult to avoid the impression that some gender equity units in education departments
> and education unions, generally, have been reluctant to openly confront boys' under-
> achievement and disengagement as an issue, perhaps for fear of undermining ongoing sup-
> port for strategies for girls. (p61)

In addition, while acknowledging that opinion among academics is divided, some
supporting the current gender-equity framework and others seeing it as
'too narrowly based on the issues that drove reform for girls [which] does not
adequately address boys' needs', the report is adamant in its rejection of the framework (p61). For example, it claims that it does not entail 'a fundamental re-
examination of the gender equity strategy intended to tackle boys' education issues
from the ground up as happened for girls' (p63). In short, it argues that the gender-
equity framework does not 'separately research and identify boys' needs' and that
'it sets boys' needs solely in the context of what still needs to be achieved for girls'
(p64). Earlier attempts to address boys' education from within such a gender-
equity framework are constituted as limited, problematic and, moreover, 'dangerous' in that' (1) they involve applying uncritically gender-equity principles
underpinning girls' education to boys' education and (2) they are based on the
desire to 'fix boys up' (p65). Thus, the logic informing the report's rejection and
critique of the framework is founded on the proposition that 'the factors limiting
boys' education achievement do not exactly parallel those that affect girls' (p65).
And yet there are some significant 'family resemblances' when considering the
ways in which social expectations around what constitutes acceptable behaviour
and 'normal' masculinity for boys affect both their educational and social outcomes in terms of participation in the broader culture and the kinds of skilling,
capacity building and training that they invest in (see Nayak and Kehily, 1996;
Gilbert and Gilbert, 1998; Davison, 2000; Francis, 2000; Martino and Pallotta-
Chiarolli, 2003, 2005; Nayak, 2003; Renold, 2003).

Advocating affirmative action for boys

The parliamentary inquiry report reiterates explicitly in Section 3.52 that a
great deal has been achieved for girls while boys' educational issues have not
been adequately addressed (p67). It claims that more girls than boys are now

participating in senior secondary schooling, but does add that 'the greatest gains for girls have been reaped by girls from higher socio-economic backgrounds', and that some problems related to lower wage-earning capacity, access to technical training, subject choice and the persistence of traditional employment trends for women are still important issues to address (see Collins *et al.,* 2000): 'Clearly the work to achieve full equality of opportunity and access in education and employment for girls is not completed' (p67). Here the report adopts a social justice approach consistent with the formulation of profeminist, equity principles in an attempt to reconcile competing new Right agendas driving the education of boys. These latter agendas position boys as the 'new disadvantaged', while profeminist approaches argue for a relational focus on gender construction, as well as the need to determine which boys and which girls are most disadvantaged (see Teese *et al.,* 1995). In attempting to resolve such tensions, however, the report refuses to acknowledge, and, in fact, rejects, the significance of gender construction in relation to boys' experiences of schooling.

This emerges explicitly in the report's critique of the Australian Education Union's position on the need to address the issue of the social construction of gender as it relates to the issue of quality teaching:

> The Australian Education Union argued that excellent teaching style 'is not dictated by gender' but a range of attitudes and abilities including an 'understanding of gender construction and its impact on students and teachers'. The Union also argued that effective male teachers 'need to understand the construction of gender and motivations for violence, and be trained in ways to intervene to deal with inappropriate behaviour. Even if this is true it places too much emphasis on gender theory and too little on the importance of the relationship between teacher and the student which is the foundation of good teaching. (p160)

This quotation highlights the inquiry's denigration of and refusal to acknowledge the impact and effects of the social construction of gender, which is not addressed in the report, despite the increasing evidence to support the very significant ways in which the social construction of gender significantly affects curriculum, pedagogical practices and relations with and between students in schools (see Gilbert and Gilbert, 1998; Mills, 2000; Lingard *et al.,* 2002; Martino and Pallotta-Chiarolli, 2003). Rather, gender theorizing is framed as detracting from a necessary focus on the significance of developing positive student–teacher relationships that help to enhance effective learning for boys. This needs to be understood within the broader political context of the report's advocacy of more male role models, which is informed by a certain degree of social conservatism and rightist appropriations of the family (see Maddox, 2005). For example, while the report acknowledges the need for a more sophisticated concept of disadvantage and that single-parent families cannot be held responsible for underachievement, it also acknowledges concerns about the *absent father* as a result of single parenthood or work commitments. This view that father absence is detrimental to boys is acknowledged as not being 'thoroughly researched' but 'generally accepted', anecdotal evidence from consultants and a principal being cited to support such a position.

These attempts to resolve these tensions and competing political agendas surface again in Section 3.53 of the report, which argues for the need to address 'a range of social indicators in addition to employment and education indicators', as is consistent with a profeminist approach that argues for 'a which boys and which girls?' approach (see Lingard *et al.*, 2002). These indicators are identified as rates of attempted and completed suicide and self-harm, drug and alcohol abuse, rates of imprisonment, involvement in petty and violent crime, rates of imprisonment and homelessness, which, it claims, 'tend to have distinct gender patterns'. On this basis, the report states that this would necessitate gender-specific strategies, but fails or rather refuses to acknowledge the crucial significance of the social construction of masculinity as an important threshold knowledge base for understanding the significance of these gendered trends. Instead, it draws on a discourse of affirmative action for boys in its support for a boys' education strategy on the basis that former gender-equity policies have not taken into consideration the distinctive educational and social needs of boys in schools.

A boys' education strategy

The report advocates a specific boys' education strategy because 'many submissions and witnesses have attested that boys respond to structure and clearly articulated purposes in learning and to easily understood methods of assessment' (p67). Such a strategy will involve stating explicitly and in positive terms, it is implied, how boys' best learn and how these principles and expectations can be best articulated and measured 'in terms of what [boys] know, what their physical and interpersonal skills are and where they end up after school' (p67). In support of this boys' education agenda, it quotes The Adelaide Declaration of the National Goals for Schooling in the Twenty-First Century to argue for the need to address active citizenship for all students and specifically boys. This is organized around the following norms quoted directly from the above declaration document:

> 1.2 Building self esteem and self-confidence etc
> 1.3 Exercising moral and ethic judgment; developing self-reflexive capacities designed to empower individuals to make sense of their world and 'to think about how things came to be the way they are, to make rational and informed decisions about their own lives, to accept responsibility for their own actions';
> 1.4 Active and informed citizenship (p68)

In light of national and international research literature on boys, masculinities and schooling – undertaken from a critical sociological and profeminist standpoint (Mac an Ghaill, 1994, 2000; Epstein *et al.*, 1998; Gilbert and Gilbert,1998; Francis, 2000; Lesko, 2000; Martino and Meyenn, 2001; Mills, 2001; Skelton, 2001; Martino and Pallotta-Chiarolli, 2003, 2005) – addressing all the above would need to involve helping boys to interrogate the social construction of masculinities in terms of how these limit and constrain boys in developing a broader repertoire of skills and capacities often considered to be the domain of the feminine and, hence, denigrated on this basis.

In short, the report compels the reader to link reticence on teaching and promoting civic and human values to the failure to address explicitly or to develop a boys' education strategy. This avoidance is then couched in terms which construct it as a human rights issue and, hence, a fundamental violation of foundational equity principles. This is the platform from which the report launches its claim of the need for the current gender-equity framework policy document to be 'recast as an overarching framework for parallel boys' and girls, education strategies'. This requires, it argues, a *recasting* of objectives in positive terms and would be in opposition, it claims, to the 'negative approach for boys implied in most of the current policy material – for example about boys not being violent, not monopolising space and equipment and not harassing girls and other boys' (p68). Thus, it is possible to understand such claims as a reactionary response to a profeminist policy document that articulates and makes explicit the uses of power and how it is gendered in terms of regimes of harassment and hierarchical social relations between boys and girls and among boys and girls (Martino and Pallotta-Chiarolli, 2005).

Rejecting 'a which boys and which girls?' approach

The report is adamant in its articulation of boys as the 'new disadvantaged'. In stating its case, it argues that boys are at risk in terms of early literacy performance, measures of attainment at Years 10 and 12, retention rates and post-school employment. While it is acknowledged that evidence has revealed 'a mixed picture of under-achievement which is influenced by characteristics such as the quality of teaching, curriculum, resources, gender, socio-economic status, racial and ethic background and location, many of which are inter-related', the report does not advocate a 'which boys and which girls?' approach to addressing gender equity in schools (p5). On the contrary, it tends to ignore evidence which foregrounds that not all boys are necessarily doing badly at school and likewise that not all girls are doing well (see Horin, 2002). In fact, it casts a 'which boys and which girls?' approach to gender-equity policy formulation as 'resistance to addressing boys' education issues' (pxvii). Such a 'gender jigsaw' approach is presented as denying the need to develop specific policies and programs that focus on the particular and distinctive educational needs of boys. In this sense, 'getting it right' within the context of the discursive limits imposed by the parliamentary inquiry report translates into devoting more attention to developing quality teacher relationships with boys and implementing a curriculum that is interesting and relevant to them:

> Of course having a relevant and interesting curriculum that is taught well is just as important for girls as it is for boys. However boys are more likely than girls to respond to dull subject matter or uninspiring teaching in an overt and challenging way that will disrupt their own and other's learning. (p72).

While acknowledging that 'a relevant and interesting curriculum' is equally important for girls, the report is insistent that there are fundamental or innate differences between boys' and girls' approaches to learning that necessitate quite a different approach to addressing the educational and social needs of boys. On this basis, the report advocates the need for curriculum content and delivery to be varied to suit the needs of students, but more specifically to 'suit particular groups of boys and girls' (p75). In addition, while stating that some boys will prefer learning styles preferred by most girls, and vice versa, it argues that there are definite orientations to learning which are the specific domain of boys as opposed to girls. Verbal, linguistic and interpersonal skills are deemed to be those usually developed and preferred by girls, while mathematical logic, spatial intelligence, kinaesthetic or physical learning, and naturalistic learning (activities related to the natural environment and tasks using sorting and classifying) are identified as being preferred by boys. A conference paper presented at the Teaching Boys, Developing Fine Men conference in 2000 is cited as supporting evidence for such claims.

Thus, within the discursive limits imposed by this report, 'effective schools' and 'good teachers' cater for and address boys' and girls' distinctive learning styles. However, the report states that both primary and secondary schools tend to favour 'passive learning' and, hence, do 'not cater well enough for those students who prefer interactive and experiential learning styles' (p79). The implication is that schools need to be more *boy-friendly* and to embrace a boys' education strategy that is committed to the realization of essentialized gender differences (see Martino *et al.*, 2004, for a critique of *boy-friendly* approaches). In short, this characterizes the ideological standpoint and rightist agenda driving the logic of boys' education, as it is inscribed within the discursive limits marked out by the parliamentary inquiry report.

Meeting the Challenge

The aim of the report entitled *Meeting the Challenge* is to document 'best practice' in schools for boys or rather to outline the 'guiding principles for success' from the Boys' Lighthouse Schools Program for stage one. A total of 110 projects involving 230 schools received funding to support the implementation of targeted boys' education programs. These programs involved a focus on one of the following:

- adapting pedagogy, curriculum and assessment to cater for boys' distinctive learning styles;
- improving literacy and communication skills for boys across the curriculum;
- addressing student engagement and motivation for at-risk boys in the mainstream classroom;
- developing effective behaviour management programs.

While it is not possible to comment on all programs implemented across the above designated categories, what does emerge in the report are certain recurrent themes and claims that are contained within unproblematized frames of reference for addressing the educational needs of boys in schools. In short, an analysis of *Meeting the Challenge*, which is concerned to report on current best practice in schools for boys, highlights the extent to which its claims have already been marked out by the limits set by the parliamentary inquiry in its capacity to authorize a certain knowledge about boys' education and an explanatory framework for making sense of what is needed to address their educational and social needs in schools. This is achieved primarily through a denial and active refutation of a body of knowledge and theorizing about the social construction of gender.

In many schools taking part in this project, the predominant focus appeared to be on catering for boys' distinctive learning styles through an emphasis on developing an activities-based or hands-on approach to curriculum development and pedagogical reform. This also entailed finding ways to provide boys with more male role models in school.

Catering for boys' different learning styles

One of the guiding principles for improving learning and educational outcomes for boys revolved around a core proposition about catering for their distinctive learning styles. This was often understood in terms of developing boys' education programs that adopt a pedagogical reform agenda with 'a practical focus and physical hands-on dimension' in addition to providing clear instructions and 'structured sessions in manageable chunks' (p137). What becomes immediately apparent in the report is that such pedagogical interventions and programs do not appear to be addressing or at least requiring boys to develop a deeper understanding about the impact and effects of hegemonic masculinities in their lives (Connell, 1995). In fact, such interventions risk reinscribing dominant masculinity through their failure to interrogate the gendered dimensions of power and how it is exercised by boys in their lives. But this would constitute, within the frames of reference delimited by the inquiry report, an approach that is 'couched in negative terms' (see House of Representatives Standing Committee, 2002). While *Meeting the Challenge* does stipulate the need to challenge stereotypical views of masculinity as one of the guiding principles for developing boys' education programs, this does not appear to be the approach emphasized or undertaken by many schools taking part in the Boys' Lighthouse Programe, which seem to be more intent on embracing an activities- based curriculum or approach to enhancing boys' self-esteem/engagement in learning.

Under the umbrella of pedagogy, curriculum and assessment, the report foregrounds the extent to which many schools are committed to developing a pedagogy which 'better matches the needs of boys' (p23). In one school, a dance program was also delivered to boys in single-sex classes to 'avoid embarrassment among some boys'. It is not surprising that a boy-friendly curriculum would necessitate or entail embracing single-sex classes, given the sort of assumptions underlying such boys' education programs (see Martino and Meyenn, 2002). What is unacknowledged are the hierarchical power relationships among boys and the nature of surveillance and enforced normalization enacted between and within particular groups of boys (Mac an Ghaill, 1994; Martino and Pallotta-Chiarolli, 2003).

Key features of programs such as the one developed by Richard Fletcher (a boys' education consultant and men's health consultant based at Newcastle University), which are informed by discourses of difference and inclusivity, are identified and designated in the report as significant guiding principles for developing and implementing educational and social welfare programs for boys. These amount quintessentially to incorporating 'boy-friendly aspects' into the curriculum and include primarily (p49):

1. *acknowledg[ing] and respond[ing] flexibly to different learning styles, including, where appropriate single sex groups;*
2. *includ[ing] more hands-on and physical activities in* class (p48);
3. providing *more practical, visual and tactile activities that emphasize physical movement and interaction to engage boys in learning* (p56).

These principles are based on the belief that 'boys learn by doing' and are more kinaesthetic in their learning styles (p51). *Meeting the Challenge* illustrates the extent to which such guiding principles underscore the rationale for developing and implementing programs in a great number of the Lighthouse schools to address the educational needs of boys. In this way, they have 'sought to link curriculum with physical activities' as a means by which to accommodate boys' learning styles. This focus on hands-on activities is endorsed by the report and framed as 'a way of learning that is authentic and engaging, and closely related to boys' values and lives' (p56).

This approach was also embraced by a number of schools who were concerned to address boys' literacy development:

> Starting from the premise that boys' literacy development is at risk, schools ... sought to create a more a more effective learning environment for boys that would engage them through hands-on activities that are practical, challenging, interesting, authentic, based on real life tasks, and that encourage safe risk-taking and use boys' resources of energy and humour. (p55)

This constitutes another exemplary instance of the essentializing and normalizing tendencies underscoring the grid of intellgibility that frame the limits for addressing the educational needs of boys.

CONCLUSION

The aim of this chapter has been to offer a critique of the limits imposed by the parliamentary inquiry report into boys' education in the Australian context. This has been significant in authorizing a certain body of knowledge and legitimating particular truth claims about the nature of how boys learn and how best to address their educational needs. While such a report needs to be understood as an attempt to settle competing interests within the context of a media-driven 'moral panic' about failing boys (Epstein, 1998; Lingard, 2003), it has been illustrated that it employs rhetorical strategies and selective *evidence* to support a particular politics founded on neo-liberal and social conservative principles which translate into inscribing boys as essentialized subjects who are predisposed to adopting particular orientations to learning. Thus, the purpose of this chapter has been to illustrate the extent to which the 'right' way to educate boys entails implementing programs and pedagogical interventions that accommodate boys' active, physical and hands-on approach to learning. It has been argued here that this constitutes the discursive limits for imposing an explanatory framework and grid of intelligibility for understanding how best to address the educational needs of boys which is grounded on a rejection of a specific form of gender theorizing informed by a threshold knowledge about the social construction of masculinities.

Meeting the Challenge, a report on a project funded by the Australian government to support the implementation of boys' education programs in schools, has also been used to demonstrate the extent to which such gender reform initiatives in school have been influenced by the terms of reference and political agenda established by the parliamentary inquiry report and its recommendations. The unfolding of this neo-liberal and neo-conservative political agenda in the Australian context has had and continues to have far-reaching consequences in terms of authorizing and legitimating a particular knowledge about how best to educate boys and to cater for their educational needs. It has been demonstrated in this chapter that this knowledge is constituted and locked within discursive regimes which perpetuate binary oppositional gender frameworks for understanding and addressing the educational needs of boys and girls in schools. Further research-based evidence about the effect of educational programs funded by the Australian government is needed with particular attention to those groups of boys and girls who are most disadvantaged and marginalized in schools. What is required is a commitment to documenting what the students involved in such gender reform agendas have to say about the effectiveness of such programs and what they have learned as a result of their participation (see Kenway *et al.*, 1997; Martino and Pallotta-Chiarolli, 2005). Until student voice is included as a legitimate form of evaluation in assessing the effectiveness of boys' education programs, particular adult-centric constructions of, and knowledge about, boys will continue to be officially sanctioned and authorized with the capacity to impact detrimentally on gender-equity policy formulation in its capacity to delimit the grid of intelligibility for addressing the educational needs of boys and girls in schools. Documenting the perspectives of a range of young people in schools who are subject to the pedagogical reforms outlined in this chapter has the potential for interrupting and disrupting the rightist agendas that continue to infiltrate and drive policy formulation and practice in boys' education in the Australian context (Martino and Pallotta-Chiarolli, 2005).

REFERENCES

Apple, M (2001) *Educating the 'right' way: markets, standards, God and inequality.* New York: RoutledgeFalmer.

Archer, L and Yamashita, H (2003) Theorising inner-city masculinities: 'race', class, gender and education. *Gender and Education,* 15: 115–32.

Arnot, M and Miles, P (2005) A reconstruction of the gender agenda: the contradictory gender dimensions in New Labour's educational and economic policy. *Oxford Review of Education,* 31: 173–89.

Buckingham, J (2005) Gender divide in road of learning. *The Australian,* 5 April www.theaustralian. news.com.au/printpage/0,5942,12755712,00.html.

Collins, C, Kenway, J and McLeod, J (2000) *Factors influencing the educational performance of males and females in school and their initial destinations after leaving school.* Canberra: Australian Commonwealth Government.

Connell, B (1995) *Masculinities.* Sydney: Allen and Unwin.

Davies, B (1993) *Shards of glass: children reading and writing beyond gender identities.* Sydney: Allen and Unwin.

Davison, K (2000) Masculinities, sexualities and the student body: sorting gender identities in school, in James, C (ed) *Experiencing difference* (44–52). Halifax, Nova Scotia: Fernwood.

DEST (Department of Education, Science and Training) (2005) *Boys' education.* www.dest.gov.au/ schools/boyseducation/sfb.htm.

DEST (Department of Education, Science and Training) (2003) *Educating boys: issues and information.* Canberra: Australian Commonwealth Government.

Epstein, D (1997) Boyz' own stories: masculinities and sexualities in schools. *Gender and Education,* 9: 105–15.

Epstein, D, Elwood, J, Hey, V and Maw, J (eds) (1998) *Failing boys? Issues in gender and achievement.* Buckingham: Open University Press.

Foster, V, Kimmell, M and Skelton, C (2001) 'What about the boys?': an overview of the debates, in Martino, W and Meyenn, B (eds) *What about the boys? Issues of masculinity and schooling.* Buckingham: Open University Press.

Francis, B (2000) *Boys, girls and achievement: addressing the Classroom issues.* London: RoutledgeFalmer.

Frank, B (1993) Straight/strait jackets for masculinity: educating for real men. *Atlantis,* 18 (1 and 2): 47–59.

Gaskell, J and Taylor, S (2003) The women's movement in Canadian and Australian education: from liberation and sexism to boys and social justice. *Gender and Education* 15: 151–68.

Gilbert, R and Gilbert, P (1998) *Masculinity goes to school.* Sydney: Allen and Unwin.

Giroux, H (1997) *Pedagogy and the politics of hope: theory, culture and schooling.* Boulder, CO: Westview Press.

hooks, b (1994) *Teaching to transgress: education as the practice of freedom.* New York: Routledge.

Horin, A (2002) Out of school, choices still favour boys. *Sydney Morning Herald,* 26 Oct.

House of Representatives Standing Committee on Education and Training (2002) *Boys' education: getting it right.* Canberra: Australian Commonwealth Government.

Kehler, MD (2004) Masculinities and resistance: high school boys (un)doing boy. *Taboo,* 8: 97–113.

Kehler, MD and Greig, C (2005) Boys can read: exploring the socially literate practices of high school young men. *International Journal of Inclusive Education,* 9: 351–70.

Kenway, J, Willis, S, Blackmore, J and Rennie, L (1997) *Answering back: girls, boys and feminism in schools.* Sydney: Allen and Unwin.

Kumashiro, K (2002) *Troubling education: queer activism and antioppressive pedagogy.* New York: RoutledgeFalmer.

Lesko, N (2000) *Masculinities at school.* Thousand Oaks, CA: Sage.

Lingard, B (2003) Where to in gender theorising and policy after recuperative masculinity politics? *International Journal of Inclusive Education,* 7: 33–56.

Lingard, B and Douglas, P (1999) *Men engaging feminisms: profeminism, backlashes and schooling.* Buckingham: Open University Press.

Lingard, B, Martino, W, Mills, M and Bahr, M (2003) *Addressing the educational needs of boys.* Canberra: Department of Education, Science and Training.

Mac an Ghaill, M (1994) *The making of men.* Buckingham: Open University Press.

Mac an Ghaill, M (2000) Rethinking (male) gendered sexualities in education: what about the British heteros? *Journal of Men's Studies,* 8: 195–212.

Maddox, M (2005) *God under Howard: the rise of the religious right in Australian politics.* Sydney: Allen and Unwin.

Mahony, P (1997) The underachievement of boys in the UK: old tunes for new fiddles? *Social Alternatives,*16: 44–51.

Mahony, P (2003) Recapturing imaginations and the gender agenda; reflections on a progressive challenge from an English perspective. *International Journal of Inclusive Education,* 7: 57–73.

Martino, W (1999) 'Cool boys', 'party animals', 'squids' and 'poofters': interrogating the dynamics and politics of adolescent masculinities in school. *British Journal of the Sociology of Education,* 20: 239–63.

Martino, W (2000) Policing masculinities: investigating the role of homophobia and heteronormativity in the lives of adolescent school boys. *Journal of Men's Studies,* 8: 213–36.

Martino, W (2004) 'The boy problem': boys, schooling and masculinity, in Transit, R (ed) *Disciplining the child via the discourse of the professions.* Springfield, IL: Charles C Thomas.

Martino, W and Meyenn, B (eds) (2001) *What about the boys? Issues of masculinity and schooling.* Buckingham: Open University Press.

Martino, W and Meyenn, B (2002) 'War, guns and cool, tough things': interrogating single-sex classes as a strategy for engaging boys in English. *Cambridge Journal of Education,* 32: 303–24.

Martino, W and Berrill, D (2003) Boys, schooling and masculinities: interrogating the 'right' way to educate boys. *Education Review,* 55: 99–118.

Martino, W and Pallotta-Chiarolli, M (2003) *So what's a boy? Addressing issues of masculinity and schooling.* Maidenhead: Open University Press.

Martino, W and Kehler, M (2006) Male teachers and the 'boy problem': an issue of recuperative masculinity politics. *McGill Journal of Education,* 41(2): 1–19.

Martino, W and Pallotta-Ciarolli, M (2005) *'Being normal is the only thing to be': boys' and girls' perspectives on school.* Sydney: UNSW Press.

Martino, W, Mills, M and Lingard, B (2004) Issues in boys' education: a question of teacher threshold knowledge. *Gender and Education,* 16: 435–54.

Martino, W, Mills, M and Lingard, B (2005) Interrogating single-sex classes as a strategy for addressing boys' educational and social needs. *Oxford Review of Education,* 31: 237–54.

Mills, M (2001) *Challenging violence in schools: an issue of masculinities.* Buckingham: Open University Press.

Mills, M (2000) Issues in implementing boys' programmes in schools: male teachers and empowerment. *Gender and Education,* 2: 221–38.

Mills, M (2003) Shaping the boys' agenda: the backlash blockbusters. *International Journal of Inclusive Education,* 7: 57–73.

Nayak, A (2003) 'Boyz to men': masculinities, schooling and labour transitions in de-industrialised times, *Educational Review,* 55: 147–60.

Nayak, A and Kehily, M (1996) Playing it straight: masculinities, homophobias and schooling. *Journal of Gender Studies,* 5: 211–30.

Plummer, D (1999) *One of the boys: masculinity, homophobia, and modern manhood.* New York: Harrington Park Press.

Reay, D (2001) 'Spice girls', 'nice girls', 'girlies' and 'tomboys': gender discourses, girls' cultures and femininities in the primary classroom. *Gender and Education,* 13: 153–66.

Renold, E (2003) 'If you don't kiss me, you're dumped': boys, boyfriends and heterosexualised masculinities in the primary school. *Educational Review,* 55: 179–94.

Salisbury, J and Jackson, D (1996) *Challenging macho values: practical ways of working with adolescent boys*. London: Falmer Press.

Skelton, C (2000) 'A passion for football': dominant masculinities and primary schooling. *Sport, Education and Society*, 5: 5–18.

Skelton, C (2001) *Schooling the boys: masculinities and primary education*. Buckingham: Open University Press.

Teese, R, Davies, M, Charlton, M and Polesel, J (1997) *Who wins at school? Boys and girls in Australian secondary education*. Canberra; Department of Education, Employment and Training.

Titus, J (2004) Boy trouble: rhetorical framing of boys' underachievement. *Discourse*, 25: 145–69.

Walker, J (1988) *Louts and legends: male youth culture in an inner-city school*. Sydney: Allen and Unwin.

Weaver-Hightower, M (2005) Dare the school build a new education for boys? *Teachers' College Record*. www.tcrecord.org/content.asp?contentid = 11743 (accessed 14 Feb 2005).

26

Constructing Femininity/Constructing Femininities

Carrie Paechter

'Femininities' is a deeply contentious term, particularly in its application to males as well as females. Specifically in relation to the school context, it has been argued (Skelton and Francis, 2002; Paechter 2006) that we should acknowledge that girls can behave in masculine and boys in feminine ways, rather than pigeonholing children into one or other grouping and failing to recognize and name the behaviour we actually see. In this chapter, however, I will follow more traditional practice and focus on the femininities constructed and practised by girls in school. I will use 'femininities' as ways of 'doing girl' (West and Zimmerman, 1987), as the variety of forms of girlhood that are constructed and taken up in the context of the school. I will thus consider masculine girls as inhabiting and performing forms of (albeit oppositional) femininity, leaving feminine boys out of my discussion on the grounds that their ways of 'doing boy' are, for these purposes at least, feminine forms of masculinity.

I will consider femininities throughout the entire school age range, but I will not do this chronologically. The femininities constructed by groups of girls change as they get older, move between schools, and develop psychologically, physically and physiologically, but they are not strictly age-banded. Nor are there particular femininities that dominate all schools in all places at particular ages or stages. I will therefore explore some of the ways in which a variety of femininities are constructed through and against schooling, in order to focus on some of the mechanisms whereby girls construct themselves and each other in the context of their schooling.

I distinguish between two related constructions: 'femininity' and 'femininities'. In school and in their peer groups, girls both construct an ideal type of what it is to be a girl (femininity), and, at the same time, develop their understandings of who they themselves are in relation to that (their individual and group femininities). Both are relational concepts, but they are relational in different ways. Femininity, while not monolithic, is much more all-encompassing, allowing girls to make generalizations (girls are like *this*, not like *that*), while at the same time constructing their individual femininities more or less in alignment with or in opposition to these ideas.

Both femininity and femininities are constructed in local communities of femininity practice. Communities of femininity practice are localized communities constituted around shared practices of girlhood or womanhood, in which girls and young women learn and construct meanings concerning what it is to be female, and develop their understandings of and ability to 'do girl' through an apprentice-like relationship with more established members, such as older girls and adult women (Wenger, 1998; Paechter, 2003a,b). Children move, as they grow older, through successive and overlapping communities, as they gradually work out what it means to be an adult man or woman in that local context. In each community of practice, there are both central and peripheral members; the latter may owe their status to their trajectory through the group (they may be in the process of joining from a younger group or leaving for an older one) or to their positioning relative to the dominant conception of femininity in the group at a particular time. Local girl communities of femininity practice are thus engaged in a constant process of constructing femininity, in relation to which individual members in turn construct their individual femininities.

A major aspect of all communities of practice is a shared understanding of what it is to be a member of that community. This is what is being developed in the construction of femininity. Lave and Wenger note that apprentices learn, among other things, 'how masters talk, walk, work, and generally conduct their lives … and what they enjoy, dislike, respect, and admire' (Lave and Wenger, 1991: 95). In developing a common conception of femininity, these factors are of central importance. As different groups of girls dominate a school class community or constellation of communities of femininity practice, as circumstances change, the collective image of the ideal typical girl will change in subtle or not-so-subtle ways. There is evidence, however, that there are at least some commonalities in these ideal typifications, and it is these that I will now discuss.

COLLECTIVE UNDERSTANDINGS OF GIRLHOOD: CONSTRUCTING FEMININITY

Schoolgirls construct femininity collectively in relation to a range of outside forces, images and representations, and through negotiation with their peer groups about what is important to girlhood. Thorne (1993) notes that groups of boys and girls engage in 'borderwork', in which gender boundaries are evoked and reified, so that

> Other social definitions get squeezed out by heightened awareness of gender as a dichotomy and of 'the girls' and 'the boys' as opposite and even antagonistic sides. (p65)

In these situations, femininity is defined directly in contraposition to masculinity, as minor differences shift into oppositional categories. At the same time, as Kehily *et al.* (2002) note, girls use talk about friendship to construct themselves both as girls and as friends, policing group femininities by defining transgressors as different and subordinate, as Other.[1] They suggest that:

> The othering of [one of the group] in a moment of group solidarity indicates the power of the peer group to regulate sex-gender identities. In recounting what is reprehensible, the group implicitly construct what they regard as desirable and acceptable. Such acts of definition can be seen as the collective negotiation of a normative femininity. (Kehily *et al.*, 2002: 171)

These shifting and interrelated internal and external influences bring about a constantly changing, localized collective view about what 'doing girl' is all about; they construct an ideal typical girl who encapsulates the ideas around which girlhood coalesces for any particular group, and whose image serves to normalize and regulate the behavior of all girls within the local community of femininity practice (Adams and Bettis, 2003). The key aspect of this group construction of femininity is that it serves to draw what for children is a particularly salient boundary: that between girls and boys. It becomes essential to know what is (locally) fundamental to being a girl, because that allows a girl to understand and convey to others that she is not a boy.

This is not to say that all girls, or even all girls in any one setting, will construct the same ideal-type femininity. Communities of femininity practice are threaded through with power relations, so that some girls are more able to influence the hegemonic view of femininity in particular circumstances and particular locations. Subordinate femininities, while being constructed against this, also contribute to the overall understanding, either through their implicit or explicit exclusion or through their included subordination. In larger schools, there may be a number of competing definitions of the feminine which coexist in a constant struggle for dominance; in this case, each of these is constructed not just in opposition to notions of masculinity but also against the other conceptions of femininity, forcing tighter definitions of what is acceptable in each broad grouping (Hey, 1997).

In arguing that girls construct group versions of femininity, I am not suggesting that these are monolithic and all-embracing. There are some aspects of group femininity, however, that, in different ways and to different degrees, cross settings, class and ethnic boundaries (Ali, 2003) with the overarching effect of distinguishing girls from boys. One major gender construction that has been found in English classrooms is the silly/sensible dichotomy identified by Francis (1998; 2000). Her research suggests that primary age children construct the two genders as oppositional, with girls being seen as sensible and selfless, boys as silly and selfish:

> Of the feminine construction, maturity, obedience and neatness are the valued 'sensible' qualities, which naturally lead to 'selflessness' – giving and facilitating. The masculine construction involves 'silly' qualities of immaturity, messiness and naughtiness, leading to 'selfishness' – taking and demanding. (Francis, 1998: 40)

These dichotomous and oppositional constructions are not only prevalent in the ways boys and girls understand femininity and masculinity, but are also common to teachers and in wider society. Indeed, Walkerdine (1990) argues that the construction of the active, exploratory, learning child as male (Walkerdine, 1984) makes it difficult for girls to take up positions as active learners in the classroom; they have quasi-teacher roles, keeping the boys in check and modelling conformist behavior. Francis (2000) argues that as children grow older, this opposition metamorphoses into one between maturity and immaturity, with femininity constructed as mature, masculinity as immature, and that this is again related to the taking up of quasi-teacher positions by girls.

A more complex but related issue is the ways in which femininity is often constructed in relation to ideas of 'niceness'. Although what constitutes niceness varies between groups of girls, it seems to be a theme that runs through many accounts of schoolgirl femininities. Kehily *et al.* (2002) note that a central criterion of belonging for the predominantly South-East Asian 9-10-year-olds they studied was that a girl 'should be nice, even when scorned, be truthful and be consistently well behaved' (p171). Similarly, Hey (1997) suggests that the public suppression of disagreement was of fundamental importance to the white, middle- class, early teenage girls in her study; to be positioned as assertive and bossy could lead to one's exclusion from the group because, 'being disagreeable (bossy and thus openly assertive) was the exact antithesis of niceness' (p56), and, as is suggested of one girl, such behavior 'undermined her claims to be suitably "nice"' (p65). Walkerdine *et al.* (2001) argue that the salience of niceness has its origins in middle-class mothering practices, as part of a strategy in which power relations between mother and daughter are masked by appeals to a child's rationality and an illusion of autonomy on the part of the child, and aggression toward the mother is regulated and contained by being labelled as 'not nice'.

Such an emphasis on 'niceness', while both important in preparing middle-class girls for social and educational success and central to group ideas about femininity, comes at a price. Not only does it involve the suppression of disagreement, but it also requires a denial of difference, particularly that originating in the achievement of academic excellence. Renold and Allan (2004), for example, found that, to fit in with their peers, high-attaining girls had constantly to position themselves 'within conventional discourses of "lack", repeatedly (in interviews) denying, downplaying, hiding and silencing their successes and achievements in school' (p7).

In addition to the construction of a femininity that, for middle-class girls, at least, requires then the suppression of individual assertiveness, there is, as girls grow older, a gradually increasing construction of femininity as physically passive and, in particular, as uninvolved in team sports. This positioning of girls as inactive and non-sporty arises from the girls themselves, from their male peers, and, in some cases, from teachers, despite the active involvement of many girls in a number of sports (Nespor, 1997). At primary school, it is not so much that girls see themselves as lacking interest in sport, but that sports are claimed so strongly as a male domain that it is difficult for girls to participate fully; boys allow them to join in as equals only if they position themselves as non-feminine (Reay, 2001). Fitzclarence and Hickey, (2001), for example, suggest that football (Australian Rules in this case) is a major site for the making of masculinity; in the oppositional world of school constructions of masculinity and femininity, this means that football[2] and related sports can have no place in collective conceptions of femininity. Furthermore, Skelton (2001) notes that male teachers repeatedly use exclusive talk and banter about sports to exclude girls through an Othering process that positions them as unable to understand or participate in sporting discourses. In primary schooling, then, although some girls remain physically active, as they get older and children's physical activity is increasingly challenged into playing sports, participation is excluded from the feminine by the Othering pressure of community conceptions of the masculine, alongside a strong construction of masculinity and femininity as exclusive and dichotomous.

As girls grow older, however, the practice of femininity seems to conform more closely to its collective conception. During puberty, girls' active play declines, at least in the school context (O'Sullivan *et al.*, 2002). At the same time, some aspects of collective femininity are constructed directly in opposition to school physical education and sports (Vertinsky, 1992; Roberts, 1996; Williams and Bedward, 2002; van Essen, 2003), despite some girls continuing with physical activities outside school (Williams and Bedward, 2002). This means that, as girls get older, collective notions of femininity involve both physical passivity and an active resistance to participation in sports. The muscular body is seen as explicitly unfeminine, and thus avoided by many girls through resistance to physical education in multiple ways.

Femininity is also constructed in relation to other aspects of the curriculum, which are labelled as masculine by both boys and girls. This is particularly the case with mathematics and physical sciences, which are consequently avoided by many girls as soon as they become optional, with boys dominating groups at advanced level. This identification of some aspects of the curriculum as masculine limits the ways in which femininity can be constructed within schooling and, indeed, education more widely. It is partly that student perceptions of these subjects epitomize some things that are specifically rejected as part of the dominant schoolgirl femininities discussed above. For example, mathematics is constructed (and often experienced (Boaler, 1997)) as highly competitive, and success at it is generally obvious, so that doing well in this area compromises the requirement not to draw attention to one's attainment. This is compounded by its perception as a difficult subject (Mendick, 2006), so that girls who succeed at mathematics, simply through their success, single themselves out as different. Hatchell (1998) argues that girls feel particularly uncomfortable about being top of a male-dominated class, such as one in advanced mathematics or physical science. Mendick also notes that some young people tell stories about mathematicians as heroes and geniuses, set apart from the rest of humanity; this reflects popular constructions of the scientist as hero, which are taken up by male science and technology workers as key aspects of their masculinities (Massey, 1995), and, again, this makes it hard to construct a femininity that includes success in these areas. Seeing mathematicians as superheroes further reinforces the subject's perceived masculinity because of the perception of superhero activity in general as masculine. Browne (2004) argues that young children see superhero roles as almost exclusively male, and it is overwhelmingly boys who engage in superhero play.

A further feature of collective constructions of femininity, and one that is important throughout school, is compulsory heterosexuality. This starts partly as a reflection of what many girls experience in their own homes; most grow up in families headed by either heterosexual couples or single parents, and acting out these roles is part of their apprenticeship to wider, adult conceptions of femininity. Walkerdine (1990) argues that girls in nursery school use domestic play to take on the role of the dominant mother in the home, thereby subverting attempts by boys to gain power through other means. As girls get older, however, an overt heterosexuality becomes increasingly important to collective ideas of femininity. One group of 9-10-year-old girls studied by Kehily *et al.* (2002), for example, used a preoccupation with erotic attachments to celebrities, teachers and boys to consolidate their group identity 'through an overtly heterosexual version of femininity' (p175). Similarly, Renold (2000) emphasizes the centrality of overt heterosexual positioning to the individual and group identities of the 10 and 11-year-old girls she studied:

> Strikingly, every girl in the study, at some time, positioned herself firmly as heterosexual. Some girls delved back to their infant days. Some constructed fantasy boyfriends. The pressure to story oneself as heterosexually desirable was overwhelming and even involved girls 'going out' with boys who were verbally abusive to them. (p315)

For older girls in particular, the collective construction of heterosexual femininity takes place in relation to media images of sexualized young women's bodies and in the context of collective readings of these through discussion of popular soap operas and magazines. Kehily (1999) suggests that magazines for young people are 'a site where heterosex can be learned' (p78), and argues that the collective reading of these magazines is an important part of the construction of teenage femininities. Girls are thus constructing ideal typical femininities that relate to those in wider society, as mediated through media images and their own discussions, interpretations and reconstructions of them.

In considering the collective construction of femininity, it is important to bear in mind that, because of its relational nature, the precise character of that femininity is a localized matter that depends on the relative positioning of other local communities of masculinity and femininity practice, including those of parents, teachers and other significant adults. Despite the commonalities discussed above, there is considerable variation between local collective conceptions of femininity. Much of this is both classed and raced, so that different groups will, for example, have different views about how overtly sexual, or even interested in boys, it is acceptable to be (Hey, 1997; Shain, 2003). There will also be effects of geographical circumstance. One study of Israeli women, for example, found a lower incidence of recalled tomboyism than is typical of Western countries; the authors argue that one explanation for this may be that Israel is a society in which many people spend a lot of time outdoors, and such activities as hiking are common to both genders (Safir *et al.*, 2003). Studies of older young people in physical education colleges have also found that, in a context in which everyone is committed to sports, collective understandings of femininity incorporate this but also put pressure on male peers to be more macho in compensation (Sherlock, 1987; Dewar, 1990). Nevertheless, within a particular location, femininity will be collectively constructed within a relatively limited frame. Girls then construct their individual identities in relation to this, in either conformist or oppositional ways.

CONSTRUCTING INDIVIDUAL FEMININITIES: SUBORDINATED AND OPPOSITIONAL GIRLHOOD

While the majority of girls construct their femininities more or less in conformity to the dominant conceptions of femininity within their particular location, many do not. Some subordinate or oppositional femininities are not well aligned with the commonalities discussed in the previous section. Thorne (1993) argues, in relation to boys, that 'the literature on "the boys' world" suffers from a "Big Man bias" akin to the skew found in anthropological research that equates male élites with men in general' (p98). Thus, there is a tendency to focus on the dominant and on those who are invested in such hegemonic conceptions of masculinity and femininity. Many girls, however, do not conform to these ideal types, either because their personal circumstances prevent this or because they actively construct oppositional femininities, openly declaring and defending their difference.

For some girls, constructing oneself as outside dominant conceptions of femininity can be very powerful, at least in the short term. Shain (2003), for example, describes a group of 'gang girls' who asserted a strong South-East Asian identity coupled with an oppositional attitude to schooling. Their collective femininity cut across a variety of aspects of both white and South-East Asian dominant and stereotypical femininities. Their strong allegiance to their South-East Asian background was highly oppositional to the dominant femininities in their schools. For example, they wore traditional clothing or modified their school uniform to meet cultural requirements, and spoke their home language publicly in school, partly as a means to resist racial abuse by explicitly excluding white students. At the same time, they transgressed stereotypes of South-East Asian girls as meek and submissive, by being prepared to defend their races, religions and modes of behavior:

> Because the girls did not passively accept racism and were prepared to defend themselves, they fell outside the dominant stereotypes associated with both white and Asian femininity. Boys were prepared to attack them physically, including punching and kicking them. The girls' willingness to fight back further reinforced their status as deserving of abuse and characterisations of them as volatile. (Shain, 2003: 60)

This strong South-East Asian identity and solidarity in defending it was a source of power for these girls. In the longer term, however, their oppositional stance lost them support from the school, particularly in pursuing future ambitions in the face of parental concerns about their potential involvement with boys if they went on to college; their lack of conformity brought them under suspicion from both parents and teachers. They faced a future as wives and mothers with a fatalism arising from both their class and cultural locations but that was compounded by their own work in constructing the conditions of their oppression; through their oppositional femininity, they rendered themselves 'dangerous' and unreliable in the eyes of both their teachers and their parents, thus severely limiting their own future lives.

Other marginal femininities can bring different problems. As was discussed above, forms of femininity constructed in school exclude confidence in one's own ability; even the cleverest girls have to play this down to avoid losing their reputation for 'niceness'. Power *et al.* (2003) found that while, middle-class, adolescent girls were able to develop 'a feminized academic identity' that was 'heavily inscribed by social class' (p76) and involved girls distancing themselves from many of their peers (see Chapter 24 in this volume). Walkerdine *et al.* (2001) also note that some high-achieving, middle-class girls are unable fully to appreciate and take pleasure in this achievement because it is seen as just what is expected by their families and schools. In this case, high attainment, but not its celebration or enjoyment, is part of the local dominant construction of femininity. Renold (2001) discusses a group of four 10-year-old, middle-class girls who were already marginalized as 'square' by to their lack of interest in popular culture and fashion, and their conformity school rules. This still failed to allow them to gain the benefits of 'owning' their academic success. While they were active in trying 'to carve out an alternative femininity that did not revolve around boys, bodies and boyfriends, and supportive dyadic friendships' (p582), they still

> feared and simultaneously struggled to be accepted as clever, where the tension between knowing and positioning themselves as a 'knower', in a social world that equates 'cleverness' and 'real understanding' with boys and masculinity, was ever-present. (p583)

These girls were consequently in a double-bind, stigmatized partly for their academic success, but unable to access the pleasure that might be expected to arise from it.

Other oppositionally constructed identities can be more straightforwardly empowering. Several reports in the literature suggest that tomboy identities among preadolescent girls can be a source of power and prestige. Extreme tomboys not only take on masculine behaviour in terms of play preference and involvement in sports, but they also tend actively to reject the feminine (Reay, 2001: 161–2). Tomboy girls are generally highly regarded by their peers; Reay notes that 'tomboy' was used as a mark of respect by both boys and girls in her study. Epstein *et al.* (2001) report a girl in one primary school, where football was 'a major signifier of successful masculinity', who had passed into myth as being 'a better football player than any of the boys' (p163). In a larger-scale study, Hemmer and Kleiber (1981) found that classmates and teachers regard tomboys as popular, cooperative, helpful, supportive of others, and leaders. Consequently, there are a number of advantages to constructing femininities that are in direct opposition to dominant modes of 'doing girl'. There are a number of disadvantages, however. Although some researchers (Plumb and Caran, 1984; Morgan, 1998) have found that tomboys expand their repertoire to embrace both masculine and feminine pursuits, other research, including my own,[3] suggests that tomboyism can be very similar to dominant masculinity. In establishing and perpetuating their role as honorary boys, more extreme tomboys can be seen as conforming to local norms of masculine behavior, demonstrating the higher value they accord to masculine practices. This may be because boys, particularly those who have power in the peer group, act as gatekeepers to tomboy behavior; only a limited number of girls are permitted to play boys' games alongside boys (McGuffey and Rich, 1999). It is thus possible that girls are deemed acceptable as regular members of boys' play groups only if they publicly reject the feminine or enact the masculine, which may involve themselves acting as gatekeepers who exclude other girls. The construction of femininity as oppositional to masculinity thus makes it difficult for girls to construct individual femininities that incorporate aspects of both; they are expected to conform either to one or to the other, however these are locally defined.

For older girls wishing to preserve some aspects of a tomboy identity, things can be much harder. As was discussed earlier, femininity in adolescent girls is often constructed in direct opposition to physical activity, with a rejection of sports and physical education. Consequently, girls who wish to preserve an interest in sport can be stigmatized; tomboys, from being admired and dominant members of the peer group, become a marginal and oppositional minority. Constructing one's own femininity in opposition to the dominant community conception can thus move from being empowering to disempowering as girls get older, particularly as adolescent boys are less likely to include girls in their games, even as honorary boys, and official sports teams are more likely to be gender segregated.

Two of the few ways to preserve a fully active lifestyle into one's teens while maintaining a hegemonic feminine identity are those that for most tomboys would seem to be anathema: ballet and cheerleading. Both allow girls to be physically active and develop a strong, muscular physique, while remaining firmly within dominant constructions of femininity. As a mass practice, ballet is generally given up by girls in middle childhood, being mainly the preserve of younger children (Griffiths, 1996), but, in the USA, cheerleading remains popular. Adams and Bettis, pointing out that it is practised by 3.3 million people a year, 97% of whom are female, suggest that:

> Operating at the juncture of all-American good looks, traditional femininity, and sports-like athleticism, contemporary cheerleading provides a culturally sanctioned space for performing the requisite traits of the ideal girl in the new millennium. ... We found ample evidence that cheerleading offers a critical space for certain girls to take risks, to try on different personas, to delight in the physicality of their bodies, and to control and revel in their own power and desire. (Adams and Bettis, 2003: 87)

Unfortunately, this comes with a version of the feminine ideal that, for those girls who have already constructed their femininities in opposition to dominant forms, is no longer accessible; it has been firmly rejected as far too 'girlie'. Girls whose femininities have been constructed through active participation in sports, may be increasingly marginalized at adolescence, as 'tomboy' becomes a stigmatized identity (Cockburn and Clarke, 2002).

Non-heterosexual femininities are similarly stigmatized in school. As noted above, even preadolescent girls can feel compelled to project heterosexuality, and the pressure becomes increasingly strong as they move through adolescence. Many secondary-school cultures, even in wider communities that are moderately tolerant, are extremely homophobic, an open lesbian identity leaving a young woman open to bullying, ostracism or even personal violence. Although, as Epstein and Johnson (1998) note, the emergence of the 'baby dyke' has made it more likely that girls will see lesbian identities as potentially fashionable, this remains rare in UK schools and is also likely to be classed and raced. Coming out at school is also likely to involve a possibly problematic parallel revelation in a young woman's family and home community. This can be particularly difficult for students who are not white and middle class; Epstein and Johnson quote one respondent as saying that she felt she 'was the only [South] Asian lesbian in the world' (p159). Young women with physical disabilities, who are in any case at a disadvantage when performing femininities that are congruent with hegemonic forms, are likely to find constructing themselves as lesbian particularly difficult; people with physical disabilities are not expected to be sexual at all (Martino and Pallotta-Chiarolli, 2003), let alone homosexual.

CONCLUSION: FEMININITY AND FEMININITIES

Girls in school construct femininity within their local adult and peer communities in a number of ways. It is constructed relationally, with respect to other local femininities and, in particular, in opposition to peer constructions of masculinity.

The result is some surprisingly common constructions, which include the silly-selfish/sensible-selfless binary, the importance of 'niceness', increasing physical passivity and compulsory heterosexuality. Together, these form a powerfully hegemonic femininity that only a few girls are able fully to resist. Where it does occur, the price of resistance may be high.

It is not so much that all schoolgirl femininities are variations on a theme, but more that significant deviation from the local dominant construction of femininity comes at a heavy cost. Schools are very intense places, and children, particularly in primary education, are stuck with a small group of peers for a significant part of the day, year after year. It is hard, in the face of this, to be different, to be a girl who frequently takes charge, who celebrates her own success or stands out against compulsory heterosexuality. Other femininities, such as those of Shain's (2003) gang girls, while useful as a short-term survival strategy that allows young women to stand up to racism or to resist labelling as 'less able' (Benjamin 2002), do not support them in developing secure, independent, longer-term futures.

Schoolgirl femininities, of course, reflect, and in some cases magnify, those to be found in wider society. Girls do not just learn how to be women from each other; they are apprenticed to their mothers, their neighbors, and to some extent their teachers. They construct femininity in relation to the media, drawing together images of girlhood and womanhood as they build collective models of the ideal typical girl. In constructing their own femininities in relation to these, they have to consider what they gain and what they lose from conformity and from resistance. If we want to intervene in such femininities, for example to help high-achieving girls to acknowledge and celebrate their attainment, active girls to continue to play sports after puberty, or young lesbians to feel comfortable in coming out, then we have to alter that balance and make resistance less risky and more worthwhile. This may involve changing how we as adult women behave in our own communities of femininity practice. We should strive to demonstrate confident femininities that also resist dominant norms, while maintaining the differences and distinctions from masculinity that are so important to girls and young women as they construct their identities.

REFERENCES

Adams, N and Bettis, P (2003) Commanding the room in short skirts: cheering as the embodiment of ideal girlhood. *Gender and Society,* 17: 73–91.

Ali, S (2003) 'To be a girl': culture and class in schools. *Gender and Education,* 15: 269–83.

Benjamin, S (2002) Reproducing traditional femininities? The social relations of special educational needs in a girls' comprehensive school. *Gender and Education,* 14: 281–94.

Boaler, J (1997) Reclaiming school mathematics: the girls fight back. *Gender and Education,* 9: 285–305.

Browne, N (2004) *Gender equity in the early years.* Maidenhead: Open University Press.

Cockburn, C and Clarke, G (2002) 'Everybody's looking at you!': girls negotiating the 'femininity deficit' they incur in physical education. *Women's Studies International Forum,* 25: 651–65.

Dewar, A (1990) Oppression and privilege in physical education: struggles in the negotiation of gender in a university programme, in Kirk, D and Tinning, R (eds) *Physical education, curriculum and culture* Basingstoke: Falmer Press.

Epstein, D and Johnson, R (1998) *Schooling sexualities.* Buckingham: Open University Press.

Epstein, DM, Kehily, M, Mac an Ghaill, M and Redman, P (2001). Boys and girls come out to play: making masculinities and femininities in school playgrounds. *Men and Masculinities,* 4: 158–72.

Fitzclarence, L and Hickey, C (2001). Real footballers don't eat quiche: old narratives in new times. *Men and Masculinities,* 4: 118–39.

Francis, B (1998) *Power plays: primary school children's conception of gender, power and adult work.* Stoke-on-Trent: Trentham Books.

Francis, B (2000) *Boys, girls and achievement: addressing the classroom issues.* London: RoutledgeFalmer.

Griffiths, V (1996) Getting in step: young girls and two dance cultures. *Women's Studies International Forum,* 19: 481–91.

Hatchell, H (1998) Girls' entry into higher secondary sciences. *Gender and Education* 10: 375–86.

Hemmer, JD and Kleiber, DA (1981) Tomboys and sissies: androgynous children? *Sex Roles,* 7: 1205–12.

Hey, V (1997) *The company she keeps: an ethnography of girls' friendship.* Buckingham: Open University Press.

Kehily, MJ (1999). More sugar? Teenage magazines, gender displays and sexual learning. *European Journal of Cultural Studies,* 2: 65–89.

Kehily, MJ, Mac an Ghaill, M, Epstein, D, and Redman, P (2002) Private girls and public worlds: producing femininities in the primary school. *Discourse,* 23: 167–77.

Lave, J and Wenger, E (1991) *Situated learning: legitimate peripheral participation.* Cambridge: Cambridge University Press.

Martino, W and Pallotta-Chiarolli, M (2003) *So what's a boy? Addressing issues of masculinity and schooling.* Maidenhead: Open University Press.

Massey, D (1995) Masculinity, dualisms and high technology. *Transactions of the Institute of British Geographers,* 20: 487–99.

McGuffey, CS and Rich, BL (1999) Playing in the gender transgression zone: race, class and hegemonic masculinity in middle childhood. *Gender and Society,* 13: 608–27.

Mendick, H (2006) *Masculinities in Mathematics* Maidenhead: Open University Press.

Morgan, BL (1998) A three generational study of tomboy behavior. *Sex Roles,* 39(9/10): 787–800.

Nespor, J (1997) *Tangled up in school.* Mahwah, NJ: Lawrence Erlbaum Associates.

Paechter, C (1998) *Educating the Other: gender, power and schooling.* London: Falmer Press.

Paechter, C (2003a) Learning masculinities and femininities: power/knowledge and legitimate peripheral participation. Gender and Education Fourth International Conference: Revisiting Feminist Perspectives on Gender and Education, University of Sheffield, UK.

Paechter, C (2003b) Masculinities and femininities as communities of practice. *Women's Studies International Forum,* 26: 69–77.

Paechter, C (2006) Reconceptualising the gendered body: learning and constructing masculinities and femininities in school. *Gender and Education,* 18: 121–35.

Plumb, P and Caran, G (1984) A developmental study of destereotyping and androgynous activity preferences of tomboys, nontomboys, and males. *Sex Roles,* 10(9/10): 703–12.

Power, S Edwards, T, Whitty, G and Wigfall, V (2003) *Education and the middle class.* Buckingham: Open University Press.

Reay, D (2001) 'Spice girls', 'nice girls', 'girlies' and 'tomboys': gender discourses, girls' cultures and femininities in the primary classroom. *Gender and Education,* 13: 153–66.

Renold, E (2000) 'Coming out': gender, (hetero)sexuality and the primary school. *Gender and Education,* 12: 309–26.

Renold, E (2001) 'Square-girls', femininity and the negotiation of academic success in the primary school. *British Educational Research Journal,* 27: 577–88.

Renold, E and Allan, A (2004) Bright and beautiful: high-achieving girls and the negotiation of young 'girlie' femininities. Paper presented at British Educational Research Association Annual Conference, 16–18 September, UMIST, Manchester, UK.

Roberts, K (1996) Young people, schools, sport and government policies. *Sport, Education and Society,* 1: 47–57.

Safir, MP, Rosenmann, A and Kloner, O (2003) Tomboyism, sexual orientation, and adult gender roles among Israeli women. *Sex Roles,* 48(9/10): 401–10.

Shain, F (2003) *The schooling and identity of Asian girls.* Stoke on Trent: Trentham Books.

Sherlock, J (1987) Issues of masculinity and femininity in British physical education. *Women's Studies International Forum* 10: 443–51.

Skelton, C (2001) *Schooling the boys: masculinities and primary education.* Buckingham: Open University Press.

Skelton, C and Francis, B (2002) 'Clever Jack and conscientious Chloe': naturally able boys and hard-working girls in the classroom. Paper presented at British Educational Research Association Annual Conference, University of Exeter, September 2002.

Thorne, B (1993) *Gender play: girls and boys in school.* Buckingham: Open University Press.

van Essen, M (2003) No issue, no problem? Co-education in Dutch secondary physical education during the twentieth century. *Gender and Education,* 15: 59–74.

Vertinsky, PA (1992) Reclaiming space, revisioning the body: the quest for gender-sensitive physical education. *Quest,* 44: 373–96.

Walkerdine, V (1984) Developmental psychology and the child-centred pedagogy: the insertion of Piaget into early education, in Henriques, J, Hollway, W, Urwin, C, Venn, C and Walkerdine V (eds) *Changing the subject.* London: Methuen.

Walkerdine, V (1990). *Schoolgirl fictions.* London: Verso.

Walkerdine, V, Lucey, H and Melody, J (2001). *Growing up girl: psychosocial explorations of gender and class.* Basingstoke: Palgrave.

Wenger, E (1998) *Communities of practice: learning, meaning and identity.* Cambridge: Cambridge University Press.

West, C and Zimmerman, DH (1987) Doing gender. *Gender and Society,* 1: 125–51.

Williams, A and Bedward, J (2002) Understanding girls' experience of physical education: relational analysis and situated learning, in Penney, D (ed) *Gender and physical education: contemporary issues and future directions.* London: Routledge.

NOTES

1. I use the term 'Other' to denote a dualistic power relation between dominant groups and those they exclude. An individual or group is positioned as Other when they are understood only as the negation of the dominant subject. The Other thus only exists in relation to and as the negative of the subject. In this context, group femininities remain cohesive through the symbolic expulsion of those who are not considered to belong; those who are othered in this way become, in effect, albeit often temporarily, non-persons (for a fuller explanation of this, see Paechter 1998).

2. The form of football this applies to varies by country. In the UK and much of Europe, soccer (along with rugby in some parts of the UK) is central dominant masculinities; in the USA, this role is taken by American football, and soccer is regarded as more feminized.

3. 'Tomboy Identities: the construction and maintenance of active girlhoods'. EESRC award number RES-00-22-1032, based at Goldsmiths College, University of London, 2005–06.

27

Appropriate Behavior? Sexualities, Schooling and Hetero-gender

David James Mellor and Debbie Epstein

INTRODUCTION

> Eight school pupils have been suspended following a protest against their headmaster's decision to ban 'canoodling'. The protest began last Friday when around 200 pupils ... refused to return to afternoon classes after being told they were not allowed to kiss, hold hands or hug. The headmaster ... said today that the ban was aimed at instilling 'appropriate behaviour'. (*The Guardian,* 6 October, 2004)[1]

The young people at this British school were disciplined for exhibiting their sexuality within a formal educational setting. As the report highlights, the head teacher clearly found the assorted acts of 'canoodling' to be disturbing and inappropriate in the educational context for which he was responsible – such acts had no place at school. It seems that such sexualized behavior fitted ill with his vision of what school pupils should be (or be like). His solution was to ban conduct that apparently disrupted both his identity as an educator and the young people's identities as students. It was, as such, an attempt to banish sexuality from their school. But to think that by stopping 'inappropriate' behavior such as kissing or holding hands, one could 'remove' sexuality from schooling is misguided, as it understands sexuality purely as biologically driven acts of intimacy and fails to recognize that sexualities are cultural and historical constructs that shape and define people's lives and identities (Weeks, 1986). Indeed, the 'appropriate behavior' required by the head teacher is, in fact, the practice of a particular kind of gendered sexuality considered correct for young people in schools. It is, moreover, a distinct type of dominant heterosexuality.

In recent years, Anglophone countries have seen a rise in abstinence campaigns that argue explicitly in favor of the postponement of sexual activity until marriage, and in so doing, promote and discipline a particularly 'straight' version of heterosexuality. The bold presumption of these campaigns is that everyone is normatively heterosexual and that this heterosexuality must be defended against the incursions of 'queer' and other non-normative versions of sexuality.[2]

CONSTRUCTING SEXUALITIES

The head teacher's attempt to control the expression of sexuality in his school assumes, as popular common sense generally does, that sexuality is biologically organized and driven in fairly uncomplicated ways. Along with most other researchers who work on sexuality, we argue that sexuality is much more than just sex. It consists of a myriad of social interactions and cultural understandings developed in particular situations and places. Sexuality, then, includes all the cultural practices adopted by people (in this chapter, children and teachers), from childhood games like 'kiss-chase', through dating and dumping practices, romantic ideals and stories, to the social and legal institutions (like marriage) through which we organize our sexual lives.

It is important to underline that sexualities are never completely stifled or removed from educational contexts and that certain sexual identities are actually openly promoted and regulated. For example, in the US context, the high-school 'prom' and, in the British context, the 'school disco' assume, require, and promote particular versions of heterosexual relating. These include dressing up in certain styles (whether formal evening wear at the prom, or the more casual, but nonetheless carefully achieved, wear appropriate to a disco), couples comprising one of each gender, and the need to be heterosexually attractive to the opposite sex. These 'ideals' are not always achieved but are very clearly understood by the young people attending such events. Even where the heterosexual presumptions underlying the organization of proms are challenged, the very extensive response (both negative and positive) to such challenges is indicative of the degree to which heterosexuality is assumed to be the only 'normal' version of sexuality.[3] Sexualities, then, are not absent from schools, but are deeply entwined within the normative discourses of education. Here, we explore the ways in which children themselves (and their teachers) form, construct, and struggle over meanings (that is discourses) in the cultural worlds of their schools. If, as many have argued, the social and cultural construction of sexualities takes place through discourse (for example, Foucault, 1978; Weeks, 1986, 1991), it follows that identities, and thus gender and sexualities, have been and continue to be shaped not by nature but by historically specific cultures. This theoretical framework has been widely used to explore sexuality in terms of people's creativity and agency, while retaining an understanding of how professionals and institutions exert considerable influence over identities (Vance, 1995). The study of sexuality in education has, generally, followed similar lines of argument (see, for example, Deacon *et al.*, 1999; Epstein, 1999; Renold, 2002; Sears, 2002; Hillier and Harrison, 2004), as we do here.

SPACE, TIME, NARRATIVE

Schools are particular discursive spaces with their own sets of (usually unstated) but widely understood regulative processes and regimes of truth. There are a number of aspects to keep in mind in this regard. First, it is worth remembering that formal schooling came into being (in the UK at least) as part of the shift from cottage industry to industrial labor.[4] This shift made it necessary to provide childcare for workers so that they could undertake paid labor in factories. Second, schooling is compulsory for children and young people (though the age of compulsory schooling varies slightly from country to country). Thus, children's presence in schools as pupils/students is coerced – they must attend (unless their parents embark on the complex process of home-schooling) whether they want to or not. Third, adults are present in schools on a voluntary basis, in so far as they have the ability to choose employment other than that of teaching or assisting teachers. Fourth, and partly because of this, adult power is institutionalized in the context of schools. While children/young people may well (and often do) resist strongly and creatively (Willis, 1977; Wyn and White, 1997), discursively and formally the adults are meant to be 'in charge'. Fifth, the underlying assumption that governs formal education is that teachers know and children learn. Thus, in what Paulo Freire (1996) identified as a 'banking model' of education, teachers are responsible for the transmission of knowledge and children are there to absorb it. In this context, the degree to which the children have become saturated with knowledge is constantly tested by both public and school-based tests and examinations. Furthermore, in the contemporary context of neo-liberal marketised education systems, schools are themselves tested, audited, and judged, often on the basis of children's success in public examinations.

This discursive field is productive of the kinds of individuals who inhabit the spaces of schools – on the one hand, adults-as-educators and, on the other hand, children-as-pupils – and this has implications for the construction of school-based sexualities. In *Discipline and Punish*, Foucault (1977) argues that schools (and the examination process) produce and depend on the regulation of what he terms 'docile bodies', defined, through discourse and surveillance, by the spaces they inhabit. Pupils' bodies are particularly subject to the disciplinary gaze of teachers and the pedagogic discourses they deploy (Walkerdine, 1990). Since sexuality is invariably embodied (as well as enculturated), it comes as no surprise that it is disciplined in gendered ways (Butler, 1993). Girls and boys are supposed to inhabit their bodies differentially and spatially (Gordon *et al.*, 2000). It therefore follows that schooling can, in no way, be divorced from the bodies of either pupils or teachers or from gendered (ethnic, classed, etc.) versions of sexuality.

Indeed, despite widespread political and common-sense support for the notion that education can and should take place *without* sexuality, many aspects of education are, in practice, concerned with educating *for* (hetero)sexuality.[5] Moreover, educational discourses can be seen to foreground a particular version of institutional, gendered (hetero)sexuality in educational sites from the nursery school or kindergarten, through secondary and high schools, to colleges and universities. It should be stressed that this 'heterosexual economy' is salient within the discursive practices and meanings of the official curriculum and the values of institutions, but also exists as a dominant regulatory force within the everyday cultures of school (Hey, 1997; Epstein *et al.*, 2002; Kehily, 2002).

As we saw at the start of the chapter, the head teacher who prohibited 'canoodling' while at school was concerned about 'appropriate behaviors'. We suggested that this was because what he saw as 'inappropriate' behaviors were disruptive of his identity as an educator and of what he thought were suitable identities for his students. Clearly, the students saw things somewhat differently. As this example shows, the playground space is much more in the control of the students than that of the classroom, and the refusal to go into class was a very symbolic action that deployed the differential discursive geographies of the school. This illustrates how schools are not singular but multiple geographical sites, and sexualities are negotiated differently in areas like the classroom, the playground, the hallways, the staff room, and the lunch hall. That is not to suggest, however, that there is freedom to choose sexual identities in any of these areas, because a combination of educational, cultural, gendered, and other discourses collude (and collide) in assembling a particularly narrow interpretation of (hetero)sexuality as 'natural' that often passes unaccredited and without criticism.

CHILDHOOD, HETERO-GENDER AND EDUCATION

Within this discursive framework, a particularly strong – even hegemonic – discourse in contemporary Western (particularly Anglophone) culture is that of 'childhood innocence'. Children, it is widely assumed, should be protected from the corrupting 'adult' world and should have as little as possible, preferably no (sexual) knowledge that, it is supposed, could damage their innocence or tempt them into experiencing forbidden practices (Kitzinger, 1988; Jenks, 1996; James and Prout, 1997). Culturally, then, children are held to be asexual or presexual persons (Jackson, 1982). Paradoxically, at the same time, children are often highly sexualized. Jackson (1999), for example, describes how young girls may be entered in beauty pageants, and Walkerdine has analyzed the sexualized discourse of very young children (Walkerdine, 1990), of young girls at the primary stage (Walkerdine, 1997), and of girls growing up to adulthood (Walkerdine et al., 2001). Similarly, boys must be 'real boys' in ways that mark them as heterosexual (Epstein, 1997; Renold, 2004). As we can see, the fixing of the boundaries of gender (Thorne, 1993) is frequently, if not invariably, achieved through hetero-normative discourses which place boys as boys and girls as girls in ways which, as Judith Butler (1990; 1993) argues, presuppose heterosexuality.

Research about children's relationship cultures has shown that the notion that children are 'innocent' and lacking in knowledge about sexuality is problematic in two, interconnected ways. First, children often do hold complex knowledges about sexuality, but they vary from and sometimes overlap adult understandings. Second, children and young people do not simply learn about sexuality, passively, but they mould and re-produce such knowledge, articulating it in diverse ways within their friendship cultures while forming their own social realities (see, for example, Kehily et al., 2002; Renold, 2005). This understanding of children's friendship groups as producers of identities differs greatly from older socialization models, where young people were seen as simply replicating the pre-existing socio-cultural order (Kehily et al., 2002).

The places where children and young people are educated and indeed all educational contexts, are widely held to be non-sexual spaces, at least in relation to processes of teaching and learning, where all present, students and educators, are cast as asexual beings – or, at least, beings whose sexuality is on temporary 'hold'. This makes the discussion of issues of sexuality in an educational space potentially a risky business.[6] There are at least two risks here. First, educators who talk with young people about sexuality may well find themselves the subject of tabloid (in the UK context) scandal, seen as 'promoting' particularly kinds of (undesirable) sexuality or of encouraging children to become sexually active by introducing them to discussions about sexuality. This may compromise their jobs and privacy. The second 'risk' is contained in the first. This is the perceived problem of young people's sexual activity at a time and in a space in which their interest in sex and sexuality is seen as illegitimate. The narrative goes that if 'society' takes one step in the direction of liberalization of sexualities (or even discussion of them), then the rest automatically follows – that is, a complete loss of all 'moral values' (especially where the only legitimate morality is seen as conservative) becomes inevitable.[7]

Adult anxieties about the behavior of young people as both endangered and dangerous to themselves and to other members of society have led to increasing levels of surveillance and regulation, such as the installation of closed-circuit TV (CCTV) in certain schools (Kelly, 2003; Bunyan, 2004) so that children can be constantly monitored by, and under surveillance from, parents, teachers, or other adults. While younger children are most often seen as at risk from others, older children are seen as a risk to others and 'decent' society. The tendency to categorize children in relation to riskiness (to themselves and/or to others) is especially marked with regard to fears about sexuality and sexual activity. Such fears run from panics about the dangers of paedophilia, to the 'epidemic' of supposedly unwanted teenage pregnancies[8] and the spread of sexually transmitted infections (STIs). This is not to suggest that these are not problematic issues or dangerous for some young people. However, the dominance they have achieved in educational discourse often leads to the exclusion of all other considerations about sexuality. In the USA, for example, sexuality education in many states constructs a model of the sexual teenager as normatively heterosexual and attends only to the risks and dangers associated with teen sex (Bay-Cheng, 2003). All this reveals a close association between sexuality and danger that is common in contemporary discourse, where both are intertwined in complex and ambiguous ways (Vance, 1984; Weeks, 1986).

This entanglement of sexuality, danger, risk, and surveillance leads to a kind of implicit and often explicit censorship of sexuality in schools, which is as often self-censorship as it is imposed by others. In one sense, this can be seen as silencing, but in practice, sexuality is very present, very loud, and very uncensored in school spaces. The very censorship itself creates the impetus for the expression of sexuality. Judith Butler (1997) suggests that censorship is not so much about silencing people as about creating the conditions of production of the self through discourse (speech and acts). For example, teachers' fears and anxieties about sexuality add to and increase the regulation and disciplining of sexuality in schools. But far from this leading to sexuality vanishing from school, what actually happens is that inherent to the discourse of the 'non-sexual school' is a strong recognition of the gendered sexualities of educators and students. Indeed, more than that, it is productive of the expression of sexualities among students/pupils and teachers alike in a whole number of ways.[9]

Paradoxically, in all this anxiety, surveillance and regulation concerning the supposed risks of sexuality to children and young people, normative ideas about gender remain largely unchallenged. The matrix of gendered practices that are undertaken daily, and the mass of naturalized gendered knowledge that informs these practices, render unnoticed the heterosexual framework by which people are compelled to live (Butler, 1990). While gender is not simply collapsible into, or a natural expression of sexuality, the compulsory and institutional nature of heterosexuality makes it appear so (Rubin, 1984). The resultant discourse of normatively gendered heterosexuality is supported by and dependent on certain narratives – stories about the way things are and should be (like romantic love) – that inform, shape, and are shaped by people as they try to make sense of the world that they live in (Bruner, 1990; Plummer, 1995). Because of the culturally pervasive discourse of gendered heterosexuality and the narratives that support it, a distinctly narrow form of hetero-gendered sexuality is privileged and sanctioned within educational institutions. This form assumes that gender is fixed in certain ways, that heterosexuality is the inevitable (and the only normal) destination for children as they grow up, and that particular modes of doing/being boys and girls are not only natural but desirable. This is what is speakable within school contexts. At the same time, other forms of sexuality, including non-normative heterosexualities, are demonized and rendered virtually unspeakable (O'Flynn and Epstein, 2005). In the context of sex education, this is maintained by a limited focus on coitus and heterosexual intimacy (Thorogood, 2000), while in other areas of the official curriculum the institutions of normative heterosexuality, such as marriage between two people of opposite sex, are positioned as natural and difficult to challenge.

CLASSROOM

Within the context of the school, classrooms constitute particular spaces of their own and have different characters at different times. They are the primary spaces for teaching and learning but are also often territorially marked as 'belonging' to a particular teacher. Generally, teachers are in control of this space in a number of important respects. They are able to control who is allowed into the space and when they may leave – notwithstanding the fact that students may sometimes barge in unceremoniously or, indeed, run out in certain circumstances, nor that senior managers and inspectors often have the run of the classroom with or without teachers' permission. The furniture is arranged in particular ways that bespeak the kind of teaching that goes on there (Walkerdine, 1984), in single file, pairs, or joined up for group work. Children are often deprived of the choice of where to sit but are given a space or refused permission to sit in another space. Thus, bodies are controlled, and this regulation often occurs in gendered and sexualized ways (Gordon *et al.*, 2000). For example, boys and girls may be made to sit next to each other in order to discipline the boys and control their behavior. Thus, boys are positioned as being active, mischievous, and/or disruptive in very bodily ways, while girls are seen as calming, mature, generally more responsible and as inhabiting quieter, stiller bodies. This leads into the common discursive framing of normative heterosexuality as dependent on active masculinity and passive femininity, which is reflected in many ideas about what and how boys and girls are 'supposed' to be.

Teachers' classroom talk with children is regulated and (self-)censored in part through the set curriculum and texts in use in the classroom. Teachers do not speak freely in classrooms, especially not about sexuality, and their classroom talk is delimited by a complex combination of personal beliefs, circumstance, and official and cultural discourses. Teachers are obliged to enact the role of the 'non-sexual educator', but in doing so, are able to draw on and deploy normatively gendered heterosexuality, positioning themselves and the children within this discourse. Thus, many heterosexual teachers will regularly make reference to their own family arrangements – children, husbands/wives, and so on (Spraggs, 1994). The point, here, is not that normatively heterosexual teachers should refrain from deploying their own lives as part of their teaching, but that it is a problem when others cannot do the same. In these ways, narratives of hetero-gender are present within many different aspects of teaching. It is these narratives that give weight and authority to the discourse of normative heterosexuality and help render alternative stories, which might open up more complex ways of understanding the world, relatively untellable.

Lessons in sex education, discussed elsewhere in this book, are not the only lessons in which sexuality is addressed overtly and directly. Lessons in science (especially biology) are clearly places where reproduction might be discussed. Equally, lessons in English, drama, and sociology, for example, may approach human relationships and sexuality as part of the curriculum. However there is, in addition, a swathe of spaces in lessons that might appear 'free' from sexuality but are not. Because teaching and learning, as supposedly non-sexual activities, rely on certain narratives about sexuality (drawn from official documents and encapsulated in and through the performed identity of the 'non-sexual' educator), particular ways of speaking about relationships are privileged, while others are seen as inappropriate or deeply problematic. Such processes can be seen in the way that, for example, traditional fairy tales are deployed in work with young children in early-years settings. In role-play, boys are regularly the 'handsome princes' rescuing the girls, who enact the damsel in distress and even when teachers may try to subvert this, the dominance of the discourse makes it difficult to achieve (Davies, 1989). As children start to do work in history, for example, they are more than likely to be taught about the heterosexual relations of famous figures (whether or not they were 'heterosexual' in any simple way). When children reach the stage of subject choice, it is well established that their choices are highly gendered (Arnot et al., 1999), but there is a relationship here, too, between the gendering of a subject and the heterosexualisation of classrooms.

We do not want to give the impression that classrooms are spaces of unproblematic or unchallenged regulation. Children are active agents in the classroom, as elsewhere, and what goes on there is the result of negotiation between and among the children and their teachers. Thus, children's own relationship cultures often (indeed usually) find many avenues for expression while they are in the classroom during formal lessons, and these cultural practices are saturated with gendered sexualities.

PLAYGROUND

If the classroom is a place where pupils are highly regulated but also active agents who may conform to and/or challenge teachers' demands, playgrounds are much more constituted as cultural spaces through the relatively unimpeded activities of the children/young people. It is often here that friendships are made, broken, and consolidated. It has been well documented that children's friendship cultures constitute a space where they exercise social control and are able to shape and construct sexual identities (Thorne, 1993; Swain, 2000; Allard, 2002; Hey, 2002; Kehily et al., 2002; McLeod, 2002; Ali, 2003; Connolly, 2004).

As these authors have shown, the impulse to present oneself as recognizable within normative heterosexuality is strongly influential within children's relationship cultures. Yet, it should be stressed that children and young people are active negotiators of sexuality discourse, many finding creative and subversive ways in which to overcome the heterosexual imperative and create positive spaces for their own sexualities (Hillier and Harrison, 2004). However, this identity work remains hard labor that runs against the grain of compulsory heterosexuality. There is, for example, an assumption that boys and girls cannot be friends, but only 'couples' from an early age (Cahill, 1998; Bhana, 2002).

One of the key issues in the playground, particularly, but also in the class-room, is the role played by homophobia in regulating both gender and sexuality. The extent of homophobic verbal and other abuse in schools has been demonstrated by a number of researchers (see, for example, Frank, 1993; Rivers, 1995; Douglas *et al.*, 1997; Kehily and Nayak, 1997; Davis, 1998; Deacon *et al.*, 1999; Duncan, 1999; Epstein, Hewitt *et al.*, 2003). The point we want to make here is that homophobia is a kind of policing activity that contributes to the difficulties young people (perhaps especially boys) may have in living out gender and sexuality in alternative ways. The quiet, studious boy or even the boy who fits gendered expectations in many ways but is hopeless at team contact sports (like soccer, rugby, or football), may well himself be the target for bullying and abuse. Epstein (1998), for example, describes the lengths that some boys go to in order to avoid being labelled as 'gay'. A further aspect of homophobia, which demonstrates its links with misogyny, is the way that boys have to demonstrate clearly that they are 'real boys'. The epithet 'girl' is frequently used, almost as an aside, in a disparaging and mocking way that some boys find extremely hurtful. However, showing that they are hurt would confirm the 'truth' of the allegation that they do not 'do boy' adequately. Finding the creativity to 'do boy' differently, in such circumstances, may be well-nigh impossible.

For girls, too, there is an imperative to be heterosexual, which generally finds expression in the demand to make the body heterosexually attractive (through diet, clothes, make-up, and so on), even though the 'tomboy' is an acceptable face of femininity, at least until the heterosexual economy of secondary schools begins in earnest (Lees, 1986, 1993; Renold, 2001). Mary Jane Kehily (1996; 2002) has shown how girls use 'teen' magazines as a resource both for exploring sexualities and for producing themselves as heterosexual (see also McRobbie, 1991, and Chapter 26 in this volume). For girls, in addition, there is the requirement to be heterosexual enough without becoming known as a 'slag', the 'local bike', or some other misogynistic designation for sexually active young women. Sue Lees' account of how girls tread a narrow line between being a 'slag' and a 'drag' (Lees, 1993) is of relevance here.[10] In spite of these constraints, the literature and our research abound with examples of children's/young people's creativity and agency in relation to sexuality and gender (among other aspects of their lives). David James Mellor has found that in some boys' friendships the strength of the 'best friend' narrative is such that boys can be close and talk about emotion and intimacy in a manner that, to some extent, overcomes the restrictive nature of the forms of heterosexual masculinity that predominated in their school. When writing stories about friendship, many of the boys would express their friendships (whether symbolic or real) in romantic terminology, where bonds between boys were secured in an instant and sustained throughout all adversity (Mellor, 2004). Boys can feel emotional closeness for each other in a manner that is often overlooked (Redman *et al.*, 2002).

We are not implying that everything has changed or is changing and that things are becoming easier for those who do not perform dominant versions of gender and of sexuality. While it is important to recognize and celebrate the creative endeavors of children/young people, it is vital that we recognize the continued existence of a dominant and limiting compulsory heterosexuality for both boys and girls.

CONCLUSION – THE CHALLENGE OF UNIVERSAL ANTI-HETEROSEXIST EDUCATIONAL PRACTICE

Throughout this chapter, we have emphasized the constructed nature of hetero-sexuality in schools, shown the way it is bolstered by official discourse, and illustrated how it is negotiated by individuals and groups. To conclude, we would like to suggest how our knowledge of compulsory heterosexuality can be used to work toward anti-heterosexist practice across the curriculum.

To begin, the gap between the academic and the everyday needs to be closed. An open discussion of how sexuality is constructed at different historical points within different cultures would open the space for students and educators to begin to think differently and to challenge dominant norms. This would aid students and educators, whether they identify as heterosexual, non-heterosexual, or queer, by helping to dissolve deep-seated heterosexism and homophobia, and thus provide greater opportunities for personal expression to all individuals regardless of sexual identification. It is important that research in the area of sexualities and schooling retains and emphasizes its focus on problematizing and de-naturalizing institutional heterosexuality and hetero-gender in educational settings. Sexuality education already exists in some areas, having replaced more traditional sex education, but this is just the beginning of what is required. Moving teaching about sexuality away from lessons strictly about biology and/or health and into the humanities and social sciences could help open up spaces for the critical reflection on the constructed nature of institutional and normative heterosexuality (Epstein, O'Flynn and Telford 2003). Such sexuality education could be a vital point of departure for challenges to both the official and unofficial curricula that cause individuals anxiety, uncertainty, and pain through the regulation and disciplining of sexual and gender identities.

One could say that the curriculum needs to be 'queered'. This does not mean trying to sexualize what young people learn but to 'excavate and interpret' the way the curriculum 'already is sexualised' (Sumara and Davis, 1999: 192; emphasis in original). As can be seen from our chapter, the dynamics for the interruption and renarration of sexual selves and sexual stories are already present within the cultural settings of education (Atkinson, 2002). One of our key arguments has been that the workings of compulsory heterosexuality in education are limiting and constraining for all involved (adults and children). A key challenge, therefore, for researchers of sexuality and education, is how to unpack and understand the nature of institutional heterosexism while working with practitioners in identifying ways of opening up the possibilities for children/young people rather than, as all too often happens, closing them down. This is an important joint project because, as Judith Butler has recently noted, 'changing the institutions by which humanly viable choice is established and maintained is a prerequisite for the exercise of self-determination' (Butler, 2004: 7). It is for the sake of the sexual self-determination of all young people and educators that research in this area will continue apace.

ACKNOWLEDGEMENTS

David James would like to thank the ESRC for funding his PhD, entitled *Playground romance: an ethnography of children's investments in romantic love* (award number PTA-030-2002-00613). Both would like to thank Emma Renold for her support since they both moved to Cardiff, and for her comments on earlier drafts of this chapter.

REFERENCES

Ali, S (2003) *Mixed-race, post-race: gender, new ethnicities, and cultural practices.* Oxford: Berg.
Allard, A (2002) 'Aussies' and 'Wogs' and the 'group in-between': Year 10 students' constructions of cross-cultural friendships. *Discourse: Journal of Theoretical Studies in Media and Culture,* 23: 193–209.
Arnot, M, David, ME and Weiner, G (1999) *Closing the gender gap: postwar education and social change.* Cambridge: Polity.
Atkinson, E (2002) Education for diversity in a multisexual society: negotiating the contradictions of contemporary discourse. *Sex Education,* 2: 119–32.
Bay-Cheng, LY (2003) The trouble of teen sex: the construction of adolescent sexuality through school-based sexuality education. *Sex Education: Sexuality, Society and Learning,* 3: 61–74.
Bhana, D (2002) Making gender in early schooling. A multi-sited ethnographic study of power and discourse: from grade one to two in Durban. Unpublished PhD thesis, University of Natal, Durban (now University of KwaZulu-Natal).
Bruner, J (1990) *Acts of meaning.* Cambridge, MA: Harvard University Press.
Bunyan, N (2004) Parents log on to watch pupils in classroom. *The Daily Telegraph,* 25 Oct, p3.
Butler, J (1990) *Gender trouble: feminism and the subversion of identity.* New York: Routledge.
Butler, J (1993) *Bodies that matter: on the discursive limits of 'sex'.* New York: Routledge.
Butler, J (1997) *The psychic life of power.* Stanford, CA: Stanford University Press.
Butler, J (2004) *Undoing gender.* New York: Routledge.
Cahill, BJ and Theilheimer, R (1998) Stonewall in the housekeeping area: gay and lesbian issues in the early childhood classroom, in Letts, WJ, IV and Sears, JT (eds) *Queering elementary education: advancing the dialogue about sexualities and schooling.* Lanham, MD: Rowman & Littlefield.
Connolly, P (2004) *Boys and schooling in the early years.* London: RoutledgeFalmer.
Davies, B. (1989) *Frogs and snails and feminist tales.* St Leonards: Allen and Unwin.

Davis, JE (1999) Forbidden fruit: Black males' constructions of transgressive sexualities in middle school, in Letts, WJ, IV and Sears, JT. (eds) *Queering elementary education: advancing the dialogue about sexualities and schooling*. Lanham, MD: Rowman & Littlefield.

Deacon, R, Morrell, R and Prinsloo, J (1999) Discipline and homophobia in South African schools: the limits of legislated transformation, in Epstein, D and Sears, JT (eds) *A dangerous knowing: sexuality, pedagogy and popular culture*. London: Cassell.

Douglas, N, Warwick, I, Kemp, S and Whitty, G (1997) *Playing it safe: responses of secondary school teachers to lesbian, gay and bisexual pupils, bullying, HIV and AIDS education and Section 28*. London: Institute of Education, University of London.

Duncan, N. (1999) *Sexual bullying: gender conflict and pupil cultures in secondary schools*. London: Routledge.

Epstein, D (1997) Boyz' own stories: masculinities and sexualities in schools. *Gender and Education,* 9: 105–15.

Epstein, D (1998) 'Real boys don't work': boys' 'underachievement', masculinities and the harassment of sissies, in Epstein, D, Elwood, J, Hey, V and Maw, J (eds) *Failing boys? Issues in gender and achievement*. Buckingham: Open University Press.

Epstein, D (1999) Sex play: romantic significations, sexism and silences in the schoolyard, in Epstein, D and Sears, JT (eds) *A dangerous knowing: sexuality, pedagogy and popular culture*. London: Cassell.

Epstein, D, Hewitt, R, Leonard, D, Mauthner, M and Watkins, C (2003) Avoiding the issue: homophobia, school policies and identities in secondary schools, in Carol V (ed), *Identity, social justice and education*. London: RoutledgeFalmer.

Epstein, D, Kehily, MJ, Mac an Ghaill, M and Redman, P (2001) Girls and boys come out to play: making masculinities and femininities in primary playgrounds. *Men and Masculinities. Disciplining and Punishing Masculinities,* 4: 158–72.

Epstein, D, O'Flynn, S and Telford, D (2002) Innocence and experience, paradoxes in sexuality and education, in Richardson, D and Seidman, S (eds) *Handbook of lesbian and gay studies*. London: Sage.

Epstein, D, O'Flynn, S and Telford, D (2003) *Silenced sexualities in schools and universities*. Stoke-on-Trent: Trentham Books.

Foucault, M (1977) *Discipline and punish: the birth of the prison* (Sheridan, A trans.). Harmondsworth: Penguin.

Foucault, M (1978) *The history of sexuality*. Vol 1, *An introduction*. Harmondsworth: Penguin.

Frank, B (1993) Straight/strait jackets for masculinity: educating for real men. *Atlantis,* 18(1 and 2): 47–59.

Freire, P (1996) *Pedagogy of the oppressed*. London: Penguin.

Gordon, T, Holland, J and Lahelma, E (2000) *Making spaces: citizenship and difference in schools*. Basingstoke: Macmillan.

Hey, V (1997) *The company she keeps: an ethnography of girls' friendships*. Buckingham: Open University Press.

Hey, V (2002) Horizontal solidarities and molten capitalism: the subject, intersubjectivity, self and other in the late modern. *Discourse: Studies in the Cultural Politics of Education,* 23: 227–41.

Hillier, L and Harrison, L (2004) Homophobia and the production of shame: young people and same sex attraction. *Culture, Health and Sexuality,* 6: 79–94.

Jackson, S (1982) *Childhood and sexuality*. Oxford: Basil Blackwell.

Jackson, S (1999) *Heterosexuality in question*. London: Sage.

James, A and Prout, A (eds) (1997) *Constructing and reconstructing childhood* (2nd edn). London: FalmerPress.

Jenks, C (1996) *Childhood*. London: Routledge.

Kehily, M (1996) More sugar? Young people, teenage magazines and sexuality. *Sex Education Matters,* 9: 7–8.

Kehily, MJ (2002) *Sexuality, gender and schooling: shifting agendas in social learning*. London: RoutledgeFalmer.

Kehily, M, Epstein, D, Mac an Ghaill, M and Redman, P (2002) Private girls and public worlds: producing femininities in the primary school. *Discourse: Studies in the Cultural Politics of Education*, Special Issue: *Theorizing friendship*.

Kehily, MJ and Nayak, A (1997) 'Lads and laughter': humour and the production of heterosexual hierarchies. *Gender and Education,* Special Issue: Griffin, C and Lees, S (eds) *Masculinities in education,* 9: 69–88.

Kelly, P (2003) Growing up as risky business? Risks, surveillance and the institutionalized mistrust of youth. *Journal of Youth Studies,* 6: 165–80.

Kenway, J, Bullen, E and Hey, V (2000) New Labour, social exclusion and educational risk management: the case of 'gymslip' mums. *British Educational Research Journal,* 26: 441–56.

Kitzinger, J (1988) Defending innocence: ideologies of childhood. *Feminist Review,* Special Issue: *Family secrets, child sexual abuse,* 28: 77–87.

Lees, S (1986) *Losing out: sexuality and adolescent girls.* London: Hutchinson.

Lees, S (1993) *Sugar and spice: sexuality and adolescent girls.* London: Penguin.

McRobbie, A (1991) *Feminism and youth culture: from 'Jackie' to 'Just Seventeen'.* London: Macmillan.

Mellor, DJ (2004) Best friends and true loves: romance in children's relationship cultures. Paper presented at 'Pleasure and Danger Revisited: Sexualities in the 21st Century' Conference, Cardiff University.

Mills, S (1997) *Discourse.* London: Routledge.

O'Flynn, S and Epstein, D (2005) Standardising sexuality: embodied knowledge, 'achievement' and 'standards', *Social Semiotics,* 15: 185–210.

Plummer, K (1995) *Telling sexual stories: power, change and social worlds.* London: Routledge.

Redman, P, Epstein, D, Kehily, MJ and Mac an Ghaill, M (2002) Boys bonding: friendship and the production of masculinities in a primary school Classroom. *Discourse: Studies in the Cultural Politics of Education,* Special Issue: *Theorizing friendship.*

Renold, E (2001) 'Square-girls', femininity and the negotiation of academic success in the primary school. *British Journal of Sociology of Education,* 27: 577–88.

Renold, E (2002) Presumed innocence: (hetero)sexual, heterosexist and homophobic harassment among primary school girls and boys. *Childhood,* 9: 415–34.

Renold, E (2004) 'Other' boys: negotiating non-hegemonic masculinities in the primary school. *Gender and Education,* 16: 247–66.

Renold, E (2005) *Girls, boys and junior sexualities: exploring children's gender and sexual relations in the primary school.* London: RoutledgeFalmer.

Rivers, I (1995) The victimisation of gay teenagers in schools: homophobia in education. *Pastoral Care,* March: 35–41.

Rubin, G (1984) Thinking sex notes for a radical theory of the politics of sexuality, in Vance, C (ed) *Pleasure and danger: exploring female sexuality.* London: Pandora. Reprinted and updated in Abelove, H, Barale, AN and Halperin, D (eds) (1993) *The lesbian and gay studies reader.* London: Routledge.

Sears, JT (2002) The institutional climate for lesbian, gay and bisexual education faculty: what is the pivotal frame of reference? *Journal of Homosexuality,* 43: 11–37.

Seidman, S (1995) Deconstructing queer theory or the under-theorisation of the social and the ethical, in Nicholson, SL, and Seidman, S (eds) *Social postmodernism: beyond identity politics.* Cambridge: Cambridge University Press.

Seidman, S (1997) *Difference troubles: queering social theory and sexual politics.* Cambridge: Cambridge University Press.

Spraggs, G (1994) Coming out in the NUT, in Epstein, D (ed) *Challenging lesbian and gay inequalities in education.* Buckingham: Open University Press.

Sumara, D and Davis, B (1999) Interrupting heteronormativity: toward a queer curriculum theory. *Curriculum Inquiry,* 29: 191–208.

Swain, J (2000) 'The money's good, the fame's good, the girls are good': the role of playground football in the construction of young boys' masculinity in a junior school. *British Journal of Sociology of Education,* 21: 95–109.

Thomson, R (2000) Dream on – the logic of sexual practice. *Journal of Youth Studies,* 4: 407–27.

Thorne, B (1993) *Gender play: boys and girls in school.* Buckingham: Open University Press (published in the USA by Rutgers University Press).

Thorogood, N (2000) Sex education as disciplinary technique: policy and practice in England and Wales. *Sexualities,* Special issue: *Sexualities and education,* 3: 425–38.

Vance, CS (ed) (1984) *Pleasure and danger: exploring female sexuality.* London: Pandora.

Vance, CS (1995) Social construction theory and sexuality, in Berger, M, Wallis, B and Watson, S (eds) *Constructing masculinity.* New York: Routledge.

Walkerdine, V (1984) Developmental psychology and the child-centred pedagogy: the insertion of Piaget into early education, in Henriques, J, Hollway, W, Urwin, C, Venn, C and Walkerdine,V (eds) *Changing the subject: psychology, social regulation and subjectivity.* London: Methuen.

Walkerdine, V (1990) *Schoolgirl fictions.* London: Verso.

Walkerdine,V (1997) *Daddy's girl: young girls and popular culture.* Basingstoke: Macmillan.

Walkerdine, V, Lucey, H and Melody, J (2001) *Growing up girl: psychosocial explorations of gender and class.* Basingstoke: Palgrave.

Warner, M (ed.) (1993) *Fear of the queer planet: queer politics and social theory.* Minneapolis, MN: University of Minnesota Press.

Weeks, J (1986) *Sexuality.* London: Tavistock.

Weeks, J (1991) *Against nature: essays on history, sexuality and identity.* London: Rivers Oram.

Willis, P (1977) *Learning to labour: how working class kids get working class jobs.* Aldershot: Saxon House.

Wyn, J and White, R (1997) *Rethinking youth.* London: Sage.

NOTES

1. The example used here is from the UK, but, as will be clear from the rest of the chapter, the disciplining of sexuality occurs in a similar vein in educational settings throughout Western Anglophone societies. It is also important to note that the news article does not say whether the students involved in the 'canoodling' were boys and girls, but the hetero-gendered silence concerning this suggests that they were.

2. The politics of using terms like 'LGBT' (lesbian, gay, bisexual, transgendered) and 'queer' is highly contested. There are many places where these politics are discussed in detail. See, for example, Warner, 1993; Seidman, 1995; Epstein *et al.,* 2003.

3. See, for example the following websites (all accessed 25 January 2005): www.ntac.org/news/01/06/18wa.html;www.pfaw.org/pfaw/general/default.aspx?oid=3385;www.egale.ca/index.asp?lang=E&menu=2002&item=275.

4. Provision of state education was, of course, also a response to the extension of the franchise.

5. 'Hetero' is placed in parentheses, here, to emphasize how certain heterosexual cultures and meanings are present in people's lives but are treated as natural and thus unproblematic. We use this form when we are representing the commonly deployed perspective that sexuality is always heterosexual.

6. This obviously also has implications for those doing research about sexualities in schools. See, for example, Kehily (2002).

7. The 2005 State of the Union address by the US president, George Bush, is a good example of this. See www.guardian.co.uk/international/story/0,1404917,00.html (accessed 7 February 2005).

8. We say 'supposedly unwanted' because it is far from clear that teenage girls who become pregnant do not want to be and, indeed, that they may not have their own rationalities in relationship to pregnancies (see, for example Kenway *et al.,* 2000; Thomson, 2000).

9. The social constructionist perspective has been enhanced by the integration of psychoanalytic theory. See, for example, Butler (1990; 1997).

10. A 'slag' is a woman who is seen as sexually promiscuous, while a 'drag' is boring (and, in this context, sexually unavailable).

28

Achieving Equity: Disability and Gender

Michael L. Wehmeyer and Harilyn Rousso

Education then, beyond all other devices of human origin, is the great equalizer of the conditions of men, the balance-wheel of the social machinery.

(Horace Mann, 1848)

Exempting Horace Mann's gender-specific language as an artifact of the nineteenth century, Mann's 'great credo of public education' articulates the critical role of education in achieving social, economic, and political equality. In an era of universal education, the importance of education as 'the great equalizer' is, perhaps, too often taken for granted by the majority. For some, however, the struggle for equity in education remains of primary importance to achieve the promise of equality. We have noted (Rousso and Wehmeyer, 2001), as have others, that 'there is a growing body of evidence that being disabled and female is a double disadvantage, placing young women with disabilities *in double jeopardy* for poverty, unemployment, and a bleak future upon leaving school' (p2), and yet issues pertaining to disability, gender, and education still receive only limited attention, particularly in countries struggling with economic hardships.

The intent of this chapter is to overview existing information about the status of educational opportunities for girls and young women with disabilities[1] and to examine issues that hinder or help girls and young women with disabilities achieve greater equity. We focus on the experiences of girls and young women because research shows that outcomes for this population are almost universally poorer than for others, including boys with disability. We note, however, that there are issues pertaining to being male and having a disability that warrant consideration, and turn to that topic specifically later in the chapter.

This is, in many ways, a daunting task for a book, much less a book chapter. First, girls and young women with disabilities are not a homogeneous group. Disability determinations vary from country to country and even within countries. We take as our reference point for defining disability the World Health Organization's International Classification of Functioning, Disability, and Health (WHO, 1999), which defines disability as an outcome of the interaction between a person's health condition and contextual factors that result in an impairment of body function or structure, capacity limitations, and/or performance or participation restrictions. This is a broad definition that acknowledges the role of biological limitations and societal barriers. Even controlling for variability by the adoption of a universal definition of disability, such as the WHO definition, however, one is left with the fact that disability occurs across multiple areas of human functioning, including cognition, mobility, and emotional and behavioral, affective, and sensory domains, and includes considerable variation within each of those human functioning domains. It is clear that the educational needs of a girl with bipolar disorder will differ considerably from those of a young woman with intellectual disabilities, whose needs, in turn, will differ from a girl who is deaf.

Second, there is a reciprocal relationship among gender, disability, and several other factors affecting equity in education, including socioeconomic status and poverty level as well as race and ethnicity. For example, there is a reciprocal relationship between poverty and disability. Poverty can cause disability, particularly in women and girls, who in the face of limited resources are more likely than their male counterparts to be deprived of basic necessities, such as food and medicine (Groce, 1997). Disability, in turn, can contribute to poverty, because of the additional expenses that it can entail or its impact on employment, discussed subsequently. Thus, disabled girls are more likely to grow up in poor families, a reality that in itself places them at an educational disadvantage. Race and ethnicity can also be a compounding factor. In the USA, for example, there are a disproportionate number of African-American students receiving special education services, reflecting, in part, the intersection of race and disability bias, and thus affecting educational equity.

Third, the educational experiences of girls and young women with disabilities must be seen in a larger context of double discrimination based on disability and gender that limits women with disabilities of all ages in all areas of their lives – home, school, workplace and community. Around the globe, on every measure of educational, vocational, financial and social success, women and girls with disabilities fare less well than their nondisabled female or disabled male counterparts. Underlying the double discrimination is double stereotyping: negative assumptions about girls and women combine with negative assumptions about people with disabilities, so that disabled women are perceived less favorably than either nondisabled women or disabled men. They are often viewed as sick, childlike, dependent, asexual, or incompetent, and their talents and assets are overlooked. The presence of discriminatory patterns in schools is particularly disheartening because of the potential of education to address social inequities.

GENDER, DISABILITY AND EDUCATION

Recognizing these complexities of our task, we first consider how many girls and young women worldwide have disabilities and then what types of educational challenges they encounter. With regard to the former, there are no completely reliable data on the number or percentage of girls with disabilities. WHO has estimated that 7–10% of the world's population has some type of disability and that 80% of these live in developing countries (WHO, 1999). UNESCO and others estimate that the number of children with disabilities under the age of 18 around the world varies from 120 to 150 million. Even assuming that girls make up somewhat less than half of all children with disabilities, as some research suggests (Groce, 1999), the number of girls with disabilities worldwide is likely to be substantial.

While we may extrapolate from what we know about gender bias and the educational experiences of all girls and reasonably suggest that these same experiences affect girls and young women with disabilities in similar ways, the truth is that there has been only limited research pertaining to how these factors affect girls and young women with disabilities. This section presents an overview of what is known about these issues. It should be obvious that the barriers to educational access vary across countries, depending upon multiple factors, including economic, social, cultural, and religious factors. We have structured these factors to align with the ecological framework proposed by Bronfenbrenner (1977). Accordingly, factors influencing access to education for girls and young women with disabilities are considered as a function of microsystem (e.g. the immediate settings and factors within which girls develop and spend their daily lives), mesosytem (linkages between microsystem variables), exosystem (settings or factors in which girls do not actually participate but through which decisions are made that affect them), and macrosystem (more global factors that influence exosystem variables) variables. We will begin with the more global factors, and then address mesosystem and microsystem factors.

MACROSYSTEM AND EXOSYSTEM VARIABLES AFFECTING THE EDUCATION OF GIRLS AND YOUNG WOMEN WITH DISABILITIES

Cultural bias against women and rigid gender roles

Internationally, the most frequently mentioned barrier to education for girls with disabilities has been cultural biases against women (Fahd *et al.*, 1997), leading to preferential treatment and allocation of resources and opportunities to male children, at the expense of their sisters (Rousso, 2003). Education is deemed less important for girls, who are expected to become wives and mothers, whereas boys, destined to become breadwinners, are given priority in schooling. Disability status does not negate this gender bias, although, as will be noted below, questions about disabled girls' potential for marriage may compound it. It is also noteworthy that this bias is not exclusive, by any means, to non-Western countries. For example, employment outcomes for women with disabilities in the USA are less positive than for disabled or nondisabled men (Rabren *et al.*, 2002), in part because of these same 'women as mothers, men as breadwinners' biases (Doren and Benz, 2001).

Such cultural biases against schooling for girls in general and girls with disabilities in particular are prevalent. In a report on gender and education to the World Bank for the UNESCO Education for All initiative, Rousso (2003) provided the following examples of these issues:

- **Kenya**: 'The African society places more value on boys than girls. So when resources are scarce, boys are given a priority. A disabled boy will be sent to school at the advantage of the girl' (Rousso, 2003: 6).

  There are similar examples from Ghana (Nyarko, 2003) and Tanzania (Macha, 2002).

- **Costa Rica**: 'There are more disabled women in Costa Rica than disabled men (51% compared to 49%), something you see in elementary school. But in secondary school and sheltered workshops there are more boys. … In our culture, girls are supposed to stay at home while boys are supposed to go out and "earn a living." Girls are more "private," boys are more "public"'. (Rousso, 2003: 7).

  A similar report came from Mexico (Rousso, 2003: 7).

- **Palestinian Territory in the Middle East**: 'The health and beauty of girls and women are a representation of family well-being, and a symbol of the good standing of the family. Female family members are not supposed to produce wealth independently; they are seen primarily as mothers, supporting the lead of fathers, brothers and ultimately their husbands. It is expected that all daughters will marry; a successfully arranged marriage is an enhancement of the family's name and prestige. Because of the norms of female beauty and the role of women in the family, a disabled woman is seen as a failure on several counts. While disabled sons can be tolerated and often married, disabled daughters are merely a drain on already stretched resources; permanent family members with no hope of future marriage or social mobility. It is quite usual for a disabled woman to be hidden by her family' (Atshan, 1997: 54).

  Activist and scholar Anita Ghai describes a similar situation in India (Hershey, 2000).

As with most factors affecting upon educational opportunities for girls and young women with disabilities, the biases and stereotypes about girls and women combine with those about people with disabilities to exacerbate the problem. Families often assume that a disabled daughter will not marry, which may add to her devaluation, since, in some cultures, the prospect of a good marriage is the primary value given to girls. In contrast, as noted, it is assumed that boys, even those with disabilities, will become breadwinners, as well as marry. In addition, in many cultures, disability is a source of stigma, so that having a disabled daughter is seen as a double liability that can lead to the devaluation of the whole family. Hence in some families, not only are girls with disabilities denied access to school, but they are also hidden away.

Poverty and economic opportunity

As we have noted, poverty and economic circumstances are intertwined with the experience of disability, as both a cause and an outcome of disability. Such economic circumstances are often intertwined with gender roles to affect access to education. In impoverished families, the limited resources available will be used to educate boys, with the expectation that they will ultimately help support the family. Girls are not likely to be educated, particularly not disabled girls, who may be more costly to send to school if they need disability-related equipment or special transportation.

Related to these issues of poverty and economic opportunity are issues of distance to education, often a problem in developing countries. Distance to school constitutes an educational barrier for many girls. Issues include safety and cultural prohibitions against females traveling unescorted. For girls with disabilities, the barriers may be intensified. In some areas, the only schools that serve students with disabilities are segregated special education schools, often located in urban centers. Students with disabilities from rural regions must travel to attend school, and often live at the school. Cultural expectations that girls stay close to home may prohibit participation by disabled girls (Fahd *et al.*, 1997).

Violence and safety

While violence is a barrier to education for all girls, it may be more of an issue for girls with disabilities. Available data suggest that people with disabilities in general and disabled girls as a group experience violence within the family, institutions, and community at higher rates than their nondisabled peers (Sobsey, 1994; Linn and Rousso, 2001). Part of this may be the disability limitations themselves, making it more difficult for some girls to assess violent situations, to defend themselves or flee, or to report incidents of violence (Khemka, 2000). However, negative attitudes may be a greater barrier. The stereotypes attributed to women with disabilities discussed previously (e.g. sick, helpless, asexual and powerless) may lead disabled girls to be seen as easy targets, a problem resulting in sexual harassment in schools (see subsequent section for discussion). They are also regularly deprived of the skills and opportunities they need to recognize and address violence, including adequate sex education (Khemka, 2000; Wehmeyer *et al.*, 2001). Finally, police and community members may fail to respond appropriately to incidents of violence against disabled girls, doubting the credibility of the reporter (Rousso, 2001).

MICROSYSTEM AND MESOSYSTEM VARIABLES AFFECTING THE EDUCATION OF GIRLS AND YOUNG WOMEN WITH DISABILITIES

It is worth noting, parenthetically, that much of the limited research on microsystem and mesosystem factors comes from more developed countries, although anecdotal information suggests that these findings may have broader implications.

Gender bias in referral and admission to special education services

To participate in school, students with disabilities may need a variety of services, from sign language interpreters, to modification in teaching methods to access to physical and occupational therapies. In more developed countries, access to services depends on being identified by school personnel as having a disability and/or 'special educational needs'. Available research suggests that gender affects who is referred.

Kedar-Voivodas (1983) noted that child-rearing practice, sex-role modeling, imitation, socialization, and a student's reaction to school influence the repertoire of behavior girls and boys perform in the classroom. Boys may learn early that adults are tolerant of their active behavior while girls are encouraged to behave in more inhibited ways; passive, quiet, obedient, and pleasant (Blackorby and Wagner, 1996). Taylor *et al.* (2001) found that when teachers viewed videotapes of students who were engaged in inappropriate behaviors, the factors most influencing teachers' perceptions of behavior were the student's gender and the teacher's gender. Therefore, one barrier to equity in education for girls with disabilities involves referral bias. Referral bias is the degree to which people responsible for referring students for evaluation for eligibility for special education services, typically teachers in regular education classrooms, make such referrals based upon personal and professional opinions rather than objective indicators.

Research suggests, however, that the problem is more complex than teachers referring males due to behavior problems. Shinn *et al.* (1987) noted two types of errors possible in teacher referrals: (1) bias, and (2) teacher inaccuracy, or 'the extent to which teachers' appraisal of pupil performance is confirmed by objective criteria' (p33). Shinn *et al.*'s (1987) study of teacher accuracy concluded that teachers were quite accurate about the reading abilities of students they referred. Across all grades and all analyses, referred students had significant reading problems when compared with local norms. However, the distribution of achievement scores for the referred students fell within the normative distribution for the measure. These authors suggested that teachers decide that not all poor readers need to be referred, but instead only those who are poor readers and have some associated school problems, such as hyperactivity or aggression, or those that 'do not meet the biases of the teacher' (p9).

MacMillan *et al.* (1996) studied the referral of students for special education services. They administered a battery of assessments to 150 students, grades 2–4, who had been nominated for special education. There was no significant difference by gender on intelligence or achievement tests for this sample, although teachers rated girls as having higher academic competence and there were statistical differences for gender on two teacher ratings of problem behaviors and social skills. Boys were rated as exhibiting more problem behaviors and lower levels of social skills than girls on one scale, and were scored higher on scales measuring conduct problems, hyperactivity, and inattentiveness on the other instrument. MacMillan and colleagues suggested that the combination of more frequent, and more severe, behavior problems combined with poor achievement led to their referral. Wehmeyer and Schwartz (2001a) conducted a records review of 695 students, six years of age and older, who had been admitted to special education for the first time during a one-year span. Consistent with national norms in the USA, boys outnumbered girls almost exactly two to one (462 boys, 233 girls). Data on biological factors that might explain the disproportionate number of boys in this sample, as well as information about behavior problems, were collected. To examine the impact of gender stereotyping on admission, data was collected on three indicators of this: age at which students were admitted to special education, IQ scores at time of admission, and type of placement. Earlier research suggested that girls are older when admitted to special education, implying they wait longer to receive assistance; girls have more significant deficits at time of admission; boys tend to have higher IQ than do girls admitted; and, once admitted for special education services, boys are more likely than boys to be placed in more segregated and restrictive classroom settings. (Singer and Osborn, 1970; Gillespie and Fink, 1974; Kratovil and Bailey, 1986).

Wehmeyer and Schwartz (2001a) found that from the total of 695 new admissions to special education, 97 student records indicated a biological explanation. For the remaining 598 students, the gender proportion remained almost 2/3 males (65% males, 35% females). Upon examination of the three indicators of gender bias, there were significant differences in two. First, girls obtained lower scores on standardized IQ tests at the time of their first admission for special education services. Second, girls were disproportionately more likely than boys to be placed in self-contained classrooms as result of their admission for special education services. It also appeared that behavioral factors were influencing referral, even when we excluded cases where higher levels of overactivity, aggression, or nonconforming behaviors had been documented. In fact, only one girl's (2.5% of all girls) record outlined behavioral reasons for her referral, while nearly 20% of boys had behavioral reasons listed on the referral sheets. Six boys had only behavior reasons provided.

In two population-based studies, Oswald *et al.* (2001) and Coutinho *et al.* (2002) found clear effects of gender on admission to special education services for students labeled as having mental retardation or learning disabilities. Essentially, boys were more likely to be admitted than girls.

In the UK, Daniels *et al.* (1999) found that among students with special education needs from 35 schools in England, boys not only outnumbered girls by nearly two to one, but also received more average hours of support per week.

Wehmeyer and Schwartz (2001a) concluded, 'the present system is inequitable, not necessarily because more boys than girls are being served, but because girls who have equivalent educational needs are not provided access to supports and services that might address those needs' (p42). The suggestion from this study was that girls, who are not as likely to be acting out, are not likely to be referred for learning problems, and thus will have to experience more significant problems to gain the support they need. Presumably, there are girls in classes who have academic needs that are comparable to boys', but who are not being referred. Girls who experience learning problems may actually be displaying more passive or withdrawn behaviors, deficits in social skills, more fearful and anxious behavior, or more obedient and conforming behaviors, and therefore may be disregarded as needing educational interventions, especially when they are 'only' having math problems (Grossman and Grossman, 1994; Lyon, 1996). As such, the problem at hand may not be male overrepresentation but, indeed, female underrepresentation. Support for this suggestion was provided by research from Share and Silva (2003) in New Zealand, whose analysis showed the predicted reading scores systematically overestimated reading disorders in boys and underestimated them in girls.

Bias in educational materials

Studies of gender bias in educational materials and resources used by students with disabilities are highly limited. However, what we know suggests that gender bias in the curriculum may be a significant issue for girls. In one of the few studies, Wehmeyer and Schwartz (2001b) examined materials developed for high-school students with disabilities and found numerous examples of gender stereotyping in the types of pictures used and in the content of materials. Other research suggests that to the extent that people with disabilities appear in instructional materials, women with disabilities are either underrepresented or stereotypically portrayed (Women and Disability Awareness Project, 1984; Council of Chief State School Officers, 1986; Shaffer and Shevitz, 2001). The lack of disabled women teachers in most school systems (Magrab, 2000) and the relative absence of women with disabilities in the media (Rousso, 2000) compound the negative effects of gender bias in the curriculum, depriving girls and young women with disabilities of positive role models.

Differences in course availability

Another area in which gender bias in education shows up is in the types and content of courses taken by girls and boys. Research has shown that both girls and boys with disabilities appear to take roughly equal numbers of vocational education courses, but differ in the types of courses they are enrolled in, with girls taking more female-stereotyped courses (home economics) or preparing for female-stereotyped jobs (cashier, childcare worker) and boys enrolled in courses leading to more traditionally 'male' roles, such as auto mechanics or carpentry (Lichtenstein, 1996; Doren and Benz, 2001). Not insignificantly, male courses also prepare attendees for higher-paying jobs, which may account for the wage gap found for young men and young women with disabilities (Lichtenstein, 1996).

Sexual harassment

Sexual harassment in school is recognized as a widespread problem for non-disabled girls (AAUW, 1993; Stein, 1993, 1996). Such harassment happens to students across gender, racial, ethnic, socioeconomic, and sexual orientation lines, and causes students to drop out, change career plans, lose friends and feel emotional anguish (Linn and Rousso, 2001). The limited data available, mainly pilot studies in the USA, that focus on sexual harassment for students/girls with disabilities, suggest that students with disabilities face higher rates of harassment in school than nondisabled students, and disabled girls face higher rates of harassment than disabled boys or nondisabled girls; girls with multiple disabilities are at particularly high risk (Joint Commission of the Chancellor and the Special Commissioner for the Prevention of Child Sexual Abuse, 1994). Reports from other countries, including Mexico, other Latin American countries, and Australia (Rousso, 2003), also acknowledge sexual and/or disability harassment in school as a barrier to learning for girls with disabilities.

ACHIEVING EQUITY

The identification of 'what we know' about gender and disability in education is a vital first step in achieving educational equity, but it is only a first step. The review of the literature reported in the first portion of this chapter leads us in two directions; first, toward the identification of what research needs to be done so that we might better understand the factors that contribute to inequitable outcomes for girls and women with disabilities, and, second, toward practices that might address these factors.

Research needs

As Wehmeyer and Rousso (2001) noted, the starting point for achieving gender equity for students with disabilities is predicated on learning more about the impact of variables that affect all girls, particularly those variables, such as teacher–student interactions, sexual harassment, or gender stereotyping in curricular materials and assessment, that have been well documented as contributing to inequity for all girls. However, to conduct separate research focused only on students with disabilities would be a mistake. The factors pertaining to disability need to be incorporated into research pertaining to gender equity for all girls. Not only must this research address gender and disability, but it must also take into account issues related to race, ethnicity, and socioeconomic status. Gender, disability, race, ethnicity, and socioeconomic status are not orthogonal variables that affect the educational process, and research needs to move from treating them as such (Wehmeyer and Schwartz, 2001: 283).

Addressing gender equity for girls with disabilities

At the macrosystem and exosystem level, a number of issues need to be addressed to achieve gender equity for girls and young women with disabilities in education. In many countries, the first step involves the establishment of policies and programs that address the educational needs of disabled girls, and provide systemic efforts to redress inequities for this group of students. In other countries, existing laws or policies need to be more vigorously enforced. To address the cultural biases that limit educational access for girls with and without disabilities, media campaigns to change attitudes and practices are important. For example, Rousso (2003) noted that activists in India succeeded in achieving more positive images of disabled women through such media-driven efforts, and similar strategies are underway in Egypt and Lebanon (Nagata, 2003). Another important strategy to change attitudes is widespread parent education that highlights the importance of education for girls and young women with disabilities and provides parents with access to successful disabled women who can serve as role models.

To address macro/exosystem and micro/mesosystem issues pertaining to violence and sexual harassment, there is a need to develop and implement more widely violence prevention awareness campaigns, as well as to provide training to medical and other professionals and to girls and young women with disabilities themselves. Such efforts are underway in many countries. For example, Rousso (2003) identified efforts by organizations in Australia to develop and disseminate a *Women with Disabilities and Violence Information Kit* that includes poetry/articles written by disabled women, research findings, annotated bibliographies, resource materials including Internet sites, and information on government programs to combat violence as an example of such initiatives. In addition, it is important that all mainstream violence and sexual harassment prevention materials incorporate issues of disability.

An important microsystem factor affecting girls and young women with disabilities involves the knowledge, attitudes, and capacity of teachers to provide gender-and-disability-equitable instruction and support. There is a need to focus more attention on teacher-preparation programs to ensure that teachers-in-training obtain information about gender bias, and its impact on girls and young women with disabilities. Many currently existing courses and resources that address gender equity – admittedly far too few – fail to incorporate disability issues.

Additionally, there is a need to focus attention on in-service training to ensure that teachers who do not receive the information in their pre-service training programs are provided such information in the context of their teaching experience. (See Rousso and Wehmeyer, 2002, for one model of an inservice training program that helps teachers develop attitudes and skills needed to address these issues.)

The above efforts will address the capacity of educators to provide gender-and-disability-equitable experiences for all students. In addition, however, the curriculum needs to be designed in such a manner as to support equity. Materials that propagate stereotyped views of women and girls or people with disabilities need to be abandoned and replaced with those that do not provide such biased perceptions. In addition, educators and administrators need to be aware of the courses students with disabilities can take, and ensure that stereotyping does not occur at that level.

Gender equity and boys with disabilities

There is ample evidence that boys outnumber girls in special education services, a finding replicated across many countries. This is, to some degree, good news in that it indicates that boys with disabilities may be getting the assistance they need to overcome limitations introduced by their disability. This is not, however, an unequivocally positive outcome. Being labeled and identified as having a disability puts one at risk of discrimination and the negative impact of stereotypes associated with disability. Flood (2001) pointed out that societal images of males as physically fit and athletic lead to perceptions of males with disabilities, many of whom have physical impairments, as weak or ineffectual and play into discriminative practices. Flood identified the following aspects of boys' experience that may relate to disability:

1. By middle school, boys are far more likely to be grade repeaters and dropouts.
2. Boys lag behind girls in reading and writing proficiency at all educational levels.
3. Boys' misbehavior results in more frequent penalties, including corporal punishment.
4. Boys comprise 71% of all students who receive school suspensions.
5. Boys comprise 80% of students with emotional and behavioral disorders
6. Boys are four times more likely to be referred to a school psychologist.
7. Boys are nine times more likely to suffer from hyperactivity and higher levels of academic stress.
8. It is estimated that one in six boys aged 5–12 is diagnosed with attention deficit disorder (ADD).
9. When they attempt suicide, boys succeed in killing themselves seven times more often than girls.
10. Though still proportionately lower than rates for white males, the suicide rate for African-American males has increased 165% over the last 12 years.
11. Gay youths account for up to 30% of all suicides.
12. The death rate from firearms use among boys aged 15–19 more than doubled (in the USA) from 1985 to 1994, now representing its highest level ever of 49.2 deaths per 100,000.

The fact is, we know next to nothing (with the exception of statistics concerning male overrepresentation in certain special needs categories) about the impact of the combination of gender and disability for boys in educational settings, yet the above referenced indicators suggest we need to do so.

CONCLUSION

Wehmeyer and Rousso (2001) suggested that teachers consider the following points when evaluating the degree to which they provide gender-and-disability-equitable educational services:

- *Know thyself*. Change starts with examining one's own practices and beliefs. Do not make assumptions about whether or not you do or do not treat students differently; step back and examine the question in an objective manner.
- *Knowledge is power*. Take advantage of resources to learn about gender-equitable practices and, if possible, arrange for training opportunities for other educators.
- *Families as partners.* Create reliable allies with parents and extended family members of children with disabilities, particularly parents of girls. Many parents of girls with disabilities share concerns about their daughters' future and if they are made aware of the many, often subtle ways that the education system discriminates against girls, and the consequences thereof, they can become powerful agents for system change.
- *Curriculum evaluation*. Curricular materials and classroom activities need to be gender fair. Identify materials that are not biased or augment existing materials to ensure equity.
- *Students as allies*. Communicate your commitment to equity to your students and bring them on as allies in your efforts. Work with students to set classroom standards for behavior and tolerance. Work within the school to ensure that students have access to orientations on issues such as sexual harassment. Be your students' ally and advocate, and be willing to listen to students.
- *Women with disabilities in the community as allies*. Draw upon the expertise of adult women with disabilities in the community to help promote gender equity in your classroom. Depending on their background and interests, they can serve as mentors and role models for students and their parents, provide invaluable information on postsecondary options and the work of work, assist with the assessment of curricula, suggest resources that more fully promote the accomplishments of women and men with disabilities, and provide a link to the national and global disabled women's movement.
- *Research to practice*. While research has been the domain of universities, there is a growing movement for participatory action research, in which practitioners have an equal role in designing, conducting, and disseminating research. If you do not have a link with a research institution, form one and suggest research activities in your classroom and campus in which you can be actively involved.

It is critical that the efforts to address gender equity and disability in education be taken worldwide. There is a paucity of such work in any country, but, particularly in countries with limited economic resources, these issues have not been addressed.

Achieving gender equity for girls and young women with disabilities will require action at all levels, from the microsystem to the macrosystem level. There are, however, promising beginnings to achieving this and, ultimately, in achieving the social, economic, and political equality embodied in the promise of education. It is important that these first steps lead to greater action on the part of educators, researchers, politicians, and policy makers.

REFERENCES

AAUW (American Association of University Women) (1993) *Hostile hallways: the AAUW survey on sexual harassment in America's schools.* Washington, DC: AAUW Foundation.

Atshan, L (1997) Disability and gender at a cross-roads: a Palestinian perspective; in Abu-Habib, L (ed) *Gender and disability. Women's experiences in the Middle* East (53–9). Dublin: Oxfam.

Blackorby, J and Wagner, M (1996) Longitudinal postschool outcomes of youth with disabilities: findings from the national longitudinal transition study. *Exceptional Children,* 62: 399–413.

Bronfenbrenner, U *(1977)* Toward an experimental ecology of human development. *American Psychologist, 32:* 513–31.

Caseau, DL, Luckasson, R and Kloth, M (1994) Special education services for girls with emotional disturbance: a case of gender bias? *Behavioral Disorders,* 20: 51–60.

Council of Chief State School Officers (1986) *Achieving equity in education programs for disabled women and girls.* Washington, DC: Author.

Coutinho, MJ, Oswald, DP and Best, AM (2002) The influence of sociodemographics and gender on the disproportionate identification of minority students as having learning disabilities. *Remedial and Special Education,* 23: 49–59.

Daniels, H, Hey, V, Leonard, D and Smith, M (1999) Issues of equity in special needs education from a gender perspective. *British Journal of Special Education,* 26: 189–95.

Doren, B and Benz, M (2001) Gender equity issues in the vocational and transition services and employment outcomes experienced by young women with disabilities, In Rousso, H and Wehmeyer, M (eds) *Double jeopardy: addressing gender equity in special education* (289–312). Albany, NY: State University of New York Press.

Fahd, N, Marji, M, Myfti, N, Masri, M and Makaran, A (1997) A double discrimination: blind girls' life chances, in Abu-Habib, L (ed) *Gender and disability. Women's experiences in the Middle* East (46–52). Dublin: Oxfam.

Flood, C (2001) Schools fail boys too: exposing the con of traditional masculinity, in Rousso, H and Wehmeyer, M (eds) *Double jeopardy: addressing gender equity in special education* (207–36). Albany, NY: State University of New York Press.

Gillespie, PH and Fink, AH (1974) The influence of sexism on the education of handicapped children. *Exceptional Children,* 41: 155–62.

Groce, N (1997) Women with disabilities in the developing world. *Journal of Disability Policy Studies,* 8: 178–92.

Groce, N (1999) *An overview of young people living with disabilities: their needs and their rights.* New York: United Nations International Children's Fund (UNICEF).

Grossman, H and Grossman, SH (1994) *Gender issues in education.* Boston, MA: Allyn & Bacon.

Hershey, L (2001) Tanzania: researcher explores lives of disabled women and girls. *Disability World,* September–October. *www.disabilityworld.org/09-10_01/women/tanzania.shtml* (accessed 13 February 2005).

Joint Commission of the Chancellor and the Special Commissioner for the Prevention of Child Sexual Abuse (1994) *Final report of the Joint Commission of the Chancellor and the Special Commissioner for the Prevention of Child Sexual Abuse.* New York: Author.

Kedar-Voivodas, G (1983) The impact of elementary children's school roles and sex roles on teacher attitudes: an interactional analysis. *Review of Educational Research,* 53: 415–37.

Khemka, I (2000) Increasing independent decision-making skills of women with mental retardation in simulated interpersonal situations of abuse. *American Journal on Mental Retardation,* 105: 387–401.

Kratovil, J and Bailey, SM (1986) Sex equity and disabled students. *Theory into Practice*, 2: 250–6.

Lichtenstein, S (1996) Gender differences in the education and employment of young adults: implications for special education. *Remedial and Special Education*, 17: 4–20.

Linn, E and Rousso, H (2001) Stopping sexual harassment in schools, in Rousso, H and Wehmeyer, M (eds) *Double jeopardy: addressing gender equity in special education* (185–206). Albany, NY: State University of New York Press.

Lyon, GR (1996) Learning disabilities. *The Future of Children: Special Education for Students with Disabilities* 6: 54–76.

Macha, E (2002) Visually impaired women and educational opportunities in Tanzania. Paper presented at the AAUW Educational Foundation Conference, International Perspectives – Global Voices for Gender Equity, 15–17 November 2002, Washington, DC.

MacMillan, DL, Gresham, FM, Lopez, MF and Bocian, KM (1996) Comparison of students nominated for prereferral interventions by ethnicity and gender. *Journal of Special Education*, 30: 133–51.

Magrab, P (2000) Special education training in thirteen OECD countries, in Savolainen, H, Kokkala, H and Alasuutari, H (eds) *Meeting special and diverse educational needs. Making inclusive education a reality*. Helsinki: Ministry for Foreign Affairs, Finland, Department of International Cooperation and Niilo Maki Institute.

Mann, H (1848) *Twelfth annual report on education*. Boston, MA: State of Massachusetts.

Nagata, KK (2003) Gender and disability in the Arab region: the challenges in the new millennium. *Asia Pacific Disability Rehabilitation Journal*, 14: 10–17.

Nyarko, V (2003) Information on disabled girls and education from GSPD in Ghana. Unpublished report.

Oswald, DP, Coutinho, MJ, Best, AM and Nguyen, N (2001) Impact of sociodemographic variables on the identification rates of minority students as having mental retardation. *Mental Retardation*, 39: 352–67.

Rabren, K, Dunn, C and Chambers, D (2002) Predictors of post-high school employment among young adults with disabilities. *Career Development for Exceptional Individuals*, 25: 25–40.

Rousso, H (2000) *Girls and women with disabilities: an international overview and summary of research.* New York: Rehabilitation International and the World Institute on Disability.

Rousso, H (2001) *Strong proud sisters: girls and young women with disabilities.* Washington, DC: Center for Women Policy Studies.

Rousso, H (2003) Education for all: a gender and disability perspective. *UNESCO Education for All Global Monitoring Report*. Paris, France: United Nations Educational, Scientific, and Cultural Organization.

Rousso, H and Wehmeyer, ML (2001) *Double jeopardy: addressing gender equity in special education.* Albany, NY: State University of New York Press.

Rousso, H and Wehmeyer, ML (2002) *Gender matters: an inservice training program for all educators working with students with disabilities.* Newton, MA: Women's Educational Equity Act Publishing Center.

Shaffer, S and Shevitz, L (2001) She bakes and he builds: gender bias in the curriculum, in Rousso, H and Wehmeyer, M (eds) *Double jeopardy: addressing gender equity in special education* (115–32). Albany, NY: State University of New York Press.

Share, DL and Silva, PA (2003) Gender bias in IQ – discrepancy and post-discrepancy definitions of reading disabilities. *Journal of Learning Disabilities*, 36: 4–14.

Shinn, MR, Tindal, GA and Spira, DA (1987) Special education referrals as an index of teacher tolerance: are teachers imperfect tests? *Exceptional Children*, 54: 32–40.

Singer, BD and Osborn, RW (1970) Social class and sex differences in admission patterns of the mentally retarded. *American Journal of Mental Deficiency*, 75: 160–2.

Sobsey, R (1994) *Violence and abuse in the lives of people with disabilities: the end of silent acceptance?* Baltimore, MD: Paul H Brookes.

Stein, N (1993) Sexual harassment in schools. *School Administrator*, 50: 14–16.

Stein, N (1996) From the margins to the mainstream: sexual harassment in K–12 schools. *Initiatives*, 57: 19–26.

Taylor, PB, Gunter, PL and Slate, JR (2001) Teachers' perceptions of inappropriate student behavior as a function of teachers' and students' gender and ethnic background. *Behavioral Disorders*, 26: 146–51.

Wehmeyer, ML and Rousso, H (2001) Addressing gender equity in special education services: an agenda for the twenty-first century, in Rousso, H and Wehmeyer, M (eds) *Double jeopardy: addressing gender equity in special education* (375–86). Albany, NY: State University of New York Press.

Wehmeyer, ML, Sands, DJ, Knowlton, E and Kozleski, E (2001) *Teaching students with mental retardation: promoting access to the general curriculum.* Baltimore, MD: Paul H Brookes.

Wehmeyer, ML and Schwartz, M (2001a) Disproportionate representation of males in special education services: biology, behavior, or bias? *Education and Treatment of Children,* 24: 28–45.

Wehmeyer, ML and Schwartz, M (2001b) Research on gender bias in special education services, in Rousso, H and Wehmeyer, M (eds) *Double jeopardy: addressing gender equity in special education* (271–87). Albany, NY: State University of New York Press.

Women and Disability Awareness Project (1984) *Building community: a manual exploring issues of women and disability.* New York: Educational Equity Concepts.

World Health Organization (WHO) (1999) *Press release WHO/68,* 12 March, International Day of Disabled Persons.

NOTE

1. We have opted to use the term '_____ with disability/ies' when referencing students who, in other disciplines may be referred to as 'disabled persons' or 'persons with impairments', as the former is the more commonly used form of 'people first language' in special education.

29

Gender Voices in the Classroom

Madeleine Arnot

The engaged voice must never be fixed and absolute but always changing, always evolving in a dialogue with a world beyond itself (bell hooks, 1994: 11 quoted in Cruddas, 2001: 62)

In this chapter, I explore the concept of gender voices and think critically about the power of such voices in educational contexts. I will refer to three different theoretical traditions which employ the concept of voice and which are highly relevant to the understanding of contemporary gender relations in classrooms today. The first tradition, I briefly describe is the feminist methodological/ epistemological tradition, which is centred on an understanding of the centrality of voice, language and identity. Feminist voice research in its many guises has been seen as the key to female liberation from male power. The second voice tradition I discuss builds on the first. Here critical sociological studies explore the often silenced, collective gendered voices of young people as a means of exposing the mythologies associated with oppressive power relations and their effects on marginalized communities and as a resource for the development of critical deconstructive critical pedagogies and transformative action. The third emergent tradition has different political antecedents. Here neo-liberalism has incorporated the concept of pupil voice to strengthen the commodification of education. In this context, pupil voice is deployed as a mechanism for school reform. The absence of an awareness of the gendered nature of student voice and the complex gender dynamics of schooling are concerns of those committed to an alternative use of student consultation as a means of democratizing education. The worry here is that neo-liberal use of student voice will aggravate class and cultural differentials in the experiences, relations and emotions associated with male and female schooling.

I have separated out these three traditions, although in effect they are not mutually exclusive. Evidence for one use of voice may well illustrate the power of voice in another tradition. But by separating them, I can describe the different objectives of research and policy related to gendered voices and some of the difficulties associated with these concepts. Unfortunately, I can only scratch the surface of this important debate but have indicated in the References where further discussion can be found.

VOICE AS A FEMINIST METHODOLOGY

Feminist research, like many critical research traditions, is heavily reliant upon the notion of voice as a powerful legitimator. Women's oppression has been understood since the 1960s as their silencing, and hence the marginalization of women's history, experience, understandings of the world, ways of knowing, values and identities. The silencing of women therefore is a key aspect of patriarchal domination and control through hegemonic male language, knowledge, values and structures. Women's silence represents, as Walkerdine (1990: 30) argued, 'psychic repression, suppression of the articulation of forbidden discourse', and/or political resistance. Not surprisingly, therefore, there has been considerable debate about the nature of the female voice. On the one hand, women's voices are shaped within male discourses and power relations; on the other hand, if elicited, their voices can challenge such discourses and power relations. And thus, 'speaking and silence, the production of language itself, become objects of regulation' (ibid.: 31). These debates have shaped feminist theory as well as feminist epistemologies and methodologies. Of central importance to such debates is the notion that feminism itself can and should construct its own definitions of social science that are primarily both *about* women and *for* women. As Walkerdine (1990) argued:

> Classic studies within feminism examining silence have concentrated on 'finding a voice'. Here, feminism was understood as providing both a place and power to speak. (Walkerdine, 1990: 30)

The analysis of 'voice' as a feminist concept has developed considerably over the last 20 years. Nevertheless it is important to acknowledge the contribution of Dale Spender, who, in 1980, published *Man Made Language*, which set the ground rules for a study of male and female language and talk. Today, her analysis would be described as a study of gender discourse with its implied power relations and constructions of subjectivities through language. Spender explored differences in when and how women and men talk, the ways in which women curtail their speech, the dominance of male talk in mixed company, and among other things, the negative representations of women as talkers. Gender differences in all the different aspects of language indicated the marginalization of women in the public world and their tentative, low self-confidence and sense of agency. The social bonds formed through gendered communication were as significant as the language used since they form the fabric of society. In the context of the classroom, Spender demonstrated the power of language in the communication between teachers and boys (then considered as 'teachers' pets') and the making invisible and silencing of girls – 'the silent bunch'. Twelve years later, Joan Swann's (1992) *Girls, Boys and Language* captures the wealth of language studies in the classroom which resulted from Spender's agenda. Her review covers as diverse a set of themes as the gendering of language use, classroom talk, the role of talk in learning, the use of language in teaching materials, the literate female, gender differences in literacy, assessing language, and the importance of language in the promotion of equal opportunities. The gendering of language is shown to be a critical element in the educational success of boys and girls, framing their experiences in the classroom, in relation to the curriculum and their social relationships in the school (see also Cameron, 1998; Graddol and Swann, 1998).

Gender language takes on new meaning in voice research, particularly within the context of feminist standpoint theory, which finds its rationale in the articulation of women's privileged insight into the nature of society. Alongside other marginalized, dispossessed and ostracized groups, women, arguably, are able to interpret the social order and thus understand the functionings of patriarchal forms. As Harding (2004) argues, standpoint theory emerged as a critical engagement with male practices of power through the production of knowledge. Since it was part of a political movement, feminist theory represents all of 'a philosophy of science, an epistemology and a methodology or method of research' (ibid.: 2). Although there are many competing views about what standpoint theory is about, there is agreement that at the core of this tradition lies the assumption that members of marginalized groups can become subjects – authors of knowledge (ibid.: 4). They could therefore speak from a particular standpoint, an experience, and a location. They could articulate their own ways of knowing and their own knowledges.

The most serious challenge to the concept of a female voice has been the development of post-structuralism and postmodernism. The category 'woman' and the concept therefore of woman's standpoint are especially problematic for post-Enlightenment anti-foundationalist theory. For example, Patti Lather's (1991) seminal text, *Getting Smart*, raises important questions about who is speaking, who is listening, and what different narratives are available. Her work challenges standpoint feminist theory to consider more than the invisibility and distortion of women's lives by deconstructing the notion of 'woman'. Using what she calls 'praxis-based research', Lather identifies the plurality of voices and the complexity of dialogue in the classroom. Learning from the hostile reception of Ellsworth's (1989) powerful critique of the canons of critical pedagogy and its use of student voice, Lather recognizes the plurality and inequalities of voice within the classroom, the unspoken, the unsaid, the hierarchies of power expressed through a diversity of voices and narratives.

The notion of voice is now more associated with post-structuralist concerns about 'identity work' – with the framing of individual and collective identities, identifications, subjectivities and discursive subject positionings. Most contemporary gender research employs qualitative interpretative methods to elicit female or male voices; however, there is also now more recognition of the power of research relationships and research dialogues in framing particular voices, eliciting some and not others. Different research methods appropriate different voices. Therefore, most feminist researchers accept that there is not a single authentic female voice – they appreciate that women's voices are internally differentiated by space, time, relation and place. Significantly, there is more recognition that even marginalized female voices (even silenced voices) can marginalize those of others.

A CRITICAL SOCIOLOGY OF SILENCED VOICES

Sociologists of education are very familiar with the dilemmas associated with interpretative, qualitative research and the issues raised about objectivity, validity, ethics and relevance. The development of critical youth cultural studies in the late 1970s, especially the publication of ground-breaking research on the resistance of male and female working-class youth in state schools, encouraged even greater interest in what particular clusters of young people could tell us about schooling and its place in their lives. The analysis of marginalization and disaffection formed the basis of a strong tradition of critical ethnography which elicited and explored the world through the eyes – in fact, the voices – of various categories of youth.

Paul Willis' (1977) much acclaimed *Learning to Labour* definitively established a tradition of critical youth cultural research. Employing neo-Marxist ethnographic methods, he befriended and listened to a group of working-class 'lads' talking about their lives, their schooling and their prospects. Through their individual and group talk, he saw what they saw – a systematic oppression of the working classes and learnt about how they resisted but also reinterpreted their destinies as manual laborers within a capitalist economy (Arnot, 2004).

This critical voice research has grown rapidly internationally. One of the strongest legacies is to be found in the USA in the work of Lois Weis and Michelle Fine. In a sequence of individual and joint books, these authors have collated a remarkable array of research on many of the groups of young men and women dispossessed by society. What these youth have in common is their status as 'Others', outside the boundaries and pathways of the dominant culture. They share what Weis and Fine (1993: 2) call 'the discursive undergrounds of students and adults at the margins of public schools'. The aim of these authors is to capture and move the 'silenced voices', or what bell hooks (1994) referred to as 'plain talk', into the public arena as a political project. The contributors in

Beyond Silenced Voices: Class, Race and Gender in United States Schools (Weis and Fine, 1993) and in *Silenced Voices and Extraordinary Conversations: Re-imaging Schools* (Fine and Weis, 2003) demonstrate the power and the poignancy of the voices of working-class young men and women, whether white, Black, Hispanic American, lesbian and gay, or truants and absentees and those excluded from school, or whether refugee or immigrant.

The gendered voices of youth position masculinity and femininity within the experience of ethnicity, sexuality, social class, marginality and poverty. Such contextualizations in themselves expose the consequences of reproduction of social inequalities in the celebration of, for example, young men's masculinities, and the associated dilemmas for young women of needing to negotiate such masculinities as well as coping with, male-ordered educational institutions. These voices of young people represent what Diane Reay and I (Arnot and Reay, in press, a) call 'identity talk', since they reveal the nature of gender identity work inside, outside and, at the margins of, schooling and their deconstructions of power.

The concept of a silenced voice can also refer to the construction of school knowledge. In the classroom, certain voices are silenced through the texts, the teaching and the dialogues between teachers and taught. So, for example, Fine's (1993) well-known piece describes the missing 'discourse of desire' in sex education classes that leaves the adolescent girls at a loss and vulnerable, without any official recognition of the realities of contemporary sexuality and the potential consequences for them of teenage pregnancies. Delpit (1988) talks about the silenced dialogue in public schools in which 'other people's children' are left – with no recognition of their culture, their learning needs, no validation of their languages and no prospect of belonging. Similarly, Nieto (1994), when analyzing the voices of a diverse group of academically successful young people from different minority ethnic backgrounds, discovers the extent of marginalization in public schools and the lack of interest in what these pupils had to say.

These authors see their political task as the transferance of such voices and their forms of resistance into the public realm – a case of moving agency from the margins to the centre (to paraphrase bell hooks, 1994). McLaughlin and Tierney (1993) describe the voiced narratives collected through autobiographies and other life history methods in their book *Naming Silenced Lives as 'Archives of Resistance'* – demonstrating how an individual or group are 'silenced by different educational arrangements' but also how they resist such silencing (p2). These critical theorists suggest that such displayed accounts can create change both individually and collectively. At the same time, authors such as Fine and Weis recognize that the elicitation of such silenced voices can be problematic. Power and privilege nurtures, sustains and legitimates the silencing of particular groups by other marginalized groups. There is a danger therefore in only collecting and listening to the silenced voices of disaffected and marginalized groups rather than understanding the power relations in schools which creates such silences. Research on the hegemonic masculinities indicates, for example, the policing of one group of boys over others, or conflicts between different ethnic masculinities

(Chapter 2 in this volume). Voice research, if not careful, can bypass such power relations *within* gender categories.

Critical sociologists tend to see schools as contradictory places in which voice can be a catalyst for political action. Despite their reproductive functions and although schools can be 'repressive and toxic' (Fine and Weis, 2003: 3), there are moments in which 'extraordinary conversations' and 'amazing talk' can take place. What Bernstein called the 'yet to be voiced' (Arnot and Reay, 2006) can be a powerful medium in creating the conditions for change. They can challenge social injustices by creating 'the very wisdom with youth and by youth that enables and even encourages and challenges social arrangements' (Fine and Weis, 2003: 3). Fine and Weiss find that there are small schools or pockets within larger schools in which 'compelling' work with youth is being conducted. Some youth are engaged in critical, rich, provocative conversations, in critical enquiry; they are involved in significant social projects and 'emerge as young scholars with civic and moral sensibilities' (ibid.: 5).

Feminist psychoanalytic research on the 'silenced voice' can also take us deeper into gender in moral/human development. A key question for educationalists is the point at which the voices of resistance, agency and confidence are silenced. Brown and Gilligan (1992), Taylor, *et al.* (1995), and Brown (1998) provide a powerful set of texts analysing the psychological health and emotional relational world of adolescent girls. Their relationships with friends, families and others are brought to life through the girls' narratives and stories. Using a 'listening guide' to uncover four different narratives within each girls' account, Brown and Gilligan (1992) expose the process with which girls silence or censor themselves in order to stay 'in relation' with others. Rather than gain in confidence, the accounts of adolescent girls record an increasingly diminished sense of self-esteem and confidence in late adolescence but also their anger and active resistance to dominant versions of femininity. The upper-middle-class girls studied initially by Brown and Gilligan suggest that by 14 years of age, the girls' resistance had been transferred into an inner voice, with the outer voice representing their compliance and obedience to gender norms of femininity and concepts of the good pupil. The subtext of Brown's (1998) book is more about raising girls' voices by exploring more carefully the 'politics of girls' anger'. These contributions encourage the view that the development of girls is reliant on their retrieving or sustaining their own voices through adolescence without being stigmatized and excluded. Not only are research strategies needed to dig deeper to hear such 'inner voices' but also quite sensitive pedagogic work around emotional and personal development is needed to help sustain girls' early feistiness.

GENDER, VOICE, CHOICE AND NEO-LIBERAL AGENDAS

In the last decade, the concept of voice has taken on a new role, which bears little relation to the feminist voice research and social/psychological study of gender identities. There is now support for the collection of student voices within the neo-liberal project – a new 'pedagogic janus' (Bernstein, 2000; quoted in Arnot and Reay, 2006b) – which has shifted the educational system toward even greater competitiveness, while emphasizing individual performativity in the name of improving education for all. By 2002, in the UK, the Labour government extended this contradictory ethos by focusing more specifically on the consumer in education and highlighting the interconnections between voice, choice and individualization.

In 2004, the then Minister for State for School Standards, David Miliband gave a speech at the Personalizing Education: The Future of Public Sector Reform conference, in which he pointed out that the conference came at 'the most important time for public services since the creation of the welfare state after 1945' (Miliband, 2004: 1). The new social democratic settlement now proposed is designed to 'make universal the life chances of the most fortunate'. Three great challenges were identified: the challenge of equity and excellence, the challenge of flexibility and accountability, and the challenge of universality and personalization. It was in relation to the third challenge that the voice, even if a 'fragmented voice' (ibid.: 2) of the consumer, should be heard by government and should now be used to hold public services accountable. Put simply – economies require flexible specialization of products and services. They also need flexible individuals:

> This leads straight to the promise of personalized learning. It means building the organization of schooling around the needs, interests and aptitudes of individual pupils: it means shaping teaching around the way different youngsters learn; it means taking the care to nurture the unique talents of every pupil. I believe it is *the* debate in education today. (Miliband, 2004: 3)

Pupils are now officially recognized as the driving force in 'whole school improvement ... [the] whole school team has to now take time to find out the needs and interests of students' (ibid.: 5). Drawing on Albert Hirschman's *Exit, Voice and Loyalty: Responses to Decline in Firms, Organizations and States* (originally about rail transportation in Nigeria), Miliband argued that *choice* and *voice* are understood to be 'strengthened by the presence of the other: ... the ability to make your voice heard provides a vital tool to the consumer who does not want to change shops, political parties every time they are unhappy'. In a key declaration, Miliband argued:

> The challenge is to ally choice with voice. Voice for the pupil. Voice for the parent. That is the new frontier for education. Personalized learning aims to engage every parent and every child in the educational experience. (Miliband, 2004: 7)

Personalized learning is associated with having an 'active demand side' to the provision of public services such as education. In this model, the aim is not to restructure public services. Instead, consumers must be able to articulate their needs, and must learn patience while their needs are being met. The voice here of pupils and parents is not the critical, deconstructivist voices of critical pedagogues. It is the 'consumer voice' (ibid.: 7). The child's voice in this context represents the empowered citizen, having, in the first instance, a 'real say' in their learning. This revived focus on student needs, interests, requirements, implies not standardized pupil types, but rather a school ethos that listens – a concept that was not new. It had already been advocated by Blair *et al.* (1999) as essential for engaging with the needs of minority ethnic pupils.

The new discursive rhetoric around 'listening to learn' (DfES, 2002) has led to the establishment of an action plan to involve children and young people in educational policy making at the centre. Goals have been set for 2006 – with young people's voices brought into the frame through surveys, focus groups and integration into the decision-making processes. A Children's Commissioner for England was established by the Children Act 2004, and Children's Trusts with strong involvement of children, young people and their families in local planning of integrated services for children and young people are being set up (www.everychildmatters.gov.uk).

Critiques of this discursive shift from progressive quasi-democratic to neo-liberal notions of child-centred policies, the involvement of children in school effectiveness and improvement, and 'customer satisfaction' are only beginning to emerge. For example, in their analysis of the South Australian Student Voice Indicator Tool, Roger Holdsworth and Pat Thomson (2002) point to the encouragement of a centrally controlled sample of student opinion rather than a commitment to 'enable and enhance a diversity of views and voices'. Student voice here becomes an 'accountability tool' within individualizing and coercive discourses and top-down management cultures. The danger is that only those students who are successful in the curriculum and school will have a voice. The 'puzzling conflation' of student voice, access and participation depends upon an ideal student:

> There is an ideal student in the text ... who likes school, negotiates, resolves conflicts, manages their own learning and constructs knowledge. Student who have 'a voice' are well behaved. Calling out, yelling, or walking out ... does not constitute 'voice'. (Holdsworth and Thomson 2002: 6)

This ideal student has certain qualities which dovetail into successful management:

> Students are expected to speak with one voice and to have one youth culture, neither of which challenge the status quo. At the same time there is a strong appeal to democratic principles of action with the agreed processes of vision, mission, planning and review – with no recognition of the potential conflicts and tensions between the mandated implementation of systemic policy and procedure and democratic 'voiced' school decision making. (Holdsworth and Thomson, 2002: 7)

The concept of 'student' in student voice policy is an abstract ideal, a mythological discourse which denies the structural inequalities already exposed by critical sociologists and psychologists (Arnot and Reay, 2006b). There is little recognition in such consultation processes that the student being consulted brings to the dialogue a range of social identities and experiences constructed within social hierarchies and power relations. Therefore, Holdsworth and Thomson (2002) argue that there are serious difficulties with student consultation mechanisms:

> In the Australian context, the notion of student voice is one that is highly problematic. In some locations it does support democratic activity, but more often than not, it is a thin conservative version of democracy in which already advantaged students are selected to erect the façade of participation and consultation. (Holdsworth and Thomson, 2002: 12)

Similarly, Fielding notes (2004) that 'so long as an undifferentiated notion of student voice is assumed or valorized' and unless power differentials are taken into account when consulting pupils, there is a significant danger that 'issues of race, gender and class are sidelined and in that process of presumed homogeneity the middle class, white view of the world conveniently emerges as the norm'. (p302)

There is no doubt that some students take to consultation initiatives more readily than others. Researchers have found that often the most articulate and academically successful students are selected for consultation (see Nieto, 1994; Peddar and McIntyre, 2003). The use of student voice in relation to school reform has tended to centre on organizational aspects paying, as Silva (2001) found,

> very little attention to the students themselves, and to the pressures, concerns and conflicts that dominate their school experiences and ultimately determine whether or not they will accept a school's invitation to participate in reform efforts. If schools intend to embrace student voice as a tenet of the decision-making and reform process, it is critical not only to examine the role of the school but also to explore how students negotiate and define their positions as participants or non-participants in the school change efforts. Particularly with respect to disturbing race- and class-based inequities in American public schools and a growing movement of related equity based reforms, it is vital to consider how and why some students choose to participate while others opt out of the school change process. (Silva, 2001: 95)

Silva's three-year ethnographic research discovered the 'powerful influence of racial, class and gender identity on student participation, particularly in the context of a school struggling to overcome a culture of inequality and division' (2001: 95). The more formal the connection between school management and a consultation outreach group, the more it seemed to encourage the participation of white, high-achieving girls. It was important for them that the consultative group was an official, legitimate part of the school. These girls had already experienced success within school rules and policies, and felt it appropriate to continue that way. For other students, any formal connection to the school was unsettling. Many of the experiences of students of color and those with the lowest level of achievement were 'harsh' and contentious. Such students were incited to participate only if they thought they could disturb traditional decision-making and reform processes rather than be part of them. Significantly, many of these students were boys.

Hannam (2001) found that there were effects of student participatory activities on students themselves. He discovered, for example, differences in the relationship between students' participation and their attitudes, attainment, attendance and exclusion rates in secondary schools that take such student participation seriously. When he asked young people whether involvement in participatory activities had affected them in any way he found that:

There appears to be a tendency for girls to have stronger perceptions of the benefits of participatory activities for their confidence, collaborative skills, communication skills and sense of efficacy. This was consistent across all the schools. There is absolutely no gender difference in the extent to which these activities make students feel 'more independent, trusted and *responsible*'. The impression was gained in the student interviews that some boys judged being too enthusiastic as 'uncool' and this might have affected the result.

(Hannam, 2002: 12)

Table 29.1 Student responses (as percentages) to involvement in participatory activities (bold: boys: italics: girls)

Has your involvement with this activity affected you in any of the following ways? Please tick the box that best describes your feelings.

		A lot	Quite a lot	Not much	Not at all
1.	Made school a more interesting place to be?	**34**	**42**	**21**	**2**
		33	*57*	*9*	*1*
2.	Helped you feel more confident in school?	**31**	**51**	**18**	**0**
		48	*38*	*12*	*2*
3.	Helped you to concentrate better in lessons?	**10**	**50**	**38**	**2**
		11	*43*	*34*	*12*
4.	Helped you to learn more in lessons?	**16**	**41**	**36**	**6**
		15	*43*	*31*	*11*
5.	Helped you to work with others?	**59**	**36**	**5**	**0**
		78	*20*	*2*	*0*
6.	Took too much time from other learning?	**1**	**1**	**48**	**50**
		0	*2*	*40*	*58*
7.	Worried your parents about your school work?	**0**	**0**	**1**	**99**
		0	*3*	*17*	*80*
8.	Made you feel proud of your achievements?	**62**	**33**	**4**	**1**
		64	*34*	*2*	*0*
9.	Helped you get on better with your teachers?	**37**	**42**	**16**	**5**
		43	*41*	*13*	*3*
10.	Caused teachers to say you were falling behind?	**1**	**1**	**15**	**83**
		0	*3*	*11*	*86*
11.	Made you more interested in the world generally?	**25**	**48**	**26**	**1**
		30	*54*	*12*	*4*
12.	Made you feel that you can improve things?	**44**	**47**	**7**	**2**
		53	*43*	*4*	*0*
13.	Helped you express yourself more clearly?	**41**	**45**	**13**	**1**
		50	*45*	*4*	*1*
14.	Made you feel more independent, trusted and responsible?	**68**	**29**	**3**	**0**
		68	*30*	*2*	*0*

Source: Hannam, 2001: 12.

When the two positive responses of 'a lot' and 'quite a lot' are combined (see Table 29.1), many of the substantial gender differences disappear. However, boys were more likely to report that such participation tended to help them concentrate better in lessons, and on the whole, girls seemed to be responding well to these participatory initiatives. They were more likely to report an effect of student participatory activities on making school a more interesting place to be, getting on better with teachers, creating more interest in world generally and being able to express themselves better. Hannam also reports 'a tendency for more girls to become involved in participatory activities than boys. In the

11 mixed schools, the ratio was approximately 4.0–4.5 boys to every 5.5–6.0 girls' (2002: 13).

In our research Diane Reay and I found that the higher-achieving, upper-middle-class girls were far more nonchalant about being consulted by teachers about their learning, possibly because they felt that, unlike less successful pupils, they had a voice and felt more in tune with the school's purposes (Arnot *et al.*, 2003; Arnot and Reay, 2006a,b). They were able to manage informal dialogue between themselves and their teachers. The most dependent learners in contrast, appeared to have difficulty achieving the levels of communicative competence required for consultations by teachers. Lower-achieving girls were worried that the teacher would become angry. They talked about being polite to teachers, not wanting to offend them and trying to keep them sweet. They were also aware of the inequalities associated with pupil consultation. Abby, for example, pointed to the language differences between pupils and teachers' preferences:

Abby: I think the teachers listen to, like who knows the most ... because the naughty people ... because they don't like care .... [then] there's people who actually want to learn; they know what to do but they just don't somehow and then there's bottom people are like 'Please help'... then the teacher's actually busy with the top group because they find it easier to talk to them instead of the others.

Qu: Why?

Abby: I think it's because of detail, because they just say the same language to the top people and then to like lower people, the bottom set, when they talk they find it harder, hard or something like that. A bit long, they have to say the same thing over and over again. (Arnot *et al.*, 2003: 5)

The problem of the lack of trust between teachers and pupils also comes regularly in the responses of lower-achieving, working-class boys in the Mandela school, an inner-city comprehensive. If teachers asked, as Leroy comments, 'obviously you can't give them your true opinion, otherwise they will dislike you and always watch out for you'. When asked whether they were ever consulted, they answered:

Leroy: No.

Kenny: 'Cos we're all seen as fools.

Leroy: Like people treat you like fools, but they still teach you.

Kenny: Teachers think – I'm the King, you are my slave. I teach you. I tell you want to do. I tell you want to get, you get it. So it's sort of like – I am the teacher, you are the pupil. I tell you what to learn and you learnt it. But it ain't that easy.

The theme of being treated fairly and with dignity ('like humans') of these working-class boys, who struggle to find some control over their learning, is clearly indicated in our data. A not dissimilar theme can be found in Cruddas and Haddock's (2003) research when they established a single-sex developmental group for girls who were defined as having special educational needs. Some of the girls in this study expressed their ambivalence about talking in such a group:

I think it's sad that we have to have this group just to voice our opinions. Don't teachers realize we've got opinions?
It's the way they (teachers) talk to us. We're not dirt, you know. (Cruddas, 2001: 63)

Cruddas and Haddock found that the girls in their study wanted a separate space to talk so as to have their voices heard. They valued being listened to, being heard above the boys, being treated as equals, having emotional space, having friends, and being supported by better pastoral systems. They wanted to have the space to work on their social and emotional issues, to investigate the complexity of their own subject positions and positioning. This strategy was not designed to essentialize girls' experience but rather to allow them to reflect on their experiences. Girls' networks were reflected in their talk – as Hey (1997) had found, girls have 'invisible, intimate and secret cultures', – their talk is 'marked by intimacy and self-disclosure' (p65) and an exploration of power and powerlessness.

Barnes (1996) argues for the importance of guiding professionals on how to talk to girls and boys. She argues that there are potential hazards in not thinking through the effects of gender classifications and social functioning of girls and boys. Reading the gender culture of different social/cultural groups can be problematic, especially if boys and girls are socialized into very different roles and identities in the family and community. Gender identities will affect their perceptions of relationships, the articulation of emotion, permission when to speak and with whom, and gender differences in terms of how to express distress and account for it (boys being more likely to blame others while girls might blame themselves). Girls might have a heightened sense of connectedness with others while boys might be more oriented toward independence and outward resilience. When consulting children, professionals such as teachers need to be sensitive to gender issues such as different forms of resistance and coping strategies. Dwivedi (1996) also highlights ethnic and cultural nuances in the ways in which boys and girls express themselves, such as body language, the language being used, self-expression, the forms of indirect and metaphorical communication, and the language style associated with gender roles in the community.

One of the key issues emerging from school-based projects which rely on pupil voice is, as Shacklock and Smyth (1997) point out, the difficulty of working with vernacular knowledge, with what Grumet (1990) called an anchored local knowledge which does not fit 'objective, hegemonic forms of knowledge' (p407). Shacklock and Smyth's own research on young people who have dropped out of school argued that this private knowledge, these new and often radically different narrations of life experience, challenge teachers' conceptualizations and explanatory frameworks. Sarah Bragg's (2001) research is an example of just how contentious such vernacular, popular voices can be. She talks about the voices 'we don't want to hear'. The pressures of needing rapid results may lead teachers to listen only or more readily to voices 'that made immediate sense' – for example, successful, articulate upper-middle-class girls. Teachers would need to have the time to deal with the voices which are anomalous, which do not fit, which talk about what is not working. She describes in moving detail the display and use of aggressive masculinity in her students' responses to her teaching of horror films on a media course. Only when she legitimated their gruesome references to heavy metal, sexual violence and their sexism by reading back their responses out loud to the class and talking about such popular cultural references with them did the male students in her class engage with her course. They could hear their own voices and also made sense of her knowledge and pedagogy. This drew on Elizabeth Ellsworth's argument that it is when you 'reflect back a difference, that it makes a difference' (Ellsworth, 1977; quoted in Bragg, 2001: 72).

CONCLUSION

There are now a number of different traditions which draw upon gendered voices in the classroom. I have indicated how feminist research has privileged the notion of voice as potentially empowering in the deconstruction of hegemonic male knowledge. That assumption can also be found in the development of critical sociological research, although, within both traditions, there are those who question what form such empowerment takes and whether 'voicing' is sufficient as a goal. The elicitation of silent, suppressed, inner and outer voices is conceptually and practically very difficult. There has not been the space here to consider the range of voice methodologies used by researchers – many of which are seen as complex multimodal strategies to uncover the layers of meaning associated with voice and narrative.

I have focused particularly on the relationship of voice to identity. However, there are other traditions, such as Bernsteinian research, which highlight the difference between the concept of voice used to describe gender, class and racial identities and the concept of a pedagogic voice – the voice which is created through the relay of power and control through educational systems. To some extent, pupils as pupils speak a common *pedagogic voice*, the language of learning. Of importance, therefore, is whether gender is a significant feature of this aspect of voice, and also what sort of impact identity talk has on pedagogic talk. In our research (Arnot and Reay, 2006b), we discriminate between different types of talk in the classroom – classroom talk, subject talk, identity talk and code talk. Researchers need to define carefully which sort of voice they are investigating. There is a concern at the moment that everything that students say is relevant, and that it is of the same genre – that is, voice. However, often, the voice is less a representation of pupils' social position and more possibly a realization of their educational experiences and the extent to which they can talk the language of schooling.

This theme is becoming more important as interest grows in metacognition – learning how to learn – and learning how to talk about learning to teachers. The more voice is associated with choice, with the commodification of schooling, and with personalized/independent learning, the more important it is that researchers explore what they mean by gender voices.

REFERENCES

Archard, D (1993) *Children rights and childhood*. London: Routledge.

Arnot, M (2004) Working class masculinities, schooling and social justice: reconsidering the sociological significance of Paul Willis' *Learning to Labour*, in Dimitriades, G and Dobly, N (eds) *Learning to labour in new times*. New York: Routledge.

Arnot, M and Reay, D (2004) The framing of pedagogic encounters: regulating the social order of classroom learning, in Muller, J, Davies B and Morais, A, (eds) *Reading Bernstein, researching Bernstein*. London: RoutledgeFalmer.

Arnot, M and Reay, D (2006) Power, pedagogic voices and pupil talk: the implications for pupil consultation as transformative practice, in Moore, R, Arnot, M, Beck, J and Daniels, H, (eds) *Knowledge, power and educational reform: applying the sociology of Basil Bernstein*. London: Routledge.

Arnot, M and Reay, D (2006b) The framing of performance pedagogies: pupil perspectives on the control of school knowledge and its acquisition, in Lauder, H, Brown, P, Dillabough, J and Halsey, A, H. (eds) *Education, globalisation and social change*. Oxford: Oxford University Press.

Arnot, M, McIntyre, D, Peddar, D and Reay, R (2003) *Consultation in the classroom: pupil perspectives on teaching and learning*. Cambridge: Pearson.

Blair, M, Kenner, C, Bourne, J, Coffin, C and Creese, A (1999) Making the difference: teaching and learning strategies in successful multi-etnic schools (Research Report). London: Prentice-Hall/Harvester Wheatsheaf.

Bragg, S (2001) Taking a joke: learning from the voices we don't want to hear. *Forum* 43: 2, 70–3.

Brown, LM (1998) *Raising their voices: the politics of girls' anger*. Cambridge, MA: Harvard University Press.

Brown, LM and Gilligan, C (1992) *Meeting at the crossroads: women's psychology and girls' development*. Cambridge, MA: Harvard University Press.

Cameron, D (ed) (1998) *The feminist critique of language*. London: Routledge.

Cruddas, L (2001) Rehearsing for reality: young women's voices and agendas for change. *Forum* 43: 62–6.

Cruddas, L and Haddock, L (2003) *Girls' voices: supporting girls' learning and emotional development*. Stoke on Trent: Trentham Books.

Delpit, L (1988) The silenced dialogue: power and pedagogy in educating other people's children. *Harvard Educational Review*, 58: 3, reprinted in Weis, L and Fine, M (eds) (1993) *Beyond silenced voices*. Albany, NY: State University of New York Press.

Department for Education and Skills (DfES) (2004) *Listening to learn*. www.dfes.gov.uk/listening to learn/ (accessed 12 August 2004)

Dwivedi, KN (1996) Race and the child's perspective, in Davie, R, Upton, G, and Varma, V (eds) *The voice of the child: a handbook for professionals*. London: Falmer Press.

Ellsworth, E (1989) Why doesn't this feel empowering? Working through the repressive myths of critical pedagogy? *Harvard Educational Review*, 59: 297–324.

Fielding, M (2004) Transformative approaches to student voice: theoretical underpinnings recalcitrant realities. *British Educational Research Journal*, 30: 295–311.

Fine, M and Weis, L (2003) *Silenced voices and extraordinary conversations: re-imagining schools*. New York: Teachers College Press.

Gorel-Barnes, G (1996) Gender issues, in Davie, R, Upton, G and Varma, V (eds) *The voice of the child: a handbook for professionals*. London: Falmer Press.

Graddol, D and Swann, J (1998) *Gender voice*. Oxford: Blackwell.

Grumet, M (1990) Voice: the search for a feminist rhetoric for educational studies. *Cambridge Journal of Education*, 20: 277–282.

Hannam, D (2001) Attitudes, attainment, attendance and exclusion in secondary schools that take student participation seriously: a pilot study. Paper presented at the ESRC Pupil Voice and Democracy seminar series, University of Cambridge 15 October 2001.

Harding, S (ed) (2004) *The feminist standpoint theory reader: intellectual and political controversies*. London: Routledge.

Hey, V (1997) *The company she keeps: an ethnography of girls' friendships*. Buckingham: Open University Press.

Holdsworth, R and Thomson, P (2002) Options with the regulation and containment of 'student voice' and/or students research and acting for change: Australian experiences. Paper presented at the AERA symposium.

hooks, b (1994) *Teaching to transgress: education as the practice of freedom*. New York: Routledge.

Lather, P (1991) *Getting smart: feminist research and pedagogy with/in the postmodern*. New York: Routledge.

McLaughlin, D and Tierney, WG (ed) (1993) *Naming silenced lives: personal narratives and processes of educational change*. New York: Routledge.

Miliband, D (2004) Choice and voice in personalised learning. Speech given at the DfES Innovation Unit/Demos/OECD conference Personalising Education: The Future of Public Sector Reform. accessed through www.standards.dfes.gov.uk/personalised learning/.

Nieto, S (1994) Lessons from students on creating a chance to dream. *Harvard Educational Review*, 64: 392–426

Peddar, D and McIntyre, D (2003) The impact of pupil consultation on classroom practice, in Arnot, M, McIntyre, D, Peddar, D and Reay, D (eds) *Consultation in the classroom: developing dialogue about teaching and learning*. Cambridge: Pearson.

Shacklock, G and Smyth, J (1997) Conceptualising and capturing voices in dropout research. Working paper on students completing schooling project. Adelaide,Flinders Institute for the Study of Teaching.

Silva, E (2001) Squeaky wheels and flat tires: a case study of students as reform participants. *Forum*, 43: 95–99.

Smyth, J and Hattam, R (2001) 'Voiced' research as a sociology for understanding 'dropping out' of school. *British Journal of Sociology of Education*, 22: 401–15.

Spender, D (1980) *Man made language*. London: Routledge and Kegan Paul.

Swann J (1992) *Girls, boys and language*. Oxford: Blackwell.

Taylor, JM, Gilligan, C and Sullivan, AM (1995) *Between voice and silence: women and girls, race and relationship*. Cambridge, MA: Harvard University Press.

Walkerdine, V (1990) On the regulation of speaking and silencing, in *Schoolgirl fictions*. London: Verso.

Weis, L and Fine, M (eds) (1993) *Beyond silenced voices: class, race, and gender in United States schools*. Cambridge, MA: Harvard University Press.

Willis, P (1977) *Learning to labour: why working class kids get working class jobs*. Farnborough: Saxon House.

Working in Schools and Colleges

INTRODUCTION

In this section, authors focus on schools as historical, social and cultural institutions within which gender is negotiated, produced and reproduced. Classrooms, primary and secondary schools, and colleges and universities are historically, politically and socially constituted institutional structures that constrain acceptable discourses of gender, self and other. Students and teachers interact with and within these institutional structures, constructing identities and relationships. The authors in this section explore several key questions, including the extent to which schools and colleges or universities reproduce existing gender discourses and/or serve as sites within which these identities and structures of power can be challenged.

In Chapter 30, Fengshu Liu describes school culture as dynamic in nature, an entity within which students produce and reproduce gendered selves. She documents how, in both Western, African and Chinese classrooms, masculinities and femininities are played out through gender segregation and teacher–student interactions. In Chapter 31, Emma Renold builds on these ideas, exploring how classroom-based studies demonstrate that classrooms are sites in which gender is produced and reproduced through social relationships. Renold describes classrooms as spaces which serve multiple purposes: they regulate interaction; they are 'dangerous spaces', within which sexual bullying and harassment occur; and they are transgressive spaces, within which students and teachers can subvert normative gender regimes.

In the remaining chapters in this section, the authors explore the experiences of teachers, administrators, and college and university professors through the lens of gender. In Chapter 32, Jane Gaskell and Ann Mullen set up the debate: are teachers powerful or powerless, autonomous or connected, knowledgeable or subordinate? Can teachers transform teaching and/or become powerful within existing (masculinist) structures? In Chapter 33, Lisa Smulyan reviews the historical construction of masculine and feminine identities within the teaching profession and explores the multiple identities crafted by teachers in schools. In Chapter 34, Sandra Acker and Michelle Webber explore the question, *Why have universities been so slow to develop gender balance and full integration of women's perspectives and participation*? Although there are more women present in colleges and universities now than 40 years ago, the proportion in adjunct and part-time positions is disproportionately high. And women faculty continue to experience tensions between their positions as women and feminists and the structures of the higher educational institutions within which they work.

Shakeshaft, in Chapter 35 examines international patterns in women's experiences as educational leaders. She finds that despite cultural and natural differences, similar barriers limit women's access to administrative positions and similar leadership styles emerge among women administrators.

30

School Culture and Gender

Fengshu Liu

INTRODUCTION

The term 'school culture' is popular and frequently used. Yet, in spite of the development of a body of research on the topic since the 1960s, there is no singly agreed meaning of 'school culture': meanings tend to be assumed but rarely articulated (Prosser, 1999: 9). Within this literature on 'school culture', identity issues such as those of gender tend to be submerged by overriding managerial discourses concerned with 'school effectiveness'.

This chapter attempts to highlight the gendered aspect of school culture. After presenting a brief conceptualization of school culture in relation to gender, I shall examine the classroom as one of the school's microcultures illustrative of the overall gendered school culture. Drawing on research conducted over half a century and around the world, the latter part of the chapter depicts and analyzes the gendered environment of the classroom, where gender segregation and gendered interactions are part and parcel of daily life.

THE GENDERED NATURE OF SCHOOL CULTURE

According to Clarke *et al.* (1975), culture is

> the peculiar and distinctive way of life of a group or class, the meanings, values and ideas embodied in institutions, in social relations, in systems of belief, in mores and customs, in the uses of objects and material life … the 'map of meanings' that make things intelligible to its members. (p10)

As such, school culture, or the 'map of meanings' in a school, constitutes the social context of schooling. This definition appears to hold greater potential for the incorporation of an analysis of gender issues than do some other conceptualizations. In this chapter, school culture is understood as both reflecting the 'wider culture' of a society and resulting from multiple interpretations and interactions by individuals and groups as active agents. The former perspective emphasizes that schools do not exist in a vacuum and therefore, cannot be considered as enclaves operating a separate reality from that outside their walls (Prosser, 1999). The latter recognizes that school culture is meanwhile the result of negotiations and interactions, as individuals and groups play their active and influential parts in shaping subcultures of the school on a daily basis (Blasé, 1991; Mahony and Hextall, 2000).

Furthermore, whereas each school may have its own particular culture, that culture tends to be gendered in nature (just as it is classed, raced, and so on). The genderedness of school culture is aptly captured in what Kessler *et al.* (1985) have termed 'gender regime'. They suggest that there is a particular 'gender regime' at work in every school (as in other institutions), and this can be defined as:

> the pattern of practices that constructs various kinds of masculinity and femininity among staff and students, orders them in terms of prestige and power, and constructs a sexual division of labour within the institution. The gender regime is a state of play rather than a permanent condition. It can be changed deliberately or otherwise, but it is no less powerful in its effects on pupils for that. It confronts them as a social fact, which they have to come to terms with somehow (Kessler *et al.*, 1985: 42).

The gender regime makes a difference in every aspect of school life such as the form of organizational management, the curriculum, disciplinary schemes, interaction, and relationships (Connell, 1996, 2000), often reflecting the dominant gender relations in the larger society. The in-group that maintains control over the resources is male-dominated and it reflects hegemonic masculinity (Connell, 1995), while the out-group is made up of female teachers and female students, non-heterosexual members, and those boys and men who choose not to or fail to embrace hegemonic masculinity. Meanwhile, schools do not merely reflect the dominant gender ideology of the wider society, but actively produce gender and heterosexual divisions (Delamont, 1990; Mac an Ghaill, 1994). The school inhabitants, especially teachers and students, serve as key 'infrastructural mechanisms', through which masculinities and femininities are mediated and lived out as they actively negotiate and reproduce gender identities for themselves and others (Mac an Ghaill, 1994: 4). Thus, just as Mac an Ghaill (1994) notes, whereas the institutional culture of the school defines gendered behavior for its inhabitants, it is through the school microcultures of managers, teachers and students that masculinities and femininities are mediated and lived out.

As with other areas of educational research on gender, investigations of the gendered aspects of school culture were initiated by feminist research exploring how femininity and females are denigrated and marginalized within educational settings; but, more recently, they have reflected a trend toward the exploration of masculinity(ies) and of the needs of boys in education. This latter focus on boys' needs is often driven by anti-feminist work that blames 'feminization' of education, women teachers, and/or feminism for the apparent 'underachievement' of boys (Skelton, 2001; Weaver-Hightower, 2003).

Significant controversy surrounds the new focus on masculinity, as critics, especially feminists, argue that it tends to de-politicize the issue of gender and draw attention away from the continued injustices faced by girls and women (Francis, 2000; Skelton, 2001; Osler and Vincent, 2003; Skelton and Francis, 2003). Furthermore, just as in earlier feminist research on girls, there is a tendency in this new focus to treat boys and girls as two homogeneous groups, thus downplaying the effect of other variables, such as social class and ethnicity, which, in effect, often mediate gender in education (Gilborn, 1997; Ball *et al.*, 2000; Osler and Vincent, 2003; Skelton and Francis, 2003). There is also a tendency to treat masculinity and femininity as isolated, rather than relational, categories (Stanley and Wise, 1993; Kelly *et al.*, 1994; Francis, 1998, 2000; Skelton and Francis, 2003). Nevertheless, like the studies on girls and education, the research on boys, masculinity and schooling that is informed by feminist perspectives does yield some important insights into the gendered nature of school culture. It has been particularly helpful in analyzing how the gendered school culture characterized by male domination may prove detrimental to both boys and girls.

THE GENDERED CLASSROOM

One of the school microcultures where the male centredness appears to be most evident is the classroom (Kelly, 1986; Delamont, 1990; Streitmatter, 1994; Francis, 2000; Kimmel, 2000). In this section, I shall examine the classroom as one of the specific sites where schools, as deeply gendered and heterosexual regimes, construct relations of domination and subordination. I shall focus on two inter-related aspects of the everyday life of classrooms: gender segregation and gendered teacher–student interactions in the classroom.

Existing reviews of research on this topic predominantly focus on work conducted in the West, especially the UK, the USA and Australia. Therefore, I shall incorporate research done in some non-Western settings. For reviews of gendered classroom culture that address topics beyond segregation and teacher–pupil interaction, see, for example, Kelly (1986), Delamont (1990), Streitmatter (1994), Howe (1997), and Skelton and Francis (2003).

Invisible but real boundaries

It is somehow ironical to begin a discussion of classroom interactions with an account of segregation. However, gender segregation is a reality in many classrooms, where invisible but real boundaries exist. As Kimmel (2000) observes:

In nursery schools and kindergarten classes, we often find the heavy blocks, trucks, airplanes, and carpentry tools in one place, and the dolls and homemaking equipment in another. While they may be officially 'open' to anyone for play, the areas are often sex-segregated by invisible but real boundaries. In the elementary school years, the informal play during out-of-school hours involves different sports, different rules, and different playground activities. .... while there are some signs of change, this nursery school experience is reproduced in every classroom in every town and city in America, every day. (pp153–4)

This phenomenon is, however, not unique to American schools. It is observed around the world that, at school and in the classrooms, boys and girls learn, and teach each other, about appropriate behaviors and experiences for boys and girls, and ensure that everyone acts accordingly (Delamont, 1992; Kimmel, 2000). In my own experience of schooling in China, throughout my primary and middle-school education, boys and girls had different games and activities to engage in, and we seldom played together. Boys typically played basketball (as football had not yet been introduced into Chinese rural schools at that time), climbing, wrestling and so on, while girls played hopscotch, skipping, battledore and shuttlecock, and other more quiet and less competitive games. One of the most unforgettable memories of my middle-school years in the early 1980s was that girls and boys in my class were hardly on greeting terms. Anyone who ventured to talk with anyone from the other sex would cause a *qihong* (roars of mocking laughter) from the boys.

My research shows that such segregation remains in many Chinese schools today (Liu, 2006). One couple in my study of parental expectations of boys and girls as only children (Liu, 2006) reported that their daughter was the only girl in a school of about 2000 students who played football and generally mixed with boys. They argued that this was because they deliberately encouraged their daughter to mix with boys so that she would become more competitive in the future society, which, the parents predicted, will still favor men. Interestingly, I found that boys and girls do play together after school, especially if they happen to live in the same neighborhood. This supports Thorne's (1993) observation that the separation of American boys and girls in play and other interactions is greater in schools than in their neighborhoods and homes. Jordan (1995) observes similar patterns in Australia. These instances may support Delamont's (1990) argument that 'schools develop and reinforce sex segregations, stereotypes, and even discriminations which exaggerate the negative aspects of sex roles in the outside world, when they could be trying to alleviate them' (p2).

Teachers also have a part to play in the gender-segregation process, and this seems most evident in the formation of groups for academic activities and the assignment of classroom chores (see Skelton and Francis, 2003). In China, teachers usually organize class activities by dividing the class into two groups: boys and girls. Moreover, in Chinese classes, such as the ones where I used to teach English, boys and girls, regardless of their age, tend to sit separately. In the Chinese context where the traditional norm that *nannu shoushou buqin* (it is just natural that there ought to be a distance between males and females) has been internalized, gender segregation is widely assumed as something desirable, rather than problematic. I have found that this norm is reinforced when children enter puberty, as parents and teachers tend to become concerned that interest in the opposite sex (note the assumption of heterosexuality) may divert the child's attention from school work (Liu, 2005b). Such concerns often lead to surveillance of interactions between boys and girls by parents and teachers.

Studies of classroom cultures in some African countries reveal that teachers' and students' assumption that girls' primary role and ambition is to be wives and mothers strongly influences how teachers treat girls (Davison and Kanyuka, 1990; Wamanhiu, 1994). And this is reflected in the pattern of task assignment found in many schools. Although boys may receive more attention during classroom instruction, when classroom responsibilities are assigned, girls assume the greatest share of the workload. This is true especially for responsibilities closely related to domestic or clerical tasks such as sweeping the floor, cleaning the board or latrines, picking up garbage, or handing out papers or supplies. In contrast, teachers more frequently assign to boys responsibilities with a measure of authority or control such as monitoring the classroom during a teacher's absence, taking message to the principal or head teacher, serving as class leaders, and assisting with the roll calling (Wamahiu, 1994). A study conducted in Burkina Faso (UNESCO, Countdown, 1997) has yielded similar findings. These forms (among others) of gender segregation may have serious consequences for children's evolving subjectivities and identities, and hence for their adult lives.

Gendered teacher–student interactions

One of the most powerful and subtle influences teachers exert over students is through teacher–student interactions. Research findings have been fairly consistent in showing that teachers' interactions with students tend to reflect gender stereotypes. In general, teacher–student interaction tends to facilitate male-centredness in classrooms, and this is manifested in both quantitative and qualitative terms.

Quantitative differences

Research conducted in classrooms suggests that, in general, boys get more attention from the teacher both in student-initiated and teacher-initiated interactions. In a comprehensive review of research on classroom interaction done in Australia, the USA, and the UK between the early 1970s and the early 1990s, Howe (1997) concludes that with the exception of some minor inconsistencies, the studies show that boys participate more than girls in whole-class interaction and that they receive more feedback from teachers on their contributions. This is true despite being conducted in three distinct parts of the world, with a wide age range, and across 20 years. This confirms the findings by the American Association of University Women (1992), which concludes that whether 'one is looking at preschool classrooms or university lecture halls … research spanning the past twenty years consistently reveals that males receive more teacher attention than do females' (p68).

Similar patterns have also been found in non-Western settings, such as Guatemala (Nunez, 1995) and Malawi (Davison and Kanyuka, 1990). Furthermore, more recent studies conducted in the West demonstrate that male students continue to dominate classroom space and teacher attention (Francis, 2000; Warrington and Younger, 2000; Skelton, 2001; Skelton and Francis, 2003). Just as Howe (1997) indicates in her above-mentioned review, two main reasons can be identified for boys' dominance of the classroom. One reason may have to do with the tendency found among teachers to perceive boys to be more reward-ing to teach, although more difficult to control than girls (Warrington and Younger, 2000; Skelton and Francis, 2003). But it may also be because teachers often have to direct more attention to boys, who tend to be more demanding and restless than girls in class, in an attempt to engage boys in work and/or discipline them so as to retain class control (Swan and Graddol, 1994; Younger et al., 1999; Skelton, 2001).

However, it is also worth noting that there may be exceptions to the above-mentioned general trend. For example, we can expect to find teacher attention allocated to boys and girls in a more balanced way in classes led by teachers who are dedicated to gender-neutral interactions aimed at gender equity. Furthermore, in spite of the general trend for boys to be more demanding, some girls can be equally, or even more, demanding and unruly (Francis, 2000; Osler and Vincent, 2003). What is interesting, however, is that girls' misbehaviors are often perceived differently from boys' bad behaviors by teachers. Girls who do not conform to conventional gender behaviors often invite harsh criticism from the teachers, whereas aggression and violence among boys may be seen as more 'natural' and hence, more understandable (Reay, 2001; Skelton, 2002; Osler and Vincent, 2003; Skelton and Francis, 2003). Moreover, teacher–student interac-tion can also be affected by the subject area being handled. According to some researchers (e.g. Alloway, 1995), teachers tend to interact more with boys when the academic topic is one that traditionally has been considered 'masculine' and more with girls when the topic is a traditionally 'feminine' one. Again, such stereotypical approaches reinforce the gendered division of labor in society.

Teacher–student interaction is also affected by other factors such as social class. My research in China (Liu, 2002) shows a distinction between higher socio-economic status (SES) families and lower SES families in children's school experiences. In contrast to those from lower SES families, the majority of the girls *and* boys from the higher SES families perceived themselves and were perceived by their parents as the teachers' favorites. In the Chinese context, this often means that they were not only appointed as class leaders (*banganbu*) but also were often dominant in class interaction with teachers.

The above-mentioned examples point to the need to caution against any sweeping generalizations about boys and girls concerning classroom behavior and interaction, just as it is necessary to guard against the tendency to treat boys and girls as two homogeneous groups in the discussion about boys' versus girls' academic attainments. Other factors, such as race, ethnicity and class, often mediate gender in students' school experiences, as has been emphasized by researchers concerned with social justice (e.g. Gilborn, 1997; Sewell, 1997; Ball *et al.*, 2000; Ferguson, 2000; Walkerdine *et al.*, 2001; Reay, 2002; Skelton and Francis, 2003).

Qualitative differences

Like quantitative differences, qualitative differences in teachers' gendered inter-action with students often reflect different teacher perceptions and expectations of boys and girls. Particularly, findings in this respect reflect a widely accepted assumption among teachers that boys are more intelligent than girls and they have greater potential for academic achievement than girls in general, and in math and science in particular (e.g. Warrington and Younger, 2000; Renold, 2001; Maynard, 2002; Liu, 2006; Skelton and Francis, 2003). Typically, teach-ers (and other adults) see boys as good at analytic thinking and girls as good at observing (Shepardson and Pizzini, 1992). In a study conducted in Israel, Ben Tsvi-Mayer *et al.* (1989) found that teachers of grades K–6 recalled significantly more boys than girls as their prominent students with the highest potential, although presenting the most discipline problems. Girls were considered as excelling in social skills and language arts. These perceptions of (middle-class) boys as 'naturally more able' are found to persist in spite of the absence of evi-dence and despite the trend toward concern with boys' apparent underachieve-ment. Thus, what Cohen (1996: 133) has termed 'the fiction of boys' potential' seems to have been perpetuated and sustained.

Teachers' differential perceptions of boys and girls concerning their academic ability and potential are often embodied in their praise and criticism of students' work. Teachers' expressions of high expectations raise students' confidence (Rosenthal and Jacobson, 1968; Weinstein, 1985, 1989). However, in their study of classroom influences on students' attitudes and beliefs, Parsons *et al.* (1982) found that teachers' praise of girls was less enthusiastic and less meaningful than that given to boys. Similarly, Elwood and Comber (1996) found that words like 'brilliant', 'flair', 'sparkle', and 'unique' often characterize descriptions of a good A-level performance by boys, while girls receive fewer such comments. Warrington and Younger's (2000) research on Year 11 students and school teach-ers in the UK also indicates that girls' work is frequently and seriously under-valued. In line with this, teachers tend to ask boys more challenging questions than they do girls, and wait longer for boys to answer. They urge boys to try harder, constantly telling boys that they can do it (Sadker and Sadker, 1994; Gordon, 1996).

By the same token, research on teachers' criticism of student work shows that teachers tend to attribute students' success or failure to different factors based on their perceptions of students' gender-based academic capacity. In particular, this seems to reflect a widespread tendency among parents and teachers to attribute girls' academic success to their hard work and boys' to their innate talent (e.g. Yee and Eccles, 1988; Walkerdine, 1989; Jussim and Eccles, 1992; Siegle and Reis, 1998; Tiedemann, 2000; Warrington and Younger, 2000; Renold, 2001; Maynard, 2002; Skelton and Francis, 2003; Liu, 2006). The underlining assumption can be summarized as follows: when girls succeed academically, it is through effort. When they fail, it is just natural; on the other hand, when boys fail academically, it is because they have not applied themselves. When they succeed, it is natural.

Likewise, research on classroom interaction conducted in some African countries has revealed that women and men teachers share these views of boys as more academically competent (VanBelle-Prouty, 1991). Their expectations of female students reflect the negative stereotypes held in the wider society of girls as lazy, gossipy and indecisive, and lacking ambition (Davison and Kanyuka, 1990; VanBelle-Prouty, 1991). This constitutes a classroom environment of discouragement for girls, which seems to be even harsher than that indicated by the examples from other parts of the world cited above. According to Anderson-Leavitt *et al.*'s (1994) study on girls' classroom experiences in Guinea, the silencing of girls by their male peers and teachers was not uncommon. Teachers made comments such as 'Oh, girls say they do not know; let's move on to boys and see', or teachers responded in a shocked manner when a girl answered correctly (p11).

This behavior may be especially evident in certain subject areas. For example, VanBelle-Prouty's (1991) research on women and education in Francophone central Africa revealed that teachers commonly called on the least capable girl students to the board in front of the class to solve maths problems. When the girls could not complete the task successfully, the teacher asked one of the most capable boys in class to assist the girls. As the girls struggled with the problem, the male teacher and boy students taunted them, suggesting that the girls were lazy and stupid. Two recent studies financed by UNESCO in Burkina Faso and Niger confirmed that boys received the most attention and encouragement during arithmetic and reading, and they were perceived by teachers as superior in maths and sciences to girls. Girls were discouraged from taking maths and sciences as these were considered unsuitable for females (UNESCO, Countdown, 1997).

For various reasons, there has been little research conducted in China on gendered classroom interactions. Nevertheless, the limited number of existing studies indicate that Chinese teachers, like parents, tend to have differential perceptions and expectations of boys and girls, similar to (or even going beyond) those as revealed by the research conducted in other countries. For example, in my study on parental expectations of boys and girls as only children (Liu, 2006), some of the parents – a few of them were teachers themselves – maintained that boys are, after all, cleverer than girls, with greater academic potential. Moreover, they told me, citing a Chinese saying, that it is not necessary to restrain boys in their activities, as one needs to do with girls, because naughty boys will surely turn out to be intelligent. A boy's mother, who was a college teacher, argued that males are good at analyzing things while females are good at memorizing things. This was, she claimed, why boys in her classes often showed more insight than girls in discussions on various topics.

Related to the above-mentioned view about girls and boys is the widely shared assumption among Chinese teachers and parents that girls tend to do better at primary school because of their relatively peaceful nature and greater commitment to school work, whereas they tend to fall behind boys as they progress through schooling (Ross, 1993). In these teachers' view, strengths and weaknesses are gender-related and biologically fixed, with strengths defined by male characteristics.

In common with research conducted around the world (e.g. Burton, 1995; Harding, 1996; Boaler, 1997; Warrington and Younger, 2000), another widespread assumption found among Chinese teachers and parents is that, generally speaking, girls are innately less likely to succeed in maths and sciences, whereas they show more talent in language and other arts subjects (*wenke*). Many of the girls in my life history research (Liu, 2005b) indicated that their teachers and/or parents helped them to choose subjects at high school or/and university that 'suit' the girls' gender, even though they had done very well in maths and sciences at school. Young people themselves also tend to internalize such notions, believing that males are naturally suited to science and maths. Some of the girls who have taken up computer sciences out of consideration for employment prospects, told me that it was not the right subject for them, as it involves much logical and abstract thinking, which, according to them, males are normally better at. The same notion has also been found among teachers in other Asian countries (e.g. Kim, 1988; cited in Namtip, 1997).

Given the relationship between teachers' differential perceptions of boys and girls and their differential treatment of male and female students, it can be argued that, generally speaking, girls at Chinese schools tend to be marginalized in the classroom like their counterparts in many other parts of the world, although there has been very little empirical documentation of gendered interactions in Chinese classrooms. However, as I have noted earlier in this chapter, in Chinese schools, as in schools elsewhere, gender may meanwhile be mediated by other factors, such as social class, race, ethnicity and locality. More research needs to be conducted into such differences.

CONCLUSION

This chapter attempts to highlight the gendered nature of school culture through an examination of gender segregation and gendered teacher–student interaction in the classroom. The literature spanning half a century and across cultures consistently indicates that the classroom is thoroughly gendered in its organization and practice. In general, the gendered classroom environment is characterized by male-centredness, whereby 'boys are found to dominate the classroom both in the positive sense as learners, as well as in a negative sense as behavioural problems' (Streitmatter, 1994: 126). This lends much empirical support to Paechter's (1998) argument that, '[d]espite improvement in girls' relative academic success at the school leaving level, and despite suggestions in the press that boys are the new underachievers, girls remain second-class citizens in education and beyond' (p5).

The gendered classroom environment, like the overall gendered school culture, may have important implications for students' evolving identities and future lives. Students in environments permeated with sexism tend to develop value systems that are gender differentiated, which in turn help perpetuate gender bias that they will carry with them into the adult world (Streitmatter, 1994). Hence students' gendered experiences at school and in classrooms 'contribute to the gender divisions found in later lives that perpetuate gender inequality, such as the choice of occupational sectors, the standing and influence within sectors, and the prioritizing of the occupational relative to the domestic' (Howe, 1997: 2).

It is important to note, however, that girls are not the only victims of the gendered school culture with its unyielding concept of what is appropriate for each gender (Delamont, 1990; Streitmatter, 1994; Gilbert and Gilbert, 1998; Kimmel, 2000). Hegemonic, heterosexist constructions of 'proper' masculinity marginalize and denigrate boys who do not conform to these constructions, as well as girls (Connell, 1995; Lesko, 2000; Skelton, 2001; Renold, 2004). Among other negative consequences, barriers are established that prevent boys and girls from learning about and from each other. Thus, rather than opening opportunities for students, gender segregation and differential treatment based on students' gender help reinforce gender-related problems in their adult lives and in the larger society.

School culture is dynamic rather than fixed. Schools reflect the dominant gender ideology of the society around them, but they do not merely mirror these in a passive manner. Rather, they actively produce and reproduce gender and heterosexual divisions (Mac an Ghaill, 1994). To recognize the dynamic nature of school culture is to recognize that schools can and ought to serve as agents of change. The classroom, as one of the school's major microcultures, where most of the teacher–student interaction takes place, can serve as an important space for such change, and teachers have a major role to play in this process. Unfortunately, as the review in this chapter shows, teachers, although largely unconsciously, often play a major part in perpetuating and reproducing the gender relations in schools, especially the classroom. A number of studies have offered classroom strategies for challenging and disrupting stereotypical gender constructions among pupils in schools (e.g. McLaughlin *et al.*, 1991; Streitmatter, 1994; Davies, 1997; Paechter, 1998; Francis, 2000; Francis *et al.*, 2002). These studies have provided valuable and practical suggestions for educators to bring about change in the classroom and schools in line with gender equity. However, I would argue that the precondition for these (and other) good suggestions to be put into practice is that teachers must be, first of all, conscious of the detrimental effects of sexism and committed to change. The review of literature in this chapter indicates the need for a greater emphasis on gender issues and on reflection on practice during teacher training and in-service training.

Moreover, in cases where there has been intervention, more research aimed at evaluating the intervention is also necessary. So far, research has yielded abundant empirical evidence illuminating the gendered environment of the classroom and the overall gendered school culture. The question remains, however, how to make better use of the research evidence for the purpose of change; for example, to awaken teacher consciousness about the consequences of gender-biased treatment of students. The fact that a vast body of research evidence coexists with continuing and prevalent sexism in the classroom and the school warrants such an enquiry.

Furthermore, it will be important to ensure that this research continues to develop analysis of the intersection of various identity factors, as well as gender, that are reflected in classroom cultures and in educational outcomes, rather than falling back on the binary views of 'girls' and 'boys' that characterize much of the earlier work reported in this chapter. This necessitates examination of femininity and masculinity as relational and mutually dependent constructions rather than as isolated categories in research on gender and education.

REFERENCES

Alloway, N (1995) *Foundation stones: the construction of gender in early childhood.* Carlton: Curriculum Corporation.

American Association of University Women (AAUW) (1992) *How schools short change girls: a study of major findings on girls and education.* Washington, DC: American Association of University Women.

Anderson-Leavitt, K, Bloch, M and Soumare, A (1994) Inside the classrooms in Guinea: girls' experience. World Bank Working Paper. Washington, DC: World Bank.

Ball, SJ, Maguire, M and Macrae, S (2000) *Choices, transitions and pathways: new youth, new economies in the global city.* London: Falmer Press.

Ben Tsvi-Mayer, S, Hertz-Lazarowitz, R and Safir, MP (1989) Teachers' selections of boys and girls as prominent students. *Sex Roles,* 21: 231–45.

Blasé, J (1991) The micropolitical perspective, in Blasé, J (ed) *The politics of life in schools. power, conflict, and cooperation.* London: Sage.

Boaler, J (1997) Reclaiming school mathematics: the girls fight back. *Gender and Education,* 9, 285–95.

Burton, L (1995) Moving towards a feminist epistemology of mathematics, in Rogers, P and Kaiser, G (ed) *Equity in mathematics education* (209–25). Lewes: Falmer Press.

Clarke, J, Hall, S, Jefferson, T and Roberts, B (1975) Subcultures, culture and subcultures, in Hall, S and Jefferson, T (ed) *Resistance through rituals: youth subcultures in post-war Britain.* London: Hutchinson.

Cohen, M (1996) Is there a space for the achieving girl?, in Murphy, P and Gipps, C (ed) *Equity in the classroom: towards effective pedagogy for girls and boys.* London: Falmer.

Connell, RW (1995) *Masculinities.* Berkeley, CA: University of California Press.

Connell, RW (1996) Teaching the boys: new research on masculinity, and gender strategies for schools. *Teachers College Record,* 98: 206–35.

Connell, RW (2000) *The men and the boys.* Berkeley, CA: University of California Press.

Davison, J and Kanyuka, M (1990) *An ethnographic study of factors affecting the education of girls in southern Malawi.* USAID.

Delamont, S (1990) *Sex roles and the school* (2nd edn). London: Routledge.

Elwood, J and Comber, C (1996) *The gender differences in examinations at 18 + project.* Nuffield Foundation/Ofsted/Equal Opportunities Commission Report.

Ferguson, AA (2000) *Bad boys: public schools in the making of black masculinity.* Ann Arbor, MI: University of Michigan Press.

Francis, B (1998) *Power plays.* Stoke-on-Trent: Trentham Books.

Francis, B (2000) *Boys, girls and achievement: addressing the classroom issues.* London: Routledge/Falmer.

Francis, B, Skelton, C and Archer, L (2002) *A systematic review of classroom strategies for reducing stereotypical gender constructions among girls and boys in mixed-sex UK primary schools* (EPPI-Center Review). Available at http://eppi.ioe.ac.uk (accessed 19 August 2005).

Gilbert, R and Gilbert, P (1998) *Masculinity goes to school.* London: Routledge.

Gilborn, D (1997) Racism and reform: new ethnicities/old inequalities. *British Educational Research Journal,* 22: 345–60.

Gordon, T (1996) Citizenship, difference and marginality in schools – spatial and embodied aspects of gender construction, in Murphy, P and Gipps, C (ed) *Equity in the classroom: towards effective pedagogy for girls and boys.* London: Falmer.

Harding, J (1996) Girls' achievements in science and technology: implications for pedagogy, in Murphy, P and Gipps, C (ed) *Equity in the classroom: towards effective pedagogy for girls and boys.* London: Falmer.

Howe, C (1997) *Gender and classroom interaction: a research review.* Scottish Council for Research in Education: SCRE Publication 138.

Jordan, E (1995) Fighting boys and fantasy play: the construction of masculinity in the early years of school. *Gender and Education,* 7: 69–85.

Jussim, L and Eccles, JS (1992) Teacher expectations. II. Construction and reflection of student achievement. *Journal of Personality and Social Psychology,* 63: 947–61.

Kelly, A (1986) Gender differences in teacher–pupil interactions: a meta-analytic review. *Research in Education,* 39: 1–23.

Kelly, L, Burton, S and Regan, L (1994) Researching women's lives or studying women's oppression? Reflections on what constitutes feminist research, in Maynard, M and Purvis, J (ed) *Researching women's lives from a feminist perspective.* London: Taylor and Francis.

Kessler, S, Ashenden, DJ, Connell, RW and Dowsett, GW (1985) Gender relations in secondary schooling. *Sociology of Education,* 58: 34–48.

Kimmel, MS (2000) *The gendered society.* New York: Oxford University Press.

Lesko, N (eds) (2000) *Masculinities at school.* Thousand Oaks, CA: Sage.

Liu, FS (2002) Parental expectations of the single child in the nuclear Chinese family: boys as single children and girls as single children. Master's thesis, Institute for Educational Research, University of Oslo.

Liu, FS (2006) Boys as only-children and girls as only-children: parental gendered expectations of the only-child in the nuclear Chinese family in present-day China. *Gender and Education.* 18(5): 491–505.

Liu, FS (2005b) Modernization as lived experiences: identity construction of first generation young-adult only-children. Unpublished manuscript.

Mac an Ghaill, M (1994) *The making of men: masculinities, sexualities, and schooling.* Buckingham: Open University Press.

Mahony, P and Hextall, I (2000) *Reconstructing teaching.* London:Routledge/Falmer.

Maynard, T (2002) *Exploring the boys and literacy issue.* London: Routledge/Falmer.

McLaughlin, C, Lodge, C and Watkins, C (eds) (1991) *Gender and pastoral care: the personal-social aspects of the whole school,* Oxford: Blackwell.

Namtip, A (1997) Gender-sensitive education for a better world. Background paper for the International Conference on Adult Education. Paris: UNESCO.

Nunez, G (1995) Research findings on interventions for promoting girls' school attendance, retention and completion and on community perceptions of public/private sector involvement in girls' education. Paper presented at the Annual Meeting of the Comparative and International Education Society, Boston.

Osler, A and Vincent, K (2003) *Girls and exclusion: rethinking the agenda.* London: Routledge/Falmer.

Paechter, CF (1998) *Educating the Other: gender, power, and schooling.* London: Falmer Press.

Parsons, JE, Kaczala, CM and Meece, JL (1982) Socialization of achievement, attitudes and beliefs: classroom influences. *Child Development,* 53: 322–39.

Prosser, J (1999) The evolution of school culture research, in Prosser, J (ed) *School culture* (1–14). London: Paul Chapman.

Reay, D (2001) 'Spice girls', 'nice girls', 'girlies' and 'tomboys': gender discourses, girls' cultures and femininities in the primary classroom. *Gender and Education,* 13: 153–66.

Reay, D (2002) Shaun's story: troubling discourses of white working-class masculinities. *Gender and Education,* 14: 221–34.

Renold, D (2001) 'Square girls', femininity and the negotiation of academic success in the primary school. *British Educational Research Journal,* 27: 577–88.

Renold, E (2004) 'Other' boys: negotiating non-hegemonic masculinities in the primary school. *Gender and Education,* 16: 247–66.

Rosenthal, R and Jacobson, L (1968) *Pygmalion in the classroom: teacher expectation and pupils' intellectual development.* New York: Holt, Rinehart & Winston.

Ross, H (1993) Growing up in a Chinese secondary school for girls: 'Do you want to know what I think or what I really think?' *Journal of Women and Gender Studies,* 4: 111–36.

Sadker, M and Sadker, D (1994) *Failing at fairness: how our schools cheat girls.* New York: Touchstone.

Sewell, T (1997) *Black masculinities and schooling: how Black boys survive modern schooling.* Stoke-on-Trent: Trentham Books.

Shepardson, DP and Pizzini, EL (1992) Gender bias in female elementary teachers' perceptions of the scientific ability of students. *Science Education,* 76: 147–53.

Siegle, D and Reis, SM (1998) Gender differences in teacher and student perceptions of gifted students' ability and effort. *Gifted Child Quarterly,* 42: 39–47.

Skelton, C (2001) *Schooling the boys: masculinities and primary education.* Buckingham: Open University Press.

Skelton, C (2002). Constructing dominant masculinity and negotiating the 'male gaze'. *International Journal of Inclusive Education,* 6: 17–31.

Skelton, C (2003) Introduction: boys and girls in the primary classroom, In Skelton, C and Francis, B (ed) *Boys and girls in the Primary Classroom* (3–25). Buckingham: Open University Press.

Stanley, L and Wise, S (1993) *Breaking out again: feminist ontology and epistemology.* London: Routledge.

Streitmatter, J (1994) *Toward gender equity in the classroom: everyday teachers' beliefs and practices.* New York: State University of New York Press.

Swann, J and Graddol, D (1994) Gender inequalities in classroom talk, in Graddol, D, Maybin, J and Stierer B (ed) *Researching language and literacy in social context* (151–67). Clevedon: Multilingual Mattters.

Thorne, B (1993) *Gender play: girls and boys at school.* Buckingham: Open University Press.

Tiedemann, J (2000) Parents' gender stereotypes and teachers' beliefs as predictors of children's concept of their mathematical ability in elementary school. *Journal of Educational Psychology,* 92: 144–51.

UNESCO (1997) Countdown, *Adult education in a polarizing world, education for all, status and trends.* Paris: UNESCO.

VanBelle-Prouty, D (1991) From the outside looking in: women and education in Francophone central Africa. PhD dissertation, Michigan State University, East Lansing.

Walkerdine, V (1989) Femininity as performance. *Oxford Review of Education,* 15: 267–79.

Walkingdine, V, Lucey, H and Melody, J (2001) *Growing up girls: psychological explorations of gender and class.* London: Macmillan.

Wamahiu, S (1994) Making the classroom friendly to the girl-child in Anglophone Africa: gender sensitivity in text-books and among teachers. Paper presented at the Seminar on Girls' Education in Anglophone Africa, Nairobi.

Warrington, M and Younger, M (2000) The other side of the gender gap. *Gender and Education*, 12: 493–508.

Weaver-Hightower, M (2003) The 'boy turn' in research on gender and education. *Review of Educational Research*, 73: 471–98.

Weinstein, R (1985) Student mediation of classroom expectancy effects, in Dusek, J (ed) *Teacher expectancies* (329–50). Hillsdale, NJ. Lawrence Erlbaum Associates.

Yee, D and Eccles, JS (1988) Parent perceptions and attributions for children's math achievement. *Sex Roles*, 19: 317–33.

Younger, M, Warrinton, M and Williams, J (1999) The gender gap and classroom interactions: reality and rhetoric? *British Journal of Sociology of Education*, 20: 325–41.

31

Gendered Classroom Experiences

Emma Renold

INTRODUCTION

Classroom-based studies have a long history in feminist research. A range of methodological and epistemological frameworks have been deployed to document and explore the gendered experiences of classroom life across nursery, infant and primary classrooms through to secondary, further and higher education classrooms. While some studies have focused exclusively on the gendered interactions within the classroom, from single qualitative case-studies to large-scale quantitative surveys, there is also a long tradition of ethnographic studies exploring the classroom as one site among many for school-based gendered experiences, via a range of multiple methods (diaries, biographical narratives, field notes, interviews, etc.). In their book, *Feminism and the Classroom Teacher*, Amanda Coffey and Sara Delamont (2000) comprehensively summarize the symbiotic relationship between different gender/feminist theories and the type of methods and substantive foci that such projects investigate (e.g. from the relationship between sex-role theory and the mapping of sex differences to the deployment of feminist post-structuralist theories to explore discursive constructions of multiple and relational gender identity work and cultures). This chapter will not rehearse these histories and linkages here. Rather, it will explore how the many classroom-based studies have each, in their own way, produced an understanding of the classroom as a powerful and intimate social site in which the micropolitics of social relations between teachers and students are charged with a range of formal and informal gendered meanings. Specifically, the chapter will pay close attention to the temporal, physical/embodied and discursive dimensions of classroom life and relations within formal and informal teacher–student and student–student relations. It will explore the extent to which the everyday gendered experiences of teachers and students shape and are shaped by the social and cultural space of the classroom in three key ways: the classroom as a regulatory and normalizing space, the classroom as a dangerous space, and the classroom as a transgressive space.

THE CLASSROOM AS A REGULATORY AND NORMALIZING SPACE

Classroom relations have long been explored in terms of the hierarchical power struggles between teachers and pupils. Early observational studies of classroom interaction have highlighted the private and isolated world of the classroom and apparent autonomy and relative power of teachers in classrooms (Jackson, 1968). However, the positioning of the teacher as autonomous professional has come under threat over the last 20 years via a range of accountability discourses and increased government centralization dictating and prescribing what and how teachers teach (see Ball, 1990; Acker, 1994). Feminist research (Walkerdine, 1990; Riddell, 1992; Steedman, 1992; Acker, 1994; Weiner, 1994) has also drawn a distinction and disjunction between autonomy and power. Coffey and Delamont (2000) summarize this relationship in their discussion of the structural power-lessness and potential isolation of female teachers:

> While teachers may have considerable autonomy in the classroom, women teachers, particularly, do not experience the same power within the school and education system generally.
>
> (2000: 16)

From the pupil perspective, the systematic imbalance of power between the adult-teacher and child-pupil endure. The production of the schoolchild as Other positions children as relatively powerless within the intergenerational adult–child binary (Paechter, 1998; Devine, 2002). The relationship between teacher and pupil, however, can shift considerably: from the feminized familialism (teacher-as-nurturer and mother) of the early/primary years to the masculinized familialism (teacher-as-authoritarian and disciplinarian) of the secondary years. Both the 'official' school and the informal or 'hidden curriculum' demand a degree of pupil passivity and obedience. Pupils are confronted with a catalogue of rules and sanctions restricting mobility and movement (e.g. from frozen bodies seated behind desks, to the relative stillness of classroom life) and regulating sound and voice (e.g. from 'fingers on lips' to 'no shouting'). Often the regulations over movement and sound intersect (e.g. pupils must raise their hands to be granted permission to speak). The regulation of embodied school identities and the ways in which time and space are tightly structured and circumscribed, are highly gendered, as Becky Francis' secondary school observations in four London-based secondary schools illustrates:

Boys moved around in the classroom and were more physically active than girls. They frequently kicked balls around, walked or ran around the classroom, pushed, slapped or hit each other, and threw things across the class … boys were substantially noisier than girls, both in terms of general noise and in terms of contributions to whole-class teaching (Francis, 2000: 31).

Classroom-based research exploring the gendered interactions and cultures of boys and girls continue to highlight how they are differently positioned and position themselves as 'pupils' within the classroom. Much of this research has focused upon exploring and explaining gender difference embedded in teacher–pupil interactions, particularly in relation to disciplinary and controlling interactions (Robinson, 1992).

Early feminist research in elementary (French and French, 1984; Paley, 1984; Evans, 1988) and secondary (Spender, 1980; Stanworth, 1981) school classrooms from the 1980s to the late 1990s and 2000s (see Fisher, 1994; Swann and Graddol, 1994; Francis, 1998, 2000) all illustrate how teachers devote a greater proportion of their time and attention to boys (usually because boys are more often reprimanded and disciplined than girls) and how boys (Evans, 1987) and men (Luke, 1994) dominate classroom talk both in whole-class discussions (teacher–pupil interactions) and mixed-gender, small-group work (pupil–pupil interactions). Fisher (1994), for example, noted how boys conversed mainly with each other when placed in mixed-gender groups and talked over and silenced girls' ideas by ignoring or overriding them. Ten years later, regardless of girls' academic successes, the ways in which girls are marginalized by their peers and teachers persist (Renold, 2001a).

While quantitative research has consistently provided evidence that teachers interact more with boys than with girls and that boys call out more and are more disruptive than girls (see Kelly, 1988), qualitative research has sought to analyze teachers' gendered perceptions of girl and boy pupils' classroom behavior and the relationship between children's social and cultural identities as 'girls' and 'boys' and their academic identities as 'pupils'.

The enduring image of the 'good pupil' as hard-working, rule-following, cooperative, conscientious and academically able is a highly gendered one. Teachers, for example, continue to identify these traits as the properties of typical 'girl pupils' (see Browne and France, 1986; MacNaughton, 2001; Reay, 2001). In contrast, the characteristics of typical 'boy pupils' are identified as dominant, disruptive, underperforming and generally challenging (Walden and Walkerdine, 1985; Epstein *et al.*, 1998; Skelton, 2001). Research has also suggested, however, that while teachers encourage (in boys) and expect (in girls) the embodiment of the 'good pupil', girls who work hard to achieve and perfect such 'goody-goody' behaviors are not necessarily thanked or perceived positively (see Francis, 1998; Renold, 2001a). Boys exhibiting challenging behaviors, on the other hand, continue to be viewed as ultimately more rewarding to teach (see Belotti, 1975; Reay, 2001). Drawing on bell hooks' concept of 'talking back' (e.g. from offering an opinion to daring to disagree with teacher authority),

Gordon *et al.* (2000) explore the ways in which 'talking back' is interpreted differently by teachers depending upon the gender of the speaker. If the speaker is a 'boy', this behavior is often interpreted as representing an active and enquiring mind. If the speaker is a 'girl', her response can represent a direct challenge to teacher authority. Indeed, research has consistently shown how girls displaying assertiveness or ambition (i.e. traditionally masculine traits) can be denigrated by their teachers as 'aggressive', 'pushy', 'spiteful', 'little madams' (see Walkerdine, 1990; Francis, 1998; Reay, 2001) and by their peers as 'bossy', 'boy-ish' and 'loud' (see Renold, 2001a). In contrast, some disruptive behavior, such as boisterousness and competitiveness in boys, can be praised (Mac an Ghaill, 1994; Skelton, 2001). Recent refocusing on school-based masculinities, however, has also illustrated how boys who stray from typical boy-pupil behavior (e.g. by being studious, quiet and settled), while rarely pathologized by their class teachers, can often be strongly pathologized by their peers as 'geeks', as 'girly' and as 'gay' (see Epstein *et al.*, 1998; Renold, 2001b; Skelton, 2001; Swain, 2003). It is also not uncommon for teachers to draw upon children's own constructions of 'boys' and 'girls' as polarized opposites as a strategy for classroom management and discipline (e.g. threatening to sit children 'boy-girl–boy-girl' if they do not 'quieten down' or 'get on with their work').

Girls' and boys' academic abilities and achievements continue to be differently interpreted. Recent research suggests that girls' high achievements continue to be undermined by their teachers as the result of 'hard work' or 'natural flair' (see Renold, 2001a), while boys' low achievements do not deter teachers from maintaining their academic potential (Maynard, 2002). Girls also continue to blame themselves and internalize failures in performance, and hide, downplay or deny rather than celebrate and improve upon their successes (Renold, 2001a, Lucey and Reay, 2002). High-achieving girls are also expected to continue their care-giving role as 'little helpers' and 'settlers' (as mini classroom assistants and pseudo-teachers) as they police boys' (naturally) disruptive behaviors and service their emotional needs and achievements (Belotti, 1975; Mahony, 1985; Thorne, 1993; Francis, 1998). While some of the early research did not pay close attention to how the gendering of pupil subject positions within the micropolitics of classroom pupil–pupil and teacher–pupil interactions and cultures operate in specific classed and racialized ways, more recent research has explored these dimensions (see Connolly, 1998; MacNaughton, 2001; Skelton, 2001; Walkerdine *et al.,* 2001; Youdell, 2003; Archer, 2003). Paying attention to the diversity of masculinities and femininities within gendered groups (thus avoiding essentializing gender differences) and drawing upon Foucaultian notions of power as diffuse and something that has to be continually achieved (rather than power as statically owned by particular groups, whether peer groups or teachers), have provided more nuanced analyses of the ways in which girl pupils and boy pupils negotiate a range of powerful and powerless positions within the classroom. Pupils' resistance and subversion of normative ways of being and doing 'pupil' is discussed in more detail below.

THE CLASSROOM AS A DANGEROUS SPACE

Feminist ethnographies of classroom life have long researched the classroom as a key social and cultural site in which both teachers and pupils produce and reproduce a range of heavily regulated and normalized gendered and sexual meanings, practices, power relations and identities. The classroom, just like any other semi-public space (such as the assembly hall, the toilets, the corridors and the cloakrooms), operates to produce and regulate a cast of covert and overt, gendered, racialized classed and sexualized performances by teachers and pupils. Paechter (1998), among others, has argued how the focus on overt forms of classroom disruption (particularly with the increasing emphasis on academic performance and outcomes) has resulted in the failure by classroom teachers and school administrations to address and combat other kinds of gendered interactions between pupils, especially the gendered nature of sexualized bullying and harassment and the informal world of classroom relations that make the classroom into an abusive and dangerous space for many pupils.

Sexual harassment, from name-calling to physical abuse, has been a central concern of feminist researchers, especially within the secondary school environment and the everyday, school-based experiences of young men and women. Early feminist research has explored young women's experiences of heterosexual harassment (Davies, 1984; Jones, 1985; Wolpe, 1988; Halson, 1989; Mahony and Jones, 1989; Lees, 1993). Later research in the 1990s and 2000s, which began exploring young people's constructions of school-based femininities, masculinities and sexualities, exposed the relationship between gender-based and sexualized forms of violence and harassment, particularly their role in the production of dominant heterosexual masculinities (Mac an Ghaill, 1994; Kehily and Nayak, 1996; Kenway and Fitzclarence, 1997; Duncan, 1999; Robinson, 2000; Sunnari *et al.*, 2002; Martino and Pallotta-Chiarolli, 2003), and in the policing of queer sexualities (Epstein, 1994; Laskey and Beavis, 1996; Epstein *et al.,* 2003; Blount, 2004).

Despite isolated incidents within the media and references within broader projects on the gendered worlds of primary schoolchildren, there are very few detailed accounts that centre the experience of pre-teenagers (but see Clark, 1990; Stein, 1996). My own research, alongside Margaret Clark (1990) in Australia and Nan Stein (1996) in the USA, reveals that such experiences are by no means peculiar or restricted to teenage girls in secondary schools. Studies have highlighted the ways in which boys unsettle and denigrate girls through sexually abusive language. Studies have also explored the physical sexual harassment of girls. Clark (1990), for example, describes reports of primary schoolboys punching girls in the breasts and Stein (1995: 149) describes 'Friday flip-up days' where 'boys in the first through to third grades flipped up the dresses of their female classmates'. Often such incidents are typically dismissed as mutual, voluntary or playful behavior or justified by boys and teachers alike through humor, as 'just mucking about' (Nayak and Kehily, 1997). And like so many reports of sexual harassment, girls tend to use discourses that serve to invalidate and undermine their experiences as a form of harassment.

Many secondary school-based studies have also illustrated how 'homophobic' talk and behaviors saturate boys' peer-group cultures, social relations and masculinity-making activities within and outside the classroom (Mac an Ghaill, 1994; Nayak and Kehily, 1997; Duncan, 1999; Sunnari *et al.,* 2002; Martino and Pallotta-Chiarolli, 2003). Each of these studies has indicated the ways in which anti-gay sentiment, such as calling a boy or his behavior 'gay', operates to produce and police dominant masculinities. More recently, primary school-based research is beginning to uncover how younger children are also drawing upon the term 'gay' in a number of different ways (Gilbert and Gilbert, 1998; Letts and Sears, 1999; Swain, 2003). Some studies, such as Jon Swain's (2003: 319) London-based ethnography of schoolboy masculinities, discovered boys' widespread use of the term 'gay' as a general form of interpersonal abuse which could encompass 'anything from being not very good to absolute rubbish'. Even trainers (sneakers) could be perceived as 'gay' if they were not sporting a designer label. In my own study in eastern England (UK), anti-gay and homophobic talk was much less prevalent and was taken up in different ways. The term 'gay' was not used as a general term of abuse but was directed at particular boys. This could include one-off comments directed at boys who got (physically) 'too close' to other boys and more persistent targeting of boys who were considered to be aligning themselves too closely with girls and femininity and/or boys who failed or chose not to access dominant masculinities (e.g. football and fighting). As shown by many other studies that have explored the ways in which sexuality and gender intersect and interact within boys' peer group cultures, any boy who dares to deviate from a normative or hegemonic masculinity is potentially subject to both gendered and sexualized attacks. Indeed, the terms 'gay' and 'girl' or 'poof' and 'sissy' are often interchangeable and illustrative of the ways in which homophobia and misogyny operate to police the Other (Kimmel, 1987).

Very rarely do girls or boys report these kinds of gendered experiences to their teachers. When I asked a group of girls who had experienced systematic verbal and physical sexual harassment by two boys in Year 6 (age 10–11 years) (see Renold, 2000) why they did not tell anyone, their responses seemed to reflect and echo wider cultural issues around denial of young girls' sexuality, girls' socialized passivity and subordination to men and authority more widely. The gender-based and anti-gay name-calling of boys was also something that boys tried to shrug off and ignore, rather than confront or challenge. All of this had the knock-on effect of reproducing the boys' behavior as 'normal' and 'natural' – constant theme in the research on schoolchildren's experiences of sexual harassment (see Martino and Pallotta-Chiarolli, 2005).

The difficulty children and young people report in disclosing experiences of gendered bullying and sexual harassment are perhaps compounded by teachers themselves (usually men teachers) who either tacitly condone the ways which girls and boys are sexually derided or are complicit in the sexual harassment of their own pupils. Much of the literature has explored male secondary schoolteachers' use of sexual joking with young women and young men as a way of establishing rapport with their pupils (see Cunnison, 1989; Riddell, 1990; Mac an Ghaill, 1994; Hey, 1997; Kehily *et al.*, 2002). Recent research has also shown that the (hetero) sexualization of teacher–pupil interactions is by no means confined to the secondary classroom. Francis and Skelton (2001) draw attention to the ways in which men teachers perform and construct their gender and sexual identities (i.e. their 'heterosexual masculinities') with their female students. The following example is an extract from Skelton's field notes of one primary schoolteacher's flirtatious behavior in which he positions himself as a 'sex object':

> The children are told to meet up in the hall for PE after they have got changed. Phillip Norris (the teacher) adds, 'You'll want to be quick, girls, because I've got my sexy shorts with me today' and he wiggles his hips (Skelton, field notes). (Francis and Skelton, 2001: 5)

In their interpretation of this extract, Francis and Skelton (2001) move beyond conceptualizing the interaction between the male teacher and 'the girls' as wholly oppressive. Rather they invite a reading which highlights how some sexual behaviors can be interpreted as simultaneously harassing and seductive, by drawing attention to the 'mixed emotions' many girls experience in feeling 'gratified by male objectification' yet also 'experiencing such behaviour as harassing'.

In relation to the ways in which men teachers interact with boys, and police and regulate normative masculinities, research has highlighted a dual process (particularly in secondary schools) in which men teachers must prove their 'masculinity' by constructing themselves as authority figures and disciplinarians, on the one hand, and 'one of the lads', on the other hand. This is mainly achieved by aligning themselves with dominant masculinities and heterosexualities and the policing and shaming of minority masculinities and sexualities. Francis and Skelton make explicit the heterosexist discourses underpinning such performances and the pressure to perform as 'properly masculine' within the 'feminized' environment of the primary school:

> [...] heterosexist discourses (reflecting homophobia and misogyny) are drawn on by men teachers in the classroom to construct their own masculinity in opposition to the boys that they are 'other' ... [T]his positioning by men teachers of themselves as 'real men' and thereby different to females and dismissive of 'the feminine' ... can be seen as one way of establishing their masculine credentials in a female profession. (Francis and Skelton, 2001: 15)

Passing and performing as 'real men' or, indeed, 'real women' can involve hiding aspects of identity that are Other to dominant gendered and (hetero) sexual scripts. Wallis and Van Every (2000) highlight how gay, lesbian and bisexual teachers who do not conform to normative gender performances (e.g. 'soft' men or 'butch' women) are targeted by pupils and teachers alike through sexual/ gender jibes and speculation as to their non-heterosexual orientation (see also Letts and Sears, 1999). The limited research on gay and lesbian teachers working at all levels of compulsory schooling suggests that in many ways identifying as lesbian or gay is either experienced or reported more widely (particularly in tabloid press) as being incompatible with being a teacher (see Epstein and Johnson, 1994). It is perhaps no surprise, then, that non-heterosexual teachers keep their sexuality private, and normative gendered performances are limited to the straightest of straight.

While the ways in which teachers police children's gender and sexual identities is well established in school-based research, research has also addressed, although more sporadically, how children themselves actively regulate their teachers' gendered sexualities. Most of this research has focused upon male students' harassment of female teachers in higher education, secondary schools (Jones, 1985; Mahony, 1985; Robinson, 2000) and even primary schools (Clark, 1990; Walkerdine, 1990; Skelton, 2001). All have illustrated how the power differential between the child student and the adult teacher can be both subverted and overturned. Robinson's (2000) research in four state high schools and two independent, single-sex schools in New South Wales suggests how most of the offensive behaviors, which ranged from verbal sexual abuse to physical and visual violations, occurred mostly during class time. Her research shows how sexual harassment is a powerful resource for boys and men to re/position themselves as powerful in an institutional context where they are often positioned as powerless.

While research has addressed the ways in which the classroom as a social and cultural site is produced and consumed as a regulatory, normalizing and dangerous space, research has also exposed the classroom as a potential site in which teachers and students actively resist, subvert and transgress gender norms and regimes.

THE CLASSROOM AS A TRANSGRESSIVE SPACE

Feminist research has provided a comprehensive history of how women teachers (Acker, 1989; Tamboukou, 2000, 2003) and queer teachers (Khayatt, 1992; Blount, 2004) benefit and are empowered by the privacy (and safety) of the classroom in a range of diverse ways, from their own identity work and personal pedagogic style to implementing an individualized feminist/queer praxis. Although the lived reality of incorporating a feminist or sexual politics is a mixed one insofar as there will always be a blurring of the classroom as a dangerous and empowering space, there are many autobiographical accounts and life history narratives each exploring the extent to which, and the costs and consequences of how, teachers draw attention to and challenge a range of gendered and sexual inequalities, silences and discriminations (Miller, 1996).

For example, the limited research on gay and lesbian teachers (especially those working within the primary and early years) suggests, unsurprisingly, that, in many ways, identifying as lesbian or gay is either experienced or reported widely (e.g. tabloid accounts) as being incompatible with being a teacher. This notion is predicated on the assumption that gay and lesbian teachers are inherently and inevitably dangerous to children insofar as they represent a corrupting influence upon children's presumed (heterosexual) innocence. Given the ways in which the staff room can operate as a prohibitive space policing non-normative gender, race and sexual identities (see Cunnison, 1989; Paechter, 1998), Amy Wallis and Jo Van Every (2000) conclude that, for many teachers, the classroom is the one remaining space where they have a certain degree of flexibility in the way they present themselves to children. However, as Epstein and Johnson (1994) highlight, for many 'out' gay teachers who seek to challenge the normalization of heterosexuality and carve out a space from which to overwrite children's own heteronormative expectations within the classroom, this becomes a difficult if not impossible task. They describe how one gay teacher's account of coming out to his class was met with disbelief and denial (see also Danish, 1998). This is particularly true of the primary school with its hetero-familial ethos, where 'even out gay teachers are read as heterosexual' (Epstein *et al.,* 2003: 30), such is the pervasiveness of children's own hetero-normative assumptions and imagined futures (see also Letts and Sears, 1999). However, Epstein also describes the reactions of a class of primary schoolchildren when their teacher 'came out' to them. Not only did they take steps to protect him, but they demonstrated a sophisticated analysis of the ways both they and he had to negotiate homophobia as a fact of everyday life.

The different ways in which students respond and either embrace or resist challenges and interventions to normative gender regimes (as lived, everyday practice or imagined futures) have been sporadically documented from individual projects on young children's mixed reactions to feminist texts which challenge traditional gendered and heterosexual storylines (see Davies, 1993) to large-scale, systematic reform programs to tackle young women's occupational aspirations and expectations (Kenway and Willis, 1998) and resources to tackle gendered school-based cultures within educational (Martino and Pallotta-Chiarolli, 2005) or health-based (e.g. HIV/AIDS) programs (see Pattman and Chege, 2003). Kenway and Willis, in particular, have drawn attention to the ways in which the micropolitics of change and transformation within classroom are increasingly strained and unsupported, as the definition of education is quashed and governmental cutbacks result in a shift away from social justice policies. Nevertheless, they do state how many students are 'hungry for change' and how both individual classroom teachers and gender reform initiatives supported students who took up counter-narratives to 'help them to build both alternative sources of strength and status and new communities of support for other ways of being male and female' (p210).

Subverting normative gendered practices can be achieved in overt ways, such as injecting verbal sexual humor and innuendo into the sanitized 'official' pedagogic discourse (Dixon, 1997; Renold, 2005) or by more covert means. Paechter (1998) highlights how 'passivity' in girls as they expertly perform 'looking busy' and 'keeping quiet' is a form of resistance, insofar as such performances can mask talk and behaviors that are far from work-related. For example, Thorne's (1993) ethnography of two primary schools in the USA explores the underground economy of cosmetics and magazine consumption and thus how some girls subvert the 'good girl' and 'asexual child' by applying lip gloss and reading about boyfriends, sex and fashion during lesson time. Moreover, where some public spaces within the school make it difficult for pupils to construct alternative or non-normative gender identities, occupying classrooms at playtime can enable children to isolate themselves from the physical and verbal abuse of their peers.

Research has also documented the ways in which boys and girls who are subject to bullying appropriate private spaces to circumvent and directly avoid the often cruel scrutiny of 'the public' (peer) gaze (see Walker, 1988; Renold, 2005). In my research, a small group of boys reappropriated the classroom at break times, usually under the guise of continuing with their class work or helping the teacher in some way. However, their motivation to occupy these spaces involved more than seeking out a safe retreat or hideaway. The privacy afforded the boys at these times and in these contexts offered them key moments to engage and interact in non-hegemonic ways – particularly in the 'trying on' and embodiment of 'soft' and 'intimate' masculinities, which in any other context (particularly within the high surveillance of the playground, which is the key arena for the posturing of hegemonic masculinities) would not have been possible. The classroom area at designated 'playtimes' was often the only space in the day free from the ritualized and heterosexist banter and subjugation by these boys' peers. Thus, while the classroom is a highly sanitized arena, producing classroom cultures that often operate to pathologize pupils that do not invest in or conform to normative masculinities or femininities, pupils have always sought out and created ways of resisting or subverting the constraints of normative practices.

SOME CONCLUSIONS

This chapter has introduced and explored the impact of past and current classroom-based research on our academic understanding of the gendering of teachers' and pupils' everyday lives in school, from the early years through to high school (see Chapters 32 and 34 in this volume for teacher/student experiences in higher education). It has specifically explored the classroom as a key social and cultural space for the production of a range of gender performances and relations and, in doing so, illustrated the productivity of methodological approaches which situate gendered classroom experiences within other sites and spaces within and beyond the school gates. Examination of the micropolitics of everyday classroom life shows that key themes are the classroom as a regulatory and normalising space (e.g. from bodies and movement to voice) and the classroom as a dangerous space (e.g. from ridicule to gendered and sexual bullying). A cross-cutting theme in both these sections was the exclusion and isolation of teachers and pupils that deviate from 'acceptable', age-appropriate, gender-appropriate, class-appropriate, racial-appropriate, and sexual-appropriate behaviors. Indeed, the hidden curriculum is far from hidden and is both troubling and troublesome. Attending equally to research that foregrounds the classroom as a transgressive space (e.g. from individual to collective resistance to gender/sexual norms), the chapter also illustrated the extent to which gendered classroom interactions operate in coercive and liberatory ways.

Perhaps one of the most disturbing findings is the durability of persistent inequalities and gender stereotypes over the last 30 years, despite major shifts and changes at the macrolevel of education policy and pedagogy (see Chapters 6 and 8). Such a finding brings home the importance of maintaining a focus on the 'hidden curriculum' and attending to the silences of both teachers' and students' everyday lives. It also necessitates a sustained focus on seeking innovative ways of creating the conditions and spaces for local, regional, national and global reforms, initiatives and change. I thus conclude this chapter with an extract from Mindy Blaise's US research exploring the gendered world of an urban kindergarten classroom:

> Madison is (…) learning about the politics of gender within the classroom and society (…) she is a 5-year-old activist, who writes and sends letters to Lego requesting more female action figures for her kindergarten classroom. (Blaise, 2005: 100)

Through the case-study of Madison, Blaise not only highlights how the drive for change starts early but also offers a contemporary interpretation of how the personal continues to be political and, central to this chapter, how the classroom continues to be taken up by students and their teachers as a site for resistance and reform.

REFERENCES

Acker, S (ed) (1989) *Teachers, gender and education.* London: Falmer.

Acker, S (1994) *Gendered education: sociological reflections on women, teaching and feminism.* Milton Keynes: Open University Press.

Archer, L (2003) *Race, masculinity and schooling: Muslim boys and education.* Buckingham: Open University press.

Ball, S (1990) *Politics and policy making in education: explorations in policy sociology.* London: Routledge.

Belotti, E (1975) *Little girls.* London: Writers and Readers Publishing Cooperative.

Bhana, D (2002) Making gender in early schooling. a multi-sited ethnographic study of power and discourse: from grade one and two in Durban. Unpublished doctoral dissertation, University of Natal, Durban.

Blaise, M (2005) A feminist poststructuralist study of children 'doing' gender in an urban kindergarten classroom. *Early Childhood Research Quarterly,* 20: 85–108.

Blount, J (2004) *Fit to teach: same-sex desire, gender and schoolwork in the twentieth century.* Albany, NY: State University of New York.

Browne, M and France, P (1983) Only cissies wear dresses: a look at sexist talk in the nursery, in Weiner, G (ed) *Just a bunch of girls.* Milton Keynes: Open University Press.

Clark, M (1990) *The great divide: gender in the primary school.* Melbourne, Curriculum Development Centre.

Coffey, A and Delamont, S (2000) *Feminism and the classroom teacher.* London: Routledge Farmer.

Connolly, P (1998) *Racism, gendered identities and young children: social relations in a multi-ethnic, inner-city primary school.* London: Routledge.

Cunnison, S (1989) Gender joking in the staffroom, in Acker, S (ed) *Teachers, gender and careers.* Lewes: Falmer Press.

Danish, B (1998) Placing children first: the importance of mutual presence in the elementary classroom, in Letts, WJ IV and Sears, JT (eds) *Queering elementary education: advancing the dialogue about sexualities and schooling.* Lanham, MD: Rowman and Littlefield.

Davies, B (1989) *Frogs and snails and feminist tales: preschool children and gender.* Sydney: Allen and Unwin.

Davies, B (1993) *Shards of glass: children reading and writing beyond genered identities.* Cresskill, NJ: Hampton Press.

Davies, L (1984) *Pupil power: deviance and gender at school.* London: Falmer Press.

Devine, D (2002) *Children, power and schooling: how childhood is structured in the primary school.* Stoke-on-Trent: Trentham Books.

Dixon, C (1997) Pete's tool: identity and sex-play in the design and technology classroom. *Gender and Education,* 9: 89–104.

Duncan, N (1999) *Sexual bullying: gender conflict and pupil culture in secondary schools.* London: Routledge.

Epstein, D (ed) (1994) *Challenging lesbian and gay inequalities in education.* Buckingham: Open University Press.

Epstein, D and Johnson, R (1994) On the straight and narrow: the heterosexual presumption, homophobias and schools, in Epstein, D (ed) *Challenging lesbian and gay inequalities in education.* Buckingham: Open University Press.

Epstein, D, Elwood, J, Hey, V and Maw, J (eds) (1998) *Failing boys? Issues in gender and achievement.* Buckingham: Open University Press.

Epstein, D, O'Flynn, S and Telford, D (2003) *Silenced sexualities in schools and universities.* Stoke-on-Trent: Trentham Books.

Evans, T (1987) *A gender agenda: a sociological study of teachers, parents and pupils in their primary schools.* Sydney: Allen and Unwin.

Fisher, J (1994) Unequal races: gender and assessment, in Graddol, D, Maybin, J and Stierer, B (eds) *Researching language and literacy in social context.* Clevedon: Multilingual Matters.

Francis, B (1998) *Power plays: primary school children's constructions of gender, power and adult work.* Stoke-on-Trent: Trentham Books.

Francis, B (2000) *Boys, girls and achievement: addressing the classroom issues.* London: RoutledgeFalmer.

Francis, B and Skelton, C (2001) Men teachers and the construction of heterosexual masculinity in the classroom. *Sex Education,* 1: 9–21.

French, J and French, P (1984) Gender imbalances in the primary classroom: an interactional account. *Educational Research,* 26: 127–36.

Gilbert, P and Gilbert, R (1998) *Masculinity goes to school.* London: Routledge.

Gordon, T, Holland, J and Lahelma, E (2000) *Making Spaces: citizenship and difference in schools.* Buckingham: Palgrave.

Halson, J (1989) The sexual harassment of young women, in Holly, L (ed) *Girls and sexuality: teaching and learning.* Milton Keynes: Open University Press.

Hey, V (1997) *The company she keeps: an ethnography of girl's friendships.* Buckingham: Open University Press.

Jackson, PW (1968) *Life in classrooms.* New York: Holt, Rinehart and Winston.

Jones, C (1985) Sexual tyranny: male violence in a mixed secondary school, in Weiner, G (ed) *Just a bunch of girls.* Milton Keynes: Open University Press.

Kehily, MJ and Nayak, A (1996) Playing it straight: masculinites, homophobias and schooling. *Journal of Gender Studies*, 5: 211–29.

Kehily, MJ and Nayak, A (1997) Lads and laughter: humour and the production of heterosexual hierarchies. *Gender and Education*, 9: 69–87.

Kehily, MJ, Epstein, E, Mac an Ghaill, M and Redman, P (2002) Private girls, public worlds: producing femininities in the primary school. *Discourse: Studies in the Cultural Politics of Education*. Special Issue: *Rethorising friendship in educational settings*, 23: 167–77.

Kelly, L (1988) Gender differences in teacher–pupil interactions: a meta-analytic review. *Research in Education*, 39: 1–23.

Kenway, J and Fitzclarence, L (1997) Masculinity, violence and schooling: challenging poisonous pedagogies. *Gender and Education*, 9: 117–33.

Kenway, J and Willis, S (1998) *Answering back: girls, boys and feminism in schools*. London: Routledge.

Khayatt, MD (1992) *Lesbian teachers: an invisible presence*. Albany, NY: State University of New York Press.

Kimmel, MS (ed) (1987) *Changing men: new directions in research on men and masculinity*. Newbury Park, CA: Sage.

Laskey, L and Beavis, C (eds) (1996) *Schooling and sexuality*. Geelong, Victoria: Deaking University Centre for Change.

Lees, S (1993) *Sugar and spice: sexuality and adolescent girls*. London: Penguin Books.

Letts, WJ, IV and Sears, JT (eds) (1999) *Queering elementary education: advancing the dialogue about sexualities and schooling*. Lanham, MD: Rowman and Littlefield.

Lucey, H and Reay, D (2002) Carrying the beacon of excellence: social class differentiation and anxiety at a time of transition. *Journal of Education Policy*, 17: 321–6.

Luke, C (1994) Women in the academy: the politics of speech and silence. *British Journal of Sociology of Education*, 15: 211–30.

Mac an Ghaill, M (1994) *The making of men: masculinities, sexualities and schooling*. Buckingham: Open University Press.

MacNaughton, G (2000) *Rethinking gender in early childhood education*. Sydney: Allen and Unwin.

MacNaughton, G (2001) 'Blushes and birthday parties': telling silences in young children's constructions of 'race'. *Journal for Australian Research in Early Childhood Education*, 8: 41–51.

Mahony, P (1985) *Schools for the boys*. London: Hutchinson.

Mahony, P and Jones, C (eds) (1989) *Learning our lines: sexuality and social control in education*. London: Women's Press.

Martino, W and Pallotta-Chiarolli, M (2003) *So what's a boy: addressing issues of masculinity and schooling*. Buckingham: Open University Press.

Martino, W and Pallotta-Chiarolli, M (2005) *Being normal is the only way to be: adolescent perspectives on gender and school*. Sydney: University of South Wales Press.

Maynard, T (2002) *Exploring the boys and literacy issue*. London: Routledge/Falmer.

Miller, J (1996) *School for women*. London: Virago Press.

Nayak, A and Kehily, MJ (1997) Masculinties and schooling: why are young men so homophobic?, in Steinberg, DL, Epstein, D and Johnson R (eds) (1997) *Border patrols: policing the boundaries of heterosexuality*. London: Cassell.

Paechter, C (1998) *Educating the Other: gender, power and schooling*. London: Falmer Press.

Paley, V (1984) *Boys and girls: superheroes in the doll corner*. Chicago, IL: University of Chicago Press.

Pattman, R and Chege, F (2003*) Finding our voices: gendered and sexual identities and HIV/AIDS in education*. Nairobi: UNICEF.

Reay, D (2001) 'Spice girls', 'nice girls', 'girlies' and 'tomboys': gender discourses, girls' cultures and femininities in the primary classroom. *Gender and Education* 13: 153–66.

Renold, E (2000) Coming out: gender, (hetero) sexuality and the primary school. *Gender and Education*, 12: 309–26.

Renold, E (2001a) 'Squre-girls', femininity and the negotiation of academic success in the primary school. *British Education Research Journal*, 27: 577–88.

Renold, E (2001b) Learning the 'hard' way: boys, hegemonic masculinity and the negotiation of learner identities in the primary school. *British Journal of Sociology of Education*, 22: 369–85.

Renold, E (2005) *Girls, boys and junior sexualities: exploring children's gender and sexual relations in the primary school*. London: Routledge: Falmer.

Riddell, S (1990) Pupils, resistance and gender codes: a study of classroom encounters. *Gender and Education*, 1: 183–97.

Riddell, S (1992) *Gender and the Politics of the Curriculum*. London: Routledge.

Robinson, K (1992) Classroom discipline: power, resistance and gender. *Gender and Education*, 4: 273–87.

Robinson, K (2000) 'Great tits, Miss!' The silencing of male students' sexual harassment of female teachers in secondary schools: a focus on gendered authority. *Discourse: Cultural Studies in the Politics of Education*, 21: 75–90.

Skelton, C (2001) *Schooling the boys: masculinities and primary education*. Buckingham: Open University Press.

Skelton, C and Francis, B (eds) (2003) *Boys and girls in the primary classroom*. Buckingham: Open University Press.

Spender, D (1982) *Invisible women: the schooling scandal*. London: Writers and Readers Cooperative.

Stanworth, M (1981) *Gender and schooling: a study of sexual divisions in the classroom*. London: Hutchinson.

Steedman, C (1990) *Childhood, culture and class in Britain: Margaret McMillan 1860–1931*. New Brunswick, NJ: Rutgers University Press.

Stein, N (1996) Sexual harassment in school: the public performance of gendered violence. *Harvard Educational Review*, 65: 145–62.

Sunnari, V, Kangasvuo, J and Heikkinen, M (2002) *Gendered and sexualised violence in educational environments*. Oulu, Finland: Oulu University Press.

Swain, J (2003) How young schoolboys become somebody: the role of the body in the construction of masculinity. *British Journal of Sociology of Education*, 24: 299–314.

Tamboukou, M (2000) The paradox of being a women teacher. *Gender and Education*, 12: 463–78.

Tamboukou, M (2003) *Women, education and the self*. Basingstoke: Palgrave Macmillan.

Thorne, B (1993) *Gender play: boys and girls in school*. Buckingham: Open University Press.

Walden R and Walkerdine, V (1985) *Girls and mathematics: from primary to secondary schooling*. London: Institute of Education, Bedford Way Press.

Walker, JC (1988) *Louts and legends: male youth culture in an inner city school*. Sydney: Allen and Unwin.

Walkerdine, V (1981) Sex, power and pedagogy. *Screen Education*, Spring 38.

Walkderine, V (1990) *Schoolgirl fictions*. London: Verso.

Walkerdine, V, Lucey, H and Melody, J (2001) *Growing up girl: psycho-social explorations of gender and class*. Basingstoke: Palgrave.

Wallis, A and VanEvery, J (2000) Sexuality in primary school. *Sexualities*, 3: 409–23.

Weiner, G (1994) *Feminisms and education: an introduction*. Milton Keynes: Open University Press.

Wolpe, AM (1988) *Within school walls: the role of discipline: sexuality and the curriculum*. London: Routledge.

Youdell, D (2003) Identity traps or how Black students fail: the interactions between biographical, sub-cultural and learner identities. *British Journal of Sociology of Education*, 24: 3–20.

32

Women in Teaching: Participation, Power and Possibility

Jane Gaskell and Ann L. Mullen

Teaching, like all occupations, has been organized, changed and framed by gender. It has been organized in a way that associates the teaching women do with low status and income, while the teaching men do garners more power and esteem. Women are more likely than men to teach younger children, to be in fields associated with women's work, and to have positions with little power or intellectual authority. While change has taken place in the number and kinds of teaching jobs that are available, and the global expansion of formal teaching jobs has opened opportunities for many women, teaching jobs have been continually reorganized and redefined so that women remain in low status positions relative to men. Women from lower social class and ethnic groups are the most disadvantaged by this dynamic. And the teaching women do has consistently been framed by images of femininity, described through maternal metaphors, and linked to social rather than intellectual tasks.

Understanding the patterns and politics of gender and teaching is important for understanding the organization of schools, colleges and universities; it is also important for understanding the history of gender. So many women have been teachers that what counts as female has been associated with teaching the young. As we look with the lens of the women's movement at the gendered hierarchies in teaching, we see a great deal about how gender works in society, and how it should be changed.

Teaching takes place in many sites, under many different conditions: in schools, universities, colleges, workplaces, literacy programs, community centers, child-care facilities and families, to name only a few of the most prominent places. In this chapter, we will discuss only teaching in formal educational institutions: in schools, colleges and universities. Most countries now insist on entry to formal schooling between the ages of 4 and 7, and make education available, with at least some public funding, through university. Students' progress through this very hierarchical and critically important system depends on the capacity and the judgment of those who teach them, and these teachers will be the focus of our analysis. Although some discussions do not include university professors in analyses of teaching, we believe that teaching in universities and colleges, like teaching in primary and secondary schools, should be seen within a hierarchy of instructional positions in educational institutions. The tendency not to consider university professors as teachers is itself a reflection of gendered conceptions of work. The teaching done in universities is higher status and more likely to be done by men; it also involves better pay, more autonomy and more association with intellectual than social development. However, one of the primary responsibilities of university professors is to teach students.

This chapter begins with an examination of women's presence in different areas and kinds of teaching. From there, we examine the processes of change that have produced these patterns. We conclude with a look at the possibilities that feminist analysis offers at a moment when more women are working as teachers than ever before, but women teachers still face patriarchal discourses about their power and authority in the classroom and the society. While our chapter is weighted toward the USA and Canada, we have included international research and statistics where available. Because the organization of schooling differs by country, we caution readers against making strict comparisons. We have also attempted to incorporate findings on race, ethnicity and social background when possible, recognizing that 'teachers' are not a unitary category, although most statistical analyses treat them as such.

THE REPRESENTATION OF WOMEN IN TEACHING

In many parts of the world, teaching is one of the most common occupations for women, making it critical for understanding women's status in any society (Anker, 1998). In a study of 41 countries, teaching ranks as one of the top nine typically 'female' occupations (Anker, 1998). Elementary teaching is the fifth leading occupation for women in Canada and the sixth for women in the USA (Seidlikoski, 2001; Padavic and Reskin, 2002). In addition, teaching around the world has become a more feminized occupation over the past two decades (Anker, 1998; Guppy and Davies, 1998). These figures, however, disguise stark patterns of vertical and horizontal segregation in the teaching profession. Like many forms of work, teaching is heavily gendered. Women are underrepresented at higher levels of education, in particular high-status subject areas like science, math and technology, and in the decision making and theorizing that shape and control teaching. Their salaries are lower, and their power is less. The patterns are consistent, although they are slowly changing as educational systems expand, and are better documented at the postsecondary level than at other levels.

Of all levels of formal teaching, women have the highest representation at the primary level. In most countries, primary education is a predominately and ever growing female occupation (Anker, 1998). In countries as varied as Argentina, Brazil, Russia, the Philippines, Austria, Germany, Hungary, Sweden, Ireland, Italy, Israel, New Zealand, the UK and the Czech Republic, women make up 80% or more of the teaching staff in public and private primary education (OECD, 2005). In Canada, women are 67% of primary teachers and in the USA 88% (OECD, 2005). Some exceptions to this pattern are China and India, where women make up 49% and 36% of primary teachers, respectively, and many African countries, where women compose less than a third of the teaching staff (Manuh, 1998; Velkoff, 1998; OECD, 2005).

Patterns of women's representation at the primary level may in part reflect vestiges of blocked opportunities for women at higher education levels. However, research shows that among recent degree recipients, women are much more likely than men to begin their teaching careers at the primary level. A 1997 study of American teachers who earned their degrees in 1992–93 found that 62% of the women taught in elementary schools, compared to just 29% of men, while 50% of men taught in secondary schools, compared to only 23% of women (the remainder taught in combined or multilevel schools) (NCES, 2000a).

At the secondary level, women and men are somewhat more evenly represented. Of the 31 OECD countries, women make up more than 60% of secondary teachers only in Canada and the Slovak Republic, and compose at least 40% of the teaching force in all other countries, except Denmark, Germany, South Korea and Switzerland (OECD, 2002). However, differentiation by field becomes pronounced at the secondary level of education. Men are more likely to teach business, math, science, history, and technology, while women are more often found in languages, home economics, and special education (Acker, 1994; NCES, 2000a). A survey of 14 countries showed that only a quarter of advanced mathematics teachers were women (Grant and Murray, 1999).

In the USA and Canada, teachers of color are underrepresented (international data on this topic are difficult to obtain). In the USA, for example, while 32% of all children in kindergarten through grade 12 are African-American, Hispanic, Asian or Native American, only 13% of teachers are non-white (Grant and Murray, 1999). Data from the Canadian census show that visible minorities are underrepresented in the teaching work force, constituting about 8.3% of the adult population but only 3.5% of elementary and kindergarten teachers and 4.3% of secondary school teachers (Guppy and Davies, 1998).

In terms of representation, while primary education is largely female dominated and secondary education more integrated, postsecondary education is still a male-dominated enterprise. At the university and college level, there are fewer women and they are in less senior positions than men. Strong patterns of gender segregation as well as discrepancies in institutional location, academic field, rank, tenure status[1] and salary can be found, paralleling those found in the broader labor market.

In Canada, 39% of all tenure-stream faculty and 27% of all tenured faculty are now women (the figures are 45% and 27%, respectively, for the USA) (NCES, 2002b, CAUT, 2005a). However, this pattern is not shared worldwide. Data collected by UNESCO reveal that women's entry into academic position varies both by region and country within region. Women have the lowest representation in the regions of South and East Asia, the Arab states, and Sub-Saharan Africa, averaging one-third or less of the positions in these regions. These figures are not surprising given that the Middle East and North Africa have the highest overall levels of occupational segregation by gender (Padavic and Reskin, 2002; UNESCO, 2004).

In addition, within Canada and the USA, the representation of female faculty is not even across races and ethnicities. In 2000, whites made up only 69% of the total population in the USA but held 89% of faculty positions, while Blacks, Hispanics, and American Indians/Alaskan Natives held far less than their proportional share (NCES, 2000b). The gender differences in faculty representation cut across race and ethnicity in the USA, with women of each group being disadvantaged in comparison to men. African-Americans are the only group that has come close to achieving gender parity, with women holding 49.7% of faculty positions. With this exception, white women hold a significant advantage over women of color in gaining access to US faculty positions (NCES, 2000b). In Canada, the Canadian Association of University Teachers (CAUT) reports that Aboriginal Canadians are seriously underrepresented among the ranks of Canadian faculty, holding only 0.7% of all faculty positions, in comparison to 2.3% of positions in the total labor force (CAUT, 2004).

In the USA, the postsecondary education system is highly stratified by quality and prestige. Research universities and doctoral granting institutions are among those institutions with the highest status and prestige, while two-year colleges are considered the lowest-prestige institutions. Within the hierarchically organized postsecondary education system, men are more likely to hold positions in high-status institutions, and women are more likely than men to be employed in the lowest-status institutions. For example, men are more likely than women to work at public doctoral granting and research universities while women are more likely to work in public two-year colleges; while only 14% of male faculty are employed in community colleges, fully one-quarter of women work at such institutions (NCES, 2000b; 2002b).

In addition to this vertical segregation of institutions and of rank within institutions, women are also horizontally segregated into fields of study. While women compose the majority of faculty in nursing (98.5%), they are only a small minority (less than a third) in fields such as engineering, history, philosophy, biological

Table 32.1   Percentage distribution of full-time instructional faculty and staff in the USA according to academic rank and gender, autumn 1998

	Full professor	Associate professor	Assistant professor	Other	Total
Men	34.4%	22.5%	20.0%	23.1%	100%
Women	15.2%	20.7%	27.6%	36.4%	100%

Source: NCES, 2002b.

sciences, physical sciences, math, computer science, social science, and occupational programs. Fully 25% of female faculty teach in either nursing or education, indicating how heavily concentrated women are in just a few fields (NCES, 2000b). These patterns are similar in Canada, where women make up 43% of faculty positions in education but only 8.6% of those in engineering and applied sciences (CAUT, 2004). These patterns reflect differences in preferences for field by gender, and may also reflect differential selection processes by universities (i.e. hiring committees may hold a gender preference in some fields).

While the system of higher education is itself hierarchically organized, faculty positions are also arranged into hierarchies within most North American institutions, ranging from non-tenure-stream positions of lecturer or instructor, to the tenure-stream positions of assistant, associate and full professor. As Table 32.1 shows, while a third (34.4%) of male academics hold the rank of full professor, less than one out of six women hold this rank. Women are more likely than men to be employed at the level of assistant professor, and over one-third of women do not hold a standard academic rank but are employed as instructors or lecturers. In Canada, this pattern repeats, with 44.7% of men at the level of full professor, but only 19.7% of women (CAUT, 2004). In addition, women in the USA (though not Canada) are more likely than men to be employed part-time rather than full-time (49% to 38%, respectively) (NCES, 2000b; CAUT, 2004).

Gender disparities can also be seen in comparisons of tenured appointments. In the USA nearly two-thirds of male academics hold tenure, compared to only 41.6% of women. Women are more likely than men either not to be in the tenure stream or to be employed at an institution without a tenure system, thus holding no prospects for rising through the academic ranks (NCES, 2002b). The patterns are similar in Canada, where in 2002–03 women made up only 27% of tenured faculty but 43% of non-tenure-stream faculty. In addition, there has been much criticism of the allocation of Canadian Research Chairs, a prestigious government program designed to retain and attract top faculty to Canada. As of 2005, women held only 15% of the tier 1 (senior) chairs and 26% of the tier 2 (junior) chairs, while the great majority of these plum positions were awarded to men (CAUT, 2005b).

In part, gender disparities of academic rank and tenure status may be explained by differences in the characteristics of men and women in the academy. On average in the USA, male academics are older, are more likely to have a doctorate degree (74.2% versus 54.3%), and have more teaching experience and more years in their current position than women. Men are also more heavily involved in research activities than women. They spend more time on research, are more likely to be engaged in funded research, and produce more publications and scholarly works (over the same span of time) than women (NCES, 2002b). However, several researchers have identified unexplained gender differentials in rank attainment in analyses controlling for experience and research productivity (Weiler, 1990; Smart, 1991; Sonnert and Holton, 1996). For example, Toutkoushian (1999), in statistical regression models controlling for highest degree; institution type; academic field; years of experience; age; race; and publication of journal articles, books, and book chapters, found that women were still significantly less likely to be tenured or promoted to full professor (though he found no disadvantage for women attaining associate status). Thus, even when women have the same credentials, experience, and qualifications as their male peers, they are still less likely to be promoted at the same rates.

It has been well documented that men in academia earn significantly more than women (Ransom and Megdal, 1993; NCES, 2000b, 2002b; CAUT, 2004). The most recent estimates for US faculty reveal that the average salary for full-time male academics was $61,680 compared to $48,370 for women. In other words, an average female professor earns only 78.4% that of the average man (NCES, 2002b), somewhat better than the average across the labor market of 72.2% (in 2000) (Padavic and Reskin, 2002). In Canada, full-time female faculty took home only 80.2% of that of the salaries of male faculty in 2002 (CAUT, 2004). Gender differences in earnings cut across race and ethnicity, with white, Black, Asian and Hispanic men all earning significantly more than women of these racial and ethnic groups (NCES, 2002b). Again, part of the gender gap in earnings can be attributed to differences in experience and research productivity as well as institution type and field of study. However, in studies accounting for these factors, researchers have consistently identified a significant unexplained gender difference in salary for faculty (Toutkoushian, 1999; NCES, 2000b). Further, a recent study shows no decrease in the salary gap between the years 1992 and 1998 (NCES, 2002b).

Though women have made considerable inroads into academic careers, when we examine how women are represented, paid, promoted, and tenured compared to men, we find striking differences. On all counts, women face considerable disadvantages. Women are less represented among the most prestigious, research-oriented universities and overrepresented in two-year colleges. Women are heavily concentrated into a small number of fields and highly underrepresented in other fields. Women are less likely than men to hold the title of full professor, be tenured, or even be in the tenure stream. Women disproportionately hold part-time and non-tenure stream faculty positions. Women earn less than men. Further, even when women are as experienced and productive as their male peers, they are still less likely to be promoted or to receive equivalent salaries, suggesting enduring patterns of discrimination impeding women's career progression within the academy.

A discussion of women in teaching would not be complete without considering their role in leadership. At the primary and secondary levels, administrative jobs are overwhelmingly held by men, especially in larger systems, and at more senior levels. In Britain in 1985, only 25% of junior schoolteachers were men, but 70% of headships were held by men. At the secondary level, men held 54% of the teaching positions and 84% of the headships (Acker, 1989). When women do hold leadership positions in educational systems, they are more likely to be in pastoral than academic areas (Cunnison, 1989). In the USA, women hold 79% of all elementary and secondary teaching positions but only 39% of principal positions (NCES, 2002a). And though the situation is slowly improving in Canada, women held only 29% of school administrator positions in 1992–93, though they held 61% of all full-time teaching positions (Canada Education Statistics Council, 1996; Guppy and Davies, 1998). Paralleling the pattern found at the primary and secondary levels, administrative jobs in colleges and universities are also largely held by men. In 1998, only 20.4% of college presidents at baccalaureate degree-granting institutions were women (Santovec, 2005), while only 25% of chief academic officers and only 13% of chief business officers were women (Chliwniak, 1997). Women are better represented at lower-status institutions, such as community colleges, where 40% of the new presidents in the last five years have been women (Santovec, 2005).

Many of the findings regarding women's positions as teachers at the primary, secondary, and postsecondary levels reflect patterns of gender segregation and the devaluing of women's work seen in the larger labor market. Occupations in most parts of the world are still highly sex segregated and the decline of sex segregation in the USA, after improving during the 1970s and 1980s, stalled in the 1990s (Padavic and Reskin, 2002). In addition, men still occupy the top ranks in most occupations and professions. Sex segregation contributes to women's lower pay and authority because occupations that are predominantly female tend to pay less than male-dominated occupations. And the devaluation of women and their work is a prime factor in the pay gap between the sexes. Thus, in higher education, average salaries are lower for faculty working in institutions and disciplines with higher proportions of women faculty (NCES, 2000b). In addition, we must question why research is more highly rewarded than teaching, when women are more likely to invest themselves more in teaching than research compared to men. At the primary level, salaries are typically lower for teachers than at the secondary level. Finally, prestige ratings of occupations show a clear hierarchy, with university professors rated as more prestigious than secondary schoolteachers, who are in turn rated more highly than elementary schoolteachers (Ingersoll, 2004).

PROCESSES OF EXPANSION, CHANGE AND REORGANIZATION IN TEACHING

An historical look at the social processes that produced these gendered patterns helps with understanding what they mean, and how they continue to change. The history of teaching in many countries has involved creating new opportunities for women, as well as limiting those opportunities through the creation and recreation of hierarchies. Women have moved into teaching jobs to extend their influence and their opportunities, but hierarchies and distinctions that preserve gendered inequalities have remained a central factor in the teaching profession.

As public systems of education expand, they require more educated workers to fill teaching positions. Public educational authorities at a time of expansion have little money for salaries; so women are pulled into the labor market as a group who have the requisite educational background and will work for lower wages. Women themselves see opportunities in these new roles, working outside the home, exerting their independence, and becoming leaders in their communities. As women enter teaching, in different countries at different times, they promote education for girls, challenge old definitions of womanhood, and shift the discourses around teaching and the purpose of education.

As schooling became compulsory and expanded in Western countries in the late nineteenth century, women took over teaching jobs in many countries (Schmuck, 1984; Prentice and Theobold, 1991). The patterns were not consistent across all western countries. Albisetti (1993) estimates that, in the early twentieth- century, women were 86% of women teachers in the USA, 75% in the UK and Russia, 50% in France, and 15% in Prussia. The degree of expansion, the strength of the forces for women's emancipation, the differential role of public and private sectors, and the funding available made a substantial difference to patterns of feminization.

Today, teaching is a profession that attracts more and more women around the world. In rural and conservative areas where literacy rates for women are low, recruiting and retaining women teachers can encourage parents to let their daughters attend school. International aid agencies and governments consider women teachers more supportive of girls' aspirations and achievements. 'Particularly in Africa and South Asia, there is a significant amount of attention paid to finding solutions to the constraints women may face in accessing training and upgrading opportunities in order to ensure there are more women teachers in schools to attract and support girls' (Kirk, 2004: 376). This of course becomes a double-edged sword for women, as the government puts responsibility for change in education on their shoulders, in the most patriarchal communities.

The leadership of women teachers in challenging gender codes, working for social change and opening up possibilities for young people from all classes and communities is a proud tale, told in several different accounts. Hoffman (2003) and Weiler (1998) document the struggles of women teachers in the USA over the last century. Many worked against racism, poverty and social injustice in their classrooms and their communities. Seller (1994) provides capsule biographies of 66 women who influenced US education and the wide variety of other fields in which they worked. She notes the energy and versatility they needed to pursue multiple careers and roles, and the range of women who were able to make a mark, including African-American, Native American, married, single, disabled and white, middle-class women. Carter (2002) shows the alliances between female teachers and feminist organizations, as women teachers struggled to better their working conditions, and forge alliances with reform organizations in the USA.

Similar struggles and successes by women teachers are documented in countries where the public school system has expanded more recently. Araujo records the 'hidden struggle' five courageous women teachers were able to engage in Portugal, under Salazar's tight political control. Ashraf's (2004) study of teachers in northern Pakistan, which has one of the largest gaps in educational attainment between men and women, points out how women who become teachers can have increased influence in their communities and begin to make changes in the traditional patriarchal norms and division of tasks. Stacki (1998; 2002) looks at the empowerment of women teachers in India, and Schultz (1994; 1998) has done the same in Nepal.

However, the struggle is not one that all women win. Concern about women's leadership in public positions, and about the threat their public employment poses to the traditional family, has meant moments of public panic about women 'taking over' educational systems, and the creation of job structures and definitions that continue to limit their possibilities. When the number of women in teaching increases, there is pressure to redefine teaching so that it remains appropriate for women, compatible with family obligations and no threat to existing gender structures. Through these processes, the teaching women do comes to be confined to subordinate roles, and associated with the emotional and moral (i.e. maternal) purposes of schooling, more than with the intellectual purposes.

In most systems, despite the progress women have made through entering teaching, their ability to progress into powerful roles is severely constrained. Married women teachers were openly discriminated against in the West until the 1960s; young, unmarried women were severely restricted by social codes and their own lack of experience. A literature that criticized 'feminized schools' and 'momism' supported the continued discrimination against women teachers (Sexton, 1969). Women were forced from their jobs when they were married, and in a later era when this became illegal, they were not allowed in classrooms when they were visibly pregnant. Elementary teachers, who were mostly women, were paid less than secondary teachers, who were mostly men. Secondary teachers were paid less than university teachers. Some of the early sociology of teaching as a 'semi-profession' paints women as a cause of the low status and wages of teaching, because they were family centered, less committed to their careers and subordinate (Simpson and Simpson, 1969; Leggatt, 1970).

Women's move into leadership positions in teaching at all levels has been contested and resisted. Affirmative-action or employment-equity policies have been introduced in some jurisdictions, with demonstrable effect. There is a considerable literature on women as educational leaders, suggesting they are more likely to emphasize relationships, collaboration and 'caring' than trouble making and change (Shakeshaft, 1987). This discourse is far too essentialized and decontextualized. Women administrators carry out their responsibilities in many ways, for 'Women who get into leadership are also trouble. Difficult and dangerous because they trouble dominant masculinities and modes of management' (Blackmore, 1999: 3).

Kirk's (2004) study of Pakistani teachers in urban, nongovernmental, English-medium schools shows how women's work as teachers gets incorporated within a patriarchal culture. These teachers describe teaching as a worthy, safe and female-friendly profession, contributing to national development and compatible with family responsibilities. Women teachers have little decision-making power, and need the consent of male family members for their activities. For women teachers, this produces complex dilemmas around how to reconcile femininity, power and educational development.

Nayar (1988) documents the same issues for women teachers in South Asia. Although teaching is by far the most socially accepted occupation for women, women teachers are constantly at risk of being seen as inadequate wives and mothers. They work to reduce this risk, as well as, sometimes, to challenge the assumptions that limit their freedom. And in China, Coleman and Yanping (1998) show how hard it is for women teachers in Shaanxi province to balance their domestic responsibilities with their work at school, and how restricted their access to management positions remains.

Changes in the organization of teaching also explain how women are marginalized. As educational systems expand, they become more complex and hierarchical. The teaching context changes from the small school, where each teacher is of necessity responsible for organizing instruction, to a larger system with a clear hierarchy, centrally designed curriculum, and more frequent visits from school inspectors (Prentice and Theobald, 1992). In this more complex system, the pressures on women to perform demanding domestic duties, as well as discriminatory beliefs about women's capacity and inclination, mean that they remain at the bottom of the hierarchy.

Rosenberg's (1982) study of the University of Chicago at the turn of the century illustrates the gender dynamics that marginalized women teachers. When women began to enter the university as students, concern that they would endanger their fertility, motherhood and therefore the home was rampant. Universities, especially places such as Chicago, which were new and relatively unknown, admitted women in order to stave off financial and political crises. This seemed to require hiring female faculty and administrators to supervise them. At Chicago, reform-minded faculty, such as Jane Addams, Marion Talbot, and Julia Lathrop, began to transform the department of sociology with their combination of political reform and scholarship. Resistance to what was described by the administration as a takeover by women led to the creation of a separate junior women's college and of a department of 'household administration', segregating women teachers and students from their male colleagues, and recreating gendered hierarchies in a form that continues through distinct disciplinary and gendered fields of study.

Women's entry into careers in postsecondary education in North America is marked in the latter part of the twentieth century. In the last 26 years, women's representation as full-time regular faculty in US colleges and universities has nearly doubled, going from 18.6% in 1975 to 34.2% in 2001 (Toutkoushian, 1999; NCES, 2002a). However, the gains experienced by North American women in attaining academic teaching careers are not shared around the world. For example, in China since the end of the Cultural Revolution, more women have entered academic positions, as universities expanded, funding diminished, and men took private-sector jobs. But women academics in China are concentrated in the teaching streams, and they are not well positioned to take advantage of international contacts and research opportunities (Hayhoe, 1996; Gaskell *et al.*, 2004).

Universities are particularly important as sites of the production and circulation of knowledge (Smith, 1975). As Luke (2001) points out, global discourses circulate through universities, and they are becoming increasingly standardized, while local experiences and opportunities shape their development and their impact on women. The marginalization of women in university-teaching positions will have consequences for the way women understand their experience and for cultural change around the world.

The expansion of teaching jobs over time has offered women an opportunity for respect, autonomy and financial independence. It has brought about social change in education, and in society, while at the same time creating teaching as a segregated and 'safe' occupation for women, blending more easily with traditional stereotypes of femininity than many other careers. As women moved into teaching, they were being paid less than men, controlled by strict gender norms, prevented from teaching when they were married or pregnant, and kept out of positions of seniority and management. The result is a continual struggle over the meaning of teaching, its autonomy, power and respect.

COMPETING DISCOURSES OF FEMININITY AND POWER: THE PROMISE OF FEMINISM

Feminism and teaching have been linked in many ways over time (Carter, 2002). As a woman's occupation, teaching has been seen as second class, and lacking in power and resources. As a result, the women's movement found a home in teachers' organizations, challenging the stereotypes and the organization of teaching, although feminist ideas have to be worked out in the context of different educational systems, and they have not often been dominant.

Walkerdine (1990) refers to the 'impossible fiction' of being a woman teacher, as the role asserts power and demands authority, while women are subordinated and marginalized. Biklen (1995) writes that teaching is so associated with femininity that it is impossible to reform teaching without taking on the gender question (p6). Her discussion of gender and teaching points to the image of the heroic male teacher in American films (such as *The Blackboard Jungle*, *Stand and Deliver*, and *Lean on Me*) and in the progressive popular literature of the early 1970s by male authors such as Jonathan Kozol, James Herndon, and Herbert Kohl. In these texts, the 'hero' is the male teacher willing to take risks and act against the norms and conventions of the (feminized) profession to serve children. These stories portray a women's field of action, mired in mediocrity, conformity and complacency, waiting for reform to come from outside, in a male form.

The voices of women teachers provide a much more complex sense of the work of teaching, and of what gender means to teachers. Biklen (1995) finds two competing feminist discourses as she interviews elementary schoolteachers in the USA. On the one hand, they comment that 'teachers are underpaid and undervalued', and that outsiders do not understand the difficulties and challenges of the work. 'Teaching looks easy from the outside' (p28). These teachers felt their work was not recognized by the general public, or by principals, district administrators, curriculum consultants and others who made decisions about what would be taught, and under what conditions. They believed the association of teaching with women undervalued its contributions and that women's status as a reserve army of labor allowed lower wages to persist.

On the other hand, these teachers valued the opportunities teaching provides for independence, personal fulfillment and social action. They enjoy working with other teachers, parents, and the community; they value caring for children, and find the struggle to connect with children's learning engaging and satisfying. They find ways to make their judgments matter, and find possibilities for social change and a voice in the public realm. Acker (1989), finds similar themes in the voices of British teachers. And Middleton (1993), talking with New Zealand teachers, emphasizes the possibilities for transformation through education, and its challenge to racial and class hierarchies, despite its lack of official power.

The competing discourses: powerful, powerless; autonomous, connected; knowledgeable, subordinate, are deployed by teachers in different ways in different contexts. They are not necessarily in opposition to each other, for they coexist. Teachers define their agency and find modes of political action in multiple ways. Gender equality and opportunities for women come in many sizes and shapes.

This makes the political agenda for feminist teachers complex. Is it to transform teaching into the model of the traditionally male professions, emphasizing definitive knowledge and autonomy, or to define new modes of career, with contingent knowledge and relational power? Does change mean embracing traditional union structures or creating a more differentiated profession? Should new structures of power in teaching have women taking over existing positions of authority, or transforming structures of power to make them more egalitarian?

These are the debates of feminist theory, and they have implications for women teachers at all levels of the system. They are debates that will not be solved for all women or for all times. Their vitality is critical for keeping a feminist analysis alive, and ensuring the welfare of women, as teachers and students, is kept on the agenda of educators everywhere.

Gender is a difference that is used to signify different things to different groups at different times. In the battle for recognition and political advantage, the difference that is made of difference changes, creating an inherent instability in its meaning (Scott, 1996). This gives feminism some of its political force and understanding, and means there are no simple victories, or definitions of equality. The context is critical to understanding what is claimed, and what its effect will be.

Two Ontario reports provide an illustration of how the context leads to different kinds of research on gender and teaching, with different intended effects. In 1970, as the second-wave women's movement gained prominence in Canada, an analysis by the Federation of Women's Teachers of Ontario (Stokes, 1970) pointed to the ways women had been marginalized in teaching, despite their numerical prominence. Stokes called for women to enter the profession on equal terms; to take leadership; and to make issues of importance to women, such as maternity leave and equal pay, central to teacher bargaining. Stokes' report, fueled by an increasing awareness of how women are marginalized in the labor force, paid less than men, and tracked into a limited number of occupations (including teaching). A call to arms for women in teaching resonated in the context of a movement that named the discrimination women faced. A feminist teachers' union, allied with a resurgent women's movement, brought about change: maternity leave became mandatory, women teachers were paid the same as men teachers, and women were allowed to teach after marriage and childbirth. Eventually, elementary teachers were paid as much as secondary teachers.

But in Ontario today, the issues facing male teachers are making the headlines. A study called *Narrowing the Gender Gap* began, 'In Ontario, across Canada, and in many nations, there is a shortage of men in the teaching profession, particularly at the elementary level' (Ontario College of Teachers, 2004: 2). The report calls for action to increase male role models in school, open up new ways of entering the profession, and change media representations of teaching, even though it recognizes that women have been the majority in teaching for a long time. No devastating effects of a feminized workforce were demonstrated: there were no studies showing that students learned less from female teachers, or that women had a negative social effect in schools. The data did not go back very far and the trends were not large; the authors did not look at any markers of difference other than gender; the analysis was based primarily on commentary by male teachers. This was not a definitive report, but it put the gender politics of teaching in the public eye, in a way quite different from Stokes' report 35 years earlier.

In early twenty-first-century Ontario, boys' failure rate on literacy tests, and their declining proportion of the university population worry the public. Jobs in traditionally male areas seem to be declining, and men are not entering traditionally female areas of employment, like teaching. The meaning of gender difference is again open for debate, and women teachers' views do not receive the same attention today that they received 30 years ago.

Research on gender in teaching has a role to play in keeping the issues of power, respect and status of teaching alive, as well as putting them in historical context. The diversity of contexts for teaching around the world, and the changing face of feminism in these many places, mean that the field will be a productive one for a long time to come. Statistics and discourses of gender will vary in ways that can be placed in historical context, and used to work toward equality for all who teach.

ACKNOWLEDGMENT

The authors would like to thank Jayne Baker and Nasr Dastgir for research assistance with this chapter.

REFERENCES

Acker, S (1989) *Teachers, gender and careers*. New York: Falmer Press.
Albisetti, J (1993) The feminization of teaching in the nineteenth century: a comparative perspective. *History of Education*, 22: 223–63.
Anker, R (1998) *Gender and jobs: sex segregation of occupations in the world*. Geneva: International Labour Office.
Araujo, D (2001) Pathways and subjectivities of Portuguese women teachers through life histories, in Weiller, K and Middleton, S (eds) *Telling women's lives: narrative inquiries into the history of women's education* (113–29). Buckingham: Open University Press.
Ashraf, D (2004) Experiences of women teachers in the northern area of Pakistan. PhD thesis, OISE/UT, University of Toronto.
Biklen, S (1995) *School work: gender and the cultural construction of teaching*. New York: Teachers College Press.
Blackmore, J (1999) *Troubling women: feminism, leadership and educational change*. Buckingham: Open University Press.
Canada Education Statistics Council (1996) *A statistical portrait of elementary and secondary education in Canada*. Ottawa: Statistics Canada.
Carter, P (2002) '*Everybody's paid but the teacher'. The teaching profession and the women's movement*. New York: Teachers College Press.
Casey, C (1993) *I answer with my life: life histories of women teachers working for social change*. New York: Routledge.
CAUT (Canadian Association of University Teachers) (2004) Closing the equity gap: a portrait of Canada's university teachers, 1996–2001. *CAUT Education Review*, 6:1–5.
CAUT (Canadian Association of University Teachers) (2005a) *Almanac of postsecondary education 2005*. Ottawa: CAUT.
CAUT (Canadian Association of University Teachers) (2005b) *Ivory towers: feminist and equity audits 2005*. Ottawa: CAUT.
Chliwniak, L (1997) Higher education leadership: analyzing the gender gap (ASHE-ERIC Higher Education Report, vol 25, no 4). Washington, DC: George Washington University, Graduate School of Education and Human Development.

Coleman, M and Yanping, QH (1998) Women in educational management in China: experiences in Shaanxi province. *Compare*, 28: 141–54.

Gaskell, J, Eichler, M, Pan, J, Xu, J and Zhang, X (2004) The participation of women faculty in Chinese universities; paradoxes of globalization. *Gender and Education*, 16: 511–29.

Grant, G and Murray, CE (1999) *Teaching in America: the slow revolution*. Cambridge, MA: Harvard University Press.

Guppy, N and Davies, S (1998) *Education in Canada: recent trends and future challenges*. Ottawa: Statistics Canada.

Hayhoe, R (1996) *China's universities 1895–1995; a century of conflict*. New York: Garland Press.

Hoffman, N (2003) *Women's 'true' profession. Voices from the history of teaching* (2nd edn) Cambridge, MA: Harvard Education Publishing Group.

Ingersoll, R (2004) The status of teaching as a profession, in Jeanne H. Ballantine, JH and Spade, JZ (eds) *Schools and society: a sociological approach to education*, (2nd edn) Belmont, CA: Thomson Wadsworth.

Kirk, J (2004) Impossible fictions: the lived experiences of women teachers in Karachi. *Comparative Education Review*, 48: 374–95.

Leggatt, T (1970) Teaching as a profession, in Jackson, J (ed) *Professions and professionalization*. Cambridge: Cambridge University Press.

Luke, C (2001) *Globalization and women in academia: north/west, south/east*. London: Lawrence Erlbaum Associates.

Manuh, T (1998) Women in Africa's development: overcoming obstacles, pushing for progress. *Africa Recovery Briefing Paper*, 11 April 1998.

Middleton, S (1993) *Educating feminists: life histories and pedagogy*. New York: Teachers College Press.

Nayar, U (1988) *Women teachers in South Asia*. Dehli: Chanakya.

NCES (National Center for Education Statistics) (2000a) *Progress through the teacher pipeline: 1992–93 college graduates and elementary/secondary school teaching as of 1997 (NCES 2000-152)*, by Henke, RR, Chen, X, Geis, S and MPR Associates, Inc. Project Officer, Paula Knepper. Washington, DC: 2002.

NCES (National Center for Education Statistics) (2000b) *Salary, promotion, and tenure status of minority and women faculty in U.S. colleges and universities, (NCES 2000-173)*, by Nettles, MT, Perna, LW and Bradburn, EM. Project Officer Linda J Zimbler. Washington, DC: 2002.

NCES (National Center for Education Statistics) (2002a) *Digest of education statistics 2001*. Washington, DC: US Department of Education.

NCES (National Center for Education Statistics) (2002b) *Gender and racial/ethnic differences in salary and other characteristics of postsecondary faculty: Fall 1998 (NCES 2002-170)*, by Bradburn, EM and Sikora, AC. Project Officer Linda J Zimbler. Washington, DC: 2002.

OECD (Organization for Economic Cooperation and Development) (2002) *Education at a glance: OECD Indicators 2002*. OECD Publishing.

OECD (Organization for Economic Cooperation and Development) (2005) *Education at a glance: OECD Indicators 2005*. OECD Publishing.

Ontario College of Teachers (2004) *Narrowing the gender gap*. Toronto: Ontario College of Teachers.

Padavic, I and Reskin, B (2002) *Women and men at work*, (2nd edn). Thousand Oaks, CA: Pine Forge Press.

Prentice, A and Theobold, M (1991) *Women who taught: perspectives on the history of women and teaching*. Toronto: University of Toronto Press.

Ransom, M and Megdal, S (1993) Sex differences in the academic labor market in the affirmative action era. *Economics of Education Review*, 12: 21–43.

Rosenberg, R (1982) *Beyond separate spheres. Intellectual roots of modern feminism*. New Haven, CT: Yale University Press.

Santovec, ML (2005) What's the trend on women getting college presidencies? *Women in Higher Education* 14: 1–3.

Schmuck, P (ed) (1984) *Women educators, employees of schools in Western countries*. Albany, NY: New York State University Press.

Schulz, LZ (1994) Your daughters are not your daughters but sons: field notes on being and becoming a women teacher in Nepal and in Canada. *Gender and Education*, 6: 183–99.

Schulz, LZ (1998) Being and becoming a woman teacher: journey through Nepal: the path taken. *Gender and Education*, 10: 163–83.

Scott, J (1996) *Only paradoxes to offer: French feminists and the rights of man.* Cambridge, MA: Harvard University Press.

Seidlikoski, WAY (2001) Women in multiple roles: characteristics of work and family that affect level of perceived time-control. Unpublished thesis.

Seller, M (ed) (1994) *Women educators in the United States: 1820–1993.* Wesport, CT: Greenwood Press.

Sexton, PC (1969) *The feminized male: classrooms, white collars, and the decline of manliness.* New York: Random House.

Shakeshaft, C (1987) *Women in educational administration.* London: Sage.

Simpson, RL and Simpson, IH (1969) Women and bureaucracy in the semi-professions, in Etzioni, A (ed) *The semi-professions and their organization.* New York: Free Press.

Smart, JC (1991) Gender equity in academic rank and salary. *Review of Higher Education*, 14:511–26.

Smith, D (1975) An analysis of ideological structures and how women are excluded: considerations for academic women. *Canadian Review of Sociology and Anthropology*, 12: 354–69.

Sonnert, G and Holton, G (1996) Career patterns of women and men in the sciences. *American Scientist*, 84: 63–71.

Stacki, SL (1998) Partnerships and processes for teacher empowerment: rays of hope for female teachers in India. Indiana University, Bloomington, PhD dissertation.

Stacki, SL (2002) Women teachers empowered in India: teacher training through a gender lens. New York: UNICEF.

Stokes, S (1970) *The shortest shadow.* Toronto: FWTAO.

Toutkoushian, RK (1999) The status of academic women in the 1990s: No longer outsiders, but not yet equals. *Quarterly Review of Economics and Finance*, 39: 679–98.

UNESCO (2004) *Global education digest 2004: comparing education statistics across the world.* Montreal: UNESCO Institute for Statistics.

Velkoff, VA (1998) Women of the world: women's education in India. Washington, DC: US Department of Commerce, Economics and Statistics Administration, Bureau of the Census.

Walkerdine, V (1990) *Schoolgirl fictions.* New York: Verso.

Weiler, K (1988) *Women teaching for change. Gender, class and power.* New York: Bergin and Garvey.

Weiler, K (1998) *Country school women: teaching in rural California 1850–1950.* Stanford, CA: Stanford University Press.

Weiler, WC (1990) Integrating rank differences into a model of male-female faculty salary discrimination. *Quarterly Review of Economics and Business*, 30: 3–15.

NOTE

1. Tenure is an employment arrangement designed to protect academic freedom that is typically granted to a faculty member after a probationary period and that protects him or her from dismissal except for reasons of incompetence, gross misconduct, or financial necessity. Generally, full and associate professors hold tenure, but not assistant professors. It is the standard in most postsecondary institutions in the USA and Canada, but is not universal in other countries.

33

Constructing Teaching Identities

Lisa Smulyan

INTRODUCTION: IMAGES OF TEACHERS AND TEACHING

In a class, I teach the topic Teachers' Lives and Work, and show film clips of teachers in popular American movies from the past 10 or 15 years. In one of the movies, *Mr Holland's Opus*, the teacher is an aspiring composer who is forced to teach to support his family. He resents the work, yet he moves from being bitter and uncaring to being an icon in the school. He is beloved as the person who engages all students, including the most unlikely, in music. Like many other male movie teachers, Mr. Holland is a hero, in part just because he is a male teacher (Biklen, 1995; Ayers, 2001).

We also discuss Miss Honey, one of the teachers in *Mathilda*. Miss Honey, as her name suggests, epitomizes nurturing and care. Led by Mathilda, an eight-year-old, Miss Honey overcomes her fears and takes on those who have constrained her in the past. She also ultimately adopts Mathilda, merging the roles of mother and teacher. Miss Honey, too, is a hero, but in a different way, one that draws on historically and culturally acceptable roles for women teachers.

Teaching, as these films illustrate, is a gendered profession. In the USA, elementary and middle-school teaching is the second largest employer of women and secondary teaching is the fourteenth (US Department of Labor, 2004). In many European countries, teaching employs the third or fourth largest number of women who work, usually 5–15%, behind health and social work, manufacturing, and retail work (European Union, 2003). In most countries in North America, South America, and Europe, and in much of Asia and the South

Pacific, women constitute up to 80% of primary or elementary school teachers and 60% of secondary teachers. In some countries in Africa, in India, Pakistan, and China, and in some Southeast Asian countries, literacy rates for girls are significantly lower than for boys, and male teachers outnumber female teachers (Ministry of Women's Affairs, 2004; UNESCO, 2004).

The statistics demonstrate both the predominance of women in teaching and the importance of teaching as an employment option for women. Within the context of these numbers and the lenses provided by popular culture, we recognize that gender frames the work of teachers, and that teaching, in turn, is an arena in which gender can be learned, defined, renegotiated, and contested.

In this chapter, I discuss the historically and culturally gendered constructions of teachers and teachers' work. In the first section, I examine studies in the field of gender and teaching that explore historical and equity-oriented questions of who taught, when, and why (e.g. Kaufman, 1984; Weiler, 1989; Fishman, 2000; Hoffman, 2003). These works often capture the previously unheard voices of (predominantly) women teachers, allowing us to trace the emergence of the images that prevail today. These studies overlap with another set, explored in the second section of the chapter, which focus on the construction of teacher identity as it interacts with gender, race, class, ethnicity, and sexuality. Every teacher constructs an identity within both historical and cultural discourses. For the most part, these constructions reproduce conservative, normatively gendered roles that mirror the images available (Britzman, 1991; Robertson, 1997). But, because they are constructions, they also contain the potential for critical change, for the possibility of feminist and critical approaches to identity and teaching.

HISTORICAL PERSPECTIVES ON GENDER AND TEACHING

In the nineteenth century, the teaching profession in the USA, parts of South America, and much of Europe experienced the influx of large numbers of women (Danylewycz *et al.*, 1987; Acker, 1995; Fishman, 2000). The statistical 'feminization of the teaching profession' (Spring, 1990; Tyack and Hansot, 1990; Skelton, 2002) resulted from changes in the field of education, shifting economic opportunities and demands, and the expansion of the definitions of womanhood that allowed women to enter the public sphere. It was also the result of women choosing to become economically self-sufficient and redefining their roles in the society.

Changes in the field of education opened up the door for women to teach. There was a growing sense that schools, although not necessarily replacing families, provided knowledge, values and skills that families might not be able to teach their children (Hoffman, 2003). There was also a call, documented in the USA, the UK, Argentina, Finland, Canada, Australia and New Zealand, for schools to take part in the preparation of citizens in a nation's changing economic and social order (Acker, 1995; Sunnari, 1997; Fishman, 2000).

In the USA, the UK and other industrialized Western countries, the call for free public schooling led to a significant demand for many new teachers at a time when shifting economic structures opened up a range of new possibilities for men (Apple, 1994; Fishman, 2000). Women could be paid less than men for the same work, were easier to supervise, and were less needed to contribute to the family economy as production and income moved outside the home (Cott, 1977; Solomon, 1985; Shakeshaft; 1989; Fishman, 2000). Schools, redefined as a continuation of the family and the place in which children developed knowledge, values, and morality, were not only acceptable places for women; they now seemed to require women teachers who could best fill these newly defined duties of teaching (Weiler, 1989). In addition, there was a growing international movement to adopt more child-centered instruction, modeled on the work of Pestalozzi and Froebel, to replace the transmission model used previously in many formal educational settings (Hilton and Hirsch, 2000). These new models mapped directly onto the acceptable domain of women's work.

Women in the nineteenth century became teachers for several reasons: they needed the income, they were anxious not to marry, they wanted to be more independent, and they were interested in fostering social, political and spiritual change (Kaufman, 1984; Solomon, 1985; Clifford, 1987; Foster, 1993; Hilton and Hirsch, 2000; Shipp, 2000; Hoffman, 2003). Women teachers came from a range of social and economic groups, many from farming and small-business-supported families, but also from élite colleges attended by middle- and upper-class women and from recently arrived immigrant families. Teaching provided women with opportunities to experience the public sphere and their own agency within it, an experience they carried over into other organizations such as the Boston Female Anti-Slavery Society, the National American Women Suffrage Association, and the Women's National Loyal League. These women, within the constraints of the social and political structures in which they lived, chose to teach and to construct the role of teacher in ways that allowed them to function as agentic individuals within the public sphere.

Male teachers also faced tensions in this historically gendered construction of teaching (Hargreaves, 1994). Schools such as Central High School in Philadelphia, a public examination school for boys that opened in 1838, hired only male teachers until well into the middle of the twentieth century, since men alone had the intellectual capacity to prepare Central graduates for their assumed positions in further education and society (Labaree, 1988). Men who taught in public elementary and secondary schools in the USA and elsewhere in the nineteenth century, however, were 'suspect'. By working with children and even adolescents, the public impression was that they were not 'real men' or that 'they were clearly doing school teaching until something better opened up for them' (Joseph, 2001: 7). This framing was experienced more by upper-class men; working-class men and women more often viewed teaching as a path into a middle-class profession (Skelton, 2001).

Parallel to the negative construction of the relationship between maleness and teaching was an historical call for more men in teaching. In Scotland in the 1890s, the lack of men in teaching was described as a 'crisis' (Acker, 1995). In the USA in the early 1900s, those warning of the 'women peril' claimed that women teachers lacked the intellectual capacity and critical ability to prepare boys to live in a modern political and economic world. These historical constructions foreshadowed current calls for more male teachers to provide role models for boys and to counter what the political backlash describes as the feminized environment of the school and classroom (Montecinos and Nielson, 1997; Connell, 2000; Skelton, 2002). They also create the model for the heroic male teacher represented by Mr Holland.

In Western countries, schools followed a pattern of early twentieth-century municipal and corporate reform and development to become more hierarchical and professional. Administrators (the specialists in this growing bureaucracy), generally men, produced, planned, and evaluated the knowledge, processes and rules that would be carried out by subservient teachers, generally women (Yeakey *et al.*, 1986; Shakeshaft, 1989; Blackmore, 1993). The management structures and styles of the developing bureaucratic and capitalistic systems of the early twentieth century carried the implicit message that, just as men controlled industry and government, so should they manage schools.

However, the twentieth century also includes images of women teachers around the world taking active public roles within these organizational structures as union leaders, suffragists, and student activists (Urban, 1982; Clifford, 1987; Cortina, 1992; Apple, 1994; Carter, 2002). Women teachers were subordinate within the bureaucracy, but they were not necessarily passive recipients of cultural constructions of subservient positions, behaviors and attitudes.

The historical framing of teaching as both appropriate for women and as women's work has contributed to the naturalistic images of women teachers as nurturing, caring, and virtuous, and as altruistic, selfless and subservient (Weiler, 1989; Acker, 1995; Joseph, 2001). There is also, in this historical construction, a thread of agency and activism: the woman teacher as social change agent. Male teachers are seen as intellectuals, as not 'real men', or as educational professionals and leaders, those who will manage the educational processes of schools. These historical assumptions are embedded in our institutions, in our discourse about teachers and teachers, in our popular culture, and in the experiences of children as students and then, perhaps, as they choose to teach. It is within these available discourses that teachers construct identities, identities in which gender intersects other aspects of self as well as institutional and cultural expectations.

CONSTRUCTING GENDERED TEACHER IDENTITIES

Teachers are both created by and create themselves within historical and cultural contexts (Levinson and Holland, 1996; Eisenhart, 2001). This section explores three areas in which researchers have explored the interactions of gender and teacher identity: women's construction of teacher identities and careers, men's construction of teacher identities, and the intersection of sexuality and teaching.

Women, identity, and teaching

All women who enter teaching negotiate their identities within existing historical, institutional, and cultural frameworks. Some do so consciously, with the goal of questioning and, at times, trying to resist constraints they see as a larger system of social injustice (Weiler, 1988; Rensinbrink, 2001; Smulyan, 2004a). Others are less aware of the ways in which they are constructed by and perhaps contribute to the construction of a gendered teacher self (Biklen, 1995; Smulyan, 2000; Walkerdine *et al.*, 2001). But all are engaged in a process of exploring and defining themselves within and through the role of teacher (Munroe, 1998).

Researchers who explore this process of negotiation often use feminist methodologies that emphasize listening to and reflecting upon previously unheard and underrepresented voices within a broad social framework (Reinharz, 1992; Franz *et al.*, 1994). As feminist historians have explored the diaries and letters of former teachers (Kaufman, 1984; Hoffman, 2003), they interview, observe, and reflect on the experiences, frameworks, and discourses available to today's women teachers. Their emphasis has shifted from examining the life stories of women teachers (e.g. Spencer, 1986) to exploring the complicated intersections between individual life histories and the historical and cultural discourses that shape dentity.

Several studies of women teachers focus on teachers who work within a feminist identity, women who choose to address oppression within their own classrooms as a way of effecting broader social change (Casey, 1993). Middleton (1994; 1993; 1989), for example, explores how feminist teachers in New Zealand use their experience of oppression and their access to theory to reflect on their lives and to shape their teaching goals. These teachers both desire and envision the possibility of change in their own lives and the lives of others. Weiler (1988) explores the lives and work of 11 feminist educators in two public high schools. She investigates how existing social and political discourse and school structures create complex sites in which feminist teachers negotiate the power of existing structures and their desire to be actors in a process of critical social change. Rensenbrink (2001) picks up on this theme in her presentation of three feminist elementary schoolteachers. Each teacher clearly defines and acts upon feminism differently in her classroom, balancing the social, institutional, and personal frameworks that constrain and define her. Like Weiler, Rensenbrink often focuses on teacher practice as a form of activism that can help children learn to challenge existing power structures. Both suggest that teachers choose to teach in ways that reflect a definition of self as agentic and political. Rensenbrink cites Harding (1991) in pointing out that these women teachers may be developing a "'traitorous identity" whereby we choose an identity that contradicts the one we were born into or find ourselves in' (Rensenbrink, 2001: 153).

Biklen (1995) weaves historical, fictional, and ethnographic materials to explore how the daily lives of teachers contribute to their definitions of themselves as teachers, and, in particular, as women teachers. The teachers with whom she worked were not 'heroic', nor were they consciously feminist or resistant to existing structures of power – unless such resistance was necessary in order to teach well. Biklen concludes that teachers themselves contribute to the gendered construction of teaching that is embedded in the discourses and structures available to them. For example, the teachers in her study sometimes found it difficult to assert themselves with mothers or male administrators, both of whom held more power within the existing hegemonic structures. At the same time, they worked hard for the children in their classrooms, were committed to their jobs, and developed collegial relationships in support of themselves and their work. Acker (1994) also describes teachers who accept, and so reproduce, gendered positions. The teachers with whom she worked did not fight the status quo but instead adopted a 'strategic fatalism' that allowed them to create workplaces in which they felt effective and supported (Acker, 1994: 120). Gender clearly played a part in their sense of themselves as teachers, but it was not an explicitly political or critically oriented element, as it may be for those teachers who define themselves as feminist.

Munroe (1998) and Smulyan (2004a) build on Weiler's work to examine how women who choose to teach 'negotiate[d] understandings of self against and with/in the dominant discourses of education and gender' (Munroe, 1998: 27). Munroe explores how the women teachers with whom she works continually define and redefine themselves within the shifting contexts and discourses available to them. Like Biklen's teachers, Munroe's teachers are not consciously or explicitly focused on gender, and yet their lives, their choices, and their narratives suggest that they do make choices that challenge historically gendered norms and expectations. Smulyan (2004a,b) examines the life and career choices of 28 college graduates, about half of whom choose to teach. Unlike the women in Munroe's study, these women describe their experiences of facing and consciously responding to the gendered stereotypes of teaching as low status, intellectually undemanding, low paying, and beneath them. They struggle, as do the teachers in all of the studies described above, with negotiating an identity within available historical and cultural frameworks that constrain who they are, where they work, how others perceive them, and how they know themselves.

Some research suggests that the traditional notion of 'career' needs re-examination when applied to many women in education (Sikes, 1985; Acker, 1989, 1994; Grant, 1989; Biklen, 1995; Smulyan, 2000). Women choose teaching, remain in teaching, and grow and change as teachers in ways that reflect both personal and social/ historical pressures on their lives. These factors differ from those affecting men, whose life patterns have been used as the norm against which women are examined.

For example, women teachers certainly feel committed to teaching, even if they take time away from work to raise a family (Biklen, 1995). Their different career paths challenge traditional notion of a linear, hierarchical career that ignores individuals' life histories or the larger social and cultural structures within which they work (Ball and Goodson, 1992; Acker, 1994; Smulyan, 2000).

Some of these studies point out that negotiating a teacher self involves navigating a complex set of discursive practices and selves; gender interacts in salient ways with discourses and structures of race, class, sexuality, and ethnicity (Biklen, 1995; Smulyan 2004). Although there have been few explicit studies of interactions between class, gender, and teaching, related research on gender, class, and identity demonstrates that the construction of a gendered self is strongly related to class-based experiences and discourses (Steedman, 1982; Walkerdine and Lucey, 1989; Walkerdine, 1990).

In the USA, 21% of white women college graduates become teachers, while 24% of African-American, 19% of Hispanic-American, and 5% of Asian-American women college graduates choose to teach (Rong and Preissle, 1997). Smulyan (2004a) found that, in some cases, ethnicity interacted with gender in supporting an individual's conception of teaching as service to children in her community; in other cases, young women who wanted to teach struggled with ethnic and class structures and community expectations that framed teaching as unacceptable because of its lower status and low pay. Rong and Preissle (1997) suggest that Asian-Americans, in particular those who have recently immigrated to the USA, are underrepresented as teachers in elementary and secondary schools. Asian women choose not to teach as a result of discrimination, parental pressure to choose other occupations, a sense of distance from the educational system, and internalized expectations that draw on all of these discourses and constraints.

Foster (1993) explores how African-American teachers' experience of racism and their work within black and white systems of education influence how they see themselves as teachers. Casey (1993), Beauboeuf (2004), and Dixon (2004) explore why black women in the USA choose to teach and how they see themselves as activist, womanist teachers. Gender and race interact within definitions of self that are inherently subversive and political:

> From the days of legally segregated schooling, Black women have been described in terms at odds with the compliance that 'good' women seek: they have been called 'transgressive' (hooks, 1994), 'subversive' (Foster 1995) educators who were likened to 'tricksters' (Jeffries, 1994) and 'quiet revolutionaries' (Wade Gayles, 1993) for engaging in 'racial uplift' (Higginbotham, 1992) through their teaching. (Beauboeuf, 2004: 4)

Research in the field of gender and identity suggests that women teachers, consciously or unconsciously, interact with the historical and cultural constructs of gender and teaching in ways that both co-construct and challenge the discourses available to them. Their identities are dynamic constructions, yielding fluid, contextual, multiple selves. They can be accepting of the gendered constructions of teaching – as caring or mothering, as less powerful in the educational bureaucracy, and as relatively low in status – because some of those constructions allow them to do the job they want to do. They can also be agentic within the constraints, trying to reconstruct definitions of woman teacher to fit their own goals and agendas. Most often, they are both defined by, and constantly redefining themselves within, existing historical and social structures.

Constructing a male teacher identity

Connell (2000) summarizes recent research on the construction of masculinity, noting that multiple masculinities, which exist in a hierarchy of power, are defined collectively within a culture and sustained through institutions such as schools. Masculinities are complex, can include contradictory desires and behaviors, and are actively produced within the constraints of historical and social conditions.

Male teachers work within the historical and cultural frameworks that define most teaching as women's work as well as those that call on men to be strong leaders and models within any social setting. Several studies have explored these tensions, some within a framework of construction, like Connell, and most within a framework that accepts existing gender regimes. Many of these latter studies accept a hegemonic binary of male and female characteristics and roles in society. They suggest that children and schools need male teachers to counter the supposedly feminized environment that results from the predominance of women teachers (Sexton, 1969; Montecinos and Nielsen, 1997; Skelton, 2001). Some men's rights proponents argue that children, especially those who grow up in single parent (mother headed) homes, need male role models and the allegedly firmer disciplinary style which men bring to their teaching (Bush, 1997; Montecinos and Nielsen, 1997; Lewis *et al.*, 1999). In some of these studies, men themselves describe their choice to teach in terms that contribute to the construction of heterosexual norms of masculinity, arguing that they provide children with important role models, fulfill valuable roles in schools in areas such as athletics and technology, and contribute a different approach to working with children that includes strong feelings of efficacy and expectations of success (DeCorse and Vogtle, 1997; Lewis *et al.*, 1999; Francis and Skelton, 2001).

These arguments assume that male teachers are needed to address the 'boy problems' of underachievement and disengagement in schools (Epstein and Johnson, 1998; Connell, 2000; Foster *et al.*, 2001). Other studies have suggested, however, that having more male teachers does not necessarily address boys' needs in school (Skelton, 2001) and that, in fact, the assumptions about masculinities male teachers bring to their work may perpetuate hegemonic notions of masculinity that interfere with boys' and girls' success and development (Mac an Ghaill, 1994; Foster *et al.*, 2001) and perpetuate constructions of schools as feminized and boys as underachievers (Skelton, 2002).

Mac an Ghaill (1994), like Connell, describes the multiple masculinities male teachers may perform, each influenced by biography, historical constructions of teaching and gender, and contextual dynamics. These multiple constructions interact in a range of ways with the masculinities and femininities, the racialized identities, and the class backgrounds being played out by male and female teachers and students at the school. These interactions complicate simplistic assumptions about the role of male teachers in schools.

King (1998, 2000) explores in more depth the tensions inherent in negotiating hegemonic constructions of 'masculinity' *and* 'teacher'. In these and other studies, male teachers (in particular male elementary schoolteachers) note that they choose to teach because they care about children. Their assumption of a stereotypically female characteristic is interpreted, by others and by themselves, as both heroic and unmasculine (Allan, 1993; DecOrse and Vogtle, 1997; Lewis *et al.*, 1999; King, 2000). These teachers are proud of doing what they and society perceive as women's work (sometimes better than the women themselves), and yet they often feel the need to defend their choice to teach. They recognize that the masculinity of male elementary teachers is always suspect, and they frequently monitor their dress and their relationships with students, teachers, and colleagues with this in mind. Both elementary and secondary male teachers may emphasize aspects of teaching that reinforce traditional constructions of masculinity; they may accept responsibility for discipline and control, become engaged in school sports, and reject less masculine behaviors in their students (Francis and Skelton, 2001). Male teachers generally do not take advantage of their position to question the masculine/teacher dichotomy, but they do experience the tensions involved in negotiating a position within it (King, 1998, 2000).

Sexuality, teaching, and identity

As noted, work on teachers, gender, and identity tends to remain within a binary heterosexual construction of masculinity and femininity. While there is a small literature on the construction of a queer teacher identity, this field has remained understudied for several reasons. First, finding subjects for such research can be difficult, since the acknowledgement of a lesbian, gay, or transgendered identity could jeopardize a teacher's job. Researchers, themselves, may be targeted, by association, for addressing topics not seen as suitable within the academy (Squirrel, 1989; Khayatt, 1992). In addition, the topic of sexuality is one that is largely ignored in schools and schooling, because of the fears and expectations that surround it (Skelton, 1994; Epstein, 2001; Fine, 2002). The work that does exist in this area, however, provides a different insight into how teachers' identity is negotiated within gendered constructs.

Historically, women teachers' sexuality was both hidden and policed. The emphasis on women's moral leadership and virtue, combined with a discourse that equated sex and sexuality with immorality and appetite, precluded any reference to women as sexual beings. When women married, they left teaching, not only to preserve a separation between private and public spheres and roles, but also to remove any implication of sexuality from the teacher role. Not until the 1950s in many districts in the USA were married women permitted to maintain their teaching positions.

Today there is still little discussion of sexuality within the more general literature on gendered teacher identities. There is even less work discussing the existence of non-heterosexual masculinities and femininities in teaching, although some of the work on male teachers, noted above, suggests that the heteronormativity of male elementary schoolteachers is questioned by colleagues, parents, students, and the male teachers themselves. This questioning becomes part of the construction of a sense of self as male and teacher for both queer and straight men (Berrill and Martino, 2002). King (1998; 2000) describes how self-identified gay men police themselves, experiencing a tension between pride in the work they do and fear of losing their jobs. The discursive conflation of homosexuality with sexuality and danger to children leads straight male teachers to assert their heterosexual masculinity and gay male teachers to stay closeted (Evans, 1998; King, 2000).

For some gay teachers, restrictions on their ability to engage personally and fully with students and peers, and the tensions and fears that accompany their need to be self-protective, make them feel less fully present and effective as teachers (Lipkin, 1999). First-hand accounts by queer teachers often focus on their need to protect and hide their private lives in order to avoid being fired, harassed, or undermined in their work (Anonymous, 1989; Khayatt, 1992; Kissen, 1996; Evans, 1998; Lipkin, 1999). Gay teachers may keep both students and colleagues at some personal distance – a choice heterosexual teachers may make for personal reasons, but that gay teachers may make out of a concern for their career and effectiveness. These barriers also take their toll emotionally and intellectually as these teachers constantly work to balance expectations of others with their desire to be good teachers.

Some gay teachers choose – or are more often forced – to be silent about their sexual orientation because of their concern that, if made public, their gay identity would overshadow all other identities they bring to their work: their feminism, their ethnicity or race, and their identity as an excellent teacher (Khayatt, 1992; Kissen, 1996; Evans, 1998). Kissen (1996) provides first-hand accounts of the experiences of gay and lesbian teachers negotiating gendered selves within powerful historical, contextual and cultural constraints. Khayatt's (1992) study of 18 Canadian lesbian teachers documents the internal and external tensions experienced by women teachers trying to negotiate multiple identities, among them teacher, woman, and lesbian. Historically constructed discourses of sexuality as dangerous (Moran, 2000), of homosexuals as sexual (and as sexual recruiters or predators) (King, 2000), and of women teachers as moral exemplars – and so asexual or nonsexual – combine to create a conflicting and often silencing framework within which queer teachers negotiate identities.

CONCLUSION

Teachers today negotiate identities within and in response to competing historical and cultural discourses about teachers, teaching, femininity, masculinity, and sexuality. Some teachers – those, for example, who describe themselves as feminists, or who consciously desire to implement social change, or those whose gender or sexuality create a disconnect with normative expectations of the teacher role – consciously explore these discourses. Others remain relatively unaware of the processes of negotiation which characterize their assumption of the teacher role. Teachers' experiences, represented in the growing literature on teachers' lives and work, demonstrate the multiple ways in which individuals can navigate the historical and cultural constructs that shape them. Just as, historically, teachers accepted and challenged their gendered expectations and institutions, so today do we see that teachers' identity constructions simultaneously reproduce and renegotiate gendered discourses around teaching.

Thus, we end up with images of teachers, in popular culture, in research and teaching, and in the minds of teachers and students, that reflect these multiple discourses. We expect teachers to care about the children they teach, but caring can be performed and interpreted as mothering, as heroic, as political, as asexual, and as sexual, depending on the individual, his or her gender and sexuality, and the context within which the teaching occurs. Teachers may be defenders of the status quo, preparing students to take on roles within the existing structures and hierarchies within the society, or, sometimes, agents of social change in their students' lives and their own. Any one teacher simultaneously reflects and contributes to these multiple frameworks, their historical and gendered constructions, and our understanding of teachers' work.

REFERENCES

Acker, S (1989) Rethinking teachers' careers, in Acker, S (ed) *Teachers, gender and careers*. Lewes: Falmer Press.

Acker, S (1994) *Gendered education*. Buckingham: Open University Press.

Acker, S (1995) Gender and teachers' work. *Review of Research in Education*, 21: 99–162.

Allan, J (1993) Male elementary school teachers: experiences and perspectives, in Williams, C (ed) *Doing women's work*. London: Sage.

Anonymous (1989) 'Miss is a lesbian'. The experience of a white lesbian teacher in a boys' school, in DeLyon, H and Migniuolo, F (eds) *Women teachers: issues and experiences*. Milton Keynes: Open University Press.

Apple, M (1994) Is change always good for teachers? Gender, class, and teaching in history, in Borman, K and Greenman, N (eds) *Changing American education: recapturing the past or inventing the future?* Albany, NY: State University of New York Press.

Ayers, W (2001) A teacher ain't nothin' but a hero: teachers and teaching in film, in Joseph, PB and Burnaford, GE (eds) *Images of schoolteachers in America*. Mahwah, NJ: Lawrence Erlbaum Associates.

Ball, S and Goodson, I (1985) *Teachers' lives and careers*. London: Falmer Press.

Beauboeuf, T (2004) Reinventing teaching: womanist lessons from Black women teachers. Paper presented at the Annual Meeting of the American Educational Research Association, San Diego, California.

Beecher, C (1851) *The true remedy for the wrongs of woman; with a history of an enterprise having that for its object*. Boston, MA: Phillips, Sampson.

Bell, C and Chase, S (1993) The underrepresentation of women in school leadership, in Marshall, C (ed) *The new politics of race and gender* (141–54). London: Falmer Press.

Berrill, D and Martino, W (2002) 'Pedophiles and deviants': exploring issues of sexuality, masculinity and normalization in the lives of male teacher candidates, in Kissen, R (ed) *Getting ready for Benjamin.* Lanham, MD: Rowman and Littlefield.

Biklen, S (1995) *School work: gender and the cultural construction of teaching.* New York: Teachers College Press.

Blackmore, J (1993) In the shadow of men: the historical construction of educational administration as a 'masculinist' enterprise, in Blackmore, J and Kenway, J (eds) *Gender matters in educational administration and policy* (27–48).

Britzman, D (1991) *Practice makes practice: a critical study of learning to teach.* Albany, NY: State University of New York Press.

Burstyn, J (1980) Historical perspectives on women in educational leadership, in Biklin, S and Brannigan, M (eds) *Women and educational leadership.* Lexington, MA: Lexington Books.

Bush, R (1997) Feminising our schools has failed our children. *Male View,* 17: 5.

Carter, P (2002) *'Everybody's paid but the teacher': the teaching profession and the women's movement.* New York: Teachers College Press.

Casey, K (1993) *I answer with my life.* New York: Routledge.

Clifford, G (1987) 'Lady teachers' and politics in the United States, 1850–1930, in Lawn, M and Grace, G (eds) *Teachers: the culture and politics of work.* London: Falmer Press.

Connell, R (2000) *The men and the boys.* Berkeley, CA: University of California Press.

Cortina, R (1992) Gender and power in the teachers' union of Mexico, in Stromquist, N (ed) *Women and education in Latin America.* Boulder, CO: Lynne Rienner.

Cott, N (1977) *The bonds of womanhood.* New Haven, CT: Yale University Press.

Danylewycz, M, Light, B and Prentice, A (1987) The evolution of the sexual division of labour in teaching: nineteenth century Ontario and Quebec case study, in Gaskell, J and McLaren, A (eds) *Women and education: a Canadian perspective.* Calgary: Detselig Enterprises, Ltd.

DeCorse, C and Vogtle, S (1997) In a complex voice: the contradictions of male elementary teachers' career choice and professional identity. *Journal of Teacher Education,* 48: 37–46.

Edson, S (1988) *Pushing the limits: the female administrative aspirant.* Albany, NY: State University of New York Press.

Eisenhart, M (2001) Changing conceptions of culture and ethnographic methodology, in Richardson, V (ed) *Handbook of research on teaching.* Washington, DC: American Educational Research Association.

Epstein, D (2001) Boyz' own stories: masculinities and sexualities in schools, in Martino, W (ed) *What about the boys?* (96–109) Buckingham: Open University Press.

Epstein, D and Johnson, R (1998) *Schooling sexualities.* Buckingham: Open University Press.

European Union, European Network of Adult Education Organizations Working on Women's Employment Issues. Statistics Information (1999–2003). Available at: www.women-employment.lt/facts/employment5.htm.

Evans, K (1999) When queer and teacher meet, in Letts, W and Sears, J (eds) *Queering elementary education.* Lanham, MD: Rowman and Littlefield.

Fishman, GE (2000) *Imagining teachers: rethinking gender dynamics in teacher education.* Lanham, MD: Rowman and Littlefield.

Foster, M (1993) Resisting racism: personal testimonies of African American teachers, in Weiss, L and Fine, M (eds) *Beyond silenced voices* (273–88). Albany, NY: State University of New York Press.

Foster, V, Kimmel, M and Skelton, C (2001) What about the boys? An overview of the debates, in Martino, W and Meyenn, B (eds) *What about the boys?* Buckingham: Open University Press.

Francis, B and Skelton, C (2001) Men teachers and the construction of heterosexual masculinity in the classroom. *Sex Education.* 1: 9–21.

Franz, C, Cole, E, Crosby, F and Stewart, A (1994) Lessons from lives, in Franz, C and Stewart, A (eds) *Women creating lives: identities, resilience, and resistance* (325–34). Boulder, CO: Westview Press.

Fueyo, V and Koorland, M (1997) Teacher as researcher: a synonym for professionalism. *Journal of Teacher Education*, 48: 336–45.

Grant, R (1989) Alternative model of 'career', in Acker, S (ed) *Teachers, gender and careers* (35–50). Lewes: Falmer Press.

Green, JE and Weaver, RA (1992) Who aspires to teach? A descriptive study of preservice teachers. *Contemporary Education*, 63: 234–8.

Hilton, M and Hirsch, P (eds) (2000) *Practical visionaries: women, education and social progress 1790–1930*. Essex: Longman.

Hoffman, N (2003) *Women's 'true' profession; voices from the history of teaching*. Boston, MA: Harvard University Press.

Joseph, PB (2001) One hundred years of schoolteaching: an invented interview, in Joseph, PB and Burnaford, GE (eds) *Images of schoolteachers in America*. Mahwah, NJ: Lawrence Erlbaum Associates.

Kaufman, P (1984) *Women teachers on the frontier*. New Haven, CT: Yale University Press.

Khayatt, M (1992) *Lesbian teachers: an invisible presence*. Albany, NY: State University of New York Press.

King, J (2000) The problem(s) of men in early education, in Lesko, N (ed) *Masculinities at school* (3–26). Thousand Oaks, CA: Sage.

King, S (1987) Feminists in teaching: the national union of women teachers, 1920–1945, in Lawn, M and Grace, G (eds) *Teachers: the culture and politics of work* (31–49). London: Falmer Press.

Kissen, R (1996) *The last closet: the real lives of lesbian and gay teachers*. Portsmouth, NH: Heinemann.

Labaree, DF (1988) *The making of an American high school: the credentials market and the Central High School of Philadelphia, 1838–1939*. New Haven, CT: Yale University Press.

Levinson, BA and Holland, D (1996) The cultural production of the educated person: an introduction, in Levinson, BA, Foley, D and Holland, D (eds) *The cultural production of the educated person* (1–56). Albany, NY: State University of New York Press.

Lewis, E, Butcher, J and Donnan, P (1999) Men in primary teaching: an endangered species. Paper presented at the Australian Association for Research in Education, Melbourne. Available at www.aare. edu.au/99pap/but99238.htm.

Lightbody, P, Sianne, G, Tait, L and Walsh, D (1997) A fulfilling career? Factors which influence women's choice of profession. *Educational Studies*, 23: 25–37.

Lipkin, A (1999) *Understanding homosexuality, changing schools: a text for teachers, counselors, and administrators*. Boulder, CO: Westview Press.

Mac an Ghill, M (1994) *The making of men: masculinities, sexualities, and schooling*. Buckingham: Open University Press.

Middleton, S (1993) *Educating feminists*. New York: Teachers College Press.

Middleton, S (1994) Schooling and radicalisation: life histories of New Zealand feminist teachers, in Stone, L (ed) *The education feminism reader* (279–299). New York: Routledge.

Ministry of Women's Afairs. Status of Women in New Zealand. Article 11, Employment (1998) Available at www.mwa.govt.nz/women/status/cedaw011.html.

Montecinos, C and Nielsen, L (1997) Gender and cohort differences in university students' decision to become elementary teacher education majors. *Journal of Teacher Education*, 48: 47–55.

Moran, J (2000) *Teaching sex: the shaping of adolescence in the 20th* century. Cambridge, MA: Harvard University Press.

Munroe, P (1998) *Subject to fiction: women teachers' life history narratives and the cultural politics of resistance*. Buckingham: Open University Press.

Reinharz, S (1992) *Feminist methods in social research*. New York: Oxford University Press.

Rensenbrink, C (2001) *All in our places: feminist challenges in elementary classrooms*. Lanham, MD: Rowman and Littlefield.

Rong, X and Preissle, J (1997) The continuing decline in Asian-American teachers. *American Educational Research Journal*, 34: 267–93.

Sexton, P (1969) *The feminized male: classrooms, white collars and the decline of manliness.* New York: Random House.

Shakeshaft, C (1989) *Women in educational administration.* Newbury Park, CA: Sage.

Sikes, P (1985) The life cycle of the teacher, in Ball, S and Goodson, I (eds) *Teachers' lives and careers* (27–60). Lewes: Falmer Press.

Skelton, C (1994) Sex, male teachers and young children. *Gender and Education,* 6: 87–93.

Skelton, C (2001) *Schooling the boys.* Buckingham: Open University Press.

Skelton, C (2002) The 'feminisation of schooling' or 'remasculinizing' primary education? *International Studies in Sociology,* 12: 77–96.

Smulyan, L (2000) *Balancing acts: women principals at work.* Albany, NY: State University of New York Press.

Smulyan, L (2004a) Choosing to teach: reflections on gender and social change. *Teachers College Record,* 106: 544–73.

Smulyan, L (2004b) Redefining self and success: becoming teachers and doctors. *Gender and Education,* 16: 225–45.

Solomon, B (1985) *In the company of educated women.* New Haven, CT: Yale University Press.

Spring, J (1990) *The American school, 1642–1990: varieties of historical interpretation of the foundations and development of American education.* New York: Longman.

Spring, J (1986) *The American school 1643–1985.* New York: Longman.

Squirrel, G (1989) In passing: teachers and sexual orientation, in Acker, S (ed) *Teachers, gender and careers.* Lewes: Falmer Press.

Steedman, C (1998) The tidy house, in Jenkins, H (ed) *The children's culture reader* (431–55). New York: New York University Press.

Sunnari, V (1997) Gendered structures and processes in primary teacher education. Doctoral thesis, University of Oulu, Finland.

Tyack, D. (1974) *The one best system.* Cambridge, MA: Harvard University Press.

Tyack, D and Hansot, E (1990) *Learning together: a history of coeducation in American schools.* New Haven, CT: Yale University Press.

UNESCO Institute for Statistics (2004) *Education statistics.* Available at: www.uis.unesco.org/ev.php?URL_ID = 5187&URL_DO = DO_TOPIC&URL_SECTION = 201.

Urban, W (1982) *Why teachers organized.* Detroit, MI: Wayne State University Press.

US Department of Labor (2004) Women's Bureau. 20 Leading occupations of employed women 22 June. Available at www.dol.gov/wb/.

Walkerdine, V (1990) *Schoolgirl fictions.* London: Virago.

Walkerdine, V and Lucey, H (1989) *Democracy in the kitchen.* London: Virago.

Walkerdine, V, Lucey, H and Melody, J (2001) *Growing up girl.* New York: New York University Press.

Weber, S and Mitchell, C (1995) *'That's funny, you don't look like a teacher'.* London: Falmer Press.

Weiler, K (1988) *Women teaching for change.* New York: Bergin and Garvey.

Weiler, K (1989) Women's history and the history of women teachers. *Journal of Education,* 171: 9–30.

Yeakey, C, Johnston, G and Adkison, J (1986) In pursuit of equity: a review of research on minorities and women in educational administration. *Educational Administration Quarterly,* 22: 110–49.

34

Women Working in Academe: Approach with Care

Sandra Acker and Michelle Webber

This chapter takes a close look, from a broadly sociological perspective, at the working lives of women academics in universities. Universities are highly complex organizations, and academics are not their only inhabitants. Most literature is concerned with students, faculty or administrators. Little has been done to study the roles of other staff members who keep the institution running through their administrative, secretarial, service and manual labor – those in the 'ivory basement', in Eveline's (2004) terminology. We, too, follow conventional practice in giving pride of place to academics. Arguably, they are key actors in the academy, even perhaps more than the students, who are temporary tenants. Charting the full intricacies of university operations remains to be done.

Both tradition and change mark the nature of academic work in any particular country. Kamau's (1996) study of Kenyan women academics, for example, identified traditional assumptions about gender that constrained possibilities for women's progress. Men academics traded information in all-male social gatherings. Similarly, Chanana (2003) found that networking, a key component of academic success (Bagilhole and Goode, 2001), was difficult for women in India, as informal cross-gender social interaction risked being misread as sexualized activity. Instances of change are readily apparent everywhere. Australia's universities were transformed through major reorganizations and restructurings in the 1980s. While women's representation among students and faculty is increasing rapidly in China, conventional ideas about gender are still pervasive and feminist approaches peripheral (Gaskell *et al.*, 2004).

Despite local variations, many commentators emphasize the global nature of recent changes in academic work (Deem, 2001). With cutbacks in federal government levels of funding, universities in many nations have seen their overall funding levels decline dramatically (Amit, 2000). Entrepreneurialism has burgeoned (Tudiver, 1999), research is being promoted as a service to business, and students are asked to evaluate courses on the basis of skills preparation for the labor market (Smith, 2004). Work for academics has intensified and come under sharper scrutiny (Morley, 2004).

A number of feminist writers focus on the new corporate academy and its effects on women faculty (e.g. Brooks and Mackinnon, 2001; Currie, *et al.*, 2002). Any retrenchment at the time women are beginning to increase their representation in the academy is a problem. On the other hand, some writers believe that rewarding competitive performance is better for women than the former workings of what passed for collegiality but could also degenerate into an old boys' network (Luke, 2001).

This preamble tells us that a single-chapter review of women faculty in academe will inevitably have limitations. The available literature, as well as our experience, is skewed toward the analysis of conditions in Western, English-speaking countries. In our discussion, we showcase Australia, the UK, Canada and the USA, with occasional reference to matters elsewhere. We concentrate on faculty, on universities, and on women. It is understood that gender operates together with race, class, age, sexual orientation and other sources of identity and positioning. Looking at women reveals much about equity commitments in academe. Questions persist: why have universities been so slow to achieve gender balance and full integration of women's perspectives and participation? What is it about these organizations that remains resistant?

Nevertheless, the changes in the past 40 years could be applauded. Women are far better represented in academic ranks than they were in the past, and they are beginning to make inroads into leadership positions (Berkowitz, 2005; Sussman and Yssaad, 2005). In many countries, the introduction of policies such as parental leaves and the abandonment of others such as antinepotism rules (which, in practice, usually meant that wives could not have permanent positions in institutions where their husbands worked) have eased their way.

In the pages that follow, we begin with a brief overview of 'where the women (academics) are'. Then, we zero in on enduring tensions for women in academe. We argue that there seems to be a 'disconnect' between the lives of women faculty and university practices, and we give two extended examples; one is the evaluation hurdles for academics, in particular, the tenure process in North America, and the other is the efforts to introduce feminist pedagogy into the university. Finally, in our conclusion, we consider shifting discourses and the prospects for women's working lives in academe.

WHERE ARE THE WOMEN?

In Canada, women's representation among full-time university faculty grew slowly from 11% in 1960–61 to 20% in 1989–90, before accelerating to 30% in 2002–03 (AUCC, 2002; Sussman and Yssaad, 2005: 6). In the same year, 35% of all full-time faculty in the UK were women (AUT, 2004; Higher Education Statistics Agency, 2004). In the USA in 2003–04, women accounted for 41% of faculty at baccalaureate and master's degree institutions, and 33% of faculty at doctoral-level institutions (AAUP, 2004). In 2004, women represented 39% of full-time and fractional (part-time expressed as full-time equivalents) faculty in Australian universities (DEST, 2004).

Small variations should not be taken to have large consequences, because not only are the systems themselves different, the figures are calculated with different conventions from one country to another. For example, in the UK, large numbers of academics who are contract researchers are included in the figures. US figures often include community colleges or are given separately (as above) for different types of institutions.

Representation alone appears to tell a success story. The trend is at least in part due to a combination of increased hiring of women at the lower ranks and older male faculty retiring (AUCC, 2002). Yet, there are many aspects of gendered trends that are less encouraging. Everywhere women are better represented in lower ranks than in higher or managerial ones; more often found in less-secure, contingent positions and less-prestigious institutions; concentrated in traditionally female subject areas; and receiving lower salaries.

In the current era of increasing corporatization of higher education, we are seeing a convergence among universities in Australia, Canada, the UK and the USA with respect to hiring practices. The use of contingent faculty (non-permanent faculty members hired on a course-by-course basis and/or for a set period of time) is a strategy to cut costs and cope with increasing enrolments. From some perspectives, the university enshrines a class system, both in terms of its own hierarchies and in terms of the lesser likelihood of people from working-class backgrounds reaching the higher status posts (Reay, 2000, 2004; Hey, 2003). When women are found disproportionately in less secure teaching and research positions, gender equity issues are also implied (Angel, 2000; Reay, 2000; Glazer-Raymo, 2003; AUT, 2004; Paul, 2004).

KEY TENSIONS FOR WOMEN IN ACADEME

Gender, regulation, and the contemporary university

Blackmore and Sachs (2001) argue that the enormous changes in universities have affected and reshaped the 'academic self'. What aspects of women's academic work need to be considered to understand this 'self'? How do academic women understand the requirements of their positions? What commitments do they undertake? What gives them the desire to continue down this pathway? What are the experiential variations *among* academic women?

Earlier studies by Acker and colleagues alert us to enduring points of tension for many women faculty: home and work, evaluation systems, and health and stress (e.g. Acker and Armenti, 2004). What we would like to argue here is that there is an endemic disconnect between the standpoint of many women academics and the typical structures and cultures of the university. By 'standpoint', we have in mind Smith's (1987) usage as a methodological positioning device that directs us to look always for the ways in which social processes and goings-on are situated in embodied subjects located in particular, local, historical settings. David (2003) provides an exemplary recent and detailed description of how her feminism developed in a social and political context over time.

Women and minority group members of both sexes occupy positions in the university that could be described as liminal – in the process of becoming something else. They are the 'outsiders within' (Hill Collins, 1986). They are unable to just 'be': they must always be 'something'. In a world dominated by men, women are inevitably hyperconscious of being female, and men, too, are hyperconscious of women being female (but not of themselves being male).

Women are never 'just' women: they have a multiplicity of additional intersecting identities. Although surveys can indicate the representation of women from diverse groups where such information is collectable, most of what we know about the experiences of minoritized academic women tends to come from personal narratives, or sometimes a small qualitative study. Auto/biographical stories illuminate the interaction of gender and other social divisions such as race or ethnicity (Walker, 1998; Carty, 1991; Mahtani, 2004), class (Morley, 1997), generation (Skelton, 2005), disability (Chouinard, 1995–96), or sexual orientation (Talburt, 2000). Identity influences pedagogy as well as career (Bannerji, 1991; Chavez Silverman, 2000; Herndl, 2003). The sense of being an outsider within is prominent throughout this literature. Hey (2003) uses the metaphor of leaving home: the outsiders within risk 'revealing a self that is thought stupid in the host culture and pretentious in your original home culture' (p326).

Even allowing for the diversity within gender groups, gender as an embracing category still operates to structure expectations and experiences. Women academics in universities find themselves in a university that was created and developed by men and with men in mind (Rich, 1979). This is not to buy into an essentialist take on men, as we know that, historically, only a minority of men have been fortunate enough to gain a university education, let alone occupy the professoriate. Yet there are certain values and styles commonly associated with men that can be easily discerned in today's universities, such as competitiveness, success, individualism, hierarchy and assertiveness (Bagilhole and Goode, 2001; Knights and Richards, 2003).

These values and styles fit well with contemporary universities. Indicators of performance are now routinely collected (Polster and Newson, 1998; Morley,

2004). What is considered 'enough' (for tenure, promotion, and prestige) is a constantly rising bar, whatever the actual conditions and constraints (both in private lives and university surroundings) may be.

Ironically, the strong beliefs in academic freedom and the enjoyment of at least a surface-level autonomy serve to obscure the controls that actually operate. Looking at the British context, where forms of external scrutiny have become particularly pervasive, Shore and Wright (2000) liken the 'audit culture' to the prison panopticon that figures in Foucault's (1977) analysis of disciplinary technologies: 'Each individual is made acutely aware that their conduct and performance is under constant scrutiny' (Shore and Wright, 2000: 77). Inmates, or in this case academics, come to internalize the criteria and the gaze, and they police themselves.

In this view of the university as a site of regulation, its denizens conform to forms of surveillance without much time to question them. As life is always full of contradictions, it is simultaneously the case that academic work affords opportunities for autonomy and pleasure beyond those experienced by most other workers (Acker, 2003). The missing piece here is the dis/connection between the gendered lives of women faculty and the parameters of the sites in which they work. Below we give two examples of such tensions, drawing on our own research as well as that of others. One is the way in which tenure and similar evaluation mechanisms are experienced by women academics. The other is the attempt by some women academics to introduce feminist principles into their teaching.

Living up to expectations

Academics are the grown-up versions of the students who worked for good grades throughout their school lives. Depending on the labor market, acquiring an academic position may itself involve arduous amounts of searching and competition and time served in the less-secure contract positions in universities. Assuming one finds what in Canada and the USA is called a 'tenure-track' academic position (i.e. one that has the potential to lead to a permanent job), the novice academic must learn to 'perform' satisfactorily according to the norms of the institution and the discipline. It has been suggested that what is required is to go beyond simple performance into 'performativity' – ensuring the performance is obvious to others (Blackmore and Sachs, 2001; Morley, 2004).

It is important to note that the tenure system is not universal. We suspect all universities (and governments) have developed ways and means of regulating academics, tenure being only one such device. Accounts from other countries of the barriers women academics face in achieving promotions or leadership positions suggest that regulatory mechanisms are often gendered, given that women suffer from 'everyday practices of exclusion' (Walker, 1998: 336; see also Mabokela, 2002, for a detailed South African example). Academic rank depends on publication, even in African countries where resources for scholarship are severely limited (Teferra and Altbach, 2004: 39). According to Altbach (2002), tenure in some European countries is very common for those who occupy senior positions (regarded as equivalent to civil servants), while nearly non-existent in Latin America, where academics work part-time and do other jobs. The North American ideal type, however, stands as an exemplar of the (self-)regulatory aspects of academe.

In this system, the new recruit is usually formally assessed after a probationary period, and then, if successful, is allowed several more years before a full tenure review is held. The process can take from 5 to 9 years or so, depending on the university. The specifics vary across universities and departments, as do the probabilities of success (generally high in Canada), but the outcome is highly consequential: the academic either has a permanent job or must leave the institution. Normally, a promotion from assistant to associate professor occurs at or about the same time as gaining tenure. Later in a career, a faculty member might be reviewed for promotion to the higher rank of full professor.

In all of the Canadian interviews with women academics conducted by Acker and colleagues (Acker and Feuerverger, 1996; Dillabough and Acker, 2002; Acker and Armenti, 2004; Acker, 2005), achieving tenure appeared as the key accomplishment in the early academic career. The older women (and men) had not found tenure problematic. Those who had been evaluated in the 1980s or later generally presented a different picture. Now a successful academic, one woman recalled: 'I had such anxiety about tenure, I was so afraid. It was a visceral, palpable fear inside me' (Acker and Armenti, 2004: 12).

In a review of studies of women academics, Wolf-Wendel and Ward (2003) comment laconically: 'significant tension exists for women who combine work and family' (p121). Perhaps as a result, women academics in tenured faculty positions in the USA have been shown to have a significantly lower chance of being married and having children (and a higher probability of being divorced) than their male counterparts (Mason and Goulden, 2004). Several North American studies have found that younger women academics were either childless or were wrestling with the simultaneity of having children and getting through tenure, that is, the conjunction of the 'tenure clock' and the 'biological clock' (Acker and Armenti, 2004; Ward and Wolf-Wendel, 2004). For those women faculty with young children, balancing the demands of children and career poses daily dilemmas. They speak of high levels of stress, exhaustion, and sleeplessness. The academic mothers in Ward and Wolf-Wendel's study 'repeatedly asserted that academic work literally never ends' (p245).

Recent research by Probert (2005) in Australia suggests that women in their forties and fifties have a constellation of family-related pressures that affect their university work. There was an unexpected drop in career success for women in mid-career. Further analysis showed that women in their forties in this institution were less likely than other groups to 'live with a partner'. This generation, especially the women, often had child-care responsibilities and sometimes caring responsibilities for aged parents, too.

For this age group, the policy improvements in universities trying to be family-friendly (day care, maternity leaves) were not relevant to the difficulties they faced. Lack of time was universally bemoaned and linked to the ever-increasing requirement to go beyond 'normal' working hours to be productive publishers. Some of these women had started out as potential stars but could no longer cope with the amount of time necessary for servicing a brilliant career (Weiner, 1996) while managing caring tasks at home.

Tenure reviews are not the only evaluation mechanism for academics. There is peer review for journals, conferences, research grants, and other attainments. Merit-award procedures, common in North America, are another form of regulation. Practices vary widely and may range from an occasional appraisal without consequences to an annual review that influences salary. Typically, the monetary rewards are relatively small, but the process keeps academics feeling that they are under continuous assessment. Wilson and Nutley (2003) see annual appraisals in the UK as a disciplinary technology, arguing additionally that individuals are assessed against an unacknowledged gendered norm. Most of the assessors (senior faculty) are men, and the reward system is biased toward research and publications rather than teaching and service. In their interviews, the 'successful academic' was described as 'someone whose first priority was research, who worked long hours, who defined themselves in terms of their work, who had experienced no break in career, and who had an uninterrupted forward movement in their career profile' (p310).

In both Australia and Britain, periodic reports need to be made on research output for external reviews. Every four or five years, Britain's Research Assessment Exercise (RAE) requires departments (and universities) to prove their productivity or risk financial adversity. Results are judged by national subject panels. Government monies for research purposes then go mainly to top-rated departments. Many academics resent the loss of collegiality and the promotion of competition involved in the exercise (Harley, 2003). Knights and Richards (2003) argue that 'academic production is shrouded in masculine norms and values surrounding the rational and competitive pursuit of knowledge that facilitates the conquest of nature and the control of populations' (p214).

University teaching has also been subject to external scrutiny in Britain and Australia. Speaking of the entire apparatus of regulation, Morley (2004) refers to the 'psychic economy of quality assurance', meaning that emotions such as guilt, pride and shame are invoked by the process and invested in it (p4). Women academics, with a shorter history in the academy than their male counterparts, may be especially motivated to prove themselves, whatever it takes (Acker and Feuerverger, 1996).

Both explicit expectations and tacit norms about what work women do in the university need examination, as it is not simply a question of women having competing commitments outside work. There is considerable evidence that women do much of what Eveline (2004) calls 'glue work', activities that keep the university functioning, but which may be not widely recognized (Fletcher,

1999). One woman administrator in Mabokela's (2003) study of South African universities described her colleagues and herself as the 'donkeys of the university'. Several studies suggest that women academics end up with taken-for-granted responsibilities for nurturing and mentoring women students (Acker and Feuerverger, 1996; Park, 1996; Barnes-Powell and Letherby, 1998). At the same time, women often enjoy and value this kind of contribution (Acker and Feuerverger, 1996). Bird *et al.* (2004) point out that women in USA universities do the work required to address gender relations in the university, for example, writing reports and collecting data on women's representation or treatment. Ethnic minority faculty have also been found to do extra nurturing and citizenship work (Tierney and Bensimon, 1996).

In her discussion of the consequences of Britain's Research Assessment Exercise, Harley (2003) brings together concerns with evaluation and women's lives. She concludes that while explicit criteria and monitoring could advantage some academic women by making their hitherto unacknowledged research contributions visible, in the long term it is unlikely to be favourable to women, given their lesser likelihood of being able to sustain unbroken productivity without career or maternity breaks and their potential discomfort with competitive individualism (p389). In this section, we have illustrated the ways in which private and public life collide, or more specifically, how women's typical life course interacts uneasily with university career requirements. Although universities have made concessions to family life, they have not done much to change the basic set of expectations around performativity. On the contrary, as the globalization literature shows us, there is a tendency to go in the other direction, toward intensified work and productivity expectations (Blackmore and Sachs, 2000; Dillabough and Acker, 2002).

Feminist teaching in the masculinist university

Our second example of the disconnect between 'women' and 'the university' concerns pedagogy. Women who identify as feminists have been for some time developing alternative models for pedagogy and curriculum. Both in women's studies classrooms and elsewhere, some academic women have considered pedagogy to be a potential route for transforming elements of the university, building what is generally termed feminist pedagogy. As detailed in Gaby Weiner's Chapter 6 in this volume, feminist pedagogues have focused primarily on classroom teaching methods, the role of personal experience in the classroom, and challenging and ultimately altering power relations in the classroom and beyond. Yet, we must ask whether it is possible to transform pedagogy in liberatory ways within an unreformed university.

Enacting feminist pedagogical principles is often done in tension with how universities are organized. A prime example is the existence of student course evaluations. From the university standpoint (and perhaps from the student one as well), course evaluations are a reasonable feature for ensuring accountability and thus quality of course provision. But course evaluations can also be seen as one of the performance indicators or surveillance mechanisms that we have suggested make up an apparatus of control over academic work (Morley, 2002). Webber's (2005a) Canadian study of feminist teaching in the academy shows that student course evaluations play an important role in how faculty, especially those without tenured positions, organize and teach their courses. The junior or contingent faculty members talked of watering down their feminist content so as not to 'offend' their students. One faculty member spoke of managing her teaching identity so as to produce a palatable persona: 'one of my tactics is to … win the Miss Congeniality prize' (p170). Taylor's (2001) Australian work notes a similar practice of instructors indulging students to avoid negative evaluations. In examining course evaluations from women's studies courses that were also cross-listed as social courses, Webber (2005a) found that the word 'feminism' only ever appeared in a negative light. For example, responding to the question, what problems if any did you encounter with this course?, one student wrote 'It was ALL feminism!!' (p236).

Thus, the feminist ideal of letting students come to 'voice' comes into conflict with the current university climate of 'quality assurance' (Morley, 2004). As Luke (1997) points out, indicators on teaching that are pulled from student course evaluations 'do not always account for students' (sceptical and often negative) perceptions of women in positions of intellectual authority' (p438). Particular teaching practices – such as avoiding overt acknowledgement of course content or pedagogy as 'feminist' – can be traced to faculty members' awareness of the impact of students' attitudes to feminist course content and their (well-founded) belief that ultimately their course evaluations might be used by administrators to evaluate their work (Webber, 2005a,b). Further, these disciplinary mechanisms often inform contract renewal or future hiring decisions, or at least non-permanent faculty members believe this to be the case.

CONCLUSION

This chapter has been concerned with (and about) the working lives of women faculty members in academe. Our central argument is that there is a disconnect between some of the typical qualities of women's lives and the often regulatory practices of universities, especially in current conditions when globalizing tendencies have increased the work, reduced the budgets, and heightened the level of scrutiny and performativity expected of academics.

Some may retort that there is no reason to equate these regulatory and competitive processes with the male-dominated university. There is no easy answer here, especially if we wish to avoid essentialist arguments about 'women' or 'men'. One idea is that we need to identify the different hegemonic masculinities that characterize universities (Harley, 2003). Collegiality, while sounding like the kind of value that some feminist writers probably would applaud, has instead often worked as male preference. Harley (2003) suggests that, in Britain, the ascendance of new managerialism and the type of surveillance described earlier is part of a transformation of the British academy, not into the inclusive or egalitarian alternative desired in feminist literature, but into a competitive-individualist, self-promoting version that inscribes a different, but still problematic, dominant masculinity.

It is a matter of debate whether things are improving or worsening for women academics. Some writers are deeply pessimistic. Currie and Thiele (2001) conclude a chapter by saying, 'the past for female academics was bleak and the future is likely to remain the same' (p112). Blackmore (1997) charges that discourses of efficiency and effectiveness have trumped those of equity. Bagilhole (2002) believes that traditional academics have sufficient autonomy to continue resisting reform.

Others stress more strongly the contradictions or the spaces within which change can happen. Acker (2005) notes that many of the academic managers she interviewed found ways to improve their situations, and some retained optimism about change overall. The Costa Rican academic women that Twombly (1998) interviewed believed themselves to be in a privileged position compared to non-academic women and saw their families not as competing with their careers but as supporting them. Krefting (2003) analyzes the intertwined discourses of gender and merit. While most of the consequences she outlines for academic women are negative, she also stresses that the contradictions and tensions within discourses leave open possibilities for resistance and destabilization (p270). Ward and Wolf-Wendel (2004) comment on 'silver linings and dark clouds' (p241) in their interviews with academic mothers. The difficulties of combining motherhood and intense academic work were spoken about in great detail (the clouds), but the pleasures of teaching and of having a family as well as a work life (the silver linings) were also described.

A recent report from the American Council on Education (2005) is interesting in that it combines an argument for gender equity with one for national competitiveness. Perhaps policy makers are more likely to listen if the issue is reframed away from being a problem of women. It contains a number of suggestions that would increase the flexibility and attractiveness of an academic career. Other recent pieces have emphasized the encouraging pace of change. A Canadian government publication charting improvements in women's representation in universities during the 1990s (Sussman and Yssaad, 2005) was described in the popular press as *Women storm Canada's ivory towers* (Brown, 2005: A2).

But are numbers enough? Using a Dutch proverb, Benschop and Brouns (2003) lament that 'adding women to unchanged academic structures and cultures is like mopping with the tap on' (p207). Taylor (2002) acknowledges the disappointment many feminist activists have felt when the university equity initiatives of the 1980s began to be dismantled in the 1990s. Yet she counsels optimism, pointing out that the struggle has to be seen in the long view, in which progress ebbs and flows. Post-structuralist feminism implies that we cannot arrive at a definitive answer to the question. In a fog of shifting discourses, perhaps it is only time that will tell.

ACKNOWLEDGEMENT

The authors would like to thank Carly Manion, PhD student at the Ontario Institute for Studies in Education of the University of Toronto, for her invaluable assistance in tracking down statistical sources and compiling references.

REFERENCES

Acker, S (2003) Living the academic life, in Dinham, S (ed) *Transforming education: engaging with complexity and diversity* (60–71). Deakin West: Australian College of Educators.

Acker, S (2005) Gender, leadership and change in faculties of education in three countries, in Collard, J and Reynolds, C (eds) *Leadership, gender and culture in education* (103–17). Maidenhead: Open University Press.

Acker, S and Armenti, C (2004) Sleepless in academia. *Gender and Education*, 16: 3–24.

Acker, S and Feuerverger, G (1996). Doing good and feeling bad: the work of women university teachers. *Cambridge Journal of Education*, 26: 401–22.

Altbach, P (2002) How are faculty faring in other countries?, in Chait, R (ed) *The questions of tenure* (160–81). Cambridge, MA: Harvard University Press.

American Association of University Professors (AAUP) (2004) *Faculty salary and faculty distribution fact sheet 2003–2004*. www.aaup/org/research/sal&distribution.htm.

American Council on Education (ACE) (2005) *An agenda for excellence: creating flexibility in tenure-track faculty careers*. Executive summary. www.acenet.edu/bookstore/pdf/2005_tenure-flex-summary.pdf.

Amit, V (2000) The university as panopticon: moral claims and attacks on academic freedom, in Strathern, M (ed) *Audit cultures* (215–35). London: Routledge.

Angel, M (2000) The glass ceiling for women in legal education: contract positions and the death of tenure. *Journal of Legal Education*, 50: 1–15.

Association of Universities and Colleges in Canada (AUCC) (2002) *Trends in higher education*. Ottawa: Publications and Communications Division, Association of Universities and Colleges of Canada.

Association of University Teachers (AUT) (2004) *The unequal academy*. www.aut.org.uk/media/pdf/aut_unequalacademy.pdf.

Bagilhole, B (2002) Challenging equal opportunities: changing and adapting male hegemony in academia. *British Journal of Sociology of Education*, 23: 19–33.

Bagilhole, B and Goode, J (2001) The contradiction of the myth of individual merit, and the reality of a patriarchal support system in academic careers. *European Journal of Women's Studies*, 8: 161–80.

Bannerji, H (1991) Re: turning the gaze. *Resources for Feminist Research*, 20(3/4): 5–11.

Barnes-Powell, T and Letherby, G (1998) All in a day's work: gendered care work in higher education, in Malina, D and Maslin-Prothero, S (eds) *Surviving the academy: feminist perspectives* (69–77). London: Falmer Press.

Benschop, Y and Brouns, M (2003) Crumbling ivory towers: academic organizing and its gender effects. *Gender, Work and Organization*, 10: 194–212.

Berkowitz, P (2005) Tipping the gender balance. *University Affairs*, 46: 36–7.

Bird, S, Litt, J and Wang, Y (2004) Creating status of women reports: institutional housekeeping as 'women's work'. *National Women's Studies Association Journal*, 16: 194–206.

Blackmore, J (1997) Disciplining feminism: a look at gender-equity struggles in Australian higher education, in Roman, L and Eyre, L (eds) *Dangerous territories: struggles for difference and equality in education* (75–96). New York: Routledge.

Blackmore, J and Sachs, J (2000) Paradoxes of leadership and management in higher education in times of change: some Australian reflections. *International Journal of Leadership in Education*, 3: 1–16.

Blackmore, J and Sachs, J (2001) Women leaders in the restructured university, in Brooks,A and Mackinnon, A (eds) *Gender and the restructured university* (45–66). Buckingham: Open University Press.

Brooks, A and Mackinnon, A (eds) (2001) *Gender and the restructured university: changing management and culture in higher education.* Buckingham: Open University Press.

Brown, L (2005) Women storm Canada's ivory towers. *Toronto Star,* 25 February, A2.

Carty, L (1991) Black women in academia: a statement from the periphery, in Bannerji, H, Carty, L, Dehli, K, Heald, S and McKenna, K *Unsettling relations: the university as a site of feminist struggles* (13–44). Toronto: Women's Press.

Chanana, K (2003) Visibility, gender, and the careers of women faculty in an Indian university. *McGill Journal of Education,* 38: 391–406.

Chavez Silverman, S (2000) Tropicalizing the liberal arts classroom, in Geok-Lin Lim, S and Merrara-sobek, M (eds) *Power, race, and gender in academe* (132–53). New York: Modern Languages Association.

Chouinard, V (1995/96) Like Alice through the looking-glass: accommodations in academia. *Resources for Feminist Research,* 24(3/4): 3–11.

Currie, J and Thiele, B (2001) Globalization and gendered work cultures in universities, in Brooks, A and Mackinnon, A (eds) *Gender and the restructured university* (90–115). Buckingham: Open University Press.

Currie, J, Thiele, B and Harris, P (2002) *Gendered universities in globalized economies.* Lanham, MD: Lexington.

David, ME (2003) *Personal and political: feminisms, sociology and family lives.* Stoke on Trent: Trentham Books.

Deem, R (2001) Globalisation, new managerialism, academic capitalism and entrepreneurialism in universities: is the local dimension still important? *Comparative Education,* 37: 7–20.

Department of Education, Science and Training (DEST) (Australia) (2004). *Staff 2004: selected higher education statistics.* www.dest.gov.au/highered/statistics/staff/2004_staff.xls.

Dillabough, J-A and Acker, S (2002) Globalisation, women's work and teacher education: a cross-national analysis. *International Studies in the Sociology of Education,* 12: 227–260.

Eveline, J (2004) *Ivory basement leadership: power and invisibility in the changing university.* Crawley: University of Western Australia Press.

Fletcher, J (1999) *Disappearing acts: gender, power, and relational practice at work.* Cambridge, MA: MIT Press.

Foucault, M (1977) *Discipline and punish.* Harmondsworth: Penguin.

Gaskell, J, Eichler, M, Pan, J, Xu, J, and Zhang, X (2004) The participation of women faculty in Chinese universities: paradoxes of globalization. *Gender and Education,* 16: 511–29.

Glazer-Raymo, J (2003) Women faculty and part-time employment: the impact of public policy, in Ropers-Huilman, B (ed) *Gendered futures in higher education* (97–109). Albany, NY: State University of New York Press.

Harley, S (2003) Research selectivity and female academics in UK universities: from gentleman's club and barrack yard to smart macho? *Gender and Education,* 15: 378–92.

Herndl, D (2003) Johnny Mnemonic meets the bimbo: feminist pedagogy and postmodern performance, in Freedman, D and Holmes, M (eds) *The teacher's body* (59–68). Albany, NY: State University of New York Press.

Hey, V (2003) Joining the club? Academia and working-class femininities. *Gender and Education,* 15: 319–35.

Higher Education Statistics Agency (HESA) (2004) *Full-time academic staff in all UK institutions by location of institution, gender, principal source of salary and clinical status.* www.hesa.ac.uk/holisdocs/pubinfo/staff/staff0203.htm.

Hill Collins, P (1986) Learning from the outsider within: the social significance of Black feminist thought. *Social Problems,* 33: S14–S32.

Kamau, MN (1996) The experiences of women academics in Kenya. Unpublished PhD dissertation, University of Toronto.

Knights, D and Richards, W (2003) Sex discrimination in UK academia. *Gender, Work and Organization,* 10: 213–38.

Krefting, L (2003) Intertwined discourses of merit and gender: evidence from academic employment in the USA. *Gender, Work and Organization,* 10: 260–78.

Luke, C (1997) Quality assurance and women in higher education. *Higher Education,* 33: 433–51.

Luke, C (2001) *Globalization and women in academia, north/west—south/east.* Mahwah, NJ: Lawrence Erlbaum.

Mabokela, RO (2002) Reflections of black women faculty in South African universities. *Review of Higher Education,* 25: 185–205.

Mabokela, RO (2003) 'Donkeys of the university': organizational culture and its impact on South African women administrators. *Higher Education,* 46: 129–45.

Mahtani, M (2004) Mapping race and gender in the academy: the experiences of women of colour faculty and graduate students in Britain, the US and Canada. *Journal of Geography in Higher Education,* 28: 91–9.

Mason, MA and Goulden, M (2004) Marriage and baby blues: redefining gender equity in the academy. *Annals of the American Academy of Political and Social Science,* 596: 86–103.

Morley, L (1997) A class of one's own: women, social class and the academy, in Mahony, P and Zmroczek, C (eds) *Class matters.* London: Taylor & Francis.

Morley, L (2002) Lifelong yearning: feminist pedagogy in the learning society, in Howie, G and Tauchert, A (eds) *Gender, teaching and research in higher education* (86–98). Aldershot: Ashgate.

Morley, L (2004) *Theorizing quality in higher education.* Bedford Way Paper no. 24. London: University of London Institute of Education.

Park, S (1996) Research, teaching, and service: why shouldn't women's work count? *Journal of Higher Education,* 67: 46–67.

Paul, LJ (2004) The untenured female academic in the corporate university, in Reimer, M (ed) *Inside corporate U: women in the academy speak out* (pp226–44). Toronto: Sumach Press.

Polster, C & Newson, J (1998) Don't count your blessings: the social accomplishments of performance indicators, in Currie, J & Newson, J (eds) *Universities and globalization: critical perspectives* (pp173–82). Thousand Oak, CA: Sage.

Probert, B (2005) 'I just couldn't fit it in': gender and unequal outcomes in academic careers. *Gender, Work and Organization,* 12: 50–72.

Reay, D (2000) 'Dim dross': marginalised women both inside and outside the academy. *Women's Studies International Forum,* 23: 13–21.

Reay, D (2004) Cultural capitalists and academic habitus: classed and gendered labour in UK higher education. *Women's Studies International Forum,* 27: 31–9.

Rich, A (1979) Toward a woman-centered university, in Rich, A *On lies, secrets and silence* (125–55) New York: WW Norton.

Shore, C and Wright, S (2000) Coercive accountability: the rise of audit culture in higher education, in Strathern, M (ed) *Audit cultures* (57–89). London: Routledge.

Skelton, C (2005) The 'self-interested' women academic: a consideration of Beck's model of the 'individualised individual'. *British Journal of Sociology of Education,* 26: 5–16.

Smith, D (1987) *The everyday world as problematic: a feminist sociology.* Boston, MA: Northeastern University Press.

Smith, D (2004) Despoiling professional autonomy: a women's perspective, in Reimer, M (ed) *Inside corporate U: women in the academy speak out* (31–42). Toronto: Sumach Press.

Sussman, D and Yssaad, L (2005) The rising profile of women academics. *Perspectives on Labour and Income,* 6: 6–19.

Talburt, S (2000) *Subject to identity: knowledge, sexuality, and academic practices in higher education.* Albany, NY: State University of New York Press.

Taylor, J (2001) The impact of performance indicators on the work of university academics: evidence from Australian universities. *Higher Education Quarterly,* 55: 42–61.

Taylor, M (2002) A few things learned, in Hannah, E, Paul, L. and Vethamany-Globus, S. (eds) *Women in the Canadian academic tundra: challenging the chill* (218–21). Montreal & Kingston: McGill-Queen's University Press.

Teferra, D and Altbach, P (2004) African higher education: challenges for the 21st century. *Higher Education*, 47: 21–50.

Tierney, W and Bensimon, E (1996) *Promotion and tenure: community and socialization in academe.* Albany, NY: State University of New York Press.

Tudiver, N (1999) *Universities for sale: resisting corporate control over Canadian higher education.* Toronto: Lorimer.

Twombly, S (1998) Women academic leaders in a Latin American university: reconciling the paradoxes of professional lives. *Higher Education*, 35: 367–97.

Walker, M (1998) Academic identities: women on a South African landscape. *British Journal of Sociology of Education*, 19: 335–54.

Ward, K and Wolf-Wendel, L (2004) Academic motherhood: managing complex roles in research universities. *Review of Higher Education*, 27: 233–57.

Webber, M (2005a) Claiming feminist space in the university: the social organization of feminist teaching. PhD dissertation, University of Toronto.

Webber, M (2005b) 'Don't be so feminist': exploring resistance to feminist approaches in a Canadian university. *Women's Studies International Forum*, 28(2–3): 181–94.

Weiner, G (1996) Which of us has a brilliant career? Notes from a higher education survivor, in Cuthbert, R (ed) *Working in higher education* (58–68). Buckingham: Open University Press.

Wilson, F and Nutley, S (2003) A critical look at staff appraisal: the case of women in Scottish universities. *Gender, Work and Organization*, 10: 310–19.

Wolf-Wendel L and Ward, K (2003) Future prospects for women faculty: negotiating work and family, in Ropers-Huilman, B (ed) *Gendered futures in higher education: critical perspectives for change* (111–34). Albany, NY: State University of New York Press.

35

Gender and Educational Management

Charol Shakeshaft

The research on gender and management begins with women's representation in formal leadership positions, explores access and barriers to access, and examines female leadership patterns. Across countries, one of the first things researchers want to know is how many and at what levels women are found in organizational management. Once women's representation has been documented, researchers pursue data that help to explain why women do not hold more positions in school management. Then, the ways women manage – often in contrast with men – are explored.

Fitzgerald (2002) notes that early studies tend to present women leaders as if they are an 'homogenized group and considerations of circumstances such as ethnicity/social class/location and beliefs have been discounted' (p10). The pioneering studies collapsed the distinctions among women partly to provide a meta-narrative. Many of the early studies assumed the norm of heterosexual, privileged, white women for all women. As research has matured, the intersections of ethnicity, culture, class, and gender have begun to be examined. Fitzgerald comments that although early studies might have included discussions of 'black women in educational management', these analyses were add-ons. 'There has not been a conscious attempt to theorize how power is exercised and differentiated in gender and race based ways' (Fitzgerald, 2002: 15).

The number of representative studies at each of these levels varies by country. In some cases, researchers are just beginning to document the lack of women in educational leadership. In other countries, this information has been in the public domain for a number of years and studies are focusing on female leadership styles and decisions.

REPRESENTATION OF WOMEN IN SCHOOL ADMINISTRATION

Trying to document the number of women in school administration worldwide is difficult: administrative titles and jobs are not comparable across countries, and few countries keep accurate records by sex of administrative office holders. Thus, there is no one study that gives a global snapshot of the number of women in school administration.

The USA is a case in point. There is no single repository for documenting the number of women in school administration. The US Department of Education collects comprehensive annual national statistics on the approximately 94,000 public elementary and secondary schools in 17,000 school districts. These statistics provide insight into many characteristics of schools and schooling, such as school size, finances, class-size, level of violence, teacher attitudes, and instructional approaches. Yet, there are no national figures documenting the number and/or proportion of women superintendents in the USA. With considerable sleuthing and access to the US Department of Education's data files, it is possible to document the proportion of women principals in a representative sample of US schools. However, determining the proportion of women superintendents or superintendents and principals by both race and gender is beyond the scope of available data. Currently, the field primarily relies upon membership counts in administrative organizations, occasional surveys by these organizations, or occasional surveys by the National Center for Education Statistics to report the percentage of women in administrative positions in US public and private schools.

There are a number of explanations for this lack of data, both in the USA and in other countries. Documentation reflects values and governments document what is important and what is valued. Numbers allow comparisons as well as accountability. Without comparable data, it is difficult to know the extent of the underrepresentation of women in educational management or if there are changes over time. Several theorists believe that failure to report proportions of leaders by sex and ethnicity indicates resistance to changing those proportions.

In the USA, women constitute approximately 75% of teachers, the pool from which principals and superintendents are selected. The most recent available figures indicate that approximately 34.5% of principals and 18% of superintendents in the USA are female (NCES, 2003).

Although not directly comparable by year or title, there are individual country-by-country accounts which document the underrepresentation of women in school management and which offer a reliable understanding of international practice. In a study of international patterns of women's educational leadership,

Cubillo and Brown (2003) from the UK note that 'the teaching profession in this country and internationally is, with few exceptions, predominated by women. However, a look at the statistics reveals that despite large numbers of women in the profession, they are greatly under-represented in positions of management' (p279). An issue of the *European Journal of Education* (vol 31, no. 4) in the mid-1990s documented that in most European countries, women were less well represented in administrative positions than they were in teaching jobs. Across most European countries, the older the student, the fewer women teachers and leaders are present.

A study of women in educational management in 10 European countries indicates that the majority of school managers are men, while the majority of teachers are women (Ruijs, 1990). This study highlights the disparity between the number of male and female school administrators:

> There is a large gap between the percentages of male teachers and principals ... In the average European country (with the exception of Greece) the percentage of female principals should be almost doubled to reflect the percentage of female teachers. This is true for primary as well as secondary education. (Ruijs, 1990: 1–2)

Women in Third World countries fare no better, according to Davies' (1990) study of women in educational management in these countries. The difference between many of these countries and Western systems is that teaching is not necessarily dominated by women. For instance, Davies reports that in the countries she studied:

> Teaching is by no means a 'feminine' profession internationally. At the primary level, 46 of the 71 countries ... have fewer than 50% women teachers; at the secondary level, 50 out of 60 countries have fewer than 50% women. The proportions of female headteachers, inspectors or senior Ministry personnel bear no relation to their proportions in the teaching force as a whole. Women are seriously underrepresented in power positions across the world, even in countries where education is seen as the prerogative of the female. (Davies, 1990: 2)

In many countries, the supply of female candidates begins to diminish in primary schools. The lack of equitable female education affects overall proportions of women in leadership positions. Lower female education leads to fewer women teachers and role models and eventually fewer female administrators. For instance, in Uganda's over 622 secondary schools with a total population of over 230,119 students, the majority (60.2%) of students and the majority (82.6%) of teachers are male. 'Girls constitute 45% of the student body in primary schools, 30% in the lower secondary ... and 20 in the upper secondary' (Brown and Ralph, 1996: 20). It is no surprise, then, that in Uganda 'female teachers are not usually promoted to higher managerial levels, especially if they are unmarried' (Brown and Ralph, 1996: 20). Table 35.1 provides some rough comparisons of the proportion of women in selected countries in educational roles. The figures from these studies illustrate that women are underrepresented in positions in school management worldwide.

Table 35.1   Women's representation in educational management

Country	Percent elementary teachers	Percent elementary principals	Percent secondary teachers	Percent secondary principals	Percent all principals
Australia					20
Belgium	75	32	55	33	
Botswana		11		9	
Brunei	66	2	49	27	
China			29	11	
Denmark	57	1		7	
Greece	49	41	48	43.5	
France	71	45	50	23	
Ireland	76	47		35	
Italy		34		27.5	
Netherlands	65	12	27	4	
Philippines	77	22	57	12	
Portugal		90		34	
Spain				19.5	
United Kingdom	78	44	50	16	
Uganda			82.6		
United States	83.5	16.9	50.1	3.5	
Zimbabwe	40	1	32	10	

BARRIERS TO WOMEN IN SCHOOL MANAGEMENT

Studies that examine the barriers that keep women from becoming school administrators document a number of reasons that have prevented women from moving into formal leadership positions in schools. Cubillo and Brown (2003) note that gaining access to positions of power transcends national borders. Theories that explain women's lack of progress of the managerial ladder have been surprisingly similar across countries and cultures.

Devaluation of women/sex discrimination/socialization

Sex discrimination in educational leadership is primarily rooted in the devaluation of women in society or the socialization of members of society into patterns and beliefs that support unequal expectations and rewards for women and men. Fitzgerald (2002) argues that Maori women in New Zealand historically represented a society in which women and men were equally valued, even if differently valued. 'One of the more powerful indications of the gender-neutral way in which the Maori world operated was that there are no personal or possessive pronouns in the Maori language that signify a hierarchy of sex' (p16). However, although gender varies across cultures, there is no culture that values women and men the same.

Across cultures, power relations within educational institutions are hierarchical and paternalistic (Acker and Feuerverger, 1996; Blackmore, 1999; Brown and

Ralph, 1996; Garrett, 1997; Heald, 1997; Court, 1998). Coleman (2000) documents resistance to female leadership in the UK that is not dissimilar to that of the experiences of women educational administrators in Uganda (Brown and Ralph, 1996) or in the USA (Shakeshaft *et al.*, in press).

The factor that explains the most about the resistance to women in positions of power in schools is the worldwide devaluation of women. Across cultures, women are seen as less than and different from men. While equity gains have been made, different expectations of and attitudes to women and men still exist. Studies indicate that negative attitudes to women by those who hire still constitute the major barrier to female advancement in school administration. Most of why women do not become school administrators can be explained by understanding that women are not valued as much as men and that this bias results in negative attitudes and practices toward women aspiring to be school administrators.

Coleman (2000) found that male teachers resented women head teachers in the UK and Wales and that women continued to have to prove themselves more than men. More than half of the women studied reported 'experiencing sexist attitudes from their male colleagues' (p23).

A study of barriers to women across nine countries – Indonesia, China, Cyprus, Greece, Kuwait, Iraq, Commonwealth of Dominica, Gambia, and Zambia – found similar patterns of stereotypic expectations and social and cultural expectations that devalued women (Cubillo and Brown, 2003). Brown and Ralph (1996) identified patriarchal patterns and male privilege as a barrier to women in Uganda, while Chisolm (2001) pointed to similar issues in South Africa. Chisolm attributed the lack of equitable representation in leadership positions of women in South Africa to the identification of competence in leadership with whiteness, masculinity and rationality.

Similarly, in a study of Catholic principals in New South Wales, Australia, women, more so than men, believed that the environment was unsupportive and that gender issues and discrimination were a primary reason that women were not principals (d'Arbon *et al.*, 2002).

Support systems

A second explanation of why women do not become school administrators is that they lack the support systems to encourage career advancement as well as to help them find and secure jobs. Successful women administrators almost always acknowledge of the importance of family support. For instance, in Cubillo and Brown's analysis of women managers from nine countries, women reported the importance of support from parents, especially fathers. Cubillo and Brown suggest that paternal support is especially important in many of the male-dominated countries they studied. 'This emphasis on paternal support may have been a consequence of the strongly patriarchal societies into which many of these women were born and socialized' (p285). Luke (1998) found a similar need for family support among women in Singapore. Luke points out that the support is two way: women need the support of their families, and women also maintain nurturing roles within their families.

In addition to family support, women need both networks and mentors. Women are much less likely than men to have formal or informal networks that let them know about jobs and help them be interviewed. They are also less likely to have mentors – whether male or female – to help them negotiate careers.

Support from networks, sponsors, and mentors is less likely to go to women than to men. Blackmore (1999) describes women managers as 'outsiders inside' working within the institution, but not in the male network. Lack of access to this network – not lack of aspiration or confidence – helps to explain women's representation at the managerial level (Cubillo, 1999). Ehrich (1994) examines the differences between networks and mentorships in Australia and argues that while both are important, mentoring is more necessary for career advancement. Citing Still and Guerin (1986), who found that males and females network differently, Ehrich concludes that 'networking is a less powerful practice for women than for men. Not only do women join less powerful formal networks (feminist and sociocultural as opposed to mainstream) but also they network more with females (who have less power than males) and they approach networking differently (i.e. they do not evaluate contacts primarily as keys to providing them with favours and help' (p7).

Stronger networks and sponsorship among men may explain why they are more likely to apply for jobs for which they are both qualified and not qualified and why females generally apply only for jobs for which they are highly qualified. Females rarely apply for positions for which they are not qualified. As a result, there are usually more male applications for a position and a male – even a less-qualified male – is likely to be hired.

When women are successful, they tend to report strong female network support as well as male support. Chisolm (2001) notes that Black women in South Africa draw upon the 'collective strength and capability of women rooted in maternal feminism' (p387).

Women report not only a lack of networks but also hostility within organizations. Cubillo and Brown (2003) found a 'lack of peer support, particularly from the men' across the women leaders they studied. These women noted male hostility toward them as well as describing the ways in which 'masculine culture was enacted to actively maintain power relationships between men and women' (p287). Coleman (2000) found that the women secondary head teachers in England and Wales that she studied were 'patronized' and that they felt 'isolated'. Many of the women reported that males had difficulty with female bosses, and more than half of the women in her studies had experienced sexist attitudes and behaviors from their male colleagues.

Family responsibilities

In most families, women are still responsible for the majority of child-care and homemaking. Women's responsibilities for family life – whether current or anticipated – slow women's progress because of both external expectations and internal accommodations.

Although there is no documentation that being a parent diminishes managerial ability, there are still many who believe that such responsibilities inhibit the ability of women to perform their jobs as school managers, and, therefore, that such responsibilities make women undesirable candidates for administrative positions.

At the same time, women sometimes say that family responsibilities keep them from applying for and assuming administrative positions, not because these women do not think they could do everything, but because they believe the costs would be too high for their families and themselves. A study of the principalship in Catholic Schools in New South Wales, Australia, indicates that family responsibilities deter both females and males (d'Arbon, *et al.*, 2002). In this study, women at both primary and secondary levels indicated that the impact of the principalship on personal and family life ranked first in importance among the reasons they were unwilling to apply for a principalship. Women and men believed that 'the role intrudes too much on personal and family life' and 'the time pressures are too stressful' (p476). The search for balance among family, work, and personal lives explains some women's reluctance to take on the public responsibilities that come with some leadership positions.

Lack of interest in the job

Some women have indicated that the tasks of administration are not of interest to them because they entered education to teach. However, as these women come to understand that administration takes many forms, they are also likely to show more interest in becoming administrators. Likewise, studies of women administrators indicate that they do the job differently than do men, focusing more on teaching, learning, and children (Shakeshaft, 1987). The more women see other women administrators incorporating the values of teaching, learning, and contact with children, the more likely women are to decide they are interested in becoming school administrators.

Preparation

Studies of the formal preparation needed to become school administrators indicate that in countries where there are certification or educational requirements, women are just as likely as men to have these qualifications. In countries where no formal managerial qualifications are required, such as the Netherlands, but where special programs in management for women have been begun, studies indicate that even when the women held advanced training in management, they were less likely to be hired than men with no training.

Lack of preparation was less likely to be the reason for women than for men for passing up opportunities for a principal's position, according to d'Arbon, *et al.* (2002) in a study of the Catholic principalship in New South Wales, Australia. Men were more likely than women to give 'lack of expertise' as the reason for not pursuing the principalship.

FEMALE LEADERSHIP STYLES

A number of researchers have noted that, historically, leadership theory is based primarily upon studies of males. Blackmore (1999), Fitzgerald (2002), Shakeshaft (1987), Theobald (1996), and Shakeshaft, *et al.* (in press) are among many researchers that have documented the male framework that dominates studies of leadership. Because of this androcentric conceptual bias, researchers – as early as the 1970s – began to examine how women lead. In the USA, many of these early studies were done to document female capability. At that time, it was important to have evidence to argue that women administrators were at least as good as, if not better than, men administrators. This research was in response to the assertions that women are unfit for administrative jobs due to their supposed inability to discipline students, work with men, 'command' respect, and possess rational and logical approaches to leadership. While these negative attitudes about women administrators have lessened, there is evidence that they are not extinguished.

In these early years, studies that did not compare women to men were deemed 'inadequate' and were not likely to be published. Critics of studies of female populations argued that findings on women were valid only if compared to findings on men. Male behavior was the measuring stick against which all studies of women were to be compared. Therefore, these early studies almost always included both females and males and were generally quantitative.

As more women moved into school administration and as scholars argued that women's styles should be researched in their own right, studies that observed, interviewed, and surveyed only women administrators emerged. These studies sought to identify the ways in which women lead as well as to describe best practice, regardless of whether or not female leadership differed from male leadership. Comparison studies by gender have continued to be published, but the bulk of the studies from 1985 to 2005 are single-sex inquiries.

Although research on women's leadership styles has grown, the norm of these 'meta-narratives' has been that of the white woman in Western countries. Among others, Fitzgerald (2002) notes that:

> discourses that universalize the complex participation of women and 'women's leadership' have produced universal and somewhat troublesome narratives that privilege 'feminine' values. In this way, categories of 'woman' and 'educational leader' have become fixed and the possibility for substantive diversity among and between women does not appear possible. (p10)

Female leadership styles

Several themes emerge from studies of female leaders. Particularly in qualitative studies that only examine female behaviors, women educational leaders are portrayed as committed to social justice, relationships, and instruction.

Social justice

Women believe that leadership will bring about change in the lives of children and families. In many studies, women describe their social justice mission as one that they carry out through education. This is a thread that runs through a number of descriptions of what motivates women to enter administration and what keeps them focused (Strachan, 1999; Sanders-Lawson, 2001; Smith-Campbell, 2002; Shapiro, 2004).

Women discuss their desire to 'make things better', right social wrongs, and increase support for underserved groups. Several studies cast women's approach as 'servant leadership' (Brunner, 1997; Alston, 1999) in which women seek to serve others by being the facilitator of the organization, bringing groups together, motivating students and staff, and connecting with outside groups. In these studies, women 'minister' to others. For instance, the 10 African descent women superintendents in Collins' (2002) study described their jobs as 'a mission'. Although not specifically identified as striving for or achieving a social justice mission, the work of Hines (1999) categorizes women administrators as transformative leaders on the Leadership Practices Inventory, and Burdick (2004) found that teachers were more likely to rate women principals, as opposed to men, as reform leaders. Coleman (2000) found that women secondary head teachers in England and Wales valued service through changing the lives of children that they could accomplish.

Spiritual

Women are more likely than men to talk about the spiritual dimensions of leadership. Several US studies document a ministerial approach to leadership that includes a spiritual dimension. This is true for both women of color (Logan, 1989; Bloom, 2001; Sanders-Lawson, 2001; Collins, 2002; Jones, 2003) and white women (Donaldson, 2000; Miller, 2000; Stiernberg, 2003).

These women administrators discuss the relationship between spirituality and the ways they model behavior and inspire others. Further, these women acknowledge the importance of their spirituality to their success and ability to push forward, often in conflictual and difficult situations.

Relational

Since Gilligan first proposed that females value relationships more than males, research on female approaches to leadership have documented a relational aspect. In these studies from the USA, the UK, Australia, New Zealand, and Canada, female administrators note the importance of relationships as evidenced in communication styles, teamwork, collaboration, and community connection

(Shakeshaft, 1987; Blackmore, 1999; Adler and Izraeli, 1994; Hall, 1996; Jirasinghe and Lyons, 1996). Several studies document women's propensity to listen to others (Bynum, 2000), whether in groups or one-on-one. Researchers have explored the themes of nurturing, emotional connections, and interpersonal relationships among women administrators, connecting these to societal expectations for women as 'mothers'. However, the research is unclear whether these 'connected' styles emerge naturally or whether they are necessary for women to be accepted. Fitzgerald (2002) describes a framework that includes the approaches of indigenous women in New Zealand that value community and connectedness. Coleman's (2000) study of female secondary head teachers in England and Wales found that more than 62% of her respondents identified their leadership style as collaborative, team related, supportive, and consultative. Gibson's (1995) cross-national study of administrators in Norway, Sweden, Australia, and the USA found that women administrators placed great emphasis on facilitating interaction among staff members.

Many, if not most, women educational leaders do not describe themselves as powerful and are uncomfortable with a discussion of their own power in the traditional sense (Formisano, 1987; Carnevale, 1994; Smith, 1996). Comfortable descriptions of power for many women cast power as the ability to help others and is conceptualized as shared (power with) as opposed to power over. For women, but not for men, sharing power is directly linked to positive relationships. For women, power used to help others strengthens relationships, while power used to control others damages relationships.

Instructional focus

A number of studies note that instruction is central to women. Women administrators are likely to introduce and support strong programs in staff development, encourage innovation, and experiment with instructional approaches. Women are likely to stress the importance of instructional competence in teachers and be attentive to task completion in terms of instructional programs. The importance of instruction overlaps the social justice agenda of many women administrators. Coleman (2002), for instance, noted that the most often cited value promoted by secondary head teachers in England and Wales was student achievement.

Striving for balance

Women's leadership styles are developed within a framework of balancing personal and professional needs and responsibilities. Women administrators often report that it is difficult for them to determine the line between personal and professional.

Gender differences in leadership

Identifying themes in the ways women lead does not necessarily mean that there are gender differences in leadership. In an examination of a number of US studies of gender differences in leadership style, the results are mixed and suggest that findings are related to the research method used (Shakeshaft *et al.*, in press). Qualitative studies are much more likely to find differences between men and women than are quantitative studies with 100% of the qualitative studies, but only 14% of the quantitative studies, reporting gender differences.

Similar to the US quantitative findings, studies in the UK (Evetts, 1994; Coleman, 2000) found no differences in leadership styles of male and female secondary head teachers. Pounder and Coleman (2002) in a review of gender differences in leadership argue that there are many additional variables that might account for differences, including national culture, socialization, workplace experiences and socialization, type of organization, and organizational demographics.

Examining gender differences across cultures may be problematic for a number of reasons. Luthar (1996) notes that many of these studies are from the USA or the UK, countries in which democracy is embedded in the national culture. Carless (1998) is skeptical of the generalizability of the leadership experiences across cultures because of this democratic frame. Pounder and Coleman (2002), referencing research in the Shaanxi province of China (Coleman *et al.*, 1998), indicated that the 'underlying patriarchal values made it very difficult for women to transcend entrenched attitudes to women and take on senior management roles in schools, despite the general approval of the idea of equality between the sexes' (p128).

Where differences are reported, women are more likely than men to be rated by both those who work with them and by themselves as instructional, task-oriented leaders (Nogay, 1995; Spencer and Kochan, 2000). Women are identified as more relational and interpersonal than are men, logging in more one-on-one contacts with staff (Counts, 1987; Perry, 1992; Nogay, 1995). Men are more likely to make contact through memos or directives and women are more likely to meet in person.

Genge (2000) found that women are more likely than men to use humor to forge relations, often making fun of themselves. Humor, as a way to lessen tension and diffuse conflict, is not atypical of women. The research contradicts the stereotype that women do not have a sense of humor.

Garfinkel (1988) reported differences in the ways in which women and men define loyal staff members. For women, a loyal staff member is first an employee who is competent. For men, the most loyal staff members are those who agree publicly.

According to Gardiner, *et al.* (2000) and Eagley and Johnson (1990), the gender context of the workplace makes a difference in leadership styles. Women are more likely to be more interpersonal than males in female-dominated workplaces, but equally interpersonal in male-dominated workplaces. Women are equally task oriented in female-dominated organizations, but more task oriented than men in male-dominated organizations. Among the 12 female secondary principals that Applewhite (2001) studied, leadership approaches were strategically chosen by the context, women sometimes using more female-identified strategies and sometimes using more male-identified strategies. Barbie (2004) and Rottler (1996) both describe a mix of traditionally male and female styles. Anatole (1997) found no specific Meyers-Briggs pattern among the high-school principals studied, although Harris (1991) determined that the female high-school principals she studied used primarily holistic or whole-brain cognitive patterns.

SUMMARY

The research on women in educational administration is remarkably similar across countries and cultures, although there are important cultural and national differences. Nevertheless, women are less likely to be represented in formal positions of leadership in schools than are men across all countries. It is noteworthy that finding statistics on gender proportions in formal leadership positions is difficult in most countries, and assembling comparable statistics across countries is not possible.

Barriers to the entrance of women into leadership positions include patriarchal societal structures and the devaluation of women within societies. These factors lead to sex discrimination and reinforced stereotypes about female inadequacy. Societal expectations that women are responsible for child-care and home maintenance increase the workload for women who work outside the home. Because of these beliefs, women are often assumed to be less available for leadership positions by those who hire. Additionally, many women make career decisions around issues of family, while many men make family decisions around issues of career.

The literature on gender differences in leadership style is mixed, with one set of literature documenting differences and another reporting no differences. Whether they are different from male administrative approaches, women's leadership styles often include a focus on communication, collaboration, teamwork, inclusiveness, and attention to instructional issues.

REFERENCES

Acker, S and Feuerverger, G (1996) Doing good and feeling bad: the work of women university teachers. *Cambridge Journal of Education*, 26: 401–22.

Adler, NJ and Izraeli, DN (1994) *Competitive frontiers: women managers in a global economy.* Cambridge, MA: Blackwell.

Alston, JA (1999) Climbing hills and mountains: Black females making it to the superintendency, in Brunner, CC (ed) *Sacred dreams: women and the superintendency,* (79–90). Albany, NY: State University of New York Press.

Anatole, MJ (1997) The characteristics of female secondary principals. Doctoral dissertation, University of Southern California.

Applewhite, AS (2001) Factors influencing Colorado female secondary principals' leadership practices. Doctoral dissertation, Colorado State University.

Barbie, JA (2004) Narratives of women's life experiences and how it informs their practice as school district superintendents. Doctoral dissertation, University of Denver.

Blackmore, J (1999) Troubling women: feminism, leadership and educational change: the upsides and downsides of leadership and the new managerialism, in Reynolds, C (ed) *Women and school leadership: international perspectives*. Albany, NY: State University of New York Press.

Bloom, CM (2001) Critical race theory and the African-American woman principal: alternative portrayals of effective leadership practice in urban schools. Doctoral dissertation, Texas A&M University.

Brown, M and Ralph, S (1996) Barriers to women managers' advancement in education in Uganda. *International Journal of Educational Management,* 10: 18–23.

Burdick, DC (2004) 'Women hold up half the sky': is principal selection based on gender and leadership style? Doctoral dissertation, Arizona State University.

Brunner, CC (1997) Working through the 'riddle of the heart': perspectives from women superintendents. *Journal of School Leadership*, 7: 138–64.

Bynum, V (2000) An investigation of female leadership characteristics. Doctoral dissertation, Capella University.

Carless, SA (1998) Gender differences in transformational leadership: an examination of superior, leader, and subordinate perspectives. *Sex Roles*, 39(11/12): 887–902.

Carnevale, P (1994) An examination of the ways women in school administration conceptualize power. Doctoral dissertation, Hofstra University.

Chisolm, L (2001) Gender and leadership in South African educational administration. *Gender and Education*, (13): 387–99.

Coleman, M (2000) The female secondary head teacher in England and Wales: leadership and management styles. *Journal of Educational Research*, 42: 13–28.

Coleman, M, Quiang, H and Yanping, L (1998) Women in educational management in China: experience in Shaanxi province. *Compare,* 8: 141–54.

Collins, PL (2002) Females of color who have served as superintendent: their journeys to the superintendency and perceptions of the office. Doctoral dissertation, Seton Hall University, College of Education and Human Services.

Counts, CD (1987) Toward a relational managerial model for schools: a study of women and men as superintendents and principals. Doctoral dissertation, Harvard University.

Court, MR (1998) Women challenging managerialism: devolution dilemmas in the establishment of co-principalships in primary schools in Aotearoa/New Zealand. *School Leadership and Management,* 18: 35–57.

Cubillo, L (1999) Gender and leadership in the NPQH: an opportunity lost? *Journal of In-Service Education*, 25: 35–57.

Cubillo L and Brown, M (2003) Women into leadership and management: international differences? *Journal of Educational Administration*, 41: 278–91.

d'Arbon, T, Duignan, P and Duncan, PJ (2002) Planning for future leadership of schools: an Australian study. *Journal of Educational Administration*, 40: 468–85.

Davies, L (1990) Women and educational management in the Third World. Paper presented at the Equal Advances in Education Management Conference, Council of Europe: Vienna, Austria, December.

Donaldson, CAM (2000) Together and alone: women seeking the principalship. Doctoral dissertation. University of Calgary (Canada).

Eagley, AH and Johnson, BT (1990) Gender and leadership style: a meta-analysis. *Psychological Bulletin*, 108: 233–56.

Ehrich, LC (1994) Mentoring and networking for women educators. *Women in Management Review*, 9: 4–10.

European Journal of Education, 31(4).

Evetts, J (1994) *Becoming a secondary headteacher*. London: Longman.

Fitzgerald, T (2002) Changing the deafening silence of indigenous women's voices in educational leadership. *Journal of Educational Administration*, 41: 9–23.

Formisano JM (1987) The approaches of female public school principals toward conflict management: a qualitative study. Doctoral dissertation, Hofstra University.

Gardiner, ME, Enomoto, E and Grogan, M (2000) *Coloring outside the lines: mentoring women into school leadership.* Albany, NY: State University of New York Press

Garfinkel, EZ (1988) An examination of the ways men and women in school administration conceptualize the administrative team. Doctoral dissertation, Hofstra University.

Garrett, V (1997) In conversation with Rosemary Whinn-Sladden, in Ribbins, P (Ed) *Leaders and leadership in the school, college, and university.* London: Cassell.

Genge, MC (2000) The development of transformational leaders: The journeys of female and male secondary school principals; alike or different? Doctoral dissertation, University of Toronto (Canada).

Gibson, CA (1995) An investigation of gender differences in leadership across four countries. *Journal of International Business Studies,* 26: 255–79.

Hall, V (1996) *Dancing on the ceiling: a study of women managers in education.* London: Paul Chapman.

Harris, PB (1991) Profiles in excellence – Leadership styles of female principals in high schools of excellence. Doctoral dissertation, University of North Carolina–Greensboro.

Heald, S (1997) Events without witness: living/teaching within the paternalistic university. *Curriculum Studies,* 5: 39–48.

Hines, JA (1999). A case study of women superintendents in the state of Ohio in their roles as transformational leaders in creating school district climate. Doctoral dissertation, University of Akron.

Jirasingh, D and Lyons, G (1996) *The competent head: a job analysis of heads' tasks and personality factors,* London: Falmer Press.

Jones, SN (2003) The praxis of Black female educational leadership from a systems thinking perspective. Doctoral dissertation, Bowling Green State University.

Logan, CBM (1989) Black and white leader perception of school culture. Doctoral dissertation, Hofstra University.

Luke, C (1998) Cultural politics and women in Singapore higher education management. *Gender and Education,* 10: 245–63.

Luthar, HK (1996) Gender differences in evaluation of performance and leadership ability: autocratic vs democratic managers. *Sex Roles,* 35(5/6): 337–61.

Miller, VJ (2000) The organizational entry and socialization of women in educational leadership positions: a case study. Doctoral dissertation, Eastern Michigan University.

National Center for Education Statistics (NCES) (2003) Schools and staffing public use data set.

Nogay, KH (1995) The relationship of the superordinate and subordinate gender to the perceptions of leadership behaviors of female secondary principals. Doctoral dissertation, Youngstown State University.

Perry AB (1992) A comparison of the ways that women and men principals supervise teachers. Doctoral dissertation, Hofstra University.

Pounder, JS and Coleman, M (2002) Women–better leaders than men? In general and educational management, it still 'all depends'. *Leadership and Organization Development Journal,* 23(3): 122–133.

Rottler, JM (1996) The women superintendents of Iowa: a 1990's analysis. Doctoral dissertation, University of Northern Iowa.

Ruijs, A (1990) Women in educational management in European countries: the statistical picture. Paper presented at the Equal Advances in Education Management Conference. Council of Europe: Vienna, Austria, December.

Sanders-Lawson, ER (2001) Black women school superintendents leading for social justice. Doctoral dissertation, Michigan State University.

Shakeshaft, C (1987) The training of women administrators. *Teacher Education Quarterly,* Spring.

Shakeshaft, C, Brown, G, Irby, B, and Grogan, M (in press) Increasing gender equity in educational leadership. *Handbook for achieving gender equity.* Mahwah, NJ: Erlbaum.

Shapiro, L (2004) Disrupting what is going on: women educational leaders make art together to transform themselves and their schools. Doctoral dissertation, Union Institute and University.

Smith, SJ (1996) Women administrators: concepts of leadership, power and ethics. Doctoral dissertation, University of Wyoming.

Smith-Campbell, SI (2002) Exploring the world of Black women middle school principals. Doctoral dissertation, Michigan State University.

Spencer, WA and Kochan, FK (2000, January 24) Gender related differences in career patterns of principals in Alabama: a statewide study. *Education Policy Analysis Archives*, 8: online ISSN 1068–2341

Stiernberg, PW (2003) The relationship between spirituality and leadership practices of female administrators in K-12 schools. Doctoral dissertation, Baylor University.

Still, LV and Guerin, C (1986) Gender aspects of career networking practices of men and women managers. *Women in management*, Series Paper no. 5, Nepean CAE School of Business Working Paper Series, May.

Strachan, J (1999) Feminist educational leadership: locating the concepts in practice. *Gender & Education*, 11: 309–23.

Theobald, M (1996) *Knowing women: origins of women's education in nineteenth century Australia.* Melbourne: Cambridge University Press.

Index